ANNUAL EDITIONS

Multicultural Education

Sixteenth Edition

P9-DNS-289

EDITOR

Nancy P. Gallavan, PhD
University of Central Arkansas

Nancy P. Gallavan, PhD, professor of teacher education at the University of Central Arkansas, earned a BS in Elementary Education from Southwest Missouri State University in 1976; an MA in curriculum and instruction from the University of Colorado, Boulder, in 1983; an elementary school administrator's certificate from the University of Colorado, Denver, in 1988; and a PhD from the University of Denver in 1994. She taught elementary school and middle level classrooms in the St. Vrain Valley and Cherry Creek School Districts in Colorado for 20 years before entering higher education at the University of Nevada, Las Vegas. She joined the University of Central Arkansas in 2006, serving first as Associate Dean and now in a faculty position. Nancy is active in the American Educational Research Association (AERA), the Association of Teacher Educators (ATE), the National Association for Multicultural Education (NAME), and the National Council for the Social Studies (NCSS). Her research focuses on the sociocultural context of teaching and learning with emphases on critical consciousness, cultural competence, and self-efficacy.

Mc Graw Hill

*Connect
Learn
Succeed*™

Connect
Learn
Succeed™

ANNUAL EDITIONS: MULTICULTURAL EDUCATION, SIXTEENTH EDITION

Published by McGraw-Hill, a business unit of The McGraw-Hill Companies, Inc., 1221 Avenue of the Americas, New York, NY 10020. Copyright © 2012 by The McGraw-Hill Companies, Inc. All rights reserved. Previous edition(s) 1994–2010. Printed in the United States of America. No part of this publication may be reproduced or distributed in any form or by any means, or stored in a database or retrieval system, without the prior written consent of The McGraw-Hill Companies, Inc., including, but not limited to, in any network or other electronic storage or transmission, or broadcast for distance learning.

Some ancillaries, including electronic and print components, may not be available to customers outside the United States.

This book is printed on acid-free paper.

Annual Editions® is a registered trademark of the McGraw-Hill Companies, Inc. Annual Editions is published by the **Contemporary Learning Series** group within the McGraw-Hill Higher Education division.

1 2 3 4 5 6 7 8 9 0 QDB/QDB 1 0 9 8 7 6 5 4 3 2 1

ISBN: 978–0–07–805109–8
MHID: 0–07–805109–6
ISSN: 1092–924X (print)
ISSN: 2162–1683 (online)

Managing Editor: *Larry Loeppke*
Developmental Editor: *Dave Welsh*
Permissions Coordinator: *DeAnna Dausener*
Marketing Specialist: *Alice Link*
Project Manager: *Connie Oertel*
Design Coordinator: *Margarite Reynolds*
Cover Graphics: *Kristine Jubeck*
Buyer: *Susan K. Culbertson*
Media Project Manager: *Sridevi Palani*

Compositor: Laserwords Private Limited
Cover Image: Blend Images/Getty Images (inset): Stock Illustration RF/Getty Images (background)

Editors/Academic Advisory Board

Members of the Academic Advisory Board are instrumental in the final selection of articles for each edition of ANNUAL EDITIONS. Their review of articles for content, level, and appropriateness provides critical direction to the editors and staff. We think that you will find their careful consideration well reflected in this volume.

ANNUAL EDITIONS: Multicultural Education 12/13
16th Edition

EDITOR

Nancy P. Gallavan
University of Central Arkansas

ACADEMIC ADVISORY BOARD MEMBERS

Preface

In publishing ANNUAL EDITIONS we recognize the enormous role played by the magazines, newspapers, and journals of the public press in providing current, first-rate educational information in a broad spectrum of interest areas. Many of these articles are appropriate for students, researchers, and professionals seeking accurate, current material to help bridge the gap between principles and theories and the real world. These articles, however, become more useful for study when those of lasting value are carefully collected, organized, indexed, and reproduced in a low-cost format, which provides easy and permanent access when the material is needed. That is the role played by ANNUAL EDITIONS.

This sixteenth edition of *Annual Editions: Multicultural Education* showcases articles that help educators in every capacity to acquire information, apply practices, appreciate research, and advocate advances that enrich and expand the current comprehension and popular approaches found in universities, schools, and classrooms. Increasing one's awareness of today's sociocultural context and taking steps to navigate cultural competence encompasses a lifelong journey that starts with awakening your critical consciousness accompanied by conducting insightful self-assessments associated with the many dynamic factors that impact your self-efficacy and sense of agency. That means you must view the world in conjunction with your role and responsibilities in ways that are *honest, natural, authentic,* and *holistic.*

To be *honest* involves sincere integrity; you want to be reliably truthful about your beliefs and intentions to yourself and to everyone around you. People want to know that your words and actions reflect the real you. Being *natural* requires accepted normalcy in yourself; you want to be comfortably relaxed in your words and interactions. People want to be assured that the image they see and hear is who you are. Being *authentic* necessitates dependable realism; you want to be transparently genuine in all your efforts and endeavors. People want to be confident that you are legitimate. To be *holistic* entails comprehensive alignment; you want to be completely integrated in your intentions and interactions. People want you to be honest, natural, and authentic at all times and with all people.

The goal is to become attuned to the presence, power, structure, and function of the learning experiences in your classroom, school, and all programs both curricular and extracurricular, so *democratic principles, educational equity, human rights,* and *social justice* are guaranteed for all students. Democratic principles include valuing each person and the person's cultural characteristics while ensuring full participation in activities and decision-making procedures in ways that are transparent and accountable. Educational equity emphasizes providing information, access, and opportunity to all students in their academic and social settings. Human rights encompass the rights and freedoms for all individuals and groups to become equal partners. Social justice empowers all individuals so they are respected and protected for their individual beliefs and choices. Not only must you ensure these factors exist for each student, your aim is for all students to understand the concepts in principle and practice as a community of learners within the interdependent global society, the context for which all teachers are preparing their learners.

My own quest to apply critical consciousness and to self-assess the teaching, learning, and schooling to enhance my self-efficacy and sense of agency led me to design the Gallavan Cultural Competence Compass (2010, Corwin Press). Like a compass rose on a map with eight compass points, the Gallavan Cultural Competence Compass (GCCC) includes eight points or directions to guide and support educators in their evolution. The eight compass points include:

N = Notice Culture and Cultural Characteristics
NE = Negotiate and Evaluate Curriculum and Content
E = Establish Community and Context
SE = Seek and Engage Collaboration and Construction
S = Spark Conversations and Climate
SW = Strengthen and Weave Together Complexities and Controversies
W = Waken Compassion and Commitment
NW = Nurture and Welcome Challenges and Changes

Noticing cultural and cultural characteristics means developing a *focus* so you comprehend what you notice and what you do not notice and being aware of the *filters* you use to control the many pieces of information and stimuli that you constantly encounter. You also want to manage the *findings* allowing you to understand the people, purpose, productivity, and pleasure when noticing culture and cultural characteristics and to *face* the realities that you discover about yourself, words, observations, and interactions.

To negotiate and evaluate curriculum and content entails fully understanding your (M) *motivation* in teaching, your (I) *implementation* style, your (N) *negotiation* techniques, and your personal (D) *dispositions.* I call this MIND over matter. You have been given a set of content standards and academic standards that you and your students must know, do, believe, and respect. Be honest about your motivation, implementation, negotiation, and dispositions that highly influence your instructional strategies and assessment tools. Cultural competence should resonate across the teaching, learning, and schooling by providing all students information, access, and opportunities.

One of the most rewarding compass points involves establishing community and context making your classroom learner-centered that *invites, ignites, excites,* and *delights* every learner. Regardless of the ages and stages that you teach, your classroom must appear safe and welcoming to invite the learner into it. Safety refers to both the physical and affective sense of place; students want to know that the teacher and their peers will accept them naturally. The learning community must engage students' thinking and participating in ways that advances their learning by igniting their imaginations and exciting their possibilities. When students can express their learning in ways that reflect their learning styles and share with their peers in ways that are authentic, the learner is delighted.

Seeking collaboration and construction presents meaningful learning experiences for you to realize that more knowledge will be learned and more tasks can be accomplished in ways that are *imaginative, insightful, positive,* and *productive* when people work with other people and co-construct the outcomes authentically. Collaboration allows you to bring your background, knowledge, and experiences to the endeavor so everyone learns about one another as they co-construct new and different results. You will benefit by finding a mentor who will partner with you; then you can replicate your discoveries with your own students. Your students' academic and social outcomes will surpass your expectations.

To spark conversations and climate offers teachers and students with unique opportunities for students to logically *inspect* and personally *connect* the learning outcomes that you academically *expect* by discussing topics and issues with *respect.* You can advance your students' levels of comprehension by introducing and moderating captivating conversations related to the content and community. Implementing techniques that bring everyone fairly into the conversation and allowing students to express differing opinions, you empower students to inspect their sources and connect their own experiences with the academic outcomes you expect in ways that help your students practice respect for both the content and one another. Sparking conversations relating the learning to people helps create a climate of acceptance and intelligence.

One point on the compass that you should readily embrace is the opportunity to strengthen and weave together complexities and controversies, since these two conditions occur frequently in classrooms and schools. The first step is to *seize* the moment and discuss curriculum from multiple perspectives to examine the complexities associated with every topic and issue. Then *integrate* controversy in both the content and your classroom management holistically allowing your students to experience critical thinking, problem solving, and decision making in immediate, real-life situations. Finally, *rationalize* possibilities through if/then scenarios so students participate in linking decisions with consequences.

In all your students, your goal is to waken compassion and commitment for both the immediate results and lifelong learning. The concept of care is somewhat abstract, elusive, and, at times, a paradox in that we care for people, places, and things both in our immediate realm as well as far away and out of sight. When teaching compassion and care, think of the word care as an acronym with C representing *concepts,* A representing *awareness,* R representing *reflection,* and E representing *education.* Teachers are encouraged to feature the concepts associated with the situation while increasing awareness of the people involved with the situation. Then inspire your students in reflecting on their own lives to infuse the concepts and awareness as part of their compassion and then guide your students in the education needed to fully understand the situation and people while making choices regarding their commitment.

The final compass point is the emphasis on nurturing and welcoming challenges and changes. Research and practices in multicultural education concentrate on the challenges experienced in schools and society throughout the history of the United States coupled with changes that teachers and students should make as you teach democratic principles, ensure educational equity, champion human rights, and promote social justice. The keys are to overcome resistance and to model resilience as you "become the change you want to see" in the world (Mahatma Gandhi, 1869–1948).

The authors of the articles included in the sixteenth edition of *Annual Editions: Multicultural Education* will impress you with their experiences and insights. Unit 1 provides a selection of articles that help you notice culture and cultural characteristics with a selection of articles that look at the world's demographics and challenges living in a globalized society. Unit 2 discusses curriculum and content in today's schools and classrooms with articles teaching about social justice and human rights for all people. Unit 3 prompts establishing a sense of place with community and context with articles addressing schools as dynamic positive systems and promoting school achievement among all populations. Unit 4 emphasizes the importance of collaboration and construction among teachers and students with articles about our professional growth to help all students find voice and choice in the classroom. Unit 5 sparks conversations and climate associated with multicultural education through language and literature. Unit 6 delves into strengthening and weaving together the complexities and controversies of cultural competence. Unit 7 inspires readers to waken compassion and commitment in themselves and their students. Unit 8 encourages readers to nurture and welcome the challenges and changes ensuring cultural competence.

We are including important *Internet References,* sites to be used to further explore article multicultural topics.

Thank you again for welcoming me as the new editor of *Annual Editions: Multicultural Education*. I also want to thank David Welsh, who has provided me the necessary guidance and support to maintain the outstanding quality we have come to expect from this outstanding publication. I have used *Annual Editions: Multicultural Education* for many years with my undergraduate and graduate teacher candidates as well as my master and doctorate candidates. Each year, the volume of articles surpasses my expectations for a well-organized and meaningful collection of research and practice that I can use with my students and to teach to my students. I am pleased with the submitted articles and encourage readers to submit more articles for future volumes. Please complete and return the form at the back of the book. We look forward to hearing from you.

Nancy P. Gallavan

Nancy P. Gallavan, PhD
Editor

The Annual Editions Series

VOLUMES AVAILABLE

Adolescent Psychology
Aging
American Foreign Policy
American Government
Anthropology
Archaeology
Assessment and Evaluation
Business Ethics
Child Growth and Development
Comparative Politics
Criminal Justice
Developing World
Drugs, Society, and Behavior
Dying, Death, and Bereavement
Early Childhood Education
Economics
Educating Children with Exceptionalities
Education
Educational Psychology
Entrepreneurship
Environment
The Family
Gender
Geography
Global Issues
Health
Homeland Security
Human Development

Human Resources
Human Sexualities
International Business
Management
Marketing
Mass Media
Microbiology
Multicultural Education
Nursing
Nutrition
Physical Anthropology
Psychology
Race and Ethnic Relations
Social Problems
Sociology
State and Local Government
Sustainability
Technologies, Social Media, and Society
United States History, Volume 1
United States History, Volume 2
Urban Society
Violence and Terrorism
Western Civilization, Volume 1
Western Civilization, Volume 2
World History, Volume 1
World History, Volume 2
World Politics

Contents

UNIT 1
Notice Cultures and Cultural Characteristics

1. **Becoming Citizens of the World,** Vivien Stewart, *Educational Leadership,*
   April 2007
   Global competence in today's world requires young people to understand the interconnectedness of economies with the rise of Asia; that science and technology are vital
   changes in the world; that health and security matters are interrelated and impact everyone everywhere; and that the *world's demographics* have accelerated *international
   migration patterns.* U.S. students must expand their world knowledge, international
   language skills, and civic values. The trends and suggestions associated with the challenges of living in a globalized society are described in detail.   **2**

2. **Colorblind to the Reality of Race in America,** Ian F. Haney López, *The
   Chronicle of Higher Education,* November 3, 2006
   The author provides an argument concerning the phenomenon of *race relations in the
   United States* and the *"color blindness"* of many white Americans and its effects on
   the lives of *persons of color.* He argues that there are efforts to ignore the reality of
   "race" in American life. Issues related to the concept of race continue to be litigated in
   the courts.   **7**

3. **"What Are You?" Biracial Children in the Classroom,** Traci P. Baxley,
   Childhood Education, June 2008
   On the 2000 U.S. Census, for the first time Americans were given the opportunity to
   identify themselves as biracial. Approximately 2.4 percent of the U.S. population or 6.8
   million people could report their heritages and *biracial identity* accurately. Biracial students comprise one of the fastest growing populations in today's schools and classrooms. Educators need to be aware of the biracial identity and practices that support
   biracial students intellectually, emotionally, and socially and promote *multicultural education* for all students in all classrooms.   **12**

4. **Beyond "Culture Clash": Understandings of Immigrant Experiences,**
   Bic Ngo, *Theory Into Practice,* 2008
   Immigrants to U.S. schools and society and their families construct cultures and identities based on their new experiences. Clashes may occur between immigrants and
   native U.S. citizens; clashes can also occur between immigrant youth and their parents
   as the youth strive to become both a part of their new peer culture and yet remain a part
   of their families. The author offers an explanation of the double movement of *identity
   development* experienced through *international migration patterns* and the need for
   redefining identity as the in-between that immigrants frequently express.   **16**

5. **Metaphors of Hope,** Mimi Brodsky Chenfield, *Phi Delta Kappan,*
   December 2004
   The author describes the promising examples of four wonderful teachers and how their
   students have responded to their teaching. Teaching since 1956, the author has traveled
   the nation observing students and teachers in *classroom interaction.*   **22**

The concepts in bold italics are developed in the article. For further expansion, please refer to the Topic Guide.

UNIT 2
Negotiate and Evaluate Curriculum and Content

The concepts in bold italics are developed in the article. For further expansion, please refer to the Topic Guide.

UNIT 3
Establish Community and Context

The concepts in bold italics are developed in the article. For further expansion, please refer to the Topic Guide.

UNIT 4
Seek and Engage Collaboration and Construction

The concepts in bold italics are developed in the article. For further expansion, please refer to the Topic Guide.

UNIT 5
Spark Conversations and Climate

The concepts in bold italics are developed in the article. For further expansion, please refer to the Topic Guide.

UNIT 6
Strengthen and Weave Together Complexities and Controversies

UNIT 7
Waken Compassion and Commitment

The concepts in bold italics are developed in the article. For further expansion, please refer to the Topic Guide.

UNIT 8
Nurture and Welcome Challenges and Changes

The concepts in bold italics are developed in the article. For further expansion, please refer to the Topic Guide.

The concepts in bold italics are developed in the article. For further expansion, please refer to the Topic Guide.

Correlation Guide

The *Annual Editions* series provides students with convenient, inexpensive access to current, carefully selected articles from the public press. **Annual Editions: Multicultural Education, 16/e** is an easy-to-use reader that presents articles on important topics such as *diversity, religion, poverty,* and many more. For more information on *Annual Editions* and other *McGraw-Hill Contemporary Learning Series* titles, visit www.mhhe.com/cls.

This convenient guide matches the units in **Annual Editions: Multicultural Education, 16/e** with the corresponding chapters in our two best-selling McGraw-Hill Multicultural Education textbooks by Cushner et al. and Kottak/Kozaitis.

Annual Editions: Multicultural Education, 16/e	Human Diversity in Education: An Integrative Approach, 7/e by Cushner et al.	On Being Different: Diversity and Multiculturalism in the North American Mainstream, 4/e by Kottak/Kozaitis
Unit 1: Notice Cultures and Cultural Characteristics	**Chapter 1:** Education in a Changing Society **Chapter 3:** Culture and the Culture-Learning Process **Chapter 9:** Religious Pluralism in Secular Classrooms	**Chapter 1:** Introduction **Chapter 2:** Culture **Chapter 3:** Globalization and Identity **Chapter 7:** Race: Its Biological Dimensions **Chapter 8:** Race: Its Social Construction
Unit 2: Negotiate and Evaluate Curriculum and Content	**Chapter 4:** Classrooms and Schools as Cultural Crossroads **Chapter 6:** Creating Classrooms That Address Race and Ethnicity	
Unit 3: Establish Community and Context	**Chapter 6:** Creating Classrooms That Address Race and Ethnicity **Chapter 13:** Improving Schools for All Children: The Role of Social Class and Social Status in Teaching and Learning	**Chapter 16:** Families
Unit 4: Seek and Engage Collaboration and Construction	**Chapter 3:** Culture and the Culture-Learning Process **Chapter 6:** Creating Classrooms That Address Race and Ethnicity **Chapter 8:** Developing Learning Communities: Language and Learning Style	**Chapter 4:** The Multicultural Society **Chapter 5:** Ethnicity **Chapter 15:** Linguistic Diversity
Unit 5: Spark Conversations and Climate	**Chapter 8:** Developing Learning Communities: Language and Learning Style	**Chapter 15:** Linguistic Diversity
Unit 6: Strengthen and Weave Together Complexities and Controversies	**Chapter 1:** Education in a Changing Society **Chapter 6:** Creating Classrooms That Address Race and Ethnicity	**Chapter 6:** Religion
Unit 7: Waken Compassion and Commitment	**Chapter 4:** Classrooms and Schools as Cultural Crossroads	**Chapter 2:** Culture
Unit 8: Nurture and Welcome Challenges and Changes	**Chapter 13:** Improving Schools for All Children: The Role of Social Class and Social Status in Teaching and Learning	**Chapter 4:** The Multicultural Way

Topic Guide

This topic guide suggests how the selections in this book relate to the subjects covered in your course. You may want to use the topics listed on these pages to search the Web more easily.

On the following pages a number of websites have been gathered specifically for this book. They are arranged to reflect the units of this Annual Editions reader. You can link to these sites by going to www.mhhe.com/cls

All the articles that relate to each topic are listed below the bold-faced term.

Internet References

The following Internet sites have been selected to support the articles found in this reader. These sites were available at the time of publication. However, because websites often change their structure and content, the information listed may no longer be available. We invite you to visit www.mhhe.com/cls for easy access to these sites.

Annual Editions: Multicultural Education 16e

General Sources

Center for Multicultural Education
http://education.washington.edu/cme

From the University of Washington, College of Education, this site provides programs, projects, and publications addressing all areas of cultural diversity.

Electronic Magazine of Multicultural Education
www.eastern.edu/publications/emme

Now succeeded by the *International Journal of Multicultural Education* (IJME) at http://ijme-journal.org/index.php/ijme, these websites provide research and practices appropriate for all classrooms and educators.

Multicultural Education
www.emtech.net/multicultural_education.html

Here you will find links to information about international cultures and guidance for effective multicultural education.

Multicultural Pavilion
www.edchange.org/multicultural

Featuring resources, research, opportunities, quotations, and activities including an awareness quiz, this website provides an extensive amount of information related to all areas of multicultural education.

Multicultural Education Internet Resource Guide
http://jan.ucc.nau.edu/~jar/Multi.html

More than 50 Internet resources are linked to this website providing an extraordinary collection of information, guidance, and support for students, teachers, administrators, professors, and families.

National Association for Multicultural Education (NAME)
www.nameorg.org

A nonprofit association founded in 1990, NAME provides guidance and support for all educators with links to information, research, conferences, and publications.

UNIT 1: Notice Cultures and Cultural Characteristics

The Big Religion Chart
www.religionfacts.com/big_religion_chart.htm
At this site you will find an incredible collection of facts about the world's 42 religions from which you can easily compare and contrast religions with one another.

Census Data
www.census.gov

To understand the population within the United States, look at the information included in this site that describes people and households, business and industry, geography, and many different special topics.

Census Bureau; International Data Base (IDB)
www.census.gov/ipc/www/idb

Here you will find population information describing the 227 countries in today's world so you can better understand a particular country in relationship to other countries.

Major Religions of the World
www.adherents.com/Religions_By_Adherents.html

Data at this site is organized into 22 religions categorized by a variety of topics allowing the reader to compare, contrast, and comprehend the complexity of each religion.

Statistical Abstract of the United States
www.census.gov/compendia/statab

This link provides statistics on the social, political, and economic organization of the United States gathered from the Census Bureau, the Bureau of Labor Statistics, the Bureau of Economic Analysis, and many other federal agencies, and provider organizations.

Tribal Government Information
www.usa.gov/Government/Tribal.shtml

An extensive collection of information and resources, this website offers background and guidance on many different topics related to tribal organization, cultural resources, and governmental services.

UNIT 2: Negotiate and Evaluate Curriculum and Content

Awesome Library for Teachers
www.awesomelibrary.org/teacher.html

Open this page for many links and access to information on many topics of interest and concern to all educators.

Library of Congress
www.loc.gov/index.html?gclid=CLTW28rd2JkCFRINDQodpgGqVA

Filled with an abundance of collections from the past and present, this informative website provides resources for students and teachers on many different topics and issues.

National Economics and Social Rights Initiative
www.nesri.org/?gclid=CIPVtYyWxJoCFRufnAodY1Q8sg

On the National Economic and Social Rights Initiative (NESRI) website, you will find information about promoting a human rights vision for the United States that ensures dignity and access to the basic resources needed for human development and civic participation.

Scholastic News-Immigration
http://teacher.scholastic.com/activities/immigration/index.htm

Stories about immigration from yesterday and today are featured on this student-centered website with many resources for curriculum and instruction, especially literature reading lists.

Internet References

Social Statistics Briefing Room
www.whitehouse.gov/briefing_room

The purpose of this website is to provide easy access to current United States statistics including demographic, safety, economic, education, and health statistics that teachers can incorporate into their curriculum and instruction.

United States Historical Census Data Browser
http://fisher.lib.virginia.edu/census

Data and terminology from the historical census data browser are organized and presented in this website to examine the U.S. census of population and housing.

UNIT 3: Establish Community and Context

National Black Child Development Institute
www.nbcdi.org

Resources for improving the quality of life for African American children through public education programs are provided at this site.

United Nations
www.un.org/en/documents/udhr

Here you will find information and links to resources and publications related to the United Nations with emphases on human rights, peace and security, development, humanitarian affairs, and international law.

United States Census Bureau and Poverty
www.census.gov/hhes/www/poverty/poverty.html

This website provides an overview, news, publications, definitions, descriptions, resources, and access to information related to poverty, issues associated with poverty, and the measurement of poverty in the United States.

United States Citizenship and Immigration Services
www.uscis.gov/portal/site/uscis

Information and links related to citizenship and immigration are provided at this website, including a general overview, services and benefits, immigration forms, laws and regulations, along with education and resources.

United States Department of Health and Human Services
www.hhs.gov/specificpopulations

Here you will find information and resources related to protecting the health of all Americans, offering insights for families and teachers related to prevention of diseases, and regulations with connections to grants, funding, and jobs.

United States Department of Justice
www.usdoj.gov/

Information and resources related to the DOJ are found here with information, archives, policies, and accessibility featured.

United States Equal Employment Opportunity Commission
www.eeoc.gov/types/race.html

An extensive collection of information related to race and race relations in the United States is located at this website including the law, areas of discrimination, concerns with compliance, and recorded statistics.

United States Immigration and Customs
www.ice.gov

The immigration and customs enforcement website contains information and links to resources related to protective services, intelligence, international affairs, and border enforcement, including news, programs, and careers.

UNIT 4: Seek and Engage Collaboration and Construction

International Programs Center (IPC)
www.census.gov/ipc/www/

Census data about the countries of the world (beginning in 1945) with additional resources are provided at this site. Demographic and sociological studies can be accessed.

Native American Facts for Kids
www.native-languages.org/kids.htm

This nonprofit organization works to preserve and promote American Indian languages with information and resources readily available for students and teachers about all American Indian tribes.

PBS: Biracial American Portraits
www.pbs.org/wgbh/pages/frontline/shows/secret/portraits

A subsection of the PBS website, here you will find descriptions and discussions related to biracial populations and cultural interactions appropriate for students and teachers. A link for searching one's family tree is featured.

Urban Education Institute
http://uei.uchicago.edu

A resource related to urban education, this website offers information and links to research and practices to reach and teach all children.

UNIT 5: Spark Conversations and Climate

American Psychological Association
www.apa.org/topics/homepage.html

Organizational information, writing guidelines, psychology topics, and research publications can be accessed at this website to inform students, teachers, administrators, parents, and professors.

Center for Global Development
www.cgdev.org/section/initiatives/_active/globalizationandinequality?gcl id=CKTYxrGWxJoCFRufnAodY1Q8sg

This website offers independent research and practical ideas for global prosperity with links to initials, research topics, publications, opinions, events, experts, and blogs.

North American Reggio Emilia Alliance
www.reggioalliance.org

Here you will find information and resources dedicated to the education and well-being of young children (up to age 6) with links to professional development and international networks.

United States Department of Education, Office of English Language Acquisition
www.ed.gov/about/offices/list/oela/index.html

This website is created to fulfill two missions: to provide national leadership (1) to help ensure that English language learners and immigrant students attain English proficiency and achieve academically and (2) to assist in building the nation's capacity in critical foreign languages with resources for students, parents, teachers, and school administrators.

UNESCO
http://unescostat.unesco.org

Themes, highlights, surveys, and statistics are featured on this website from the United Nations Organization for Education, Science, and Culture equipping educators with facts and policies.

Internet References

United States Government
www.firstgov.gov

This government-sponsored website provides news, resources, and services for all aspects of the United States government appropriate for all teachers, learners, businesses, employees, and visitors.

UNIT 6: Strengthen and Weave Together Complexities and Controversies

Association for Moral Education
www.amenetwork.org

This website provides an interdisciplinary forum for professionals interested in the moral dimensions of educational theory and practice with links for education, grants, publications, and conferences.

Center for Social Justice
http://csj.georgetown.edu

Located at Georgetown University in Washington, DC, this site offers information and support related to infusing social justice in all research, teaching, and service.

Human Rights Watch
www.hrw.org/

Focused on international events, this website provides news, publications, and multimedia related to ensuring human rights around the world.

Hunger and World Poverty
www.poverty.com

This site connects poverty and hunger as global challenges by linking the concerns with diseases that impact everyone internationally.

UNIT 7: Waken Compassion and Commitment

Education World
www.education-world.com

This website connects the reader to seemingly endless resources related to teaching, learning, and schooling more effectively and efficiently.

Infonation
www.un.org/Pubs/CyberSchoolBus/infonation/e_infonation.htm

Here you will find information related to developing curriculum and building community in the classroom with respect for multicultural education.

National Association of Social Workers
www.socialworkers.org/pressroom/features/issue/peace.asp

To promote social justice in schools and classrooms, this website extends the knowledge, skills, and dispositions from the field of social work into education to guide teachers, administrators, families, and professors.

UNIT 8: Nurture and Welcome Challenges and Changes

Centers for Disease Control and Prevention/National Center for Health Statistics
www.cdc.gov/nchswww

This site provides an extensive examination of the health of the U.S. population, noting changes over time and the impact their knowledge, practices, and attitudes make on the world.

Demographic and Healthy Surveys
www.measuredhs.com

Here you will find quality information about the world's population and health situations with data reported from residents in more than 75 countries.

State of the World's Children
www.unicef.org/apublic

Well-known to many educators, UNICEF is an organization that provides goods and services for less fortunate children around the world. From this site, the reader can review past endeavors as well as view current enterprises and future efforts.

The World Bank
http://web.worldbank.org

Look here to find insightful data describing the wealth indices from more than 186 countries with financial and technical assistance for third-world countries. This organization is made up of two groups: the International Bank for Reconstruction and Development (IBRD) and the International Development Association (IDA) collaborating to advance the vision of inclusive and sustainable globalization.

UNIT 1

Notice Cultures and Cultural Characteristics

Unit Selections

Learning Outcomes

After reading this unit, you will be able to:

• Describe today's world citizens, their cultural characteristics, and the interconnectedness of issues.

• Expound on global trends that impact all of the world's citizens.

• Explain race relations in the United States and how "color blindness" impacts everyone.

• Detail biracial identity and the practices that support biracial students.

• Discuss international migration patterns and the challenges immigrants to the United States face.

• Review ways teachers prepare themselves and today's youth to be culturally competent.

Student Website

www.mhhe.com/cls

Internet References

The Big Religion Chart
www.religionfacts.com/big_religion_chart.htm
Census Data
www.census.gov
Census Bureau; International Data Base (IDB)
www.census.gov/ipc/www/idb
Major Religions of the World
www.adherents.com/Religions_By_Adherents.html
Statistical Abstract of the United States
www.census.gov/compendia/statab
Tribal Government Information
www.usa.gov/Government/Tribal.shtm

Many years ago, similar types of people could be described as a particular group of individuals living in an isolated geographic location, speaking their own language, maintaining a unique way of life, and sharing a specific collection of characteristics, qualities, and beliefs. Long before modern inventions impacting transportation and communication were developed and distributed, people were known primarily for their geography, both physical and cultural. Groups created their own language and lifestyles that became their culture and how they were identified. However, far too often, groups of people did not interact cooperatively with one another; frequently, their clashes were based more on their perceptions and fears rather than on the realities and facts. People's perceptions were founded on actual or perceived barriers associated with control, power, and privilege. People around the world would focus more on their differences and dominance rather than their similarities and support.

Over time, many of the people of the world have changed. Today's world has become much more interconnected through technological advancements and cultural concerns. All kinds of people live, work, and play in all kinds of places, and people frequently move in search of new and better opportunities for themselves and their families. Individuals often travel near and far for business and pleasure. Through film and television, we see people, places, and events from the past, the present, and projected into the future at our fingertips and from multiple perspectives. Thanks to the Internet, people communicate instantly with one another all around the world. Some people say that the world is a smaller place due to technological advances. Perhaps the world seems like a smaller place because there are more people sharing the space and we are quickly realizing the importance of cooperating with one another for the future of people and the perils of the planet.

The paradox becomes evident that while most people want to maintain their special characteristics, qualities, and beliefs that allow them to bond with other people with similar characteristics, qualities, and beliefs, most people also want to live in harmony with and show respect for people whom they consider different from themselves. However, given the prevalent historical influences associated with our (mis)perceptions for not trusting or honoring one another based on our perceptions of our differences rather than the realities of our similarities, relationships within and among classrooms, schools, neighborhoods, regions, and countries continue to challenge the citizens of the world.

This societal dilemma is complicated by two vital factors: (1) Groups of people no longer share all aspects of their once-common historical identities, and (2) many people no longer want to be identified solely by their perceived historical identifications. As people have migrated, the world has become a multiracial, multiethnic, multilingual, multireligious, multi-interest . . .

© Thinkstock Images / JupiterImages

multicultural society. Many people are comfortable wherever they are, and they want to help everyone to understand and appreciate one another for the sake of all humans and the Earth. Coexistence has become more than a philosophy; it has become a pathway through life and all aspects of life.

Today's world involves a vibrant society seeking information about everyone, everywhere, and everything. People around the world want equal access and unlimited opportunities to fulfill their lives. Classroom teachers and school administrators serve as the gatekeepers who can open (limit or close) the gates of information, access, and opportunity to the young people and students of today in their journeys in their preparation to be the adults and leaders of tomorrow. Through their messages and modeling, teachers guide and empower their students to ask meaningful questions, search for assorted answers, and try various approaches for expressing learning and experiencing living. When teachers introduce their students to a range of possibilities, they equip their students with tools for life. Their students experience multiple views and multicultural education for themselves; and students' new perceptions become the realities that transform their sense of cultural competence and coexistence.

The articles in Unit 1 introduce the reader to notice culture and cultural characteristics. Readers should begin to recognize and accept all students with respect for their individual and shared cultural characteristics; provide all students with information, access, and opportunities to learn more about themselves, one another, and society in the context of culture; and ensure that all learning connects with individual academic and cultural backgrounds. Additionally, readers should be learning more about their own individual cultural characteristics and about the cultural characteristics of the students and families in their school communities.

Becoming Citizens of the World

The future is here. It's multiethnic, multicultural, and multilingual. But are students ready for it?

VIVIEN STEWART

The world into which today's high school students will graduate is fundamentally different from the one in which many of us grew up. We're increasingly living in a globalized society that has a whole new set of challenges. Four trends have brought us here.

The first trend is economic. The globalization of economies and the rise of Asia are central facts of the early 21st century. Since 1990, 3 billion people in China, India, and the former Soviet Union have moved from closed economies into a global one. The economies of China, India, and Japan, which represented 18 percent of the world's gross domestic product (GDP) in 2004, are expected to represent 50 percent of the world's GDP within 30 years (Wilson, 2005). One in five U.S. jobs is now tied to international trade, a proportion that will continue to increase (U.S. Census Bureau, 2004). Moreover, most U.S. companies expect the majority of their growth to be in overseas markets, which means they will increasingly require a workforce with international competence. According to the Committee for Economic Development (2006),

> To compete successfully in the global marketplace, both U.S.-based multinational corporations as well as small businesses increasingly need employees with knowledge of foreign languages and cultures to market products to customers around the globe and to work effectively with foreign employees and partners in other countries.

Science and technology are changing the world and represent a second trend. In *The World Is Flat,* Thomas Friedman (2005) describes how the "wiring of the world" and the digitization of production since 1998 are making it possible for people to do increasing amounts of work anywhere and anytime. Global production teams are becoming commonplace in business. In addition, scientific research, a key driver of innovation, will increasingly be conducted by international teams as other countries ramp-up their scientific capacity.

The third trend involves health and security matters. Every major issue that people face—from environmental degradation and global warming, to pandemic diseases, to energy and water shortages, to terrorism and weapons proliferation—has

an international dimension. Solving these problems will require international cooperation among governments, professional organizations, and corporations. Also, as the line between domestic and international affairs blurs, U.S. citizens will increasingly vote and act on issues—such as alternative energy sources or security measures linked to terrorism—that require a greater knowledge of the world. In response to this need, a 2006 report from the National Association of State Boards of Education recommends infusing classroom instruction with a strong global perspective and incorporating discussions of current local, national, and international issues and events.

The fourth trend is changing demographics. Globalization has accelerated international migration. New immigrants from such regions as Asia and Central and South America are generating a diversity in U.S. communities that mirrors the diversity of the world. Knowledge of other cultures will help students understand and respect classmates from different countries and will promote effective leadership abroad.

In short, U.S. high school graduates will

- Sell to the world.
- Buy from the world.
- Work for international companies.
- Manage employees from other cultures and countries.
- Collaborate with people all over the world in joint ventures.
- Compete with people on the other side of the world for jobs and markets.
- Tackle global problems, such as AIDS, avian flu, pollution, and disaster recovery (Center for International Understanding, 2005).

However, U.S. schools are not adequately preparing students for these challenges. Surveys conducted by the Asia Society (2002) and National Geographic-Roper (2002) indicated that, compared with students in nine other industrialized countries, U.S. students lack knowledge of world geography, history, and current events. And shockingly few U.S. students learn languages that large numbers of people speak, such as Chinese (1.3 billion speakers) and Arabic (246 million speakers).

Many countries in Europe and Asia are preparing their students for the global age by raising their levels of education attainment; emphasizing international knowledge, skills, and language acquisition; and fostering respect for other cultures. The United States must create its own education response to globalization, which should include raising standards, increasing high school and college graduation rates, and modernizing and internationalizing the curriculum.

What Global Competence Looks Like

The new skill set that students will need goes well beyond the United States' current focus on the basics and on math, science, and technology. These skills are necessary, of course, but to be successful global citizens, workers, and leaders, students will need to be knowledgeable about the world, be able to communicate in languages other than English, and be informed and active citizens.

World Knowledge

Teaching about the rest of the world in U.S. schools has often focused on the superficial: food, fun, and festivals. Today, we need deeper knowledge, such as understanding significant global trends in science and technology, how regions and cultures have developed and how they interconnect, and how international trade and the global economy work. For example, students might consider how increasing the supply of fresh water or changing forms of energy use in one country could have major effects on another country.

In a world in which knowledge is changing rapidly and technology is providing access to vast amounts of information, our challenge is not merely to give students more facts about geography, customs, or particular conflicts. Rather, our challenge is to hone students' critical-thinking skills and to familiarize students with key concepts that they can apply to new situations. In this way, they can make sense of the explosion of information from different sources around the world and put factual information into perspective and context. Only then can this information become meaningful.

Teaching students about the world is not a subject in itself, separate from other content areas, but should be an integral part of *all* subjects taught. We need to open global gateways and inspire students to explore beyond their national borders. Programs like iLEARN and Global Learning and Observations to Benefit the Environment (GLOBE) make it possible for students to work collaboratively with peers in other countries. School-to-school partnerships enable both real and virtual exchanges.

U.S. students are global teenagers, similar in many ways to their technology-enabled peers around the world. Adding an international dimension to subjects and encouraging students to reach out to peers in other countries are powerful ways to make the curriculum relevant and engaging to today's youth.

Language Skills

Only about one-half of U.S. high school students study a foreign language. The majority never go beyond the introductory level, and 70 percent study Spanish (Draper & Hicks, 2002). This results in a serious lack of capacity in such languages as Arabic and Chinese, both of which are crucial to the prosperity and security of the United States.

The United States should do as other industrialized countries in Europe and Asia do—start offering foreign languages in the elementary grades, where research has shown that language learning is most effective (Pufahl, Rhodes, & Christian, 2001), and continue the emphasis in secondary school to create pipelines of proficient language speakers. U.S. students need opportunities to learn a broader range of languages, as in Australia, where 25 percent of students now learn an Asian language (Asia Society, 2002). Heritage communities in the United States—communities in which a non-English language is spoken at home, such as Spanish or Navajo—provide rich sources of teachers, students, and cultural experiences (National Language Conference, 2005). Specific practices, such as immersion experiences, can greatly enhance language proficiency.

> **As the line between domestic and international affairs blurs, U.S. citizens will increasingly vote and act on issues that require a greater knowledge of the world.**

The growing interest in learning Chinese, as shown by the fact that 2,400 U.S. high schools expressed interest in offering the new advanced placement course in Mandarin, suggests that parents and teachers are realizing the importance of communication skills in a multilingual, multicultural world (see www.AskAsia.org/Chinese). Even if graduates don't use a second language at work, quite possibly they will work in cross-cultural teams and environments.

Civic Values

U.S. students need to extend traditional American values into the global arena. These include a concern for human rights and respect for cultures that differ from the United States. By learning to understand other perspectives, students can develop critical-thinking skills and enhance their creativity.

Students should focus on becoming active and engaged citizens in both their local and global environments. Schools can promote civic engagement by weaving discussions of current events throughout the school day and through participatory forms of education, such as Model UN or the Capitol Forum on America's Future, in which high school students voice their opinions on current international issues. Schools should use technology to connect students directly to peers in other parts of the world and promote service learning projects on issues that students can address at both the local and international levels, such as alleviating hunger, providing education support to students in poverty, and improving the environment.

What Schools Can Do

Across the United States, many schools already define their mission as producing students who are prepared for work, citizenship, and leadership in the global era. These schools have found that internationalizing the curriculum creates a more exciting environment for students and teachers alike (Bell-Rose & Desai, 2005). Several approaches have proven successful.

Have a large vision of what you want to achieve, but start slowly, one course or grade level at a time.

Introducing an international studies requirement for graduation. More than a decade ago, the school board of Evanston Township, Illinois, introduced an international studies requirement for graduation and asked the high school's teachers to develop the necessary courses. Now, every sophomore in this diverse Chicago suburb must complete the one-year international studies requirement. Students choose from a series of in-depth humanities courses on the history, literature, and art of Asia, Africa, Latin America, and the Middle East. Simulations and participatory projects are central to instruction, and partnerships with local universities ensure that teachers have ongoing professional development in international affairs.

Creating an elementary school immersion program. After surveying parents and local businesses about the future needs of the community—they cited skills in English, Spanish, and Japanese as important—Seattle public schools created the John Stanford International School, a public elementary bilingual immersion school. Students spend half the day studying math, science, culture, and literacy in either Japanese or Spanish; they spend the other half of the day learning reading, writing, and social studies in English. The school also offers English as a second language courses for immigrant students and after-school courses for their parents. As a result of the school's success, the city of Seattle has recently decided to open 10 more internationally oriented schools.

Developing international schools-within-schools. The Eugene International High School is a school-within-a-school on four high school campuses in Eugene, Oregon. The school is open to all interested students. The four-year sequence of courses centers thematically on culture, history, and the political, economic, and belief systems of different world regions, such as Asia, Africa, the Middle East, and Latin America. The school also emphasizes independent research courses to give students the tools to address global issues. An extended essay and a community-service requirement in 11th and 12th grade both have an international focus. For example, one student wrote a 4,000-word research essay on hydrogen cars and their place in the world economy. Students volunteer at such places as Centro Latino Americano, University of Oregon International Education and Exchange, and Holt International Children's Services. Finally, students have the option of pursuing the International Baccalaureate.

Teaching crucial language skills to prepare for the global economy. With strong support from Mayor Richard M. Daley, whose goal is to make Chicago a hub for international trade, the city has created the largest Chinese-language program in the United States. Twenty public schools teach Mandarin, from an all-black school on the West Side to a nearly all-Hispanic school on the South Side to more diverse schools throughout the city. For many of these students, Chinese is their third language after English and Spanish. The program resulted from partnerships among political, business, school, and community leaders and the Chinese Ministry of Education, which provides Chinese teachers and organizes a summer cultural program for Chicago educators in China.

Redesigning urban secondary schools with an international focus. Using the International High School of the Americas in San Antonio, Texas, and the Metropolitan Learning Center in Hartford, Connecticut, as anchor schools, the Asia Society has created a network of small, internationally themed secondary schools across the United States (see www.international studiesschools.org/). The mission of each school is to prepare low-income students for college and to promote their knowledge of world regions and international issues. Each public or charter school incorporates international content across the curriculum, offers both Asian and European languages, provides international exchange opportunities, and provides links to international organizations and community-service opportunities. To date, 10 schools have opened in New York City; Los Angeles; Charlotte, North Carolina; Denver, Colorado; and Houston, Texas. Additional schools are slated to open in other locations, such as Mathis and Austin, Texas, and Philadelphia, Pennsylvania.

Using student-faculty exchanges to promote curriculum change. Two public high schools in Newton, Massachusetts—Newton North and Newton South—run an exchange program with the Jingshan School in Beijing, China. Created by two teachers in 1979, the exchange enables U.S. and Chinese teachers and students to spend time in one another's schools every year. The program has served as a catalyst for districtwide curriculum change, bringing the study of Asian cultures into various academic disciplines, from social studies to science, and adding Chinese to the district's broad array of language options. The leaders of this exchange now help schools around the United States develop exchange programs with China as a way to internationalize their curriculums.

Using a K–12 foreign language sequence to promote excellence. The Glastonbury School District in Connecticut has long promoted language study, beginning with a K–8 language requirement. Ninety-three percent of students study at least one foreign language, and 30 percent study more than one. The foreign language curriculum is thematic and interdisciplinary, integrating both foreign language and world history standards. All high school students take a one-semester history course on a non-Western geographic/cultural region and a civics/current issues course that includes international content. The school district's reputation for languages and international studies is a major draw for families moving to the area.

These and other pioneering schools offer models that all schools can replicate. What are the lessons learned? Have a large vision of what you want to achieve, but start slowly, one course or grade level at a time. Involve parents as well as business and community leaders in planning and supporting international education and world languages. Focus on professional development for teachers, including partnerships with local colleges, so teachers can broaden and deepen their international knowledge. Include a focus on mastery of languages, including nontraditional languages, and start at the lowest grade levels possible. Use international exchanges, both real and virtual, to enable students to gain firsthand knowledge of the culture they are studying. If it is unfeasible for students to travel, try technology-based alternatives, such as classroom-to-classroom linkages, global science projects, and videoconferences (Sachar, 2004).

What Policymakers Can Do

Recognizing that future economic development and jobs in their states will be linked to success in the global economy, many states are developing innovations to promote international knowledge and skills. Nineteen states have been working together through the Asia Society's States Network on International Education in the Schools. States have developed commissions (North Carolina, Vermont); statewide summits (Delaware, Indiana, Massachusetts, Washington); and reports to assess the status of international education in their state (North Carolina, New Jersey, Wisconsin, West Virginia). They have created mechanisms, such as International or Global Education Councils (Ohio, Indiana, Wisconsin), and appointed International Education Coordinators to develop new policies and action plans (Delaware, Indiana, Ohio, New Jersey, Wisconsin). They are revising standards (Delaware, Idaho) or high school graduation requirements (New Mexico, Virginia) to incorporate international content. Some states are offering professional development (Oklahoma); initiating new language programs (Connecticut, Delaware, Illinois, Minnesota, Wisconsin, Wyoming); engaging in school exchanges with China (Connecticut, Massachusetts); adding crucial foreign language courses to their virtual high schools (Kentucky); and adding an international dimension to science, technology, engineering, and math (STEM) schools (Ohio, Texas). Finally, some (Arizona, Massachusetts, North Carolina, Washington) have introduced state legislation to provide additional funds to incorporate a global dimension into their schools (see http://Internationaled.org/states).

Many states recognize that future economic development and jobs in their states will be linked to success in the global economy.

In 2006, the National Governors Association held a session on International Education at its annual meeting. In addition, the Council of Chief State School Officers recently adopted a new policy statement on global education (2007). These state efforts are a good start, but the United States has yet to make international knowledge and skills a policy priority on the federal level and develop the systems and supports necessary to get high-quality international content into U.S. classrooms.

States need to pursue four policy goals to make this happen. They should

- Redesign high schools and create new graduation requirements to motivate higher achievement and promote important international knowledge and key skills.
- Expand teacher training to deliver rigorous study in world history and cultures, economics, world regions, and global challenges.
- Develop world language pipelines from primary school to college that focus on crucial languages, such as Chinese, and that address the acute shortage of language teachers.
- Use technology in innovative ways to expand the availability of international courses and ensure that every school in the United States has an ongoing virtual link to schools in other countries.

For almost 50 years, the U.S. government has played a crucial role in fostering foreign languages and international education in *higher* education. We need to extend this commitment to K–12 education and make it an urgent priority. By doing so, we can improve students' international knowledge and skills and increase both the competitive edge and security of the United States.

In his 2006 report, *The Economics of Knowledge: Why Education Is Key for Europe's Success*, Andreas Schleicher from the Organisation for Economic Cooperation and Development wrote,

The world is indifferent to tradition and past reputations, unforgiving of frailty and ignorant of custom or practice. Success will go to those individuals and countries which are swift to adapt, slow to complain, and open to change.

Part of the great strength of the United States is its adaptability. U.S. schools adapted to the agrarian age, then to the industrial age. It's time to open to change once more and adapt to the global age.

References

Asia Society. (2002). *States institute on international education in the schools: Institute report, November* 20–22, 2002. New York: Author.

Bell-Rose, S., & Desai, V. N. (2005). *Educating leaders for a global society.* New York: Goldman Sachs Foundation.

Center for International Understanding. (2005). *North Carolina in the world: A plan to increase student knowledge and skills about the world.* Raleigh, NC: Author.

Committee for Economic Development. (2006). *Education for global leadership: The importance of international studies and foreign language education for U.S. economic and national security.* Washington, DC: Author. Available: www.ced.org/docs/report/report_foreignlanguages.pdf

Council of Chief State School Officers. (2007). *Global education policy statement.* Washington, DC: Author. Available: www .ccsso.org/projects/International_Education/Global_Education_ Policy_Statement/

Draper, J. B., & Hicks, J. H. (2002). *Foreign language enrollments in secondary schools, fall 2000.* Washington, DC: American Council on the Teaching of Foreign Languages. Available: http:// actfl.org/files/public/Enroll2000.pdf

Friedman, T. L. (2005). *The world is flat: A brief history of the twenty-first century.* New York: Farrar, Straus, and Giroux.

National Association of State Boards of Education. (2006). *Citizens for the 21st century: Revitalizing the civic mission of schools.* Alexandria, VA: Author. Available: www.nasbe .org/publications/Civic_Ed/civic_ed.html

National Geographic-Roper. (2002). *2002 global geographic literacy survey.* Washington, DC: Author.

National Language Conference. (2005). *A call to action for national foreign language capabilities.* Washington, DC: Author. Available: www.nlconference.org/docs/White_Paper.pdf

Pufahl, I., Rhodes, N. C., & Christian, N. (2001). *What we can learn from foreign language teaching in other countries.* Washington, DC: Center for Applied Linguistics.

Sachar, E. (2004). *Schools for the global age: Promising practices in international education.* New York: Asia Society.

Schleicher, A. (2006). *The economics of knowledge: Why education is key for Europe's success.* Brussels: Lisbon Council. Available: www.oecd.org/dataoecd/43/11/36278531.pdf

U.S. Census Bureau. (2004). Table 2. In *Exports from manufacturing establishments: 2001* (p. 8). Washington, DC: U.S. Department of Commerce.

Wilson, W. T. (2005). *The dawn of the India century: Why India is poised to challenge China and the United States for global economic hegemony in the 21st century.* Chicago: Keystone India. Available: www.keystone-india.com/pdfs/The%20 India%20Century.pdf

Critical Thinking

1. What does global competence look like?

2. How can schools internationalize the curriculum?

3. What else can policymakers do?

4. Why is it critical to help today's students to become citizens of the world?

VIVIEN STEWART is Vice President, Education, at the Asia Society, 725 Park Ave., New York, New York, 10021; vstewart@asiasoc.org.

Colorblind to the Reality of Race in America

Ian F. Haney López

How will race as a social practice evolve in the United States over the next few decades? The American public, and indeed many scholars, increasingly believe that the country is leaving race and racism behind. Some credit Brown v. Board of Education, the revered 1954 U.S. Supreme Court decision pronouncing segregated schools unequal, and the broad civil-rights movement of which the decision was a part, with turning the nation away from segregation and toward equality. Others point to changing demographics, emphasizing the rising number of mixed-race marriages and the increasing Asian and Hispanic populations that are blurring the historic black-white divide.

My sense of our racial future differs. Not only do I fear that race will continue to fundamentally skew American society over the coming decades, but I worry that the belief in the diminished salience of race makes that more likely rather than less. I suspect that the laws supposedly protecting against racial discrimination are partly to blame, for they no longer contribute to racial justice but instead legitimate continued inequality. We find ourselves now in the midst of a racial era marked by what I term "colorblind white dominance," in which a public consensus committed to formal antiracism deters effective remediation of racial inequality, protecting the racial status quo while insulating new forms of racism and xenophobia.

The Jefferson County school district, in Kentucky, covers Louisville and surrounding suburbs. A target of decades of litigation to eradicate Jim Crow school segregation and its vestiges, the district has since 2001 voluntarily pursued efforts to maintain what is now one of the most integrated school systems in the country. But not everyone supports those efforts, especially when they involve taking race into consideration in pupil assignments. In 2004 a white lawyer named Teddy B. Gordon ran for a seat on the Jefferson County School Board, promising to end endeavors to maintain integrated schools. He finished dead last, behind three other candidates. Indifferent to public repudiation, he is back—this time in the courtroom. Gordon's argument is seductively simple: Brown forbids all governmental uses of race, even if designed to achieve or maintain an integrated society.

He has already lost at the trial level and before an appellate court, as have two other sets of plaintiffs challenging similar integration-preserving efforts by school districts in Seattle and in Lynn, Mass. But Gordon and the conservative think tanks and advocacy groups that back him, including the self-styled Center for Equal Opportunity, are not without hope. To begin with, over the past three decades the courts have come ever closer to fully embracing a colorblind Constitution—colorblind in the sense of disfavoring all uses of race, irrespective of whether they are intended to perpetuate or ameliorate racial oppression. More immediately, last June the Supreme Court voted to review the Louisville and Seattle cases—Meredith v. Jefferson County Board of Education and Parents Involved in Community Schools v. Seattle School District.

Roger Clegg, president and general counsel of the Center for Equal Opportunity, is thrilled. As he gleefully noted in *The National Review,* there's an old saw that the court does not hear cases it plans to affirm. The Bush administration, too, supports Gordon and his efforts. The U.S. solicitor general recently submitted a friend-of-the-court brief urging the justices to prevent school districts across the country from paying attention to race.

At issue is a legally backed ideology of colorblindness that could have implications beyond schools—for higher education and the wider society. Yes, in a narrowly tailored decision three years ago, the Supreme Court allowed the University of Michigan to consider race as one factor in law-school admissions. But since then, conservative advocacy groups have used the threat of lawsuits to intimidate many institutions into halting race-based college financial-aid and orientation programs, as well as graduate stipends and fellowships, and those groups are now taking aim at faculty hiring procedures. This month Michigan voters will decide whether to amend the state constitution to ban racial and gender preferences wherever practiced. And looming on the horizon are renewed efforts to enact legislation forbidding the federal and state governments from collecting statistics that track racial disparities, efforts that are themselves part of a broader campaign to expunge race from the national vocabulary.

Gordon predicts that if he prevails, Louisville schools will rapidly resegregate. He is sanguine about the prospect. "We're a diverse society, a multiethnic society, a colorblind society," he told *The New York Times.* "Race is history."

But the past is never really past, especially not when one talks about race and the law in the United States. We remain a racially stratified country, though for some that constitutes an argument for rather than against colorblindness. Given the long and sorry history of racial subordination, there is tremendous rhetorical appeal to Justice John Marshall Harlan's famous dissent in Plessy v. Ferguson, the 1896 case upholding segregated railway cars: "Our Constitution is color-blind, and neither knows nor tolerates classes among citizens."

Contemporary proponents of colorblindness almost invariably draw a straight line from that dissent to their own impassioned advocacy for being blind to race today. But in doing so, partisans excise Harlan's acknowledgment of white superiority in the very paragraph in which he extolled colorblindness: "The white race deems itself to be the dominant race in this country. And so it is, in prestige, in achievements, in education, in wealth and in power. So, I doubt not, it will continue to be for all time." That omission obscures a more significant elision: Harlan objected not to all governmental uses of race, but to those he thought would unduly oppress black people.

As viewed by Harlan and the court, the central question was where to place limits on government support for the separation of racial groups that were understood to be unequal by nature (hence Harlan's comfortable endorsement of white superiority). He and the majority agreed that the state could enforce racial separation in the "social" but not in the "civil" arenas; they differed on the contours of the spheres. Harlan believed that segregated train cars limited the capacity of black people to participate as full citizens in civic life, while the majority saw such segregation only as a regulation of social relations sanctioned by custom. The scope of the civil arena mattered so greatly precisely because state exclusions from public life threatened to once again reduce the recently emancipated to an inferior caste defined by law.

For the first half of the 20th century, colorblindness represented the radical and wholly unrealized aspiration of dismantling de jure racial subordination. Thus Thurgood Marshall, as counsel to the National Association for the Advancement of Colored People in the late 1940s and early 1950s, cited Harlan's celebration of colorblindness to argue that racial distinctions are "contrary to our Constitution and laws." But neither society nor the courts embraced colorblindness when doing so might have sped the demise of white supremacy. Even during the civil-rights era, colorblindness as a strategy for racial emancipation did not take hold. Congress and the courts dismantled Jim Crow segregation and proscribed egregious forms of private discrimination in a piecemeal manner, banning only the most noxious misuses of race, not any reference to race whatsoever.

In the wake of the civil-rights movement's limited but significant triumphs, the relationship between colorblindness and racial reform changed markedly. The greatest potency of colorblindness came to lie in preserving, rather than challenging, the racial status quo. When the end of explicit race-based subordination did not eradicate stubborn racial inequalities, progressives increasingly recognized the need for state and private actors to intervene along racial lines. Rather than call for colorblindness, they began to insist on the need for affirmative race-conscious remedies. In that new context, colorblindness appealed to those opposing racial integration. Enshrouded with the moral raiment of the civil-rights movement, colorblindness provided cover for opposition to racial reform.

Within a year of Brown, Southern school districts and courts had recognized that they could forestall integration by insisting that the Constitution allowed them to use only "race neutral" means to end segregation—school-choice plans that predictably produced virtually no integration whatsoever. In 1965 a federal court in South Carolina put it squarely: "The Constitution is color-blind; it should no more be violated to attempt integration than to preserve segregation."

Wielding the ideal of colorblindness as a sword, in the past three decades racial conservatives on the Supreme Court have increasingly refought the battles lost during the civil-rights era, cutting back on protections against racial discrimination as well as severely limiting race-conscious remedies. In several cases in the 1970s—including North Carolina State Board of Education v. Swann, upholding school-assignment plans, and Regents of the University of California v. Bakke—the court ruled that the need to redress the legacy of segregation made strict colorblindness impossible. But as the 1980s went on, in other cases—McCleskey v. Kemp, which upheld Georgia's death penalty despite uncontroverted statistical evidence that African-Americans convicted of murder were 22 times as likely to be sentenced to death if their victims were white rather than black, and City of Richmond v. Croson, which rejected a city affirmative-action program steering some construction dollars to minority-owned companies despite the fact that otherwise only two-thirds of 1 percent of city contracts went to minority companies in a city 50 percent African-American—the court presented race as a phenomenon called into existence just when someone employed a racial term. Discrimination existed only but every time someone used racial language. Thus the court found no harm in Georgia's penal system, because no evidence surfaced of a specific bad actor muttering racial epithets, while it espied racism in Richmond's affirmative-action program because it set aside contracts for "minorities."

That approach ignores the continuing power of race as a society-altering category. The civil-rights movement changed the racial zeitgeist of the nation by rendering illegitimate all explicit invocations of white supremacy, a shift that surely marked an important step toward a more egalitarian society. But it did not bring into actual existence that ideal, as white people remain dominant across virtually every social, political, and economic domain. In 2003 the poverty rate was 24 percent among African-Americans, 23 percent among Latinos, and 8 percent among white people. That same year, an estimated 20 percent of African-Americans and 33 percent of Latinos had no health insurance, while 11 percent of white people were uninsured. Discrepancies in incarceration rates are particularly staggering, with African-American men vastly more likely to spend time in prison than white men are.

Or forget the numbers and recall for a moment the graphic parade of images from Hurricane Katrina. Or consider access to country clubs and gated communities, in-group preferences for jobs and housing, the moral certainty shared by many white folks regarding their civic belonging and fundamental goodness. Or, to tie back to Louisville, reflect on what you already know about the vast, racially correlated disparities in resources available to public (and still more to private) schools across the country. Racial dominance by white people continues as a central element of our society.

What may be changing, however, is how membership in the white group is defined. The term "white" has a far more complicated—and fluid—history in the United States than people commonly recognize. For most of our history, whiteness stood in contrast to the nonwhite identities imposed upon Africans, American Indians, Mexican peoples of the Southwest, and Asian immigrants, marking one pole in the racial hierarchy. Simultaneously, however, putative "racial" divisions separated Europeans, so that in the United States presumptions of gross racial inferiority were removed from Germans only in the 1840s through 1860s, the Irish in the 1850s through 1880s, and Eastern and Southern Europeans in the 1900s to 1920s. The melding of various European groups into the monolithic, undifferentiated "white" category we recognize today is a recent innovation, only fully consolidated in the mid-20th century. Now white identity may be expanding to include persons and groups with ancestors far beyond Europe.

Perhaps we should distinguish here among three sorts of white identity. Consider first persons who are "fully white," in the sense that, with all of the racially relevant facts about them widely known, they would generally be considered white by the community at large. (Obviously, racial identity is a matter not of biology but of social understandings, although those may give great weight to purportedly salient differences in morphology and ancestry.) In contrast to that group, there have long been those "passing as white"—people whose physical appearance allowed them to claim a white identity when social custom would have assigned them to a nonwhite group had their ancestry been widely known. Of people of Irish and Jewish descent in the United States, for example, one might say that while initially some were able to pass as white, now all are fully white.

Today a new group is emerging, perhaps best described as "honorary whites." Apartheid South Africa first formally crafted this identity: Seeking to engage in trade and commerce with nations cast as inferior by apartheid logic, particularly Japan, South Africa extended to individuals from such countries the status of honorary white people, allowing them to travel, reside, relax, and conduct business in South African venues that were otherwise strictly "whites only." Persons who pass as white hide racially relevant parts of their identity; honorary whites are extended the status of whiteness despite the public recognition that, from a bioracial perspective, they are not fully white.

In the United States, honorary-white status seems increasingly to exist for certain people and groups. The quintessential example is certain Asian-Americans, particularly East Asians.

Although Asians have long been racialized as nonwhite as a matter of law and social practice, the model-minority myth and professional success have combined to free some Asian-Americans from the most pernicious negative beliefs regarding their racial character. In part this trend represents a shift toward a socially based, as opposed to biologically based, definition of race. Individuals and communities with the highest levels of acculturation, achievement, and wealth increasingly find themselves functioning as white, at least as measured by professional integration, residential patterns, and intermarriage rates.

Latinos also have access to honorary-white identity, although their situation differs from that of Asian-Americans. Unlike the latter, and also unlike African-Americans, Latinos in the United States have long been on the cusp between white and nonwhite. Despite pervasive and often violent racial prejudice against Mexicans in the Southwest and Puerto Ricans and other Hispanic groups elsewhere, the most elite Latin Americans in the United States have historically been accepted as fully white. With no clear identity under the continental theory of race (which at its most basic identifies blacks as from Africa, whites from Europe, reds from the Americas, and yellows from Asia), and with a tremendous range of somatic features marking this heterogeneous population, there has long been relatively more room for the use of social rather than strictly biological factors in the imputation of race to particular Hispanic individuals and groups.

It seems likely that an increasing number of Latinos—those who have fair features, material wealth, and high social status, aided also by Anglo surnames—will both claim and be accorded a position in U.S. society as fully white. Simultaneously, many more—similarly situated in terms of material and status position, but perhaps with slightly darker features or a surname or accent suggesting Latin-American origins—will become honorary whites. Meanwhile, the majority of Latinos will continue to be relegated to nonwhite categories.

The continuing evolution in who counts as white is neither particularly startling nor especially felicitous. Not only have racial categories and ideologies always mutated, but race has long turned on questions of wealth, professional attainment, and social position. A developing scholarship now impressively demonstrates that even during and immediately after slavery, at a time when racial identity in the United States was presumably most rigidly fixed in terms of biological difference and descent, and even in the hyperformal legal setting of the courtroom, determinations of racial identity often took place on the basis of social indicia like the nature of one's employment or one's choice of sexual partners.

Nor will categories like black, brown, white, yellow, and red soon disappear. Buttressed by the continued belief in continental racial divisions, physical features those divisions supposedly connote will remain foundational to racial classification. The stain of African ancestry—so central to the elaboration of race in the United States—ensures a persistent special stigma for black people. Honorary-white status will be available only to the most exceptional—and the most light-skinned—African-Americans,

9

and on terms far more restrictive than those on which whiteness will be extended to many Latinos and Asian-Americans.

Those many in our society who are darker, poorer, more identifiably foreign will continue to suffer the poverty, marginalization, immiseration, incarceration, and exclusion historically accorded to those whose skin and other features socially mark them as nonwhite. Even under a redefined white category, racial hierarchy will continue as the links are strengthened between nonwhite identity and social disadvantage on the one hand, and whiteness and privilege on the other. Under antebellum racial logic, those black people with the fairest features were sometimes described as "light, bright, and damn near white." If today we switch out "damn near" for "honorary" and fold in a few other minorities, how much has really changed?

In the face of continued racial hierarchy, it is crucial that we understand the colorblind ideology at issue in the school cases before the Supreme Court. "In the eyes of government, we are just one race here," Justice Antonin Scalia intoned in 1995. "It is American." That sentiment is stirring as an aspiration, but disheartening as a description of reality, and even more so as a prescription for racial policies. All persons of good will aspire to a society free from racial hierarchy. We should embrace colorblindness—in the sense of holding it up as an ideal. But however far the civil-rights struggle has moved us, we remain far from a racially egalitarian utopia.

In this context, the value of repudiating all governmental uses of race must depend on a demonstrated ability to remedy racial hierarchy. Colorblindness as a policy prescription merits neither fealty nor moral stature by virtue of the attractiveness of colorblindness as an ideal. In the hands of a Thurgood Marshall, who sought to end Jim Crow segregation and to foster an integrated society, colorblindness was a transformative, progressive practice. But when Teddy Gordon, Roger Clegg, the Bush administration, and the conservative justices on the Supreme Court call for banning governmental uses of race, they aim to end the efforts of local majorities to respond constructively to racial inequality. In so doing, they are making their version of colorblindness a reactionary doctrine.

Contemporary colorblindness is a set of understandings—buttressed by law and the courts, and reinforcing racial patterns of white dominance—that define how people comprehend, rationalize, and act on race. As applied, however much some people genuinely believe that the best way to get beyond racism is to get beyond race, colorblindness continues to retard racial progress. It does so for a simple reason: It focuses on the surface, on the bare fact of racial classification, rather than looking down into the nature of social practices. It gets racism and racial remediation exactly backward, and insulates new forms of race baiting.

White dominance continues with few open appeals to race. Consider the harms wrought by segregated schools today. Schools in predominantly white suburbs are far more likely to have adequate buildings, teachers, and books, while the schools serving mainly minority children are more commonly underfinanced, unsafe, and in a state of disrepair. Such harms acccumulate, encouraging white flight to avoid the expected deterioration in schools and the violence that is supposedly second nature to "them," only to precipitate the collapse in the tax base that in fact ensures a decline not only in schools but also in a range of social services. Such material differences in turn buttress seemingly common-sense ideas about disparate groups, so that we tend to see pristine schools and suburbs as a testament to white accomplishment and values. When violence does erupt, it is laid at the feet of alienated and troubled teenagers, not a dysfunctional culture. Yet we see the metal detectors guarding entrances to minority schoolhouses (harbingers of the prison bars to come) as evidence not of the social dynamics of exclusion and privilege, but of innate pathologies. No one need talk about the dynamics of privilege and exclusion. No one need cite white-supremacist arguments nor openly refer to race—race exists in the concrete of our gated communities and barrios, in government policies and programs, in cultural norms and beliefs, and in the way Americans lead their lives.

Colorblindness badly errs when it excuses racially correlated inequality in our society as unproblematic so long as no one uses a racial epithet. It also egregiously fails when it tars every explicit reference to race. To break the interlocking patterns of racial hierarchy, there is no other way but to focus on, talk about, and put into effect constructive policies explicitly engaged with race. To be sure, inequality in wealth is a major and increasing challenge for our society, but class is not a substitute for a racial analysis—though, likewise, racial oppression cannot be lessened without sustained attention to poverty. It's no accident that the poorest schools in the country warehouse minorities, while the richest serve whites; the national education crisis reflects deeply intertwined racial and class politics. One does not deny the imbrication of race and class by insisting on the importance of race-conscious remedies: The best strategies for social repair will give explicit attention to race as well as to other sources of inequality, and to their complex interrelationship.

The claim that race and racism exist only when specifically mentioned allows colorblindness to protect a new racial politics from criticism. The mobilization of public fears along racial lines has continued over the past several decades under the guise of interlinked panics about criminals, welfare cheats, terrorists, and—most immediately in this political season—illegal immigrants. Attacks ostensibly targeting "culture" or "behavior" rather than "race" now define the diatribes of today's racial reactionaries. Samuel P. Huntington's jeremiad against Latino immigration in his book *Who Are We?: The Challenges to America's National Identity* rejects older forms of white supremacy, but it promotes the idea of a superior Anglo-Protestant culture. Patrick J. Buchanan defends his latest screed attacking "illegal immigrants," *State of Emergency: The Third World Invasion and Conquest of America,* against the charge of racism by insisting that he's indifferent to race but outraged by those with different cultures who violate our laws. My point is not simply that culture and behavior provide coded language for old prejudices, but that colorblindness excuses and insulates this recrudescence of xenophobia by insisting that only the explicit use of racial nomenclature counts as racism.

Contemporary colorblindness loudly proclaims its antiracist pretensions. To actually move toward a racially egalitarian society, however, requires that we forthrightly respond to racial inequality today. The alternative is the continuation of colorblind white dominance. As Justice Harry Blackmun enjoined in defending affirmative action in Bakke: "In order to get beyond racism, we must first take account of race. There is no other way."

Critical Thinking

1. What does the author mean by "colorblind to the reality of race"?
2. How does this issue impact schools?
3. What can you do in your classroom?
4. Why is this issue critical in today's society?

IAN F. HANEY LÓPEZ is a professor at the Boalt Hall School of Law at the University of California at Berkeley. New York University Press has just issued a 10th-anniversary edition of his *White by Law: The Legal Construction of Race,* with a new chapter on colorblind white dominance.

To actually move toward a racially egalitarian society requires that we forthrightly respond to racial inequality today. The alternative is the continuation of colorblind white dominance.

As seen in the *Chronicle of Higher Education,* November 3, 2006, pp. B6–B9. Excerpted from WHITE BY LAW, 10th Anniversary edition (New York University Press, 2006)
Copyright © 2006 by Ian F. Haney López. Reproduced with permission of the author.

"What Are You?" Biracial Children in the Classroom

Traci P. Baxley

Over the last 30 years, biracial individuals have become one of the fastest growing populations in the United States. Despite this rapid growth, these citizens are only slowly beginning to be acknowledged among monoracial groups and in academia ("New Way," 2001; Root, 1996; Wardle, 2007). Because biracial identities "potentially disrupt the white/ 'of color' dichotomy, and thus call into question the assumptions on which racial inequality is based," society has a difficult time acknowledging this section of the population (Dutro, Kazemi, & Balf 2005, p. 98).

Biracial heritage can mean mixed parentage of any kind. This can include, but is not limited to, African American, white, Latino, Asian, and Native American. "Biracial," "interracial," "multiracial," and "mixed-race" are used interchangeably and are often self-prescribed by individuals and their families (McClain, 2004; Root, 1996; Wardle, 1992). As this group increases in the general population, teachers are beginning to see more of these children in their classrooms. How are biracial children different from monoracial children? How do biracial children challenge us to think differently about racial identity and curricular issues in our classrooms?

Historical Glance at Biracial Children

Biracial children and their families are often marginalized by members of monoracial heritage, and specifically by leaders of minority communities (Root, 1996; Wardle, 2006). According to Brunsma (2005), biracial people have always been an issue for U.S. society, because they go against the structure of American's racial order and white privilege preservation. Many white slave owners and enslaved black women produced light-skinned offspring, known as "mulattoes," who sometimes looked more like the fathers than their mothers. Having a biracial heritage was not a choice at the time and these children were categorized not by their appearance, but rather by the "one drop rule," meaning if one had *any* known African ancestry, one was considered black both legally and socially (Tatum, 1997). The "one drop rule" was established by the U.S. Census Bureau. Before the 1920s, the Census count categorized "mulatto" and "pure Negro." Between the 1920s and 1960s, the previous categories were dropped and replaced with "black," as defined by the "one drop rule."

In 1967, a Supreme Court ruling in the case of *Loving v. Virginia* overturned the remaining laws prohibiting interracial marriages (FindLaw, 2007). The ruling not only helped remove the legal taboo, it may have increased acceptance of, and therefore the number of, interracial marriages in the United States.

Not until the 2000 Census, however, were Americans given the opportunity to identify themselves as multiracial (CensusScope, n.d.; "New Way," 2001). About 2.4 percent of Americans (equal to about 6.8 million people) were able to validate all of their heritages. The four most commonly reported interracial categories were white and some other race—white and American Indian, white and Asian, and white and black. From the multiracial community's perspective, this was a giant step in the right direction. However, many minority groups, including the National Association for the Advancement of Colored People and the National Asian Pacific American Legal Consortium, were not in favor of this new Census category because of the possibility of jeopardizing federal funds, civil rights laws, and voting rights issues ("New Way," 2001). Selecting more than one race can affect the number of people who previously checked one of the single minority boxes.

Biracial Identity

Experts recognize that biracial identity development is different from that of white and minority children (Tatum, 1997; Wardle, 1992). Multiple factors should be considered when racial identity is developing, including individual personalities and phenotype, familial relationships and racial identities, and geographical locations and local communities (Root, 1996; Tatum, 1997). Root (1996) recognizes five possible options for biracial identity: 1) accept the racial identity given by society; 2) identify with the minority race; 3) identify as white, if the individual physical features allow; 4) identify as "biracial" (no individual race identified); and 5) identify with more than one race. Root (1996) states that any of these choices can be positive if the individual makes that choice and if that individual doesn't feel compromised or marginalized by his/her choice.

Earlier studies concluded that biracial children were confused about their identity due to their lack of ability to connect completely to either of their heritages (Brandell, 1988; Gibbs, 1987; Herring, 1992). More recently, researchers believe that unresolved identity issues remain for biracial children because their unique heritages are not acknowledged by schools or society in general (Tatum, 1997; Wardle, 1992). In spite of this resistance from society, biracial citizens have demonstrated a sense of achievement, positive self-awareness, and emotional well-being (Tatum, 1997; Tizard & Phoenix, 1995).

Wardle (2007), when analyzing current child development textbooks, found that only two of 12 books addressed multiracial children at all. Wardle also addressed the absence of biracial people in many multicultural education books that focus solely on monoracial and monoethnic groups of people. Wardle suggests that biracial children are not included within the diversity construct of academia because multicultural and diversity experts view America as a "salad bowl" with separate racial/ethnic contributions, view diversity from a narrow-minded American viewpoint, and rely on one critical theory—the ownership of power—that requires each race/ethnic group to be completely separate in a hierarchically oppressed system.

Classroom Practices to Support Biracial Children

The 2000 Census revealed that approximately 4 percent of all children under 18 in the United States are multiracial, and that there are 1.6 million interracial married couples (CensusScope, n.d.). This cannot be ignored when it comes to classroom practices. Teachers who say they treat everyone in the class "the same" need to re-evaluate the idea of equity, ensuring that *every* student is afforded opportunities for academic excellence, and begin to acknowledge their own misconceptions and discomforts when addressing racial issues and identity in their classrooms. This includes investigating their personal stance regarding biracial children (Wardle, 1992). When conducting a self-analysis, a teacher might ask such questions as: How do I feel about interracial marriages? What preconceived notions do I have about biracial people? What have my experiences been with biracial people? Do these experiences impact my perceptions about biracial people? If so, what can I do about it? (Harris, 2002; Tatum, 1997). Biracial parents often feel as if "at best, teachers do not know how to support their children's healthy identity development in the classroom and, at worst, force them to identify with their parent of color, or parent of lowest status" (Wardle & Cruz-Janzen, 2004, p. 13).

In 2002, Harris found that school personnel who were actively engaged in cultural diversity and awareness programs held more accurate perceptions of biracial children. Ignoring students' racial identities and being "color blind" is actually a disservice, not only to biracial students, but also to all students. Biracial individuals may begin their schooling having embraced their double heritage and possessing positive self-images; however, their monoracial classmates may not understand them, and, even worse, may have preconceived notions regarding race. Biracial children who appear to "look black" may be taunted by monoracial black students for being light-skinned and having curly hair. Similarly, a biracial child who appears to be more "white" may receive negative comments from peers when her black parent enters the classroom. Living in a racially and culturally conscious society dictates that the classroom climate should deal fairly with racially charged issues and enable students to work toward positive solutions.

The parents of biracial children hold various views regarding their children's identity. Therefore, it is imperative that teachers communicate with these parents and ask them what racial designation they feel most appropriately conveys their child's heritage. More and more parents are teaching their children to embrace the term "biracial" in order to identify with both heritages (Tatum, 1997). Teachers can develop appropriate activities for their curriculum by listening to parents' suggestions regarding ways to increase awareness of biracial children.

The growth in the number of biracial students in classrooms requires educators to examine their instructional practices and evaluate any adjustments in order to acknowledge and accommodate this population. According to Wardle and Cruz-Janzen (2004), biracial students are "totally invisible in the schools' curriculum: no stories, pictures, articles and reports, books or textbook items that reflect their unique family experiences" (p. 13). Biracial students present a distinctive challenge to educators partly because of prevailing stereotypes that surround their identity. One stereotype is that biracial children must *choose* to identify with one racial heritage only, usually that of a minority heritage (Harris, 2002; Wardle, 2006). Although this practice may have held sway in the past, thereby causing feelings of guilt over the rejection of the other parent, the last 30 years have given biracial children more choices. Biracial youth are proud of their heritages and are becoming more proactive in speaking out against the racism and opposition around them. Organizations, such as the Association of Multi-Ethnic Americans (AMEA), have sprung up as resources to support multiracial families while educating people from monoracial backgrounds. Teachers who want to address issues regarding biracial students can find a wealth of information from these organizations.

Another stereotype is that biracial students do not want to talk about their racial identity or that they have racial identity issues (Harris, 2002; Tatum, 1997; Wardle, 2006). While some may find it difficult to discuss these issues, educators need to make certain that their questions are sincere and nonjudgmental (Harris, 2002). Many families of biracial children are proactive in communicating to their children who they are and teaching them to have pride in their background (Wardle & Cruz-Janzen, 2004). Teachers need to include an extensive array of approaches and practices in their instruction in order to encourage peers to acknowledge and accept biracial children, as well as to support biracial children in developing positive identities. In addition, teachers should model appropriate ways to engage in discussions focused on people's similarities and differences.

We must move beyond what Banks (2003) calls the "heroes and holidays" approach to teaching multicultural education, in which only surface level concepts are being taught but the mainstream curriculum remains the same. According to Wardle and Cruz-Janzen

(2004), this approach "marginalizes and trivializes" non-mainstream white cultures (p. 40). Instead, teachers need to encourage students to shift to Banks' (2003) social action approach. This approach is more comprehensive and means that students must engage in problem-solving and critical thinking activities that require them to *evaluate* and *take action* on social issues.

Balf's 4th- and 5th-grade class was assigned a critical literacy culture project in which three biracial students were able to reveal both parts of their heritage and discuss it with their peers (Dutro, Kazemi, & Balf 2005). Most classmates were not aware of the students' backgrounds. From this assignment, subsequent whole-group discussions became necessary in order for the biracial students to articulate how they felt, both positively and negatively, about being biracial. Ultimately, these discussions became insightful for the researchers, the teacher, and the other students. More important, it changed the way the monoracial students viewed the biracial students in the class.

Biracial students should see themselves in the curriculum through famous biracial or multiracial historical individuals, such as George Washington Carver, Frederick Douglass, W. E. B. DuBois, as well as more contemporary ones, such as Bob Marley, Tiger Woods, Colin Powell, Halle Berry, Derek Jeter, Alicia Keys, and Barack Obama. Also, inviting members from the local community into schools to reinforce the presence of biracial role models not only validates racial identity for biracial students, but also helps white and other minority children recognize the growing number of biracial and multiracial people around them. Having real role models is crucial to students' overall success and positive racial identity (Wardle & Cruz-Janzen, 2004).

Finally, teachers should supply their classroom libraries with picture books, adolescent novels, and reference books that focus on biracial children. This requires effort on the teachers' part, due to many schools' and libraries' lack of resources about biracial children. The following list of resources may be helpful in supporting teachers as they incorporate culturally responsive practices in their classrooms.

Reference Books

Dalmage, H. M. (2000). *Tripping on the color line: Black-white multiracial families in a racially divided world.* New Brunswick, NJ: Rutgers University Press.

Gaskins, P. F. (1999). *What are you?: Voices of mixed-race young people.* New York: Henry Holt & Company.

Nissel, A. (2006). *Mixed: My life in black & white.* New York: Random House Publishing Group.

Rockquemore, K. (2005). *Raising biracial children.* New York: AltaMira Press.

Wright, M. A. (1998). *I'm chocolate, you're vanilla: Raising healthy black and biracial children in a race-conscious world.* San Francisco: Jossey-Bass.

Picture Books

Ada, A. F. *I love Saturdays y Domingos.* New York: Atheneum.
Adoff, A. (1973). *Black is brown is tan.* New York: Harper.
Adoff, A. (1991). *Hard to be six.* New York: Lothrop.

Cheng, A. (2000). *Grandfather counts.* New York: Lee & Low.
Cisneros, S. (1994). *Hairs/Pelitos.* New York: Knopf.
Cole, H., & Vogl, N. (2005). *Am I a color too?* Bellevue, WA: Illumination Arts Publishing Company.
Davol, M. W. (1993). *Black, white, just right.* Morton Grove, IL: Albert Whitman & Company.
Edmonds, L. (2004). *An African princess.* Cambridge, MA: Candlewick Press.
Friedman, I. (1984). *How my parents learned to eat.* New York: Houghton.
Hoffman, M. (1990). *Nancy no-size.* New York: Mammoth.
Igus, T., & Sisnett, A. (1996). *Two Mrs. Gibsons.* New York: Little Book Press.
Johnson, A. (1996). *The aunt in our house.* New York: Orchard Books.
Katz, K. (1999). *The color of us.* New York: Henry Holt & Company.
Lamperti, N. (2000). *Brown like me.* Norwich, VT: New Victoria Publisher.
Little, O. M. (1996). *Yoshiko and the foreigner.* New York: Farrar Straus & Giroux.
Mills, C. (1992). *A visit to Amy-Claire.* New York: Macmillan.
Monk, I. (1998). *Hope.* New York: Carolrhoda Books.
Rattigan, J. K. (1993). *Dumpling soup.* New York: Little, Brown Books.
Ringgold, F. (1996). *Bonjour, Lonnie.* New York: Hyperion.
Spohn, D. (1991). *Winter wood.* New York: Lothrop.
Straight, S. (1995). *Bear E. Bear.* New York: Hyperion.
Wing, N. (1999). *Jalapeno bagels.* New York: Atheneum.
Wyeth, D. S. (1996). *Ginger brown: Too many houses.* New York: Random House.

Adolescent Books

Curry, J. (2005). *Black canary.* New York: Simon & Schuster Children's Publishing Division.
Forrester, S. (1999). *Dust from old bones.* New York: HarperCollins.
Meyer, C. (2007). *Jubilee journey.* New York: Harcourt.
Nash, R. D. (1995). *Coping as a biracial/ biethnic teen.* New York: The Rosen Publishing Group.
Viglucci, C. P. (1996). *Sun dance at turtle rock.* Rochester, NY: Stone Pine Books.
Woodson, J. (2003). *The house you pass on the way.* New York: Puffin Books.
Wyeth, D. S. (1995). *The world of daughter McGuire.* New York: Yearling Books.

Websites

Association of Multi-Ethnic Americans (AMEA): www.ameasite.org
Center for the Study of Biracial Children: www.csbc.cncfamily.com/
Interracial Voices: www.interracialvoice.com
The Multiracial Activist: www.multiracial.com
New People E-Magazine: www.newpeoplemagazine.com
Representation of Mixed Race People: www.mixedfolks.com

References

Banks, J. A. (2003). *Teaching strategies for ethnic studies* (7th ed.). New York: Pearson Education Group.

Brandell, J. R. (1988). Treatment of the biracial child: Theoretical and clinical issues. *Journal of Multicultural Counseling and Development, 16,* 176–187.

Brunsma, D. L. (2005). Interracial families and the racial identification of mixed-raced children: Evidence from the early childhood longitudinal study. *Social Forces, 84*(2), 1131–1157.

CensusScope. (n.d.). Retrieved September 29, 2007, from www .censusscope.org/us/chart_multi.html

Dutro, E., Kazemi, E., & Balf, R. (2005). The aftermath of "you're only half": Multiracial identities in the literacy classroom. *Language Arts, 83*(2), 96–106.

FindLaw. (2007). *The fortieth anniversary of Loving v. Virginia: The personal and cultural legacy of the case that ended legal prohibitions on interracial marriage.* Retrieved September 27, 2007, from http://communities.justicetalking.org/blogs/ findlaw/archive/2007/05/29/the-fortieth-anniversary-of-loving- v-virginia-the-personal-and-cultural-legacy-of-the-case-that- ended-legal-prohibitions-on-interracial-marriage-part-one-in-a- two-part-series.aspx

Gibbs, J. T. (1987). Identity and marginality: Issues in the treatment of biracial adolescents. *American Journal of Orthopsychiatry, 57,* 265–278.

Harris, H. (2002). School counselors' perceptions of biracial children: Pilot study. *Professional School Counseling Online.* Retrieved October 6, 2007, from http://findarticles.com/p/articles/mi_ m0KOC/is_2_6/ai_96194762

Herring, P. D. (1992). Biracial children: An increasing concern for elementary and middle school counselors. *Elementary School Guidance and Counseling, 27,* 123–130.

Lanier, S. (2000). *Jefferson's children: The story of one American family.* New York: Random House Books for Young Readers.

McClain, C. S. (2004). Black by choice: Identity preferences of Americans of black/white parentage. *The Black Scholar, 34*(2), 43–54.

New way to measure America. (2001). Retrieved September 8, 2007, from www.tolerance.org/news/article_print .jsp?id=140

Root, M. (1996). A bill of rights for racially mixed people. In M. Root (Ed.), *The multiracial experience: Racial boarders as the new frontier.* Thousand Oaks, CA: Sage.

Tatum, B. D. (1997). *"Why are all the black kids sitting together in the cafeteria?" And other conversations about race.* New York: Basic Books.

Tizard, B., & Phoenix, A. (1995). The identity of mixed parentage adolescents. *Journal of Child Psychology and Psychiatry, 36,* 1399–1410.

Wardle, F. (1992). Supporting the biracial children in the school setting. *Education & Treatment of Children, 15*(2), 163.

Wardle, F. (2006). *Myths and realities.* Retrieved September 13, 2007, from http://csbchome.org

Wardle, F. (2007). *Why diversity experts hate the multiracial movement.* Retrieved September 13, 2007, from http://csbchome .org

Wardle, F., & Cruz-Janzen, M. I. (2004). *Meeting the needs of multiethnic and multiracial children in schools.* New York: Pearson Education.

Critical Thinking

1. What is biracial identity?

2. How do current classroom practices help and hinder biracial students?

3. What transformational practices help all students?

4. Why do you need to address biracial identities specifically?

TRACI P. BAXLEY is Assistant Professor of Literacy, Department of Teaching and Learning, Florida Atlantic University, Boca Raton.

Author Note—Traci P. Baxley is the mother of four biracial children.

Beyond "Culture Clash": Understandings of Immigrant Experiences

This article addresses the ways in which the experiences of immigrant youth and families in U.S. schools and society have been conceptualized primarily as conflicts between immigrant cultures and dominant U.S. culture. Exemplified by the discourse of culture clash or of immigrants being torn between two worlds, this prevalent understanding structures the experiences, cultures, and identities of immigrants as unchanging and fixed in time. This article illustrates the ways that culture and identity are constructed within the double movement of discourse and representation. It offers examples of how dominant representations create simplistic understandings of the identities of immigrant youth, as well as the ways youth are constructing new identities.

BIC NGO

As a researcher interested in the experiences of immigrant families in the United States, I try to pay attention to news stories about immigrants. More often than not, these stories highlight the *clash of cultures,* or the ways that immigrant youth are torn or caught between two worlds with ubiquitous headlines such as "Generation 1.5: Young immigrants in two worlds" (Feagans, 2006), "Taking on two worlds" (Do, 2002), and "Mother's Fray: Culture clash puts special strain on immigrant moms and daughters" (Wax, 1998). One dimension of this focus on cultural conflict emphasizes the differences between immigrant cultures (East) and U.S. culture (West). In the practices of the popular press, we see dualisms of traditional/modern or rural/urban in explanations of immigrant culture and U.S. culture. For example, in a series highlighting the ways that Hmong girls have been *Shamed into Silence* by Hmong culture, Louwagie and Browning (2005a, 2005b) pointed out that "culture clash can stymie help" (2005b, p. 11A) for Hmong girls who have been raped by Hmong gang members. In their explication of the culture clash, the journalists highlighted the contrast, "Adapting any non-Western culture to the United States is a formidable task. For the Hmong community, which hails from isolated mountain villages in Laos and refugee camps in Thailand, settling in urban areas such as St. Paul has meant a bigger change" (Louwagie & Browning, 2005b, p. 11A). Here, the identity and culture—beliefs, behaviors, and values—of immigrants such as the Hmong are characterized as traditional, patriarchal, and rural, in contrast to a highly modern and civilized U.S. society.

Another dimension of the culture clash discourse emphasizes the differences between the first-generation (parents) and second-generation (youth). This dichotomy results in a preoccupation with intergenerational conflict where arguments that immigrant youth and adults have over clothes or dating restrictions are construed to be clashes between the traditional values of immigrant parents versus modern values of youth who are influenced by contemporary U.S. practices. Again, the *Shamed into Silence* series is illustrative: "The problem comes in mixing Hmong traditions with American culture, many agree. While Hmong refugees are struggling to survive in a culture foreign to them, their children are adapting more quickly and disobeying what they see as their parents' antiquated rules" (Louwagie & Browning, 2005b, p. 11A). Implicitly and explicitly, the values and practices of Hmong immigrants are depicted as backward or stuck in time.

In education, the cultural difference model for explaining immigrant student achievement problematically positions educational outcomes as a product of the cultural practices of immigrants. At one extreme, explanations of low achievement point to bad cultural practices for the under-achievement of immigrant students (S. J. Lee, 1997; Ngo, 2002). Hmong students' decisions to drop out of school to marry, for instance, are viewed as choices that are tied to traditional values—rather than as a response to oppressive social structures (Ngo, 2002). At the other extreme, cultural values based on Buddhist and Confucian beliefs are used to account for educational progress and attainment. Vietnamese students' high success is attributed to a strong work ethic and family support (Zhou & Bankston, 2001).

As a result of this either–or framework, immigrant students are viewed as gangsters and delinquents or as academic superstars and model minorities. Immigrant families are viewed as supportive and functional or as unsupportive and dysfunctional.

Even though I want to recognize the importance of the cultural difference research in drawing attention to the struggles of immigrants, I also want to point out the insidious effects of a singular focus on cultural conflict. The cultural difference model for understanding immigrant experiences sets up binary oppositions between tradition and modernity, East and West, and First World and Third World, among others. This oppositional framework is problematic for at least two reasons. First, the emphasis on traditional cultural values reifies the notion of culture, positioning it as some thing that is fixed or a given, rather than as a social process that finds meaning within social relationships and practices. Second, binary oppositions inscribe judgment and a pecking order (i.e., good/bad, ours/theirs) into cultural practices and values. Moreover, as Lowe (1996) convincingly argued, "the reduction of the cultural politics of racialized ethnic groups, like Asian Americans, to first-generation/second-generation struggles displaces social differences into a privatized familial opposition" (p. 63). The challenges faced by immigrant youth and adults are relegated to the private sphere of the home. This focus on intergenerational conflict problematically absolves institutions of education, labor, and government of responsibility, and deflects attention from exclusionary historical practices as well as discrimination immigrants continue to face (Jaret, 1999; Olneck, 2003).

In order to account for the complexity of immigrant students' and families' experiences, and the ever-changing nature of culture and identity, we need to move beyond discrete understandings of culture and identity as good/bad, traditional/modern, us/them. In this article, I suggest that we move toward seeing the changes or the *in-between* (Bhabha, 1994) of culture and identity. To do so, I illustrate the ways that culture and identity are constructed within discourse and representation. In the following section, I explicate an understanding of identity that accounts for its dynamic, contested, and messy nature that moves beyond the fixity of binary categories. I then offer examples from my work with Lao American immigrant students to illustrate how this plays out in students' lives.

Understanding Culture and Identity as Dynamic

The work of cultural studies theorists such as Hall (1989, 1990) and Bhabha (1994) provides a foundation for understanding culture and identity that takes into account the continuous process of change and negotiation. These theorists reject the definition of cultural identity based on an understanding of a singular, shared culture of a collective *one true self* shared by people of a common history and ancestry (Hall, 1990). Drawing on this work, I understand *identity* as constructed through discourse and representation and involving the play of power (Hall, 1996). Rather than whole, seamless, or naturally-occurring, culture and identity are the result of differentiation in social relations

precisely because identities are constructed within, not outside discourse, we need to understand them as produced in specific historical and institutional sites within specific discursive formations and practices, by specific enunciative strategies. Moreover, they emerge within the play of specific modalities of power, and thus are more the product of the marking of difference and exclusion, than they are the sign of an identical, naturally-constituted unity. (Hall, 1996, p. 4)

Because identity is constructed through the "play of specific modalities of power, and thus are more the product of the marking of difference and exclusion," (Hall, 1996, p. 4) identity is a *positioning*—political and negotiated.

I understand *discourse* to mean the spoken and written language and images used in popular and academic arenas. Discourse is more than simply a collection of statements or images, but is a set of historically grounded (yet evolving) statements and images that function to create a certain reality (Gee, 1996).[1] For example, the dominant discourse about Asian Americans highlights their status as a model minority. This image of success emphasizes the role of hard work, family support, and cultural values in the high educational attainment of Asian Americans (S. J. Lee, 1996). This dominant discourse of the Asian American model minority positions Asian Americans as the poster-child of American meritocracy, as it simultaneously blames other groups (e.g., African Americans, Latino Americans) for their underachievement (Osajima, 1987).

An important assumption of this understanding of discourse is that some discourses have been so ingrained through repetition that they seem to be natural and have become dominant. The repetition and naturalization of dominant discourses have masked their social and continuous construction. These dominant discourses conceal the existence of competing discourses. From the above example, the dominant discourse of Asian American success masks discourses that account for the struggles of Southeast Asians such as the Lao and Hmong (Ngo, 2006). Because identity is reflective of power and takes place within discursive relations, characterizations of immigrants as traditional, patriarchal, and resistant to assimilationist demands are neither neutral nor harmless. They reflect political positions, values, and social practices (Hall, 1990; Kumashiro, 2002).

From this understanding of *identity* and *discourse,* identity construction involves a double movement, where we are identified by a history of discourses—ideas and images of who we are—and identify ourselves by responding to the representations that have already identified us (Hall, 1996). The ways we respond may repeat, resist, or contradict how we have been identified. As we draw on discourses to make meaning for ourselves, others also use discourses that are available to understand or identify us. For instance, as a person of Vietnamese heritage who has lived in the United States for most of my life, I might identify myself as an Asian American. However, others may identify me as Chinese because my physical appearance matches with what they know about people of Chinese descent. This double movement creates an identity that is "fragmented and fractured; never singular but multiply constructed across different, often intersecting and antagonistic, discourses, practices and positions" (Hall, 1996, p. 4). This understanding of identity as shaped through discourse and representation allows for sites to continuously open for reexpression (Bhabha, 1994; Hall, 1990). Bhabha called the space that opens up for negotiation and change the third space, ambivalent space, or *in-between*. He maintained that "we should remember that it is the 'inter'—the cutting edge of translation and negotiation, the *in-between* space—that carries the burden of the meaning of culture" (Bhabha, 1994, p. 38).

By looking in the *in-between,* we may see how immigrant students work with or rework discourses that have already identified them. Next I draw on data from an ethnographic study[2] with Lao American students at an urban public high school, to illustrate the double movement of identity and the *in-between* of Lao immigrant students' identity.

The Double Movement of Identity
Dominant Discourses at Work: Lumping Lao Students as "Chinese"

One way to think about dominant discourses is to think about the stereotypes or myths that exist and are circulated about different immigrant groups. For immigrants in general, these dominant discourses or stereotypes include the perception that immigrants are a burden on the U.S. economy or take jobs from so-called real Americans. For Asian immigrants in particular, some stereotypes include the perception that Asian immigrants are all computer geniuses, good at math, passive and quiet, or martial arts experts.[3] An important characteristic of stereotypes or dominant discourses is that they lump individuals into one-dimensional, generalizing categories that ignore the complexity of their lives and experiences.

This was the case in my research with Lao immigrant students at Dynamic High School.[4] Dynamic was an urban public high school that enrolled approximately 1,482 students from across the city. The majority of the students were either African American (43%), Asian American (mostly Hmong American) (38%), and White (16%). According to the school brochure, its richness in cultural and ethnic diversity was notable in the 41 languages and dialects spoken by students and staff. Of the large number of Asian American students, the majority were Hmong. Even though the non-Asian students and teachers at Dynamic knew that most of the Asian American students were Hmong, many still referred to all Asian students as Chinese.

The lack of understanding and acknowledgment of the differences within Asian ethnic groups at Dynamic High reflects the dominant ways in which Asian immigrants are represented and understood within the popular imagination, as a homogeneous group who are all the same (S. J. Lee, 1996).[5] Problematically, this obscures the diversity of Asian groups and the variation in immigration experiences, educational attainment, and economic status (Ngo, 2006). Although Asian Americans are comprised of numerous groups, including those of Cambodian, Chinese, East Indian, Filipino, Guamanian, Hawaiian, Hmong, Indonesian, Japanese, Korean, Laotian, Samoan, Taiwanese, and Vietnamese

heritages[6] (Pang, 1990), dominant discourses mask this enormous variety. Individuals of Asian descent are all lumped into simplistic categories such as *Chinese* or *Japanese.*

For example, at Dynamic High, despite the fact that school records revealed that although none of the students were Chinese, all Asian students were labeled as Chinese. Consider what Chintana, one of my Lao student participants, said when I asked her if students and staff knew the difference between Hmong and Lao students:

Chintana: A lot of people like call Asian people like just Chinese or something. I hear it all the time . . . I've heard it like they'll say "That Chinese boy." And I'm sitting here thinking, "He's not Chinese." 'Cause I can tell the difference almost all the time.

Researcher: They don't say he's Hmong or they're all Hmong?

Chintana: No. Some of them say it, because then most of them think that everybody here is Hmong. But most of them think it's like Chinese or something (laughs).

Two discourses about the culture and identity of Asian students dominated at Dynamic High. The first racialized and identified all Asian ethnic groups (e.g., Lao, Hmong, Cambodian) as Asian; and the second identified all Asian students as Chinese. This occurred even though most of the students knew that the majority of the students at the school were Hmong. The remarks of Ms. Anderson, an ESL teacher, highlight the role of the media in framing the identities of Asian immigrant students:

Okay, students who are Hmong obviously know that the Lao kids are Lao. And other Asian kids know. But I think that as far as, if you look at the African kids, they have no idea. No idea who's Hmong and who's Lao and who's Chinese. I mean I've had a lot of the kids in my 6th hour who refer to all Hmong as Chinese. And like Jackie Chan is like their sort of national hero.

In these remarks, Ms. Anderson reiterated the identification of all Asian students as Chinese. Her reference to how non-Asian students perceived Jackie Chan as the national hero for the Asian American students also alludes to the role of popular culture in defining Asian identity and heritage. Informed by popular representation, this understanding exemplifies two stereotypes about individuals of Asian heritage: all Asians look the same and all Asians know martial arts or kung fu (R. Lee, 1999). Such understandings about Asian American students and families do little to capture the change and complexities of their lives in the United States.

Conflicting Discourses: Redefining Identity in the In-Between

In the double movement of identity, our identities are not exclusively determined by dominant discourses of other people. Because culture and identity are shaped within social relationships (Hall, 1996), the work of identity construction is fraught with tensions and disagreements that are belied by notions of identity construction and negotiation that allude to a trouble-free process (West, 2002). At the same time that others use discourses to identify us, we also draw on discourses to make meaning for ourselves. In the *in-between* (Bhabha, 1994) of culture and identity, expectations from others of who we are or should be may collide and conflict with how we want to identify ourselves. Although discourses of the experiences of immigrant families frame the choices and struggles of culture and identity within East/West or immigrant/nonimmigrant binaries, my work with Lao students revealed the salience of "different, often intersecting and antagonistic, discourses, practices and positions" (Hall, 1996, p. 4).

I found that the tensions that arose in students' identity work came from expectations by non-Lao students, as well as family members and Lao peers. For example, in Mindy's case, her association with the Hmong students at the school was problematic to her identity as Lao. As she shared: "I think my friends are getting mad at me 'cause I'm hanging out with too many Hmong people. . . . I think that they think I'm becoming one of them." Friends as well as family accused her of wanting to be Hmong. According to Mindy, her parents asked "Why you trying to be like Hmong people, dying your hair and stuff like that?" Her parents particularly worried that she would "turn out bad":

Mindy: It's like they think if I hang out with Hmong people I'm going to be bad, right? But to me, I hang out with different kind of people, you know and I don't turn out bad. I know what's right and what's wrong sometime.
Researcher: What are your parents afraid of? Like when you say they're afraid you're going to turn out bad—what are they afraid of?
Mindy: Like becoming a slut, like kind of forgetting your own race kind of.
Researcher: What does that mean?
Mindy: Like I would talk American, English at home a lot. They be like "Don't talk American, you're going to forget your own race, you're going to be American" and stuff like that.

In Mindy's experience, her identity work was problematic for her parents and Lao friends in at least two ways. First, speaking English or "American" was an activity that would lead to her forgetting her identity as a Lao person. Second, having Hmong American friends meant that she was choosing a Hmong identity over her Lao identity. This emphasis on her Lao identity is remarkable because she is half Lao and half Vietnamese.

In addition, the presence of multiple discourses at play in Mindy's experiences with her parents is especially notable. From Mindy's account, her parents associated being Hmong with conceptions of Americanization that included putting red or blonde streaks in her long black hair and "turn[ing] out bad." Turning out bad included "forgetting your own race" and being sexually promiscuous or "becoming a slut." This understanding of Hmong culture and identity is also noteworthy because in some ways it echoes popular discourses of Hmong immigrants that emphasize the role of Hmong traditional practices in contributing to the high rate of pregnancy and marriage among

Hmong teenage girls (S. J. Lee, 1997; Ngo, 2002). In other ways, it contradicts the dominant discourse that frames Hmong culture and identity as rooted in tradition. From the perspective of Mindy's Lao parents, what it means to be Hmong links Hmong culture and identity to the harmful influences of Americanization and practices of Western society rather than notions of tradition.

Conclusion

In the social construction of identity, a Lao student may consider herself Asian American, her parents may consider her Lao, and non-Lao students may consider her as Chinese or Asian. The double movement of identity opens up a space of change and negotiation. Here, the identity that individuals such as Lao American students may want to claim is not recognized or misrecognized by others because it disrupts ingrained discourses of who they should be. In Mindy's case, who she thinks she is and the way she wants to represent herself are at odds with perceptions and expectations of friends and family. The culture and identity of immigrant students and families thus cannot be conceptualized simply as something that is static, passed from one generation to the next. Notions of immigrant experiences must move beyond an either–or paradigm (i.e., either one is traditional or modern), toward an understanding of the *in-between* (Bhabha, 1994). In the *in-between* of culture and identity, students such as Mindy are changing what it means to look and behave as a Lao American. Accordingly, perceptions about immigrants must move beyond a culture clash understanding in order to account for the work of immigrants to redefine and reexpress what it means to be parents and youth in U.S. schools and society.

As educators, community members, and policymakers, this means attending to the dominant discourses that we invoke to understand immigrant families. Paying attention to these discourses will allow us to question the assumptions and representations underlying them. For example, we might ask ourselves:

1. What are the binary discourses that we use to understand the educational experiences of immigrant students and families?
2. What are alternative discourses or explanations for understanding the experiences and actions of immigrant students and parents?
3. How might we look at the *in-between* to account for changes as it relates to issues such as gender roles, family authority, identity, and economic survival?

For educators interested in moving beyond a culture clash understanding of immigrant experiences and toward a notion of *in-between,* there are a few practical recommendations to keep in mind. First, it is important to learn about and address the dominant representations or stereotypes of immigrants in general and specific immigrant groups in particular. For example, class lessons might examine the various stereotypes of immigrants, such as the ever-present myth that immigrants are a burden on the U.S. economy.[7] Second, because identity and representation have political underpinnings, it is important to learn and teach about the motivations and contexts for the representations. For instance, stereotypes of Asian Americans as the *yellow peril* and model minority have historical roots in U.S. labor and civil rights movements respectively (R. Lee, 1999). Finally, because culture and identity are in a continuous process of change, it is important to address how this is occurring in the everyday practices, interests, and experiences of immigrant youth and families. Class lessons that delve into the outside school interests of students might reveal, for example, that immigrant adolescents are identifying as hip-hop spoken-word artists.

Additionally, it is important to remember that all discourses are political. All discourses position individuals within specific power relations, and prompt us to attend to certain issues but ignore others. Understanding immigrants as *traditional* positions immigrant youth and families as backward, failing to assimilate, and thwarting assistance (Louwagie & Browning, 2005a, 2005b). This has implications for how we view immigrant students and families, and the types of services and assistance we provide as educators. Consequently, we need to ask: What kinds of educational initiatives are possible by our discourses or understandings? What kinds of initiatives are possible when we position Muslim immigrants as patriarchal and sexist? What kinds of initiatives are possible when we position Vietnamese parents as deeply committed to their children's education? These questions are critical for recognizing the political and educational implications of what we choose to emphasize as educators and researchers—because different discourses make possible different ways of teaching individual students and organizing schools.

Notes

1. See Fairclough (1992), Gee (1996), Mills (1997), Popkewitz and Brennan (1998), and Wodak (1996) for more extensive discussions of discourse.

2. See Ngo (2003) for more information about the study and methods.

3. For a thorough explanation of the dominant stereotypes of Asian Americans, see R. Lee's (1999) *Orientals: Asian Americans in Popular Culture.*

4. All names of people and places are pseudonyms.

5. A resource that examines this stereotype is Soe's film (1986), *All Orientals Look the Same.*

6. Additionally, the U.S. Bureau of the Census included smaller Asian American groups within the category of "All Other Asians" in the 1980 Census: Bangladeshi, Bhutanese, Bornean, Burmese, Celbesian, Cernan, Indochinese, Iwo-Jiman, Javanese, Malayan, Maldivian, Nepali, Okinawan, Sikkimese, Singaporean, and Sri Lankan (Pang, 1990).

7. For resources, see websites such as http://immigrationforum.org/ and http://www.mnadvocates.org.

References

Bhabha, H. (1994). *The location of culture.* New York: Routledge.

Do, A. (2002, January 11). Taking on two worlds. *Orange County Register.* Retrieved November 15, 2006, from http://www.proquest.umi.com.

Fairclough, N. (1992). *Discourse and social change.* Cambridge, England: Polity Press.

Feagans, B. (2006, September 3). Generation 1.5: Young immigrants in two worlds. *The Atlanta Journal—Constitution.* Retrieved November 15, 2006, from http://www.proquest.umi.com

Gee, J. (1996). *Social linguistics and literacies: Ideology and discourses* (2nd ed.). Philadelphia: Falmer Press.

Hall, S. (1989). New ethnicities. In D. Morley & K. H. Chen (Eds.), *Stuart Hall: Critical dialogues in cultural studies* (pp. 441–449). London: Routledge.

Hall, S. (1990). Cultural identity and diaspora. In J. Rutherford (Ed.), *Identity: Community, culture, difference* (pp. 222–239). London: Lawrence and Wishart.

Hall, S. (1996). Introduction: Who needs 'identity'? In S. Hall & P. du Gay (Eds.), *Questions of cultural identity* (pp. 1–17). Thousand Oaks, CA: Sage.

Jaret, C. (1999). Troubled by newcomers: Anti-immigrant attitudes and action during two eras of mass immigration to the United States. *Journal of American Ethnic History, 18,* 9–39.

Kumashiro, K. (2002). Against repetition: Addressing resistance to anti-oppressive change in the practices of learning, teaching, supervising and researching. *Harvard Educational Review, 72,* 67–92.

Lee, R. (1999). *Orientals: Asian Americans in popular culture.* Philadelphia, PA: Temple University Press.

Lee, S. J. (1996). *Unraveling the "model minority" stereotype: Listening to Asian American youth.* New York: Teachers College Press.

Lee, S. J. (1997). The road to college: Hmong American women's pursuit of higher education. *Harvard Educational Review, 67,* 803–827.

Louwagie, P., & Browning, D. (2005a, October 9). Shamed into silence. *Star Tribune.* Retrieved November 15, 2006, from http://www.proquest.umi.com

Louwagie, P., & Browning, D. (2005b, October 10). Shamed into silence: Culture clash can stymie help. *Star Tribune.* Retrieved November 15, 2006, from http://www.proquest.umi.com

Lowe, L. (1996). *Immigrant acts: On Asian American cultural politics.* Durham, NC: Duke University Press.

Mills, S. (1997). *Discourse.* New York: Routledge.

Ngo, B. (2002). Contesting "culture": The perspectives of Hmong American female students on early marriage. *Anthropology and Education Quarterly, 33,* 163–188.

Ngo, B. (2003). Citing discourses: Making sense of homophobia and heteronormativity at Dynamic High School. *Equity and Excellence in Education, 36,* 115–124.

Ngo, B. (2006). Learning from the margins: Southeast and South Asian education in context. *Race, Ethnicity and Education, 9,* 51–65.

Olneck, M. (2003). Immigrants and education in the United States. In J. A. Banks & C. M. Banks (Eds.), *Handbook of research on multicultural education* (pp. 381–403). New York: Macmillan.

Osajima, K. (1987). Asian Americans as the model minority: An analysis of the popular press image in the 1960s and 1980s. In G. Y. Okihiro, S. Hune, A. A. Hansen, & J. M. Lie (Eds.), *Reflections on shattered windows: Promises and prospects for Asian Americans studies* (pp. 166–174). Pullman: Washington State University Press.

Pang, V. (1990). Asian American children: A diverse population. In T. Nakanishi & T. Nishida (Eds.), *The Asian American educational experience* (pp. 167–179). New York: Routledge.

Popkewitz, T., & Brennan, M. (1998). Restructuring of social and political theory in education: Foucault and a social epistemology of school practices. In T. Popkewitz & M. Brennan (Eds.), *Foucault's challenge: Discourse, knowledge and power in education* (pp. 3–35). New York: Teachers College.

Soe, V. (Producer/Director). (1986). *All orientals look the same* [Experimental/Documentary]. Available from the Center for Asian American Media: http://www.asianamericanmedia.org

Wax, E. (1998, May 10). Mother's fray: Culture clash puts special strain on immigrant moms and daughters. *Newsday.* Retrieved November 15, 2006, from http://www.proquest.umi.com

West, T. R. (2002). *Signs of struggle: The rhetorical politics of cultural difference.* New York: SUNY Press.

Wodak, R. (1996). *Disorders of discourse.* New York: Longman Press.

Zhou, M., & Bankston, C. L. (1998). *Growing up American: How Vietnamese children adapt to life in the United States.* New York: Russell Sage Foundation.

Critical Thinking

1. What are the culture clashes that occur to and among immigrants?
2. How do culture clashes occur in schools and classrooms?
3. What are today immigrant students experiencing that other students are not experiencing?
4. Why are initiatives essential to introduce to education for today's immigrant students?

BIC NGO is an assistant professor of immigrant education at the University of Minnesota.

Correspondence should be sent to Bic Ngo, Assistant Professor, Immigrant Education, University of Minnesota, Department of Curriculum and Instruction, 152C Peik Hall, 159 Pillsbury Drive SE, Minneapolis, MN 55455. E-mail: bcngo@umn.edu.

Metaphors of Hope

Refusing to be disheartened by all the negative press surrounding education today, Ms. Chenfeld travels the country and encounters one inspiring educator after another. She tells four of their stories here.

Mimi Brodsky Chenfeld

On the Big Island of Hawaii, there's a forest of lava-crusted hills and bare corpses of trees called Devastation Trail. Old volcanic eruptions burnt the Ohia trees and left this once-lush terrain barren and ashen.

Walking on the wooden paths through the devastation, one could easily miss the tiny flowers remarkably pushing through the charred earth. The markers that identify these flowers read: Thimbleberry, Swordfern, Creeping Dayflower, and Nutgrass. While others aimed their cameras at the stark, mysterious lava hills, I focused on the flowers. In the midst of such a desolate scene, these perky "signs of life" seemed to be symbols of courage and persistence.

Reading daily the bleak headlines and articles that stress the stress by focusing on bullying, violence, gangs and cliques, and numerous random acts of unkindness and hostility in our seemingly devastated educational landscape, one could easily sink into despair. However, as a stubborn optimist, I always search for markers of thimbleberry, swordfern, creeping dayflower, and nutgrass—metaphors of hope!

When Mr. T (also known as Tom Tenerovich) was moved upstairs after years of teaching kindergarten classes, he observed that second-graders were more vocal, more argumentative, more opinionated! A voracious reader of books about education, he was familiar with many theories and programs. *But reading about ideas is different from doing.*

One idea that intrigued Mr. T was that of Town Meeting. He and his students discussed building a structure that would enable all voices to be heard, problems to be solved, and good listening habits to be formed.[1]

The class added mayor and assistant mayor to the list of jobs on their classroom helpers board. During the year, every student would be assigned to these jobs for a one-week term of office.

The Town Meeting works this way: each week, the mayor and assistant mayor, along with Tom, write an agenda for two, 30- to 40-minute Town Meetings. Any student can submit a proposal for discussion, but it has to be written and include name, date, and the issue to be discussed. Some of the issues concerning the students have included changing seats, playground rules,

classmates being hurtful, picking team members, and activities for "Fun Fridays."

At the Town Meeting, the class discusses the topic and votes to resolve the issue. "Even if they disagree, it's so sweet to hear how they disagree," Tom reports. "They're really beginning to listen to each other." He continues,

> It's amazing the way it works out. None of the kids are bossy when they become mayor. Even our most timid children became good mayors. Believe it or not, one of my most high-maintenance tough kids was the best mayor! He took charge in a fair way—he knew what to do—he behaved appropriately.
>
> Even I became an agenda issue! One of the kids reminded me that I hadn't done something I promised. That was important to the children, and I had to remedy it.

Committees formed from discussions: academic committees, playground committees (to see that no students were left out of games or weren't chosen for teams), and classroom improvement committees. Tom was thrilled to see how the twice-weekly Town Meetings honoring the feelings and agendas of the students carried over into the everyday life of the group. "This really is democracy in action! Points of view are freely expressed. All opinions are valued and respected. You can see and feel the increase of courtesy and kindness."

The school mascot is a bobcat. Tom and his second-graders added the idea of Bobcat Purrs to their Town Meeting. Like "warm fuzzies," pats on the back, recognition of positive acts, observations of improvements, Bobcat Purrs were "built into our meetings," Tom explains, "and became part of our culture. Children wrote up a 'purr,' decorated it, and handed it to the mayor, who read it and presented it. No one was ever left out. We promised *not* to just recognize our best friends. Children looked for what their classmates were doing well. They were very specific."

One student, who had experienced alienation, low self-image, and loneliness in earlier years and whose posture defined his feelings, received a Bobcat Purr during a Town Meeting that stated how proudly he was standing. He was standing up straight! The boy beamed!

Another student who had difficulty finishing her work received a Bobcat Purr from a classmate honoring her for finishing *all* of her work. Everyone rejoiced.

When children live in a climate that accentuates the positive, their eagle eyes catch the flickering light of flames that are almost burnt out.

The picture I want to snap for my Album of Hope is of a proud second-grader standing up straight with the mayor, assistant mayor, his teacher, and all of his classmates honoring him with a Bobcat Purr during the Town Meeting.[2]

Swordfern: Cathy

Cathy Arment and her first-graders are not involved in the building of structures like Town Meetings. With their teacher, this group of students from diverse cultures, races, and religions works hard and plays hard together. Cathy described a memorable scene in a telephone message: "I was reading the children Jonathan London's *Froggy's First Kiss*—you know, for Valentine week. Mim, I looked up from the story to see the children sitting in clusters, their arms around each other, their eyes wide as I turned the pages, so totally involved. I almost began to weep at the sight of their beauty."

Here we have students with Ethiopian, Mexican, Appalachian, Southeast Asian, and African American backgrounds. How did such a diverse group of children learn to love one another?

Here we have students with Ethiopian, Mexican, Appalachian, Southeast Asian, and African American backgrounds—children who are newcomers, some from dysfunctional homes, some from foster homes, some with hardship home lives, some at risk. How did such a diverse group of children learn to love one another?

Cathy and I talked at length. With all the realities of alienation, anxiety, insecurity, and mean-spiritedness that these students face, *how is such a warm and loving environment created?* What is the strategy? What are the techniques? Cathy thought long and hard about these questions. She realized that she did not have a preconceived plan for helping her students build positive classroom relationships. She hadn't adopted a program specifically aimed at such outcomes. Nowhere in her plan book were consciously chosen activities based on proven behavior management theories. *She just did what she did because of who she was and what she believed.* Reviewing her ideas, she said:

All I can think of is that from day one, we are together. We verbalize feelings—good and bad. We're not afraid to share. From our first moment together, we talked about respecting everyone. Some of my children have heavy accents. They are "different." Many of them have been

made fun of. We talk about how hurtful it is to be teased, to put people down and to be put down. We begin to listen to each other. To care about each other. *My children never, ever tease!* And—I'm a human being, too—I share with them. They'll ask me, "Teacher, what did YOU read? What did YOU do over the weekend? Did YOU have a fun holiday?" When a child has a low day, we all try to cheer that child. Sometimes I have a gray day. The kids will go out of their way to brighten me. They know we stick together, that I care for them very deeply. They know that we are all safe in our room.

When the children wrote and illustrated their "I Have A Dream" papers inspired by Dr. Martin Luther King, Jr.'s famous speech, many of them expressed the warm feelings they experienced in the classroom and wrote dreams like these: "I have a dream to be with my family and to give love to everybody and to care about everybody" (Abigail). "I have a dream that people would be nice to other people and, if people are hurt, other people could help them just like other people help me" (Carissa).

The Israeli-Yemenite dancer Margolith Ovid once said, "The greatest technique in the universe is the technique in the human heart."

The picture I would snap for my Album of Hope is of Cathy's kids, arms around each other, sitting in clusters, listening to Froggy's First Kiss.[3]

Creeping Dayflower: Ms. Gibson

Before the new school year even begins, Dee Gibson sends warm *Welcome to the Family* cards to her future students! These fortunate first-graders know— from everything said and done, from words and actions, activities and discussions, planning and projects—that their class is a second family in which each and every family member is important and connected to everyone else. This is not a theme or a curriculum item or a subject area—*it's the way it is* in Ms. Gibson's class. Because she is passionate, articulate, and committed to creating, with her children and families, a safe, encouraging, caring community that really is a second family (and for some children over the years, a first family!), the experiences of her students are very special. They help one another. They cooperate. They plan and talk together. They are totally involved in the life they share together in this home away from home.

We can't take the environment for granted. We are the architects of the culture of the school, of the program.

When the children were asked such questions as "What is it like being in this kind of class family? What do you do? How do you feel?" the responses were honest and forthcoming:

We're all together. We get in pods. We work together. If two kids are having an argument, the whole class stops till we work it out. We really feel like everyone cares about each other.—*Jay*

***

We're like teamwork. We help each other with work and to pick up. Everyone here sticks together —*Lauri*

***

All the kids are friends. Arguing doesn't really happen much—everyone cooperates.—*Ryan*

***

Our teacher treats people fair. The other kids act very kind together. She teaches us how to work together.—*Barrett*

***

We don't really get in fights!—*Nikki*

***

Everybody is nice to each other, and they act like a family. Ms. Gibson is like one of the family.—*Danielle*

The language in this class is the language of respect, acceptance, courtesy, responsibility, and cooperation. It's not limited to a week's celebration of a theme! It's the vocabulary of a close-knit family. That's an everyday reality.

The picture I want to take for my Album of Hope is of the children holding up their summer "Welcome to the Family" cards. A sequel to that picture is of children discovering that the welcome cards were not a gimmick! They were the real thing.[4]

Nutgrass: Anne and Claudette

Partners in Educating All Children Equally (PEACE), Anne Price and Claudette Cole travel to schools, programs, and conferences, spreading very simple messages—especially to administrators who too often don't attend workshops that are aimed directly at the heart. Anne and Claudette remind those directors, managers, principals, and superintendents that their influence in the creation of positive, life-affirming school climates is immeasurable. They *really can* make the difference between the life and death of an entire program or school.

Claudette and Anne discuss ways of helping teachers to develop positive relationships with their students and to motivate the students to develop caring and respectful relationships with one another. What are some suggestions for doing so? Usually, without hesitation, most of the administrators offer such actions as recognizing students, paying attention to them, appreciating their talents and efforts, encouraging them to cooperate with and be considerate of one another, and inviting students to share ideas and input so that they are directly involved in the success of the school.

Claudette and Anne gently turn these ideas around, directing them to the administrators. "Just as we advocate developmentally appropriate practices for teaching children, so we have to apply those ideas to our staff." Anne explains their simple, direct approach: "It's our responsibility to pay attention to the needs of staff so they can meet the children's needs."

What are some of the greatest trouble spots in the dynamics of any school or program? Absenteeism, turnover, bullying, discipline problems, low morale, lack of trust, miscommunication—to name just a few. It's so obvious to Anne and Claudette that these problems, often reflecting a disconnected and resentful staff, carry over to the students and poison the atmosphere. (Think lava!)

Think of ways to inspire and create a healthy workplace for all who spend time there. Claudette asks, "Does the staff feel appreciated? Respected? Do they feel they have ownership of and an investment in the success of the program? Are their efforts and contributions valued? Do we keep all avenues of communication open? Do we trust enough to be honest with each other without fear of reprisal?"

Anne reminds participants in her workshops that we can't take the environment for granted. *We are the architects of the culture of the school, of the program.* "You'll see the difference in an environment where children, staff, families, and communities are nurtured and respected. Ideas flow freely, teamwork flourishes, staff feels open and trusting with each other and with the administration—now, will the turnover be as great? The absenteeism? The low morale?" She challenges her groups to talk honestly about these vital components that make for a healthy, positive school culture.

"And," she warns, "you can't give it if it's not in you to give. That's why we constantly have to think about our commitments, beliefs, and goals. How we feel about those deeper questions will generate our behavior."

Claudette and Anne inspire those who lead to look deeply into their own hearts and souls and honestly find whether their beliefs, actions, and words are in harmony. Their decisions will shape the culture of their schools, affecting children, staff, families, and neighbors.

The image for my Album of Hope is a group of administrators exchanging ideas and experiences, sharing feelings, and being energized by the process and promise of making a real difference in the lives of those they guide.[5]

These are just four examples of courageous, confident, hopeful educators who, like our four brave little flowers, insist on growing through hardened and lava-crusted times! I must tell you, I have gathered hundreds and hundreds of examples of educators throughout the land who inspire and nurture caring, compassionate communities of learners.

All of them give themselves wholly to this "holy" process. Their words aren't slogans. Their promises are not bulletin-board displays or mottos. Their commitments are demonstrated every day by how they meet and greet, listen and talk, share and care in their numerous interactions with children and adults.

They know that nothing is to be taken for granted. Tom's Town Meeting is not guaranteed to succeed. A teacher who does not teach in the "key of life," who doesn't listen to or respect the students, who is rigid and devoid of joy and humor, can follow the recipe for a Town Meeting to the last syllable, but it will yield nothing that will teach the children, *through doing,* the art of building positive classroom relationships.

I have gathered hundreds and hundreds of examples of educators throughout the land who inspire and nurture caring, compassionate communities of learners.

Cathy didn't adopt a specific program. She and her children *are* the program, and their mutuality, kindness, and concern for one another are expressed in everything they do. There is no place for bullying in the safe place of Cathy's classroom. She teaches by heart!

Unless one believes it deeply and demonstrates that belief in everything he or she does (from the smallest acts to the largest), even a stellar concept like *family* will be another act of betrayal. Dee Gibson truly believes in establishing a second family with her children. This is not a once-a-month, set-aside time slot; it's the air they breathe and everything they do. Children are acutely alert to hypocrisy. They know when their teachers speak empty words. Lip service is disservice! They learn those lessons well.

Anne and Claudette, in their workshops, invite administrators to examine their own beliefs, motivations, and actions. Joanne Rooney, in her excellent article "Principals Who Care: A Personal Reflection," wrote:

> Good principals model care. Their words and behavior explicitly show that caring is not optional. Nothing can substitute for this leadership. Phoniness doesn't cut it. No principal can ask any teacher, student, or parent to travel down the uncertain path of caring if the principal will not lead the way.[6]

The way through these often grim times is through dedication and commitment, courage, persistence and fierce optimism. Just as Swordfern, Nutgrass, Creeping Dayflower, and Thimbleberry push their bright colors through seemingly solid lava, countless teachers and administrators shine their lights—brightening the sacred spaces they influence, dotting the charred landscape with blossoms of hope.

Notes

1. Tom was inspired by A. S. Neill, *Summerhill School* (New York: St. Martin's Griffin, 1992).

2. Tom Tenerovich and his second-graders enjoyed their Town Meetings at the Royal Palm Beach Elementary School, Royal Palm Beach, Fla. Tom currently teaches second grade at Equestrian Trails Elementary school in Wellington, Fla.

3. Cathy Arment and her loving first-graders listened to *Froggy's First Kiss* at the Etna Road School, Whitehall-Yearling Public Schools, Whitehall, Ohio, where she was voted Teacher of the Year 2004.

4. Dee Gibson and her family of first-graders thrive in the Walden School, Deerfield Public Schools, Deerfield, Ill. Dee was featured in my guest editorial, "Welcome to the Family," *Early Childhood Education Journal,* Summer 2003, pp. 201–2.

5. Anne Price and Claudette Cole are PEACEmakers in Cleveland, Ohio. You can contact Anne and Claudette at www.peaceeducation.com.

6. Joanne Rooney, "Principals Who Care: A Personal Reflection," *Educational Leadership,* March 2003, p. 77.

Critical Thinking

1. List steps that can be taken to remove bullying behavior from the playground, classroom, and away from school.

2. Give examples from your experience of teachers who inspire learning in their students. What was their "magic"?

3. Give some examples of how staff can be supported in their efforts to educate their students.

MIMI BRODSKY CHENFELD began teaching in 1956. She works and plays with people of all ages and grade levels throughout the country. Among her books are *Teaching in the Key of Life* (National Association for the Education of Young Children, 1993), *Teaching by Heart* (Redleaf Press, 2001), and *Creative Experiences for Young Children,* 3rd ed. (Heinemann, 2002). She lives in Columbus, Ohio. She dedicates this article to the memory of Pauline Gough, whose life's work, brightening the way for educators and children, is a stellar example of metaphors of hope.

From *Phi Delta Kappan,* by Mimi Brodsky Chenfeld, December 2004, pp. 271–275. Copyright © 2004 by Phi Delta Kappan. Reprinted by permission of the publisher and author. Mimi Brodsky Chenfeld, teacher/author, has also published TEACHING IN THE KEY of LIFE (NAEYC), TEACHER BY HEART (Redleaf), and CREATIVE EXPERIENCES FOR YOUNG CHILDREN (Heinemann).

UNIT 2

Negotiate and Evaluate Curriculum and Content

Unit Selections

Learning Outcomes

After reading this unit, you will be able to:

- Retell the lessons learned by a novice teacher from the assassination of Dr. Martin Luther King, Jr.

- Describe the research conducted in two mid-south elementary schools to honor the life and legacy of Dr. King.

- Expand upon the importance for and practices of fairness and equity in today's schools and classrooms.

- Discuss the phenomenological methods of inquiry applicable to curriculum and content.

- Summarize how culture shapes curriculum.

- Explain the roles and responsibilities of curriculum and instruction on student learning.

Student Website
www.mhhe.com/cls

Internet References

Awesome Library for Teachers
www.awesomelibrary.org/teacher.html

Library of Congress
www.loc.gov/index.html?gclid=CLTW28rd2JkCFRINDQodpgGqVA

National Economics and Social Rights Initiative
www.nesri.org/?gclid=CIPVtYyWxJoCFRufnAodY1Q8sg

Scholastic News-Immigration
http://teacher.scholastic.com/activities/immigration/index.htm

Social Statistics Briefing Room
www.whitehouse.gov/briefing_room

United States Historical Census Data Browser
http://fisher.lib.virginia.edu/census

Most teachers are responsible for developing curriculum that is standards based and content intense. Members of every academic discipline have dedicated much time, money, and energy crafting the minimal expectations that all students should know, do, and believe related to a particular subject area. The outcomes have been prioritized and ordered so curriculum offers both a comprehensive scope within each grade level or course of study coordinated with a smooth sequence so all students are exposed to all expectations during one's academic career. Ideally, curriculum developers collaborate with instructional strategies so the academic content and pedagogical practices fit together seamlessly, equipping teachers to facilitate student-centered learning that engages each student in developmentally appropriate activities and assignments. The curriculum and instruction should align with the classroom assessments that are established clearly in advance of the teaching and learning so teachers, students, and students' families know what is supposed to occur, how it is going to occur, why it is going to occur, who is responsible, and when events will occur or are due. By starting with the end product, the teacher can work backwards to design instruction to effectively guide the process and support each learner to achieve the learner's potential. When teaching and learning are assessed frequently and properly, teachers' decisions and student growth are both data-driven and purposeful.

However, in order for learning to be student-centered, the teacher needs to become fully acquainted with each individual student. Understanding each student via the cognitive, physical, affective, and social domains of learning for every subject area presents an overwhelming task for even the most seasoned, accomplished educator. Yet teachers must attempt to achieve this goal so they can choreograph the most effective and efficient teaching and learning environments multiple times per day.

Too often, the phrase that today's classrooms are more challenging, particularly with the increase in diverse student populations, is repeated. Some teachers defer to this unsound analysis to account for their success and satisfaction. Yet many more teachers enter the classroom every day fully aware that every classroom is filled with diverse student populations and that all classrooms have always been filled with diverse student populations.

Becoming acquainted with each student in all four domains of learning means recognizing and accepting all forms of diversity; it is the student's cultural characteristics that frame the student's world and, thus, the student's learning. Each student's cultural characteristics are a combination of nature and nurture: the characteristics with which one is born and the influences one receives from interactions with families, communities, and opportunities that happen by chance and by choice through life. Students mature at individual rates into a range of unique individuals, all of whom comprise our multicultural world. Thus, classrooms are filled with diverse student populations even if the teacher believes that everyone in the classroom seems to be the same.

The concept of multiculturalism is essential for educators to develop curriculum and design instruction that is culturally competent. Teachers must organize and prepare their course content and pedagogical strategies so all students are motivated to learn, are fully engaged in the learning, connect the learning to their own backgrounds, collaborate with their peers, express the learning through their individual learning styles and strengths, exchange discoveries with peers, and assess their own progress and assess the progress of their peers. These guidelines apply to all students; teachers cannot decide who will receive the more effective and efficient educations and who will not.

© Ariel Skelley/Getty Images

To achieve cultural competence, teachers must infuse multicultural education across the curriculum and instruction too. All students need to learn about all people. The curricular content must infuse information related to all cultures; the content cannot be limited to the dominant culture represented of selected cultural characteristics. The pedagogical strategies must offer students learning experiences to build upon their strengths and fortify their weaker areas so learning is balanced. Teachers cannot decide in advance the curriculum and instruction that are appropriate for particular students; all students are entitled to the same opportunities to learn and grow.

Unit 2 articles prompt the reader to negotiate and evaluate the curriculum and content. Readers must ensure that they teach all students about their own and other cultures in all parts of the curriculum. Likewise readers must set high standards for all students with instructional guidance and support for students to demonstrate achievement through the curriculum. All students must be provided a variety of avenues of expression, alongside opportunities to exchange discoveries and outcomes with peers aligned with multiple forms of assessment. Readers must examine textbooks and supplementary materials to infuse cultural connections in the curriculum and content as well as updated instructional strategies that ensure culturally relevant pedagogy is available for all students at all times.

A Letter Long Overdue

Dr. Michael L. Fischler

Dear Coretta:

I'm sorry this letter has taken so long to write, but you have been on my mind. When I awoke on January 31st and heard of your passing, I filled with sadness. I closed my eyes and thought of you. I remembered your dignity. I bore witness to your beauty, I reflected (as I have so many times before) on your principles. I hurt, not unlike I hurt some 38 years ago, as I envisioned the horror that you and your family experienced on that fateful day when you lost your husband. I flashed on your adult children, recognizing that they would once again mourn the loss of a parent. I mourned too, not only because of your loss, but because I never shared with you how the direction of my life was profoundly altered, as was your, by the death of your beloved husband. I never told you because I feared that my private story, compared to the important stories that fill your days, did not merit your attention. I now wish I had found the courage to have shared my story with you. Please consider this "sharing" as my attempt to, on some level, connect, and offer gratitude for the gift of wisdom your husband gave me when I, a young junior high school student teacher, struggled on April 5, 1968, to find a way to come to terms with his passing . . .

Friday, April 5th had been reserved for testing. The exams were copied, and my plans carefully scheduled each event of the day. But exams and routine plans had lost their significance due to the previous evening's events. I walked into the junior high a little afraid and a little ashamed. I was afraid that being white, in an all-black Southern school, I would in some way be blamed for Dr. King's assassination. I was ashamed that such a crime could be committed in my country. I felt that in some way I shared the burden of guilt.

The day was one for discussion and understanding—a day to contemplate the tragedy and grope for truths or lessons. It was an emotional day, a day for letting off steam, a day to realize that a disease existed in our country.

I expected hostility and found apathy. I decided to read Walt Whitman's *"O Captain! My Captain!"* and to ask the class what special significance could be found in the poem.

The first two classes were unmoved by the recitation and sleepily answered questions as to why today was different from any other day.

By the third period I was puzzled by the lack of concern. Optimistically, I again read the poem and questioned the class.

"Why is today of special significance?"
"Dr. King was killed last night," the class said.

"Who is the captain in the poem?"
"Abraham Lincoln."

"Who are we comparing him to?"
"Dr. King."

"Who killed Dr, King?"
"The white people."

"White people?" I asked. *"Is that who killed Dr, King?"*
"Yes," the class answered.

Suddenly I saw my opportunity. I asked a student to go to the board and write the heading "White Person." I then told the class that I didn't know what a "white person" was and asked them to tell me. They answered, "Whites have all the opportunities; white people take advantage of black people; white people have the better jobs." And so it went. When the list was completed, there were 10 similar statements.

I then asked the student to put the heading "Black" on the board. *"What's a black?"* I asked. They answered, "A black works hard; a black is honest; a black is taken advantage of by the whites." And so this list went. As the activity slackened, I asked the group if they could add anything to the list headed "White Person." One stated that "white people are cheap." Another student quickly corrected him, asserting that "Not all white people are cheap, just Jews!" I realized that another opportunity had presented itself. I asked, *"Is there a special kind of white person called a Jew?"* To this I heard a resounding "Yes!" So I put up the word "Jew" as a category.

"Now tell me what you feel a Jew is."

Suddenly the class came alive. People told stories of how "the Jews" took advantage of them, how they cheated them, how they never gave them a fair opportunity, and how they were always rich. I laughed at the tales along with my students, seeking to have them realize as definite a commitment to their stereotyped ideas as they possibly could. The list grew to twice the size of the preceding two, and was twice as virulent.

I then entered the final phase of the improvisation. With three lists on the blackboard, the fourth was to be "me, Mr. Fischler." *"What am I?"* I asked.

Although a game-like attitude had permeated the room, the students were afraid to answer this question. *"Tell it like it is,"* I said. *"I'm only a student teacher, I don't know what I am; this is the only way I can improve myself! I won't punish you for anything you say—just be serious."*

The responses I got were meager at best, so I took the initiative and asked the class to answer questions about me. I read from the list under the heading "Jew," and asked how I compared with it.

"Am I rich?"
"No." So "not rich" went up on the board.

"Do I give you a fair opportunity in my class?"
"Yes," they answered. So this went up.

"Am I cheap?"
"No." So "not cheap" was included.

I went through the entire list without the class realizing what I had done. Without exception, even to "not having a big nose," it read exactly the opposite of the list of Jewish characteristics.

I explained that what they had done was called "stereotyping." I told them that a similar class full of white students might be guilty of the very same reaction if asked to give black people's characteristics. I told them that for many years segments of the white community had envisioned blacks as being "untrustworthy and lazy." They saw that these terms did not agree with those that they had listed to describe their race.

I asked, "Is it possible that the man who shot Dr. King felt he was ridding the world of a tyrant who represented an unworthy people? All of us are guilty of stereotyping; it is the easy way out. Perhaps now you can understand what was in the mind of the man who killed Dr. King. The same poison can be found to one degree or another in all of us. You did the same thing to the Jews that you accuse the white people of doing to you. Look at the blackboard."

The bell rang, and I asked them to hold their seats for another minute. *"I want you to know"* I said, *"that I am a Jew and by your own admission I don't fit even one of your Jewish characteristics. My parents are Jews, and so are many of my friends. None of them fits this image that you have created. Think about your words. Think about the reasons why people hate other people. Don't let the lesson we learned today go to waste."*

Coretta, I never forgot that lesson. I carried Martin with me (or was it Martin carrying me?) through advanced study, 35 years in higher education, and into every interaction I have had where I have chosen love and compassion over anger and arrogance, It was no accident that I chose to focus my professional life on teaching and supporting principles related to diversity, compassion and human rights, and have carried forth that message to thousands of students. You need to know that in the remarkable life you chose to live, where daily you carried the weight of your husband's teachings, you were never alone. Many of us, often anonymously and in seemingly unimportant ways, share and will continue to share your commitment to actualizing your husband's dream.

Most Sincerely,

Michael L. Fischler

Critical Thinking

1. What did the novice teacher do to his lesson plan in 1968?

2. How have the events of 1968 changed the teacher over time?

3. What are the anticipated impacts of the modified lesson plan?

4. Why has the author written a letter to Coretta Scott King at this point in time?

Status of the Dream: A Study of Dr. King in Little Rock and Memphis Classrooms

ANGELA WEBSTER-SMITH

Introduction

The author was present for what would become the last speech of Dr. Martin Luther King, Jr., (MLK) when she was an elementary school student in Memphis, Tennessee, in 1968. Being present for such a historical event was life-altering in shaping her views on equity with reference to what is known as *the American dream* (Webster-Smith, in press). Today, as a professor of leadership studies who helps to prepare and develop school leaders, she continues to see the significance of this watershed moment in history as it relates to what is believed to be the new American civil right: education. Dr. King's influence extends far beyond U.S. borders and offers a model for peace around the world.

Over 40 years after his death in 1968, the author investigated a total of 50 elementary school teachers in Little Rock, Arkansas, and in Memphis, Tennessee, regarding the life and legacy of Dr. King in contemporary classrooms. Selecting populations of teachers from these venues was important because both cities attracted national attention and fashioned defining moments during the Civil Rights era. The Little Rock crisis involved high school students known as the Little Rock Nine who were initially prevented from entering a racially segregated Little Rock Central High School, whereas the Memphis emergency concerned the Sanitation Strike of 1968 that culminated with Dr. King's death. Because the investigator was born, reared, and lived in the greater Memphis area for many years but currently lives in the greater Little Rock area, often she has wondered about the contemporary effects of Dr. King's legacy on instruction in schools in areas where civil rights battles were fought publically.

This paper acquaints the reader with how the MLK dream is operationalized in the personal and professional lives of a small sample of modern-day teachers.

Specifically, this paper speaks to the ways in which elementary school teachers are honoring a piece of American history in their classrooms and will offer implications for teacher education.

Literature Review

The National Council for the Social Studies (NCSS, 2010) defines social studies as an integrated study of the social sciences and humanities to promote civic competence in K-12 and college/university settings. Its framework consists of 10 themes including culture, change, people, places, environment, institutions, power, authority, governance, society, global connections, civic ideals, and practices. In alignment with these precepts, elementary school teachers must routinely help their students understand the relevance and significance that everyday citizens have on the symbols, icons, and traditions of American history. The teachers must chronicle the events, protocols, laws, and the basic structures of American life, how those procedures came to be and how such systems affect contemporary living.

Teachers must be able to give credence to Americans who take risks to secure the liberties that are enjoyed in this land of the free. When honoring the nation's heroes, teachers should include individuals from a diverse group of populations. Furthermore, teachers of social studies have the responsibility of engaging students in the processes of critical thinking, ethical decision making, and social participation because these tenets are necessary for democratic living (Ligon, 2005). Principles of the democratic ideal should be taught in ways that allow students to become more conscious of civic life and to see themselves as actors in history (Ayers, Kumashiro, Meiners, Quinn, & Stovall, 2010). Critical reflection and critical discourse are especially important in classrooms where minority students are taught as these instructional methods engage the learner in the process of intellectual border-crossing in that the students can move beyond the borders that have been constructed throughout the course of history through political (power, privilege, and policy) and social contexts (norms, culture, and ethos) (Ingram & Waters, 2007).

Additionally, ideals that educators have for themselves and for their students should include those that pertain to the character and courage that strengthen democracy, equity, and social justice in classrooms and throughout the school (Gallavan, 2011). Freire (1970) purported that education is a practice of freedom and necessary to experience the fullness of humanity; without education, people do not make their own way. They merely become what history makes for them. So, in order to ensure consistent and widespread implementation of teaching democracy, it is important that teachers become comfortable, confident, and competent in designing and presenting lessons to and about a multicultural America and a multicultural world.

Standards for the National Council for Accreditation of Teacher Education (2008) compels colleges and universities to ensure that teacher candidates as well as leadership candidates demonstrate their abilities to apply proficiencies related to diversity and to develop classrooms that value diversity. Therefore, institutions of higher education must offer experiences that help candidates confront issues of diversity and inclusiveness that affect teaching effectiveness and improves student learning. Such experiences would afford candidates opportunities to practice the integration of multiple perspectives in their disciplines and to connect curriculum and instruction to their students' experiences and cultures. These informed practices include knowing how to explain, in developmentally appropriate contexts, the effects of cultural and historical events on general and minority populations for the success of all students and the good will of the nation (Banks, 2007; Davis, 2009; Gay, 2000; Grant & Sleeter, 2007; Irvine, 2007).

Multicultural education is a broad concept that calls for school wide transformation for an empowering, inclusive, and equitable school culture and social structure. It also promotes a leadership team that works with teachers from all disciplines to understand and prepare for their highly interrelated roles (Banks, 2007). While developing students' consciousness and building democratic participation are building blocks in multicultural education (Grant & Sleeter, 2007), curriculum and instruction are crucial components. To that end, teachers must discern the confluence of culture and academic achievement on their roles as effective teachers (Banks, 2007; Davis, 2009; Gay, 2000; Grant & Sleeter, 2007; Irvine, 2007).

For all intents and purposes, teachers should be able to employ culturally responsive pedagogy (Gay, 2000) with consistency and confidence. Of the key elements of multicultural education is the consideration of various approaches and perspectives with an appreciation of how such interpretations are based upon beliefs and social identity (Davis, 2009). Banks (2007) recommends the transformative approach to multicultural education. In this approach, the overall framework of the curriculum is structured such that concepts, issues, and themes are considered from a variety of perspectives. Accepting knowledge as a social construction, teachers present diverse understandings, explanations, and interpretations of the same event.

When used by teachers, the social construction practice helps students understand how the knowledge that is constructed is influenced by the ethnic, racial, and social-class backgrounds of the people constructing that knowledge. In view of the growing diversity in America's schools, this study captures a snapshot of how a small group of teachers integrates the NCSS social studies frameworks that offer a concept map, the NCATE diversity standards that guide best practice and prevailing multicultural education principles that offer practical applications for teaching.

Conceptual Framework

This study was conducted specifically to explore the vitality of Dr. King's dream in contemporary classrooms. Of the many possible approaches for framing these phenomena, the author chose to use integrated lines of investigation to construct and to contextualize this study with respect to its place and connection to key, related standards for teaching. The conceptual framework also honors the influence of phenomenology and phenomenology of practice (van Manen, 2007) as it affords teachers a means of considering what they believe and how that translates into how they act in everyday situations.

Phenomenological research gives credence to individuals and how they make sense of their lived experiences. Through this approach, individuals are also given conceptual space to address the significance of events, time, self, and others as they are experienced (Stanford Encyclopedia of Philosophy, 2008). In addition, the idea context for this study provides insights into how individuals build bridges between how they think and feel with how they act as much as it connects who they are with who they may become (van Manen, 2007).

On one hand, the study utilized direct examination by simply recording what occurred around a single organizing principle such as valuing diversity in the classroom. On the other hand, the investigator considered multiple ideologies such as developing civic competence and advancing multicultural education. Using a naturalistic, interpretive approach, the investigator prioritized explaining the phenomenon in terms of participants' meanings and perspectives. For example, the approach allows for teachers' personal presuppositions and interpretations of the concept, aka Dr. King's dream, and how their personal meanings of the concept intersect with its place in the contemporary elementary school classroom.

This approach gives conceptual space for examining whether it should be taught, when it should be taught, and how often it should be taught. Therefore, this qualitative study has the freedom to emerge with its own themes.

Lastly, this conceptual framework was selected to develop the necessary structures to tell a story about the concept of Dr. King's dream and its relationship to 21st century schools and to teacher education with regards to the implications for how colleges of education prepare practicing teachers, provide professional development, and collaborate with schools.

Every learning environment takes into account knowledge of general and individual stages of child development and learning plus educational effectiveness. When teaching about the dream of Dr. Martin Luther King, Jr., teachers are guided by at least three plausible systems: the NCSS social studies standards, NCATE accreditation standards for valuing diversity, and Bank's transformative approach to multicultural education. The conceptual map (see Figure 1) offers a visual display expanding the social studies standards as the constructs grounding Dr. King's dream. The conceptual map also shows the integrated relationships among the concepts.

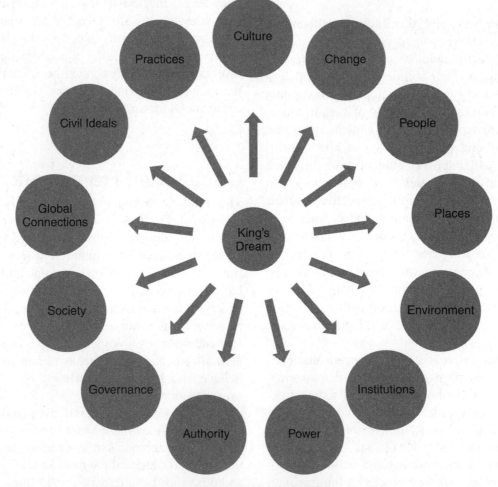

Figure 1   Conceptual Map Expanding the NCSS Themes

Dr. King's dream is at the core of the concept map. The tendrils represent preparation for democratic citizenry, a respect for diversity, as well as the incorporation of multiple perspectives for teaching and learning. This system of concepts frames the expectations for how teachers might honor this building block in the pillars of American history.

Methodology

Subsequent to the 40-year commemoration of Dr. King's death was an appropriate juncture in time to examine the status of Dr. King's dream in America's classrooms. This study was conducted using a qualitative research paradigm as it is useful for studying a limited number of participants. Qualitative research is also valuable for describing complex phenomena and for understanding and describing participants' personal experiences of the phenomenon in question related to Dr. King's dream. The qualitative approach allows for describing this phenomenon as situated and embedded in local contexts (Johnson & Onwuegbuzi, 2004).

In 2008, Americans commemorated the 40th anniversary of Dr. King's death and the 45th centenary since his *I Have a Dream* speech. During Dr. King's lifetime, the American Civil Rights Movement targeted ideals such as integration, justice, and equal access. The movement received notable mention for its victories in Little Rock, Arkansas, and in Memphis, Tennessee. In the 21st century, education is considered to be the new civil right; therefore, the author focused the spotlight on a school in each of these cities to catch a glimpse of how teachers commemorate that moment in American history with regards to its significance and relationship to the life and times of current students.

Participating Cities

During the time of the study, the city of Little Rock proper was managed by a Caucasian mayor with an approximate population of 184,000, while the city of Memphis proper was governed by an African American mayor with an estimated population of 646,000 (Little Rock Community Profile, n.d.; Memphis Community Profile, n.d.). To revisit the Little Rock Nine situation, one can find the Little Rock Central High School Museum and Visitor's Center across the street from the continuously vibrant Little Rock Central High School as well as a memorial on the grounds of the state Capitol. Additionally, the street where the Capitol complex resides was renamed in honor of Dr. Martin Luther King, Jr. To memorialize the Memphis emergency, one can find the National Civil Rights Museum located in the, now defunct, hotel where Dr. King was slain. Each city hosts special events to celebrate the life of Dr. Martin Luther King, Jr., and across the United States the third Monday in January honors his life as the first national holiday that specifically honors the life of an African American.

Participating Schools

The participating schools and school districts in this study are located approximately 200 miles apart. At the time of the study, both school districts employed African American superintendents and both schools were lead by African American principals. The majority of students at each school received free and/or reduced meals. Both schools were elementary schools serving students in grades PK-5. The Little Rock elementary school enrolled approximately 400 mostly Caucasian students while the Memphis elementary school enrolled approximately 1,000 mostly African American students. At the time of the study, the participating Little Rock elementary school was rated as "meets standards" according to the *No Child Left Behind Act* (NCLB), and the participating Memphis elementary school was rated as having a "good" NCLB standing.

Participating Teachers

The participating teachers included 18 teachers from the Little Rock elementary school and 32 teachers from the Memphis elementary school. The Little Rock teachers included 1 African American, 16 Caucasians, and 1 Native American. The only male teacher in the study was in Memphis with 22 African American teachers, 1 Asian teacher, and 9 Caucasian teachers. Credentials of the Little Rock teachers included mostly master's degrees averaging 20 years of experience whereas Memphis teachers held mostly graduate degrees (master's degrees and doctorates) with an average of 12 years of teaching experience. The majority of Little Rock teachers were over age 40 while the majority of Memphis teachers were under age 40. The majority of teachers at both venues reported living in either urban or suburban neighborhoods. Teachers of language arts/literacy/literature, science, mathematics, social studies, music, and art participated from both schools. Other participants in the study included the counselor, speech pathologist/therapist and English Language Learning (ELL) teacher. All grade levels, Pre-K

Table 1 Teacher Demographics

| | Teachers (N=50) | | |
	Little Rock	Memphis	Totals
Gender			
Female	17	32	49
Male	1	0	1
Credentials			
Bachelors	6	12	18
Master's	4	10	14
Master's +	8	8	16
Doctorate	0	2	2
Age Range			
Under 30	3	3	6
31–40	3	14	17
41–50	4	5	9
51 +	8	10	18
Ethnicity			
African American	1	22	23
Asian	0	1	1
Caucasian	16	9	25
Native American	1	0	1
Home Residence			
Suburban	12	18	30
Rural	2	1	3
Unincorporated	1	1	2
Urban/City	3	12	15

through 5th grade, were represented among the participants. Teacher demographics are displayed in Table 1.

Procedures

The investigator employed the three basic stages of research. She declared the research objective, collected the data, and analyzed and interpreted the data (Johnson & Onwuegbuzi, 2004). Before data were collected, written, site permission was granted in each case by the lead school administrator. Thereafter, surveys were placed in the U.S. mail to the school principal with a self-addressed envelope and necessary postage. Upon receipt, the administrator at each school placed the surveys in the faculty lounge with instructions for interested, volunteer teachers to complete and return to the envelope.

Teachers were provided an informed consent form notifying them of the potential benefits, that their participation was voluntary, and that the estimated time investment for completing the survey instrument was approximately 30 minutes. Teachers also were informed that they could refuse to participate, stop participation at anytime without penalty, or they could indicate their withdrawal by simply discontinuing their responses to the questions and returning the participation packet to the envelope or to the investigator. Teachers were further notified of confidentiality in that the data were not associated with their names and that their data would not be withdrawn from the study after it had been collected.

Instrumentation

The survey instrument was created by the investigator (see Appendix A). In order to determine a sufficiently valid and adequately reliable method of approaching the research questions, the investigator considered the types of information being pursued, uses of the information, individuals to be helped by receiving the information, the timeliness of the project, and the available resources (Krathwohl, 1993; Mathison, 1988; Patton, 1990). To those ends, this design was primarily selected for its potential to provide understanding and reasonable generalizability. As the chief interest of this study lay in exploring ways contemporary teachers honor the life of Dr. King, both qualitative and quantitative data were collected.

The survey questions were arranged with the intention of taking each participant through the same sequence and asking each participant the same questions using the same words. This method minimized variation in the questions posed thus affording data that are more systematic and thorough. The different kinds of inquiries helped to capture patterns and differences, attempting to understand the reasons for those differences and where they existed (Krathwohl, 1993; Mathison, 1988; Patton, 1990). The qualitative inquiries were particularly important in gaining insight into learning how teachers honored the life and legacy of Dr. King in the classroom, while the queries also aided in capturing the emotions of the participants on the subject.

The survey questions included what the MLK dream means to participants, the ways they celebrate the MLK holiday, the parts of the MLK dream they believe are important enough to integrate and model for students throughout the academic year, if the participants have taught lessons on the dream, the instructional approach(es) or practice(s) they used, and the ways that participants believe the MLK legacy should be preserved in school settings. The quantitative inquiries were represented in questions pertaining to culture, gender, age, years of teaching experience, subjects they teach, geographical residence, and degree of education.

Limitations

The investigator does not know the reasons that the 50 participating elementary school teachers were motivated to complete the survey. Ultimately, 72 percent of the teachers from the Little Rock elementary school participated and 66 percent of the teachers from the Memphis elementary school participated. While the majority of teachers from each school participated, it is possible that only the teachers who were interested in the MLK legacy took the time to complete survey. Those teachers who chose not to complete the survey may or may not be sending a message. Neither interviews nor observations were conducted in the schools, methods that could have added to the depth, interplay, and interpretation of teacher practices. Because the data are contextualized and unique to the relatively few people included in the research study, the findings may not necessarily generalize to other people or other settings (Johnson & Onwuegbuzi, 2004).

Moreover, the principals at each location were not surveyed to denote their support or indifference about the study or its results. Contingent upon the liberties and/or reluctance of the participants, additional limitations may exist. The quantitative inquiries offered a number of predetermined response categories so that the experiences and perspectives of participants were measured in a standard fashion. Although the investigator used primarily a qualitative approach, the demographic data allowed comparison and descriptive measures as well as a generalizable set of succinctly presented findings.

Results

The data are based on the participants' own categories of meaning. In reporting the results of the study, the investigator used direct quotes and fragments of quotes in order to represent participants' opinions, approaches, and methods in their own terms while capturing the heart of their experiences in their own words. Participant perspectives yielded the emerging themes of equality, justice, fairness, peace, character, respect for, and celebration of cultures. The perspectives are presented in terms of their personal phenomenology, school practices, their phenomenology of practice, and their curricula ideals.

Teacher Phenomenology

Critical reflection has long been a staple of teacher education (Dewey, 1933) as a means for teachers to grapple with the historical, political, and cultural contexts of their work. Hence, this study asked teachers to describe what MLK's dream meant to them personally. The primary theme that teachers expressed related to equality. Teachers in Little Rock reported such sentiments as *it is a reinforcement of Christian beliefs that all people are of equal value and precious in God's sight;* that *all people can live and work together as equals; equal opportunity;* and that it represents *a society in which "color" plays no part.* Teachers in Memphis reported similar sentiments with statements such as *all people were created equal in the eyes of God;* the *end of segregation; equal access;* and that now *people can be judged by their character not their race.*

With respect to observing the MLK holiday in their personal or professional life, one group of teachers reported general activities whereas the other group of teachers reported highly specific events. In this study, 70 percent of the Little Rock participants reported having observed the MLK holiday with *church services* and nonspecific *celebrations in his honor.* Other teachers reported observations *in college only.* Additionally, 80 percent of Memphis teachers reported observation of the MLK holiday with attendance at *parades, speeches, the Civil Rights Museum, prayer breakfast, MLK Annual Walk, Gandhi-King Conference,* and *rallies.* Other teachers reported taking time to reflect on his life or talking about how they can follow his example.

School Practices

As the principles of multicultural education call for an overarching school structure that goes beyond curriculum and instruction (Banks, 2007), teachers were asked about ways that the MLK holiday is acknowledged at their schools. The teachers at one elementary school reported many more signs of recognition than the teachers at the other elementary school. Little Rock teachers reported that their school only acknowledges the MLK holiday in the *morning* via the *school news/announcements.* At this school, there are no school wide activities that address the life of MLK. Memphis teachers reported that their school acknowledges the MLK holiday by *reading the MLK dream over the intercom,* hosting an *assembly,* and by pointing it out in their *news/announcements.* The teachers also noted having *related music, displays of artwork, projects,* and examining his life through *Black history studies* that *extend throughout the year, not just in February.*

Phenomenology of Practice

In a sense, all phenomenology is pragmatic and lends itself to the practice of living (van Manen, 2007). Besides, praxis is the culmination and application of the knowledge, skills, and dispositions that define the substance of teaching (Ingram & Waters, 2007); therefore, teachers were asked if they had ever taught lessons on the MLK dream.

In this study, 80 percent of the teachers in the Little Rock elementary school reported affirmatively while 75 percent of the teachers in the Memphis elementary school reported affirmatively. Lessons from both groups of teachers can be primarily categorized as social studies, language arts, and art lessons. Miscellaneous activities also were reported. Little Rock teachers reported the following types of activities. In social studies, teachers led discussions on *MLK's contributions to society* and his *influence, equality, civil rights,* and the *historical* context of what Dr. King did. These teachers also reported *watching a history channel documentary,* watching a *video on united streaming,* and *visiting the MLK website using the data projector.* In language arts, teachers reviewed related *vocabulary words;* students wrote their own *I Have a Dream* papers, devised an *I Have a Dream* pledge, participated in various *writing* and *journaling* activities, and *read books about MLK.* In art classes, students *designed a medallion to wear all day; they made booklets, made a Dream Mobile* and other unnamed *art activities.* These miscellaneous activities included *visiting the Central High Museum,* listening to the *I Have a Dream speech on tape,* and completing *diversity activity worksheets.*

The Memphis elementary school teachers reported other types of MLK activities. In social studies, teachers led *discussions on MLK's life as a child and his education* so that students could identify with him more readily as a child and student and not always as the adult hero. Students *wrote reports* and *watched films.* They also *studied a unit on MLK's life and legacy* that included the use of PowerPoint presentations, videos, and work sheets. *Students memorized parts of the dream that were important to them.* Further, one class *held a party to celebrate his birthday.* In language arts, students *made a booklet to celebrate the day, read related books,* and *read his autobiography.* In addition, students *recorded their own dreams then stood at the classroom podium and read their dreams to their classmates.* In art classes, students *participated in role play, drew their own dream; made a web of how to achieve their personal dreams, listened to his speech,* and *sang songs about Dr. King's life.* Miscellaneous activities included *visiting the Civil Rights Museum,* integrating *MLK's dream at the beginning of the academic year when students were generating their dreams and goals for the year,* and routinely holding *lessons on fairness* throughout the school year.

When teachers had taught lessons on the MLK dream, elementary school teachers in both Little Rock and Memphis reported that they designed their own lessons. Their schools did not provide related lessons in their designated curricula.

When asked about the educational settings where they learned multicultural approaches to instruction, teachers at both elementary schools reported learning about multicultural approaches to instruction from all five of the sources in the survey. They gained knowledge while enrolled in either their undergraduate or graduate programs or from professional development workshops offered by their schools.

Curricula Ideals

Curricula in multicultural education should interweave inclusiveness in ways that acknowledge and celebrate a multifocal, relational view of the human experience (Tetreault, 2007). To that end, teachers' opinions were sought concerning the parts of the MLK dream that are important enough to integrate and model for students throughout the academic year. Similar sentiments were expressed by each teacher in the categories of fairness, justice, equality, life success, peace, and character. The Little Rock elementary school teachers mentioned that *color should not influence discipline or learning;* that students are *free to be anything they want to be if they make good choices;* that *injustices happen and are wrong; being able to speak and write are important;* people should find *peaceful ways of solving problems and injustices;* that *character is about the person, not the color of skin;* that *trustworthiness and honesty count.* The Memphis elementary school teachers mentioned that people must *treat other people with dignity and worth;* that students must be encouraged to *follow their dreams* and *work hard so students can achieve.* The principles that were consistently mentioned were *fairness, justice,* and *equality.* Other regular comments supported the presence of *diversity in the curriculum,* the promotion of *non-violent/peaceful disagreement* and that *character is what matters.*

Teachers reported that the most ideal ways of preserving MLK's legacy/dream in a school setting included the significance and impact of MLK's life, justice, fairness, coming together, respect and celebration of cultures, peace, and character. The Little Rock teachers recommended the promotion of the *historical import* of the MLK legacy through the *discussion of diversity and what that looks like in schools today versus diversity before* the Civil Rights Movement. These teachers expressed their beliefs that there should be more *student based projects, presentations, posters,* etc., that capture the essence of MLK's impact. These teachers also shared that they want to remain cognizant of the fact that *all students have the same right to learn and be offered various teaching strategies in order to reach them all.* They promoted *working together, diversity, fairness, acceptance, patience, and celebrating cultures* plus *teaching conflict resolution and character to promote respect for all.*

The Memphis teachers recommended a more consistent means of effectively *presenting MLK's legacy* and *the study of the Civil Rights Movement* with *developmental appropriateness.* They also desired to routinely *teach children to have respect for all cultures and races* and to provide students with *opportunities to come together with different groups of people so that differences can be noticed but celebrated.* These teachers reported that they would appreciate *more school-wide observances and celebrations* so that their students could see *MLK's legacy as an everyday philosophy* modeled by all *teachers throughout the year* so that *some will not just focus on it in January and February only.* They also noted that they believe that *teaching the significance of character* and *encouraging students to dream* would be ideal as well.

Discussion

In examining the participating cities, schools, and teachers, similarities as well as differences were reported. Clearly, one city offers more MLK activities than the other city. The death of Dr. King in Memphis might explain the reasons that city has more related MLK activities and stimulates more involvement of its students and citizenry than the Little Rock school and community. Memphis may possibly have more activities than any other community besides Atlanta, where Dr. King lived during the height of the Civil Rights Movement. Likewise, the Memphis school, noticeably, may give more school wide attention to the MLK holiday and attempt to extend the MLK legacy more broadly.

The results of this study were uplifting and revealed a sense of agreement and forward thinking among the teachers who completed the survey from both locations. The findings are even more interesting considering that the participating teachers in the Little Rock elementary school are older and have many more years of teaching, on the average, than the more youthful teachers at the Memphis elementary school. What is consistent with conventional wisdom is that teachers are on the front lines in classrooms every day, and their attitudes and aspirations can make a difference in what lessons are prepared and the ways in which they are led.

The ideals of equality, justice, fairness, peace, character, respect for, and celebration of cultures that emerged as themes from the participating teachers in both locations are noteworthy. The teachers' philosophies seem to be aligned with that of the current U.S. Secretary of

Education, Arne Duncan, who asserts that education is a daily fight for social justice while it promotes opportunity and reduces inequality and that every child is entitled to a quality public education regardless of race, creed, or zip code (Duncan, 2009).

The participating teachers also demonstrated consistency with their ideals and serve as good role models for students when they attend community events that symbolize honor and respect for Dr. King's leadership. These teachers not only locate or design lessons that highlight the MLK dream, they also expressed strong beliefs that such principles are integrated and highlighted in instruction throughout the academic year employing pedagogy that is developmentally appropriate. When considering the ideal instruction of Dr. King's dream, teachers indicated use of many of the standards noted on the concept map. Some standards were used more often and in more depth than other standards, and a few standards such as environment, power, authority, governance, and global connections were not given much attention. This finding might speak to a need that colleges of education can fill.

Implications

The commentaries collected in this study represent a strident call to teacher educators that affirm NCATE obligations. Hence, colleges of education should customarily give teacher candidates opportunities and guidance in developing lessons about diverse populations as well as lessons that recount history from multiple perspectives. In order for teacher candidates and classroom teachers to gain the comfort, confidence, and competence they need to consistently demonstrate value for diversity, their education programs must routinely provide guidance in and practice with this topic that is compelling, meaningful, reflective, and related. It is valuable to know that, although the elementary schools in this study did not provide a curriculum for MLK activities, teachers were able to use what they learned about multicultural approaches from their respective colleges of education and their school districts' professional development opportunities. Perchance if candidates received more practice during their teacher preparation programs, more of them would attempt such lessons and they might be able to carry them out with even greater creativity, diplomacy, and teaching and learning effectiveness.

21st Century Colleges of Education

As America's public schools are increasingly more culturally diverse and aware of their diversity, colleges of education must rethink and reexamine their teacher education programs to ensure that they are able to prepare candidates for the populations that await them. For instance, colleges of education must ensure that their faculty are recalibrated to ensure that every instructor is up-to-date and prepared to integrate multicultural principles into their courses. Instructors must also hold students accountable for adopting multicultural practices and look for evidence of competency in assignments, field experiences, and internship appointments.

Basic multicultural principles and cultural understandings are important because instructional and curricular practices that employ a singular perspective are destined to disengage students (Irvine, 2003). More specifically, all teachers must teach with appreciation that communication of knowledge is conveyed through language and language is highly influenced by culture. Learning must be contextualized as opposed to decontextualized much like it is presented for the purposes of taking standardized achievement tests. When information is separated from students' realities rather than intertwined with their cultures, when instruction is misaligned with students' learning preferences, and when concepts and practices are void of everyday cultural experiences and students' ways of knowing and perceiving, then meaning is not constructed by the learner (Irvine, 2003). Without meaning, the relationships that connect new information with already stored information are splintered as is comprehension (Ormrod, 2009). Where there is no construction of knowledge, learners are merely consumers of knowledge absent ownership and equity.

Another critical consideration in multicultural education is that learning, for some cultures, is a social event, not necessarily an individual one (Irvine, 2003). Therefore, teachers must build in time for students to cooperate and collaborate; teachers must be prepared to indulge in repetition; teachers must initiate highly emotional engagement, lively discussions, stimulating instruction, controversy, creative analogies, symbolisms, and aphorisms (Irvine, 2003). Various assessments must be conducted over time that demonstrate verify competencies through traditional and unconventional means. Teachers must also generously extend encouraging gestures.

In essence, colleges of education should prepare candidates to take their place in the community as nation builders by empowering them to personalize and own the craft of teaching. Teacher education programs must combine critical theory with reflection and experiences that parlay theory into practice through practical and habitual application (Freire, 1970). This combination empowers teachers to become involved in the work of social transformation. According to Freire (1970), this is when teaching truly becomes praxis.

Conclusions

Although the sample of teachers surveyed in this study is small, the investigator believes that this study provides insight and implications for colleges of education that correspond to NCATE directives and relate to the optimal preparation of candidates for comfort, confidence and competence in 21st century classrooms. It is heartening, nonetheless, that such a beautiful American dream remains alive in 21st century classrooms through social studies, language arts, the arts, and through interdisciplinary means. Even though teachers must remain faithful to mandatory frameworks and state academic standards, teachers are finding creative ways to bring historical context to elementary school students so that American ideals can be planted in their hearts and, thereby, extended into following generations. In terms of the status of the dream, it is promising.

References

Ayers, W., Kumashiro, K., Meiners, E., Quinn, T., & Stovall, D. (2010). *Teaching toward democracy: Educators as agents of change.* Boulder, CO: Paradigm Publishers.

Banks, J. (2007). Multicultural education: Characteristics and goals. In J. A. Banks & C. A. McGee Banks (Eds.), *Multicultural education: Issues and perspectives* (pp. 3–30). Hoboken, NJ: John Wiley & Sons.

Davis, B. (2009). *Tools for teaching.* San Francisco: John Wiley and Sons.

Dewey, J. (1933). *How we think: A restatement of the relation of reflective thinking to the educative process.* Boston, MA: Heath.

Duncan, A. (2009). *A call to teach: Secretary Arne Duncan's remarks at The Rotunda at the University of Virginia.* Retrieved from http://www.edgovblogs.org/duncan/2009/10/a-call-to-teach/

Freire, P. (1970). *The pedagogy of the oppressed.* New York: Seabury Press.

Gallavan, N. P. (2011). *Navigating cultural competence in grades K-5: A compass for teachers.* Thousand Oaks, CA: Corwin Press.

Gay, G. (2000). *Culturally responsive teaching: Theory, research, & practice.* New York: Teachers College Press.

Grant, C., & Sleeter, C. (2007). *Doing multicultural education for achievement and equity.* New York: Taylor and Francis Group.

Ingram , I., & Waters, T. (2007). A critical reflection model to teach diversity and social justice. *Journal of Praxis in Multicultural Education, 2(1),* 23–41.

Irvine, J. (2003). *Educating teachers for a diverse society: Seeing with the cultural eye.* New York: Teachers College Press.

Johnson, R. B., & Onwuegbuzi, A. J. (2004). Mixed methods research: A research paradigm whose time has come. *Educational Research, 33(7),* 14–26.

Krathwohl, D. (1993). Methods of educational and social science research. New York: Longman Publishing Group.

Ligon, J. (2005). Transforming schools into democratic sites. In A. Pearl & C. Pryor (Eds.), *Democratic practices in education: Implications for teacher education* (pp. 1–8). Lanham, MD: Rowman & Littlefield.

Little Rock Community Profile. (n.d.). Retrieved from http://www
.epodunk.com/cgi-bin/genInfo.php?locIndex=11591

Mathison, S. (1988). Why triangulate? *Educational Researcher,*
17(2), 13–17.

Memphis Community Profile. (n.d.). Retrieved from http://www
.epodunk.com/cgi-bin/genInfo.php?locIndex=1256

National Council for Accreditation of Teacher Education. (2008).
Professional standards for the accreditation of schools, colleges,
and departments of education. Washington, DC: Author.

National Council for the Social Studies. (2010). *National curriculum*
standards for the social studies: Executive summary. Retrieved
from http://www.socialstudies.org/standards/execsummary

Ormrod, J. (2009). *Educational psychology: Developing learners,*
Upper Saddle River, NJ: Pearson Education, Inc.

Patton, M. (1990). *Qualitative evaluation and research methods.*
Newberry Park: CA: Sage Publications.

Stanford Encyclopedia of Philosophy (2008). *Phenomenology.*
Retrieved from http://plato.stanford.edu/entries/phenomenology

Tetreault, M. (2007). Classrooms for diversity: Rethinking curriculum
and pedagogy. In J. A. Banks & C. A. McGee Banks (Eds.).
Multicultural education: Issues and perspectives (pp. 159–181).
Hoboken, NJ: John Wiley & Sons.

van Manen, M. (2007). Phenomenology of practice. *Phenomenology*
& Practice, 1(1), 11–30.

Webster-Smith, A. (in press). *One night with a king.* Louisville, KY:
Innovative Press.

Critical Thinking

1. What is the author's connection with Dr. Martin Luther King, Jr.?
2. How does this research reveal racial dynamics related to the reported outcomes?
3. What is the author/investigator seeking to learn in this research?
4. Why is this research important?

Appendix A
Status of the Dream Survey

Check one response or fill-in-the-blank for items 1-11. Write a response for items 12a-12j.

1. Gender   ____ Female ____Male

2. Age   ____ Under 30   ____ 31-40 ____41-50 ____51+

3. Your culture   __African American __Latino __Caucasian __Asian __Native American

4. School district _____

5. The community in which you live is most defined as __urban ___suburban __rural

6. Years of teaching experience_____

7. Your education: Bachelor's____ Master's ____ Master's+____ Doctorate____

8. Grade levels you teach this academic year_____

9. Subjects/academic disciplines you teach this academic year_____

10. Estimate the percentage of culturally diverse students you teach who identify as:

    __African American __Latin Descent __Caucasian __Asian Descent __Native American

11. Principal's Culture __African American __Latino __Caucasian __Asian __Native American

12. Please answer the following questions in the space given, on the back or on additional paper.

    a. Have you ever observed the Dr. Martin Luther King (MLK) holiday in your personal or professional life? If so, describe how.

    b. Do your students report ways in which they have observed the MLK holiday in their personal lives? If so, describe how.

    c. What does MLK's *dream* mean to you personally?

    d. What parts of the *MLK dream* are important enough to integrate and model for students throughout the academic year?

    e. Have you ever taught lessons on the dream of Dr. Martin Luther King? If so, give a brief example of the lesson.

    f. If you taught a lesson on the dream of Dr. Martin Luther King, was it part of your school's
    curriculum? _____Yes _____ No
    OR did you design the lesson? _____ Yes _____No

    g. In what educational settings have you learned multicultural approaches to instruction? Check all that apply.
    _____ Undergraduate _____ Master's_____ Master's+
    _____ Doctorate _____ Professional Development

    h. In addition to having a day away from school, are there acknowledgements of the MLK holiday at your school? If so, describe the acknowledgements.

    i. What do you think is an ideal way of preserving MLK's legacy/dream in a school setting?

    j. Are there MLK holiday activities in the community where you live? If so, give brief examples.

Teaching for Social Justice in Multicultural Urban Schools: Conceptualization and Classroom Implication

JOSE LALAS

Presumably, everyone shares the understanding that teaching for social justice means providing students with a supportive learning environment that is just, fair, democratic, and even compassionate. In reality, people are probably using this term to mean many things without actually embracing it as a perspective for educating students in urban school settings.

Is teaching for social justice a process of conveying a set of radical beliefs related to equity, diversity, and racial differences? Does it mean taking a political stand and becoming a change agent in diminishing the inequities in schools? Is it a virtue? Is it possessing certain abilities and knowing certain kinds of knowledge to do certain things in the classroom that reflect equality?

In this article, I examine the different definitions and conceptualizations offered by a number of educator-researchers on teaching and learning for social justice and identify the common principles that are applicable, relevant, and translatable into classroom practice. I then offer a personal perspective on how the notion of teaching for social justice can develop, evolve, and become part of an ideological and political commitment for educational advocacy and activism.

A Glimpse of Urban School Reality

One has to be aware of the demographic situation in urban areas and the social reality of isolation and poverty faced by its residents to make the connection how these conditions affect urban schools and why there is a need to teach for social justice in an attempt to raise the students' identity, provide equitable access to appropriate curriculum and instruction, and remedy any existing harmful inequities.

Jean Anyon (1997) documented that most residents of large urban areas across the United States are African American or Latino. They can be found in New York (57%), Chicago (62%), Los Angeles (63%), Atlanta (70%), Detroit (79%), and Miami (88%). More than half African American, Latino, and Asian reside in the cities of Baltimore, Cleveland, El Paso, Memphis, San Antonio, San Francisco, San Jose, and Washington, D.C. The relatively poorer urban residents who mostly belong to minority populations are isolated from the economic mainstream of middle class jobs and not provided adequate social services because of the impoverished situations of many city governments.

Urban schools are directly affected by the overall political and economic conditions in urban areas and provide what Anyon termed "ghetto schooling" to its diverse student population (Anyon, 1997). Kozol (2005) described the "savage inequities" in inner-city schools further by reporting that nowadays scripted rote-and-drill drill curricula, prepackaged lessons, standard-naming and numbering rituals, display of standards in bulletin boards, rewards and sanctions, and other forms of control on every intellectual activity are prevalent. He also observed that "the more experienced instructors teach the children of the privileged and the least experienced are sent to teach the children of minorities" (p. 275).

Kozol cited Gary Orfield and his colleagues at the Civil Rights Project at Harvard University who reported that "almost three-fourths of Black and Latino students attend schools that are predominantly minority . . . attend schools which we call apartheid schools (in which 99% to 100% of students are non-white). Kozol (2005) concluded that "these are confections of apartheid, and no matter by what arguments of urgency or practicality they have been justified, they cannot fail to further deepen the divisions of society" (p. 275).

Kincheloe (2004) asserted that "urban education is always in crisis—yesterday, today, and certainly in the near future" and that we need to develop a powerful urban pedagogy and a rigorous urban education. In an essay "What Is Urban Education in an Age of Standardization and Scripted Learning?" Hill (2004) writes:

> Urban, we know, is the environment of a city: a complex hub of human endeavor, a place of dense population of diverse peoples, an important location for financial and governmental affairs, and a rich center of cultural imagination and artistic creation. Urban environments are some of the most contradictory areas of our world, where the extremes of our civilization coexist—the richest of the rich and the poorest of the poor, the most privileged and the most disenfranchised, live and work here in large concentrations. (p. 119)

In summary, urban schools serve a big, complex, and diverse group of students in areas marked by profound socioeconomic disparity, ethnic diversity, and higher immigrant populations. Inner-city schools are also more susceptible to educational mandates and sanctions, usually called "reforms," that are monitored carefully for their strict adherence to regulated curricula, technical standards, standardized evaluations, and high-stakes testing preparation and performance.

Educational Inequities in Urban Schools

Clearly, "teaching for social justice" at this point sounds essential for all children in the increasingly diverse urban schools in the United States, where inequities seem to abound and where the majority are refugee students, English language learners, and students of color attend (Goldenberg, 2004; McBrien, 2005).

Rumberger and Gandara (2004) explained with thorough documentation the "seven inequitable conditions" existing in California schools that affect the opportunities of the English learners (ELs) to learn and contribute to the academic gap between them and their English-only counterparts: (1) inequitable access to appropriately trained teachers—25 percent of teachers of ELs were not fully certified and thus ELs are significantly less likely to have a fully credentialed teacher than other low-income non-EL peers; (2) inadequate professional development opportunities for teachers—very little support with only 7% to 10% of reported professional development time focused on the instruction of ELs; (3) inequitable access to appropriate assessment—the only measures of achievement for ELs are tests administered in English with an exclusive reliance on an English-language norm-referenced achievement test for ELs; (4) inadequate instructional time—a great deal of instructional time is lost while ELs are in the structured English immersion program and waiting for their permanent classroom to be assigned, and classrooms with large numbers of ELs have fewer assistants in them to help; (5) inequitable access to

instructional materials and curriculum—75% of the teachers surveyed said that they use the same textbooks for their ELs and English-only students with no materials adapted to their linguistic needs, and teachers with high percentages of ELs are less likely than teachers with low percentages of ELs to have access to appropriate textbooks and instructional materials; (6) inequitable access to adequate facilities—schools with a high concentration of ELs have overcrowded classrooms, poorer working conditions for teachers, less parental involvement, and more neighborhood crime; and (7) intense segregation into schools and classrooms that place them at high risk for educational failure—55% of all elementary-aged ELs in California are enrolled in schools with large concentrations of ELs, two-thirds of ELs attended classrooms in which more than 50% of their classmates were ELs, thus denying them the opportunity to interact with peers who could be English language models and who are achieving at high or even moderate levels.

As you can see from the reported educational inequities in California, that are consciously or unconsciously created and perpetuated, the English language learners are very far from receiving a just, equitable, and fair education in urban schools.

Similarly, McBrien (2005) explained that as children of refugees from usually war-torn countries settle in and attend high-poverty urban areas, they often end up in "a negative, subtractive assimilation pattern, rejecting their family and cultural ties in hopes of being accepted by American peers" (p. 355). Her research warned that "misunderstanding the dire situations of parents, the role of trauma in refugees' behaviors, cultural differences, and best practices in language acquisition has caused many school personnel to hold prejudiced attitudes that lead to discrimination" (p. 356).

In a related study, Lalas and Valle (2005) in a narrative inquiry described the set of inequities perceived by students of color in their school experiences in inner-city schools. Their perceived inequities included interracial differences, racial segregation, racial violence, stereotyping, bullying, religious intolerance, gender segregation, unfair treatment, language barriers, cultural clash, drug and alcohol abuse, gangs, and low income. Lalas and Valle concluded that students' voices need to be heard so teachers can understand their students and "create a caring environment to pave the path for social justice."

While many more recent studies have supported the assertion that students in urban schools, indeed, face many challenges associated with race, ethnicity, and poverty (Haycock, Jerald, & Huang, 2001; Singham, 2003), many educational reforms have also been primarily initiated to improve the academic performance and achievement of inner-city students. Some of these reforms included joint-decision making among teachers and administrators, flexible scheduling, core planning in individual schools, teaming of teachers, integration of curriculum, class size reduction, parental involvement, new forms of assessment, corporate models, and many other research-based approaches.

However, Rothstein (2004) explained that school reforms alone including higher standards, better teachers, more accountability, better discipline, and other effective practices are not enough to overcome the effect of the "social-class characteristics" in widening the academic gap between White, middle class students and their minority and lower-class counterparts. I therefore suggest in this article that teachers and teacher educators must play key roles in the reform effort because reforms are, in the final analysis, classroom reforms that are directly in their hands and the inner-city students they interact with. But can teachers do it alone?

Teachers for Social Justice: Key to Classroom Reforms

It has been well-documented and well-argued that educational reforms are mitigated by urban poverty and cannot transform inequities in schools without thinking about restructuring the "city environment itself, which produces these students and the failing schools" (Anyon, 1997, p. 13). In fact, Anyon (2005) showed that "job, wage, housing, tax, and transportation policies maintain minority poverty in urban neighborhoods, and thereby create environments that overwhelm the potential of educational policy to create systemic, sustained improvements in the schools" (p. 66).

However, classroom teachers are the most essential element because they have the ultimate responsibility to navigate the curriculum and instruction with their students in the classroom. They can examine the impact of race, ethnicity, class, gender, sexual orientation, disability, and poverty itself on the educational outcomes of students in urban schools. They have the intellectual and critical capacity to analyze the purposes, practices, and policies of schools and the impact on students' life opportunities. They may not be able to transform the society's fundamental inequities, but they can contribute in many practical ways by raising the level of social awareness of their students and guiding the curriculum for social justice instruction.

It is imperative that both pre-service and in-service teachers be assisted and guided in developing their content knowledge, pedagogical skills, and advocacy for social justice to improve the overall education of their students in urban schools. However, Cochran-Smith (2004) asserted that there are multiple paths for pursuing the social justice agenda and she called for a broad participation of school- and university-based educators, including classroom teachers, teacher educators, and community advocates who are willing to "rethink beliefs and attitudes about difference, privilege, diversity, and culture" and work "together as teachers but also learners, and as educators but also activists" (p. 156).

What Does It Really Mean to Teach for Social Justice?

Generally, educators may view teaching for social justice as a way of recognizing, respecting, and valuing differences in race, cultural beliefs, social norms, intellectual flexibility, and personal perspectives and dispositions among students in a typically multicultural classroom in urban schools. Many classroom teachers may believe that social justice can be cultivated in the classroom by appreciating diversity, promoting equity, advancing broad-mindedness, and encouraging voice and expression (Brooks & Thompson, 2005). Recently, urban school counselors relate an emphasis in social justice as an essential skill in assuming an advocacy role as part of their work and paying attention to social, political, and economic realities of students and families (Bemak & Chung, 2005).

According to Brown (2004), being administrators and leaders for social justice requires grounding in learning theories, transformative pedagogy, and critical discourse and reflection, and aims "to perceive social, political, and economic contradictions, and to take action against the oppressive elements of reality."

Whatever lens is used in explaining the term, a compelling argument needs to be made for "the necessity of a social justice agenda in a democratic and increasingly diverse society" (Cochran-Smith, 2004, p. 168). Some experts believe that it is quite ironic and a sad statement on the moral responsibility of our schools that one has to even advocate for teaching for social justice (Kohl, 2001; Shamsher & Decker, 2004).

Teaching for social justice can be also defined as a set of beliefs that emphasizes equity, ethical values, justice, care, and respect (Marshall & Oliva, 2006). Practically, it can also translate to making the necessary instructional adaptations for diverse and special needs students to remedy any problem in securing equitable access to instruction and assessment for them (Solomon, Lalas, & Franklin, 2006).

Others frame learning to teach for social justice as a lifelong undertaking that involves:

> coming to understand oneself in relation to others; examining how society constructs privilege and inequality and how this affects one's own opportunities as well as those of different people; exploring the experiences of others and appreciating how those inform their worldviews, perspectives, and opportunities; and evaluating how schools and classrooms operate and can be structured to value diverse human experiences and to enable learning for all students. (Darling-Hammond, 2005, p. 201)

As you can surmise from the definition she uses in working with her teacher candidates, Darling-Hammond (2005) suggests that teachers for social justice need to understand one's identity, other people's background and their worldviews, and the sources of inequities and privileges. Sensitivity to these issues will be helpful in facilitating the learning of students authentically and making a difference in the their lives.

Bell (1997) explains in an even more global and philosophical sense that teaching for social justice means providing all groups in a society full and equal participation in meeting their needs:

Social justice includes a vision of society in which the distribution of resources is equitable and all members are physically and psychologically safe and secure . . . Social justice involves social actors who have a sense of their own agency as well as a sense of social responsibility toward and with others and the society as a whole. (p.1)

It is clear from Bell's conceptualization that teachers, both pre-service and in-service, who would like to practice social justice, need to understand that all individuals in the society must be responsible to each other and deserve to enjoy equity, security, safety, and involvement in their interaction and dealing with others and the society.

Cochran-Smith (2004) frames teaching for social justice as connected to teacher preparation when she asserts in her book that:

the conception of teaching and learning to teach that underlie the social justice agenda include learning to represent complex knowledge in accessible and culturally responsive ways, learning to ask good questions, use diversified forms of assessment to shape curriculum and instruction, develop relationships with students that support and sustain learning, work with—not against—parents and community members, collaborate with other professionals, interpret multiple data sources in support of pupils' learning, maintain high academic standards for students of all abilities and backgrounds, engage in classroom inquiry in the service of pupil and teacher learning, and join with others in larger movements for educational and social equity. (p. 159)

In this description of the "social justice agenda," Cochran-Smith outlines the knowledge, skills, abilities, and disposition that teachers need to develop to move this agenda forward, which include culturally responsive teaching, making content comprehensible and accessible, effective and purposeful questioning, use of different forms assessment to inform instruction, support for students, collaboration with parents, community members, and other professionals, knowing how to interpret data, maintaining high academic standards, being a teacher-researcher, and strong advocacy for equity.

Cochran-Smith (2000) also explains emphatically that teachers and teacher educators, to be effective, need "to struggle to unlearn racism itself" and understand that teaching does not require content knowledge and verbal ability alone in raising pupils' test scores and academic achievement. Teaching, from a social justice perspective, is not a matter simply of transmitting knowledge and equating pupil learning to higher scores on high-stakes tests, but rather engaging pupils in "developing critical habits of mind, understanding and sorting out multiple perspectives, and learning to participate in and contribute to a democratic society by developing both the skill and the inclination for civic engagement" (Cochran-Smith, 2004, p. 159).

Aside from democratic citizenship and a focus on democracy, others suggest that teaching for social justice also includes "anti-oppression education" which highlights diversity in schools and proposes different ways of confronting the inequities faced by students in urban multicultural environments (Brandes & Kelly, 2004).

Many classroom practitioners have also begun designing and implementing instruction that reflects social justice instruction and critical teaching through students' personal stories, use of literature, critical literacy as comprehension (McLaughlin & DeVoogd, 2004), "acting for justice" lessons (Christensen, 2001), thematic units (Beale, 2004), service learning (Lucas, 2005), cooperative learning (Sapon-Shevin, 2004), and other learning strategies across differences (Shor & Pari, 1999).

Classroom Implications

In summary, the conceptualizations of teaching for social justice by several educator-researchers described in this article reveal some common principles that are relevant, appropriate, and translatable to classroom teaching. At this point, it is essential to understand that the teaching and learning processes that occur are facilitated by the on-going dynamic interaction of three major components—namely, the learner, teacher, and the classroom context, as clearly described in the sociocognitive interaction model of meaning construction in reading formulated by Ruddell and Unrau (2004). In this meaning-construction process, both the learner and the teacher use their life experiences, personal values and beliefs, personal and world knowledge, abilities to construct, monitor, and represent knowledge, and personal meaning construction and decision-making disposition in the instructional context of the classroom.

The classroom context where the interaction, generation, and negotiation of meaningful experiences happen is broadly defined here to include the physical classroom arrangement, classroom discipline, key sources of authority where meanings reside, textbooks, assessment instruments, assignments, and many other visual and supplementary materials. Thus, it is through the dynamic interchange of the learner, teacher, and classroom context that the following teaching and learning principles drawn from the teaching for social justice conceptualizations can be applied:

1. Understanding oneself in relation to other individual or group of individuals.
2. Appreciating diversity and promoting equity.
3. Recognizing inequities and how to diminish them.
4. Equitable participation and allocation of resources.
5. Creating a caring and culturally responsive learning environment.
6. Working together as a learning community.
7. Engagement in classroom inquiry.
8. Critical thinking and reflection.
9. Using varied forms of assessment for equitable and fair monitoring of student progress.

This list of common principles implies the significant roles that a classroom teacher and learner must play as he or she interacts, shares, negotiates, and generates knowledge in the classroom context. The infusion of these principles in the classroom occurs only when the teacher, the learner, and the classroom context are joined together as significant variables and consciously relied upon as meaningful and influential sources in the construction and acquisition of knowledge. The student and the teacher not only bring their own personal, social, cultural, economic, and political values from prior beliefs and experiences into the classroom, they also interpret the classroom culture and social life they find there.

As such, providing teaching and learning contexts to students in urban schools and preparing teachers to work in diverse classroom will continue to challenge pre-service and in-service teachers and teacher educators because, as Cochran-Smith (2004) declares with authority, teacher education for social justice is a "learning problem" and a "political problem."

As she suggests, it is not just knowing a content area or body of knowledge, and possessing the pedagogical skills to deliver it, but it is also being reflective and critical as "part of community where the participants deliberately claim the role of educator as well as activist, based on ideological commitment to diminishing the inequities of American life" (p. 19).

References

Adams, M., Bell, L., & Griffin, P. (Eds.) (1997). *Teaching for diversity and social justice.* New York: Routledge.

Anyon, J. (1997). *Ghetto schooling: A political economy of urban educational reform.* New York: Teachers College Press.

Anyon, J. (2005). What "counts" as educational policy? Notes toward a new paradigm. *Harvard Educational Review, 75*(1), 65–88.

Beale, U. (2004). Family is someone to tuck you into bed: Teaching a unit on family diversity. In M. Shamnsher, E. Decker, G. Brandes & D. Kelly (Eds.), *Teaching for social justice.* Vancouver, BC: British Columbia Teachers' Federation.

Bell, L. (1997). Theoretical foundations for social justice education. In M. Adams., L. Bell & P. Griffin (Eds.), *Teaching for diversity and social justice.* New York: Routledge.

Brandes, G. & Kelly, D. (2004). Teaching for social justice: Teachers inquire into their practice. In M. Shamnsher, E. Decker, G. Brandes & D. Kelly (Eds.), *Teaching for social justice.* Vancouver, BC: British Columbia Teachers' Federation.

Bemak, F. & Chung, R. (2005). Advocacy as a critical role for urban school counselors: Working toward equity and social justice. *ASCA Professional School Counseling,* February 2005, 196–202.

Brooks, J., & Thompson, E. (2005). Social justice in the classroom. *Educational Leadership,* September 2005, 48–52.

Brown, K. (2004). Leadership for social justice and equity: Weaving a transformative framework and pedagogy. *Educational Administration Quarterly, 40*(1), 77–108.

Christensen, L. (2001). Acting for justice. *Rethinking Schools Online, 15*(2), Winter.

Cochran-Smith, M. (2000). Blind vision: Unlearning racism in teacher education. *Harvard Educational Review, 70*(2), 157–190.

Cochran-Smith, M. (2004). *Walking the road: Race, diversity, and social justice.* New York: Teachers College Press.

Darling-Hammond, L., French, J., & Garcia-Lopez, S. (Eds.). (2002). *Learning to teach for social justice.* New York: Teachers College Press.

Genesee, F., Lindholm-Leary, K., Saunders, W., & Christian, D. English language learners in U.S. schools: An overview of research findings. *Journal of Education for Students Placed at Risk, 10*(4), 363–385.

Goldenberg, C. (2004). Literacy for all children in the increasingly diverse schools of the United States. In R. Ruddell & N. Unrau (Eds.), *Theoretical models and processes of reading, fifth edition.* Newark, DE: International Reading Association.

Haycock, K., Jerald, C., & Huang, S. (2001). Closing the gap: Done in a decade. *Thinking K-16,* Spring 2001. Washington, DC: Education Trust.

Hill, J. (2004). What is urban education in an age of standardization and scripted learning? In S. Steinberg & K. Kincheloe (Eds.), *19 Urban questions: Teaching in the city.* New York: Peter Lang.

Kincheloe, J. (2004). Why a book on urban education? In S. Steinberg & K. Kincheloe (Eds.), *19 Urban questions: Teaching in the city.* New York: Peter Lang.

Kohl, H. (2001). Teaching for social justice. *Rethinking Schools Online, 15*(2), Winter.

Kozol, J. (2005). Confections of apartheid: A stick-and-carrot pedagogy for the children of our inner-city poor. *Phi Delta Kappan, 87*(4), 265–275.

Lalas, J. & Valle, M.E., (2005). Paving the path for social justice in teacher education: Responding to urban student voices. Unpublished manuscript, presented at the Educational Leadership for Social Justice Institute: University of Redlands.

Lucas, T. (2005). Fostering a commitment to social justice through service learning in a teacher education course. In N. Michelli & D. Keiser (Eds.), *Teacher education for democracy and social justice.* New York and London: Routledge.

Marshall, C., & Oliva, M. (2006). *Leadership for social justice: Making revolutions in education.* Boston: Pearson Allyn & Bacon.

McBrien, J. (2005). Educational needs and barriers for refugee students in the United States: A review of the literature. *Review of Educational Research, 75*(3), 329–364.

McLaughlin, M. & Devoogd, G. (2004). Critical literacy as comprehension: Expanding reader response. *The Reading Teacher, 48,* 52–62.

Michelli, N., & Keiser, D. (Eds.). (2005). *Teacher education for democracy and social justice.* New York and London: Routledge.

Rothstein, R. (2004). A wider lens on the Black-White achievement gap. *Phi Delta Kappan, 86*(2), 104–113.

Ruddell, R. & Unrau, N. (2004). Reading as a meaning-construction process: The reader, the text, and the teacher. In R. Ruddell & N. Unrau (Eds.), *Theoretical models and processes of reading.* Newark, DE: International Reading Association.

Rumberger, R., & Gandara, P. (2004). Seeking equity in the education of California's English learners. *Teachers College Record, 106*(10), 2032–2056.

Rusch, E. (2004). Gender and race in leadership preparation: A constrained discourse. *Educational Administration Quarterly, 40*(1), 14–46.

Shamsher, M., & Decker E. (2004). Editors' foreword. In M. Shamnsher, E. Decker, G. Brandes & D. Kelly (Eds.), *Teaching for social justice.* Vancouver, BC: British Columbia Teachers' Federation.

Shamsher M., Decker, E., Brandes, G., & Kelly, D. (Eds.). (2004). *Teaching for social justice.* Vancouver, BC: British Columbia Teachers' Federation.

Shields, C. (2004). Dialogic leadership for social justice: Overcoming pathologies of silence. *Educational Administration Quarterly, 40*(1), 109–132.

Shor, I., & Pari, C. (1999). *Education is politics: Critical teaching across differences.* Portsmouth, NH: Heinemann.

Singham, M. (2003). The achievement gap: Myths and reality. *Phi Delta Kappan, 84,* 586–591.

Solomon, M., Lalas, J., & Franklin, C. (2006). Making instructional adaptations for English learners in the mainstream classroom: is it good enough? *Multicultural Education, 13*(3), 42–45.

Critical Thinking

1. What is social justice?
2. How can classroom teachers promote social justice in their curricula and classrooms?
3. What are the benefits for the students?
4. Why is it important to teach social justice?

Jose Lalas is associate dean, professor of literacy, and director of teacher education with the School of Education at the University of Redlands, Redlands, California.

From *Multicultural Education,* Spring 2007, pp. 17–21. Copyright © 2007 by Caddo Gap Press. Reprinted by permission.

The Human Right to Education
Freedom and Empowerment

CAETANO PIMENTEL

Introduction

Education is widely understood as the gradual process of acquiring knowledge or the process of training through which one teaches or learns specific skills; furthermore, it can be understood as disciplining the character. It is undoubtedly the spread of knowledge and information but, more than this, the imparting of experience, knowledge, and wisdom. One of the fundamental goals of education is the transmission of culture between generations.

In a broader sense, education begins with life itself[1] and goes beyond formal or informal schooling, encompassing the struggles and triumphs of daily life. It is essential both for children and adults—in the case of the latter, to replace or prolong initial education in schools, colleges, and universities as well as in apprenticeship.[2]

Religious values, political needs, and the system of production have always determined the standards of education. Indeed, education has always been subordinated to the expectations concerning the roles individuals would perform in their social group.

But the importance of education has been acknowledged in a much broader sense:

Dakar Framework for Action:

6. (. . .)[Education] is the key to sustainable development and peace and stability within and among countries, and thus an indispensable means for effective participation in the societies and economies of the twenty-first century, which are affected by rapid globalization.(. . .)

Indeed, as a human right, education is the acknowledgement of the individual's rights rather than his or her role in the capitalist goals of the economic growth; the human right to education is the way through which one can conquer freedom and become a genuine individuated[3] being, self-aware and yet deeply and truly connected to others.

The Brazilian educator Paulo Freire formulated ideas concerning literacy (and the learning process as a whole) which became influential internationally. According to Freire, the process of learning necessarily goes along with the learner's ever-increasing awareness of his/her existential condition and of the possibility of acting independently to change it—with individuals reflecting on their values, their concern for a more equitable society, and their willingness to support others in the community. Learning process is what Freire called 'conscientization,' an empowerment of the individual.

Freire expanded education's technical-pedagogic dimension to a political one, which demands a major shift of the education paradigm into 'praxis': reflection plus action, which highlights the importance of learners becoming active subjects in the learning process, taking a position of agents.

Education throughout History[4]

Education has taken as many forms as cultural, political, and religious values have been created by human kind. In Egypt and Mesopotamia (3000 B.C.), the first formal group education appeared as Scribal schools. In primitive societies of hunters and gatherers, learning process was based on watching and imitating. Jewish religious education was a way to glorify God. In Greece, a man-centered approach to education was available to a privileged male few, both at home and in State schools—but, still, the whole purpose of education was to subordinate the individual to the needs of the State.

Medieval education was an evolution of Catholic catechetical schools of the second century—Monasteries were both for those preparing for a monastic vocation (oblati) and those whose aims were secular (extend); the later Middle Ages witnessed the rise of the great cathedral schools followed by the ascendancy of the universities and the complexities of scholasticism.

During the Renaissance, there was a turn back to humanistic cultural values of Classical Greece and Rome. Based mainly on parish church provisions and also found in some monasteries and palaces, primary schools were mostly limited to elites. Changes in economical relations arising at the time led to the education of some new skills, such as computation and bookkeeping.

In the following centuries, complex changes on economic, political, technological, religious, scientific, and aesthetic levels demanded a substantial increase in provisions for schooling and the access to schools. The fullest expression of the need to broaden formal educational opportunity came in calls for universal schooling. Convictions and trends moved in the direction of enlarged access despite the persistence of some conservative medieval opposition. These convictions and trends meant increasing the number of schools and putting them near potential student populations in towns and villages—and a big challenge was to find a sufficient number of competent schoolmasters.

The 18th century gave way to the emergence of the idea that schools should be instruments of social reform (Samuel Hartlib, John Dury, John Comenius), and access to them should be increased. Social and religious reforms, nationalism, commerce and industry, colonization, and scientific methods of inquiry and technological innovations were responsible for the development of a number of theories concerning education and school access, amongst them the ideas of secular universal elementary schooling and the development of critical rational thinking.

The North American colonies along the Atlantic coast (17th–18th centuries) transplanted the ideas of Renaissance (South), Reformation (North), and Enlightenment (Franklin and Jefferson), whereas earlier settlements established by Spain and France maintained a parish organization of schools. Private schools (Franklin), free public school for all (Jefferson), language teaching, and the diffusion of knowledge were some of the trends concerning education for white boys and girls.

In Brazil, Asia, and Africa, Jesuit Priests were in charge of the catechisation of natives and the children of the first colonisers. Particularly in Brazil, their mission was to teach them to read, perform labor, and organize themselves in order to protect the land occupied, which led the native culture to be nearly extinguished. The Jesuits remained in Brazil until 1759, when they were sent away from the country by Marques de Pombal, whose goals were to create an administrative elite and increase the production of raw materials and commodities (e.g., sugar) to be traded by Portugal.

Major social, political, cultural, and economical changes arose after the French and American revolutions, when four major trends to modern western democracies were established: the rise of nation states, urbanization and industrialization, secularization, and popular participation.

Nation states, with their enormous power to gather and focus both human and material resources, have come to interfere increasingly in the definition of educational policy and schooling. Industrialization and urbanization resulted in a concentration of human populations more and more diverse. Secularization has meant an augmenting emphasis on rational/empirical modes of explanation. Popular participation refers to an enlarging access to involvement in the governance of public life.

These trends have not and do not come about in a linear way, nor are they alike everywhere, either in timing or scope. Changes are still operating in many western and eastern countries today, and as a result we can find four major issues that modern states are yet to sort out: social stratification and class interests, religion and ideology, race and ethnicity, and geography (i.e., localism, regionalism).

The Right to Education— A Historical Background

Educational process implies a number of actors: those who receive education, those who provide education, and those who are responsible for the ones who receive education.[5] The first legislation on educational issues were an attempt to balance the complex relations between these actors. The social, cultural, political, and economical changes brought about in the modern age by the emancipation of the individual have had a great impact on the relationship between the individual and the state. The recognition of rights of individuals and duties of state are both a reflection and a consequence of these changes.

Although we may find today the right to education enshrined in many provisions of human rights law, none of the classical civil instruments such as the British Bill of Rights of 1689, the Virginia Declaration of Rights of 1776, the American Declaration of Independence of 1776, and the French Declaration of Rights of Man contained any language specifically related to the right to education, although some recognised the freedom of teaching from state interference. Indeed,

> Public education was perceived as a means to realising the egalitarian ideals upon which these revolutions were based (. . .).[6]

Child labor in England had been subject to legal regulation since the first Factory Act in 1802 (Health and Morals of Apprentices Act), but it was not until the Factory Act of 1833 that legal provisions imposed restrictions on child labor and created the obligation of school attendance—first in textile establishments, and then the Mines Act came later in 1842.

The Constitution of the State of Indiana (1816), in its article IX, recognized the importance of education to the preservation of free government (sect. 1) and also stated goals to provide for a general system of education, free and equally open to all (sect. 2).[7]

The socialist ideas of a paternal state, drafted by Marx and Engels, and the liberal anti-clerical concepts of freedom (of science, research and teaching, among others) also influenced the definition of the educational rights by means of compulsory school attendance and similar measures. In the latter half of the 19th century the Constitution of the German Empire contained a section entitled "Basic Rights of German People," and the German Weimar Constitution of 1919 included a section on "Education and Schooling."[8]

The first provision on the human right to education with a corresponding duty of the state to provide education was in Stalin's Soviet Constitution of 1936. As a matter of fact, the right to education has been a major fundamental right in all constitutions of socialist states.[9]

As a major interest of the state and society, education turned out to be a right of the individual, rather than solely a duty of state or parents. And in the 20th century, many international and regional instruments and a number of national constitutions have recognized the right to education, which thus has become a fundamental human right.

At the international level, peaceful resolution of conflicts has always been a major concern: the International Peace Conference (The Hague, 1899), the League of Nations (Versailles, 1919), and the Declaration by United Nations (1942) to support the fight against the Axis Powers were the expression of nations' concern about peace and security.

When the Second World War was over, representatives of 50 countries met in San Francisco, in 1945, to draft the United Nations Charter. The purpose of the United Nations, set forth by the charter, comprehends not only peace and security goals, but a broader scope of actions and international cooperation efforts concerning economic, social, cultural, and humanitarian problems and, above all,

> to reaffirm faith in fundamental human rights, in the dignity and worth of the human person, in the equal rights of men and women end of nations large and small (. . .).[10]

UNESCO, the United Nations Educational, Scientific, and Cultural Organization, was born in the same year. Peace and security, justice, the rule of law and the human rights, and fundamental freedoms are clearly expressed in its declaration of purpose.

The United Nations' Universal Declaration of Human Rights (UDHR) (1948) enshrines, in its Article 26, the right of everyone to free and compulsory education and recognizes the role of education in the development of the human personality and the respect for human rights and fundamental freedoms.

The process of positivization of the rights contained in the UDHR at the international level started with the two covenants adopted in 1966. Concerning education, the International Covenant on Economic, Social, and Cultural Rights spells out in more detail the right to education, in its articles 13 and 14, including the right to free compulsory primary education, adult education, freedom to choose education, and recognition of the role of education in enabling all persons to participate effectively in a free society.

Education as a Human Right

Emphasising education as a basic human right shifts the focus from simply concentrating on the contribution that education can make to economic development. The focus on education as a fundamental human right is that the internationally agreed Human Right treaties form a common platform for enshrining equal rights to education for all citizens. In this perspective the individual in society is viewed as a stakeholder with rights and not an object of charity or investment.[11]

The international community has embraced education as a basic human right, as major international and regional instruments disclose a number of important State obligations.

The right to education is recognized as the one which empowers individuals to cope with basic needs, such as health and dignity, and which enables the full and free development of his or her personality. Also, education is required for the implementation of the collective right to development—which means that any society depends on the education of its members to enjoy satisfactory conditions of life and fully achieve its goals, to assure that they will be able to fulfill personal needs such as housing, health, and food.

Education is now recognized as the pathway to freedom, and free democratic society depends on its members' abilities to freely choose, think, and express themselves, and to actively contribute to the political and social processes in pursuit of their interests.

Education is assigned to the "second generation" of human rights, those related to equality. The nature of second generation rights is fundamentally social, economic, and cultural. In social terms, they ensure different members of the community equal conditions and treatment, securing the ability of the individual to lead a self-directed life and to pursue the development of his or her personality.[12]

Second generation Human Rights are mostly positive rights, "rights (or guarantees) to," as opposed to negative rights which are "rights from," usually freedom from abuse or oppression by others. Hence, education must be provided by a series of positive actions by others: school systems, teachers, and materials must be actively provided in order for such a right to be fulfilled, representing things that the State is required to provide to the people under its jurisdiction.

But the Right to Education can also be linked to first generation (freedom) rights, for it entitles individuals to a certain degree of liberty and autonomy before states and their institutions (the right to choose education), and to third generation (solidarity) rights: the right to self-determination, to economic and social development, and to participate in the common heritage of mankind,[13] aspiring ultimately to the full respect for and protection of all human rights. The article 8(1) of the Declaration on the Right to Development reads as follows:

> States should undertake, at the national level, all necessary measures for the realization of the right to development and shall ensure, *inter alia*, equality of opportunity for all in their access to basic resources, education, health services, food, housing, employment and the fair distribution of income. Effective measures should be undertaken to ensure that women have an active role in the development process. Appropriate economic and social reforms should be carried out with a view to eradicating all social injustices.[14] (emphasis added)

The right to education is complex and demands strong commitments at many levels to be implemented. As a result, many different aspects of the right to education have been emphasized by the international community since the Universal Declaration of Human Rights, perhaps due to a lack of full commitment to the principles related to this multifaceted right.[15]

In the subjective dimension of the right to education, we can take the definition given by Canotilho[16] to social rights:

> Social rights are subjective rights inherent to the portion of space where the citizen lives, independently of immediate justitiability or exequibility. (. . .) Neither the state nor third parties can damage re-entrant juridical positions in the ambit of protection of these rights.

In the objective dimension, the right to education, as any other social right, according to Canotilho, can be put into practice through lawmaking processes, in order to create material and institutional conditions for these rights to be granted to individuals. In addition, it must be provided as a materialization of the subjective dimension of these rights and a duty of the state to comply with its institutional obligations. These obligations range from minimum guarantees inspired by neoliberal principles to the full wide-ranging welfare model adopted by social-democracies in northern Europe, for instance.

Education Today

Albeit the repeated affirmation and recognition of education as a human right, one hundred and thirteen million children around the world are not enrolled in school and many more than that drop out before being able to read or do simple mathematics. These figures will add to the ranks of 880 million illiterate adults in the world[17] and to escalating unemployment, poverty, and income disparities. A lot has changed since the rise of nation-states, but educational policies are still ruled by economical and political interests.

Since 1950, the estimated illiteracy rates have significantly declined,[18] but as a complex right which consists of quantitative and qualitative aspects, these numbers fall short on describing how well all the purposes comprised by the Article 26 of the Universal Declaration have been fulfilled. On this matter, Joel Samoff has stated:

> The most important measures of success of an education programme are the learning that has taken place and the attitudes and values that have been developed. There is little point in reducing the cost of 'delivering education services' without attention to whether or not learning is taking place. Assessing learning and socialization is both complex and difficult. That it is difficult makes it all the more important that it be addressed systematically and critically.[19]

Although in most countries primary education is compulsory by law, it is rarely enforced. From the Proclamation of Teheran, in 1968, to the World Declaration on Education for All adopted by the World Conference on Education for All in Jomtien, Thailand in 1990, and the Dakar Framework for Action of 2000, many changes took place, especially with regard to the focus of education.[20]

Basic principles, such as "free education" and "primary education," have been distorted to exempt governments from the duty of implementing education as set by international and national law. In contrast, statements concerning the international community's agreement on the education's purpose have been considerably broadened:

> Taking into account all of the above, the vision of education's aims and purposes that has emerged over the past several decades is essentially focused on two inter-related themes. The first, which can be broadly labelled as 'Education for peace, human rights and democracy', is directly linked to—indeed, has largely been inspired by—the aims and purposes proclaimed in Article 26 of the Universal Declaration. The second, which can be broadly labelled as 'Education for development,' is linked to Article 26 in a more complex way.[21]

Right to Education v. Access to Education

According to the Annual Report 2004 by the UN Special Rapporteur on the Right to Education, Professor Katarina Tomasevski, there are many obstacles to the full realization of the right to education: the commercial approach to education (rather than a human-right approach), gender discrimination, and school drop-out are the ones which deserve special attention.

The liberalization of education, under the World Trade Organization GATS (General Agreement on Trade in Services), is within the concept of free market and competitiveness, raising a conflict between trade law and human rights law.[22] Deregulation, privatization, and reduction of public spending leads to the elimination of public funding or subsidy to public services—and that includes education. The underlying philosophy of this process leads to a change of perception from public and community good to individualism and individual responsibility.[23]

In this context, education is not regarded as a right which must be made freely available, accessible, acceptable, and adaptable. It is reflected in an altered vocabulary, as pointed out by Prof. Tomasevski, in which "access" to education does not grant free education funded by the government.[24] Education is no longer provided by the entitlement to rights; it is determined by purchasing power and the rules of self-regulation of the market, as a part of a creeping privatization of education that causes the transference of education costs to poor families. An astonishing array of education charges, from direct school fees to indirect costs for books, pencils, uniforms, and transportation, are supposed to be afforded by family units worldwide.[25]

We must take into account that the expansion of private education is creating a two-tiered system that creates inequities rooted in social class, caste, and gender—where public education, in very poor condition due to lack of resources, is only used by those who cannot afford to pay for better quality schooling provided by private institutions. This dual education system creates and perpetuates a divided society, and this division goes beyond purchasing power, for this inequality also reflects discrimination on the basis of religion, language, race, and gender.

Moreover, not every family can afford having one or more of their children going to school instead of helping the family earn more income. Very often, costs are cited by parents as the major factor in deciding to keep children out of school.[26]

Education is the way to break out of the poverty cycle: through education children, particularly girls, can ultimately help increase the family income, and stay healthier. Education is definitely the foundation for equitable human and economic development.

In developing countries, the education crisis is also a crisis of education quality. Those children who do attend school in the world's poor countries face enormous obstacles to their learning. A chronic teacher shortage most of the time results in large-sized classes, multi-graded or divided by shifts. Another problem is the inadequate supply of basic materials, such as books, desks, and benches, not to mention the lack of transportation for students and the too-often empty stomach.

Gender Inequalities

Gender issues concerning education are also a major concern,[27] for very large gender inequalities still exist in the majority of developing countries. Education not only provides basic knowledge and skills to improve health and income, but it empowers women to take their rightful place in society and the development process. It gives them status and confidence to influence household decisions—women who have been to school tend to marry later and have smaller families. Their children are better nourished and are far more likely to do well at school. Educated women can overcome cultural and social factors, such as lack of family planning and the spread of disease, which contribute to the cycle of poverty.[28]

But girls are needed at home and they contribute largely to the family income: they look after siblings, nurse sick relatives (e.g., in the context of HIV/AIDS in Africa), and do domestic tasks. Besides that, the low number of government schools and the limited public transport make distance a barrier for both boys and girls, but for reasons of safety and security, most parents are reluctant to let their daughters walk long distances to school. In some African countries, sexual abuse of girl pupils—at school and on the way to school—is one of the main reasons parents withdraw their daughters from school.[29]

Girls and women have been victimized by economic factors not only in the realm of education, as it has been pointed out by Prof. Tomasevski.[30] A major shift on many other factors is equally necessary to ensure employment and political representation opportunities—but equal access to education is a significant start to achieve gender equality.[31]

Inclusive Education

Another step in universal education goals is inclusive education: a strategy contributing towards the ultimate goal of promoting an inclusive society, one which enables all children/adults, whatever their gender, age, ability, ethnicity, refugee status, impairment or HIV status, to participate in and contribute to that society. Difference is respected and valued. Discrimination and prejudice must be actively combated in policies, institutions and behavior.[32]

Within schools inclusive education is an approach which aims to develop a child-focus by acknowledging that all children/adults are individuals with different learning needs and speeds. It leads people to learn about themselves and understand their strengths and limitations, which makes them better able to recognize and understand not only individual health and physical conditions, but also the political, economic, and social conditions that surround them. One must view oneself positively in order to move from passive to active participation.

School Drop-Out

Providing schools is only part of the problem—a huge one for sure, but still only a part of it; the drop-out phenomenon poses another challenge to schools, families, and governments, as well as to the quality of education provided in many countries.[33]

According to Paulo Freire,[34] society itself prevents students from having access to and remaining at school; indeed, dropout is nothing but "school push-out," i.e., children/adults are expelled from school for a number of social, economic, and cultural factors.

The causes that give rise to the dropout/push-out of students are many, such as to help their families, course failure, pregnancy, lack of interest, addiction to drug/alcohol, financial reasons, gender and ethnic discrimination, not getting along with teachers and/or other students, or criminality. School drop-out/push-out is an issue which concerns both developed and underdeveloped countries—and it does not refer only to minority groups such as immigrants and indigenous populations.

Effective and relevant education is important to combat school dropout/push-out. It helps the promotion of the personal development of the individual, ensuring that educational content, method, and scheduling are appropriate to the different needs and circumstances of each person—as in the case of rural areas, where harvest season can make children and adults prioritize work rather than school,[35] or school-dropout caused by the student's mere lack of interest.

Indeed, concerning this problem in China and Colombia, Prof. Tomasevski stated in her Annual Report 2004:

> (. . .) an important reason for children's dropping out of school was their dislike of the education provided them. That many children, when asked whether they liked school—rarely as this happens—answered in the negative is a sobering lesson for education authorities.

From sub-Saharan Africa to Canada, from rich to poor, from eastern to western culture countries, the world cannot refrain from dealing with education issues—such as exclusion and poor quality education—raised by many cultural, religious, ethnic, social, or economic factors, and their impact on the educational process.

The Dakar Framework for Action affirms:

> 43. Evidence over the past decade has shown that efforts to expand enrollment must be accompanied by attempts to enhance educational quality if children are to be attracted to school, stay there, and achieve meaningful learning outcomes.

To address these problems, it is necessary to promote a shift in the education paradigm. Students are not supposed to be coadjuvants to education process and schools should not be an instrument of dominant economic and political purposes.

All students in school is inclusive education in the broadest sense—regardless of their strengths or weaknesses in any area, they become part of the school community. They are included in the feeling of belonging among other students, teachers, and support staff.[36]

A New Approach to Education

The strategic objectives of UNESCO's Medium-Term Strategy for 2002–2007 provide a new vision and a new profile for education, as follows:

- Promoting education as a fundamental right in accordance with the Universal Declaration of Human Rights;
- Improving the quality of education through the diversification of contents and methods and the promotion of universally shared values;
- Promoting experimentation, innovation and the diffusion and sharing of information and best practices as well as policy dialogue in education.

It is important to highlight the concern towards the methods and contents of education, an important issue which has been raised in recent years in order to achieve the higher purpose of education, that is to say, the learner's achievement and development.

In addition, there must be developed a deeper understanding of literacy, a core educational issue, which is widely seen as essential for enabling a person to function fully in his/her society and is often reduced to the ability to read and write in the official language.

This narrow understanding of literacy, developed in the last two centuries with the formation of the nation state, industrialization, and mass schooling, does not recognize the role it plays as a key to developing a critical mind—which does not rely merely on the development of such skills, but on the liberation and full development of the individual.

Human Rights Education

Human rights education has been proclaimed in various global and regional legal instruments, such as The Charter of the United Nations, which reads:

> To achieve international co-operation in solving international problems of an economic, social, cultural, or humanitarian character, and in *promoting and encouraging respect for human rights and for fundamental freedoms* for all without distinction as to race, sex, language, or religion; (. . .)[37] (emphasis added)

Moreover, the Universal Declaration of Human Rights proclaimed

> as a common standard of achievement for all peoples and all nations, to the end that every individual and every organ of society, keeping this Declaration constantly in mind, shall strive by *teaching and education to promote respect for these rights and freedoms* (. . .)[38] (emphasis added)

At the regional level, the African Charter on Human and Peoples' Rights, in its article 25, explicitly calls on African states to

> promote and ensure *through teaching, education and publication, the respect for the rights and freedoms contained in the present Charter* and to see to it that these freedoms and rights as well as corresponding obligations and duties are understood, (emphasis added)

In 1994, the General Assembly of the United Nations proclaimed the United Nations Decade for Human Rights Education (1996–2004), on recommendation of the World Conference on Human Rights (Vienna, June 1994).

The recognition of education as a major instrument to promote and enforce human rights is based on the conviction that we all have the right to know our rights—and it can only be enforced when we learn and understand about the human rights enshrined in national constitutions and in all international human rights instruments.

People are empowered to act when they learn about their human rights and can actively defend themselves from abuses, overcoming their lack of concern towards politics. In addition, imparting of knowledge and skills regarding human rights promotes

a. The strengthening of respect for human rights and fundamental freedoms;

b. The full development of the human personality and the sense of its dignity;

c. The promotion of understanding, tolerance, gender equality and friendship among all nations, indigenous peoples and racial, national, ethnic, religious, and linguistic groups;

d. The enabling of all persons to participate effectively in a free society;

e. The furtherance of the activities of the United Nations for the maintenance of peace.[39]

Empowerment through human rights education develops the individual's awareness of rights and obligations regarding his/her human condition and includes everyone in the citizenry; it charges people with the responsibility of claiming rights for themselves and others, as well as respecting those rights. People become aware of the difference individuals can make and the importance of joining efforts to do so. Additionally, human rights can become more tangible when related to people's own life experiences, which strengthens the power of these rights in the process of building a more equitable, just, and peaceful world.

The implementation of human rights education goes beyond inclusion in the schools' curricula, for it involves a whole commitment to human rights, from the training of teachers to a safe and healthy learning environment. Human rights education is not only a set of contents to be transmitted to learners, but also understandings of how and where it will be done. Schools' staff must be fully aware of human rights, which should be incorporated in all strategies, procedures, and activities developed and performed by them.

Finally, human rights education should be an integral part of the right to education,[40] both in formal and non-formal schooling.

Sex Education

Education on sexuality, relationships, and reproductive health is deeply connected with women's and girls' rights. The Convention on the Elimination of All Forms of Discrimination against Women (CEDAW) and the recommendations of the General Comments of the related Committee are clear on the importance of sex education.[41] Nevertheless, sexuality is inherent to human beings and men and women, boys and girls, every person should have the right to be educated on sexual health, and the Committee of the Rights of the Child states that

> Adequate measures to address HIV/AIDS can be undertaken only if the rights of children and adolescents are fully respected. The most relevant rights in this regard, in addition to those enumerated in paragraph 5 above, are the following: (. . .) the right to preventive health care, sex education and family planning education and services(. . .).[42]

Sex education is the process of acquiring knowledge and skills concerning sexual behaviour (which comprises sexual orientation, relationships, birth control, and disease prevention), empowering individuals to make decisions, assert their choices, and protect their physical, emotional, and moral integrity. As a result, individuals learn when and how to seek help and become better able to engage in healthier relationships, exert control over their own lives, and recognize other people's rights, cultural differences, and attitudes towards sexuality—mainly regarding sensitive issues such as sexual orientation, contraception methods, abortion, and gender roles.[43]

One could never emphasise enough the core importance of sex education to children—especially girls—with regards to HIV/AIDS prevention, family planning, and elimination of gender discrimination. The right to sex education should be realized with the inclusion of sex education in the curricula worldwide, despite large obstacles such as cultural, religious, and political factors which might tend to prevent schools and educational authorities from enforcing such education.

Education Paradigm Shift

Independently of the reasons, be they economic, social, or cultural, a major change in the pedagogical approach is necessary to deal with the current education crisis. Curriculum adaptation, special programs, acknowledgement of cultural peculiarities, and flexible school schedules are many of the potential solutions for such educational problems as large classes, uncaring and untrained teachers, passive teaching methods, inappropriate curriculum, inappropriate testing/student retention, and lack of parent involvement.

A *Manual on Rights-Based Education* has been developed as a result of collaboration between UNESCO Bangkok and the UN Special Rapporteur. Such an approach recognizes that human rights are interdependent and inter-related and seeks to protect and put them into effect. Human rights are the means, the ends, the mechanisms of evaluation, and the focal point of Rights-Based Education. The manual is based on international human rights law, aiming to bring human rights standards into educational practice, encompassing health, nutrition, safety, and protection from abuse and violence.

One of the issues addressed in the manual is the quality of education, which should be learner-centred and relevant to learners, as well as respectful to human rights, such as privacy, gender equality, freedom of expression, and the participation of learners in the education process.[44] This means that both content and pedagogical approach are crucial to quality of education.

Furthermore, the content should be related to real-life experiences and learners' cultural and social context, encouraging full participation of all parties involved, enforcing their fundamental rights of freedom of expression, access to information, privacy, and health, among others. The importance of education content has also been recognised by the Committee of the Rights of the Child.[45]

A propos, Freire had always stressed the need to change the traditional schooling system, which treats students as objects and contributes to the marginalization of minorities, as opposed to "liberatory" pedagogy, one that uses the dialogical method to facilitate the growth of humanization and empowerment[46] and enforces the principle of equality while respecting differences. The focus must be on education for equity, transformation, and inclusion of all individuals through the development of consciousness and critical thinking.

Freire has based his work on the belief in the power of education to change the world for the better, supporting freedom from oppression and inclusion of all individuals. In his book *Pedagogia da Autonomia* (Pedagogy for Autonomy), he enunciates the three pillar concepts of teaching:

1. there is no teaching without learning;
2. to teach is not to transmit knowledge; and
3. the process of education is a human peculiarity.[47]

Freire's pedagogy requires a whole new approach to the exercise of power over education; responsibility is to be shared between all parties involved (teachers, learners, those responsible for learners, and the community at large) from the curriculum planning to the process of learning. The dialogical process resulting herein comes about from the recognition of and respect for each individual's personal knowledge and skills, which enables all to participate equally in the organization and development of education.

Teachers and learners share equally the experience of learning through questioning, reflecting, and participating; as a result, this process contributes to the enforcement of infinitely diverse human potentials, instead of refuting, weakening, distorting, or repressing them.

Such a pedagogical approach builds up to the formation of critical consciousness and allows people to question the nature of their historical and social situation—to "read their world"—becoming more than a mere passive object to the information disseminated by others.[48]

The schooling system is not supposed to be limited to reproducing a dominant ideology, to teach a truth that is not true for all, fostering impossible dreams and hopes in the learners; but at the same time it must allow them to dream. It requires an affectionate—yet scientific—posture by the teacher.[49]

The role of the teacher is crucial, but s/he cannot be just an individual in the world, rather than an individual with the world and with other people, sharing the experience of being in "quest"—in a permanent process of questioning, changing, growing, learning, improving, and finding new directions.[50]

Teachers become educators when they get fully aware of the surrounding world's influence on every individual. And, most of all, they must be open to the reality of learners, get acquainted with their way of being, adhere to their right to be. Educators choose to change the world with learners.[51]

Being actively aware of the world, the teacher becomes better able to do more than just disciplining the process through which the world gets into the students, imitating the world, filling their empty vessels with chunks of knowledge.[52]

In an ever-increasing globalized world, learning processes must recognize and value differences; teachers must be prepared to deal with diversity in every level (cultural, social, economic, religious, ethnic, and linguistic) and schools must be prepared to cultivate a joyful environment to foster this get-together. Learning is to celebrate the communication and interaction between people.

Conclusion

The future of humankind relies on the fulfillment of the right to education: equality, freedom, dignity, equitable social and economic development, sustainable development, and peace are highly dependent on successful universal education policies.

Nevertheless, just providing universal formal schooling is not a guarantee of an educational system that prepares the individuals to be free. Although it is clear that a lot of work needs to be done until every individual is provided education worldwide, the process of learning can always be improved to achieve its goals of preparing people to participate actively and consciously in the society of which they are part. And education must be respectful of every individual's cultural background so that each person can make the most of it in their personal journey and in their interaction with others.

A rights-based approach to education requires respect for the human rights of all individuals involved in the learning process; it offers education as an entitlement, rather than as a privilege, and does not exempt any actor of the learning process from his/her responsibility for the full protection and fulfilment of any other fundamental right.

Such an approach to education takes place when learners are respected for their autonomy and dignity; moreover, they must be provided all things necessary for them to take part actively in the learning process and to develop their awareness of reality. They learn about their past, understand their present, and acknowledge their power to fight for their future.

Education requires dialogue and affection between teachers and learners. The learning process involves joy, beauty, affection, ethics, equality, mutual respect, and faith in a better world.

Notes

1. World Declaration on Education For All, Jomtien, 1990, article 6. Learning begins at birth. This calls for early childhood care and initial education. These can be provided through arrangements involving families, communities, or institutional programmes, as appropriate.

2. CRC General Comments General Comment no. 1: The Aims of Education, Article 29 (1).

3. According to Jung, individuation is "a process by which individual beings are being formed and differentiated . . . having as its goal the development of the individual personality" (Jung, C.W. 6: par. 767), bearing in mind that "As the individual is not just a single, separate being, but by his very existence presupposes a collective relationship, it follows that the process of individuation must lead to more intense and broader collective relationships and not to isolation." (CW 6, par. 768) "Individuation does not shut one out from the world, but gathers the world to itself." (CW 8, par. 432) quoted in Sharp, 1991.

4. Bowen, 2003.

5. Nowak, 2001:190.

6. Hodgson, 1998:8.

7. "Article 9: sect. 1st. Knowledge and learning generally diffused, through a community, being essential to the preservation of a free Government, and spreading the opportunities, and advantages of education through the various parts of the Country, (. . .) shall be and remain a fund for the exclusive purpose of promoting the interest of Literature, and the sciences, and for the support of seminaries and public schools.(. . .); sect. 2. It shall be the duty of the General assembly, as soon as circumstances will permit, to provide, by law, for a general system of education, ascending in a regular gradation, from township schools to a state university, wherein tuition shall be gratis, and equally open to all." As in http://www.in.gov/icpr/archives/constitution/1816.html#art9

8. Hodgson, 1998:8.

9. Nowak, 2001:192.

10. United Nations Charter, Preamble.

11. Education, Democracy and Human Rights in Swedish development co-operation, Swedish International Development Cooperation Agency, 2004: p. 17.

12. Nowak, 2001:196.

13. As in http://www.fact-index.eom/t/th/three_generations_of_human_right8.html

14. Declaration on the Right to Development, adopted by the General Assembly in 1986.

15. World Education Report 2000:23.

16. Gomes Canotilho, 1998:434.

17. Dakar Framework for Action-Education For All: Meeting Our Collective Commitments Text adopted by the World Education Forum-Dakar, Senegal, 26–28 April 2000: 6. (. . .) it is unacceptable in the year 2000 that more than 113 million children have no access to primary education, 880 million adults are illiterate, gender discrimination continues to permeate education systems, and the quality of learning and the acquisition of human values and skills fall far short of the aspirations and needs of individuals and societies.(. . .)

18. World Education Report 2000:17.

19. J. Samofi; Education for What? Education for Whom? Guidelines for National Policy Reports in Education, UNESCO, Paris, 1994, p. 28. quoted in Special Raporteur's Annual Report 2004.

20. "Every person—child, youth, and adult—shall be able to benefit from educational opportunities designed to meet their basic learning needs. These needs comprise both essential learning tools (such as literacy, oral expression, numeracy, and problem

solving) and the basic learning content (such as knowledge, skills, values, and attitudes) required by human beings to be able to survive, to develop their full capacities, to live and work in dignity, to participate fully in development, to improve the quality of their lives, to make informed decisions, and to continue learning. . . ." (Jomtien Declaration, 1990: article 1)

21. World Education Report 2000:76.

22. Special Rapporteur Annual Report 2004, par. 15.

23. As seen in http://campus.northpark.edu/history/Koeller/ ModWorld/Development/neoliberalism.htm; website on longer on line.

24. Special Rapporteur Annual Report 2004, par. 8.

25. OXFAM Briefing Paper 3, "A Tax on Human Development", 2001:2.

26. Not surprisingly, social protection is one of the prevention measures of International Programme on the Elimination of Child Labour of the ILO, so that families do not have to rely on their children's workforce to pay for their living.

27. World Declaration on Education For All, Jomtien, 1990: Article 3 (3) The most urgent priority is to ensure access to, and improve the quality of, education for girls and women, and to remove every obstacle that hampers their active participation. All gender stereotyping in education should be eliminated.

28. A Fair Chance, Global Campaign for Education, April 2003:2.

29. Ibid, p. 25.

30. Special Rapporteur Annual Report 2004, par. 32.

31. As seen in http://www.unesco.org/education/ educnews/20_12_12/gender.htm; website on longer on line.

32. As seen in http://www.eenet.org.uk/theory_ practice/whatisit .shtml; website no longer on line.

33. World Declaration on Education For AU, Jomtien, 1990, Preamble: "More than 100 million children and countless adults fail to complete basic education programmes; millions more satisfy the attendance requirements but do not acquire essential knowledge and skills; (. . .)"

34. Freire, 2000:50–51.

35. A Fair Chance, Global Campaign for Education, April 2003: 24.

36. Dakar Framework for Action, par. 67: There is an urgent need to adopt effective strategies to identify and include the socially, culturally and economically excluded. This requires participatory analysis of exclusion at household, community and school levels, and the development of diverse, flexible, and innovative approaches to learning and an environment that fosters mutual respect and trust."

37. Charter of the United Nations, article 1(3).

38. Universal Declaration of Human Rights, proclamation.

39. Report of the United Nations High Commissioner for Human Rights on the implementation of the Plan of Action for the United Nations Decade for Human Rights Education, Appendix, par. 2.

40. UNESCO Executive Board 165th Session-Elements for an Overall Unesco Strategy on Human Rights, par. 31.

41. CEDAW, Article 10(h): "Access to specific educational information to help to ensure the health and well-being of families, including information and advice on family planning." General Recommendations of the Committee, 21: "In order to make an informed decision about safe and reliable contraceptive measures, women must have information about contraceptive measures and their use, and guaranteed access to sex education and family planning services, as provided in article 10 (h) of the Convention." Recommendations for government action, par. 31: "States parties should also, in particular: (c) Prioritize the prevention of unwanted pregnancy through family planning and sex education."

42. Committee of the Rights of the Child, General Comments 3, par. 6.

43. As in http://www.avert.org/sexedu.htm

44. *Manual on Rights-Based Education.* Collaborative project between Katarina Tomasevski (UN. Special Rapporteur on the Right to Education) and UNESCO Asia and Pacific Regional Bureau for Education, Bangkok, Thailand.

45. General Comment no. 1 (on the article 29 [I]) "The Aims of Education", par. 3: "The child's right to education is not only a matter of access (CRC—art. 28) but also of content. (. . .)"

46. Freire, 1970: 43.

47. Freire, 1998.

48. Freire, 1970: 68.

49. Freire, 1998.

50. Freire, ibid.

51. Freire, ibid.

52. Freire, 1970: 36.

References

Bowen, James (2003), *A History of Western Education,* Vol. I–III, Routledge.

Canotilho, J.J. Gomes (1998), *Direito Constitucional e Teoria da Constituicão,* Almedina.

Freire, Paulo (1970), *Pedagogia do Oprimido,* Paz e Terra, versão.

Freire, Paulo (1997) *Pedagogia da Autonomia: Saberes necessaries à pratica educativa,* Paz e Terra, versão e-book.

Freire, Paulo (2000), *A Educaçao na Cidade.*Cortez, versao e-book.

Hodgson, Douglas (1998), *The Human Right to Education.* Ashgate.

Nowak, Manfred (2001). The Right to Education. In Asbjorn Eide, Catarina Krause, & Allan Rosas, *Economic, Social and Cultural Rights—A Textbook,* Martinus Nifhoff Publishers, pp. 189–211.

Critical Thinking

1. What are human rights?

2. How can human rights be integrated in the curriculum?

3. What teaching techniques model the value of human rights?

4. Why is it important to teach human rights?

CAETANO PIMENTEL resides in Rio de Janeiro, Brazil. This article is based on a monograph he wrote for a post-graduation course on Human Rights and Democracy at the University of Coimbra, Coimbra, Portugal.

An Investigation of How Culture Shapes Curriculum in Early Care and Education Programs on a Native American Indian Reservation

The drum is considered the heartbeat of the community.

JENNIFER L. GILLIARD AND RITA A. MOORE

Introduction

Instruction informed by children's home and community culture is critical to supporting a sense of belongingness that ultimately impacts academic achievement (Banks, 2002; Osterman, 2000). American school populations are increasingly diversified with immigrants and English language learners; but American teachers are over 90% European American (Nieto, 2000). Educators who are from different cultural perspectives than those present in the families and communities of the children they teach, "may render it difficult to "see" the cultural identities shaping the behaviors and achievement of their students" (Moore, 2004a). How then do we prepare the predominantly European American teaching force to strengthen the connection between home and school cultures for children of diverse backgrounds?

Many researchers have examined schooling or education in culture, affording opportunities for educators to broaden their knowledge base and learn about delivering curriculum from multiple cultural perspectives (Bullock, 2005; Lee & Walsh, 2005; Luo & Gilliard, 2006; Nagayama & Gilliard, 2005; Walsh, 2002). For example, Nagayama and Gilliard (2005) investigated similarities and differences in curriculum in early childhood programs in Japan and in the United States. The present study extends these efforts to understand education and culture in early learning programs on a Native American Indian Reservation.

The purpose of this study was to explore the presence of family and community culture in curriculum at three tribal early care and education programs. Classroom observations and open-ended interview questions with eight early childhood teachers were conducted at three early learning programs, two infant and toddler programs and one toddler and preschool program on the Flathead Indian Reservation. Data were collected by four preservice early childhood

teachers as a culminating field experience for a special topic university course called Cultures and Communities, in which the preservice teachers were enrolled. Two university professors served as investigators for this study, one of whom taught the course and accompanied the preservice teachers on the field experience that resulted in data collection.

Culture and education in the three tribal early learning programs were explored in this study through teacher responses to interview questions, field notes taken during classroom observations, and journals written by the preservice teachers who collected the data. The research question that guided the study was: How does the culture of the family and community shape curriculum?

Rationale and Conceptual Framework

In an essay exploring the dynamics between the school and home culture in addition to a transformative approach to bringing family and community culture into the schools, Moore (2004a) suggested two issues emerged: the treatment of a child's personal, social, and cultural literacies within school cultures affects the child's sense of belonging as well as achievement (Osterman, 2000), and the fact that most educators are unprepared to work with cultural values different from their own (Banks, 2002; Nieto, 2002).

Children experience a sense of belongingness when their home culture is not alienated from the school culture (Osterman, 2000). When the school culture that reflects the culture of a teaching force that is 90% European American (Nieto, 2000) is the dominant culture, there is potential for the marginalization of children from cultural and linguistic minorities (Moll, 1992). To provide maximum learning opportunities for all children, "School and home connections should work toward establishing a network of interactions and authentic learning situations that draw immediately from student background, language, and culture" (Moore, 2004a, p. 23). Skilled educators motivate students to learn by inviting participation of multiple cultures and perspectives, providing students with opportunities to connect curriculum with their own funds of knowledge (Allen & Labbo, 2001; Moll, 1992; Moore with Seeger, 2005).

The notion of children having a sense of belongingness within school cultures is clearly demonstrated in many Native American communities, especially in tribal K-12 schools on reservations, where the majority of teachers are of European American descent. For example, according to the Department Head of Tribal Education on the Flathead Reservation, the vast majority of teachers in the public tribal schools are women, middle class, and Anglo. She suggested that the educators have little or no training in dealing with a culture different from their own which has a negative effect on the social belongingness and academic achievement of Native children (J. Silverstone, personal communication, January 23, 2003). It is interesting to note that this fact did not hold true for the early childhood teacher participants in this study; all but one of the teachers were registered tribal members and all seemed motivated to provide early learning curriculum within the context of family and community culture.

It is often difficult for educators who do not share their students' culture to provide curriculum within the context of their students' family and community cultures (McIntosh, 1989; Moore with Seeger, 2005). The education literature suggests that a successful strategy for teaching children from diverse cultures and languages is teachers exploring who their students are in order to understand their students' family and community contexts (Jones & Derman-Sparks, 1992; Luo & Gilliard, 2006; Moore, 2004a; Van Horn & Segal, 2000; Yang & McMullen, 2003) as well as educators examining their cultural identities and how their cultural lens affects their teaching (Allen & Labbo, 2001; Grossman, 1999; McIntosh, 1989; Moore, 2004a; Van Horn & Segal, 2000).

The purpose of this study was to explore the presence of family and community culture in curriculum at three tribal early care and education programs on the Flathead Indian Reservation. The present study extends the literature that focuses on examining education in culture providing opportunities for educators to expand their knowledge base through learning about delivering curriculum from multiple cultural perspectives (Bullock, 2005; Lee & Walsh, 2005; Luo & Gilliard, 2006; Nagayama & Gilliard, 2005; Walsh, 2002).

Overview of the Study and Method

The Participants and Setting

The participants of the study were eight female early childhood educators with at least three years of experience. Three of the teachers earned Associate's degrees in Early Childhood Education, three earned Bachelor's degrees in Education or a related field,

and two earned Child Development Associate Certificates (CDAs). Seven out of eight were registered members of the Salish or Kootenai tribes, or were descendants of another American Indian tribe. Four female preservice teachers enrolled in an early childhood education Associate's degree program in a small university in Montana collected the data. Data were collected as a culminating research project for a special topic course: Cultures and Communities. Two university professors, both teacher educators, served as investigators for the study. One of the investigators, L. Jennifer, was also the instructor for the course in which the preservice teachers were enrolled and for which the data for the present study were collected.

The study took place on the Flathead Indian Reservation. Two infant-toddler centers and one toddler-preschool center located on the Flathead Reservation were sites for the study. One of the programs was located on the campus of a small four-year degree granting tribal college, and two of the programs were located in nearby tribal early learning facilities. Many of the families enrolled in the programs were members or descendants of the Salish and Kootenai tribes or members or descendants of other American Indian tribes; and they were defined as being of low socioeconomic status.

The Flathead Indian Reservation located in Montana is home to the Confederated Salish and Kootenai tribes. The tribes are a combination of the Salish, Pend d'Oreille, and Kootenai and have lived in this region for thousands of years (Travel Montana, 2006). As of July 2003, the 1.2 million acre reservation had 4,457 enrolled tribal members living on the reservation, accounting for 17% of the population on the reservation, and 2,481 enrolled members living off the reservation (First Class News, 2003).

Additionally, Montana is ranked 48th in the United States in terms of unemployment: in some Montana counties the unemployment rate is between 5–10% and on the Flathead Reservation the unemployment rate is 41%. Of those who are employed on the Flathead Indian Reservation, 38–48% access poverty-based services on a seasonal basis (First Class News, 2003). In 2001, Montana had the fifth lowest per capita income among all 50 states and the average personal income was $22,532. The Montana reservations' per capita income in 2000 was estimated at a low of $7,100 and a high of $22,754, with the average per capita income $14,738 (First Class News, 2003).

Research Questions and Data Sources

The research was guided by the following question: How does the culture of the family and community shape curriculum in the investigated tribal early childhood programs?

Prior to the study, the preservice teachers were instructed by their professor on a phenomenological approach to qualitative research (Valle & King, 1978) along with interview and observation procedures and qualitative research design (Creswell, 1998; Moore, 2004b). In addition, the preservice teachers engaged in multiple class activities and read from multiple sources that explored background information and knowledge on how cultures influence communities and schooling.

Data were collected at the end of two full days of observation and interviews. Data sources for the study included the following:

Table 1   Interview Questions

What is your work title and the name of the school/institution for which you work?

Please describe any training or education you have had to prepare you for your job as an early childhood educator. Have you taken some college courses or hold a degree or CDA? If so, in what area is your degree?

Would you please describe your culture and ethnicity?

Please describe the children you teach. How old are they? Do they have special learning needs? Describe their culture and ethnicity. Would you describe your teaching philosophy or beliefs? How are aspects of culture or multiple cultures included in your curriculum?

Please describe a typical day in your classroom.

How are parents included in your program/classroom?

Do you believe that your culture has influenced your teaching or instruction? If so, how?

Do you believe that the culture of the children you teach has influenced your teaching? If so, how?

How do you individualize instruction around the culture of the children you teach?

What are some cultural issues that might impact learning in your classroom?

What do you believe is important for teachers to know about instructing children from diverse cultures or backgrounds?

Is there anything else you would like to tell me that might be helpful to me as an early childhood teacher who is interested in adapting instruction to cultural differences of learners?

(1) the reflective journals in which the preservice teachers wrote responses to what they were learning about home and school culture in the tribal early childhood programs; (2) interview responses from the early childhood teachers; and (3) field notes of the principal investigator and the preservice teachers. A copy of the interview questions is provided in Table 1.

Procedures

Classroom observations and open-ended questions with eight early childhood teachers were conducted by preservice teachers at three tribal early learning programs, two infant-toddler centers and one toddler-preschool center on the Flathead Indian Reservation. Interview sessions were tape recorded and transcribed by interviewers. The study occurred near the end of the university's May interim session, 2006, as a culminating field experience for a course about cultures and communities.

Prior to the study, the preservice teachers were asked to respond to a survey prompting them to think about how their culture and their perceptions of diverse cultures might influence their teaching beliefs and actions. During the two-day study, preservice teachers were instructed to write reflective journals in which they wrote responses to what they were learning about home and school culture in the tribal early childhood programs and to keep detailed field notes of their classroom observations. At the end of the observation and interview period, preservice teachers submitted transcribed interviews, field notes of observations, and reflective journals to the course instructor. Jennifer, the investigator who also taught the communities and cultures course, regularly visited the classrooms to which the preservice teachers were assigned, writing field notes during each visit.

Data Analysis

At the end of the course, the investigators, Jennifer and Rita, sorted the data by color coding pertinent responses to the research question. Separately, we each color coded the responses from the three data sources: preservice teachers and Jennifer's field notes; preservice teachers' reflective journals; and transcribed interview responses of the early childhood teachers.

Next, we compared our coded data for accuracy, discussing any variations. We then read the data another time for the purpose of developing clarifying themes within the research question. Themes were determined by noting whether at least eight responses from the three data sources alluded to the main concept of the theme (Lincoln & Guba, 1985).

After that, we re-read the data, marking categorization changes as needed. After discussion of meaning, minimal modifications were made involving interpretation of responses. Trustworthiness was established through careful triangulation of data in which at least three data sources cross checked the findings for the research question. To be considered relevant to the question, a similar response from each data source had to be sorted to a question at least five times (Lincoln & Guba, 1985).

Results of the Study

The results of the study are grouped below according to the research question. They are examined through themes that consistently emerged under the question.

Question

How does the culture of the family and the community shape curriculum in the early learning programs we investigated on the Flathead Indian Reservation? The theme focusing this question was: different ways of understanding and defining culture. Three distinct categories emerged within this theme: respect of children, families, and community, building a sense of belongingness and community through ritual, and the importance of family values and beliefs.

Data sources used to support this theme were preservice teachers' journals, Jennifer and the preservice teachers' field notes, and the early educators' responses to interview questions.

Different Ways of Understanding and Defining Culture

The early educators interviewed in this study did not define their interactions with the children and families with whom they worked as necessarily influenced by culture but rather by respect and understanding. They described their part in honoring and perpetuating the day-to-day rituals, routines, and beliefs of the place in which they lived.

Three categories within this theme consistently emerged. Categories were: respect of children, families, and community, building a sense of belongingness and community through ritual, and the importance of family values and beliefs.

Respect of Children, Families, and Community

The data suggested that respect was central to the early learning curriculum in these programs. Stated beliefs and observed interactions revealed that the early educators approached their interactions with children, families, and community in a reflective and respectful fashion. For example, one preservice teacher wrote in her journal:

> The parents' personal wishes, beliefs, and ideas about child care are honored and respected in the classroom. . . . The providers are doing an excellent job researching parents' values and keeping so much of it at the heart of learning for the children in these environments.

Another topic that emerged regarding respect was the early childhood teachers' acceptance of the tribal tradition of honoring life in death. Death is considered a celebration of life on the reservation and the entire family, including children, and community comes together for a week to support each other and remember and honor the one who died. The educators' acceptance of family and community practices around death is illustrated in the following statement made by one of the teachers during her interview:

> Another thing I've noticed in the classroom, and it also involves death, is that if there is a death in the family or community everybody goes and so they will miss about a week of school. I am very accepting of that.

Another example of respect that consistently surfaced in the data was awareness of what curricular activities may offend certain tribes. For example, telling of the "Coyote Stories" (Confederated Salish & Kootenai Tribes, 1999), children's tribal stories passed down by elders, came up repeatedly as an activity that some tribes believe should only occur during the winter. Thus the early educators in these tribal programs ask parents before they proceed with many curricular activities such as the telling of the "Coyote Stories" so they do not offend any of the families by going against their beliefs. As one teacher indicated in her interview:

> Because we do have so many different tribal cultures represented in the classroom, one of the things you have to be aware of is doing something that one tribe thinks is okay and another does not. The "Coyote Story" is an example of that. Around here they are only told during the winter so it would be totally inappropriate for us to read one during late spring. And, you need to check before you do something like that.

Last, all of the reflective journals contained descriptions of how soft, quiet and gentle the interactions were between educators and children. One preservice teacher wrote, "The words spoken were kind and tender, the touches and sounds were reassuring and encouraging."

Building a Sense of Belongingness and Community through Ritual

The data revealed a number of rituals that served to bring together the children, parents and teachers as well as the community. The ritual that was common to all three data sources was the powwow. Powwows, common to most American Indian tribal customs, bring together the tribal community both in preparation for the event and for the actual powwow; they are festive, cultural celebrations of life. (Schultz, 2001).

Interviews and observations for this study were conducted one week after an annual powwow celebration on the Flathead Reservation so teachers were rich with stories about the event. Preparation for the powwow consisted of teachers, children and parents working together to make the children Native outfits including moccasins, ribbon shirts and dresses, as well as shawls. At the center and in their homes, the older children were encouraged to dance, sing and drum together in preparation for the event. Some parents showed the older children dances they knew at the centers; dances vary depending on a person's tribe so children were exposed to different ways of celebrating through dance. During her interview one teacher described the powwow:

> We had a powwow. We do this every year. It is usually the first Friday of May. Each child is given a pair of moccasins for the powwow. This year, our center and parents decided to make their own outfits, so we had someone (from the community) come in and help with ribbon dresses and the parents helped with that, too. And, some of them decided to do their own moccasins. So, the parents are really involved.

The ritual of drumming and music was clearly associated with daily classroom curriculum. Drums were found in all programs and children were encouraged to play the drums, dance and sing to drumming plus come together for group activities when teachers drummed. As a non-native teacher at one program stated:

> One of the things I do notice is that every tribe has the drum as the center of their music and dancing and I didn't realize when I first started teaching how much it draws people into the circle and it does. The drum is the heartbeat and it does draw the children in.

Similarly, one of the preservice teachers wrote in her daily journal, "The drum is considered the heartbeat of the community."

Other rituals described in the data were as follows: community work days; the tribal celebration of life in death; the practice of swaddling infants and teaching swaddling of infants; families bringing or wearing different patterns marked on their clothing or as decoration; and regularly planned feasts such as the Bitterroot Feast. For this feast the community comes together to commemorate the beginning of spring through digging the bitterroot for medicinal purposes and through sharing in a celebratory feast.

Importance of Family Values and Beliefs

The data in this category showed that the early educators valued parent involvement in their program curricula. All of the educators gave examples of including parents, and even extended family, in program activities and events. For example, all three programs requested that parents participate in social gatherings that provided meals so families could get to know each other and so teachers and families could spend time conversing. Parents were invited to participate in: regularly scheduled center meals including breakfast and lunch; special holiday meals or celebrations; the day-to-day classroom activities; for example, some teen parents spend 40 minutes a day in the classroom, feeding and playing with their infants and toddlers; field trips; special cooking and dancing demonstrations; and preparation for powwows.

Data reflecting the day-to-day interactions between parents and teachers revealed that although educators included families in the curriculum through a more traditional additive fashion as defined by the parent involvement activities above, they also worked to connect home and school culture through a more transformative approach (Moore with Seeger, 2005) where understanding of parents' beliefs and values was sought and this understanding was used to transform curriculum. That is, daily respectful interactions provided families with voice to shape and extend curriculum in their children's programs. As one educator suggested:

I think you just need to be aware . . . there are many different cultures and many different ways to do different things . . . and just don't learn about the culture, a little bit. You could talk with the family and learn about what their beliefs are. You know, the way they do things.

The data provide several examples of parent voice in the early learning programs. For example, an interview with one teacher revealed that parents in her program had day-to-day decision-making power through voting on and planning curriculum activities. Parents decided what types of special activities the children would do around holiday and cultural celebrations. For example, in one program, parents decided that the children would make their own moccasins for the annual powwow.

Another instance of parent voice was the fact that parents could bring their family's tribal language into the center through word labels, music, and modeling of their language. Most of the programs taught the Salish language but many of the children were members of or descendants of other tribes and spoke a variety of tribal languages. Educators were very respectful and asked parents clarifying questions about each child's home language or languages. Although challenging, educators tried to reinforce for children the importance of speaking in their various tribal languages.

An additional case of respectfully discussing parent values while taking into account the caretaking needs of the educators was as follows: a mother brought her child to the center secured to a cradle board to help the child grow and maintain strength. This was a family tradition for this mother and the elders in her family believed strongly that this was a necessary custom when raising an infant. The educators were respectful of the mother's values, allowing the infant to be secured to a cradle board while at the center, but presented her with their concerns of not being able to burp or hold the infant, or help him quickly enough if he choked. After a few days of these respectful discussions, the mother elected to leave the cradle board at home.

Limitations of the Investigation

The authors acknowledge that the participants were able to observe and conduct interviews for only two days; however, funding for the field experience was limited. Consequently, the number of participants was limited to eight and the number of programs studied was limited to three.

Discussion

The literature suggests that the largely European American teaching force is unprepared to work with an increasing population of ethnically diverse children (Banks, 2002; Nieto, 2002). Thus educators fail to link home and community culture to school culture, failing to foster a sense of belongingness in children that promotes academic achievement (Moore, 2004a; Osterman, 2000). However, the early educators in this study seemed sensitive to the need to link home and community culture to school curriculum and worked on a daily basis through respectful and thoughtful planning and interactions to learn about as well as to honor parent beliefs and values.

Interestingly, seven of the eight early childhood teacher participants were members of the Salish or Kootenai tribes or descendants of the tribes. The majority of K-12 teachers on the Flathead Indian Reservation are Anglo according to the Department Head of Tribal Education (J. Silverstone, personal communication, January 23, 2003). It is also noteworthy that these Native early educators did not define their teaching or actions within the context of culture but rather as acts of respect and knowing. One teacher stated in response to a question regarding whether or not the culture of the children and families affected her teaching, "No, because I'm pretty much the same . . . I don't think what I do is cultural." Another educator described herself as being more sensitive to cultural issues because she, too, is Native.

The early childhood teachers were able to clearly describe how they thought children learned as well as what defined their teaching practices such as valuing children's knowledge, learning by listening or by watching someone who wants to pass down knowledge, and learning through hands-on experience; however, they did not associate their beliefs as cultural or unique to a Native American classroom. Lee and Walsh (2005) defined folk pedagogy as "the taken-for-granted practices that emerge from deeply embedded cultural beliefs about how children learn and how teachers should teach" (p. 60). Perhaps the Native teachers were steered by a folk pedagogy that was in synch with the home and community culture of the children they taught. However, the educators did make several references to diverse tribal beliefs and practices as "something to watch out for," or "something to be aware of" indicating their awareness of variations between their culture and the home and community culture of the children they taught.

The data clearly revealed the relevance of ritual in building a sense of belongingness and community within the early childhood programs we studied. Ritual and customs are integral to the perpetuation of culture (Banks, 2002) and we saw, in this study, the richness of educators, children, families and community participating in unison in various tribal traditions such as preparation for and partaking in a powwow. The powwow brought family and community members into the children's school environment to craft outfits along with practice singing and dancing. Mutual involvement in cultural rituals provided for a seamless connection between school culture and the community and home cultures of the children in these early learning programs.

Perhaps the most consistent finding in the data was the strong evidence of the teachers' commitment to honoring family beliefs and practices. All of the teachers emphasized the importance of involving parents and even extended family in curriculum development and instruction. The teachers not only suggested that they believed that the children's parents are their most important teachers, their practice of consistently seeking information and understanding about home cultures through day-to-day interactions with parents demonstrated congruence between their beliefs and their actions. The teachers did not describe parents' wishes as frustrating or inconvenient as is often the case with educators who offer a fixed or static curriculum (Goldstein, 2003; Moore with Seeger, 2005); but rather, they welcomed family input and saw the care and education of the children in their programs as a partnership between themselves and the parents.

Fostering a child's sense of belonging and ultimately his or her academic achievement requires congruence between the school culture with the home and community culture of the children we teach (Nieto, 2002; Osterman, 2000). Given the lack of preparedness of a largely European American teaching force to educate children from diverse cultural backgrounds (Nieto, 2002), English language learners and ethnically diverse children are at risk of being marginalized in our American classrooms (Moll, 1992). Studying ethnically diverse classrooms and educators such as the classrooms and educators in this research may offer early educators lessons that will enable them to bridge the gap between the culture of their classrooms and the home and community culture of the ethnically diverse children they teach.

The findings from this study suggest the following implications for early educators for connecting the culture of their school or classroom with the home and community culture of the children they teach: the value of respecting and honoring parents' beliefs and wishes in a way that transforms curriculum, and the significance of building belongingness through authentic school participation in family and community cultural rituals.

References

Allen, J., & Labbo, L. (2001). Giving it a second thought: Making culturally engaged teaching culturally engaging. *Language Arts, 79*(1), 40–52.

Banks, J. (2002). *Teaching strategies for ethnic studies* (7th ed.). Boston: Allyn & Bacon.

Bullock, J. (2005). Early care, education, and family life in rural Fiji: Experiences and reflections. *Early Childhood Education Journal, 33*(1), 47–52.

Confederated Salish & Kootenai Tribes. (1999). *Coyote stories of the Montana Salish Indians.* Helena, MT: Montana Historical Press.

Creswell, J. W. (1998). *Qualitative inquiry and research design: Choosing among five traditions.* Thousand Oaks, CA: Sage Publications.

First Class News. (2003). Retrieved September 3, 2006, from http://72.14.203.104/search?q=cache:StkQ_jRYYeIJ:firstclass.skc.edu/news/0000D3A8-80000002/S004061D3-004061DF.2/Carol%2520Juneau%2520-%2520information.doc+Flathead+Indian+Reservation+average+Income+2002&hl=en&gl=us&ct=clnk&cd=2.

Goldstein, L. S. (2003). Preservice teachers, caring communities, and parent partnerships: challenges and possibilities for early childhood teacher education. *Journal of Early Childhood Teacher Education, 24,* 61–71.

Grossman, S. (1999). Examining the origins of our beliefs about parents. *Childhood Education, 76*(1), 24–27.

Jones, E., & Derman-Sparks, D. (1992). Meeting the challenge of diversity. *Young Children, 47*(2), 12–18.

Lee, K., & Walsh, D. J. (2005). Independence and community: Teaching Midwestern. *Journal of Early Childhood Teacher Education, 26,* 59–77.

Lincoln, Y., & Guba, E. (1985). *Naturalistic inquiry.* London: Sage.

Luo, N., & Gilliard, J. L. (2006). Crossing the cultural divide in early childhood teacher education programs: A study of Chinese graduate students' perceptions of American early care and education. *Journal of Early Childhood Teacher Education, 27:* 171–183.

McIntosh, P. (1989). White privilege: Unpacking the invisible knapsack. *Peace and Freedom, 49*(4), 10–12.

Moll, L. (1992). Bilingual classroom studies and community analysis: Some recent trends. *Educational Researcher, 2*(2), 20–24.

Moore, R. A. (2004a). The impact of community and culture on literacy teaching and learning: We know the problems but we don't understand them. *Journal of Reading Education, 29(30),* 19–27.

Moore, R. A. (2004b). Classroom research for teachers: A practical guide. Norwood, MA: Christopher Gordon.

Moore, R. A., with Seger, V. (2005). Rich or poor? Examining the image of family literacy in the K-6 curriculum. *Language and Literacy Spectrum, 15*(3), 53–61.

Nagayama, M., & Gilliard, J. L. (2005). An investigation of Japanese and American early care and education. *Early Childhood Education Journal, 33*(3), 137–143.

Nieto, S. (2000). Placing equity front and center: Some thoughts on transforming teacher education for a new century. *Journal of Teacher Education, 51*(3), 180–187.

Nieto, S. (2002). *Language, culture, and teaching: critical perspectives for a new century.* Mahwah, NJ: Erlbaum.

Osterman, K. (2000). Students' need for belongingness in the school community. *Review of Educational Research, 70,* 323–367.

Schultz, B. A. (2001) Powwow power. Retrieved July 29, 2006, from http://www.powwoww-power.com/powwow history.html.

Travel Montana. (2006). Retrieved September 3, 2006, from http://montanakids.com/db_engine/presentations/presentation.asp?pid=170&sub=Tribal+Histories. Retrieved September 3, 2006.

VanHorn, J., & Segal, P. (2000). Talk to your baby: Honoring diversity while practicing from an evidence base. *Zero to Three, 23*(5), 33–35.

Valle, R. S., & King, M. (1978). *Existential phenomenological alternatives for psychology.* New York: Oxford University Press.

Walsh, D. J. (2002). The development of self in Japanese preschools: Negotiating space. In L. Bresler & A. Ardichvili (Eds.), *Research in international education, Experience, theory, and practice* (pp. 213–245). New York: Peter Lang.

Yang, H., & McMullen, M. B. (2003). Understanding the relationships among American primary-grade teachers and Korean mothers: The role of communication and cultural sensitivity in the linguistically diverse classroom. *Early Childhood Research and Practice, 5*(1), 1–19.

Critical Thinking

1. What is the role of culture and cultural characteristics on curriculum and school?

2. How do Native American Indian students express themselves at school?

3. What can all teachers glean from this research to help them in their own classrooms?

4. Why is the presence of family and community vital to learning?

JENNIFER L. GILLIARD is in Department of Education, Early Childhood Division, The University of Montana—Western, 710 S. Atlantic Street, Dillon, MT 59725, USA. **RITA A. MOORE** is in Department of Education, The University of Montana—Western, 710 S. Atlantic Street, Dillon, MT 59725, USA.

Correspondence should be directed to Jennifer L. Gilliard, Department of Education, Early Childhood Division, The University of Montana—Western, 710 S. Atlantic Street, Dillon, MT 59725, USA., e-mail: j_gilliard@umwestern.edu.

UNIT 3

Establish Community and Context

Unit Selections

Learning Outcomes

After reading this unit, you will be able to:

• Describe the practices and beliefs educators held to help sustain high student performance.

• Summarize the Native American students' perceptions on their schooling and achievement.

• Discuss the author's suggestions for improving student achievement.

• Expound upon the deficit model.

• Explain the role of arts in the classroom to enhance awareness, community relations, and parental involvement.

• Support community-based learning in teacher education.

Student Website

www.mhhe.com/cls

Internet References

National Black Child Development Institute
　　www.nbcdi.org
United Nations
　　www.un.org/en/documents/udhr
United States Census Bureau and Poverty
　　www.census.gov/hhes/www/poverty/poverty.html
United States Citizenship and Immigration Services
　　www.uscis.gov/portal/site/uscis
United States Department of Health and Human Services
　　www.hhs.gov/specificpopulations
United States Department of Justice
　　www.usdoj.gov/
United States Equal Employment Opportunity Commission
　　www.eeoc.gov/types/race.html
United States Immigration and Customs
　　www.ice.gov

Classrooms and schools encapsulate hope and promise for the future. Young people come to school every day wanting to understand themselves, one another, and the greater society. They are eager to interact with their friends, investigate the world around them, and try new experiences. It may seem like students are preoccupied, distracted, and resistant to learning; remember they are attempting to balance acceptance by their peers, compliance with their parents, and respect for their teachers. Fortunately, multicultural education provides the ways, means, and purposes for achieving the balance.

Every school and classroom is a microcosm of the world. People may talk in terms of degrees of diversity, but the references are unsound and unclear. Every group of learners includes individuals who share similarities and offer differences. No two learners are identical in every way, even identical twins. Our cultural characteristics, qualities, and beliefs consist of one's race, ethnicity, gender, social class, religion, nationality, geography, language, size, sexual orientation, abilities, education, interests, and so forth. The list is endless and we customize the categories and descriptors to accommodate our individual situation and need.

Some aspects of our cultural identities remain the same throughout our lives either by chance or by choice. Some aspects of our cultural identities change throughout our lives, again by chance and by choice. Some aspects of our cultural identities are selected for us; some aspects we select ourselves. And, sometimes we make new or different choices as we grow older, move, and experience changes through our lives.

The blend of static and dynamic qualities combined with choice and chance creates our individual being. Choice is the key element. No one is born with bias, prejudice, or stereotyping. These are learned behaviors, and, sadly, they are learned from the people most of us hold near and dear to us: our parents, grandparents, teachers, religious leaders, and community members. Children as young as kindergarten students arrive at school with a predetermined set of beliefs about themselves, one another, and the world. Reflect on your own elementary school days and you, too, can recall understanding your peers' cultural characteristics, qualities, and beliefs.

Classrooms and schools may offer the only places where young people can go to safely and comfortably learn about multicultural education in ways that value cultural diversity to enhance their cultural competence. To achieve these outcomes, classroom teachers and school administrators must understand multicultural education in ways that value cultural diversity to ensure cultural competence for everyone, everywhere, and all of the time. This charge is neither quick nor easy. Educators are people who bring their own set of biases, prejudices, and stereotypes learned from an early age from people they love and honor. Educators may or may not have experienced an effective course during their university preparation programs to equip them with the tools and techniques necessary to ensure democratic principles and social justice in various educational contexts.

© Photodisc Collection/Getty Images

And, unfortunately, educators may be expected to follow an agenda imposed on them by their immediate communities, or they may bring their own agendas that usurp cultural competence. These agendas may be overt, meaning that everyone is fully aware of the expectations, or these agendas may be covert meaning that the agendas are not public, they are covered or hidden to fulfill expectations for selected individuals with public awareness. For many years in the United States, classrooms and schools operated with overt agendas that segregated students, teachers, and families. Frequently, information, access, and opportunities were limited to the cultural dominant members of society.

Today, covert agendas can be detected in classrooms and schools. Educators may or may not even realize that they are promoting inequities. Although educators are expected to fulfill state academic standards, classroom teachers and school administrators are the ones who develop their own content curricula, select their instructional strategies, align their assessment techniques, and establish their learning communities. Too often, all school services are not provided to all students. Questions arise related to the students who are placed in special services and detention.

Perhaps classrooms and schools need to examine their practices so all students feel safe, welcomed, and wanted.

U.S. schools are a long way from achieving a teaching force that replicates the country's demographics in the P-12th grade classrooms as well as in higher education. This means that every teacher in every educational setting must ensure equity and excellence for all students. Teacher education programs must focus on providing specific courses that examine cultural competence accompanied with pedagogy for valuing cultural diversity effectively. Multicultural education must be present in the curriculum, taught directly to all students at all ages and stages, infused into all courses, and modeled by all educators. Extensive, not selective, cultural competence must be present in all formal and informal, direct and indirect exchanges in all educational settings. Teacher educators must accept their responsibilities for preparing teacher candidates for today's world; school administrators must ensure that the cultural competence is demonstrated in all communities of learning and systems of classroom management and school disciplinary programs.

The articles in Unit 3 provide the reader with the importance to establish community and context in all learning environments. All students must feel safe, welcomed, and wanted at school and in the classrooms; the classrooms must be student centered and learner driven; multiple opportunities for students to contribute to and participate in classroom conversations and activities as well as school and community functions must be available for all students. Readers may benefit by visiting a classroom that is focused on establishing learning communities and/or attending a workshop or university course dedicated to the concepts, research, vocabulary, and practices associated with effective learning communities.

The Need to Reestablish Schools as Dynamic Positive Human Energy Systems That Are Non-Linear and Self-Organizing

The Learning Partnership Tree

MICHELE ACKER-HOCEVAR ET AL.

Introduction

With the *No Child Left Behind Act of 2001* (NCLB) all states are required to implement some iteration of standards-based, accountability-driven reform. In the United States NCLB is the primary federal policy tool to deliver educational services to children of low socioeconomic (low-SES) status and limited English proficiency (LEP), otherwise called English Language Learners (ELL). Florida has embarked upon this mandated, educational reform movement with high-stakes testing at its center. Although each state has the prerogative of creating its own accountability system, Florida has chosen a punitive system based on the Sunshine State Standards. Known as the *A + Plan,* and primarily based on the Florida Comprehensive Achievement Test (FCAT), this plan determines how schools are assigned letter grades on an "A" through "F" scale.

This scale is a fundamental tenet of *Florida's System of School Improvement and Accountability,* which reports annually schools' accomplishments. Low performing schools, designated "D" or "F," typically have disproportionately high numbers of low-SES students, racial and ethnic minority student (students of color and LEP/ELL) (Yan, 1999) and rarely attain "C" or above (Acker-Hocevar & Touchton, 2002). The dearth of research on schools attaining high performance with students who typically underperform their more affluent and native English-speaking peers (Valdés, 1996) led to this study. As such, this study is of great interest to policymakers and educators. Given the politics of high-stakes testing, and the fact that few other educators (Carter, 2000; Charles A. Dana Center, 1999; Scheurich, 1998 for exceptions) have been able to accomplish what these high-performing schools have (Education Commission of the States, 1998), the study provides glimpses into internal practices which have sustained these schools' reform efforts and, offers a description of how these practices work synergistically in a model. This article is the second of two reporting the findings; the first laid out the initial framework for the study (Schoon, Wilson, Walker, Cruz-Janzen, Acker-Hocevar, & Brown, 2003).

Method
Selection of Schools

Nine schools met the following criteria: 1) sustained achievement in reading and math for three consecutive FCAT years; 2) competence in these disciplines for three years at grades 3, 4, and 5; 3) 50% or greater low-SES students as defined by Title I; and 4) 10% or greater LEP students as defined by Title VII and the Multicultural Education Training Advocacy (META). LEP/ELL students receiving English for Speakers of Other Languages (ESOL) services for two years or less were not part of the reported scores.

Sustained achievement is depicted in Table 1. Although the State criteria have changed every year, making comparisons impractical, trends can be noted.

Design

The Interview Protocol was developed to elicit information regarding best practices at the school and classroom levels and about the schools' perceptions of best practices at the district level in relation to the schools. Questions were grouped according to 10 constructs linked to student achievement and grounded on school effectiveness literature (Edmonds, 1979; Purkey & Smith, 1993; Spillane & Seashore Louis, 2002; Teddlie & Reynolds, 2000; Wiggins & McTighe, 1998). Constructs were organized as a two-dimensional model with outer and inner cores (Schoon et al., 2003). The outer core represented constructs deemed pivotal to standards-based school effectiveness: Information Management, Accountability, Personnel, Instruction, and Resources (Carter, 1997; Siegel, 2003). The inner core represented constructs deemed integral, yet not viewed as the driving force behind

Table 1 Summary of High-Performing School Grades by Year and School

School[1]	1998–99	1999–00	2000–01	2001–02	2002–03
X 1	A	C	A	B	A
X 2	C	B	A	A	A
X 3	C	A	B	A	A
X 4	C	A	A	A	A
X 5	C	B	A	A	A
X 6	B	A	A	A	B
X 7	C	C	A	A	A
X 8	D	C	C	A	A
X 9	D	C	C	B	A

[1]Note. State of Florida (2003).

standards-based school reform: Leadership, Decision Making, Culture and Climate, Communication, and Parent and Community Involvement (Elmore, 2000; Scheurich & Skrla, 2003; Scribner, Young, & Pedroza, 1999; Sergiovanni, 1994; Snyder, Acker-Hocevar, & Snyder, 2000; Spillane, Halverson, & Diamond, 2001). According to this model, the inner core provides the impetus for changes but the outer core is the most direct link to school effectiveness and improvement. This was called the Systems Alignment Model (SAM) (Schoon et al., 2003).

Ron Edmonds (1979) demonstrated that schools can attain high academic achievement with low-SES students and students of color, laying a foundation for other scholars to further identify practices affecting student achievement positively. As researchers, we sought to answer three questions:

What theories-in-use seem to sustain school progress over time?

What practices lend credibility to the initial conceptual lenses for this study?

Do practices in high-performing schools confirm or reject the Systems Alignment Model?

Site visits were conducted in fall of 2002 and spring of 2003. During the two-day site visits interviews were held with individual principals, assistant principals, in several instances with both, and separately with groups of teachers and parents. The interviews were recorded, transcribed, and coded by two independent researchers. Once agreement was reached the codes served to examine practices across schools (Merriam, 2001).

Theories-In-Use

Three theories-in-use emerged from the findings and provide a backdrop for interpretation and discussion of results. First, systems theory frames how these schools worked in collaborative partnerships to shape and improve their "work systems and services and to assess the quality of effects on those being served" (Snyder, Acker-Hocevar, & Snyder, 2000, p. 211). Next, power theories clarify how educators constructed "partnership power beliefs" within their unique settings. Last, "additive schooling" explains how these schools were able to sustain high achievement over time with diverse populations.

The schools used information systems to respond to changes in their environment in natural ways. Organizational theorists (Senge, 1990; Wheatley, 1992) suggest that healthy systems can promote disequilibria in natural ways through the sharing of information and ongoing dialogue. Information can be used to respond to subtle environmental changes, stimulating variable and adaptive growth. This ability is more likely to happen when power is disbursed and shared broadly throughout the organization.

Drawing on a metaphor of power, "The Power River" illustrates power relationships along four places: Power over, Power to, Power with and Power through (Snyder et al., 2000). *Power over* and *Power to* are set within a bureaucratic and dominator framework, while *Power with* and *Power through* are set within a contrasting framework of partnership and community power socially constructed between educators and communities.

The first place on the river is Power over, the most limited use of power, with restricted access to resources and opportunities within a hierarchical, top-down, controlling, and bureaucratic perspective. Power over is increasingly exercised through federal and state threats of punishment for districts' and schools' failure to produce changes within acceptable levels and timelines.

Power to represents the dominator bureaucratic power framework that begins to unleash its hold over resources and opportunities to develop the skills of others and share some access to resources; power appears more widely shared than it is. Only when the Power River shifts its energy and direction beyond the bureaucratic and dominator paradigm does power give way to *Power with*. This changes dramatically the way people work together to solve problems and extends access to the broader community. There is an underlying belief in the expertise of the internal community that builds a collective sense of purpose.

Finally, *Power through* is enacted when power is loosely coupled with everyone, including parents and the community, working as partners to build learning communities through shared expertise and vision. There is an ethic of care and concern for each person connected to this broader community vision.

Partnership practices seem to underpin additive schooling, the third theory-in-use within the schools. The focus of the nine schools was on the community's culture(s) and language(s). This was termed additive schooling by the researchers. Drawing on the work of Valenzuela (1999), the assumptions underpinning subtractive schooling, and its converse: additive schooling, were examined. Subtractive schooling posits that today's schools work to fracture communities' cultural and social capital.

Several well-established notions drive additive schooling. First, it has been demonstrated that schoolwork cultures do make a difference in "the lives of children and also in a school's ability to meet accountability requirements" (Cummins, 1996; Espinoza-Herold, 2003; Snyder et al., 2000, p. 202). Further, cultural and language minority students perform better in nurturing environments that embrace and affirm their heritages (Beck, 1994). The goal must be to narrow the gap between teachers' and students' social and cultural differences (Banks, 2001; Nieto, 2001; Sleeter, 1992). As long as those in charge are uneducated on the needs of either ELL or culturally marginalized students, schooling has the potential to continue to subtract resources from them (Valenzuela, 1999).

Embracing students' and communities' cultural and social capital as integral components of the schools' network leads to a joint and reciprocal effort to educate everyone in the organization; children, community members, and school personnel (Valenzuela, 1999). Mutual trust is guided by the belief that both schools and parents have genuine interest and agency in children's educational and social competency. Parents must trust schools as places where their children are safe and educated as wholesome individuals who value themselves and their communities, and others in the world beyond (Espinoza-Herold, 2003; Valenzuela, 1999).

A New Model Emerges

This study found support for schools as non-linear, less bureaucratic, living systems capable of self-organization (Meier, 1995). Learning organizations are enabling, capacity building, human energy systems empowered to mediate external controls. Although the schools existed within a *Power Over* paradigm, they were organized around partnership and constructivist relationships. The original Systems Alignment Model had to be reconceptualized to account for the theories-in-use. The new model depicts both sets of constructs as interconnected, interactive, and interdependent parts of a dynamic living system.

The Outer Core was reclassified as Organizing Variables. The Inner Core was renamed Sustaining Variables when it was found that while these variables often function in less observable and quantifiable ways, they are essential for the healthy life of the entire learning organization and were, in fact, the synergy driving the entire system. In the words of Deborah Meier (1995), it would take a "strong storm" to "uproot or break" strong learning organizations. The Sustaining Variables, then, are the fuel driving the Organizing Variables. They create the synergy to transform the Organizing Variables into practices that better meet the needs of students. The Organizing and Sustaining Variables became the lenses through which beliefs and practices were examined.

Organizing Variables: School Practices

Accountability in these schools is driven by the internal core values and vision of the organization. In one school, this is expressed as, "You never settle for what you have, but always strive to be better." The school works together to analyze the needs of students and look broadly at what is required to help them achieve. Most of the information gathered internally assists to evaluate student achievement. Monitoring techniques include pretests, progress checks, performance assessments, portfolios, weekly progress report, and pacing charts for long range planning. In several of the schools, survey feedback keeps the pulse on the academic climate to see what resources are needed in classrooms, including professional development, and/or planning time. Sharing high expectations built a culture where learning was central to how teachers, principals, and parents talked about the school, particularly student learning. Accountability for excellence was one of the internal norms bonding everyone. Teachers considered their commitment and dedication to collegiality as contributing to their success. The schools educated parents on what standards meant for their child's learning.

At school #X8 "There is one teacher assigned to make sure that they are working on the standards and that they have the techniques and materials to do so." Most of the schools relied heavily on the knowledge and expertise of teachers within the building. In all the schools standards were aligned across grade levels, along with the grades above and below. Notably, when principals were asked how they held teachers accountable, they stated that they ensured teachers had the necessary resources and professional development to be successful. The focus was not on surveillance, or monitoring, but direct instructional assistance when students were not achieving. It was clear that all educators shared a common sense of accountability and responsibility for successfully educating all children, including working with the child and the child's family. Principals kept books in their offices and freely gave them to parents. School media centers were open into the evenings for parents and students. "The priority is that students are going to succeed regardless of what it takes for the administration, faculty and parents" (School #X2).

Resources. Although districts provide a so-called "operating budget," all the schools agreed that, the district, state, or federal government did not generally fund "A or D," schools adequately. After paying for staff, supplies, materials, and operational expenses, very little is left. As funds dwindle each passing year schools have a harder time purchasing basic instructional materials. All schools reported budget cuts forcing program and instructional personnel reductions with increased class sizes. Although all the schools received "FCAT Merit" funds, as reward for high marks according to the A+ Plan, most reported using these funds to purchase basic instructional materials and support tutorial programs, especially with 3rd graders, who risk mandatory retention if they fail the FCAT.

All schools reported that their allocated budgets were insufficient to maintain and upgrade technology. Although expected to integrate technology in instruction, most stated that districts generally did not fund technology sufficiently to stay current. Schools varied widely on their technology programs and ability to obtain outside funding for technology. School #X9 had few computers and even lacked Internet. Moreover, some of the principals reported funding teacher, student, and parent recognition awards from personal income. The principal at School #X2 personally conducted her school's Saturday tutorial because they had no funds to pay teachers. The role of principals and leadership teams has expanded to include, in the words of a respondent, "begging"—"I never thought that being a principal meant begging."

Criteria for school effectiveness have grown to include individual schools' ability to aggressively secure external funding. For many schools this really means balancing the negative equation created by deficit funding; not to enhance, but survive. This assault on schools' financial viability escalates as higher SES communities add significantly to their school's budgets, even doubling it through monetary and in-kind contributions.

All the schools depended on volunteers to supplement insufficient staffing, assist classrooms, and tutor. The ability to secure volunteers is tied to the community's resources as well as parents' work and family demands. Schools in communities that cannot contribute significantly, financially or in-kind, were forced to secure resources through grants and/or partnerships. Although many districts have partnerships with local businesses, contributions tend to be limited (food, school supplies, etc.) and are chased by far too many needy schools. Add to this the reality that external funding is closely related to the skills and connections of leadership team members, and a truly disproportionate picture unfolds. Some educational leaders, be they teachers, parents, or principals, become adept at grant writing and/or hold personal connections to external funding sources (Brown & Cornwall, 2000).

Some schools attracted funding by establishing reputations as effective spenders. School #X7, which had already secured an excess of $1.3 million dollars in grants over a three-year period, received an additional $10,000 when a district agency discovered unspent money. This school leader received an unanticipated phone call and asked to spend the money before weeks' end. In his words: "I was called because people knew I could spend money well. Many other schools cannot put together a spending plan that quickly." Although all the schools agreed that what really matters in school effectiveness and student achievement was teacher quality, many openly expressed that schools perceived as having the most resources and community support, tended to attract and retain the best teachers.

Instruction. Each of the nine schools stated vehemently that they "don't teach to the FCAT," but rather teach students to think. To quote a principal, "Schools that teach to the FCAT are not going to be really successful." While all the schools agreed that the FCAT provided them with information, they overwhelmingly disagreed with how it was used to penalize students and schools. Schools aligned their curriculum and assessments with the district's standards, which in turn aligned their standards to the State's. These schools, however, consistently developed curriculum beyond the core academics and agreed: "Students need

the arts, the fitness; the intra-personal and the inter-personal." Schools offered before, during, and after school programs that included tutorials, fine arts, dance, chorus, chess, videography, cheerleading, etc. An important observation was that the schools consistently related the curriculum to students' lives and needs, and their future as productive, socially conscientious citizens. This made the curriculum relevant to empower students as problem-solvers within their own communities and beyond. Instruction included environmental concerns, as well as local, national, and geopolitical and economic issues (Meier, 1995).

Schools employed many assessment strategies and tools, including teacher-developed tests and, in fact, indicated that they were already utilizing a variety of assessments, particularly authentic assessments, to monitor student progress and self-reflect about their own organizational effectiveness, before the FCAT. Some of the externally mandated assessments were described as content-based or specific strategy-based and not accurate measures of students' critical thinking. Schools geared much of their in-house assessments at higher order thinking, and targeted various forms of intelligences. Schools focused on literacy across all the content areas. Although districts heavily controlled instructional programs and materials, these schools selected strategies that supported the unique needs of their students. ELL students were supported through numerous research-based strategies and assessments that, while effective with most students, have been demonstrated as uniquely valuable with second language learners. Most of the schools indicated that their teachers had much instructional flexibility: "If you want to teach in a tree and that works, you can teach in a tree."

These schools promoted infused multiculturalism on a daily basis throughout the school year to affirm students' cultural assets and validate other cultures (Banks, 2001; Sleeter, 1992). Many had multicultural committees to implement special programs as assemblies and festivals. Teachers purchased culturally authentic materials and libraries held a wide variety of books by authors of diverse backgrounds. The schools hired sufficient teachers proficient in students' native languages to provide self-contained bilingual and/or content area education, especially in math, science, and social studies along with English literacy. Two-Way bilingual education was found in the majority of the schools. They also mainstreamed LEP/ELL students with additional English instruction. The least effective model was not employed in any of the schools. This model, used widely in the State, is the traditional ESOL pullout program with no support in the student's native language. Team-teaching and articulation within and between grades ensured that Bilingual/ESOL and regular students were instructed in the same content and with the same grade-level materials and expectations—the curriculum was not "watered down."

Because of mandatory 3rd grade retention, disproportionately impacting ELL students, whose FCAT scores count after only one year of Bilingual/ESOL education, retention is often used district-wide to coerce a focus on English language skills, even at the expense of other content areas. Yet, in this study's schools, retention was neither used to coerce nor punish; once the teacher ensured that the student is ready to move on, the school promotes the child without forcing the child to spend an entire school year in that grade. Thus, while adhering to the state's 3rd grade retention law, learning is recognized for ELL students.

Information management. The ability to have a good information management system was directly related schools' ability to be accountable and responsive. This fostered autonomy and flexibility for success beyond the status quo and compliance requirements. Schools demonstrated valuing information/data as part of their ongoing self-assessment and improvement. Accountability was driven by the internal core values and vision linked to information management. One principal states, "So in addition to whatever the district has identified we also decided what tools we were going to use and how we were going to use them. But we have done it for us." Schools employed numerous methods and formats, including quantitative and qualitative, to obtain a broad range of credible, relevant, and timely information/data from within and outside. Members became their own internal evaluators. Self-assessment included School Climate Surveys for teachers and parents. Although assessment data drove instruction, decisions on students were made on an individual basis. All the schools had already established information management processes before the FCAT was mandated. Data provided through the State and district was viewed as additional information to support organizational growth.

Personnel. Across most districts, principals are assigned and can be re-assigned or removed at any time. Although schools are given some flexibility in the selection of instructional staff, it is not uncommon for excessed teachers to be assigned to schools, regardless. Principals expressed looking for teachers wanting to be part of a community, and for "someone that had a real need to see children succeed. I don't think that I can mention anyone on the staff that wouldn't give their all" (School #X8). Most schools experienced very low teacher turnover. Teachers described schools as families supportive of them and their work. In school #X3, teachers left only when promoted. Then, the staff commiserated on how much the person was missed. These schools made a conscious effort to blur the boundaries of seniority between faculty with newly hired faculty immersed into the school culture at once.

Teachers saw themselves as life-long learners, involved in providing in-house professional development, and attending state and national conferences. Repeatedly, teachers stated that their professional development was linked to student learning and needs. They were encouraged to try new things as team teaching, looping, and observing peers. The school cultures encouraged inclusiveness, consensus building, openness, and sharing. Teachers talked about feeling motivated to seek creative and alternative ways of reaching students, and to assume greater personal responsibility for the school's well being. A teacher in school #X2 said, "The principal just fosters that; she gives you the encouragement to just succeed at anything for your students and at a personal and professional level."

Sustaining Variables: School Practices

Culture and climate. The core culture of learning organizations is reciprocally shaped by the sustaining variables, and particularly the organizational leadership style. All schools demonstrated a culture unified by common family/team spirit where each member is a valuable and essential asset and leader, whether openly designated or not. Teachers addressed themselves and were addressed as professional by the school's designated leaders and parents. A strong sense of collegiality permeated the school culture. Teachers expressed high levels of ethical and professional expectations, standards, and motivation. This was matched with high expectations for everyone in the learning organization, especially students. They openly affirmed each other's expertise in numerous areas and willingness to work collaboratively. Teachers mentored new faculty and each other and were not inhibited and/or threatened by visiting each other's classrooms to provide support. While everyone recognized that their job was "very tough" and "even harder than most other schools," they defined it within a positive challenge paradigm, seeing the numerous obstacles as challenges they could overcome through teamwork. All of this led to productive synergy sustained through incentives and celebrations of achievement, even approximations. Continually, teachers, students, and parents were recognized.

A significant finding in all schools was a strong sense that the students and communities were an asset, including their culture(s) and language(s) (Cummins, 1996; Nieto, 2000; Valenzuela, 1999). Relationships with students and communities were premised on authentic caring. Our findings demonstrated that to the extent the schools embraced and validated students' cultural and linguistic background, respect and trust were reciprocally established between schools and communities.

Leadership. The formal leadership in schools was affirming, nurturing, inclusive, and willing to share power with teachers and/or parents. In all but one of the schools, teachers described leaders as democratic, consensus builders, and participatory. Principals were attuned to moving their schools forward, rather than resting on their laurels. Instead, they sustained the energy for ongoing improvement through professional dialogue and collaboration. Teachers were given common planning times within and cross grade levels, and with feeder schools. Repeatedly, parents commented on the schools' access to them and willingness to respond quickly to their needs. One parent talked about how in a previous school, it took weeks for the teacher or principal to get back to her. In these schools, however, teachers and principal were in daily contact with parents and responded to concerns immediately.

Principals recognized teachers were key to successful learning cultures in all of the schools. There was an expressed view of teachers as capable. "I like to find the strengths in the teachers and build on that. . . ." School leadership was not vested in the principal. The administrators at school #X2 described the leadership like this:

We have a leadership team. Everyone basically in the school is a leader . . . I think that, very quickly when you come into this

Table 2 School Ratings and Power Relations between the Administration with Teachers and Parents

School[1]	98–99	99–00	00–01	01–02	02–03	Power Relations	
						Teachers	Parents
X1	A	C	A	B	A	Through	With
X2	C	B	A	A	A	To	Over
X3	C	A	B	A	A	Through	Through
X4	C	A	A	A	A	Through	With
X5	C	B	A	A	A	Through	With
X6	B	A	A	A	B	Through	With
X7	C	C	A	A	A	Through	With
X8	D	C	C	A	A	With	To
X9	D	C	C	B	A	With	To

[1]Note. School grade data are from The Florida School Report (State of Florida, 2003).

building you realize that this is a building where, everyone is expected to bring something to the table, and they are allowed to share what they feel would be the best course. And so it's very expected and very welcomed when people bring ideas to the table. . . .

Leaders encouraged teachers to talk about the school, not just their individual classrooms. This collective vision evoked language such as "we are all in this together" and "we work hard on school improvement here." Teachers were willing to share resources, prioritize them based on school needs, and dispense with the idea that everyone getting whatever resources they needed was equitable. Leadership was seen as collective accountability for student learning.

Decision making. Staff perceptions were valued over external judgments. Table 2 reflects how power was enacted within schools and communities.

It was not surprising that schools #X8 and #X9 had the least developed Cultures/Climates and Core Values, as well as the most fragile levels of achievement. Both had the least finely honed practices of shared power with parents. School #X2, had a second year principal who moved the school's relationship with parents from *power with* to *power over*. The school culture acquiesced to the principal's dominating power and relationships with teachers also shifted from *power with* to *power to*. These parents were the most ignorant of school leadership processes, decisions, and the school mission and improvement plan. They expressed that their involvement in decision-making was minimal and limited to a small group of parents. Teachers expressed a shift from the previous administrator's practices of more involvement. School #X3 had the most developed partnership culture. The principal envisioned a "break-the-mold" school of empowered staff, minimal bureaucracy, and achievement focused on integrating multiple intelligences into all aspects of the curriculum. The vision focused on democratic processes and consensus. The leadership team was comprised of administration, a secretary, a paraprofessional, a cafeteria worker, a custodian, two teachers, two parents, and a member-at-large.

Communication. Communication with parents was strong in all schools. Information was sent home in student's native language and English. Parents often attributed few discipline problems to the robust communication. "Most of the parents agree with the teachers. They want their kids to come to school; they want their kids to learn. If their child is misbehaving, they want to know and they put an end to that" (School #X8). Teachers communicated to parents that they cared about their students. Frequently, parents commented on the accessibility of the teachers and administrators: "They are always at school." Teachers displayed student work prominently, communicated weekly student progress, held frequent parent-teacher conferences, and generally created openness for parents. Parents could verbalize the missions and knew how decisions were made in all schools but one. Parents and teachers shared how their input was always welcomed, if not sought, except in school #X2.

Parent and community involvement. Research supports that students whose parents are consistently involved in their education attain higher academic achievement levels. Programs with high parent involvement are more successful than those with less involvement. The effects of parental involvement linger through the middle school level (Decker & Decker, 2000). Learning organizations ensure significant parent and community involvement. All the schools supported bilingual communication with parents, including translations during meetings. Parent and community involvement specialists, which included school counselors, made home visits, arranged workshops for parents, and secured speakers from the community. Parents were provided opportunities to enhance their native language literacy, English literacy through ESOL, computer skills, parenting, and behavior management. Parents in all schools were provided instructional materials and strategies to support their children at home. All the schools indicated willingness to teach parents how to get involved in an equitable manner to the maximum extent possible according to their work and family responsibilities. With one exception, all schools continually worked to augment parents' abilities to participate in decision-making.

Training included information about how the school and district works, and where information is located about their child.

All schools encouraged parents to continue speaking and reading to their children in their native languages. They believed that parents were essential partners in developing foundational concepts in the native language that could transfer later into English. Support for the home language sent a strong message to students that they were valued and respected.

Establishing Schools as Learning Partnerships

The Learning Partnership Tree

The emergent framework, termed the Learning Partnership Tree, describes how the Organizing and Sustaining Variables were found to work in concert in the nine schools (see Figure 1). There was little, if any, vertical alignment between districts and schools on the Organizing Variables except for Information Management and Accountability. Schools perceived that the Sustaining Variables were not considered as significant within the state-mandated framework that sought to focus on the quantifiable constructs and centered on Accountability and Information Management.

Contrary to the state focus, the framework that emerged from the findings is grounded on strong vertical and horizontal alignments between internal accountability measures reflecting how beliefs were constructed and power shared within these systems. Externally mandated accountability measures were integrated within the core beliefs and selectively negotiated by each school to serve its unique needs and objectives.

Represented as a tree, above the ground is the trunk (Organizational Core Values) supporting the branches (Organizing Variables) and canopy. The trunk (Core Values) must be structurally strong to support the branches and entire system upright. The Organizing Variables, while essential to the system, fluctuate at different times, depending on the system's interaction with its surroundings. All the Organizing Variables are interrelated, interdependent, and aligned at the juncture with the Core Values, signifying the system's internal determination of when and how to access the Organizing Variables according to priorities mediated through its Core Values. The Organizing Variables are the parts of the system most visible, concrete, and quantifiable, and thus, most focused on today.

Below the ground is the taproot (Culture/Climate) with its branching secondary root system (Sustaining Variables). The Sustaining Variables, while also essential to the system, exist in fluctuating proportions at different times and act in response to numerous factors found in the underground environment. Often, these components are less focused on, as they tend to be less visible, more abstract, and less quantifiable. All the Sustaining Variables are interrelated and interdependent and aligned at the juncture with the grounding organizational Culture/Climate. This juncture signifies the point where incoming nutrients merge to sustain the taproot (Culture/Climate) and develop into the Core Values that contributed to additive schooling.

While all the variables are essential to the whole system's health, the system is critically dependent on the Sustaining Variables, which provide the nutrients essential for a strong Culture/Climate. As the taproot grows, so does the trunk and vice versa. As the Core Values evolve through interaction with the outside environment, the organizational Culture/Climate responds in tandem. The upper part of the system reaches out to the surrounding environment and it too receives sustaining nutrients. Healthy systems use information and resources to move flexibly; failure to do so could destroy them.

What must not be ignored is that the overall health of the upper tree cannot be sustained without a strong root system. Often, what surprises unaware observers is that the root system (i.e., an organization's Culture/Climate and other Sustaining Variables) must be equally as large (or even larger) and equally as strong (or even stronger) as the parts above the ground. Another surprising aspect of this interrelationship is that as long as the root system remains healthy and strong, it can often re-sprout to re-create the tree. An extension of this to the upper tree is not always the case; for a trunk and branches cannot often re-sprout roots.

There exists an interrelated and interdependent connection between Organizing and Sustaining Variables. The trunk and canopy cannot continue growing indefinitely without the growth of the roots. And so, schools' Organizing Variables cannot be sustained without strong structural and supportive Core Values grounded by a strong Culture/Climate. Additionally, the Organizing Variables cannot be imposed on the system without the existence of this strong structuring and grounding.

Discussion and Conclusions

This study supports the view of schools as living, natural systems that cannot be dissected into isolated parts (Snyder et al., 2000). When we engage in educational reform, we must look at the entire system and not simply those parts that are most apparent and quantifiable.

A principal's knowledge is no longer "sufficient to actuate change" (Snyder et al., 2000). Effective change is created and sustained through team effort and shared leadership. Leadership requires principals working through democratic processes and consensus. Power must be distributed; accountability shared, and work equitable and collaborative.

Evidence of collegial norms encompassing attitudes and beliefs of support, trust, and openness to learning, with dedication to collective responsibility and accountability, seemed to assist these schools in adapting their work context to high stakes testing and standards based instruction. Yet, the traditional role of principals remains entrenched in a bureaucratic, managerial, model that most districts reinforce by not accepting a more distributed leadership model. By holding principals accountable for "running" the building and answering for all the decisions made in the school, the power of synergy among parents, teachers, and leaders is ignored.

Furthermore, the view of schools as natural human systems requires relationship building, self-reflection, mutual respect, and core values grounded on "inquiry as well as responsibility"

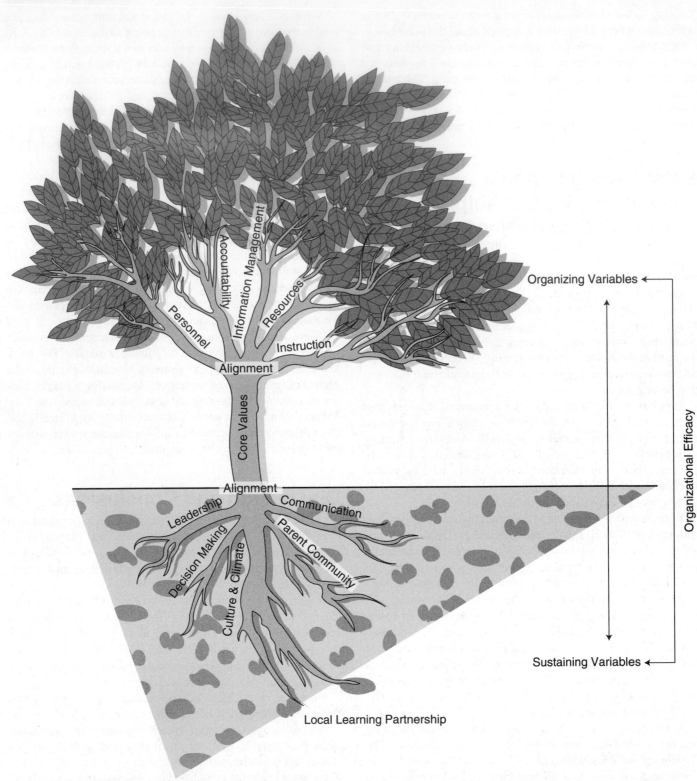

Figure 1 Learning partnership tree.

(Meier, 1995). It is evident that this is crucial for low performing schools where principal turnover occurs with abnormal frequency. With each new principal, there is also staff turnover and the anticipation, with the remaining staff, of surviving yet another principal. Such schools are not able to establish supportive organizational core values and stable shared leadership.

Two major, albeit misguided, assumptions undergird the current state-mandated framework. First, that school improvement must be driven by top-down and external vertical alignment of the Organizing Variables between districts and schools. Specifically, this means that the District superimposes, for example, an information management system, and so forth, for each of the Organizing Variables. Significantly, this hierarchical approach also assumes that while both sets of variables are necessary for school effectiveness and improvement, the Organizing Variables take the front seat in educational reform and school effectiveness, particularly Information Management and Accountability.

A second major assumption is that school improvement is then driven by increased external domination and supervision over schools and classrooms through the Organizing Variables, particularly Accountability and Information Management Systems, perceived as being responsible for "tightening the screws" on educators. This ignores all the other variables that make schools successful and is conceived narrowly within a highly technical and rational "power over" system of control. This contributes to the dysfunctional fragmentation of today's educational systems. A hidden, highly detrimental, assumption of the statemandated model is that schools lack the know-how and/or motivation to effectuate improvement on their own. This perception reinforces negative perceptions of those at the bottom of the education pyramid: teachers, students, and parents.

The classroom is left straddled with the most direct, massive, and cumulative effects of external demands. Systems alignment has meant "teaching to the test," forcing schools and teachers to work in isolation, and competing rather than collaborating. Teacher isolation hinders problem solving, creation of supportive networks, and collective self-reflection (Sleeter, 1992).

This study supports the notion that what appears to be most important is what happens at the school level and how the district can support the school site. Sleeter (1992), among other educational researchers, sees the school rather than individual teachers, as the center of reform and recommends shifting the focus to the organizational arrangements, conditions, and processes at each building. She suggests turning the lens at the collective, people who work in schools, and the culture/climate they create, within the broader external context in which schools exist.

Further, this study reaffirms that educational reform must be grounded within individual schools and classrooms that need increased autonomy from external domination (Meier, 1995; Snyder et al., 2000), particularly domination based on fear. In the words of Meier (1995), it may be possible to have "schools that work" but that requires abandonment of the "stance of outsiders."

The state and districts appear primarily concerned with supervision of FCAT scores, rather than the Instruction, Resources, and Personnel required for effective school improvement. It was clearly perceived by the schools that the Sustaining Variables were not deemed as significant within the statemandated framework. The emergent framework is grounded on high vertical and horizontal alignment of internal accountability measures within each school. These schools had begun establishing these internal alignments and accountability networks before the statemandates, meaning that strong structural and supportive Core Values, grounded by a strong Culture/Climate, orchestrated the Organizing and Sustaining Variables. Rather than focusing initial and immediate attention on the upper parts of the tree, the findings of this study suggest priority development of strong and supportive root systems.

Further, since little vertical alignment was found between these high-performing schools and districts in the area of Instruction, one might presume that districts do not want to intervene in a system of instruction that worked well. In fact, it was found that in these high-performing schools educators had more autonomy, which empowered them to negotiate external intrusion and even "massage" instructional plans to fit their unique needs and reduce massive, regimented, student testing. While local autonomy is a requirement for school effectiveness, schools that do not meet externally imposed standards of achievement are indeed the ones most straddled with external domination and little ability to self-organize. Districts tend to reduce the demands placed on high-performing schools, allowing them more freedom to grow internally. Ironically, most high-performing schools tend to represent more affluent and mainstream White/Caucasian student populations that continue to enjoy greater self-determination and autonomy.

This study supports a holistic approach to school effectiveness and educational reform focusing deeply below the surface, on those not-so-apparent structures and processes, which hold the sustaining nutrients to keep the entire system moving in responsive directions. Those rushing to control and punish schools, teachers, and children simply do not understand the nature of schools as human energy systems, the significance of power relations in establishing healthy and strong core values, or the notion of schools as learning partnerships. They fail to understand that the nutrients of sustainable school progress are found in positive relationships, sharing of power and information, the valuing of others, and the building of strong, stable, and trusting relationships. They do not understand that there are no fixed recipes for success, only a philosophy that promotes additive schooling, includes professional respect and dedication, supports shared leadership, and the building of collective expertise (Neumann, King, & Rigdon, 1997).

References

Acker-Hocevar, M., & Touchton, D. (2002). How principals level the playing field of accountability in Florida's high poverty/low-performing schools: Part I: The intersection of high-stakes testing and effects of poverty on teaching and learning. *International Journal of Educational Reform, 11*(2), 106–24.

Banks, J. A. (2001). *Cultural diversity and education: Foundations, curriculum, and teaching.* Boston, MA: Allyn and Bacon.

Beck, L. (1994). *Reclaiming educational administration as a caring profession.* New York: Teachers College Press.

Brown, R. J., & Cornwall, J. R. (2000). *The entrepreneurial educator.* Lanham, MD: Scarecrow Press.

Carter, D. (1997). Information management for site based decision making in school improvement and change. *International Journal of Education Reform, 6,* 174–188.

Carter, S. C. (2000). *No excuses: Lessons from 21 high-performing, high poverty schools.* Washington, DC: Heritage Foundation.

Charles A. Dana Center, University of Texas at Austin. (1999). *Hope for urban education: A study of nine high-performing, high-poverty, urban elementary schools.* Washington, DC: U.S. Department of Education, Planning, and Evaluation Service.

Cummins, J. (1996). *Negotiating identities: Education for empowerment in a diverse society.* Ontario, CA: California Association for Bilingual Education.

Decker, L. & Decker, V. A. (2000). *Engaging families and communities: Pathways to educational success.* Fairfax, VA: National Community Education Association.

Edmonds, R. R. (1979). Some schools work and more can. *Social Policy, 9*(2), 28–32.

Education Commission of the States. (1998). *Turning around low-performing schools: A guide for state and local leaders:* Denver, CO: Author.

Elmore, R. F. (2000). *Building a new structure for school leadership.* Washington, DC: Albert Shanker Institute.

Espinoza-Herold, M. (2003). *Issues in Latino education: Race, school culture and the politics of academic success.* Boston, MA: Allyn and Bacon.

Meier, D. (1995). *The power of their ideas: A fiery manifesto for the salvation of public education.* Boston, MA: Beacon Press.

Merriam, S. B. (2001). *Qualitative research and case study applications in education.* San Francisco: Jossey-Bass.

Neumann, F. M., King, M. B., & Rigdon, M. (1997). Accountability and school performance: Implications from restructuring schools. *Harvard Educational Review, 67*(1), 41–74.

Nieto, S. (2001). *Affirming diversity* (3rd ed.). New York: Longman.

No Child Left Behind. Retrieved April 13, 2003 from www.NoChildLeftBehind.gov

Purkey, S. C., & Smith, M. S. (1993). Effective schools: A review. *Elementary School Journal, 83,* 427–452.

Scheurich, J. J. (1998). Highly successful and loving public elementary schools populated mainly by low-SES children of color. Core beliefs and cultural characteristics. *Urban Education, 33*(4), 451–491.

Scheurich, J. J. & Skrla, L. (2003). *Leadership for equity and excellence: Creating high-achievement classrooms, schools, and districts.*

Schoon, P., Wilson, C. L., Walker, D., Cruz-Janzen, M. I., & Acker-Hocevar, M. (2003). A systems alignment model for examining school practices that sustain standards based reforms in high poverty and English language learner schools. Paper presented at annual international conference of the American Educational Research Association (AERA), Chicago, Illinois.

Scribner, J. D., Young, M. D., & Pedroza, A. (1999). Building collaborative relationships with parents. In P. Reyes, J. D. Scribner, & A. Paredes Scribner (Eds.), *Lessons from high-performing Hispanic schools: Creating learning communities* (pp. 36–60). New York: Teachers College Press.

Senge, P. M. (1990). The fifth discipline: The art and practice of the learning organizations. New York: Doubleday.

Sergiovanni, T. J. (1994). *Building community in schools.* San Francisco: Jossey-Bass.

Siegel, D. (2003). *Performance-driven budgeting: The example of New York City's schools* (Report No. EDO-EA-03-05). East Lansing, MI: National Center for Research on Teacher Learning. (ERIC Document Reproduction Service No. ED474305).

Sleeter, C. (1992). *Keepers of the American dream: A study of staff development and multicultural education.* Washington, DC: The Falmer Press.

Snyder, K. J., Acker-Hocevar, M., & Snyder, K. M. (2000). *Living on the edge of chaos: Leading schools into the global age.* Milwaukee, WI: ASQ.

Spillane, J. P., Halverson, R., & Diamond, J. B. (2001). Investigating school leadership practice: A distributed perspective. *Educational Researcher, 30*(3), 23–38.

Spillane, J. P., & Seashore Louis, K. (2002). School improvement processes and practices: Professional learning for building instructional capacity. In J. Murphy (Ed.), *The Educational Leadership Challenge: Redefining Leadership for the 21st Century* (pp. 83–104). Chicago, IL: The University of Chicago Press.

State of Florida. (2003). *Florida school report.* Retrieved August 6, 2003, from http://www.firm.edu/doe/evaluation/home0018.htm

Teddlie, C., & Reynolds, D. (2000). *The international handbook of school effectiveness research.* New York: Falmer.

Valdés, G. (1996). *Con respeto: Bridging the distance between culturally diverse families and schools.* New York: Teachers College Press.

Valenzuela, A. (1999). *Subtractive schooling: U.S.-Mexican youth and the politics of caring.* Albany: State University of New York.

Wheatly, M. (1992). Leadership and the new science: Learning about organization from an orderly universe. San Francisco, CA: Berrett-Koehler.

Wiggins, G. P., & McTighe, J. (1998). *Understanding by design.* Alexandria, VA: ASCD.

Yan, J. (1999). *What affects test scores?* Miami: Applied Sciences and Technology.

Critical Thinking

1. What are educators' beliefs and practices that help to sustain high student performance?

2. How can school faculties increase their capacity building?

3. What are ways that teacher educators can help their candidates to understand internal cultures?

4. Why are internal cultural curriculum difficult to start?

DR MICHELE ACKER-HOCEVAR Research focus on school organizations, school development, instructional leadership, and altering power relations, most especially for disadvantaged schools and communities. DR. MARTA CRUZ-JANZEN Research focus on impact of P/K-12 curricula on self-concept and academic achievement of students of color, reform of teacher preparation, and Latino racial identity development. DR. CYNTHIA L. WILSON Research interests include preparation for pre-service teachers and professional development for in-service teachers. Primary focus is literacy achievement of at risk-students and students with mild disabilities. DR. PERRY SCHOON Research interests in the area of mental modeling and expert systems. Co-author of "Instructional Technology, Process and Product." DR. DAVID WALKER Research interests in areas of research methodology, statistics, and K-12 teaching and learning reform.

From *International Journal of Learning,* vol. 12, no. 10, 2005/2006, pp. 255–266. Copyright © 2006 by Common Ground Publishing, Melbourne Australia. Reprinted by permission.

Promoting School Achievement among American Indian Students throughout the School Years

As American Indian children develop, they gain social awareness and their cultural identity becomes stronger; thus, they become more cognizant of the cultural disconnect between their non-Indian school and their Indian culture.

KRISTIN POWERS

American Indian students as a population are not achieving high academic standards. For example, only 57 percent of American Indians who took the 8th-grade National Assessment of Educational Progress reading test in 2003 scored at or above the basic level, and only 16 percent scored at or above the proficient reading level (versus 83 percent and 41 percent, respectively, of white students) (National Center for Education Statistics, 2004). Yet school failure appears to be acquired rather than inherent at the onset of schooling. Many researchers have reported that American Indian children function at an average range academically until the 4th grade; by 10th grade, however, they are, on average, three years behind their non-Native peers (Hornett, 1990; Rampaul, Singh, & Didyk, 1984; Safran, Safran, & Pirozak, 1994). The reasons for this "crossover" effect are not clear, although a combination of school, family, and student characteristics most likely is at work.

Underachievement among Native students often is attributed to culturally incongruent school settings. At school, many American Indian students must negotiate unfamiliar discipline, instruction and evaluation methods, rules for forming interpersonal relationships, and curricula that diverge from those promoted by their family, tribe, and community (Chrisjohn, Towson, & Peters, 1988; Lomawaima, 1995; Snipp, 1995). If cultural differences between home and school are the source of academic failure among American Indian students, the decline in achievement would suggest that these differences widen as youth age. Elementary curricula and instructional methods may be more aligned to Native cultural values (e.g., cooperation, thematic or holistic learning, oral recital) than those in the later grades. Hornett (1990) suggests that developmental changes within the child contribute to the cultural gap. He argued that as

American Indian children develop, they gain social awareness and their cultural identity becomes stronger; thus, they become more cognizant of the cultural disconnect between their non-Indian school and their Indian culture. The challenge, therefore, is determining how to bridge the cultural gap while maintaining high standards and promoting a positive climate for school learning.

The Research Project

Extant survey data collected from 240 urban American Indian youth (primarily Ojibwa, Lakota, and Dakota) from two large urban Midwestern cities, ages 9 to 18, were examined to identify educational variables that were negatively correlated with students' age (Geenen, 1998). Fifty-eight survey items were combined into 11 scales that measured 10 educational variables (e.g., student achievement, home-school collaboration, and achievement motivation) and the respondents' affiliation with their Native culture.

A negative correlation between age and student achievement ($r = -.379$; $p \leq .001$), as measured by self-reported grades and overall achievement, was found, which supports the "crossover" effect. Similarly, American Indian students' school attendance and participation were negatively correlated with age ($r = -.248$; $p \leq .001$). Thus, older American Indian students were less likely than younger American Indian students to report passing grades, consistent attendance, and high levels of engagement with school activities—all important indicators of educational attainment and success.

The hypothesis that declining student achievement is associated with increasing discontinuity between the culture of the school and home was not supported by these data. Neither the respondents' affiliation with their Native culture (e.g., how important Indian values are, speaking a tribal language in the home, participation in traditional activities and rituals) nor the extent to which their school embraced Native culture (e.g., teaching Indian cultural values, history, stories, and tribal languages at school; attending school with other Native youth) was correlated with age. While this study is very preliminary and based only on cross-sectional survey data, it does suggest that the crossover effect is not simply a result of cultural discontinuity. Some of the educational factors that were negatively correlated to age may deserve greater attention as school personnel attempt to combat underachievement among older American Indian students. These efforts are described next.

Student Achievement Motivation

Like non-Native students, American Indian students' achievement motivation is central to their academic achievement and persistence in school (McInerney & Swisher, 1995). McInerney and Swisher hypothesized that the presence of achievement motivation may indicate that American Indian students have successfully negotiated the cultural discontinuity of the school by adopting some of the mainstream strategies for school success without feeling that they have abandoned their cultural heritage. Conversely, the absence of a desire to achieve, attend, and participate in school may be symptomatic of what Ogbu (1981) described as the demand to develop alternative competencies. Faced with a long history of racial discrimination, some American Indian adolescents may discredit the importance of school and develop alternative competencies and motivations that are in opposition to school values.

In the present study, student achievement motivation, as measured by such items as "I try to do my best at school" and "It is important to me to be proud of my school work," was negatively correlated with student age ($r = -.169$; $p = .009$). This suggests that American Indian students may become less motivated to do well in school as they age. Therefore, primary, elementary, and secondary teachers should strive to provide engaging instruction for their American Indian students by adhering to universal principles of effective instruction while incorporating native culture and content into the curriculum (Powers, in press). Culture-based educational programs, such as the Kamehameha Early Education Program (KEEP) (Goldenberg & Gallimore, 1989) or the inquiry-based Rough Rock program (McCarthy, Wallace, Lynch, & Benally, 1991), which incorporate Native themes, languages, and Elders in the content and delivery of instruction, may serve as viable models for keeping American Indian students academically motivated. Efforts to increase student achievement motivation also should be directed at decreasing remediation. Repeated exposure to remedial activities that lack a cognitive and a cultural emphasis is likely to deplete students' desire to commit to academic tasks.

Teacher Expectations

Some evidence suggests that teacher expectations for American Indian students' success declines as the students progress through the grades (Rampaul, Singh, & Didyk, 1984). In the present study, students were asked whether they thought their school work was too easy, too hard, or just right; whether people at their school expect them to do well; and whether the adults at their school encourage them to do the best that they can. The American Indian students' responses to this teacher expectation scale were not correlated with age, suggesting that youth of all ages in this sample reported similarly about teacher expectations. Ideally, this finding would indicate that teachers maintain high and attainable expectations for their American Indian students across the various grades. Yet, failure to find a statistically significant correlation between teachers' expectations and age may also be due to either insufficient sample size or indicate low teacher expectations across the age groups. Teachers of American Indian students should constantly ask themselves: "Am I holding my American Indian students to the same rigorous standards that I expect from my other students?" Again, an overreliance on remediation activities rather than in-depth, inquiry-based instructional activities should be a signal to teachers to reconsider their expectations for American Indian students.

Teacher Supportiveness

American Indian students' ability to access the social capital of school personnel also may be compromised by their divergent cultural competencies. Plank's (1994) in-depth study of Navajo reservation school teachers illustrates how intercultural communication differences impede social bonding between teachers and students. For example, an experienced teacher of Navajo students stated:

> If I'm walking with . . . a Navajo, we may not say anything, and they are comfortable with that. Me, on the one (sic) hand, I feel like I should be saying something (Plank, 1994, p. 8).

Teachers may misread American Indian students as being uninterested in developing a relationship with them, or as overly shy, rude, or immature; this misperception is likely to impede the formation of interpersonal relationships between school staff and Indian students (Hornett, 1990; Kasten, 1992; Plank, 1994). A lack of interpersonal relationships with school personnel puts American Indian students at a disadvantage because those social bonds are critical to fostering a sense of belonging to school that leads to students' confidence in their own academic abilities and the availability of educators to provide academic support (Finn, 1989; Goodenow, 1993). Corner (1984) has observed that "when the school staff fail to permit positive attachment and identification, attachment and identification take place in a negative way" (p. 327). Interviews conducted with American Indian dropouts suggest that de-identification with school personnel and the norms of the school is a part of the drop-out process (Dehyle, 1992). The cross-over effect in American Indian student achievement may be the result of declines in school staff accessibility and supportiveness as American Indian students develop.

In the present study, teacher supportiveness was negatively correlated with student age ($r = -.183$, $p = .004$), which suggests that older youth found their teachers to be less available and supportive than younger youth. Items on this scale include: "Do you get along with your teachers?" "Has a teacher gotten to know you really well?" "Would you turn to a teacher for help if you were depressed?" These results raise the possibility that improved interpersonal relationships with teachers may help middle childhood and adolescent students remain committed to school. Teachers' and students' relationships will be strengthened through meaningful mentoring, extracurricular, and community-based programs, such as the American Indian Reservation Project, in which student teachers provide "academic tutoring, companionship and role modeling" while boarding with their Navajo students (Stachowski, 1998).

Family Involvement

Parents' presence and participation at school may buffer American Indian students from declining teacher expectations, supportiveness, and accessibility by promoting greater cultural consistency within academic programs and by offering additional academic assistance. Parental involvement is critical to assisting American Indian students in negotiating the mainstream culture of public school (Friedel, 1999). Surprisingly, older American Indian students did not report lower rates of parental involvement in school than younger students in the present study. It is possible that the attempts made by the districts in this study to incorporate Native culture into the curricula and instruction fostered greater parental involvement. For example, most of the respondents indicated that they had learned about Indian culture (86 percent) and Indian legends (75 percent) at school.

> **A lack of interpersonal relationships with school personnel puts American Indian students at a disadvantage, because those social bonds are critical to fostering a sense of belonging to school that leads to students' confidence in their own academic abilities.**

Including Native American culture in the curriculum design and instruction may entice American Indian parents to remain involved in home-school collaborations as their children develop; yet, some American Indian parents may need assistance in helping their older youth meet academic demands. Historically low rates of educational attainment among American Indians make it more likely that American Indian parents lack the content skills necessary to assist their children as the curriculum becomes more advanced. For example, a study of over a thousand 5th- and 6th-grade students found American Indians to be twice as likely as African American or Anglo students to report that they had no one to ask for help on their mathematics homework (Mather, 1997).

Safe and Drug-Free Schools

Older students in this study reported the occurrence of much more fighting and alcohol and drug use than did younger students. Urban American Indian youth may experience even greater risks associated with violence and alcohol and drug use than their rural or reservation dwelling peers because they have lost the support of extended kin who often assist in mentoring and disciplining adolescents (Machamer & Gruber, 1998). Parental involvement and a sense of belonging to the culture and norms of the school protect adolescents from deviant and potentially harmful behaviors such as alcohol, tobacco, and other drug (ATOD) use (Hawkins, Guo, Hill, Battin-Pearson, & Abbott, 2001). Rather than embracing "zero tolerance" policies, which Watts and Erevelles (2004) argue give "schools new ways to justify the expulsion, exclusion, shaming and labeling of students who need professional help rather than punishment" (p. 281), schools should improve parental involvement and students' sense of belonging to the culture and norms of the school in order to protect American Indian adolescents from school violence and ATOD use (Hawkins et al., 2001).

Implications for School Personnel

Teachers should consider, first and foremost, strengthening their interpersonal connections with their American Indian students. Strong relationships between students and teachers promote a sense of belonging, freedom to take academic risks, and investment in academic learning (i.e., academic motivation), and may help American Indian students negotiate cultural discontinuities between school and home. Teacher training on Native cultural competencies is a positive step toward increasing teachers' understanding and commitment to forming positive relationships with their students. School-wide anti-bullying, anger management, and substance abuse programs also may curb declines in student achievement. Finally, school-wide screenings may be effective in identifying American Indian students before underachievement becomes entrenched. An individualized intervention plan for American Indian students when they begin to fall behind in achievement or attendance should be implemented, monitored, and revised until the desired outcomes are achieved. This plan should be based on ecological assessments that consider developmental imperatives and individual assets (e.g., native cultural affiliation, parent support for learning) and vulnerabilities (e.g., insufficient teacher support, violence, and ATOD use at school) in selecting from among various intervention options.

Achievement data on sub-populations of students, such as American Indian students, should be examined regularly for signs of underperformance at each grade level. However, school personnel should understand that not all American Indian students identify with their Native culture in the same way. Cultural differences exist within and among the different tribes; thus, some students, particularly urban students who are three or four generations removed from their tribal homeland, may identify more with the mainstream culture of their school than with their Native culture. Accordingly, addressing cultural discontinuity may or may not improve achievement among older American Indian students. However, sufficient access to meaningful learning opportunities, supportive teachers, and safe schools is likely to propagate school success.

References

Chrisjohn, R., Towson, S., & Peters, M. (1988). Indian achievement in school: Adaptation to hostile environments. In J. W. Berry, S. H. Irvine, & E. B. Hunt (Eds.), *Indigenous cognition: Functioning in cultural context* (pp. 257–283). Dordrecht, The Netherlands: Marinus Nijhoff.

Comer, J. P. (1984). Home-school relationships as they affect the academic success of children. *Education and Urban Society, 16*(3), 323–337.

Dehyle, D. (1992). Constructing failure and maintaining cultural identity: Navajo and Ute school leavers. *Journal of American Indian Education, 31*(2), 24–47.

Finn, J. D. (1989). Withdrawing from school. *Review of Educational Research, 59*(2), 117–142.

Friedel, T. L. (1999). The role of Aboriginal parents in public education: Barriers to change in an urban setting. *Canadian Journal of Native Education, 23*(2), 139–157.

Geenen, K. (1998). *A model of school learning for American Indian Youth* (Doctoral dissertation, University of Minnesota, Minneapolis, 1998). Retrieved August 30, 2004, from Digital Dissertation at www.lib.umi.com/dissertations/.

Goldenberg, C., & Gallimore, R. (1989). Teaching California's diverse student population: The common ground between educational and cultural research. *California Public Schools Forum, 3*, 41–56.

Goodenow, C. (1993). The psychological sense of school membership among adolescents: Scale development and educational correlates. *Psychology in the Schools, 30*(1), 79–90.

Hawkins, J. D., Guo, J., Hill, K. G., Battin-Pearson, S., & Abbott, R. D. (2001). Long-term effects of the Seattle Social Development intervention on school bonding trajectories. *Applied Developmental Science, 5*(4), 225–236.

Hornett, D. M. (1990). Elementary-age tasks, cultural identity, and the academic performance of young American Indian children. *Action in Teacher Education, 12*(3), 43–49.

Kasten, W. C. (1992). Bridging the horizon: American Indian beliefs and whole language learning. *Anthropology, and Education Quarterly, 23*, 108–119.

Lomawaima, K. T. (1995). Educating Native Americans. In J. A. Banks & C. A. M. Banks (Eds.), *The handbook of research on multicultural education* (pp. 331–345). New York: Macmillan.

Machamer, A. M., & Gruber, E. (1998). Secondary school, family and educational risk: Comparing American Indian adolescents and their peers. *Journal of Educational Research, 91*(6), 357–370.

Mather, J. R. C. (1997). How do American Indian fifth and sixth graders perceive mathematics and the mathematics classroom? *Journal of American Indian Education, 36*(2), 39–48.

McCarthy, T. L., Wallace, S., Lynch, R. H., & Benally, A. (1991). Classroom inquiry and Navajo learning styles: A call for reassessment. *Anthropology and Education Quarterly, 22*(1), 42–59.

McInerney, D. M., & Swisher, K. G. (1995). Exploring Navajo motivation in school settings. *Journal of American Indian Education, 36*(3), 28–51.

National Center for Education Statistics. (2003). *Percentage of students, by reading achievement level and race/ethnicity, grade 4: 1992–2003*. Retrieved August 25, 2004, from http://nces.ed.gov/nationsreportcard/reading/results2003/natachieve-re-g4.asp

Ogbu, J. (1981). Origins of human competence: A cultural-ecological perspective. *Child Development, 52*, 413–429.

Plank, G. A. (1994). What silence means for educators of American Indian children. *Journal of American Indian Education, 34*(1), 3–19.

Powers, K. (in press). An exploratory study of cultural identify and culture-based educational programs for urban American Indian students. *Urban Education.*

Rampaul, W. E., Singh, M., & Didyk, J. (1984). The relationship between academic achievement, self-concept, creativity, and teacher expectations among Native children in a northern Manitoba school. *The Alberta Journal of Educational Research, 30*(3), 213–225.

Safran, S. P., Safran, J. S., & Pirozak, E. (1994). Native American youth: Meeting their needs in a multicultural society. *Journal of Humanistic Education and Development, 33*(2), 50–57.

Snipp, C. M. (1995). American Indian Studies. In J. A. Banks & C. A. McGee Banks (Eds.), *Handbook of research on multicultural education* (pp. 245–258). New York: Macmillan.

Stachowski, L. L. (1998). Student teachers' efforts to promote self-esteem in Navajo pupils. *The Educational Forum, 62*, 341–346.

Watts, I. E., & Erevelles, N. (2004). These deadly times: Reconceptualizing school violence by using critical race theory and disability studies. *American Educational Research Journal, 41*(2), 271–299.

Critical Thinking

1. What are the perceptions of Native American Indians' schooling experiences?

2. How can teachers help their Native American Indian students?

3. What are ways that teachers can improve their relationships with Native American Indian students?

4. Why are relationships essential for students to take ownership of their learning?

KRISTIN POWERS is Assistant Professor, College of Education, California State University Long Beach.

Discarding the Deficit Model

Ambiguity and subjectivity contribute to the disproportionate placement of minorities in special education.

BETH HARRY AND JANETTE KLINGNER

Many authors in this issue of *Educational Leadership* describe students as having "learning needs" and "learning challenges." How we wish this language truly reflected the common approach to students who have difficulty mastering the information and skills that schools value! Many students have special learning needs, and many experience challenges learning school material. But does this mean they have *disabilities?* Can we help students without undermining their self-confidence and stigmatizing them with a label? Does it matter whether we use the word *disability* instead of *need* and *challenge?*

Language in itself is not the problem. What *is* problematic is the belief system that this language represents. The provision of special education services under U.S. law—the Education for All Handicapped Children Act in 1975 and the Individuals with Disabilities Education Improvement Act in 2004—ensured that schools could no longer turn away students on the basis of perceived developmental, sensory, physical, or cognitive limitations. However, the downside of the law is that it has historically relied on identifying a disability thought to exist within a child. The main criterion for eligibility for special education services, then, has been *proof of intrinsic deficit.* There are two problems with this focus: First, defining and identifying high-incidence disabilities are ambiguous and subjective processes. Second, the focus on disability has become so intertwined with the historical devaluing of minorities in the United States that these two deficit lenses now deeply influence the special education placement process.

We recently completed a three-year study that throws some light on the issue (Harry & Klingner, 2006). We looked at the special education placement process for black and Hispanic students in a large urban school district in a southeastern U.S. state. The 12 elementary schools involved represented a range of ethnicities, socioeconomic statuses, and rates of special education placement. On the basis of data we gathered from classroom observations, school-based conferences, interviews with school personnel and family members, and examination of student documents (such as individualized education programs, behavioral referrals, and evaluation reports), we found that several conditions seriously marred the placement process. These included lack of adequate classroom instruction prior to the student's referral, inconsistencies in policy implementation, and arbitrary referrals and assessment decisions. It was also clear that students in poor neighborhoods were at risk of receiving poor schooling, which increased their risk of failing and of being placed in special education.

Minorities in Special Ed

The disproportionate placement of some minority groups in special education continues to be a central problem in the field. As noted in a report by the National Research Council (2002), the categories with the highest incidence of disproportionate minority-group placement are also those categories whose criteria are based on clinical judgment: Educable Mental Retardation, Emotional/Behavioral Disorders, and Learning Disability. The categories whose criteria are based on biologically verifiable conditions—such as deafness or visual impairment—do not show disproportionality by ethnicity.

Across the United States, African American students are represented in the category of Educable Mental Retardation at twice the rate of their white peers; in the category of Emotional/Behavioral Disorders, they are represented at one and one-half times the rate of their white peers. In some states, Native American and Hispanic students are overrepresented in the Learning Disability category (National Research Council, 2002).

The roots of this problem lie deep in U.S. history. Looking at how the mandate for school integration intertwined with special education, Ferri and Connor (2006) analyzed public documents and newspaper articles dating from *Brown v. Board of Education* in 1954 to the inception of the Education for All Handicapped Children Act in 1975. The authors show how African American students entering public schools through forced integration were subject to low expectations and intense efforts to keep them separate from the white mainstream. As the provision of services for students with disabilities became a legal mandate, clear patterns of overrepresentation of Mexican American and African American students in special education programs emerged. Plagued by ambiguous definitions and subjectivity in clinical judgments, these categories often have more to do with administrative, curricular, and instructional decisions than with students' inherent abilities.

Dilemmas of LD and EMR

The label of Learning Disability (LD) used to be assigned mainly to white and middle-class students. African American students—and in some states, Hispanic and Native American students—were more likely to be disproportionately assigned to the more severe category of Educable Mental Retardation (EMR). More than two decades ago, various scholars offered thoughtful analyses of these patterns. Sleeter (1986) argued that the Learning Disability category came into being to create a space for students from predominantly white and middle-class homes who were not living up to family and community expectations. She noted that the other side of this coin was that students with learning difficulties who were from low-income homes were more likely to end up in the Educable Mental Retardation category.

In a careful examination of how the construction of the Learning Disability category affected African American students, Collins and Camblin (1983) argued that the definition of *learning disability* and the means of identifying it guaranteed this pattern. First, the requirement for a discrepancy between IQ score and academic achievement was designed to indicate that the student was unexpectedly achieving below his or her measured potential. This requirement was intended to ensure that the learning difficulty was the result of a specific, not generalized, learning disability. In other words, the student was capable of higher achievement, as evidenced by his or her IQ score, but some specific disability seemed to be holding him or her back.

But how do we measure cognitive potential? Through IQ tests. It is widely acknowledged that IQ tests are really "tests of general achievement, reflecting broad, culturally rooted ways of thinking and problem solving" (Donovan & Cross, 2002, p. 284). It is not surprising, therefore, that if we measure intelligence this way, then groups with inadequate exposure to the skills and knowledge required to do well on these tests will score lower than their mainstream counterparts. Thus, as Collins and Camblin pointed out, African American students' lower scores on IQ tests make it more unlikely that their scores will reflect the "discrepancy" required for admittance into the Learning Disability category.

Collins and Camblin's second argument focused on the "exclusionary clause" of the Learning Disability definition. In addition to ensuring that the student does not have some other intrinsic limitation, such as mental retardation or sensory impairments, the exclusionary clause requires that school personnel establish that the source of the problem inheres in the student, not in his or her environment or experience. Consequently, African American students living in poor socioeconomic circumstances were less likely to receive the Learning Disability label because their environments tended to exclude them from this category.

This brings us to the paradoxical impact of the Learning Disability category on minority students. On the one hand, the underrepresentation of poor and minority students in this category—also known as a pattern of false negatives—is a problem if it means that students fall between the cracks and do not receive appropriate instruction. Further, there are benefits associated with the Learning Disability label. For example, students in this category can receive accommodations on secondary and college-level testing, which many middle-class white families continue to take advantage of.

On the other hand, the number of minorities represented in this category has begun to increase. We might now face the possibility of overrepresentation of minorities—or false positives—in the Learning Disability group. Some researchers have argued that many students currently in the category should actually qualify for Educable Mental Retardation (MacMillan, Gresham, & Bocian, 1998). Moreover, our research showed that some psychologists use the Learning Disability label to protect a student from the more stigmatizing and isolating label of Emotional/Behavioral Disorders (Harry & Klingner, 2006).

The real problem is the arbitrariness and stigmatizing effects of the entire process. Students shouldn't need a false disability label to receive appropriate support. They also shouldn't acquire that label because they had inappropriate or inadequate opportunities to learn. And they shouldn't end up in programs that don't offer the truly specialized instruction they need.

Students shouldn't need a false disability label to receive appropriate support.

Dilemmas of EBD

The use of the Emotional/Behavioral Disorders (EBD) label grew by 500 percent between 1974 and 1998, from just over 1 percent in 1974 to just over 5 percent in 1998 (National Research Council, 2002). This category is plagued by as much ambiguity as the Learning Disability category is. To qualify for the EBD label, a student must display inappropriate behaviors to a "marked degree" and for a "length of time." These criteria depend on subjective judgment.

Also, decisions about what evaluation instruments to use vary widely across states (Hosp & Reschly, 2002). Some states use projective tests, which are well known for their inherent subjectivity. Students respond to stimuli, such as pictures or sentences, and then a psychologist interprets their responses as a projection of their feelings. Other states rely on checklists, which are equally subjective. Our research revealed that different teachers using the same instrument rated the same student very differently. For example, using a behavioral checklist to rate a 2nd grade African American boy, one teacher checked four items relating to poor self-concept as occurring "excessively" (more than 50 percent of the time), whereas another teacher checked those same items as occurring "seldom" (1–10 percent of the time).

One teacher in the study commented, "They're not disturbed. They're just a pain in the neck!" As many scholars have observed, it's often difficult to tell whether the behavior is mostly troubling to school personnel or whether it reflects a troubled child.

Two Distorting Lenses

The intertwining of race and perceptions of disability are so deeply embedded in our way of thinking that many people are not even aware of how one concept influences the other. Let's consider how this works in light of the study we conducted.

The Disability Deficit Lens

Many teachers in the study saw disability as a simple fact. One teacher noted, "These children have disabilities, just like some children have blue eyes." When a student experiences continued difficulty mastering academic skills, all too often the first question someone asks is, "Does this student have a disability?" The Learning Disability label requires that we exclude potential environmental reasons for the student's difficulties. But barring obvious developmental limitations, how can we separate a student from his or her social and cultural experience?

Let's consider some environmental experiences that could interfere with a student's learning. Most often, the experiences cited as exclusionary include poverty, detrimental home and community environments, or lack of opportunity to learn. In and of itself, poverty does not cause learning difficulties. Most children from poor homes have effectively mastered the usual developmental childhood tasks of motor and language skills, and they have learned the values and social practices of their homes and neighborhoods. But they often haven't learned particular forms of the language or the ways in which schools use that language to the extent that their middle-income peers have.

For example, in a study of African American preschoolers' language development, Brice-Heath (1983) demonstrated how their social environments prepared students for an imaginative form of storytelling but not for answering the testlike, factual questions prevalent in schools. Moreover, the students' vocabularies may not be as extensive or as sophisticated as those of children growing up in middle-class homes. Students may also not have had extensive experience handling printed materials or listening to stories told in the linear fashion so common to many children's books. Their lack of experience in some of these areas can make children seem unprepared for academic learning.

Absence from school as well as poor instruction in the early years can also be sources of a student's low achievement. Our research found that school personnel were always ready to blame the students' home contexts but seldom examined the school context. Even when students were referred for special education evaluation, members of the placement teams seldom asked whether poor classroom climate or instruction contributed to the students' difficulties or whether peer pressures could be the source of their withdrawal or acting out.

School personnel were always ready to blame the students' home contexts but seldom examined the school context.

The Social/Cultural Deficit Lens

When a habit of looking for intrinsic deficit intertwines with a habit of interpreting cultural and racial difference as a deficit, the deck is powerfully loaded against poor students of color. Speaking about her African American 1st graders, one teacher in the study pointed out that "they don't know how to walk, talk, or sit in a chair. It's cultural!" Comments like this really don't refer to whether the students can or cannot do these things. Instead, they show that the manner in which the students do these things is unacceptable to the teacher. The teacher's focus on deficiencies predisposed her to see the students as limited by their culture and, ultimately, to refer almost one-half of her class of normally developing children for evaluation for special education.

If it is evident that students' early home and community experiences have not prepared them well for schooling, what do schools do? Do the schools then provide the students with adequate and appropriate opportunities to learn? Does instruction begin where the students are? Does it move at a pace that enables them to become accustomed to the new norms and expectations? Are the students made to feel that the school values the knowledge they bring from their homes and communities? Do teachers build on these "funds of knowledge" (Moll, 1990), or do they see only deficits in the students?

Variation, Not Pathology

Beyond the fact that these processes affect minorities unduly, the steady and dramatic increase in the use of disability labels in our schools is a cause for serious concern. The figures are startling. According to the National Research Council (2002), the risk of *any* student (averaged across ethnic groups) being identified as having Specific Learning Disabilities has increased from 1.21 percent in 1974 to 6.02 percent in 1998.

The truth is that the law's provision of disability categories for students who have learning and behavioral difficulties has become a way for schools to dodge their responsibility to provide high-quality general education. The deficit model is based on the normative development of students whose homes and communities have prepared them for schooling long before they enter school. Children who come to school without that preparation, and without the continuing home support of family members who can reinforce the goals of schooling, face expectations that they have not had the opportunity to fulfill. All too quickly the students become candidates for suspected "disability." Further, the special education programs into which they are placed are disproportionately of low quality in terms of curriculum, instruction, and ratio of students to teachers.

So why can't we see students' difficulties as "human variation rather than pathology" (Reid & Valle, 2004, p. 473)? Some encouraging trends are under way. The recent reauthorization of the Individuals with Disabilities Education Act allows for a change in the discrepancy model. The law now recommends tiered interventions by which schools can screen students early for signs of difficulty and provide more intensive and individualized instruction in needed areas without applying a special education label. The recent reauthorization enables schools to spend 15 percent of their special education funds on early intervention services.

The three-tiered Response to Intervention (RTI) model is currently receiving great attention in the field (Klingner & Edwards, 2006). The first tier involves quality instruction and ongoing monitoring within the general education classroom. In the second tier, schools provide intensive intervention support for students who have not met expected benchmarks. In the final tier, students who do not respond to second-tier interventions are evaluated for possible placement in special education.

The RTI model holds promise for preventing academic failure. It also provides support for culturally and linguistically diverse students before they underachieve. Educators are becoming increasingly aware that they need to apply the model in culturally responsive ways (see Klingner & Edwards, 2006). This might mean considering whether suggested instructional interventions have proven effective with *all* students, including English language learners. Also, educators should avoid a one-size-fits-all approach because culturally diverse students or English language learners may require different tier-one or tier-two interventions.

The law also calls for increased and specific efforts to include parents in all phases of the placement process. Schools must ensure that parents understand the proceedings of individualized education program (IEP) meetings and provide an interpreter if necessary. They also must notify parents early on about meetings to help ensure attendance and provide parents with a copy of the IEP.

These changes in the law signal a need for revising the concept of "disability" as the single criterion for eligibility for specialized and intensive services. We need a new vision of special education—one that reserves the notion of disability for students with clear-cut diagnoses of biological or psychological limitations and uses the categorization only for the purpose of delivering intensive, specialized services in the least restrictive education environment possible. Students who have no clear-cut diagnoses but who struggle to master school-based tasks should be eligible for specialized services according to explicit criteria based on level of achievement. The Response to Intervention model monitors the progress of all students so that teachers can provide extra support—within the general education context—to those students who are not making adequate progress.

Rather than devoting extensive resources to finding out whether students "have" disabilities, we should devote those resources to assessing students' exact instructional needs using models like Response to Intervention. Schools will need to provide this instruction through collaboration between general and special education personnel to ensure that all students continue to have full access to the general curriculum. As Lisa Delpit (2006) noted, let's stop looking for disabilities and just "teach the children what they need to know" (p. 3).

References

Brice-Heath, S. (1983). *Ways with words: Language, life, and work in communities and classrooms.* Cambridge, UK: Cambridge University Press.

Collins, R., & Camblin, L. D. (1983). The politics and science of learning disability classification: Implications for black children. *Contemporary Education, 54*(2), 113–118.

Delpit, L. (2006). Foreword. In B. Harry & J. K. Klingner, *Why are so many minority students in special education? Understanding race and disability in schools.* New York: Teachers College Press.

Donovan, S., & Cross, C. (2002). *Minority students in special and gifted education.* Washington, DC: National Academies Press.

Ferri, B. A., & Connor, D. J. (2006). *Reading resistance: Discourses of exclusion in desegregation and inclusion debates.* New York: Peter Lang.

Harry, B., & Klingner, J. K. (2006). *Why are so many minority students in special education? Understanding race and disability in schools.* New York: Teachers College Press.

Hosp, J. L., & Reschly, D. J. (2002). Regional differences in school psychology practice. *School Psychology Review, 31,* 11–29.

Klingner, J. K., & Edwards, P. (2006). Cultural considerations with response-to-intervention models. *Reading Research Quarterly, 41,*108–117.

MacMillan, D. L., Gresham, F. M., & Bocian, K. M. (1998). Discrepancy between definitions of learning disabilities and school practices: An empirical investigation. *Journal of Learning Disabilities, 31,* 314–326.

Moll, L. C. (Ed.). (1990). *Vygotsky and education: Instructional implications and applications of socio-historical psychology.* Cambridge, UK: Cambridge University Press.

National Research Council. (2002). *Minority students in special and gifted education.* Washington, DC: National Academies Press.

Reid, K., & Valle, J. W. (2004). The discursive practice of learning disability: Implications for instruction and parent-school relations. *Journal of Learning Disabilities, 37*(6), 466–481.

Sleeter, C. (1986). Learning disabilities: The social construction of a special education category. *Exceptional Children, 53,* 46–54.

Critical Thinking

1. What is the deficit model?
2. How do teachers identify students needing assistance?
3. What can teachers do to support their students needing assistance?
4. Why are more resources necessary to expand curriculum and communities?

BETH HARRY is Professor in the Department of Teaching and Learning at the University of Miami, Florida; 305–284–5363; bebeharry@aol.com. **JANETTE KLINGNER** is Associate Professor in Bilingual Special Education in the Division for Educational Equity and Cultural Diversity at the University of Colorado, Boulder; 303–492–0773; jkklingner@aol.com.

From *Educational Leadership*, February 2007, pp. 16–21. Copyright © 2007 by ASCD. Reprinted by permission. The Association for Supervision and Curriculum Development is a worldwide community of educators advocating sound policies and sharing best practices to achieve the success of each learner. To learn more, visit ASCD at www.ascd.org

Arts in the Classroom

"La Llave" (The Key) to Awareness, Community Relations, and Parental Involvement

Margarita Machado-Casas
University of North Carolina at Chapel Hill

As a teacher and a person of color, I am committed to social justice, equity, and meaningful teaching that takes students' cultural heritage into consideration in the workplace. Yet this is not easy in American schools. When entering the classroom we are expected to act as if we are blind to the social-economic issues our students struggle with daily. We are expected to teach only academic subjects and not deal with what school really is about—an extension of home and preparation for real life situations that are more complex than just dealing with character education. When in the classroom we are trained to be authoritative beings that control through "regimentation," "depositing," and "manipulation." As teachers we become our students' oppressors (Freire, 1970, p. 107). Being and acting as teacher the oppressor is harmful for all students but particularly for immigrants who on top of having to learn a new language, and a new educational system, have to suppress their cultural being,—all they have known in order to fit into American schools.

I was born in Nicaragua, from which seven in my family and I fled to Panama escaping from war and an oppressive government. We lived in Panama for five and a half years before political instability caused turmoil in that country as well. Having experienced this oppression before, my father courageously opted to bring the family to the United States. I arrived in California at the age of 14. Knowing less than basic English I was enrolled in a middle school in Fullerton, California, where I was placed in an ESL (Sheltered English class). My initial school experience was devastating. I not only did not know the language enough to communicate my thoughts and feelings in an understandable manner, but I was also having to re-learn school and the behaviors one is to display when in school. For example, back in both Nicaragua and Panama, students were expected to have an opinion and to express it without raising their hands.

As a child in the U.S., I was often the translator, the bridge between my parents and schools, the one person who in the process of translating became responsible for getting the message across properly. My parents were never invited to school events and were too busy working to get involved. Schools did nothing to encourage parental involvement of immigrant parents. As a student my experience, life, language, and family were ignored. I was being told in school that "Yo" (me) was not good enough for this society, and I had to change. This sudden alienation became an everyday event; one that persisted throughout my school years. I felt culturally and cognitively abused, "Whether urbane or harsh, cultural invasion is thus always an act of violence against the persons of the invaded culture, who lose their originality or face the threat of losing it" (Freire, p. 133).

Being successful in our current educational system means being able to acculturate to the dominant culture (Credit Nieto, 1999, pg. 75), and, now with accountability, demands it means being able to successfully pass a test. When I came into the country as an immigrant child, I remember the struggles I went through, I was invisible, my "real" life experiences were ignored. In my case, I came to see "real" life experiences as those we live daily, e.g., encounters with strangers, family members, friends, and community members that make us happy and/or sad. I also saw real life in our homes and school, where we saw, touched, smelled, and used our other senses. Reality, to me, included reactions with and from others; looks we are given and names we are called; pains, struggles, faces that make sad; actions, mannerism that make us who we are; love, interactions with others; what we eat; what we dance to; the languages we speak; and the way we act and think in the world. I would have been better prepared to deal with these struggles if I had had a school environment where school was an extension of home, real life, a place where acculturation was not the goal, but rather self-exploration, critical thinking, and exposure to real life situations to bring about "concientization" (Freire, 1970, p. 140) to promote action. Creating this kind of environment would have allowed me to break the current mold of thinking and begin to create new ways of thinking. As a teacher, I wanted my students to have what I did not. In my own classroom I wanted to create new ways of thinking that addressed students' different life situations. I began thinking about what I had that I could use. I realized the starting points were the classroom and myself.

I wanted the classroom to be an open-safe-respectful environment where all cultures, races, and ethnic differences were celebrated and promoted and where the home culture and school experience came together in significant ways. I learned this was revolutionary, "Revolution is achieved with neither verbalism or activism, but rather with praxis, that is, with reflection and action directed at the structures to be transformed" (Freire, p. 107). I began to organize my classroom into a community that was very much connected with home and real life situations. I wanted to make real life social justice issues accessible, visible, and practiced. Yet, I was in need of the "La llave" [the key] that would enable all this, and arts integration became "mi llave" [my key].

What constitutes arts? I define arts by not just a drawing, song, dance, but rather by those everyday experiences that lead us to thinking, questioning, talking, communicating with others, communicating our feelings, doing, hurting, loving, but most importantly feeling and voice/expression. Why the arts? We are surrounded by arts. We breathe them, live them, touch them, and experience the arts daily, both consciously and unconsciously. From the time we are born we are invaded with artistic gestures that portray love, affection, beauty, pain, suffering, and everyday life: "Experiences in the arts richly augment our ordinary life experiences and by doing so, often lead us to tactical understanding of the deeper meaning of our existence, our culture, and our world" (Fisher & McDonald, 2002, p. 1). Through the "arts," students and parents in my classroom began cooperating with their children. This, in turn, created reflection and action in both the classroom and community. Arts created a praxis that allowed students and parents to engage in dialogue and to get involved in school and acting.

Thinking about Being the Teacher

The teacher is a sociocultural mediator when she or he "becomes the link between the child's sociocultural experiences at home and school. That is the teacher becomes the sociocultural, sociohistorical mediator of important formal and informal knowledge about the culture and society in which children develop" (Diaz & Flores, 2000). Therefore, taking the role of a teacher as a sociocultural mediator involves making connections with students and those who impact student's lives. Teachers have the power to

bring students and parents into a three-way relationship I call *sociocultural triangulation* (See Figure 1).

Sociocultural triangulation assumes all three are equal and equally responsible to promote a child's progress. The role of the teacher in this triangulation process is to start the communication between student, parent or guardian and teacher that will promote sociocultural acceptance and inclusion in the classroom. The role of the teacher in this case is redefined and restructured to give up control in order to allow dialogue, thinking, and reflection to occur, "If the true commitment to the people, involving transformation of the reality by which they are oppressed, required a theory of transforming action, this theory cannot fail to assign the people a fundamental role in the transformation process" (Freire, p. 108).

In this article I describe how arts integration enabled me to develop such triangulation that resulted in shifting of the roles of the parties involved. Further, I will explain the ways in which organized art activities helped create a classroom environment where relationships between student and parents or guardians evolved in order to promote individuality, cultural inclusion, "conscientization," and equity. By utilizing arts as the "llave" [key] we began to create a cultural platform between a diverse classroom and an equally diverse community. In order to illuminate this, I will explore three areas I organized to achieve these goals: my classroom, my teachings, and community connections. Along with arts integration these three connections (which also lead to sociocultural triangulation) were essential to the creation of a new platform that connected the community and school in a new way of thinking about learning through the arts.

The Classroom

My classroom was a 4th grade two-way immersion classroom in which instruction in the fourth grade was provided in both English and Spanish. Fifty percent of the time instruction was provided in English and fifty percent of the time in Spanish. Half of the students were minorities, mostly Latino/a and Chicano/a, and the other half of the class was White or other ethnicities. The class was considerably from a low socioeconomic background as well as considerably diverse. Class diversity was represented both economically and socially. Parents' occupations ranged from housewives, "campesinos" [farm workers], factory workers, teachers, and professionals working for the government.

When walking into the classroom one would immediately notice how the classroom was divided into different sections or walls. Looking south was the children's international diversity

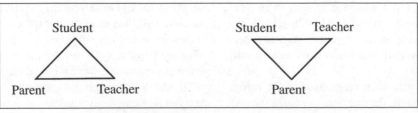

Figure 1 Sociocultural triangulation*

*This triangulation can be initiated by anyone and no one is the head or controller of this process.

wall, which included pictures of children from around the world. Each picture was enlarged and it included a narrative written by the child or an adult about that child's experience. This wall was of great success in the classroom. Both students and parents enjoyed looking at the pictures and reading the narratives. Still on the south side of the wall, immediately after that wall was a calendar wall, which was in both English and Spanish and more pictures and narratives of children from all over the world. North of the international diversity wall was the social studies wall that presented issues related to subjects being studied in class. The wall contained writing samples of all children. East of the room was the creative wall, this wall was initially designed to give children the opportunity to post drawings, but after I began the sociocultural triangulation process through arts it became the most important wall in the classroom—one both students and parents helped design and maintain.

The classroom was not solely mine, but instead a more collective community space where students, parents, guardians, and I were responsible to make sure the classroom was running smoothly. Before the school year started I contacted all parents via telephone or correspondence. I introduced myself and told them a little bit about my life; this gave parents the opportunity to get to know my life experiences and me. I then proceeded to tell parents that there was an "open door" policy, and that they were welcomed and encouraged to come to volunteer in the classroom. I invited them over to the classroom prior to school starting. Many came and we talked about what they saw as the struggles their children have had, frustrations they have had, and ways in which I could help them both. At this time I informed parents that I was going to be calling them every Friday to give them updates and reports of how the classroom was going. They seemed both shocked, and doubtful; I later found out that the majority of them did not think I was going to be actually calling them every Friday.

As I came from a working class family, I am aware of parents' busy schedules as well as the necessity to sometimes carry more than one job to sustain a family. To that end, I explained to parents that *how* they are involved with their child's schooling is more important than the *amount* of involvement. I wanted parents to be able to express their experiences with their children and me (optional). I wanted parents to begin dialogue, to talk to their children about their struggles when they bring an issue home, to ask their children about school, to share their qualities (those things they are good at), whatever they might be, and most importantly to talk and reflect with them. Some parents expressed concerns that they "Did not have anything they were good at, many of us are just housewives or factory workers, 'campesinos' (farm workers)." I reiterated that everyone has something they are good at and that I was sure that if I asked their children what their parents or guardians were good at they could tell me in a second. I reinforced the concept that children appreciate any interaction with parents; and the most important interaction was one that started dialogue and reflection. I explained to parents that I was committed to doing all that was in my power to inform parents and guardians of what we were doing in class, that I saw them as colleagues, so input given to me was appreciated and encouraged. By being including and welcoming, parents and guardians

and students began to feel comfortable around the classroom, with me, and with other students. They began to trust me and the classroom environment.

As I wanted my classroom to be an extension of home, of real life experiences, I needed a way for parents to participate. Moreover, I wanted this participation to be something that was special and not something that would merely help the teacher with her tasks. It seemed to me that one way to accomplish this was to build a partnership with parents through arts. I began to do this by assigning creative projects to students that involved math, social studies, language arts, and arts. The assignments consisted of students going home and finding things around the classroom and/or neighborhood that had to do with school activities. The goal was for students and parents to look around their world, their reality and find beauty and art within it. For example, when we discussed geometric shapes in the classroom I asked students to go home and with parental or guardian help they were to find an object that would match the shapes we were studying. If they could not find one like it, they had to select objects that when connected to others, created that shape. It was a project that everyone seemed to enjoy. One student could not find the shape of a trapezoid, so his father helped him create one with old car parts. Along with the parent, the student sketched each part of the car where it was taken from and explained the process of figuring out what parts would fit together to create a trapezoid. The student also talked about the process of how the metal was bent, welded, and put together. The student brought it to class to share his invention along with an explanation of how he did it. I used that moment to explain to students that arts does not only involve drawing and coloring but also creating new things out of old ones; arts involves everyday experiences and objects that surround us.

My Teaching

Arts have been one of my favorite tools in the classroom. It was a great source of release when I was a child, as it was through the arts I that was able to express many emotions, feelings, and thoughts. For this reason, I felt that including arts in the classroom and in my lessons was imperative. Initially, arts were used in the classroom as a way to express or retell what students were writing or working on. As in the trapezoid example mentioned above, this was very superficial, and it did not require much critical thinking. I began thinking about my intentions and what art expression meant to me while growing up as an immigrant. With that in mind, I began to think about my goal and about changing my role as a teacher. My goal was to promote critical thinking, a sense of commonality, transcendence of time, connection with real life situations, and recognition of power structures that affected characters in the past and that are still affecting many today. After I had a vision of what could be achieved and my role as the sociocultural mediator, I began to think about ways in which I could utilize the arts to raise awareness, promote critical thinking, equity, and social justice. I had my work cut out for me!

Children are always really excited to read about others' experiences, lives, and struggles. Therefore, I chose several biographies and gave students a summary of the biographies that included some of the accomplishments of the characters. I asked the class to choose one biography and write why they wanted to read that particular biography. Students then took the biographies home and shared with their parents the choices they had. Many children returned to class with their favorites and their parents' favorites. Students were also instructed to draw a picture that predicted events which they thought were going to take place in the story; they were to do this with only the information I provided for them. Some parents wrote their favorites on a piece a paper along with the reasons why they liked that particular biography. Some parents wrote it in Spanish and others in English. This allowed them to be included regardless of the language they spoke. I explained to students that I asked them to come up with reasons as to why we should read these biographies in order for them to begin to think about social-political and cultural issues they and their parents are interested in. I then asked for volunteers to discuss their prediction drawings. They were to explain what it was and why they chose those colors, background, and the meaning behind the scene. This became a wonderful artistic activity and experience given that every student had a different interpretation of each of the stories, and therefore colors, background, and scene were and had different meaning. The three biographies they chose were Frida Kahlo, Anne Frank, and Biddy Mason. Frida Kahlo was read in English, Anne Frank in Spanish, and Biddy Mason in Spanish. We began by reading Anne Frank. To save space here, I will only discuss Anne Frank.

The story of Anne Frank is a book that is filled with socio-political issues. First, we began the unit by reading the book and talking about Germany during that time. I provided the class with historical information about Hitler, the Jewish community, and Germany. None of these historical facts included pictures of Hitler. They were then asked to create a portrait of Germany during those times. The portrait was to include the feeling, struggles, and emotions students thought were being felt by either Germans, Jews, or Hitler. Many drew either a picture of Hitler or included Hitler in their portraits; surprisingly enough almost all but two students drew Hitler with blond hair and blue eyes. When asked to share their portraits with the class many expressed that Hitler was blond with blue eyes because he liked people who were "like him, blond with blue eyes." Here students began to make a connection to their own life experiences, their feeling comfortable or liking people who were like them. So, if Hitler liked people who were blond with blue eyes, then he must be blond and have blue eyes. When they all finished presenting their portraits, I showed them several pictures of Hitler. They were all shocked to find out that Hitler was not blond, nor did he have blue eyes. I also told them that Hitler's mother was Jewish. And they suddenly began to think. Their eyes were wide open; they were in deep thought. We talked about why it was more acceptable for Hitler to be blond with blue eyes than for him to have dark hair and brown eyes. I got responses such as, "If he was just like the Jews, brown hair, and dark eyes, then why did he dislike them?" "He must not like himself." "I know some people who are mean to many who are like them; like Latinos hurting Latinos."

We talked about what life was about during that time, and what it was to be a young woman without the opportunity to experience "la vida" (life). This conversation about Anne Frank was happening in the classroom and at home. I asked parents to begin a portrait of the Anne Frank story at home. I explained to them that as the story proceeded they were to add something to the portrait. I felt this was a great opportunity to get parents involved and share their experiences their "vida" (life). I asked parents to share how their experiences were similar to those of Anne Frank. Hence, together with their children, many parents worked on the Anne Frank portrait. As the story proceeded they were to add whatever from Anne's life or their life they thought was important to the portrait.

Although this story was one that touched them, they were still responding superficially to the story. I wanted them to feel like the key person in the story, to put their feet in Anne Frank's shoes. Therefore, I asked them to literally take their shoes off and to share them with the person next to them and to put each other's shoes on. I too had to exchange shoes with a student. They were all really excited about doing this. I moved the desks, dimmed the lights, and had students close their eyes. I began playing German classical music and we all began to "walk in someone else's shoes." I asked the class to think about their feelings, emotions, to imagine being a teenager during the holocaust and not being able to enjoy life fully, to imagine being imprisoned, trapped, and scared because of persecution. After the exercise was completed, they were quiet, and some raised their hands. They shared how it felt to imagine being someone else. Many talked about being powerless or "sin poder," frightened, trapped, and caged "como un animal." This activity provided students with a more creative way of looking at the arts. It was the arts that involved movement, sense of one's place, and thinking about others while being here. For fourth graders this was a unique way of feeling the arts—seeing beauty, pain, and otherness.

I asked them to think about the way they felt and to portray their feelings in any way they wanted to. They could do this by singing, acting, drawing, or creating a mini-book. Two created sketches, one sang, and the rest created portraits of what they experienced while being in someone else's shoes. One child drew a portrait of Anne as a girl crying, in one corner was the Star of David and on the other side were armed forces. The side of the face that had armed forces was white with blue eyes and blond hair and the side with the Star of David was brown with black eyes and dark hair. Bars imprisoned the girl, and a tear was coming out of her eye. In the writing description, it said, "The Hitler army wants her to be white, blond with blue eyes, but she has black hair and dark eyes, and that is why she is in a prison; the attic of that home. Anne was an amazing girl who was proud of who she was and who wrote those letters to let us know what not to do and to take people like they are." One child performed a sketch that connected her own personal experiences with those of Anne Frank. The sketch was a moving and sad story of her grandmother and her family running away from Mexico, away from the threat of being killed. This skit created an interesting conversation between the entire class. Children began to talk about oppression, ethnicity, race, power, powerlessness, discrimination, racism, genocide, social political implications, survival, and what it means to us now. Since many of them did not know the terminology, they only expressed themselves through experiences and examples. As they were giving me examples I began to provide them with the terms that described that particular situation. For example, Hitler killed thousands of people and this is called genocide. We talked about color and preconceived notions many have about a particular race because of the color of their skin. Another student began to sing about class differences, which lead us to talk about privilege and poverty. Many students could relate to this given that many had felt mistreatment because of their social class.

They all had wonderful examples of artistic expressions; their feelings and reactions showed they understood how struggle is painful regardless of when it happens. With this activity, it did not matter if you could draw, sing, or dance. Any form of artistic expression was accepted; it became the universal language of acceptance. Arts became a universal voice that was open and accessible to all.

Community

As parents began to get involved and informed about what was going on in the classroom, other family members became involved as well. Many parents were immigrants and their migration experiences as well as their struggles with a life in a new country had valuable lessons for their children. Being an immigrant whose experiences were ignored, I reiterated to parents that their experiences were valuable and appreciated. Parents became involved in helping to create portraits, giving children ideas, and sharing their own stories. They were dialoguing, communicating, and reflecting on their experiences together. Students began sharing their family stories with the class to find out that many of our stories were similar.

I noticed that children were really interested in other children's stories, in their own family stories, and the way each child expressed their stories through the use the art. Because I was aware that "men and women . . . [are] beings who cannot be truly human apart from communication, for they are essentially communicative creatures" and that "to impede communication is to reduce men to the status of 'things'" (Freire, p. 109), I decided to invite parents, grandparents, guardians, uncles, friends and anyone who wanted to share their struggles, motivations, purpose, moments of feeling powerless, and the sources of their strengths to participate. Parents were encouraged to create or do something artistic with their children to bring them to class and also present with their son or daughter. I announced this activity a month or two in advance just as I began to make home visits. During home visits we began to share life experiences, anecdotes, and stories. I asked parents, guardians, grandparents, and other family members if they would be willing to share their stories and argued it was important for them to tell children their "whys." Most importantly, I wanted them to share the "whys" for their being in this country and what their motivations and hopes were. In addition, they were asked to share what the lack of opportunities and struggles were that motivated them to flee their own countries. Visiting with them at home and calling parents every Friday worked well and helped me schedule the

first couple of presentations. Prior to parents presenting, I sent a bulletin home that included some of the portraits students had created along with a brief description of what we were doing in class. In the bulletin I invited parents to come in and observe other parents' presentations, and I told them I was going to provide snacks and drinks for students and parents.

More than half of the parents showed up that afternoon to hear the presentations. They brought multi-ethnic foods and drinks. One even brought "taquitos" for the entire class. Since it was my idea to do this, I decided to begin the presentations. I talked to the class about coming to the United States, learning the language, and the struggles my parents overcame in this country. I told them about my going to college and trying to be a good teacher who promotes social justice. I showed pictures of my country, my family, and sang for the class. An immigrant mother who had only been in the United States for three years gave the second presentation. She had been a teacher in Mexico and was a factory worker here. She had two jobs and the father of the family had three jobs. The mother and son had created a collage of pictures and portraits that illustrated their story. The son introduced his mother. "This is 'mi Jefa' (my boss or mother), and she is going to share our story with you. Please listen to her; she does not know English, but I will tell you what she is telling and our teacher will help me if need help." The mother began to share that they were a middle class family in Mexico; they owned a house, two cows, and at least three-dozen chickens. The animals enabled them to survive while growing up. She got up every morning to work on the farm, went to school, and then came back after school to work some more. She loved books and really wanted to be a teacher; so she begged her parents to let her go to school. They agreed but only if she continued helping with the animals on the farm. When she started attending university, she took a bus for two hours to get to classes everyday. After graduation, her father became ill. Since she could not support the farm with her salary, and they lost everything. She and her husband were the only two working. She was making less than fifty dollars a month, and her husband made even less. They were really struggling. She said that she wanted her children to go to college and have a better life.

So, they came to this country hoping to be able to do better here. Indeed she had hoped she could teach here. She was shocked when she found out that her degree was worth nothing here and her skills were not appreciated. She decided to place her children in the dual immersion program my class was part of because she wanted to be able to communicate with the teacher. But most importantly she wanted her children to maintain their language. They shared the collage they had created and the portraits of "el ranchito" they had in Mexico. The mother shared that she was not a very artistic person, but creating a collage gave her a new way to look at art. She called it "el arte de mis recuerdos" [the art of my memories]. The son then proceeded to talk about why it was so important for him to go to school. He said, "I need to go to school so that I can buy 'mi jefa un ranchito.'"

Third, an Anglo family of three (mother, father, and son) presented. They spoke only English so their son translated into Spanish. They brought a song to share with the class. Both parents were professionals who lived in an upper middle class neighborhood. They wanted their children to be in the two-way immersion program because they wanted their children to be culturally well rounded, not racist, and to speak a second language. They shared with the class that in their neighborhood there are not any minorities, and they thought it was important for their children to experience being with other children. They also mentioned that three generations before their parents came from Germany not knowing the language and struggling like many of the parents and guardians who are in the class. They also brought black and white pictures of their family in Germany and talked about how excited they were to have children who are bilingual when they are not. They then began to sing a song they sang at home, as a family. This family song had become the way to connect past with present, to maintain their history and to keep their ancestors alive.

These community meetings became the high points of the school year. They became events where the parents and guardians shared their culinary arts and a time for us to learn about foods and experiences from different parts of the world. The classroom became a larger community that consisted of students, teacher, and family members. It was a community in which everyday diversity, differences, struggles, achievements, and pains were shared and respected. Many of the students and parents had known each other only briefly and did not even know that they had so much in common. Some became good friends and started talking on the phone. Others just began to understand many of the struggles others parents had gone through. Others collaborated in creating arts projects with other families who had similar experiences or who were neighbors. Some parents united to bring issues pertaining to them and their children to school officials and school board meetings. They began to have voice. These meetings continued throughout the year as a way to share what is so natural if explored: artistic expression.

Conclusion

Being a teacher of color means being a political being (Apple, 1990). Yet, "la llave," a key, is needed to invite parents and guardians into the education of their students. The arts became a means to begin dialogue where students and parents and guardians could communicate, express themselves, and connect their personal experiences. Arts became an expression of their lives, a way to see the world, and a way to understand different points of view. Through the arts they expressed their desires and needs. They also came to see school differently. Their children were engaged in their real lives as actors and critics.

Students were not just making pictures. Rather they began to experience differences of opinions through arts. They began to explore their own beliefs and those beliefs of their parents and guardians. They began to think critically about the sociopolitical implications mentioned in Anne Frank and other biographies, and how these implications apply to them today. Students began to recognize the difficulties of walking in other people's shoes and found the arts as a way to accomplish this. Art also was used to make writing more interesting, fun, and to make it theirs: to own it.

Arts also became the way for parents to communicate with their children, to talk, to share, to work together, to get to know each other. Parents also learned about each other's families and the reasons why they were in a two-way immersion program and, for some, in this country. It gave students the opportunity to feel proud of their cultural heritage, their family, and their classmates. It provided all of us with a community where social justice, critical thinking, respect, and consciousness were valued. It provided parents, students and me, the teacher, with a process of critical pedagogy. This process was discovery oriented and used the arts as a way of looking at differences. An arts pedagogy was used as a platform to provide a safe method and space for different groups to express traditions and perspectives, to articulate social injustices, to ultimately dialogue, think, reflect and act. Parents and students empowered themselves through their artistic expression. The arts are "La llave" [the key] that teachers can use to create a classroom where all children and their parents and guardians are accepted, respected, and seen as powerful political beings.

References

Diaz, E., & Flores, B. (2000). Teacher as sociocultural mediator: Teaching to the potential. In M. de la cruz Reyes & J. Halcon (Eds.), *Best for Latino children: Critical literacy perspectives.* New York: Teachers College Press.

Fisher, D. & McDonald, N. (2002). *Developing arts-loving readers: Top 10 questions teachers are asking about integrated arts education.* Maryland: Scarecrow Press.

Freire, P. (1970). *Pedagogy of the oppressed.* New York: Seabury.

Nieto, S. (1999). *The light in their eyes: Creating multicultural learning communities.* New York: Teachers College Press.

Critical Thinking

1. What are Freire's ideas about critical theory?
2. How can teachers use the arts to promote community and context?
3. What are students' responses to arts in the classroom?
4. Why are the arts key to awareness, community relations, and parental involvement?

Strengthening the Case for Community-Based Learning in Teacher Education

Jewell E. Cooper

Cultural disconnections between teachers and their students have led, in some cases, to teachers and administrators communicating poorly with students. Particularly in high-poverty schools, lack of effective communication has translated to teachers teaching students with a deficit model in mind.

We have evidence from previous studies (i.e., Cabello & Burstein, 1995; Wiest, 1998; Zeichner & Melnick, 1996) that community-based experiences are effective in creating in middle-class preservice teachers an awareness of the cultural strengths of students and their families. However, such home/community experiences are not yet a part of most teacher education programs. Consequently, this article is designed to demonstrate that activities can be developed to engage preservice teachers in the home communities of their learners. Furthermore, such activities can encourage a change in preservice teachers' conceptions and dispositions about students and their families, which further substantiates the need for teacher educators to incorporate such practices as a routine part of teacher education programs.

Theoretical Background

Researchers remind us of what we already see—that White middle-class females will most likely teach our nation's growing number of native-born ethnic majority, ethnic minority, and immigrant children (Banks, 2000; Cabello & Burstein, 1995; Hodgkinson, 2002; Sleeter, 2001; Zeichner, 1996). Therefore, we need to transform how we prepare our preservice teachers (Garibaldi, 1992). Those ways include understanding and learning about other cultures.

Three major reasons support the need for such an understanding. First, both in-service and preservice teachers hold stereotypic views of certain ethnic groups based on media representations, interpretations of history, and previously held beliefs passed down by family members and significant others (Gollnick & Chinn, 2001; McIntyre, 1997). For example, preservice teachers of diverse learners in Terrill and Mark's (2000) study indicated that they were afraid to visit the homes of culturally diverse students, expected more discipline problems, saw their students as victims of abuse, perceived that they were rarely gifted or talented, and believed that they lacked motivation and parental support.

Second, many in-service and preservice teachers may not consider themselves to be cultural beings, and do not often understand discrimination (Gay, 2001; King, 1991; Tatum, 1997; Wright, 2004). Therefore, they may not comprehend discriminatory practices as perceived by culturally diverse persons, chiefly because they have not explored their own ethnic identities (McIntyre, 1997). In her study, McIntyre discovered that because preservice teachers did not consider themselves to be as a significant part of a culture, they believed culturally diverse students were deficient. The preservice teachers' "innocent ignorance" or "conscious avoidance" (my terms) became a form of "dysconscious racism" (King, 1991), that may or may not be understood by those who do not have the power (Delpit, 1995).

Third, preservice teachers may engage in avoidance and choose to teach in less-challenging settings. In the Terrill and Mark (2000) study, preservice teachers were questioned about their preferences for student teaching placements. Many of them provided socially acceptable answers and stated that they would willingly teach in schools with high enrollments of children of color—in this case, Hispanic children. However, when these same preservice teachers realized that their preferences would determine placement, they recanted and requested placement in suburban schools where White students were in the majority.

In an effort to better prepare preservice teachers to teach culturally diverse student populations, multicultural education courses have been added to teacher education programs. They have included topics such as the recognition and acknowledgment of White privilege (Jordan & Rice, 1995, Lawrence & Bunche, 1996; McFalls & Cobb-Roberts, 2001; Pewewardy, 2005). These courses have been met, at times, with resistance by students (Brown, 2004), but changes in attitudes can occur (VanGunten & Martin, 2001).

Community-Based Learning

Community-based learning has also been advocated as a powerful way to teach preservice teachers about other cultures (Boyle-Baise & Sleeter, 1998; Sleeter, 2000). In her review of the literature, Sleeter (2001) noted that there is value in cultural-immersion programs (those where preservice teachers live/actively participate in the communities in which they student teach and/or volunteer). Further, cultural-immersion experiences allow preservice teachers to view, experience, reflect upon, and change perspectives of how others respond to and make sense of their worlds (Cabello & Burstein, 1995; Wiest, 1998; Zeichner & Melnick, 1996). Sleeter, however, recognized that convincing teacher educators to include such programs and activities in teacher-preparation programs is "difficult without a stronger research base" (p. 4).

It is not that we totally lack evidence in the effectiveness of community-based learning experiences. In fact, field experiences in culturally diverse schools have been cited as being most beneficial and having great potential to influence the choices of where preservice teachers ultimately desire to teach (Burant & Kirby, 2002; Colville-Hall, McDonald, & Smolen, 1995; Grant & Secada, 1990; Ladson-Billings, 2000, 2001; Olmedo, 1997; Zeichner, 1996). Not only do these experiences allow preservice teachers to acquire experience being with diverse learners in the classroom before and while they student teach, but they also provide opportunities to change ways of thinking about their learners. For instance, the prospective teachers in Olmedo's (1997) study found out that inner-city children did want to learn, that good teaching could take place, that there was diversity within diversity, and that purporting to be "colorblind" was disadvantageous to their teaching.

The purpose of this study is intended to strengthen that research base in two ways: (a) by demonstrating that carefully staged community experiences, structured developmentally and sequentially, can be incorporated in teacher education programs; and (b) by providing evidence that cultural-immersion experiences can challenge preservice teachers' preconceived beliefs about students who are very different from themselves.

What We Did
Context

The study took place at a southeastern public university that has approximately 14,300 students. The university is 1 of 14 campuses that house a state Teaching Fellows Program. This statewide program awards scholarship loans to outstanding high school seniors who are committed to teaching in K-12 state public schools after they graduate. In addition to acceptance of the scholarship loan, Teaching Fellows (TFs) have to attend weekly seminars every year during their tenure at the university, among other required activities. Each seminar has an established theme. The theme for the junior-year seminar is "Diversity."

Development of the Community-Based Program for Preservice Teacher Education

When I first began to teach the junior-year seminar, I recognized that when the topic of diversity arose, TFs commonly said, "we hear diversity to death." Their repeated statements caused me to question their conscious recognition of their places among diverse populations. Considering their responses and reactions to earlier activities, as well as mandates of accrediting bodies for teacher education candidate preparation, the TFs' campus director and I decided to develop and implement a diversity-awareness program component of the teacher education program in the junior TF seminar. The three goals of the seminar became (a) to help TFs experience diversity or "otherness" themselves; (b) to provide sequentially connected experiences for cultural engagement that went beyond the schools where TFs were completing internships; and (c) to discover community/human assets in each community explored. Over the course of an academic year, the TFs' director and I planned six activities. Note that the first four activities took place during the Fall semester; the last two activities took place during the Spring semester. The activities are as follows:

Written autobiography—The autobiography included important events that led up to the TFs' decision to teach. This served as initial fact statements of themselves, the "factual me." At least five written pages were required; however, students in this study turned in between 5 and 22 pages.

Bio-Poem—In contrast to the autobiography, this exercise allowed TFs to be "the me I want others to see." A 10-line formula poetry strategy, the Bio-Poem, includes the following directions: Person's First Name, Title, Four adjectives that describe the person, Lover of three or more things or ideas, Who believes (one or more ideas), Who wanted (three things), Who used (three things or methods), Who gave (three things), Who said (a quote), and Person's Last Name.

Privilege Walk—The purpose of this identity-based sequenced activity was for students to discover the diversity within themselves, as well as to experience how preconceived notions and beliefs about people, particularly their friends, affected how they view them. Two examples of the directions for this "step forward-step back" activity are: "If there were people of color who worked in your household as servants, gardeners, etc., take one step forward" and "If you studied the culture of your ancestors in elementary school, take one step forward." Additionally, this activity gave definition to "the me I am but don't want others to see." More information about this activity can be found at http://www.msu.edu/-bailey22/Privilege_Exercise.htm.

Camera Safari—In groups of two or three, TFs were provided with a disposable camera, and when they visited one of their school feeder communities, one from which ethnic minority students were bussed or walked, they took pictures to answer 10 questions related to the community: something historical that you weren't aware of; something that shows the natural beauty of the area; a scenic or panoramic view; something that shows the area is changing; something that could be used in a tourism brochure to advertise this part of the school community to entice people to come to the community; something that shows growth in the area; something that is "kid-friendly'; something that you or your group feels could be improved about the area; something that surprised you or your group about the area; and other scenes that you would like to add. These pictures were then presented by the groups and discussed with the entire class. This activity was originally created by an area leadership organization and was used with permission. We tailored it to better meet our needs.

Walking a Mile in Another's Shoes—This activity included real-life scenarios for TFs to enact that involved experiences in which their students' families might engage. Each student was given a scenario that included experiences such as using public transportation to apply for an hourly wage job, applying for subsidized childcare and subsidized housing, eating at a homeless shelter, applying for food stamps, taking a police ride, having physical disabilities, enrolling a child in school as a gay couple, being low income and seeking health care, attending an Alcoholics Anonymous meeting, seeking services as an immigrant, and seeking resources while living in public housing. It is important to note here that I assigned TFs to each activity. Each written scenario included a set of reflective questions that related to it. Of course, we contacted officials of the agencies that the TFs would be visiting so that they (the officials) would not actually allocate the resources to them; however, we requested that TFs receive the same kind of treatment that actual applicants received. These activities were also used with permission from the leadership organization and adapted accordingly.

Debunking the Community—TFs were required to attend at least two different services at the predominant center of worship in their school community, make purchases and spend time in the community grocery store at least twice, but not in the same week, and participate in at least one recreational experience with community members, etc. TFs were also required to make a home visit, accompanied by their cooperating teacher, if possible, or make a telephone call to the parent or guardian of a struggling student with whom they had been working. Explicit instructions were given on how to make home visits. For 6 weeks, TFs participated in the school feeder community in which the "Camera Safari" took place, or they could choose the neighborhood or community from which their students came to complete these last two activities.

Sequencing the activities was imperative, for I purposely arranged the order of the activities so that the TFs would journey from self-interrogation within themselves and discovery to outside of themselves by engagement in the communities where their students lived.

Participants

Forty-two junior-level TFs participated in these six diversity activities. Thirty-seven were White (27 female, 10 male), four were African American (3 female, 1 male), and one was Puerto-Rican (female). One student was hearing impaired. More specifically, among these were prospective teachers from the following disciplines: birth-K (1), elementary (15), middle grades (2), and high school—English (2), math (1), social studies (6), biology (1). Among the class, K-12 disciplines were also represented: art (2), music (4), theatre (1), speech (2), psychology (1), health (2), and foreign language (2). Before this diversity seminar, none of the students had taken a course specifically directed toward diversity. However, diversity had been included as a topic in previous coursework.

Data Sources and Collection

I functioned as both seminar leader and as participant observer, recording notes immediately after discussing/processing each event throughout the year. Across the junior-year experience, I collected data from five writing sources: TFs' autobiographies (AB), Bio-Poems (BP), fast writes (FW)—written immediately after activities were completed, responses to reflection wheels completed after the "Privilege Walk" (PW), and anonymous "Blackboard reflections" of TFs' experiences (BB). My field notes (FN) and group visual representations of the activity, "Walking a Mile in Another's Shoes," (VR) that were shared and discussed with the class served as another source for data collection. One year later, at an end-of-year senior retreat, I was provided an opportunity for a follow-up group interview (GI) that was audiotaped and transcribed. TFs reflected globally on the activities of the junior year, and how the knowledge constructed from those activities might have affected their year-long senior field-based experience.

Data Analysis

I inductively analyzed these data in three phases. First, I analyzed data received from each writing source. For example, in the fast writes from the "Privilege Walk," I noted words and phrases such as "nervous," "fear," and "isolation," and counted the number of times such words or related words were mentioned. Second, I began to identify patterns across each of the data sources. For instance, safety and fear of the unknown—more specifically, how TFs felt they would be received—were written as concerns 21 times in their various writings. In the third phase of analysis, I began to generate categories that were formed from clusters of patterns. Examples of those emerging categories were emotions, fear, resistance, surprise, and transformation. Just as the activities were sequentially arranged and completed, the revelation of categories also emerged in a sequential fashion that seemed related to the activities experienced. Finally, I renamed the categories as themes. They became: (a) "I second that emotion" of privilege, (b) fear and resistance, (c) surprise patrol, and (d) "was blind but now I see"—transformations in the making. My field notes and data from the senior retreat assisted me in triangulating these data as TFs reiterated these themes when reflecting on their experiences. Based on the categories, I selected quotations that demonstrated the themes to provide illustrations. In the text that follows, these quotations are noted as to the TF, data source, and date. For example, the first citation (JEC, FN, 10/01) shows that the quote was taken from my (JEC) field notes (FN) dated October, 2001.

Findings

The first two activities, the personal autobiography and the Bio-Poem, served as activities that allowed the preservice teachers to investigate the person they knew best—themselves. The four remaining activities were revealed by themes as students moved from intrapersonal to transformational perspectives.

As revealed through their autobiographies, all 42 TFs acknowledged that they were from suburban and rural backgrounds. They lived in two-parent and single-parent homes, and had endured the aftermath of divorce, transience, and survival on minimal amounts of money. Although TFs admitted experiencing family hardship at times, they also recognized the power to overcome difficult and even "impossible circumstances" through the strong work ethic of their parents. Overwhelmingly, 29 TFs described themselves as "being blessed" (AB, 8/01). Those "blessings" were also expressed in their Bio-Poems (BP, 9/01). Only 3 of the 42 students identified themselves ethnically.

Theme 1: "I Second That Emotion" of Privilege

All of the activities conjured up emotions in the TFs, particularly the "Privilege Walk." This activity required that participants should stand shoulder to shoulder in a straight line without talking and take steps forward or backward in response to statements related to privilege or disadvantage. Thirty-five such directives were given and students moved accordingly, resulting in a wide distribution of positions across the room. I documented the emotional responses in my field notes.

Immediately after the completion of the activity, the group returned to the class to process the event. Blank stares confronted me; some students' eyes could not meet mine. Water-glazed eyes filled. One student broke down in tears. (JEC, FN, 10/01)

In fast writes following this activity, students wrote that the "Privilege Walk" was "very cathartic," made them "nervous," "confused," "isolated," "distanced," and that it "evoked bad memories" (PW, FW, 10/01). The activity aroused feelings of positionality, isolation, and marginalization. Three students echoed the thoughts of others in this way:

Consistently I felt nervous and confused throughout the privilege activity. As many of my classmates began to move ahead of me, I felt isolated and distanced by their lack of shared experiences. At times, as I stepped further and further back, I felt guilty and wished to be in the middle (not the front, as guilt would also result from extreme privilege). Ultimately I left sad and angry at the visual representation of my isolation and marginalization. Perhaps I feel cheated that some part of me results in such a multitude of negative experiences. (AN, FW, 10/01)

This activity was hard for me to participate in. . . . I must admit that this activity made me ashamed and I did not want others to know things about me. Even as I sit here now I feel like others think differently about me. I feel like the way I have built up has crumbled and I am not very comfortable with that. (JM, FW, 10/01)

The privilege activity made me feel upset and awkward. I was at the back of the group and felt bad with everyone looking at me. . . . Also, answering those questions brought up a lot of bad memories for me. (EW, FW 10/01)

Seminar members reflected on how different they were from others in the class. Some of those differences had not been anticipated; in fact, the person in the back of the group astounded everyone, including me. Field notes stated:

the Town and Country [name of an upscale fashion magazine] girl stood out noticeably like a lone ranger far from the others in the front or in the middle. She was actually standing in the back alone. When I looked at her, the tears began to stream down her face. She murmured that she did not want to remember what she had tried so hard to mask and forget. (JEC, FN, 10/01)

After I engaged them in dialogue about the definition of White privilege, its daily enactments, the possible responses to these enactments from those on the receiving end, and the lenses through which their students and their families may view them as teachers, "the entire class was left speechless after the revelation of 'the me I am but don't want others to see'." (JEC, FN, 10/01)

Theme 2: Fear and Resistance

Thirty-seven students did not want to complete or were hesitant about completing the "Camera Safari" and "Walking a Mile in Another's Shoes." From excuses about not having the time to commit to such activities to being apprehensive about going into

unfamiliar territory, TFs repeatedly mentioned their fear of the unknown. For one particular TF, the "Camera Safari" process was one that "I hated. Getting together with people I didn't know, going somewhere I didn't want to go seemed worthless" (DC, FW, 11/01). Safety remained a central issue. One TF was "very nervous about getting out of the car to talk to people. I was scared to walk down the street" (SO, FW, 11/01). Another "thanked God I brought along my friend. I figured I'd be safe" (JH, FW, 11/01). Still other TFs were quite concerned about how they would be received in the communities that they visited. One voiced:

As we walked into the community to complete the project, I wondered what the people of the community would think of us—four White student teachers wandering around the local projects with a disposable camera. I wondered if we would be asked to leave or even approached by the community leader or police officer. I was not afraid to be there, but I was a little self-conscious about our conspicuousness. (AB1, BB, 11/01)

Three TFs echoed concern about how their group would be received by others in the community. However, fear did not stop participants from being inquisitive and wanting to know about community members' lives.

Actually, going into—[name of public housing community] had me really scared. I remember myself and my group members discussing leaving on our internship tags so maybe people wouldn't think we were being nosey and intrusive. I was scared of the people I'd come across and the reactions we would receive. (RM, BB, 11/01)

I felt entirely out of place. I walked the street with camera in hand. I was terrified that some half-drunk man would come stumbling out of his home yelling at me to get the Hell out of his neighborhood. Would the people be afraid of me? Would they feel different, like lab rats up for inspection? (AN, BB, 11/01)

I felt like an outsider. I felt dressed-up, even though I wasn't. I felt a little uncomfortable, like an animal on edge in another's turf. Would anyone ask me to leave or inquire about my reasons for taking the pictures? Would they be offended? There sure weren't many people outside. I wanted to see what it was like inside the homes, but I was scared to knock on any doors. (MG, BB, 11/01)

In response to a "Walking a Mile in Another's Shoes" scenario, one TF wrote that "I didn't want to do the food stamps activity. . . . I didn't know what to expect. While I was completing the activity I just kept thinking, I hope I don't have to ever go through this" (AM, FW, 03/02). Other TFs who applied for subsidized housing did not understand why they were chosen for the activity. Fear and confusion consumed them for a while. Although the police ride excited three of four of the TFs assigned to do it, one did not want to take the excursion because "it would be a waste of my time, to be honest" (AB1, FW, 03/02). Going to the Department of Social Services (DSS) made another TF feel "frustrated." It would be a "waste of my time and a waste of DSS's time as well" (MG, VR, 03/02). Even to a TF of color, thinking about taking public transportation—riding the bus to apply for a job—was not exciting:

Buses to me have always been . . . icky . . . I didn't want to get on. I didn't want all those people staring at me. Applying for a job as a single mom in need of daycare wasn't my idea of fun either. I had always had less patience for "those kinds of people." (AB3, BB, 03/02)

Though begun with resistance, the two previous activities paved the way for students to participate in "Debunking the Community" with less fear and opposition. In class discussions, they related their increasing comfort in doing the assignment because they had been with their classrooms or tutored students for a longer period of time. In fact, 10 of the TFs talked with their tutees and students about community playgrounds, grocery stores, and churches in the area, and were invited to attend.

Theme 3: Surprise Patrol

Even with the aforementioned resistance and fear of initially beginning the activities, once students were engaged in the explorations, new experiences yielded surprise revelations from them. The residents and appearances of the communities astonished the TFs most, especially while they were doing the "Camera Safari" and "Debunking the Community." Thirty-seven of 42 TFs were surprised at what they found in the communities in which they interacted. A neighborhood with a welcoming atmosphere was definitely not expected. One TF "was surprised by how friendly the people were to me. I expected them to shun me" (AT, FW, 11/01). Two others described their group's experience:

As we walked through the neighborhood, we were welcomed by some of our students and their parents. Before getting too far into the project, we visited the main office of the housing community and got some information from the woman there, who was only too happy to tell us everything we wanted to know. (JG, FW, 11/01)

I was shocked at this point, at the sense of pride I felt swelling up in the community. The more time I spent there, the more it seemed that this was a good place to live. (AB2, FW, 11/01)

Once TFs were comfortable enough in the communities to "let my guard down" (JEC, FN, 11/01), they were surprised at "how cultural and religious these people are. They are anything but lazy" (JEC, FN, 11/01). They were also surprised to find historic sites near public housing and "attempts of the community to improve their environment" (JEC, FN, 11/01). Expecting media representations of public housing as unkempt and boisterous, one TF was "shocked by how small but neat the yards were" (JH1, FW, 11/01). "The neighborhood was pretty quiet even though there were several people out in the yards" (JH2, FW, 11/01). Nonetheless, the reality of school busing and the face of segregation were observed. One TF questioned, "Why are these children being bused so far from home to go to school? That is ridiculous! Why are they traveling so far?" (RM1, FW, 11/01). Another TF's expectation was shattered by some students going one way and others going another:

I was definitely surprised about the area! I expected to see that stereotypical Mayberry, middle-class neighborhood. I did not expect to see a particular race of people dominating the area because of the highly diverse population of the school. When I saw White children get off a bus and exit

to the right, and all others exit to the left, I was stunned! I thought the fight against segregation had gone further than that. (AM, FW, 11/01)

Theme 4: "Was Blind but Now I See"— Transformations in the Making

All of the activities allowed TFs to "step outside my comfort zone" (DM, FW, 04/02) and see and experience how "the other" lives. In class discussions, members shared that they feared the African American population most, and generally held the most negative stereotypical beliefs about them. These beliefs were chiefly based on media portrayals, both print and electronic, and word-of-mouth descriptions expressed in personal encounters. Twenty TFs thought that African American parents more often than White parents did not respond to academic inquiries from teachers or other school personnel concerning their children. After engaging in these activities, TFs shared discoveries about themselves, some of which shattered long-held predispositions. After making two telephone calls with her cooperating teacher to two students, one TF acknowledged that one parent requested advisement about managing her son's school attendance. The other parent was on the defensive about the teacher calling regarding her son. Later, the parent apologized for her behavior. The cooperating teacher explicitly instructed the preservice teacher on how to make a telephone call to parents (JEC, FN, 04/09). From those telephone interactions, the TF learned that:

. . . Students' backgrounds have a great deal to do with their habits. As teachers, we need to be the model for them through our actions. Students learn so much more by our actions than just what they hear us say. There is an endless amount of nonverbal communication present that teachers need to be aware of. We can't give up on their parents, though, and think that they don't care about their children. (KC, BB, 04/02)

The "Debunking the Community" activity encouraged some TFs to appreciate students' backgrounds more. Home visits allowed TFs to personally learn more about students they were teaching. However, two TFs found out that their cooperating teachers refused to visit some of the neighborhoods of their students. Undaunted, the TFs were determined to complete their assignment so they went anyway. When they got lost, they asked the police patrolman for directions. He questioned their presence in the community and told them that "that is not a neighborhood for them to go in" (JG, CC/JEC, FN, 04/02). The TFs were appalled at his reaction. They went anyway.

Ten TFs recognized that more vocal methods of praise are demonstrated by some religious denominations practiced by African Americans. Specifically, one TF linked this lively style of worship with schooling and noted that:

. . . I enjoyed joining in on the enthusiastic praises of the Baptist and Pentecostal churches. Students who attend these churches are accustomed to services that are more active and, therefore, they will become bored in classes that they do not feel a part of. Teachers should remember to keep the students involved and active to keep their attention. No matter what belief a person holds, whom they worship, or where and when, their background and attitudes are shaped by these beliefs. Teachers need to be aware of the strong attachments that students have to their houses of worship to understand where their students come from. (JH1, BB, 04/02)

Another recognized the sense of community that the church offers to the African American ethnic group.

At first I was SO frustrated that I had been sitting in a pew for three hours. How do these people do it every week and then some, I wondered? As we sang and hollered and clapped and HUGGED—I have never been hugged by so many strangers in my life—I realized that the church is really a place of safety for its members. See if you are struggling to make it and you are faced with classism and racism combined into so much struggle, you need a place to go where you can let go, feel energized, be loved, and be encouraged to keep on keepin' on. And, this place needs to be SAFE—physically and spiritually . . . And there is community amongst these people. This church is a place where people can express themselves without fear of ridicule and where they can truly BELONG. (AH, BB, 04/02)

Admitting those predispositions became a powerful step forward. The risk was worthwhile. Admitted one TF, "I took a risk going. I never would have gone unless required or if I knew someone in the vicinity. I learned I live behind a pale veil, being downtown and privileged" (TW, BB, 04/02). Two others discovered that:

The more time I spent there, the more it seemed that this was a good place to live. As I adopted this philosophy, I began to see the hurt of injustice—powers' view of the community, windowless homes, and threatening signs from city government. I became sad and angry. Through this activity, I found that I have prejudices. As much as I try to value all people, I have deep-seated prejudices. (JM2, BB, 04/02)

I found out that although I like to say that I am an open-minded, unbiased individual I fell right into being judgmental and maybe even prejudiced. Such a strong word but it really opened up my eyes, and although hard to say about oneself but if you judge others on stereotypes—that's what being prejudiced is. (JN, BB, 04/02)

Thirty-five TFs expressed a stronger commitment to understanding and helping their students. Among their reflections, one "found out that I CAN go wherever I need to go for the sake of my students. I can feel okay, if not comfortable, anywhere they are because I know it means so much to them that I came" (AT, BB, 04/02). Another gained new vision. "Now I see that I need to go a little further if I want to really know how my students live day to day. Going into their communities is a good way to do that" (CC, BB, 04/02).

Conclusion

This study demonstrated that activities can be incorporated into teacher education to move preservice teachers from their assigned schools into the communities of their learners. In doing so, it provides more evidence that cultural-immersion experiences can challenge preservice teachers' prior beliefs and stereotypes about the students they teach, their students' families, and the locations of their home communities.

Through seminar requirements, TFs were able to engage in connected, sequential activities that first allowed them to learn (a) who they are, (b) who they want to appear to be, and (c) who they are but do not want others to see. The last three activities all involved cultural immersion through community-based experiences. Fear of the unknown led to strong resistance initially, which has been cited by other researchers (Brown, 2004; McFalls & Cobb-Roberts, 2001). However, in this case, as the TFs engaged in the community-based activities, their perceptions about their students began to change. One year later at the senior retreat, one TF revealed:

I'm more sensitive to people's environments. I taught at a 'White flight' high school. I hear, 'that's so ghetto,' or 'that's so gay.' I take time to explain [to the class] what they're really saying and that it is not acceptable to me. (JN, GI, 04/02)

In addition, there appears to be a case for the developmental sequencing of such activities. Allowing TFs to explore themselves first and then slowly engaging them in community activities they had never encountered before was effective. As a result, they saw themselves, their students, and their students' families through a lens of strength instead of one filled with deficits.

Therefore, I recommend that other teacher educators include such activities in their courses. Three points are important. First, although the "Privilege Walk" was uncomfortable and even unsettling for some, completing this activity or a similar one was vital to prepare TFs for the community-based learning activities that followed. Second, I knew that the TFs would resist going into the communities of their learners with the "Camera Safari" activity; it became my greatest challenge (Gallavan, 2000). Therefore, for those groups most resistant and/or afraid, I accompanied them. I investigated and became familiar with the neighborhoods the TFs chose to visit. After all, how could I ask my students to do something that I would not do myself! But doing the "Camera Safari" first made it easier to complete the "Debunking the Community" exercise. Except for the time commitment involved, I detected much less resistance in completing the final activity because, as one TF stated, "I've already been there. I am not afraid" (SO, BB 04/02). Third, I had no apprehensions about including the activities in their seminar course. In the days of forced integration of the South's public schools, I often wondered why we, as students, had to be bussed into other neighborhoods. If we were brave enough to face such a challenge, then it is about time that others came to see the strengths of who we were, of who we are.

Finally, if institutions of teacher education want preservice teachers to teach all children, they should consider incorporating community-based learning into the formal preparation process. To do so would not only help preservice teachers know how to most effectively deliver their content because they know their students better, but it would also assist them in correcting misperceptions about and in building relationships with students, their families, and members of the greater school community.

References

Banks, J. A. (2000). *Cultural diversity and education: Foundations, curriculum, and teaching.* Boston: Allyn & Bacon.

Boyle-Baise, M., & Sleeter, C. E. (1998). *Community service learning, for multicultural teacher education.* Washington, DC: Education Resources Information Center. (ERIC Document Reproduction Service No. ED 429925)

Brown, E. L. (2004). What precipitates change in cultural diversity awareness during a multicultural course: The message or the method? *Journal of Teacher Education, 55,* 325–340.

Burant, T. J., & Kirby, D. (2002). Beyond classroom-based early field experiences: understanding an "educative practicum" in an urban school and community. *Teaching and Teacher Education, 18,* 561–575.

Cabello, B., & Burstein, N. D. (1995). Examining teachers' beliefs about teaching ill culturally diverse classrooms. *Journal of Teacher Education, 46,* 285–294.

Colville-Hall, S., MacDonald, S., & Smolen, L. (1995). Preparing preservice teachers for diversity in learners. *Journal of Teacher Education, 46,* 295–303.

Delpit, L. (1995). *Other people's children: Cultural conflict in the classroom.* New York: New Press.

Gallavan, N. P. (2000). Multicultural education at the academy: Teacher educators' challenges, conflicts, and coping skills. *Equity and Excellence in Education, 33*(3), 5–11.

Garibaldi, A. (1992). Preparing teachers for culturally diverse classrooms. In M. E. Dilworth (Ed.), *Diversity in teacher education: New expectations* (pp. 23–29). San Francisco: Jossey-Bass.

Gay, G. (2001). *Culturally responsive teaching.* New York: Teachers College Press.

Gollnick, D., & Chinn, P. (2001). *Multicultural education in a pluralistic society* (6th ed.). New York: Prentice Hall.

Grant, C. A., & Secada, W. G. (1990). Preparing teachers for diversity. In W. R. Houston (Ed.), *Handbook of research on teacher education* (pp. 403–422). New York: Macmillan.

Hodgkinson, H. (2002). Demographics and teacher education: An overview. *Journal of Teacher Education, 53,* 102–104.

Jordan, M., & Rice, L. (1995). Reflections on the challenges, possibilities, and perplexities of preparing preservice teachers for culturally diverse classrooms. *Journal of Teacher Education, 46,* 369–374.

King, J. (1991). Dysconscious racism: Ideology, identity, and the miseducation of teachers. *Journal of Negro Education, 60,* 133–146.

Ladson-Billings, G. (2000). Fighting for our lives. *Journal of Teacher Education, 51,* 206–214.

Ladson-Billings, G. (2001). Multicultural teacher education: Research, practice, and policy. In J. Banks & C. M. Banks (Eds.), *Handbook of research on multicultural education* (pp. 747–759). San Francisco: Jossey-Bass.

Lawrence, S. M., & Bunche, T. (1996). Feeling and dealing: Teaching White students about racial privilege. *Teaching and Teacher Education, 12,* 531–542.

McFalls, E. L., & Cobb-Roberts, D. (2001). Reducing resistance to diversity through cognitive dissonance instruction: Implications for teacher education. *Journal of Teacher Education, 52,* 164–172.

McIntyre, A. (1997). *Making meaning of Whiteness: Exploring racial identity with White teachers.* Albany, NY: State University of New York.

Olmedo, I. M. (1997). Challenging old assumptions: Preparing teachers for inner city schools. *Teaching and Teacher Education, 13,* 245–258.

Pewewardy, C. (2005). Shared Journaling: A methodology for engaging White preservice students into multicultural education discourse. *Teacher Education Quarterly, 32*(1), 41–60.

Sleeter, C. (2000). Strengthening multicultural education with community-based service learning. In C. R. O'Grady (Ed.), *Integrating service learning and multicultural education in colleges and universities* (pp. 263–276). Mahwah, NJ: Lawrence Erlbaum.

Sleeter, C. (2001). Preparing teachers for culturally diverse schools: Research and the overwhelming presence of whiteness. *Journal of Teacher Education, 52,* 94–106.

Tatum, B. (1997). *Why are all the Black kids sitting together in the cafeteria? And other conversations on race.* New York: Basic Books.

Terrill, M. M., & Mark, D. L. (2000). Preservice teachers' expectations for schools with children of color and second-language learners. *Journal of Teacher Education, 51,* 149–155.

VanGunten, D. M., & Martin, R. J. (2001). Complexities and contradictions: A study of teacher education courses that address multicultural issues. *Journal of Intergroup Relations, 28*(1), 31–42.

Wiest, L. R. (1998). Using immersion experiences to shake up preservice teachers' views about cultural differences. *Journal of Teacher Education, 49,* 358–365.

Wright, J. (2004). Culture's role in teacher identity: Prompting teachers to explore their cultural background. *Action in Teacher Education, 25*(4), 9–13.

Zeichner, K. (1996). Educating teachers for cultural diversity. In K. Zeichner, S. Melnick, & M. L. Gomez (Eds.), *Currents of reform in preservice teacher education* (pp. 133–175). New York: Teachers College Press.

Zeichner, K., & Melnick, S. (1996). The role of community field experiences in preparing teachers for cultural diversity. In K. Zeichner, S. Melnick, & M. L. Gomez (Eds.), *Currents of reform in preservice teacher education* (pp. 176–196). New York: Teachers College Press.

Critical Thinking

1. What is community-based learning?
2. How is community-based learning integrated into the classroom?
3. What are the positive outcomes on the learning community and context?
4. Why do teacher candidates need authentic experiences to understand community-based learning?

JEWELL E. COOPER is an assistant professor in the School of Education at The University of North Carolina at Greensboro, where she teaches diversity courses and secondary teacher education courses to undergraduate and graduate students. Her research interests include the practice of equity education through the inclusion of community-based learning in teacher education programs, culturally responsive teaching, and secondary school reform.

Author's note—The author gratefully acknowledges the constructive feedback provided to her by Barbara B. Levin, Gerald G. Duffy, and David B. Strahan, on versions of this manuscript.

UNIT 4

Seek and Engage Collaboration and Construction

Unit Selections

Learning Outcomes

After reading this unit, you will be able to:

- Describe the five phases of professional development to help ensure social justice in schools.

- Summarize cultural issues that influence school dropout rates in urban settings.

- Expound upon the effects of remedial and unchallenging school work for Latino/a students.

- Explain critical voices and intellectual capacities needed to empower all students.

- Detail the reading levels of Vietnamese American students.

- Discuss the guidelines and resources needed to unlearn prior behaviors to institute change.

Student Website
www.mhhe.com/cls

Internet References

International Programs Center (IPC)
www.census.gov/ipc/www/
Native American Facts for Kids
www.native-languages.org/kids.htm
PBS: Biracial American Portraits
www.pbs.org/wgbh/pages/frontline/shows/secret/portraits
Urban Education Institute
http://uei.uchicago.edu

Education in the United States is not only a right, it is a responsibility of each state's government to guarantee that the people living in each state are offered an education and become educated. The majority of each state's revenue is dedicated to education costs. Yet, over time the federal government has become more involved legally and financially for education. Policies and regulations have changed many times and in many ways since the United States and each state were established.

Educating all students presents myriad challenges for everyone. Issues impacting education are not relegated to students currently enrolled in the P–12th grades and the students' families. Every person living in the state and across the United States is a stakeholder in education. The social, political, and economic well-being of each state and the United States relies upon the continuation of an educated population.

That means that everyone is responsible for educating all students; we are all in this endeavor together. And we need for all students to be educated to their maximum potential with clear evidence of cognitive, physical, affective, and social growth and development. Educators and most of society acknowledge that there are multiple ways of learning and expressing one's learning. We all know that people acquire knowledge, skills, and dispositions about many different topics and issues. The term, "multiple intelligences," is an established part of the popular contemporary culture. Thanks to our recognition of multiple intelligences, educators are equipped with avenues to reach each student so the citizenry is prepared with people possessing all kinds of strengths to contribute to society.

However, when individuals study both the history and the current operations within their states and the country, their investigations reveal that education has not been offered to all people throughout time in ways that would be considered equal or excellent. Not all schools and classrooms are equipped with the best materials, resources, tools, and technologies. Not all teachers are prepared the same, not all teachers facilitate teaching and learning the same, and not all teachers are rewarded the same. So all students are not taught the same.

One might retort that schools are funded primarily by local tax dollars, so, therefore, if the local region is less wealthy, the school will have fewer resources and cannot hire the best or the brightest teachers. This summation raises many questions: Why do state governments continue to function this way? Is this design useful in any way? Why would a population purposely deny the right of education to children because their parents and families live in geographic regions where there is less wealth? Are we not continuing to restrict the opportunity to people to advance their economic situation to better not only themselves but to improve the region? Let's say you are injured through no fault of your own and

© Medioimages/Photodisc/Getty Images

severely enough that you should seek medical attention. The wound needs to be treated and you need to fill a procoription so you return to your former fully functioning self. However, instead of treating the wound, you buy items to pamper other parts of your body. Rather than attending to the area needing help, you focus on areas that do not need help. Your injury does not heal; soon it becomes infected and much worse. The infection spreads, and the whole body becomes quite ill, requiring major intervention.

This analogy reflects what happens in education. The classrooms, schools, and districts who need attention are not always assisted or with enough treatment for them to heal. Other classrooms, schools, and districts who appear to be quite healthy receive attention and thrive. Many states need major intervention to help their education systems. Too many students are not becoming educated; the chances are strong that these students will not become contributing members of society. The citizenry will experience the "generational perpetuation of practice" as young adults continue the low expectations of their children repeating the low expectations asked of them as children and students at school.

The lowering of expectations lies with many educators too. For years, educators claimed that they were not raised with people generally unlike themselves physically, intellectually, socially, economically, and so forth. These educators ascribed to the belief that they did not know students and families unlike themselves or how to teach students unlike their own children. Therefore, teacher education programs created courses in multicultural education and infused multicultural education curriculum and instruction throughout their program courses. These changes were initiated during the 1990s and teacher education programs have been held accountable for their progress.

Yet, educators still purport that they do not understand how to reach all students. And too often, educators infer that it is "those students" who are not learning. Results from studies conducted by many different educational researchers reveal that some educators not only tend to resist learning about culturally competence, some educators resist changing their practices and becoming culturally competent. Evidence of bias, stereotyping, and prejudice can be found in every state across the United States in classrooms, schools, school districts, and government agencies.

Think again about your injury. If you are not healing, then you change the medication. Therefore, if students are not learning, then the teaching needs to change.

Unit 4 articles persuade the reader to seek and engage in collaboration and construction. Readers should teach their students the processes and encourage the students to construct new learning collaboratively, group their students so they learn more information about one another and society, and show their students the procedures for interacting appropriately with people both like and unlike themselves. Readers should seek and engage in collaborative activities themselves with a teammate on a special project and read professional literature to learn more about collaborating with their students.

As Diversity Grows, So Must We

Schools that experience rapid demographic shifts can meet the challenge by implementing five phases of professional development.

GARY R. HOWARD

Many school districts nationwide are experiencing rapid growth in the number of students of color, culturally and linguistically diverse students, and students from low-income families. From my work with education leaders in some of these diversity-enhanced school districts, I know they are places of vibrant opportunity—places that call us to meaningful and exciting work. In these "welcome-to-America" schools, the global community shows up in our classrooms every day, inviting us—even requiring us—to grow as we learn from and with our students and their families.

The Need for Growth

All is not well, however, in these rapidly transitioning schools. Some teachers, administrators, and parents view their schools' increasing diversity as a problem rather than an opportunity. For example, in a school district on the West Coast where the number of Latino students has quadrupled in the past 10 years, a teacher recently asked me, "Why are they sending these kids to our school?" In another district outside New York City—where the student population was once predominantly rich, white, and Jewish but is now about 90 percent low-income kids of color, mostly from the Caribbean and Latin America—a principal remarked in one workshop, "These kids don't value education, and their parents aren't helping either. They don't seem to care about their children's future." In a school district near Minneapolis with a rapidly increasing black population, a white parent remarked, "Students who are coming here now don't have much respect for authority. That's why we have so many discipline problems."

Diversity-enhanced schools are places of vibrant opportunity—places that call us as educators to meaningful and exciting work.

Other educators and parents, although less negative, still feel uneasy about their schools' new demographics. In a high school outside Washington, D.C., where the Latino immigrant population is increasing rapidly, a teacher told me that he was disappointed in himself for not feeling comfortable engaging his students in a discussion of immigration issues, a hot topic in the community in spring 2006. "I knew the kids needed to talk, but I just couldn't go there." And a black teacher who taught French successfully for many years in predominantly white suburban schools told me recently, "When I first found myself teaching classes of mostly black kids, I went home frustrated every night because I knew I wasn't getting through to them, and they were giving me a hard time. It only started getting better when I finally figured out that I had to reexamine everything I was doing."

This teacher has it right. As educators in rapidly transitioning schools, we need to reexamine everything we're doing. Continuing with business as usual will mean failure or mediocrity for too many of our students, as the data related to racial, cultural, linguistic, and economic achievement gaps demonstrate (National Center for Education Statistics, 2005). Rapidly changing demographics demand that we engage in a vigorous, ongoing, and systemic process of professional development to prepare all educators in the school to function effectively in a highly diverse environment.

Many education leaders in diversity-enhanced schools are moving beyond blame and befuddlement and working to transform themselves and their schools to serve all their students well. From observing and collaborating with them, I have learned that this transformative work proceeds best in five phases: (1) building trust, (2) engaging personal culture, (3) confronting issues of social dominance and social justice, (4) transforming instructional practices, and (5) engaging the entire school community

Phase 1: Building Trust

Ninety percent of U.S. public school teachers are white; most grew up and attended school in middle-class, English-speaking, predominantly white communities and received their teacher preparation in predominantly white colleges and universities (Gay, Dingus, Jackson, 2003). Thus, many white educators simply have not acquired the experiential and education background that would prepare them for the growing diversity of their students (Ladson-Billings, 2002; Vavrus, 2002).

The first priority in the trust phase is to acknowledge this challenge in a positive, inclusive, and honest way. School leaders should base initial discussions on the following assumptions:

- Inequities in diverse schools are not, for the most part, a function of intentional discrimination.
- Educators of *all* racial and cultural groups need to develop new competencies and pedagogies to successfully engage our changing populations.
- White teachers have their own cultural connections and unique personal narratives that are legitimate aspects of the overall mix of school diversity

School leaders should also model for their colleagues inclusive and nonjudgmental discussion, reflection, and engagement strategies that teachers can use to establish positive learning communities in their classrooms.

For example, school leaders in the Apple Valley Unified School District in Southern California, where racial, cultural, and linguistic diversity is rapidly increasing, have invested considerable time and resources in creating a climate of openness and trust. They recently implemented four days of intensive work with teams from each school, including principals, teacher leaders, union representatives, parents, clergy, business leaders, and community activists from the NAACP and other organizations.

One essential outcome in this initial phase of the conversation is to establish that racial, cultural, and economic differences are real—and that they make a difference in education outcomes. Said one Apple Valley participant, "I have become aware that the issue of race needs to be dealt with, not minimized." Said another, "I need to move beyond being color-blind." A second key outcome is to establish the need for a personal and professional journey toward greater awareness. As an Apple Valley educator noted, "There were a lot of different stories and viewpoints shared at this inservice, but the one thing we can agree on is that everyone needs to improve in certain areas." A third key outcome in the trust phase is to demonstrate that difficult topics can be discussed in an environment that is honest, safe, and productive. One Apple Valley teacher commented, "We were able to talk about all of the issues and not worry about being politically correct."

Through this work, Apple Valley educators and community leaders established a climate of constructive collaboration that can be directed toward addressing the district's new challenges. From the perspective of the school superintendent, "This is a conversation our community is not used to having, so we had to build a positive climate before moving to the harder questions of action."

Phase 2: Engaging Personal Culture

Change has to start with educators before it can realistically begin to take place with students. The central aim of the second phase of the work is building educators' *cultural*

competence—their ability to form authentic and effective relationships across differences.

Young people, particularly those from historically marginalized groups, have sensitive antennae for authenticity. I recently asked a group of racially and culturally diverse high school students to name the teachers in their school who really cared about them, respected them, and enjoyed getting to know them as people. Forty students pooling their answers could name only 10 teachers from a faculty of 120, which may be one reason this high school has a 50 percent dropout rate for students of color.

Aronson and Steele's (2005) work on stereotype threat demonstrates that intellectual performance, rather than being a fixed and constant quality, is quite fragile and can vary greatly depending on the social and interpersonal context of learning. In repeated studies, these researchers found that three factors have a major effect on students' motivation and performance: their feelings of belonging, their trust in the people around them, and their belief that teachers value their intellectual competence. This research suggests that the capacity of adults in the school to form trusting relationships with and supportive learning environments for their students can greatly influence achievement outcomes.

Leaders in the Metropolitan School District of Lawrence Township, outside Indianapolis, have taken this perspective seriously. Clear data showed gaps among ethnic groups in achievement, participation in higher-level courses, discipline referrals, and dropout rates. In response, district teachers and administrators engaged in a vigorous and ongoing process of self-examination and personal growth related to cultural competence.

Central-office and building administrators started with themselves. Along with selected teachers from each school, they engaged in a multiyear program of shared reading, reflective conversations, professional development activities, and joint planning to increase their own and their colleagues' levels of cultural competence. They studied and practiced Margaret Wheatley's (2002) principles of conversation, with particular emphasis on her admonitions to expect things to be messy and to be willing to be disturbed. They designed their own Socratic seminars using chapters from *We Can't Teach What We Don't Know* (Howard, 2006) and used the stages of personal identity development model from that book as a foundation for ongoing reflective conversations about their own journeys toward cultural competence.

As this work among leaders began to be applied in various school buildings, one principal observed, "We are talking about things that we were afraid to talk about before—like our own prejudices and the biases in some of our curriculum materials." In another school, educators' discussions led to a decision to move parent-teacher conferences out of the school building and into the apartment complexes where their black and Latino students live.

Phase 3: Confronting Social Dominance and Social Justice

When we look at school outcome data, the history of racism, classism, and exclusion in the United States stares us in the face. Systems of privilege and preference often create enclaves of exclusivity in schools, in which certain demographic groups are served well while others languish in failure or mediocrity. As diversity grows in rapidly transitioning school districts, demographic gaps become increasingly apparent.

Educators of *all* racial and cultural groups need to develop new competencies and pedagogies to successfully engage our changing populations.

In phase three, educators directly confront the current and historical inequities that affect education. The central purpose of this phase is to construct a compelling narrative of social justice that will inform, inspire, and sustain educators in their work, without falling into the rhetoric of shame and blame. School leaders and teachers engage in a lively conversation about race, class, gender, sexual orientation, immigration, and other dimensions of diversity and social dominance. David Koyama, principal of a diversity-enhanced elementary school outside Seattle, said, "One of my most important functions as a school leader is to transform political jargon like 'no child left behind' into a moral imperative that inspires teachers to work toward justice, not mere compliance."

Unraveling social dominance takes courage—the kind of courage shown by the central office and school leadership team in the Roseville Area School District outside the twin cities of Minneapolis and St. Paul. Roseville is in the midst of a rapid demographic shift. As we approached this phase of the work, I asked Roseville leaders to examine how issues of privilege, power, and dominance might be functioning in their schools to shape educators' assumptions and beliefs about students and create inequitable outcomes.

One of the workshop activities engaged participants in a forced-choice simulation requiring them to choose which aspects of their identity they would give up or deny for the sake of personal survival in a hostile environment. Choosing from such identities as race, ethnicity, language, religion, values, and vocation, many white educators were quick to give up race. Among the Roseville administrative team, which is 95 percent white, the one white principal who chose to keep his racial identity during the simulation said during the debriefing discussion, "I seriously challenge my white colleagues who so easily gave up their race. I think if we are honest with ourselves, few would choose to lose the privilege and power that come with being white in the United States."

As an outgrowth of the authentic and sometimes contentious conversations that emerged from this and other activities, several core leaders and the superintendent identified a need to craft a strong Equity Vision statement for the district. The Equity Vision now headlines all opening-of-school events each year and is publicly displayed in district offices and schools. It reads,

Roseville Area Schools is committed to ensuring an equitable and respectful educational experience for every student, family, and staff member, regardless of race,

gender, sexual orientation, socioeconomic status, ability, home or first language, religion, national origin, or age.

As a result of the increased consciousness about issues of dominance and social justice, several schools have formed Equity Teams of teachers and students, and an Equity Parent Group has begun to meet. The district is looking seriously at how many students from dominant and subordinate groups are in its gifted and AP classes and is conscientiously working for more balance.

Like Roseville, other diversity-enhanced districts must establish clear public markers that unambiguously state, "This is who we are, this is what we believe, and this is what we will do." Any approach to school reform that does not honestly engage issues of power, privilege, and social dominance is naive, ungrounded in history, and unlikely to yield the deep changes needed to make schools more inclusive and equitable.

Phase 4: Transforming Instructional Practices

In this phase, schools assess and, where necessary, transform the way they carry out instruction to become more responsive to diversity. For teachers, this means examining pedagogy and curriculum, as well as expectations and interaction patterns with students. It means looking honestly at outcome data and creating new strategies designed to serve the students whom current instruction is not reaching. For school leaders, this often means facing the limits of their own knowledge and skills and becoming colearners with teachers to find ways to transform classroom practices.

In Loudoun County Public Schools, outside Washington, D.C., teachers and school leaders are taking this work seriously. One of the fastest-growing school systems in the United States, Loudoun County is experiencing rapid increases in racial, cultural, linguistic, and economic diversity on its eastern edge, closer to the city, while remaining more monocultural to the west. Six of Loudoun's most diverse schools have formed leadership teams to promote the following essential elements of culturally responsive teaching (CRT):

- Forming authentic and caring relationships with students.
- Using curriculum that honors each student's culture and life experience.
- Shifting instructional strategies to meet the diverse learning needs of students.
- Communicating respect for each student's intelligence.
- Holding consistent and high expectations for all learners. (Gay, 2000; Ladson-Billings, 1994; McKinley, 2005; Shade, Kelly, & Oberg, 1997)

CRT teams vary in size and membership but usually include principals, assistant principals, counselors, lead teachers, specialists, and, in some cases, parents. In addition to engaging deeply in the phases outlined above, these teams have begun to work with their broader school faculties to transform instruction. At Loudoun County's Sugarland Elementary, teacher members of the CRT team have designed student-based action research projects. They selected individual students from their most academically challenged demographic groups and then used the principles of CRT to plan new interventions to engage these students and track their progress.

As educators in rapidly transitioning schools, we need to reexamine everything we're doing.

In one action research project, a 5th grade teacher focused on a Latino student, an English language learner who "couldn't put two sentences together, let alone write the five-paragraph essay that is required to pass our 5th grade assessment." The teacher's first reaction was to ask, "How was this student allowed to slip by all these years without learning anything beyond 2nd grade writing skills?" When the teacher launched her CRT project, however, her perspective became more proactive. She realized that she couldn't just deliver the 5th grade curriculum—she had to meet this student where he was. She built a personal connection with the student, learned about his family culture and interests (a fascination with monkeys was a major access point), and used this relationship to reinforce his academic development. The student responded to her high expectations and passed his 5th grade writing assessment. And after missing its No Child Left Behind compliance goals in past years, Sugarland recently achieved adequate yearly progress for all subgroups in its highly diverse student population.

This phase requires a crucial paradigm shift, in which teachers and other school professionals stop blaming students and their families for gaps in academic achievement. Instead of pointing fingers, educators in Loudoun schools are placing their energies where they will have the most impact—in changing their *own* attitudes, beliefs, expectations, and practices. I frequently ask teachers and school leaders, "Of all the many factors that determine school success for our students, where can we as educators have the most influence?" After educators participate in the work outlined here, the answer is always, "Changing ourselves."

Phase 5: Engaging the Entire School Community

Changing demographics have profound implications for all levels and functions of the school system. To create welcoming and equitable learning environments for diverse students and their families, school leaders must engage the entire school community.

Leaders in the East Ramapo Central School District in New York State have committed themselves to just such a system-wide initiative. The school district, which lies across the Tappan Zee Bridge from New York City, has experienced a dramatic shift in student population in the past 15 years as low-income Haitian, Jamaican, Dominican, Latino, and black families from

the city have moved into the community and middle-class white families have, unfortunately but predictably, fled to private schools or other less diverse districts.

In the midst of this demographic revolution, East Ramapo's broad-based diversity initiative has engaged all groups and constituencies in the school district community, not just teachers and administrators. For example, the district has provided workshops to help classified employees acknowledge their powerful role in setting a welcoming tone and creating an inclusive climate for students, parents, and colleagues in school offices, lunchrooms, hallways, and on the playground. For bus drivers, this work has meant gaining cultural competence skills for managing their immense safety responsibilities while communicating clearly and compassionately across many languages and cultures on their buses.

In one session that I led with school secretaries, we worked through their confusion and frustration related to all the diverse languages being spoken in the school offices and, in some cases, their feelings of anger and resentment about the demographic changes that had taken place in "their" schools. Asked what they learned from the session, participants commented, "I saw the frustration people can have, especially if they are from another country." "We all basically have the same feelings about family, pride in our culture, and the importance of getting along." "I learned from white people that they can also sometimes feel like a minority." In addition to these sessions, East Ramapo has created learning opportunities for school board members, parents, students, counselors, and special education classroom assistants. The district has convened regular community forums focusing on student achievement and creating conversations across many diverse cultures. White parents who have kept their children in the public schools because they see the value of diversity in their education have been significant participants in these conversations.

As a result of East Ramapo's efforts, the achievement gaps in test scores along ethnic and economic lines have significantly narrowed. In the six years since the district consciously began implementing the professional development model discussed here, the pass rate for black and Hispanic students combined on the New York State elementary language arts test increased from 43 percent in 2000 to 54 percent in 2006; on the math test, the pass rate increased from 40 percent to 61 percent. During that same period, the gap between black and Hispanic students (combined) and white and Asian students (combined) decreased by 6 percentage points in language arts and 23 percentage points in math. The achievement gap between low-income elementary students and the general population decreased by 10 points in language arts and 6 points in math—results that are particularly impressive, given that the proportion of economically disadvantaged students grew from 51 percent in 2000 to 72 percent in 2006.

A Journey toward Awareness

Professional development for creating inclusive, equitable, and excellent schools is a long-term process. The school districts described here are at various stages in the process. Everyone involved would agree that the work is messier and more complex than can be communicated in this brief overview. However, one central leadership commitment is clear in all of these rapidly transitioning districts: When diversity comes to town, we are all challenged to grow.

References

Aronson, J., & Steele, C. M. (2005). Stereotypes and the fragility of human competence, motivation, and self-concept. In C. Dweck & E. Elliot (Eds.), *Handbook of competence and motivation* (pp. 436–456). New York: Guilford.

Gay, G. (2000). *Culturally responsive teaching: Theory, research, and practice.* New York: Teachers College Press.

Gay, G., Dingus, J. E., & Jackson, C. W. (2003, July). *The presence and performance of teachers of color in the profession.* Unpublished report prepared for the National Collaborative on Diversity in the Teaching Force, Washington, DC.

Howard, G. (2006). *We can't teach what we don't know: White teachers in multiracial schools* (2nd ed.). New York: Teachers College Press.

Ladson-Billings, G. (1994). *The dreamkeepers: Successful teachers of African American students.* San Francisco: Jossey-Bass.

Ladson-Billings, G. (2002). *Crossing over to Canaan: The journey of new teachers in diverse classrooms.* San Francisco: Jossey-Bass.

McKinley, J. H. (2005, March). *Culturally responsive teaching and learning.* Paper presented at the Annual State Conference of the Washington Alliance of Black School Educators, Bellevue, WA.

National Center for Education Statistics. (2005). *The nation's report card.* Washington, DC: Author.

Shade, B. J., Kelly, C., & Oberg, M. (1997). *Creating culturally responsive classrooms.* Washington, DC: American Psychological Association.

Vavrus, M. (2002). *Transforming the multiculrural education of teachers: Theory, research and practice.* New York: Teachers College Press.

Wheatley, M. (2002). *Turning to one another: Simple conversations to restore hope to the future.* San Francisco: Barrett-Koehler.

Critical Thinking

1. What are the five phases of professional development to help ensure social justice in schools?

2. How can teachers participate in all five phases of professional development?

3. What are the benefits of participating in the five phases of professional development?

4. Why are these five phases of professional development still a proposal and not the procedures?

GARY R. HOWARD is Founder and President of the REACH Center for Multicultural Education in Seattle (www.reachctr.org); 206-634-2073; garyhoward@earthlink.net. He is the author of *We Can't Teach What We Don't Know: White Teachers, Multiracial Schools* (Teachers College Press, 2nd ed., 2006).

From *Educational Leadership,* March 2007, pp. 16–22. Copyright © 2007 by ASCD. Reprinted by permission. The Association for Supervision and Curriculum Development is a worldwide community of educators advocating sound policies and sharing best practices to achieve the success of each learner. To learn more, visit ASCD at www.ascd.org

In Urban America, Many Students Fail to Finish High School

Faced with a deteriorating pipeline of students, colleges in cities like Compton, Calif., struggle to serve their local neighborhoods.

KARIN FISCHER

Edith J. Negrete's big dreams defy her modest means. In those dreams, Ms. Negrete is an anesthesiologist, earning a comfortable salary that pays for a fancy car and a nice home for her 8-year-old son, Joshua.

Her reality is more complicated. Ms. Negrete, who dropped out of high school at age 15 to get married, recently lost her job as a clerk at a moving company here and has moved in with her father to make ends meet. Now 27, she is raising Joshua on her own and getting a divorce from her husband, who is in prison.

But Ms. Negrete says she has hope for the future, in the form of the local community college, El Camino College Compton Center. Inspired by a former co-worker, who studied for a psychology degree during lunch breaks, Ms. Negrete enrolled at the college three years ago. Eventually, she wants to transfer to the University of California at Los Angeles.

"As you get older, you really know what you want," says Ms. Negrete, who is the first in her family to attend college. "Once you have an education, have a paper in your hand, then a lot of doors open."

The situation Ms. Negrete faced mirrors what is happening in low-income urban centers across America. Hindered by poor-performing public schools, many residents drop out before earning a high-school diploma, and with it, the all-important ticket to the bevy of higher-education institutions often located in and around urban areas.

In this Southern California city, part of an arc of low-income neighborhoods on Los Angeles' southern tier, only one-third of residents 25 years or older are high-school graduates; fewer than seven in 100 have a bachelor's degree. Nationwide, 84 percent of Americans hold a high-school diploma, and 27 percent are four-year-college graduates.

Faced with that deteriorating pipeline, urban colleges, both two-year and four-year, have struggled to serve large swaths of their local neighborhoods. Just 382 Compton students attend the nearest California State University campus, at Dominguez Hills, making up about 4 percent of the undergraduate population

there, while 134 go to the campus in Long Beach, accounting for less than 1 percent of its student body. As for UCLA, Ms. Negrete's top choice, just seven of the university's nearly 25,000 undergraduates are from Compton.

Even as a college degree becomes an ever more indispensable vehicle out of poverty, the share of English-language learners, members of racial and ethnic minorities, and other groups historically underrepresented in higher education is growing in inner-city schools. The small number of students who enroll in college often struggle to succeed, battling poor preparation and juggling work and family responsibilities. And factors outside the classroom can also depress scholastic achievement. This fall alone, Compton's public-school district was notified of 460 new foster-care placements among its students.

"Increasingly, there is a gulf between the haves and the have-nots," says Houston D. Davis, project director for the national Educational Needs Index, which paints a county-by-county portrait based on educational, economic, and population data. "In cities . . . there are pockets, there are populations, that have very real needs, and those needs are getting greater."

Changing Expectations

The Compton Unified School District's slogan is "excellence in progress," and, by many measures, the city schools have far to go. The district's graduation rate lags behind the statewide average. Twenty-five percent of students drop out before graduation day. Fewer than a quarter of high-school seniors complete requirements for admission to either of California's two public-university systems, and just 27 percent of students who graduated last spring went on to a four-year college.

Despite those daunting numbers, Jesse L. Gonzales, the district's superintendent, says he wants to send the message that a college degree can open doors beyond Compton, where the unemployment rate is 11 percent, well above the national average. Partnerships have been established with local colleges, and liaisons have been appointed at each of the district's three high schools to help parents, most of whom never attended college, understand the college application process. When Mr. Gonzales visits Compton elementary schools, he says, his question to students is, "Where are you going to college?"

"It is better to set standards too high and miss them," he says, "than to set them too low and hit them."

On the face of it, Compton graduates have a multitude of postsecondary options—after all, Los Angeles County is home to more than 50 two- and four-year colleges.

But the factors holding inner-city students back can be both practical and parochial. Many Compton students are illegal residents and are not eligible for state or federal financial aid. For others, earning an immediate paycheck is more important than an eventual degree, while some struggle to balance work schedules, child care, and a three-bus commute.

For first-generation students, the "nuts and bolts" of applying for college admission and financial aid can also be a deterrent, says Robert L. Caret, president of the Coalition of Urban and Metropolitan Universities, a group of colleges that are located in, and primarily draw from, metropolitan areas.

"No one in their family or their peer group has done it, and they don't know how to begin," says Mr. Caret, who is president of Towson University, near Baltimore.

Beating the Odds

At Compton High School, every morning before classes begin, the principal, Jesse Jones, stands outside its gates, greeting each student with a booming "Good morning." He says he never misses a day.

"Many of these kids have no stability in their lives," says Mr. Jones, who came out of retirement three years ago to run the school. "It's about the image you are sending. They have to start believing in you."

The students streaming onto the campus look very much like the population of Compton as a whole. Nearly 69 percent are Hispanic, and 29 percent are black. One-third speak English as a second language.

Originally a predominantly white, middle-class community, which counts the former president George H.W. Bush among its past residents, the complexion of the area has changed significantly in recent decades. By the 1970s, the city's population was largely African-American. Today an influx of immigrants, mainly from Mexico, and the migration of Latino families from elsewhere in the Los Angeles metropolitan region have led to rapid growth of the Hispanic population, especially among school-age children.

Compton's changing demographics have brought special challenges. Although the student body is now predominantly Latino, much of the district's staff is black. In some cases, that has meant retraining teachers to adjust to students' new learning styles.

Under the now five-year watch of Mr. Gonzales, the superintendent, more Advanced Placement and college-preparatory classes have been added to the curricula of the high schools, while the most academically at-risk ninth-grade students have been singled out for extra instruction in reading and mathematics.

Students in kindergarten through the third grade have two hours of "protected" reading time each day.

There is some evidence that Mr. Gonzales's efforts are working: Since 2002, Compton students have shown improvement on California's two statewide accountability assessments.

Second Chances

Ms. Negrete says she didn't get that kind of encouragement when she went to public school here. Now she is trying to give her son the kind of support she never received. Joshua, she says proudly, is at the top of his class and wants to be an archaeologist. Occasionally, when her aunt cannot watch him, Joshua comes with her to classes at El Camino College Compton Center.

"Sometimes he complains," she says, "but I tell him that if you want to succeed, you have to have a degree."

With busy schedules and sometimes unreliable child care, Ms. Negrete is not alone in bringing a child with her to classes on the campus. On a recent sunny day, students' children darted across the college's sunny courtyard as a live band played a rollicking beat. The occasion was Fiesta Latina, part study break, part celebration of the college's continued existence after its predecessor, Compton Community College, lost its accreditation last July. Faculty and staff members joined the queue for homemade tostadas and pupusas, gathering in small clusters to scoop the food off paper plates.

"It would have been a disaster if the college had closed," says Hilda Gaytan, president of the student government, which sponsored the event. Ms. Gaytan, 50 and a Mexican immigrant, came to Compton Community College after she lost her job in the garment industry three years ago. "We all came here for a second chance."

The community college has been providing second chances to students in Compton and the surrounding towns for nearly 80 years. The community's pride in the college is palpable. Everyone, it seems, knows a young person who appeared destined to go down the wrong path but was turned around by Compton Community College professors. At night, residents stroll the parklike campus, a safety zone in a city that last year ranked as one of the nation's deadliest, with 72 murders for 97,833 residents.

In 2002, voters in Compton, where the per capita income is just $12,617, voted overwhelmingly for a $100-million bond, essentially taxing themselves for the next two decades to pay for new classroom buildings and a tutoring facility on the campus. But the amount of revenue from all sources that Compton is able to spend is about 10 percent below that of other California community colleges.

A Community's College

Community colleges in urban areas often face a struggle to make ends meet, says Alicia C. Dowd, an assistant professor of education at the University of Southern California. Ms. Dowd has found that community colleges in large cities have per-student revenues 13 percent to 18 percent lower than two-year colleges elsewhere.

Part of the reason for that, she says, is that urban colleges often lack the political clout to fight for larger state appropriations. They also might not have skilled administrators who can compete for grants from private foundations or federal and state governments.

Federal student-aid policy can also work against some types of urban postsecondary institutions, says John B. Lee, an education consultant. He notes that for-profit colleges have been pulling out of central cities since a change in financial-aid rules in the 1990s made serving at-risk students with high student-loan default rates too costly. The percentage of full-time students enrolled in proprietary schools in cities declined by 11 percent between 1996 and 2000. Meanwhile, enrollments at for-profit institutions in suburban areas increased 18 percent during the same period.

Mr. Lee says he is concerned that the loss of these institutions, which frequently offered training programs that lasted just a few months, leaves inner-city students with fewer educational options. "I worry these students are being abandoned," he says.

In Compton, an agreement to combine Compton Community College with El Camino College ensured a continued local higher-education presence in the city. The accreditation fight ended in July when Compton officials decided to drop their appeal of the decision a year earlier by the Western Association of Schools and Colleges' Accrediting Commission for Community and Junior Colleges. But that battle the subsequent merger have left a bitter taste with some city residents. They question whether El Camino, with its largely middle-class, transfer-oriented student body, can be sensitive to the needs and to the challenges of the Compton community, where students are far more likely to be pursuing a vocational degree or certification.

Because only courses approved for El Camino can be offered at the Compton center, this fall's session began without a number of basic-skills and English-language courses or its popular licensed vocational nurse-training program. (The center has since entered into an agreement with another area college, Los Angeles Trade-Technical College, to offer the practical-nursing program, and El Camino is fast-tracking approval of about 20 courses before the next semester.)

"This is our community's college," says Bruce A. Boyden, a graduate of the college and a member of the Committee to Save the Compton Community College District, a group that pushed for the college to remain independent. "Compton took disenfranchised young people and empowered them to become employable in the community in which they live. At El Camino, they are preparing doctors, lawyers, and Indian chiefs."

A Basic-Skills Gauntlet

But if Compton is the community's college, it is also a reflection of the community's struggles.

One out of every five courses taken at the college is a basic-skills course. In all of California, by contrast, remedial math and writing courses account for only about 7 percent of community-college enrollment. What's more, many students appear to become mired in these remedial courses without ever making it to for-credit course work. Only about one-quarter of Compton College students who took a basic-skills class in their first year took and passed a college-level course in the same subject area within three years.

The last three years for Ms. Negrete, for instance, have largely been catching up. She is also pursuing her general-equivalency diploma and estimates it will take her another two years before she has earned the credits to transfer to a four-year college.

Becoming bogged down in remedial courses can discourage students from earning a community-college degree or going on to a four-year university, says Estela Mara Bensimon, director of the Center for Urban Education at the University of Southern California.

"The biggest barrier to success for black and Latino community-college students is basic skills," says Ms. Bensimon. "Basic skills is a gantlet."

At Compton Community College, that problem was exacerbated because writing was not integrated throughout the curriculum, says Toni Wasserberger, a professor of English at the college. Instead, many faculty members would rely on other measures of assessment, such as multiple-choice exams or short-answer responses.

As a solution, college officials decided to pair a number of courses in the English department, including some at the basic-skills level, with some in other disciplines, including history, psychology, and even math. Students take the paired courses, which have complementary syllabi and writing assignments that reinforce each other, during the same semester. The two professors leading each course review students' papers and general progress together.

With the upheaval at the college over the last two years, it is difficult to accurately measure the success of the linked courses, says Ms. Wasserberger, a tiny woman with hip eyeglasses and energy to spare. Some students, she notes, had to drop out of the linked program because of the difficulty of taking two classes while working full time.

Still, for Ms. Wasserberger, who has been at the college since 1970, helping at-risk community-college students succeed seems to be as much of an art as a science.

A student wanders into the English department's outer office, interrupting Ms. Wasserberger midthought. "Just a minute," she says, "I've got to go give this student a hug."

The student, a slender woman who appears to be in her late 20s, is equally effusive. "You're my mentor," she says, before seeking some advice on English course offerings. After she leaves, Ms. Wasserberger returns to her seat.

"She was in my class," Ms. Wasserberger says of the student. "She literally could not write a sentence."

"You don't make up for what they didn't have," she says. "You make progress."

Critical Thinking

1. What are the cultural issues influencing school dropout rates in urban settings?
2. How are dropout rates different in urban settings?
3. What can teachers to do promote school completion?
4. Why is reducing the school dropout rate in urban settings important to the U.S. citizenry?

A Critically Compassionate Intellectualism for Latina/o Students

Raising Voices above the Silencing in Our Schools

JULIO CAMMAROTA AND AUGUSTINE ROMERO

Latina/o students often experience coursework that is remedial and unchallenging—benign at best, a dumbing-down at worst (Solórzano & Yosso, 2001). This potential limiting curriculum is not only failing to provide Latinas/os with the credentials necessary to advance economically, but their education denies them the opportunity to develop the critical voices and intellectual capacities necessary to do something about it. To borrow the words of Carter G. Woodson (1977), there is a "mis-education of Latinas/os," in which their voices and potentialities to challenge an unjust world is suppressed by the consistent battery of standardized tests, rote learning, and curricular content that has little bearing on their everyday struggles as young people of color.

Thus, the standard educational experience for young Latinas/os tends to submerge them into silence, where they are taught to be quiet and avoid independent and critical thinking. This is a dangerous lesson for them to learn, and it is dangerous for everyone. Young Latinas/os are the next generation that will significantly change the composition of our society. And if they are encouraged to become silent adults, this new burgeoning majority will not have the capacity to effect social change that moves toward an egalitarian reality for all people.

In this article, we present an educational model based on a critically compassionate intellectualism that can foster the liberation of Latinas/os as well as other students of color from the oppression of silencing they currently experience in school. A teacher following critically compassionate intellectualism implements the educational trilogy of critical pedagogy (Freire, 1993), authentic caring (Valenzuela, 1999), and a social justice centered curriculum (Ginwright & Cammarota, 2002). For students of color, critical pedagogy affords them the opportunity to become critical agents of social and structural transformation. Authentic caring promotes student-teacher relationships characterized by respect, admiration, and love and inspires young Latinas/os to better themselves and their communities. A social justice curriculum dispels ideological notions of racial inferiority while cultivating the intellectual capacities of students of color.

We argue that the trilogy's elements—critical pedagogy, authentic caring, and social justice curriculum—must be implemented simultaneously in the classroom to present the most effective preparation for Latina/o students to participate in the development of a truly democratic society. Each element becomes stronger and more effective with the integration and reinforcement of the additional constituent elements. In critically compassionate intellectualism, the sum is much greater than its separate educational parts, and the individual parts become greater when they are combined in a collective, tripartite approach.

The Silencing of Latina/o Students

Studying a cohort of Latino students at different grade levels, Quiroz (1997, 2001) compares their autobiographical narratives written in the 8th grade and then again in the 11th grade, noticing that silencing was a common theme throughout the texts. She discovers that the students' reactions to silencing change over time, with the effects becoming more profound toward the end of their grade school tenure. In the 8th grade, students respond by engaging "in self-denigration, internalizing failure in school and directing anger at themselves instead of at those responsible for their failure" (2001, p. 340). By the 11th grade, they are more familiar with the institutional factors behind their marginalization and adhere to "perceptions of apathy, injustice, and racism, as students recognize how profoundly these conditions affect their educational lives, and many are convinced of teachers' general lack of interest in their educational progress" (2001, p. 339).

The eventual outcome of the "schoolsponsored silencing" (2001, p. 328) is the students' widely held belief that academic success is unattainable for them. Quiroz argues that such beliefs explain "why the majority of these students disengage from schooling or only perform intermittently" (1997, p. 14). The irony, as Quiroz (2001, p. 328) points out, is that these Latina/o students could communicate in more than one language, yet "had no voice, at least in matters related to their schooling. They spoke through their narratives but no one listened."

The Uses of Power in School-Sponsored Silencing

The urban, low-track curriculum emphasizes order and discipline, and as Michelle Fine (1991) argues, it also actively silences young people by treating them and their intellectual capacities as insignificant. Principally, it is through "power" that educational institutions "nurture, sustain, and legitimate silencing" (Weiss, Fine, & Lareau, 1992, p. 1). The power in school-sponsored silencing is exercised and experienced through the curriculum, teacher and student relationships, and racist discourse.

Regarding power in the curriculum, Bourdieu (1977a, 1977b) argues that educational content based on the achievements of the dominant group actively silences the cultural capital[1] and thus intellectual contributions of subordinate groups. Schools accomplish silencing by rendering certain curricular processes, such as the acquisition and exposition of "valid" school knowledge, appear universally available and possible for every student. However, Bourdieu argues that educational institutions, which are invested in maintaining certain power relations, elide the fact that "valid" school knowledge is culturally specific and thus not universally available. Bourdieu (1977a, p. 494) states:

> By doing away with giving explicitly to everyone what it implicitly demands of everyone, the educational system demands of everyone alike that they have what it does not give. This consists mainly of . . . cultural competence and that relationship of familiarity with culture which can only be produced by family upbringing when it transmits the dominant culture.

Knowledge acquisition is easier, in most societies, for one social group—the group that has the power to control educational institutions. In reality, access to "valid" school knowledge is an arbitrary process related to one's social and cultural location. If a student is a member of the dominant group, he or she will display all the mannerisms, codes, and communication patterns that symbolize, according to the dominant group's criteria, someone who is knowledgeable. The opposite is true for students from subordinate groups. Educational institutions silence—through curricula highlighting the contributions of the dominant group—the subordinate group's knowledge and intellectual capacities.

Freire (1993, 1998) writes extensively about the traditional teacher and student relationship, and how it might contribute to the silencing of students. In the traditional educational format, which he categorizes as "banking education," the teacher is perceived as the only true authority of knowledge while the student is perceived as an unknowing subject that should passively accept, without questioning, the knowledge disseminated by the "legitimate" authority within the pedagogical process. Freire (1998, p. 71) illustrates the practice and effects of banking education:

The teacher's task is to . . . "fill" the student by making deposits of information which he or she considers to constitute true knowledge. And since people "receive" the world as passive entities, education should make them more passive still . . . Translated into practice, this concept is well suited to the purposes of the oppressors, whose tranquility rests on how well people fit the world the oppressors have created, and how little they question it.

Although Freire wrote about banking education some 30 years ago, the practice is still prevalent in our schools today. The primary assumption holds true; teachers supposedly possess all the knowledge, and their job is to fill students' supposedly blank minds with the state's official perception and understanding of the world. The result of such direct, one-way depositing of information is the cultivation of students who are taught to accept the conditions of their existence "as is" and forced into a marginal space where racial discourse maintains a silence about their potential to rectify problems of injustice. They are left thinking that their world will never change, or more importantly, that they can never change it. Thus, their realities become nihilistic states of suffering and distress whereby they believe that nothing can be done but accept the way things are—including the inequities that cause the suffering of many, and in some situations, themselves.

Although acts of power experienced through the curriculum and pedagogy may impede the academic progress of Latina/o students, everyday racism in society and schools has enough impact, in and of itself, to present serious impediments to success. For example, teachers who believe that Latina/o students are hopelessly and helplessly uneducable could countermand the positive effects of a democratic pedagogy and culturally competent curriculum. Thus, the effects of racism upon teachers who then transmit racist ideas to their students can stand alone and have a destructive impact on academic outcomes (Reyes & Rios, 2003).

The historical backdrop, according to Pollock (2001, p. 9), of "American racism" consists of "naturalizing a racial hierarchy of academic and intellectual potential ever since racial categories were created and solidified with pseudo-science." This nefarious racial dynamic of the American past is still active today in the consistent and widespread expectation and acceptance that racial differences in achievement are part of the normal outcomes of education (Pollock, 2001; Spring, 2001). Thus, racism in schools reinforces a racialization process that constructs a hierarchical order of social groups. This stratified racial order corresponds to capitalist imperatives for subordinate classes that are in turn exploited economically by a dominant ruling class (Darder & Torres, 2004). A certain economic utility underpins the schools' production of racial differences in academic outcomes.

Governments, districts, officials, administrators, teachers, parents, and even students often internalize the belief that people who are phenotypically light tend to be smarter than their darker-skinned counterparts. Although biological explanations for racial differences in achievement are somewhat passé, current theories harboring assumptions about deficiencies in the culture, normative structures, and environments of non-White communities not only have a similar ring but have attained significant currency in many educational settings (Valencia & Black, 2002).

For example, in Pollock's (2001) study of racial achievement patterns in a California high school, she discusses how teachers and administrators often cite "culture" and "parents" as explanations for the failure of students of color. These culturally based explanations contribute to racist ideology because they do nothing more than point to the putative "foibles" in certain races while avoiding the real systemic problems of racism, White supremacy, and White privilege.

In short, power is enacted through the curriculum, through pedagogy, as well as racist ideologies. Power issued through these particular forms foments a practice of silencing that can permeate attitudes, policies, and actions and thus instigate the treatment of students of color as intellectually inferior and ultimately uneducable. These abuses of power in education invariably impel students to withdraw, either permanently by dropping out or partially by "checking out" mentally and becoming silent.

The Social Justice Class in Tucson

We have the opportunity to implement and develop an alternative, social justice pedagogy in a high school located in Tucson, Arizona. The school principal allowed us to work with a cohort of 20 Latina/o students during their junior and senior years, teaching them the state's social studies requirements but adjusting the content and pedagogy in ways that facilitated the students' critical consciousness around racial inequalities affecting their educational and general life experiences. The students participated in this social justice curriculum for two years and received credit for all high school graduation requirements in U.S. History and U.S. Government.

More importantly, these students were afforded the opportunity to cultivate the skills and knowledge to address everyday injustices that limit their own future opportunities, and those of other Latina/o youth. Our goal was to help students' raise their own voices above the silencing of traditional schooling. In addition, we hoped that they would become active citizens armed with a critical consciousness that could lead them toward the transformation of educational and social structures presently failing to meet their specific needs.

The location for the social justice education course is Cerro High School.[2] The socioeconomic status of many Latino families served by Cerro is among the lowest in the Tucson metropolitan area. Consequently, two-thirds of all Cerro students receive free lunch, a rate that is more than 25% higher than the Tucson district-wide average of 39%. Student Achievement Accountability for Results (STAAR)—a set of standardized tests measuring academic performance—reports that Cerro has the lowest ranking in standardized test scores of any public high school in Tucson. Furthermore, in 2004–05, Cerro offered only seven Advanced Placement (AP) courses, while the most

predominately White (64% White to 20% Latina/o) school in the district, Ultimate High School, offered 62 advanced placement courses.

The history of racial inequality at Cerro makes for interesting dynamics in implementing social justice education. Latinas/os represent 62% of the Cerro student population, and they are more likely to fill the lower ranks of the school's academic hierarchy. Sixty percent of the Latina/o students at Cerro write below a level denoted as "standard" by the state, while White students are the highest performing group on campus. Whites represent 51% of the students enrolled in AP courses while comprising only 18% of the student population. A counselor at Cerro mentioned that the special magnet program at Cerro, which offers many of the advance placements courses, has only 20 Latinas/os enrolled out of 400 students. The overwhelming majority consists of White students.

In addition, White students receive most college scholarships given to Cerro graduates. Although Latinas/os are more than 60% of the student population, they received only 31.3% of the college scholarship money given to graduates in 2002. Some 60% of this scholarship money goes to White students. Cerro High School has been more efficient at guiding these students into academic tracks and on to college.

A Critically Compassionate Intellectualism

Drawing from our experiences in the social justice class and from the voices of the social justice students, we have developed an approach to educating Latina/o students that can help them to deflect the institutional power maintaining their silence. This approach follows a trilogy of educational practice, combining the essential characteristics of critical pedagogy, compassionate student/teacher relationships, and social justice content. We call this pedagogical trilogy *critically compassionate intellectualism,* and it is our belief that educators who implement this learning process will provide their students with the opportunity to counter the institutional silencing that prevents their full and active participation in shaping their futures.

The following sections will delineate the parameters for a critically compassionate intellectualism while showing how each part of the trilogy is inextricably related to the others and necessary in combination for breaking through the silence and promoting critically engaged citizenship among students of color.

Critical Consciousness in Education

In the social justice education course, our experiences with the students have been both encouraging and troubling. On the one hand, the curriculum has been effective in raising the students' consciousness with regards to racial inequalities. On the other hand, the innovative instruction has also revealed the failure of the standard public school curriculum to help young people evolve into critically minded citizens who actively work toward improving conditions in their communities and society at large.

This failure became evident during a student photo presentation on the challenges for Chicano/Latino students. The students chose to take photos and develop attendant slide presentations on topics related to a critical study of their educational experiences. For two weeks, students roamed around their high school campus with disposable cameras and took pictures related to racial stereotypes, cultural oppression, misrepresentation of students of color, and critical thinking vs. passivity in education. It was during the slide presentation on critical thinking vs. passivity and comments made by a specific student that we realized the standard education for many Latinas/os at this school was practically barren of any content encouraging critical thinking.

High school student Kati Diaz showed a slide of students in the auto-shop class, who were primarily Latino males. At first we didn't know what this slide had to do with critical thinking, but Kati made these comments.

> In advanced placement [AP] classes, students are always being challenged . . . always using your brain, you are always moving a step ahead. And how critical can auto shop be? And I don't see any difference between the people here and the people in AP classes except race.

Kati's comments parallel the analysis that education scholar Jeannie Oakes (1985) reported in her book, *Keeping Track.* Oakes states that Latinas/os as well as African Americans tend to fill the ranks of the lower academic tracks, which focus more on remedial or vocational education. In contrast, White students are more apt to be placed in the advanced placement classes, preparing them for the best universities in the country. One of the most interesting findings in Oakes' study was that:

> . . . teachers of high-track classes were more likely to emphasize such behaviors as critical thinking, independent work, active participation, self-direction, and creativity. At the same time, teachers of low-track classes were more likely than others to emphasize student conformity, students getting along with one another, working quietly . . . being punctual, and conforming to classroom rules and expectations. (1985, p. 85)

These habits of conformity and complacence encouraged in lower tracks stifle students' expression and thinking, and lead to the passive silence evident in the education of Latino/a students at Cerro.

Another student in our social justice course, Sandra Sanchez, is concerned about her classmates' perceptions of their own muteness and concomitant inefficacy. Similar to the juniors in Quiroz' study (2001), Sandra started to comprehend the impact of racism and injustice on her education, as well as that of other students of color. She spoke about racial bias evident in news reports on Tucson schools. In her low-income community, reports tend to focus on negative traits, such as poor performance on standardized tests, whereas the media represents schools located in whiter and wealthier areas in the most positive light. She adds, "We are good students and we are very respectful compared to other schools, but I don't think we show them how great we are by test scores. We could show them in many other ways. But the difference is, will they listen?" Sandra recognizes the injustices around her, but feels her words on these matters would fall on deaf ears.

A Pedagogy of Critical Literacy

In the social justice education course, our pedagogical approach is greatly influenced by the work of education scholar Paulo Freire. We design lessons from the framework of critical pedagogy and related non-banking education approaches to teaching. This framework is based on the key premise that the high school students should be equal partners in the construction of knowledge, identification of problems of social injustice, and implementation of solutions to these problems.

Therefore, we offer the students a curriculum that closely follows Freire's concept of critical literacy, which encourages students to adopt "an attitude of creation and re-creation, a self-transformation producing a stance of intervention in one's context" (Freire, 1998, p. 86). Critical literacy renders both students and educators as subjects of knowledge, collaborative creators of knowledge that can be used to transform the oppressive conditions of reality.

To establish this type of a learning partnership—knowledge production through collaboration—between high school students and classroom coordinators (high school teacher of record and university researchers), we structure lessons so that we (students and coordinators) are consistently engaged in dialogue. Our first dialogical exercise involved having students and coordinators write poems about their identities. The poems, or what we call *I Am Poems,* gave us the opportunity to understand the students' realities, to see where they were coming from and how they comprehend the issues and problems most relevant to their lives.

As Freire states, "the starting point for a political-pedagogical project must be precisely at the level of the people's aspirations and dreams, their understanding of reality and their forms of action and struggle" (Freire, 1998, p. 214). The coordinators and students shared their own dreams and realities by writing poems that they presented to the entire class. See Figure 1 for an example of an "I Am" poem.

The coordinators used generative themes and issues discovered in the poems to create questionnaires for the students to fill out. We studied their responses and created a list of potential topics that could function in many ways as particular lenses for the students to conduct a class research project on inequalities in education. The students and coordinators dialogued and came up with the four research topics: *cultural assimilation, critical thinking vs. passivity in education, racial and gender stereotypes of students, media representations of students of color.* These topics became the basis for student research and subsequent presentations to the school, district officials, academics, educators and community members, with the intent of making recommendations to improve education for students of color in their district.

The back-and-forth dialogue between students and coordinators lasted for over two months; this lengthy process was necessary to empower students to become equal partners in the research project. Otherwise we would be guilty of establishing a learning process that would amount to no more than another

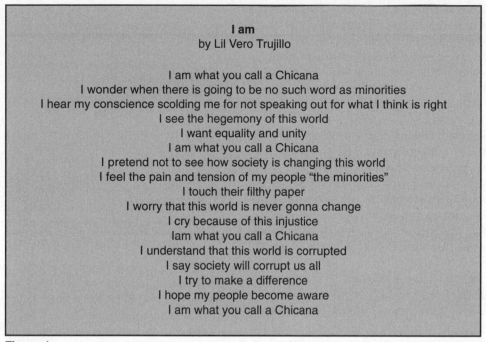

I am
by Lil Vero Trujillo

I am what you call a Chicana
I wonder when there is going to be no such word as minorities
I hear my conscience scolding me for not speaking out for what I think is right
I see the hegemony of this world
I want equality and unity
I am what you call a Chicana
I pretend not to see how society is changing this world
I feel the pain and tension of my people "the minorities"
I touch their filthy paper
I worry that this world is never gonna change
I cry because of this injustice
Iam what you call a Chicana
I understand that this world is corrupted
I say society will corrupt us all
I try to make a difference
I hope my people become aware
I am what you call a Chicana

Figure 1

form of oppression. According to Freire, "coordinators must be converted to dialogue in order to carry out education rather than domestication. Dialogue is an I-Thou relationship, and thus necessarily a relationship between two Subjects. Each time the 'thou' is changed into an object, an 'it,' dialogue is subverted and education is changed to deformation" (1998, p. 89). We wanted to avoid providing the students yet another experience of being the static objects of learning, stuffing information into them without having them criticize, discuss, or question what is being taught. Such educational experiences represent the norm for these students and force them to be uncritical and tolerant of a life of subordination.

Because students are more familiar with banking education, encouraging them to think critically, to voice their opinions, and to contribute to the construction of knowledge are challenging tasks. Most of their educational experiences have revolved around the banking mode of learning. Many students recount how they have experienced years and years of banking education: teachers constantly telling them what to do, what they should learn, and never asking them about their opinions or asking them for their input, suggestions, comments, feedback, or thoughts about their education. The students said they are conditioned to learn within that type of education.

So now, in the social justice class, when we ask them to speak up, give their opinions and think critically, they really have a hard time. In fact, Sandra Sanchez said that if we don't tell them what to do, "crack the whip," and get on them to make sure things are done, they will just sit there and not do anything. She added that they do not know how to take the initiative to become responsible for their own education, have input on what they learn, or participate in the construction of their own knowledge.

We are amazed how Freire (1993) was right in terms of the oppressive and stifling effects of colonization. According

to Freire, liberation from the silencing force of oppression is extremely difficult for the colonized, because they tend to gravitate toward the model of living imposed by the dominant class. The model emphasizes the tacit acceptance of the established hierarchical order of domination and subordination. Because this model is so pervasive—so entrenched in the psyche of the oppressed—they have difficulty acting differently or deviating from it. The students first needed to *unlearn* the myriad lessons of banking education to feel confident and capable voicing their opinions and engaging in dialogue.

Although the challenges of establishing a critical pedagogy seem overwhelming at times, educators must stay on task to avoid failure and the continued subordination of their students. The stakes are too high to loosen the commitment to critical pedagogy. Latino students can no longer remain silent; becoming vocal is imperative for them to attain some faith in their intellectual abilities. It is important to note that the silencing they experience in school does more than keep them quiet.

We stated earlier that school silencing encompasses enactments of power through the curriculum, traditional pedagogy, and racist ideology, with the intended effect of erasing the intellectual potential of students of color. Therefore, learning to speak one's voice is vital for advancement to the higher levels of education and society. The converse leads us towards the depths of oppression wherein Latinas/os are abysmally exploited for capitalistic gains (Delgado, 1999).

Compassionate Relationships between Students and Teachers

After struggling with the numerous days of silent students, we realized compassion was necessary to establish a strong and trusting relationship between students and coordinators, which in turn would lay the foundation for free-flowing dialogue. The need for compassion in education became apparent when a student, Kati Diaz, told us after class that perhaps we (classroom coordinators) would have an easier time getting the students to talk if we would open up and let them know us personally.

She suggested that we start talking about ourselves as people. In essence, the students wanted to know something about our lives and family experiences. According to Kati, students wanted to trust us first before talking and communicating with us. We, in positions of institutional power, had to take the first step before we could expect the students to open up.

We took the first step by sharing our feelings and concerns. Students needed to see us as complete human beings and interact with us on an emotional level before engaging with us intellectually.

Our response to this student's request was to create and read our own "I Am" poems. The poem in Figure 2 reflects one of the author's experiences as a Puerto Rican male, and the personal and social struggles that have captivated his attention and energy throughout his life.

We realized that a critical yet humanizing pedagogy was crucial for generating dialogue and a sense of ownership among the students. The following is an excerpt from an exit interview conducted with two students who graduated from the social justice class. Their words demonstrate how a humanizing pedagogy can help students to feel they are knowledgeable Subjects that guide the educational process.

Vanessa Acosta: The social justice class was interesting because we had a part in it. And usually we don't have a voice in nothing. So that's why it interested us and plus what it was about. And plus all our subjects. And plus our teachers were cool too.

Julio Cammarota: Was it interesting for you because you were looking at some of the problems in society and trying to find out solutions for the problems?

VA: We got to explain to other people. To teachers what was going on. We got to tell them.

Maria Perez: We got to teach them.

VA: Yeah. And they loved it. And they loved us. And that was bad [meaning 'good'] too.

MP: And some of them said they didn't even realize that we were teenagers.

VA: They loved us.

MP: We are loved.

JC: Did you have any other opportunities like this in other classes?

MP: No.

VA: In other classes its like open your book. "Do this." "That's it." "Write this."

JC: Tell you what to do?

VA: Yeah. You couldn't be like, "well could I do this?" "No." I think that if we had more classes like the social justice class then a lot more kids would be interested in school. They would want to learn.

I hear, sometimes, voices of family and friends who have passed away. My Titi Elsa, Abuelo julio, Cunado Renzo, and mi Chavalo Fabricio, who died from broken hearts and gunshots. But appear to me when I need strength and, guidance to overcome obstacles of self-doubt arising from that imposed inferiority.

I see faces of people who I don't know... but I will know, maybe not now, but in the future or in the past that is still unknown to me. I want peace, justice, equality for all people who suffer from oppression, from poverty, from the pain of having one's heart, mind, and soul be invisible to those willing to sacrifice their hearts, minds, and souls for the power to dominate and control.

Figure 2

When they presented their social justice research to educators, administrators, and other members of their community, the students' sense of empowerment extended beyond the classroom. The presentations in the community and at academic and youth conferences offered them the rare opportunity to see themselves as knowledgeable Subjects. In contrast, the standard educational system treats them as empty slates ready to be carved and etched on by teachers. In the presentations, they were carving and etching out knowledge. Our deepest hope was that the students would gain a 'voice' in the class and carry their confidence and sense of efficacy to the world outside the classroom walls.

Thus, dialogue—real discussion for generating ideas that construct knowledge—occurs through a humanizing as well as critical pedagogy, in which genuine and compassionate relationships form between students and educators. Freire states:

Love is at the same time the foundation of dialogue and dialogue itself. . . . Dialogue cannot exist, however, in the absence of a profound love for the world and for people. The naming of the world, which is an act of creation and re-creation, is not possible if it is not infused with love . . . because love is an act of courage, not of fear, love is commitment to others. (1993, p. 70)

A humanizing pedagogy is accomplished by educators interacting with students on an emotional level and sharing their deepest concerns and feelings about life. What must be avoided at all costs is treating students solely as empty receptacles that must be filled with academic skills. An educator should not only reveal what he or she cares about personally but also show the students that he or she loves them in the caring sense and shares similar concerns about the world. Compassion is another crucial step for enacting a critical pedagogy and ultimately a critically compassionate intellectualism.

The idea of a critical yet humanizing pedagogy correlates with the caring literature in education (Noddings, 1984, 1992; Valenzuela, 1999). Valenzuela (1999) claims that the lack of care and respect in teacher/student relationships may be a key factor behind the failure of Latina/o students. Her study is based on research conducted at a high school in Texas with primarily Mexican American and Mexican immigrant student populations.

At this school, she noticed two types of teaching methods: authentic caring and aesthetic caring. Valenzuela (1999, p. 61) states that authentic caring is a "form of caring that emphasizes relations of reciprocity between teachers and students." That is, the teacher establishes that emotional, human connection with his or her students and demonstrates a real interest with the students' overall wellbeing. Aesthetic caring is tantamount to treating students like objects, seeing them only as blank slates that need to be inscribed with academic skills, and not as complete people with real-life problems.

Lalo Garcia, a classroom teacher from our social justice course, engages in authentic caring. We observed this while he was consulting with a student about his future academic plans. Nestor wants so badly to drop out of Cerro, because school is not engaging him. He is failing in his classes, and wants and needs to move on in life. His mother is leaving Tucson and moving in with her boyfriend who lives in California. Nestor has the option of moving with her, but he has so many ties in Tucson that he is preparing to stay. He states, "I need a full-time job to support myself, because I will be on my own."

There is an opportunity cost for Nestor: stay in school where he is failing or drop out to find a job to support himself. He understands that life will be harder for him without a high school education, so he says that when he drops out he will obtain a GED. Lalo spoke with him earnestly. He said that he understood Nestor's situation. He gave Nestor several options to stay in Tucson—making up credits at charter schools or staying at Cerro to graduate. Nestor said that's a possibility but he preferred getting a GED and to start working full-time.

We noticed how Lalo was talking with Nestor. He listened to Nestor and his words and actions were filled with love and respect. Lalo figuratively had become a father figure. Nestor's body language indicated that he was taking Lalo's words seriously. He seemed relaxed in the chair, although a bit pensive about his situation. His posture indicated that perhaps a positive outcome would result from the conversation, because he was conversing with someone who genuinely cares about his fate. We liked how Lalo didn't refute or put down Nestor's ideas. He said that they were good ideas and possibilities, but also mentioned others, such as charter or weekend school, that Nestor might consider.

Lalo's interaction with Nestor is a good example of authentic caring in action. He was able to give Nestor authentic advice, because he developed a caring relationship with him. Lalo acknowledged the social and economic conditions impacting Nestor's life. Therefore, Lalo could provide advice formulated from a viewpoint that emerges from Nestor's reality. Listening to the students' problems and showing some compassion for their situation may be necessary actions for educators to improve relationships with their students.

Unfortunately, at Cerro High School, most teachers or teaching styles fall under the category of aesthetic caring, being concerned with only the technical (i.e., skill level) side of their students' experiences. With the current climate in education, resulting from high-stakes testing policies such as No Child Left Behind (NCLB), aesthetic caring is becoming more prevalent in schools such as Cerro High. Because of the fear of being labeled "under-performing" as a result of standardized tests, Cerro High and the school district pressure teachers to barrage students with test content. The students in our social justice course consistently speak of how they are inundated with a curriculum that prepares them solely for standardized tests.

These test-based lessons, called "focus lessons," review test content in multiple subjects (math, English, etc.), and usually it is the same exact focus lesson reviewed repeatedly in every class throughout the school day. Furthermore, the increased focus or state-mandated testing forces an aesthetic pedagogy upon the teachers. Cerro student Validia Tejerina says,

> Focus lesson usually takes the whole period. It's the same thing over and over and over. With the focus lesson you go from one period to another learning the same thing: It's usually like . . . before the AIMS [Arizona Instrument for Measuring Standards] test [is administered] here . . . the whole week is just focused on focus lessons, you know, they are just reading it over and over and over. Each period. So that when the test comes along you can remember. You don't learn anything.

Validia asserts that the boredom of the focus lesson has the tendency to disengage students from their education.

Social Justice Content in Education

Social justice educational content is the basis for promoting authentic caring. Teaching to the test—course work that drills students on academic skills—will create a chasm that places teachers and students miles apart from each other. On the other hand, teachers will make strong connections with students when the educational content is based on matters most significant and meaningful to the students' lives. And what matters a great deal to many of the students in our social justice course is determining how to challenge social forms of oppression that limit opportunities for themselves, their families, and communities.

At Cerro High School, students are familiar with oppression produced by racist ideology. Suggestions of racial inferiority besiege students of color on a regular basis. Conversations with Cerro students reveal this consistent burden of injustice. Validia Tejerina mentions how teachers regularly tell Latina/o students that they are incapable of academic success and should drop out. She talks about a specific event in which she was supposed to turn in a report to her teacher but forgot to bring it to school on the due date. When the teacher asked for the report, she said she forgot. The teacher then said, "You should just drop out of school and work in a restaurant and wash dishes."

Validia interprets these comments as racist. First, by telling her that she should drop out, the teacher indicates that she has no belief in Validia's intellectual capacity. Second, because she suggests Validia should work as a dishwasher, the teacher implies that is all Validia is capable of accomplishing in life. Validia adds that when she was a freshman, a science teacher told her the same thing—that she should drop out of school. Arturo Reyes said that he had the same teacher who told Validia to become a dishwasher, and this teacher told Arturo that he shouldn't even bother trying to pass this class and he should drop out of school.

We must recognize how racist ideology engenders conflict between students and teachers and prevents them from forming strong meaningful relationships. Indeed, Freire emphasizes that oppression prevents us from realizing our full humanity, and oppression must be challenged to reach the point of seeing the full humanity in others and in ourselves. It is at this point of mutual recognition and respect for each other's humanity that strong human connections are established.

Teachers cannot become authentic caregivers to students of color unless they merge their caring with counter-hegemonic content that dispels notions of racial inferiority and recognizes the wealth of knowledge, culture, and understanding of every student who walks into the classroom. This is the moment when caring evolves into compassion for the student's social and economic situation that may render him or her less than human and thus deny him or her any possibility for self-determination.

The Practice of Critically Compassionate Intellectualism

Educators can attain a liberating education for Latina/o students by combining three approaches to learning into one educational framework—critically compassionate intellectualism. The following represents the three components of critically compassionate intellectualism:

1. *Critical Pedagogy*—elevating students to the status of Subjects in the creation of knowledge.
2. *Authentic Caring*—treating students as full and complete human beings.
3. *Social Justice Content*—teaching content that directly counters racism and racist stereotypes through epistemological contextualization of the students' social, economic, and cultural realities.

To facilitate critically compassionate intellectualism, we recommend that a social justice perspective feed into and guide all educational practices. That is, we suggest progressing beyond the ordinary multicultural approach that at best validates the cultural capital of marginalized groups (Banks, 2002; Nieto, 2000; Sleeter, 1996). Although elevating the cultural capital of such groups is essential, students should focus on the injustices that engender marginalization in the first place, and then develop remedies for palliating them. This has been our approach in the social justice course.

For instance, this course provided Latina/o students with the opportunity to discuss their experiences with the state's oppressive language policies that have essentially banned bilingual education. In effect, the state of Arizona's Proposition 203 has followed in the footsteps of California's Proposition 227 by rendering English the only instructional language in the school system. Our students have spent numerous hours discussing the direct and subtle effects of this proposition.

Students contend that Spanish speakers are now more likely to drop out, because teachers cannot by law speak to them in any language except English. Since these Spanish-speaking students do not understand what's happening in the classroom, they simply disengage, biding time until they leave school altogether. The students of our social justice course have decided to bring this problem to the Tucson school board, and recommend the development of a waiver program that expands outreach to Latina/o communities and supports administrators and teachers who wish to adequately serve their Spanish-speaking students by implementing bilingual education.

The study of language and cultural politics via Proposition 203 served as a vehicle for critically compassionate intellectualism. By positioning the students' experiences with anti-bilingual language policy as the centerpiece for knowledge acquisition, students share the status of co-investigators—equal with the project coordinators. Students and coordinators both become Subjects and equal partners in the construction of knowledge. In addition, focusing on language and cultural oppression meant that the students' education related to something that mattered to them. It matters to them, their families, and their younger brothers and sisters, because they perceive Proposition 203 as an attempt at eradicating a language essential for the development and advancement of Latina/o communities—their communities.

By examining ways to preserve the vitality of the Spanish language, students recognize our intentions as sincerely demonstrating compassion for them and their families' futures. Finally, the students engage in social justice work by taking their concerns to policymakers (i.e., the school board) with the hope of rectifying a problem that threatens the academic success as well as the intellectual development of many Latina/o students. Critically compassionate intellectualism involves more than discussing problems of inequality; it requires students to engage in activities that promote social justice in their own context.

Concluding Remarks

We will end our discussion on critically compassionate intellectualism with Bell Hooks' description of teachers she had while attending segregated schools in the South. Her description highlights the importance of a pedagogy of liberation, and suggests that other factors—beyond lack of resources—may impede the progress of students of color. In particular, schools often fail to prepare these students to deal with a society that treats them as racially inferior. Our sense is that the teachers from Bell Hooks' childhood engaged in critically compassionate intellectualism, because they achieved authentic caring through a critical yet humanizing pedagogy that promoted a social justice perspective. Adopting this perspective counters notions of inferiority that result from the institutional dehumanization of children of color. hooks describes how:

The work of all our progressive teachers, was not to teach us solely the knowledge in books, but to teach us an oppositional world view—different from that of our exploiters and oppressors, a world view that would enable us to see ourselves not through the lens of racism or racist stereotypes but one that would enable us to focus clearly and succinctly . . . to see ourselves first and foremost as striving for wholeness, for unity of heart, mind, body, and spirit. (1989, p. 49)

Despite a lack of resources, these teachers instilled in their students a critical perspective on the hegemony they experienced, as well as a belief in their own humanity.

It is essential that we implement an education for Latina/o students that follows critically compassionate intellectualism by drawing on critical pedagogy, authentic caring, and social justice content. This educational trilogy may elevate the voices of Latina/o students and expand their rights in this society. We live in precarious times in which apartheid is looming on the horizon. Latinas/os are one of the fastest growing racial groups in the country, yet Whites still hold onto the key positions of power in state institutions. The net effect of such an unfair distribution of power is that Whites will continue to fill the classroom seats of the most privileged universities, while Latinas/os will more likely fill the service jobs (janitors, cooks, etc.) at these same privileged universities.

Educational disparities have other frightening consequences. As the U.S. government and corporate leaders wage their wars for global dominance, it is young Brown and Black blood they trade for brown and black oil. It is in our best interest to transform the education of our people so that our blood is no longer used to grease the wheels of global capitalist greed.

Notes

1. Cultural capital refers to the mannerisms, style, dispositions, customs, and cultural knowledge that symbolize and confer a certain degree of social currency or value. That is, cultural capital has social values or "symbolic value" that distinguishes a person's different and higher social standing in relation to others (Bourdieu, 1977b.).

2. The names of schools have been changed for reasons of confidentiality.

References

Banks, J. A. (2002). *An introduction to multicultural education.* Boston: Allyn & Bacon.

Bourdieu, P. (1977a). Cultural reproduction and social reproduction. In J. Karabel & A. H. Halsey (Eds.), *Power and ideology in education.* Oxford, UK: Oxford University Press.

Bourdieu, P. (1977b). *Outline of a theory of practice.* Cambridge, UK: Cambridge University Press.

Darder, A. & Torres, R. (2004). *After race: Racism after multiculturalism.* New York: New York University Press.

Delgado, R. (1999). *When equality ends: Stories about race and resistance.* Boulder: CO. Westview Press.

Fine, M. (1991). *Framing dropouts: Notes on the politics of an urban public high school.* Albany, NY: State University of New York Press.

Freire, P. (1993). *Pedagogy of the oppressed.* New York: Continuum.

Freire, P. (1998). *The Paulo Freire reader.* A. M. Freire & D. Macedo (Eds.). New York: The Continuum Press.

Ginwright, S., & Cammarota, J. (2002). New terrain in youth development: The promise of a social justice approach. *Social Justice, 29*(4), 82.

hooks, b. (1989). *Talking back: Thinking feminist, thinking Black.* Boston: South End Press.

Nieto, S. (2000). *Affirming diversity: The sociopolitical context of multicultural education.* New York: Longman.

Noddings, N. (1984). *Caring: A feminine approach to ethics and moral education.* Berkeley, CA: University of California Press.

Noddings, N. (1992). *The challenge to care in schools: An alternative approach to education.* New York: Teachers College Press.

Oakes, J. (1985). *Keeping track: How schools structure inequality.* New Haven, CT: Yale University Press.

Pollock, M. (2001). How the question we ask most about race in education is the very question we most suppress. *Educational Researcher, 30*(9), 2–11.

Quiroz, P. A. (1997). The "silencing" of the lambs: How Latino students lose their "voice" in school. ISRI Working Paper No. 31. East Lansing, MI: Michigan State University, Julian Samora Research Institute.

Quiroz, P. A. (2001). The silencing of the Latino student "voice": Puerto Rican and Mexican narratives in eighth grade and high school. *Anthropology & Education Quarterly, 32*(3): 326–349.

Reyes, X. A., & Rios, D. I. (2003). Imaging teachers: In fact and in the mass media. *Journal of Latinos and Education, 2*(1), 3–11.

Sleeter, C. E. (1996). *Multicultural education as social activism.* Albany, NY: State University of New York Press.

Solórzano, D. G., & Yosso, T. J. (2001). From racial stereotyping and deficit discourse toward a critical race theory in teacher education. *Multicultural Education, 9*(1), 2–8.

Steele, C. M. (1992). Race and the schooling of Black Americans. *The Atlantic Monthly, 269*(4), 68–78.

Spring, J. H. (2001). *Deculturalization and the struggle for equality: A brief history of the education of dominated cultures in the United States.* Boston: McGraw-Hill.

Valencia, & Black. (2002). Mexican Americans don't value education. *Journal of Latinos and Education, 1*(2), 81–103.

Valenzuela, A. (1999). *Subtractive schooling: U.S.-Mexican youth and the politics of caring.* Albany, NY: State University of New York Press.

Weis, L., Fine, M., & Lareau, A. (1992). *Schooling and the silenced "others": Race and class in schools.* Special studies in teaching and teacher education, Number Seven. Buffalo: State University of New York, Buffalo, Graduate School of Education, 1–81.

Woodson, C. G. (1977). *The mis-education of the Negro.* New York: AMS Press.

Related Articles

Julio Cammarota and Augustine Romeo. (2004). Reflexiones Pedagogicas: A Critically Compassionate Pedagogy for Latino Youth. *Latino Studies, 4,* 305–312.

Julio Cammarota. (2006). Disappearing in the Houdini Tradition: The Experience of Race and Invisibility among Latina/o Students. *Multicultural Education, 14*(1), 2–10.

Critical Thinking

1. What guidelines will help teachers reach Latina/o students?

2. How are Latina/o students currently disenfranchised?

3. What roles do critical voices and intellectual capacities play for students?

4. Why are teachers resistant to helping all students equitably?

JULIO CAMMAROTA is an assistant professor and **AUGUSTINE ROMERO,** is a graduate student in the Bureau of Applied Research in Anthropology and the Mexican-American Studies and Research Center at the University of Arizona, Tucson, Arizona.

From *Multicultural Education,* Winter 2006, pp. 16–23. Copyright © 2006 by Caddo Gap Press. Reprinted by permission.

Educating Vietnamese American Students

HUONG TRAN NGUYEN

Promotion of English proficiency for students from disadvantaged backgrounds was one of the major provisions of the *No Child Left Behind* federal act of 2001. This act mandated that limited English proficient (LEP) students or English language learners (ELL) "learn English as quickly and effectively as possible," and receive instruction "through scientifically based teaching methods" delivered by "high quality" teachers in every core content classroom (U.S. Department of Education, Major Provisions of the Conference Report to H.R. 1, the NCLB Act, August 23, 2003).

In California the teacher population is 74.2% Caucasian and 25.8% ethnic minority, but the students they teach are 32% Caucasian and 68% ethnic minority. Over 1.5 million of those students are ELL (California State Department of Education, 2001–2002).

Many ELL students struggle to function in English-only classes and to compete with their native English-speaking peers, and tend not to fare well on high-stakes testing (Cummins, 2000). Regardless of student demographics, locales, staffing, and available resources, schools must, by law, provide necessary means for all students to achieve.

City Middle School

At City Middle School (a pseudonym) we identified 14 Vietnamese American students whose reading levels ranged from an alarming 1.5 to 4 (mid-year first grade to fourth grade), and English language development (ELD) from level 1 (beginning) to level 3 (Intermediate). Although there were far more ELL middle schoolers in need, there were only three pre-service teachers available to help, so we had to identify the most needy, which amounted to 14. What support would these middle school students (MSS) need in order to function in their English-only classes?

Although their *basic interpersonal communicative skills* (BICS) in English were passable, their *cognitive academic language proficiency* (CALP) severely lagged behind that of their native English-speaking peers (Cummins, 2000). The school administration, some of the teachers, and the MSS themselves recognized that they had been experiencing difficulty in their English-only core subject classes.

In order for these ELL students to become proficient in English (L2) and in content area knowledge, it would be logical and theoretically sound that instruction be delivered in their heritage language (L1), a language with which they would be more familiar. Reading and writing skills acquired through L1 provide a foundation for L2 development, being that academic skills and knowledge transfer across languages (Cummins, 2000).

Standardized tests have placed undue pressure on school administrators and teachers to push their ELL students to gain speedy English acquisition, overlooking the fact that it takes three to five years to develop oral proficiency and four to seven years for academic proficiency (Cummins, 2000).

Under Proposition 227 in California, ELL students would receive English-only *structured immersion* or *sheltered English immersion* (SEI) instruction for just one year. Rossell (2004–2005) reported that most immigrant children in mainstream classrooms ". . . seem to swim, not sink" (p. 36) after one year of SEI instruction. However, Hakuta, Butler, and Witt (2000) argued that the one-year time period of "sheltered English immersion" (SEI) was "wildly unrealistic" (p. 13). This arbitrary one-year period was a broad-brush determination, but it does not paint an accurate English acquisition picture for many ELL students, including the fourteen middle school students described below.

Context for My Involvement at City Middle School

In addition to teaching required core courses at a local university for CLAD (Crosscultural, Language, and Academic Development) certification in the Single Subject Credential Program, I have also been supervising the practicum of Multiple Subject Credential Program pre-service teachers (PST)—also known as student teachers—for CLAD and BCLAD (Bilingual Crosscultural, Language, and Academic Development) certification at various schools in different school districts.

The administration and school achievement teacher (SAT) at City Middle School sought my guidance regarding fourteen "at risk" students from grades 6 to 8 in need of support (I had worked with this administration in the past). Three out of five of the PSTs under my supervision were placed at City Middle School to fulfill their CLAD certification practicum; thus, it made sense for these three PSTs to work with the fourteen MSS and fulfill their BCLAD certification practicum hours at the same site as well.

Based on the school's needs and schedule, I recommended an after-school program with class sessions meeting twice a week, totaling to four hours, to which the administration agreed. The administration, the teachers in charge, the PSTs, and I realized that it would be unrealistic to expect formidable growth results from the MSS after a brief semester in terms of their CALP, but the MSS could use some assistance.

With data provided by the ELD teacher (in charge of all of the school's ELL population) and in consultation with me, the PSTs developed lessons and activities collaboratively based on the English language arts content standards. Each PST was responsible for the instruction of her own group of MSS in English and in Vietnamese, but a few sessions were conducted with all fourteen MSS together. Each PST took turns in teaching those lessons and activities during said sessions, which gave the MSS an opportunity to work with their peers and the PSTs to become acquainted with all fourteen MSS, both in a small group and a large group setting.

Twelve of the MMS were born in Vietnam, one in Oslo (Norway), and one in Malaysia. All arrived in the United States with their families from various destinations, one in 2001, one in 2002, three in 2003, one in 2004, and eight in 2005. Similar to the background of their MSS, all three PSTs were born in Vietnam and arrived in the U.S. with their families as refugees in 1975. Two of the PSTs started pre-school in the U.S.; the third was French-schooled in Vietnam and resumed her education in the U.S. in 11th grade. She made a career move in her mid-forties.

In addition to informal conversations, a writing sample, student interactions, and class discussions, the PSTs and I hoped to learn more about the MSS, so we designed a 20-item survey (in English and in Vietnamese) and administered it to the MSS at the end of the after-school program.

Survey

The survey (see Table 1) consisted of three parts. The first set of three items (1-3) consisted of fill-in-the-blank statements or questions regarding personal information about the participants' initial U.S. arrival and schooling experience both in the U.S. and the country of origin. In the second set of ten items (4-13), participants responded to statements of a quantitative nature based on a rating scale (*agree, strongly agree, disagree, to strongly disagree*), culminating in Table 2. The last set of six items (14-19) consisted of open-ended questions asking participants to elaborate on specific questions, and the last item (20) was reserved for any additional comments. Although there were 14 MSS enrolled in this after-school program, three were absent on the day this survey was administered. Respondents had the option to write their answers in English, Vietnamese or both; seven did so in English, the other four in Vietnamese, and all remained anonymous.

Discussion of Survey Results

Items 4-7 aimed at finding out how MSS felt about Vietnamese and English. Respondents unanimously agreed that Vietnamese was their predominant language of oral communication in their respective families (items 4 and 5). However, since items 6 and 7 included speaking *and* writing skills, the responses varied from those in the previous items.

For example, seven MSS agreed or strongly agreed that they were more comfortable speaking and writing in English, but four disagreed. The latter four were more truthful in their self-assessment in indicating that their oral proficiency (BICS) in English was functional, but their academic proficiency (CALP) was another matter altogether. (Judging by the written responses on the survey by the other seven respondents, it was clear that their CALP needed much refinement).

This is consistent with Cummins' (2000) finding that it takes three to five years to develop oral proficiency and four to seven years for academic proficiency, and that the one-year time period of sheltered English immersion (SEI) as proposed by Proposition 227 was inadequate for ELL to acquire academic proficiency (Hakuta, Butler, & Witt, 2000).

In terms of the importance of English and Vietnamese, ten out of eleven students were in agreement that these languages were equal in that regard (item 8). As far as being taught by the PST, all MSS unanimously agreed or strongly agreed that they liked the additional assistance they received (item 9), which they felt have helped them to improve in their regular English-only classes (item 10).

Insofar as items 11-13 were concerned, the notion of respect (in the students' cultural frame of understanding) often came up in informal discussions with the MSS or among themselves. All of them agreed or strongly agreed that students should demonstrate respect toward their teachers but believed that the reverse should hold true as well.

Interestingly, the group observed that "American" teachers did not have the same level of respect as their teachers did in Vietnam (item 13). The MSS shed light on the meaning of respect, elaborating on how important it was to them and to their parents who insisted that they respected their teachers (and elders) and looked to them for directions and sage advice (items 14-19).

Hence, they were surprised to find that respect was not as valued in U.S. classrooms and that "American" teachers tolerated disrespectful behavior from students far more often than they should have. According to the MSS, such student behavior would not have been tolerated in Vietnam and would result in severe punishment.

In terms of L1 support from the PSTs, the MSS benefited from having abstract concepts and ideas explicated in Vietnamese and supported with relevant examples deriving from familiar cultural practices which made learning refreshing, less intimidating, and more comprehensible. For example, in a story some of the MSS had read in their regular class, the author described a family's harvesting and preparation of an authentic dish with potatoes, unique to a U.S. region. The MSS were unfamiliar with that American dish, potatoes, and the region where this story took place.

117

Table 1 The Survey

Survey Items 1–3: Personal Information

1. I arrived in the U.S. on _____ (date/month), in _____ (year) with _____ (family members or others).
2. I was born in _____ (city & country) in _____ (year).
3. The first school I attended in the U.S. was _____ (name) in the city of _____ and the sate of _____ .

Survey Items 4–14: Quantitative Section

(Based on a rating scale of: Agree, Strongly Agree, Disagree, Strongly Disagree)

4. I speak more <u>Vietnamese</u> than English with my parents, brothers, and sisters at home.
5. I speak more <u>English</u> than Vietnamese with my parents, brothers, and sisters at home.
6. I am more comfortable speaking and writing in <u>Vietnamese</u> than in English.
7. I am more comfortable speaking and writing in <u>English</u> than in Vietnamese.
8. In my opinion, English <u>and</u> Vietnamese are <u>equally</u> important.
9. I like to be taught by the three Vietnamese American student teachers.
10. Having a Vietnamese teacher helps me to learn my subject matter and do better in my regular classes.
11. Students must always show respect to their teachers.
12. Teachers must also demonstrate respect toward their students.
13. Respect for teachers in Vietnam means the same as respect for teachers in the U.S.

Survey Items 14–19: Qualitative Section

14. What did you learn from your parents about respect for others?
15. In what ways have the Vietnamese American student teachers helped you with learning your subject matter?
16. Of the lessons and/or activities that the Vietnamese American student teachers taught you, which one(s) did you like the most and why? the least and why?
17. What do you think about the style of teaching of the Vietnamese American student teachers?

Survey Item 20

You are invited to write any additional comments. Thank you for your input and participation.

Table 2 Results of the Quantitative Section Questions

Question	Agree	Strongly Agree	Disagree	Strongly Disagree
4. I speak more Vietnamese than English with my parents, brothers, and sisters at home.	5	6	0	0
5. I speak more English than Vietnamese with my parents, brothers, and sisters at home.	1	1	9	0
6. I am more comfortable speaking and writing in Vietnamese than in English.	4	2	5	0
7. I am more comfortable speaking and writing in English than in Vietnamese.	5	2	4	0
8. In my opinion, English and Vietnamese are equally important.	7	3	1	0
9. I like to be taught by the three Vietnamese American pre-service teachers.	6	5	0	0
10. Having a Vietnamese teacher helps me to learn my subject matter and do better in my regular class.	1	10	0	0
11. Students must always show respect to their teachers.	2	9	0	0
12. Teachers must also demonstrate respect toward their students.	7	4	0	0
13. Respect for teachers in Vietnam means the same as respect for teachers in the U.S.	0	0	1	10

The PSTs contextualized the story by referring to a U.S. map, pointing to the region in question, and explaining that it the farming community relied on its own harvest to sustain its families. When translating "potato" to "khoai," (a term in Vietnamese), the PST brought realia (real objects) such as a potato and other roots (e.g., yam, sweet potato, taro), and paralleled this American dish to other Vietnamese stew-like recipes that used a couple of these roots, but that potatoes could have be substituted.

The MSS were excited about this lesson because it tapped into their prior knowledge. They each wanted to share a mouthwatering dish that their mother used to prepare with these ingredients. This is an example of making learning relevant to students' lives by connecting the story to the students' experience made possible because the PSTs and MSS shared a similar background and cultural practice.

Through L1 support, the MSS were able to ask the PSTs for clarification or elaboration without the anxiety of formulating questions in English instantaneously while monitoring their pronunciation, proper vocabulary and syntactical usage (items 15-16). Moreover, the MS discussed how the hands-on approach to teaching (e.g., visuals, manipulatives, Total Physical Response or TPR, and so on) helped them tremendously, particularly when it came to figurative language (e.g., idioms, metaphors, analogies, inference) often found in literature. Through the analogy below, a PST described how she viewed Specially Designed Academic Instruction in English (SDAIE) strategies:

As an umbrella shelters a pedestrian in a rain storm, the SDAIE techniques or sheltered classes offer these ELL students some protection from the storms of concepts and language, thus giving them an opportunity to progress academically, as they are still acquiring the language and U.S. cultural ways. [JT_5-17-06]

Although one could not claim that this brief after-school program will have a long-term impact on the learning outcomes of these middle school students, it would be difficult to disregard the apparent joy with which these students bonded and related to one another and the PST in charge and pride in using their L1. It appeared that the MSS were comfortable with disclosing their struggle with balancing between being an American teenager and adopting U.S. values and being a Vietnamese son/daughter bound by traditional familial values.

Seven Key Factors

What factors should teachers take into account when working with students of a similar language and culture as these Vietnamese Americans?

Develop Students' Background Knowledge and Foundation of Subject Matter

It would be dangerous for teachers to assume that ELL students entering their classrooms would have had a literacy base in their heritage language (L1) and/or in English (L2) as well as adequate exposure to using L2 in conversational and academic settings. Therefore, teachers would need to provide ELL students with basic knowledge and foundation of the subject matter being taught, including the usage of SDAIE (e.g., slower speech, clear enunciation, quality visuals, gestures, facial expressions, and contextualized vocabulary, and so on).

If the classroom teacher was bilingual or had a bilingual aide, the use of L1 to support student comprehension of subject matter would be ideal. In this case, concepts would be previewed in L1, followed by the teacher's direct instruction in L2, then reviewed in L1 to make certain that the ELL students understood key concepts and ideas and asked related questions.

Recognize and Build upon Students' Dual Identity

Being a bilingual individual (including U.S. born) means to be part of both cultures. Many ELL students struggled with being perceived as less intelligent and less capable because they had not adequately demonstrated strong command of English, familiarity with cultural ways of the U.S., and difficulty with fitting into the total school population. Build on what they know. Validate who they are and the familial resources they bring. Never insist on their shedding their L1 in order to acquire their L2.

Allow for Think Time and Wait Time

Though many ELL students have been considered as conscientious and hard working by some of their teachers, they often felt shy and uncomfortable about classroom participation. Slow in raising their hands, they had to process the question and the answer in English as well as the terminology in that subject matter, and tended to become frustrated when their classmates' hands went up immediately after the teacher had posed a question.

If longer think and wait time had been allowed, these ELL students would have stood a better chance of formulating their answers before making their responses public and risking "losing face" in front of others. How about signaling to ELL students that they would be called on and giving them appropriate time to get ready? What about broadening the definition of "participation" to include other ways of responding to questions to include writing assignments, small group discussion, pair-share, use of post-it notes, thumbs up/thumbs down, or individual erasable white boards as part of participation? Lack of verbal participation may not necessarily equate to lack of understanding.

Deliver Instruction at a Slower Pace

For ELL students, instruction and class discussion in English-only classes seemed to occur at a-mile-a-minute pace, leaving them inundated with information and overwhelmed with English "noise." How about verbally communicating key concepts and terminology and write these ideas on the board (supported by relevant examples)? Guide students in taking notes of important ideas and in making sense of essential concepts in order for them to demonstrate their understanding of the material in course assignments, discussions, and examinations.

For instance, content standards are written in such a way that even teachers can find them confounding and ambiguous. Therefore, break content standards into smaller chunks and help students to read between the lines in terms of what teachers are expected to teach and students are to learn and be able to do.

Emphasize Note Taking and Organization

Teachers often assumed that by the time students, including ELL students, arrived in middle school, they would already have learned how to take proper notes from class lectures and organize them into folders/binders from one class period to the next. However, some may not have mastered these skills. If a teacher taught her students how to take notes from a reading assignment, students would be able to focus attention on key concepts and ideas in order to study for exams.

Furthermore, it is important for teachers to make a habit of reminding students when and what to take notes of so that it becomes a pattern for them. For ELL students, this process may take some time. How about assigning a percentage of the total course grade to note taking and organization?

Maximize Multiple Learning Modalities

To minimize teacher talk and to increase student understanding of material taught, teachers might employ visual, tactile, and kinesthetic modalities (Kellough & Roberts, 2002) in order to tap upon the multiple intelligences of learners (Gardner, 1983) and to allow more than one way for students to demonstrate knowledge. Strategies such as TPR and SDAIE should be used as much as possible to make input comprehensible and concepts less abstract (Asher, 1965; Krashen, 1995), thus benefiting not only ELL students but other students as well.

Establish a Support System

Besides the teacher, an older student, an English-proficient classmate, a teacher/college aide, a parent or a community volunteer could also assist the ELL students with class work by supplementing, not supplanting, the teacher's role. Hence, the *zone of proximal development* (ZPD) of the ELL students would be "stretched" from their current level of understanding to their potential state of development (Vygotsky, 1962).

One of the reasons ELL students hesitated to raise their hands was because they preferred not to call attention to themselves for fear of being labeled as "braggers" or "know it alls" by their classmates. Furthermore, ELL students rarely asked questions even if they did not understand. Why show others what they did not know?

Teachers should make time to talk to and connect with ELL students personally as much as possible. For many ELL students, group success is far more important than individual success. Teachers do affect the lives of students who cross their paths and to ensure that giving up should not be an option for teachers or students. No child should be left behind.

References

Asher, J. (1966). The strategy of the total physical response: A review. *Modern Language Journal, 50,* 79–84.

Bielenberg, B., & Fillmore, L. W. (December 2004-January 2005). The English they need for the test. *Association for Supervision and Curriculum Development, 62*(4), 45–49.

Cummins, J. (2000). *Language, power and pedagogy: Bilingual children in the crossfire.* Clevedon, UK: Multilingual Matters.

Gardner, J. (1983). *Frames of mind.* New York: Basic Books.

Hakuta, K., Butler, Y. G., & Witt, D. (2000). *How long does it take English learners to attain proficiency?* Santa Barbara, CA: University of California Linguistic Minority Research Institute.

Krashen, S (1995). *Principles and practice in second language acquisition.* New York: Phoenix ELT.

Kellough, R. D., & Roberts, P. (2002). *A resource guide for elementary school teaching: Planning for competence* (5th Ed.). Upper Saddle River, NJ: Merrill Prentice Hall.

Rossell, C. (December 2004-January 2005). Teaching English through English. *Association for Supervision and Curriculum Development, 62*(4), 32–36.

Vygotsky, L. S. (1962). *Thought and language.* Cambridge, MA: MIT Press.

Critical Thinking

1. What unique conditions impact Vietnamese American students?

2. How can teachers help Vietnamese American students with their reading proficiencies?

3. What approaches are helpful for all students needing assistance?

4. Why are English Language Learners a major concern in U.S. schools?

HUONG TRAN NGUYEN is an assistant professor in the Department of Teacher Education, College of Education, California State University, Long Beach, Long Beach, California.

From *Multicultural Education,* Fall 2007, pp. 23–26. Copyright © 2007 by Caddo Gap Press. Reprinted by permission.

The Diversity Merry-Go-Around: Planning and Working in Concert to Establish a Culture of Acceptance and Respect in the University

RAPHAEL C. HEAGGANS AND WALTER W. POLKA

Introduction

The following poem (Polka, 2007) provides a conceptual framework for educational planners to consider when designing programs, projects, strategies, and activities that accentuate diversity and promote the appreciation of differences:

Our Quest
Several individuals have searched diligently for
Similar
patterns, structures, and expressions among
Diverse
people, things, and ideas,
In their quest for simple understanding.

Numerous others have made substantial plans to
Standardize
access, activities, and incentives among
Diverse
people, things, and ideas,
In their quest for simple understanding.

Many others have implemented forcibly with
Precision
programs, models, and assessments among
Diverse
people, things, and ideas,
In their quest for simple understanding.

Some others have evaluated wrongly, and
Rigidly
knowledge, attitudes, and skills among
Diverse
people, things, and ideas,
In their quest for simple understanding.

Others have self-righteously worked to
Homogenize
languages, cultures, and beliefs among
Diverse
people, things, and ideas,
In their quest for simple understanding.

Thus, all of us must begin now to
Humanize
Histories, realities, and futures among
Diverse
people, things, and ideas,
In our quest for enriched understanding.

And, each of us must genuinely try to
Appreciate
difference, uniqueness, and individuality among
Diverse
people, things, and ideas,
In our grand quest for enlightened understanding.

Background Information

Heagolka University, a pseudonymous university, is in an area that is overwhelmingly White in racial composition and middle-class in socio-economic status. Members of its various academic and administrative departments allege that they cannot diversify the campus given the challenges to attracting more ethnic minorities within its faculty, staff, or student body. University leadership note that 95% of the faculty and 90% of the staff are White. Only 2% of the faculty of color is tenured. There has been a history of litigation at the University from ethnic minority faculty and staff on grounds of discrimination.

The University administration asserts that it is "colorblind"; it aims to hire faculty and staff who are well qualified and to admit students who meet its admissions criteria (which has not been overhauled since the 1960s). Yet, the admissions and hiring criteria have an adverse impact on candidates of color.

The University leaders believe that being colorblind provides equitable access to the University; they cannot comprehend why there is not a greater presence of faculty, staff, and students from underrepresented backgrounds. These leaders assert that they are in favor of diversity. But being in "favor of diversity" does not make anyone embrace diversity, just as being for humor does not make one laugh (Bullard, 1996). Accepting and celebrating diversity in the workplace is an on-going process. Too often university campuses take a carnivalesque approach to celebrating diversity. They believe it is a part of diversity awareness. This approach does not lead one to analyze his or her beliefs on diversity, and it does not trigger self-assessment practices that strongly convey the university supports diversity. Further, awareness is a benign, somewhat amorphous state of being without specific action or agency. One may be aware of a person's presence in a room without knowing the person's approximate height, weight, color of hair, or body frame. Thus, awareness can occur without actually focusing on the person at all.

That example raises the specter of people who treat diversity as an incantation, seeking instantaneous results for their campus as opposed to those who wish to confront the issues that foster and nurture diversity as the norm, not exception. Part of any university's underlying goal is to recruit, retain, and graduate students who have developed intellectually, personally, ethnically, and culturally. In light of this commitment, faculty, administrators, staff, and all other persons affiliated with a university have an obligation to prepare students for the diverse world they will face upon graduating (Banks, 1999; Blum, 2002; Cortez, 1999; Morbarak, 2005).

In order for Heagolka University and others like it to make diversity an endemic part of its organization, all employees have to engage in an exploration of the collective prejudices, values, beliefs, attitudes, and stereotypical notions they hold about persons from underrepresented groups (Maltbia & Power, 2008). It may be a discomforting process, but this discomfort may be a necessary factor in the evolution of the university's community. It is an on-going process. Rather than making overly generalized statements about diversity or trying to avoid discussion of diversity, the process of becoming a diverse university should be constructed in a way that enables discomforting conversations to take place in a secure and supportive work environment (Page, 2007). This paper examines proactive approaches that may be employed at universities as a part of a process of enhancing diversity initiatives.

Before any initiative is operationalized, the university must establish a strategic plan and apply quality management principles during and after its implementation. Kaufman, Herman, and Watters (2002) contend that, "strategic planning and quality management are two useful processes when applied consistently and correctly" (p. 173). The authors added that strategic planning involves establishing, modifying, or collapsing new objectives as a part of direction finding, while quality management enrolls

all organizational members—everyone—to deliver total client satisfaction and quality. Each person in the organization strives to continuously improve everything they use, do, and deliver. Individuals and organizations learn from mistakes, and use performance data to improve, not blame. (p. 175)

Doing Some *Unlearning*

Just because Heagolka University is located in Anywhere, USA where the area is 95% majority population, does not mean that diversity does not exist in the community. As is often the case, a one-dimensional view of diversity exists on this campus, suggesting that diversity is just about race. It is imperative, however, for university stakeholders who desire to begin the diversity appreciation focus to uncover the various human and cultural differences that already exist within the university community. Figure 1 attempts to capture the range of diversity that is found at a university like Heagolka and within its respective community.

Essential university-wide attitudinal changes are more likely to occur as the result of longer-term diversity educational programs where everyone benefits. Reforms should not assume that there is no need for diversity discussions just because there are no blatantly negative comments made about underrepresented groups or because people are openly nice to each other.

Before any university can begin designing an initiative that demonstrates a comprehensive commitment to diversity, the specific needs related to the contextual human and cultural differences should be clearly articulated (Morbarak, 2005; Page, 2007). In addition, as noted by Hoy and Tarter (2008), the overall pattern of organizational decision making needs to center on the following four streams of events:

Problems . . . points of dissatisfaction that need attention, but are independent of solutions and choices. A problem may or may not lead to a solution, and problems may or may not be solved when a solution is accepted.

Solutions . . . ideas proposed for adoption, but they can sometimes exist independently of problems. In fact, the attractiveness of an idea can stimulate a search for a problem to justify the idea.

Participants . . . organizational members who come and go. Problems and their solutions can change quickly because personnel can change rapidly.

Choice opportunities . . . occasions when organizations are expected to make decisions. Contracts must be signed, people hired and fired, money expanded, and resources allocated. (p. 59)

Heagolka University certainly has its share of problems that do not have quick solutions. The University's participants—administrators, professors, support staff, students, alumni, and the community-at-large—can collectively assist in viewing

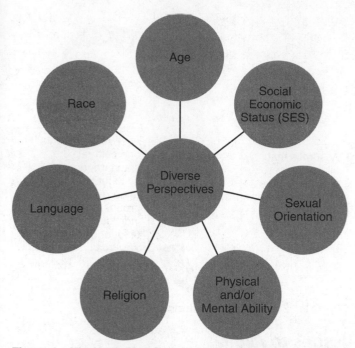

Figure 1   Kinds of diversity within Heagolka University and any other community

the problems as choice opportunities. To assist in defining the issues at Heagolka University, the following questions, synthesized from ten diversity evaluation questions originally posed by Shireman (2003), may be useful: *What kind of students does our university attract? Why?* Key university personnel—or the leadership of departments within them—should investigate who chooses to matriculate at the institution. In doing so, the first part of the investigation should include analyzing the demographic profiles of: (1) the counselors from secondary schools who recommend the university to students, (2) the students who obtained information about the University via the Internet, (3) the students who visited the University, and (4) the students who spoke with employers who hired University graduates. Institutional development personnel should then compare the results of the profiles to those students who actually applied, were admitted, and enrolled. Subsequently in this vein, personnel in the office of multicultural affairs can work together with other auxiliary staff at the University to attract more qualified students from various backgrounds to apply for admission.

How socially and academically successful are the students? Key university personnel—or the leadership of departments within them—need to analyze the answers to the following questions: (1) Who are the students that actively participate in leadership positions on campus? (2) Who are the students that are typically on academic probation? (3) Who are the students applying and admitted to graduate school? (4) Why is it that some students do not participate in any of the activities held on campus? (5) What are the differences in graduation rates of White students versus ethnic minority students? and (6) How does the university work with the community to create social events inclusive of culturally diverse perspectives?

What are some ways the university is spreading the news about the positive things it is doing in relation to diversity? When it is stated that, "Heagolka University is located in Anywhere, USA," what stereotypes about the community does that statement instantly create? University leaders need to work together to dispel the stereotypes. If the students are applicants mainly from Anywhere and its surrounding area, dispelling the stereotype to enhance the university's potential for attracting qualified ethnic minority students may be a more difficult task. The University director of multicultural or international affairs should play an intricate role in recruiting students inside and outside of Anywhere and working to keep them successfully matriculating at Heagolka.

Some university personnel may ask, "Why is it necessary to travel to various places to recruit students?" It is essential for the University leadership to regionalize and nationalize the positive diversity efforts of its organization to make them known in other places outside of Anywhere, USA. By highlighting the accomplishments and strategic plans related to diversity efforts, the university leaders may be able to dismantle stereotypes and attract potential faculty, students, and staff to Anywhere.

Who are our faculty, staff, and administrative leaders within the university? Heagolka University, as similar real world institutions, may have a fine faculty, staff, and administrative team; however, like every university, there is always room for enhancement. Any person can be a positive role model for students; however, the experience at Heagolka University may be more difficult for individuals from underrepresented groups who have limited faculty, staff, or administration with similar human and cultural perspectives. The extent to which the leadership of Heagolka University attracts and retains faculty, staff, and administrators from underrepresented groups may be a primary indicator of the degree the University faculty, staff, and administration have fully embraced diversity outside of tokenism.

What are the racial and ethnic minority students and faculty saying about their experience at Heagolka University? Racial and ethnic minority faculty and students are some of the best recruiters of other racial and ethnic minority faculty and students. Heagolka should unite with the community to determine strategic ways to meet the cultural needs of these faculty and students. Given that the University is in an isolated area in Anywhere, USA, ethnic minority students need to feel connected with the Anywhere community. Most persons want to be around groups of people who share commonalities. Heagolka must be mindful that diversity celebrates difference but also *sameness.*

Presenting a Case for Diversity

Change is a difficult process. But, as the adage goes, that if [university leaders] do what they have always done, they will get what they always got. Heagolka is aware of their problems with attracting and retaining ethnic minority faculty, staff, and students. Barclay (1996) posits that institutional leaders cannot ignore these problems, hoping they will resolve themselves and disappear. One must wonder if our historical patterns of exclusion and differential treatment are so deeply ingrained in the fabric of [the Heagolka University] society that they will hinder [it] from capitalizing on the strength of [its] growing diversity. (p. 49)

Figure 2 illustrates the cycle of negative effects of colorblindness. These effects of colorblindedness have lead Heagolka to place a bandage on that which actually requires surgery. The first director of multicultural affairs was recently hired at Heagolka to be a part of the president's cabinet in its 150-year history. That is a positive step in overcoming the diversity malaise that has impacted that university. The director and her respective strategic planning team, consisting of students, faculty, administrators, alumni, members of the community, members outside of the community, and others, can develop a proposal to the president's cabinet and board to pursue an ongoing diversity recruiting initiative. Some elements of that plan may include emphasizing:

1. The "Past Prouds"
2. Issues to avoid
3. Becoming diversity-smart

Change is rarely an easy process, but it is a process that begins with individuals and then spreads throughout the organization (Flanagan & Booth, 2002). Some persons within an organization, however, do not wish to disrupt the status quo (Thomas, 2007). The task of the diversity strategic planning team is to convince the president's cabinet and board of the necessity of change to enhance all diversity initiatives (Maltbia & Power, 2008).

Emphasizing the Past Prouds

No university wishes to be known as one that discriminates on the basis of race, religion, gender, age, and so on. But an absence of blatant acts of racism, religionism, sexism, and/or ageism does not mean that these *isms* do not exist. The University has to assess its institution-wide discriminatory practices. Further, Kirkham (1996) suggests:

The reporting relationships, business practices, policies, and even the physical structure of any workplace are based on the cumulative experiences of that organization: the people who have made up the workforce over time, the larger culture they have created, and the total context in which the organization operates. (p. 25)

Heagolka University's mission statement states that it does not discriminate on the basis of race, creed, or sexual orientation, but it took the University 150 years to hire a director of multicultural affairs. But focusing on the University's deficits does not make the president's cabinet or the community naysayers feel empowered to change the future. It is one reason why the *past prouds* should be emphasized. Heagolka University has had strong programs and recognition from the *ABC World Report*. It has increased its ethnic-minority enrollment by 2% within the past year, and it is affordable. These elements may be emphasized to set a foundation for the issues the diversity strategic planning team may wish to address (Konrad, 2006).

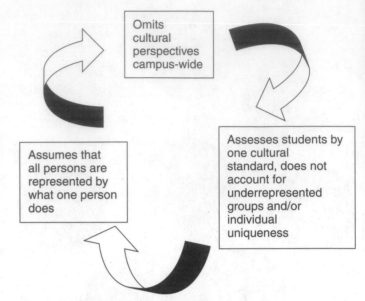

Figure 2 **Effects of colorblindness**

Issues to Avoid

Oftentimes, the people in the Heagolka community, as in similar communities throughout the United States, have a challenging time breaking the paradigm of an institutionally discriminatory culture (Dulio, O'Brien, & Klemanski, 2008). The University, as an institution, is directionless about what to do. Barclay (1996) asserts "there is still a reluctance to admit the deep-rooted nature of discrimination, prejudice, racism, and sexism that continue to pervade our society. Until we can admit this reality, developing a solution becomes very difficult" (p. 49). The director of multicultural affairs and strategic planning team must help the University by addressing, not avoiding, these issues.

In making a case to the president's cabinet of Heagolka University, the director of multicultural affairs and the strategic planning team members should present the issues the University wishes to avoid, which are: attrition, withdrawal of alumni support, litigation, under-preparation of students, and an unfavorable reputation.

All of Heagolka's students benefit from diverse perspectives being present on campus; otherwise, the University creates a campus atmosphere of diversity *unawareness*. The effects of it are cultural blindness, bad publicity, litigation, "fudging" of accreditation information related to diversity, and a loss of tuition revenue. For example, if ethnic minorities perceive that Heagolka University is discriminatory in its practices, those students may not apply or withdraw, resulting in lost tuition revenue. Subsequently, Heagolka's ethnic minority and some White alum may withdraw their financial support of the University, perceiving that diversity and the appreciation of difference is not welcomed. This, leads to negative perceptions about the University, which can, in turn, reduce student applications. Yet, more importantly, losing students from ethnic minority groups leads to the under-preparation of all students for the diverse world that exists around them.

Some faculty members may be aware of the litigious history associated with this University. It has been hit with multiple lawsuits by *qualified* ethnic minorities who applied for positions but were not considered for an interview; or obtained an interview, but, were denied an offer for the position, as the position was given to another who was clearly less qualified. In this instance, diversity unawareness can create a litigious work environment, further damaging the University's reputation.

Becoming Diversity-Smart

Corporations benefit from having a diverse workforce. Any university that does not have a diverse student body, faculty, staff, and administrators is suffering from the effects of *diversity disregard*. Diversity disregard can lead to bad publicity, litigation misleading student organizations, disingenuously reporting accreditation information as it relates to diversity, and a loss of money.

General Motors provides a vivid example of the impact of diversity disregard. The company attempts to sell the car model *Nova* in Spanish-speaking countries. Yet, *"No va* means 'no go' in Spanish. Had even one employee who knew Spanish and Spanish culture been present to provide guidance, GM could have saved a great deal of money" (Hayles & Russell, 1997, p. 2). Another example Hayles and Russell noted is: "The team that marketed Gerber baby food in Africa made the picture on the label a black-skinned baby, yet sales in Africa were very few. Customers there expected labels that pictured the product, not the consumer. Gerber's losses were substantial" (p. 2). In our contemporary "Global Village" it is imperative that all cultural perspectives are considered and that students are well prepared to appreciate differences between and among people (Brief, 2008; Brislin, 2008).

As with the two examples from business, Heagolka University's losses have been substantial. Recruiting ethnic minorities to the University would mean (a) more tuition dollars, (b) increased enrollment, (c) the potential of greater alumni support, (d) greater diversity, and (e) enhanced public reputation. The enhanced diversity would help the students learn more about persons from underrepresented groups and vice versa. The accrediting agencies that review the programs of Heagolka include diversity components within their evaluation criteria. It is quite difficult for universities that do not take a proactive approach to integrating diversity to meet the standards of their accrediting bodies. Therefore, it is critical that the strategic planning team articulate and record their plans and actions to improve the appreciation of differences. Previously the information reported was misleading to give an appearance of diversity, but, in reality, it was not incorporated into university functions nor assimilated into the university's culture.

So in sum, some of Heagolka's current issues are: (a) developing means to attract qualified diverse faculty, staff, administrators, and students; (b) providing finding/scholarships to qualified White and ethnic minorities; (c) analyzing the relationships between White faculty and diverse students across academic, social, professional and interactive ends; and, (d) retaining diverse faculty and students. This is in an effort to eradicate lawsuits. This University needs to revisit its vision and mission statement on diversity and then develop diversity-related goals and institutional policies and procedures to: (a) increase recruitment efforts and enrollment of students of color; (b) develop more culturally competent graduates; and, (c) establish a strategic planning committee at the grassroots level to monitor growth via the change process.

Sometimes the strategic planning decisions may connect by chance to the appropriate diversity solutions. Cohen, March and Olsen (1972) initially labeled such a chance decision-making model as the "garbage can" approach. Hoy and Tarter (2008) further extended the applications of the "garbage can" approach in their guide to solving problems of practice in education. They contend that sometimes educational change agents will find solutions to problems by realizing that previous attempts at problem-solving in their respective institutions created a series of solutions that may not have been used initially but are still "in the hopper" waiting for the right problem to emerge. Hoy and Tarter further clarified this concept of chance in problem-solving by positing,

> Actually a hope-chest metaphor rather than the garbage-can metaphor may be more apt because these ideas are not garbage but rather good ideas that teachers and administrators hope will be implemented. Therefore, they are kept alive in the hope chest, not buried in the garbage can. (p. 63)

Consistent with the above hope chest metaphor, a sincere commitment can be demonstrated by the educational leaders at Heagolka University for establishing a diversity curriculum, initiating a comprehensive focus on appreciating differences of all kinds, working with other university doctoral programs that have ethnic minorities to attract them to consider Heagolka for employment post-graduation, and providing on-going diversity workshops (Clements & Jones, 2002; Morbarak, 2005) as part of their diversity "hope-chest." In addition, to make their diversity hopes become reality and to set the climate for change at Heagolka University, the members of the president's cabinet may be specifically assigned to complete the following tasks:

Subsequently, the university administration would be strategically planning to improve the diversity at its institution using the "hope-chest" approach to solve non-inclusive historical practices. Even if the desired changes in diversity are slow and meet expected resistance, at least solutions have been identified and may be used sometime in the future (Thomas, 2007). And, as Hoy and Tarter stated, "Although the garbage-can [read "hope-chest"] metaphor is an apt description of the ways some decisions are reached, it may not be as common in most public elementary and secondary schools as in universities . . ." (p. 64). But, they contended that, "The *garbage-can model* suggested that, especially in organizations where uncertainty is high and coordination loose, fortuitous events often influence the way decisions are made" (p. 74).

Hopefully, diversity improvement ideas, such as provided in Figure 3, "float" for only a brief time until people agree that the above solutions are good for institutional diversity problems and a fortuitous match is made (Hoy & Tarter). Consequently, the hope-chest ideas for diversity will then have served a useful purpose.

Job Title	Diversity Charge
President	Circulate diversity directives to the institution as they relate to the vision and mission of the University. Lead a review and revision of all University policies and procedures to promulgate an authentic appreciation of human and cultural differences throughout the University.
Vice President	Provide the Director of Multicultural Affairs entrée to faculty to assess what diversity-themed courses exist and how to develop more; require all freshman students to take a designated minimum number of credit hours in diversity-themed courses, beginning with their first semester.
Director of Institutional Development	Assist analyzing/presenting diversity data campus wide; work with Media Relations in developing strategies for presenting diversity data.
Director of Multicultural Affairs	Facilitate diversity initiatives; assist admissions officers with recruiting diverse students.
Director of Enrollment Management	Develop an ethnic minority recruitment plan (outside of Anywhere, USA); assist in promoting learning opportunities leading to the success and retention of diverse students.
Director of Media Relations	Highlight the accomplishments of diverse faculty, staff, and students; analyze how effective the multicultural initiatives are in the regional marketing campaign.

Figure 3   Example of President's and Cabinet's responsibilities pertaining to diversity

The Bottom Line

Heagolka has to examine the environment it has created over the years and ensure that their "middle-class, dominant culture students see their own taken-for-granted values and styles and the institutional arrangements with which they are so familiar as simply illustrations of 'culture in action'" (Lalkin, 1995). Vogt (1997) states "although education has a general tendency to promote tolerance by increasing commitment to civil liberties, it also promotes commitment to orderly, nondisruptive political procedures and to the values of white-collar, educated people" (p. 62). Overcoming prejudicial attitudes involves analyzing our beliefs about people, things and ideas that we perceive are different from us (Harvey & Allard, 2008). How is it possible for students to analyze some of their beliefs about racism, ageism, sexism and other human and cultural discriminations when some university administrators, faculty, and staff who are perceived by their students to be role models, avoid teaching about these matters as part of Heagolka culture?

Thoughts to Consider

Reverend Martin Niemoller provided sound words of advice: "In Germany, the Nazis first came for the Communists, and I didn't speak up because I was not a Communist. Then they came for the Jews, and I didn't speak up, because I wasn't a Jew. Then they came for the trade unionist, and I didn't speak up because I wasn't a trade unionist. Then they came for the Catholics, and I didn't speak up because I was Protestant. Then they came for me, and by that time, there was no one left to speak for me" (Niemoller, 1945). Universities have to begin asking themselves: If we were put on trial for our commitment to diversity, would there be enough evidence to convict us? (Clements & Jones, 2002).

Another valued reference for this paper is the following pledge from the Anti-Defamation League that could and should be the first action that authentic diversity-minded individuals and institutional strategic planning teams recite, agree to, and internalize in order to make our university and world a better place for ALL:

A World of Difference

I pledge from this day onward to do my best to interrupt prejudice and to stop those who, because of hate, would hurt, harass or violate the civil rights of anyone. I will try at all times to be aware of my own biases against people who are different from myself. I will ask questions about cultures, religions and races that I don't understand. I will speak out against anyone who mocks, seeks to intimidate or actually hurts someone of a different race, religion, ethnic group or sexual orientation. I will reach out to support those who are targets of harassment. I will think about specific ways my school, other students, and my community can promote respect for people and create a prejudice-free zone. I firmly believe that one person can make a difference and that no person can be an "innocent bystander" when it comes to opposing hate.

By subscribing to this pledge, I recognize that respect for individual dignity, achieving equality, and opposing anti-Semitism, racism, ethnic bigotry, homophobia, or any other form of hatred is a non-negotiable responsibility of all people. (Anti-Defamation League, 1999)

Summary and Diversity Strategic Planning Resources

Each of us, as educational planners and community leaders, must authentically embrace the appreciation of our human and cultural differences so as to serve as genuine role models and to facilitate a more civilized culture wherein individuals are not discriminated against because they are "different" (Clements & Jones; Cox, 2001; Davidson & Fielden, 2003). We each possess the "Power of One" and each of us can make a difference in our world by internalizing the values of diversity and recognizing the inherent dangers associated with the perspectives of homogeneity and standardization. We need to reflect upon the various ways that underrepresented groups have been maltreated and disrespected at our various institutions and in our specific workplace and we must individually pledge to do something about it. If not, the contemporary mini-holocausts of hate may, again, evolve into another major holocaust. History has a habit of repeating itself unless we individually and collectively intervene to change the course.

As planners and leaders we have the power and the responsibility to provide valuable service to others who are working in their contexts to change discriminatory mindsets. We have the experience and the resources to help others make a difference and, thus, continue to advance a more humane world. The following note from a Nazis Holocaust survivor given to a teacher on the first day of a new school year sums up our view of the significance of valuing an appreciative humane approach to education:

> Dear Teacher,
> I am a survivor of a concentration camp. My eyes saw what no man should witness:
> Gas chambers built by learned engineers.
> Children poisoned by educated physicians.
> Infants killed by trained nurses.
> Women and babies shot and burned by high school and college graduates.
> So I am suspicious of education.
> My request is: Help your students become human. Your efforts must never produce learned monsters, skilled psychopaths, educated Eichmanns. . .
> Reading, writing, arithmetic are important
> Only if they serve to make children more humane. (Author Anonymous)

To assist you in planning to make a difference at your institutions and work places, we have provided a listing of some valuable diversity references, in addition to those used for this paper, which we have found to be very helpful in developing programs, projects, strategies and/or activities that accentuate diversity and promote the appreciation of difference. Of course, our recommended list is limited by our own experiences so we encourage you to assist us in facilitating a more respectful and appreciative world by adding references that you have used to our list and communicating them to us via e-mail so that we may continue to develop a veritable diversity resource cornucopia we may all use in our quest for enlightened understanding.

References

Anti-Defamation League. (1999). Retrieved February 20, 2008 from the website: http://www.adl. org/prejudice/prejudice.pledge .html.

Banks, J. (1999). *An introduction to multicultural education.* Massachusetts: Allyn and Bacon.

Barclay, D. (1996). Allies or enemies?: Affirmative action and management diversity. In E. Cross and M. White (Eds.), *The diversity factor: Capturing the competitive advantage of a changing workforce.* Boston: McGraw-Hill.

Bell, M. (2006). *Diversity in organizations.* New York: South-Western Publishers.

Blum, L. (2002). *I'm not a racist but. . .: The moral quandary of race.* New York: Cornell University Press.

Boutte, G. (1999). *Multicultural education: Raising consciousness.* California: Wadsworth Publishing Co.

Brief, A. (Ed.). (2008). *Diversity at work.* Cambridge, England: Cambridge University Press.

Brislin, R. (2008). *Working with cultural differences: Dealing effectively with diversity in the workplace.* New York: Praeger Pub.

Bullard, S. (1996). *Teaching tolerance: Raising open-minded empathetic children.* New York: Doubleday.

Clements, P., & Jones, J. (2002). *The diversity training handbook.* Sterling, VA: Stylus Publishing.

Cohen, D., March, J., & Olsen, J.(1972). A garbage-can model of organizational choice. *Administrative Science Quarterly,* 17, 1–25.

Cox, T. (2001). *Creating the multicultural organization: A strategy for capturing the power of diversity.* San Francisco: Jossey-Bass, Inc.

Davidson, M., & Fielden, S. (Eds.). (2003). *Individual diversity & psychology in organisations.* New York: John Wiley & Sons Inc.

Dulio, D., O'Brien, E., & Klemanski. J. (Eds.). (2008). *Diversity in contemporary American politics and government.* New York: Longman Publishers.

Flanagan, M., & Booth, A. (2002). *Reload: Rethinking women + cyberculture.* Cambridge, MA: MIT Press.

Harvey, C., & Allard. M. (2008). *Understanding and managing diversity: Readings, cases, and exercises.* New York: Prentice Hall.

Hayles, R., & Russell, A. (1997). *The diversity directive: Why some initiatives fail and what to do about it.* New York: McGraw-Hill.

Heaggans, R. (2003). *A tolerance initiative versus multicultural education: Portraits of teachers in action.* Unpublished dissertation. West Virginia University.

Hoy, W., & Tarter, C. (2008). *Administrators solving the problems of practice.* Boston: Allyn & Bacon.

Kaufman, R., Herman, J., & Watters, K. (2002). *Educational planning: Strategic, tactical, and operational.* Maryland: Scarecrow Press.

Kirkham, K. (1996). Managing in a diverse workforce: From incident to "ism". In E. Cross and M. White (Eds.), *The diversity factor: Capturing the competitive advantage of a changing workforce.* Boston: McGraw-Hill.

Konrad, A. (2006). *Cases in gender and diversity in organizations.* Thousand Oaks, CA; Sage.

Larkin, J. (1995). Curriculum themes and issues in multicultural teacher education programs. In J. Larkin & C. Sleeter (Eds.) *Developing multicultural teacher education curricula.* New York: State University of New York Press.

Maltbia, T., & Power, A. (2005). *A leader's guide to leveraging diversity: Strategic learning capabilities for breakthrough performance.* New York: Butterworth-Heinemann.

Morbarak, M. (2005). *Managing diversity: Toward a globally inclusive workplace.* Thousand Oaks, CA: Sage Publications.

Niemoller, M. (1945). Retrieved, September 23, 2008 from the website: http://www.hobes.com/Fireblade/Politics/niemoller/

Nieto, S. (2000). *Affirming diversity: The sociopolitical context of multicultural education.* (3rd ed). New York: Longman.

Page, S. (2007). *The difference: How the power of diversity creates better groups, firms, schools, and societies.* Princeton, NJ: Princeton University Press.

Polka, W. (2007). Our Quest. In A. Foster (Ed.), *NINER News,* 4(1), 7. National Network for Education Renewal. Seattle, WA: University of Washington.

Shireman, R. (2003, August 15). 10 Questions College Officials Should Ask About Diversity. *Chronicle of Higher Education,* 49(49), B10.

Thomas, K. (Ed.). (2007). *Diversity resistance in organizations.* New York: Psychology Press.

Vogt, P. (1997). *Tolerance & education: Learning to live with diversity and diference.* Thousand Oaks, CA: Sage Publications.

Other Recommended Resources to Promote Respecting Differences

Aghion, P., & Williamson, J. (Eds.). (1998). *Growth, inequality, and globalization: Theory, history, and policy.* Cambridge, UK: Cambridge University Press.

Asakawa, K., & Csikszentmihalyi, M. (1998). The quality of experiences of Asian American adolescents related to future goals. *Journal of Youth and Adolescence, 27*(2), 141–163.

Banks, J., Cookson, P., Gay, G., Hawley, W., Irvine, J., Nieto, S., Schofield, J., & Stephan, W. (2001). Diversity within unity: Essential principles for teaching and learning in a multicultural society. *Phi Delta Kappan.*

Cardi, J. (1997). *Faculty stance toward multiculturalism and multicultural education: A Qualitative study.* Unpublished doctoral dissertation. West Virginia University.

Cortes, C. (2000). *The children are watching: How the media teach about diversity.* New York: Teachers College Press.

Delpit, L. (1995). *Other people's children.* New York: The New Press.

Dunn, R., Gemake, J., Jalai, F., Zenhausern, R., Quinn, P., & Spiridakis, J. (1990). Cross-cultural differences in learning styles of elementary-age children from four ethnic backgrounds. *Journal of Multicultural Counseling and Development 18,* 68–93.

Fine, M. (1997). *Framing dropouts: Notes on the politics of an urban high school.* New York: State University of New York Press.

Gay, G. (1994). At *the essence of learning: Multicultural education.* Indiana: Kappa Delta Pi.

Gay, G. (2002). Preparing for culturally responsive teaching. *Journal of Teacher Education, 53*(2).

Graybill, S. (1997). Questions of race and culture: How they relate to the classroom for African-American students. *The Clearing House, 70*(6), 311–318.

Giroux, H. (1992). *Border crossings: Cultural workers and the politics of education.* New York: Routledge Press.

Guild, P. (1994). The culture/learning style connection: Educating for diversity. *Educational Leadership,* 447–452.

Gurung, R., & Prieto, L. (2009). *Getting culture: Incorporating diversity across the curriculum.* Sterling, VA: Stylus Publishers Llc.

Haberman, M. (1995). Selecting "Star" teachers for children and youth in urban poverty. *Phi Delta Kappa,* 44–50.

Hate-Benson, J. (1986). *Black children: Their roots, culture and learning styles.* Baltimore: Johns Hopkins University Press.

Harvard Business Press. (2009). *Managing diversity: Expert solutions to everyday challenges.* Boston: Harvard University Press.

Haycock, K., & Jerald, C. (2002, November/December). Closing the gap. *Principal,* 20–23.

Hilliard, A. (1990). Misunderstanding and testing intelligence. In J. I. Goodlad and P. Keating (Eds.), *Access to knowledge: An agenda for our nation's schools.* New York: College Entrance Examination Board.

Hillis, M. (1993). Multicultural education and curriculum transformation. *The Educational Forum, 58*(1), 50–56.

Hodgkinson, H. (2002, November/December). The politics of diversity. *Principal,* 15–18.

Hogan, K., & Pressley, M. (1997). *Scaffolding student learning: Instructional approaches and issues.* Brookline Books, Inc.: Cambridge, MA.

Howard, G. (1999). *We can't teach what we don't know: White teachers, multiracial schools.* New York: Teachers College Press.

Hubbard, E. (2003). *The diversity scorecard: Evaluating the impact of diversity in organizational performance.* New York: Butterworth-Heinemann.

Hyde, C., & Hopkins, K. (2004). Diversity climates in human services agencies: An exploratory assessment. *Journal of Ethnic & Cultural diversity in social work, 13,* 25–43.

Irvine, J. (1990). *Black students and school: Policies, practices, and prescriptions.* New York: Greenwood Press.

Johnson, L. (2002). My eyes have been opened: White teachers and racial awareness. *Journal of Teacher Education, 53*(2).

Jonas, R. (2002, October). Defining diversity. *American School Board Journal. 189*(10), 18–23.

Kendall, F. (1983). *Diversity in the classroom: A Multicultural approach to the education of young children.* New York: Teachers College Press.

Kennedy, R. (2002). *Nigger: The strange career of a troublesome word.* New York: Panthaeon Books.

Kochman, T. (1981). *Black and white styles in conflict.* Chicago: The University of Chicago Press.

Kressel, N. (2002). *Mass hate: The global rise of genocide and terror.* New York: Westview Press.

Krupat, A. (2002). *Red matters: Native American studies.* Philadelphia, PA: University of Pennsylvania Press.

Ladson-Billings, G. (1994). The *dreamkeepers: Successful teachers of African-American children.* San Francisco: Jossey-Bass Publishers.

Lessow-Hurley, J. (1986). *The foundations of dual language instruction.* Second Edition. Nerv York: Longman.

Lipman, P. (1998). *Race, class and power in school restructuring.* New York: State University of New York.

Milner, R. (Ed.). (2009). *Diversity and education: Teachers, teaching, and teacher education.* London: Charles C. Thomas Pub. Ltd.

Manning, M. (1994). *Celebrating diversity: Multicultural education in the middle level schools.* US: National Middle School Association.

Manning, M., & Baruth, L. (2000). *Multicultural education of children and adolescents.* Massachusetts: Allyn & Bacon.

Oakes, J. (1985). *Keeping track: How schools structure inequality.* New Haven, CT: Yale University Press.

Oberdiek, H. (2001). *Tolerance: Between forbearance and acceptance.* Lanham, MD: Rowman & Littlefield Press.

Ozbilgin, M., & Tatli, A. (2008). *Global diversity management: An evidence-base approach.* New York: Palgrave Macmillan.

Page, R. (1991). *Lower-track Classrooms: A curricular and cultural perspective.* New York: Teachers College Press.

Phatak, A., Bhagat, R., & Kashlak, R. (2008). *International management: Managing in a diverse and dynamic global environment.* New York: McGraw-Hill College.

Quisenberry, N., & McIntyre, J. (Eds.). (1999). *Educators healing racism.* Reston, VA: Association of Teacher Educators & Association fro Childhood Education International.

Rasool, J., & Curtis, C. (2000). *Multicultural education in middle secondary classrooms: Meeting the challenge of diversity and change.* California: Wadsworth.

Ravitch, D. (1990). Multiculturalism: e pluribus plures. *The key reporter, 56*(l), 1–4.

Roediger, D. (2002). *Colored white: Transcending the racial past.* Los Angeles: University of California Press.

San Juan, E. (2002). *Racism and cultural studies: Critiques of multiculturalist ideology and the politics of difference.* Durham, NC: Duke University Press.

Shade, B. (1992). *Afro-American patterns of cognition.* Madison: University of Wisconsin Press.

Sleeter, C. (1996). White racism. *Multicultural Education, 1*(4), 5–8, 39.

Sleeter, C., & Grant, C. (1998). *Turning on learning: Five approaches for multicultural teaching plans for race, class, gender, and disability.* New Jersey: Prentice-Hall.

Southern Poverty Law Center. Retrieved February 29, 2008 from http://www.splcenter.org/

Stotsky, S. (1999, May) Multicultural illiteracy. *The School Administrator, 56*(6), 443–446.

Viet, T. (2002). *Race and resistance: Literature and politics in Asian America.* New York: Oxford University Press.

Yao, E. (1988). Working effectively with Asian immigrant parents. *Phi Delta Kappan, 70,* 223–225.

Critical Thinking

1. What changes need to occur on university campuses to make diversity an endemic part of the institution?

2. How can unlearning replace the prior learning?

3. What can teachers glean from this process to benefit their classrooms?

4. Why are universities and P-12 schools challenged with cultural acceptance?

UNIT 5

Spark Conversations and Climate

Unit Selections

Learning Outcomes

After reading this unit, you will be able to:

• Describe the teacher's role as community organizer to develop collective classroom efficacy.

• Explain the importance for developing cultural competence particularly when teaching world languages.

• Summarize the three themes of sociolinguistic conversations.

• Detail the vocabulary, concepts, and practices that help students create a sociocultural context.

• Discuss the efforts to promote cultural pluralism with Arab children's literature.

• Expound on the benefits for students using multicultural literature.

Student Website

www.mhhe.com/cls

Internet Reference

American Psychological Association
www.apa.org/topics/homepage.html
Center for Global Development
www.cgdev.org/section/initiatives/_active/globalizationandinequality?gclid=CKTYxrGWxJoCFRufnAodY1Q8sg
North American Reggio Emilia Alliance
www.reggioalliance.org
United States Department of Education, Office of English Language Acquisition
www.ed.gov/about/offices/list/oela/index.html
UNESCO
http://unescostat.unesco.org
United States Government
www.firstgov.gov

Language development and communication proficiency entail one's ability to think, view, listen, speak, read, and write. Learning requires a great amount of vocabulary and articulation as we acquire new knowledge, skills, and dispositions in multiple contexts; apply the newness to our individual lives at school, at home, at work, at play, to solve immediate problems, and for future reference. We appreciate the fresh information, access, and opportunities that open doors for us cognitively, physically, affectively, and socially. We expand our language development and communication proficiency every day through the ideas and insights gained from formal and informal interactions along with various forms of text and text connections to express and exchange our discoveries. Through language and communication individuals find strengths, success, and satisfaction.

Every person is engaged in language development throughout his or her life. Not only is the wealth of words in the English language overflowing, new words are added to our vocabularies every day. Given the sundry registers of language allowing us to communicate effectively and efficiently at formal functions, during informal interactions, with job-specific jargon, and so forth, everyone is constantly discovering new words to learn, use, and enjoy.

In the United States, the English language incorporates words from many other languages. As we enrich our abilities to speak English, we realize that we have acquired vocabulary from around the world. Some words commonly used in the English language have no translation from their original languages, so English speakers incorporate those words comfortably and competently. The same outcomes occur as we expand our language and communications through the cell phone and Internet. Likewise, we have developed an abundance of words, phrases, accents, and dialects that are unique to specific groups of people, careers, and geographic areas found across the United States. For example, we readily detect someone from Massachusetts, Georgia, or Texas. Although we are attempting to communicate with one another and frequently share the same message, the phrases used on the East Coast, mid South, Deep South, the Southwest, and the West Coast may differ from one another. It can be both fun and frustrating to glean the meaning.

The United States is filled with people from many countries; the country began as a refuge for immigrants. Thus, there are many people who speak many different languages. When young people who do not speak English proficiently go to school, the teachers must employ their expertise in providing specific instruction. Many teacher education programs are expanding to include/require courses in English language learning so teachers can help all learners. Young people who have immigrated to the United States are challenged in their abilities to communicate with people in their new communities. Like everyone else in the United States, English language learners are attempting to balance maintenance of their own cultures and family structures while learning new customs and community structures. The challenges for the learners, their families, the schools, and the teachers are intense; the conversations have escalated to involve educators, communities, and politicians and will continue into the future.

© SW Productions / Photodisc / Getty Images

The conversations related to ELL is not limited to immigrants. Sadly, although native English speakers, many people in the United States are weak in their abilities to use the English language well and communicate effectively. Again, through the power of the "generational perpetuation of practice," young people tend to acquire their primary abilities to develop language and communicate proficiently from their parents and families rather from their teachers and other educated role models. Young people echo the dialects, vocabulary, and communication skills found in their immediate circles and cultures. Teachers may attempt to introduce new vocabulary and expand upon young people's abilities to express themselves effectively, but familial influences tend to dominate.

To experience language development and communication proficiency first hand, people should read a wide variety of texts. The sources are endless. By reading both nonfiction and fiction, we explore spaces from the past, present, and future, delving into the lives of many different people, real and imaginary. Through literature, we experience the descriptions and adventures firsthand, as if we were there. We see exactly what the characters see or what the author wants us to see; we hear their conversations and language or what the author wants us to hear. When the literature is accompanied by a reader or a recording, we get to hear the dialogue, vocabulary, and accents exactly as the author meant for the story to be understood. The same discoveries apply to the photographs, drawings, and illustrations found in the literature. We are provided more clues to better comprehending the communication.

Literature of all kinds should be used in all classrooms to inform, instruct, and inspire students. Textbooks are read primarily to inform students about content knowledge. Assignments usually include instructions for students as they practice specific skills. And literature, in all its various forms, is used to inspire students. Most students find it much easier to read a fictional story or book to contextualize and comprehend all of the details associated with people, places, things, and events, especially people, places, things, and events with which we are not familiar or do not understand from reading a textbook. For example, the social studies textbook may include a page about World War II and the dropping of the bombs on Japan. However, reading the books *Hiroshima* (1954) by John Hersey or *Sadako* (1993) written by Eleanor Coerr and illustrated by Ed Young gives the reader more insight, satisfying all the senses to another place and times that most social studies textbooks and teachers cannot convey.

Integrating literature with social studies, teachers can incorporate literacy by asking students to write one of many different kinds of assignments. Math, science, technology, the fine arts, and multicultural education all fit with this unit too. The learning becomes much more inviting, exciting, and igniting as students connect with the various forms of text and one another to express and exchange their new learning.

The articles in Unit 5 inspire the reader to spark conversations and climate by teaching all students about bias, prejudice, and stereotyping as part of the curriculum, instruction, and assessments as well as featured in their classroom management and community of learners. All students should learn about and practice democratic practices, educational equity, human rights, and social justice. All students must be given voice, choice, and ownership or agency to take responsibility for their own learning. The reader should attend workshops or conferences to become more aware of and reduce bias in the classroom. Visiting an agency focused on human rights to learn more about culturally competent content and practices would be beneficial, too.

Developing Collective Classroom Efficacy: The Teacher's Role as Community Organizer

LeAnn G. Putney[1] and Suzanne H. Broughton[2]

Scenario of a fifth-grade classroom:

As a university researcher who became the resident classroom ethnographer in Ms. Falls's fifth-grade classroom, I entered the classroom on a day in mid-October with a visiting faculty candidate who was interested in seeing the classroom in action. The students were in reading groups, pouring over their assigned novels. After introducing the visitor to Ms. Falls, we went to sit in the back of the room, just to observe.

We were approached by Bethany who offered to introduce us to the class, and who asked Ms. Falls if it was ok to tell the visitor about their reading response activities. Ms. Falls agreed, and the students began to talk about the various kinds of reading response formats. What was common to all of these students was that they had to become the characters and perform the ideas from the novels they were reading. As they were trying to explain, Beto exclaimed, "This is too hard to explain, we need to just do it!" Bethany agreed and called for "Fishbowl" with the group reading *Pedro's Journal*.

Immediately the group sprang into action, moving chairs to the center of the room. Beto assigned students to sit in close as they were the "evaluators" of the performance. Ms. Falls reminded the others that they were to get ready to ask "probing questions." Jaz said, "You know, the kind of questions that make us say 'why' something happened." As the students continued into their performance, I caught the look from our visitor that indicated something special was happening here. On our way out of the school, she asked, "How did that group of kids get to be so independent that they could just take control of their learning in that way?"

The question posed by the visitor to this classroom creates an interesting area of inquiry related to classroom instruction and learning. As part of an ongoing ethnographic study

with this classroom teacher, we noted that in each of the four years studied the participants constructed a community in which student responsibility appeared to be central to the learning environment. At the same time, this was not the first person visiting the classroom who expressed admiration for the way the "class runs itself."

In sifting through the research journals of the resident classroom ethnographer, we read such comments anecdotally from other visitors she had taken into the classroom, from other classroom teachers at the same school, from the principal of the school, from substitute teachers who left notes to the teacher, and in interviews with preservice teachers. The bigger questions for us as researchers at that moment became, how did this sense of collective responsibility develop over time, and how was it promoted through participation in classroom activities? Was the sense of responsibility and belonging also related in any way to collective efficacy?

The central tenets of collective efficacy relate to how well group members respond and relate to one another as they work toward common goals. They also relate to the resilience of a group and the willingness of group members to continue to work through difficult situations (Goddard, Hoy, & Hoy, 2004). Knowing these central tenets led us to question whether collective efficacy could be examined through a sociocultural lens, which focuses on the learning and development of individuals through their participation in a cultural collective. Could using a Vygotskian (1986) approach provide a means to demonstrate how teachers and students establish a cohesive sense of responsibility toward their learning and toward each other that result in performance capability?

Our intention is to examine collective classroom efficacy as a construct that is socially constructed and that develops over time between members in a classroom context. To do so we needed to combine the initial construct of student self-efficacy and collective efficacy from Bandura's (1997) work with a perspective that allows us to examine

[1]University of Nevada, Las Vegas, Las Vegas, NV
[2]Utah State University, Logan, UT

collective functioning from its genesis to its realization, which Vygotsky provides. It is as if we were shining two spotlights from different angles onto the same stage to better illuminate what the classroom participants are playing out through their dialogic interactions.

Sociocultural Theory

A Vygotskian perspective allows us to understand learning and development of the individual as part of a collective. One goal of a sociocultural approach is to make visible relationships between human mental functioning and the cultural, institutional, and historical situations in which this functioning occurs (Wertsch, del Rio, & Alvarez, 1995). Hence, the individual is as much part of the collective as the collective is made up of individuals.

Vygotsky's representation of development presumes "two dimensions of development: one that resides in the individual and the other in the collectivity" (Souza-Lima, 1995, pp. 447–448). Thus, development is not linear, nor is it totally predictable. Learning and development are in a reflexive relationship that is recursive, transformational, and primarily socially enacted. In other words, it involves a transformation of people and the world as they know it through productive activity. In this sense, knowing means to purposefully change the world and oneself, whereas knowledge is the practice of change rather than merely a discrete body of facts, concepts, or rules that can be transferred from one situation to another (Vygotsky, 1978, 1986).

Neo-Vygotskian scholars have examined the notion of distributed cognition to suggest that "human thinking is not reducible to individual properties or traits. Instead, it is always mediated and distributed among persons, artifacts, activities, and settings" (Moll, 2000, p. 265). Along with the construct of distributed cognition, the work of Lave and Wenger (1991) examined how learners in a community of practice shared in the learning process. From their framework of legitimate peripheral participation, learning occurs as newcomers participate in various peripheral roles alongside more experienced or competent members in community practice. In their work together, the less experienced members gradually become able to fully participate in such contexts. As related by Mercer (2000), sociocultural psychologists have primarily examined the shared thinking of adults and children to determine its influence on individual children's development. He suggests that "we should also try to explain children's development as *interthinkers*" by examining how experienced community members act as "discourse guides" as they guide novices into "ways of using language for thinking collectively" (Mercer, 2000, p. 170).

In his construct of the zone of proximal development, Vygotsky (1978) theorized that participants working together to solve a problem are able to accomplish collaboratively what they would not yet be able to do on their own. It is through their dialogic work that classroom participants provide opportunity for students to reformulate problems and possible solutions in their own words. What began as a collective work has the potential to be transformed as students actively internalize the common language and knowledge of the collective. In other words, students who are working together on a shared text in an inquiry-based situation have the opportunity to construct knowledge that has potential for becoming both collective knowledge as well as individual knowledge (Edwards & Mercer, 1987; John-Steiner & Meehan, 2000; Mercer, 2000; Putney, Green, Dixon, Duran, & Yeager, 2000). This pedagogical stance offers opportunities for education to be an avenue for creating a classroom culture in which all students can contribute to the collective knowledge and development (Bruner, 1986). Likewise, this pedagogical stance offers opportunities for a classroom culture in which students can develop self- and collective efficacy. As suggested by Wheatley (2005), researchers can more closely examine this process through direct observation and dialogic interpretation as opposed to self-report surveys.

Self- and Collective Efficacy

Researchers have studied at length the influence of self-efficacy on academic achievement (Bandura, 1993; Goddard, Hoy, & Woolfolk Hoy, 2000; Schunk, 1990), including math and reading achievement (Pajares, 2001; Pajares & Valiante, 2006). In addition, efficacy researchers have focused on the efficacious beliefs of a group and how those beliefs affect performance (cf. Goddard & Goddard, 2001; Tschannen-Moran, Woolfolk Hoy, & Hoy, 1998). Much of this research at the collective level has investigated teacher beliefs for schoolwide student achievement.

However, as noted by Wheatley (2005), several gaps exist in the literature on teacher and collective efficacy. One area that has not yet been closely examined, but is of importance to the present study, is the view that efficacy is a continuous variable, developing over time, rather than a dichotomous, all-or-nothing variable. Another gap is the focus on how to use the efficacy literature in a way that enhances teacher education and the subsequent impact on classroom pedagogy. Also missing from the efficacy research is the opportunity for more democratic teaching practices to be understood. Wheatley (2005) asserted,

> As it is currently operationalized, collective teacher efficacy measures do not clearly assess the co-construction of teaching and learning. Thus, while many "democratic" approaches to education portray some social distribution of agency in teaching, neither teacher efficacy nor collective teacher efficacy measures explicitly assess such agency. (p. 754)

By focusing on how the teacher helps students develop a sense of collective responsibility and belief in their accomplishments, we may begin to help fill one gap in the literature on how collective classroom efficacy can be developed and enhanced through collective action on the part of the classroom members.

In what follows we briefly describe some of the seminal work on self-efficacy in academic settings as well as the more contemporary research on teacher and collective efficacy at the school level. What has been less well defined is the construct of collective efficacy at the micro level of the classroom, which we are calling collective classroom efficacy. The purpose of this study is to begin to explore collective classroom efficacy and how it can be developed and facilitated by the classroom participants. By examining discursive classroom interactions, we will make visible how teachers' instructional practice can promote collective classroom efficacy.

Self-Efficacy

Self-efficacy, as conceptualized by Bandura (1997), is a belief in one's capabilities to organize and accomplish a given task. Students possessing high levels of perceived self-efficacy are more likely to persevere through challenging activities, demonstrate resilience to adversity, have high aspirations, and believe they can accomplish a task (Bandura, 1993; Schunk, 1995). Thus, self-efficacy is task specific and is based in part on past experience. In addition, self-efficacy is linked closely to initial task engagement, persistence, analytical thinking, and successful performance (Bandura, 1993; Pajares, 1996). Compared with less efficacious students, those higher in self-efficacy are more likely to select challenging tasks, expend more effort, and persist when encountering difficulties (Bandura, 1997; Pajares, 1996).

Schunk (2003) cautions that self-efficacy is one of multiple factors influencing academic achievement. When students lack the requisite skills and knowledge, high self-efficacy will not necessarily result in academic achievement. In addition, motivation researchers have found that students who view ability as being changeable with effort and who focus on learning goals rather than on proving their ability to others do not rely on confidence (Dweck, 2000). In other words, students with low efficacy beliefs who also believe that ability can be changed with effort are often just as persistent as those with more confidence (Dweck & Leggett, 1988).

Sources of Self-Efficacy

Bandura (1997) illustrated four sources of self-efficacy: enactive mastery experience, vicarious experience, verbal persuasion, and psychological and affective states. First, enactive mastery experiences are those that provide the most authentic evidence of individual success that then build the belief in personal efficacy. Mastery does not presume that all experiences are immediately successful. Rather, facing some difficulties, enactive mastery experiences can result in resilience with opportunities to learn how to exercise better control over events by encouraging perseverance.

As a second source, vicarious experiences (Bandura, 1997) are those in which individuals may rely on modeling from more proficient others to improve their own capabilities.

Although individuals attempt to maintain a sense of efficacy during a struggle with difficulties, it may be easier to do so if others use the third source, verbal persuasion, to encourage the individual to continue in the task. Through verbal persuasion, individuals may try harder to succeed if the positive appraisal is realistic and they believe that they will be able to produce positive effects through their efforts.

The fourth source of self-efficacy, physiological and affective states, recognizes that people can actually produce a negative performance through their stress reactions to a situation (Bandura, 1997). For example, if students can be persuaded to control emotional reactions through mastery experiences that demonstrate their capabilities, they will be less likely to feel vulnerable in a testing situation. These four sources relate to self-efficacy on an individual basis; however, researchers have expanded their investigations of self-efficacy to examine efficacy as a group construct. In what follows we unfold the definition of collective efficacy as it has been identified currently by researchers.

Collective Efficacy

The construct of self-efficacy has expanded to include individual teacher efficacy and collective efficacy, which focuses on "the performance capability of a social system as a whole" (Bandura, 1997, p. 469). Similar to self-efficacy, collective efficacy relates to the goals of a group and how well members of the group work together toward those goals (Goddard et al., 2004). Collective efficacy also has been associated with the group's resilience and willingness to persist in difficult situations (Goddard, 2002; Goddard & Goddard, 2001; Tschannen-Moran et al., 1998; Woolfolk & Hoy, 1990).

Since collective efficacy has been translated at a school level to individual teachers' judgments concerning the faculty's ability to plan effectively and implement lessons that result in positive student achievement (Goddard, 2001), we now refer to this construct as teacher collective efficacy beliefs. The emphasis of that research has been to identify characteristics and resulting relationships of teachers and schools with high levels of collective efficacy. Although these studies examined teachers' beliefs about their ability to have a positive impact on student academic achievement at a schoolwide level, the measures did not examine whether teachers worked together in a synergistic effort to accomplish that goal (Wheatley, 2005). An additional gap in the teacher collective efficacy beliefs literature is that these studies did not include an examination of the synergistic relationship of teachers and students in classrooms. In general, these sources of self-efficacy relate to the individual and the individual's responses in particular situations according to Bandura's perspective.

Analogous to this rich body of research on teacher collective efficacy beliefs at the macro or school level is the potential of examining how individuals at the micro or classroom level operate both personally and collectively in terms of these sources of self-efficacy. As asserted by Bandura (1993) in studying Vygotsky (1962), "Children's intellectual development cannot be isolated from the social relations within which it is embedded and from its interpersonal effects. It must be analyzed from a social perspective" (p. 120). Therefore, in this research we explore the genesis of collective classroom efficacy through dialogic activities among classroom participants in their social setting.

Teacher as Guide and Community Organizer

To understand the synergistic relationship among teachers and students as it relates to collective classroom efficacy, we need to make visible the role of the teacher in setting expectations for classroom interactions. Vygotsky advocated for the role of the teacher to be one of instructional guide in a classroom in which the teacher and students are active with one another through the curriculum (Vygotsky, 1997). In a similar fashion, Goddard and Goddard (2001) described the role of highly efficacious teachers as one of helping students arrive at appropriate answers without giving them the answer directly. In addition, highly efficacious teachers utilize activities that foster positive affect while promoting high expectations for achievement (Ashton & Webb, 1986). Bandura (1997) noted the role of community organizer in terms of collective efficacy, stating,

> The role of a community organizer is not to solve people's problems for them but to help develop their capabilities to operate as a continuing potent force for bettering their lives and upholding their sense of self-worth and dignity. The organizer serves as the community enabler rather than as the implementer of action plans. (p. 501)

The initial task of community organizer is to select and develop local leaders to unite the collective for a common cause. In the case of democratic classrooms, students serve as local leaders, and the common cause is overall academic achievement and responsibility for self and others. The collective establishes a social community that shapes its efforts to achieve its common academic and personal goals. One primary task of the classroom community organizer is to construct a self-directing collective that unifies, enables, and motivates its participants to recognize that many of their academic issues are shared issues that can be alleviated primarily by working together. Also important is the ability of the classroom community organizer to establish a learning environment where warm interpersonal relationships are constructed throughout the academic and social activities (Ashton & Webb, 1986). Our goal is to illustrate ways in which the classroom teacher becomes classroom community organizer, especially as relating to the development of collective classroom efficacy.

Research Questions

In this article, our purpose is to examine collective classroom efficacy during the classroom collaborative activities and through the interactional discourse, with the teacher in the role of community organizer. As indicated by Moll (2000) normative research often does not capture all of the diversity of life. Indeed, Vygotsky (1986) argued,

> Psychology cannot limit itself to direct evidence.... Psychological inquiry is investigation, and like the criminal investigator, the psychologist must take into account indirect evidence and circumstantial clues—which in practice means that works of art, philosophical arguments and anthropological data are no less important for psychology than direct evidence. (pp. xv–xvi)

Furthermore, Gumperz (2003) argued that survey research attempts to measure objectively constructs such as self- and collective efficacy. However, survey research produces self-report data and does not allow for understanding the dynamic and interactive classroom context surrounding those individuals. In examining classroom key events, we make visible what participants place in the public sphere through their talk and actions. When examined through focused ethnographic inquiry, across events and over time, we begin to build "replicable information on relevant beliefs and values" (Gumperz, 2003, p. 215). These interactions among classroom participants have the potential to make visible a classroom version of collective efficacy as a construct associated with how classroom members view themselves within their classroom collective and in relation to their learning and development with one another.

Our research question to unfold the social construction of collective classroom efficacy was, in what ways can collective classroom efficacy be evidenced through an ethnographic inquiry of interactional discourse? More specifically, how does collective classroom efficacy develop with the teacher as classroom community organizer and students as local leaders?

Method

Participants and Setting

The data for this exploration were culled from an extensive ethnographic data set from one teacher's fifth-grade classroom over four years. The orienting approach of interactional ethnography was selected to frame the study and to make visible the constructed patterns of beliefs and practices over the length of the academic year (Castanheira, Crawford, Green, & Dixon, 2000; Putney et al., 2000). Interactional ethnography also contains a component of sociolinguistic and critical discourse analysis, which makes it possible to examine how these beliefs and practices were constructed in particular moments by members.

The first author was the resident university ethnographer during those four years. The classroom in which this study took place was in an elementary (K-5) public school in partnership with, and located at, an urban university in the southwestern United States. At the time of the data collection, the school was conducted as a year-round school, meaning that the school calendar started the fourth week of August and ran until the second week of August of the next year. Students and teachers were assigned to one of five calendar-based tracks (time periods) that were scheduled to run with periodic three-week breaks scheduled throughout the year.

Of the school's nearly 900 students, 85% were participating in the free and/or reduced lunch program. The official transience rate was 65%, with a school population of 50% Hispanic, 29% Anglo-American, 14% African American, 6% Asian, 1% Native American, 15% special education, and 46% limited English proficient. The particular classroom selected also reflected these demographics. The teacher in this classroom, Ms. Falls, had more than 10 years of experience in urban elementary classroom settings and was well known by her colleagues as a teacher who incorporated inclusive practices with excellent classroom management techniques.

Table 1 Domain Analysis: X Is What Teacher Holds Constant in the Classroom Setting

Classroom management	Class election of executive council
Personal accountability	Constructing a class constitution
	Constructing norms
	Authentic class jobs
	Team and individual responsibilities
	Work ethic rubric
	Role models for the school
	Really getting to know each other
	Goal setting and extending
	Bottomliners—respect, responsibility, caring, collaboration
Teacher role	Guide
	Leader
	Facilitator
	Initiator
Student role	Problem solving
	Asking probing questions
	Clarifying for each other
	Supporting ideas with evidence
	Negotiating meaning
	Valuing and supporting each other
	Responsibly governing

Data Analysis

The classroom events in the four year data set had been videotaped on a regular basis: daily for the first three weeks of the school year then at least twice monthly thereafter. At the teacher's request, additional videotaping, interviewing, and data sessions took place to capture particular classroom activities. Anecdotal evidence across the four years suggested that this classroom teacher was consistently successful in fostering a strong sense of interdependence among students as an avenue in building a democratic classroom. For example, we encountered comments about how well the "class ran itself" from classroom visitors, other classroom teachers at the same school, the principal, and substitute teachers who left notes to the classroom teacher and in interviews with preservice teachers.

In examining the entire data set, we looked for evidence beyond the anecdotal data that could theoretically illustrate the construct of interest to us, collective classroom efficacy. After selecting the data set from Year 4 as a telling case, or one that makes visible a theoretical construct (Mitchell, 1984), we further examined that data set for examples that illustrated different elements of collective classroom efficacy. We selected the classroom as the unit of analysis because from a Vygotskian perspective, development takes place both as an individual as well as collective process. In addition, we were examining interactions among teacher and students that added to the knowledge base of both individuals and the collective unit as suggested by Edwards and Mercer (1987).

We examined field notes, interview transcripts, and video data to construct the telling case of developing collective classroom efficacy. We relied on various formats of triangulation. In one aspect of triangulation, the data analysis consisted of utilizing both primary and secondary researchers (Putney & Broughton, 2007). The first author as classroom ethnographer could bring forward the context of the classroom because of her past experience of researching with the classroom teacher. The secondary researcher brought forward her expertise as a former classroom teacher as well as her researcher lens in examining data that she did not collect but with which she became highly familiar. Bringing together these distinct yet complementary angles of vision allowed us to validate the findings and co-construct the telling case through our dialogic interactions about the data.

A second aspect of triangulation involved juxtaposing different forms of data from the data set. For example, we purposefully selected an interview with the teacher that revealed her teaching philosophy. We then chose a segment of classroom interaction from the first days of school involving the teacher and students discussing the construction of the classroom norms that reflected her democratic teaching philosophy. To examine more closely the democratic interdependence among classroom participants, we chose a particular activity, Visible and Invisible Walls, as a series of discursive events in one related content area of social studies. This multileveled analysis demonstrates the format of instruction, the teacher role and expectations, and participant interactions as a form of triangulation.

The field notes and transcripts were coded for evidence of the co-construction of collective classroom efficacy through both interpersonal and academic events. Juxtaposing the social skill building against the academic knowledge building within key classroom events becomes what we are calling dialogic triangulation. This micro analysis makes visible the potential for co-construction of the interdependence and shared academic knowledge among classroom participants.

The ethnographic data across four years with this classroom teacher indicate that she held certain classroom values constant as cornerstones of her curriculum and classroom management. At the same time the particular content changed each year as students jointly constructed knowledge together in the classroom. The domain analysis (Table 1) illustrates the values related to classroom management, personal accountability, teacher role, and student role that the teacher held in common across the four years.

As part of her role as community organizer, the teacher gradually shifted the classroom management over time from teacher-driven to a student-led governance system in which they jointly constructed their norms for living and working together. Although the community each year began to solidify by the third week of school, they continually reviewed their norms and assessed their behavior and their academic work on a regular basis using a "work ethic rubric" scale from zero to four (Putney, 2007). By keeping these classroom values constant, the teacher maintained a classroom style that supported a strong community identity through personal and academic accountability.

Although the value of student governance stayed relatively constant across the four years, what changed year by year was the curricular focus of the major classroom project. These projects consisted of conducting classroom businesses in Years 1 and 2, with a shift in focus to an interest apprenticeship program in Year 3 in which students worked with local community mentors to improve their artistic skills. The focus in Year 4, illustrated in this article, was Visible and Invisible Walls: Examining Tolerance, to examine the use of walls throughout history to oppress people. Across the four years, even though the curricular focus changed, what did not change was the teacher's insistence that students work together responsibly to construct their learning.

We selected Year 4 because of the richness of the data set in relation to the construct of classroom collective efficacy. We surveyed data across the year and initially constructed domains of activity that related to the following themes: developing classroom community, establishing norms, teacher role, student role, life skills (respect, responsibility, caring, and collaboration), types of learning activities, and developing tolerance. From the initial domains, we further analyzed the data to see what the elements within the domains had in common. The common elements formed into subsets that we placed into tree diagrams or taxonomies, in

particular one related to participant roles that subsumed both domains of teacher and student roles.

As we examined the teacher role in more detail, we began to notice a trend supporting Bandura's notion of the role of community organizer as part of collective classroom efficacy. These roles included developing self-improvement capabilities, upholding sense of self-worth and dignity, serving as the community facilitator, constructing a self-directing collective, promoting unity, and motivating interdependence in solving shared issues. Although Bandura initiated the construct of community organizer in a more global sense, we could see the application of such at the classroom level. In the results section, we illustrate how the teacher in the classroom was enacting the characteristics of community organizer while promoting individual and collective learning and development (Putney et al., 2000; Vygotsky, 1986). We further examined the synergistic effort among classroom participants in co-constructing an interdependent classroom community.

Results

We examined the role of teacher as community organizer because this role is central to fostering a sense of collective among the individual members of the group (Bandura, 1997). Data from an interview with the teacher about her teaching philosophy illustrated her role as a classroom community organizer. As detailed by Bandura, a community organizer is one who does not seek to solve people's problems. What the community organizer does is to foster capabilities of the members by promoting self-worth and dignity. The community organizer must also foster local leaders who can unite the collective for a common cause. In the case of Ms. Falls, we quickly recognized her take-up of the role of community organizer, as will be made visible in the following excerpt from her interview:

> This is my definition, based on what I do. My classroom is one that develops, nurtures, and extends the social and academic potentials and interests of all members within the class. It is a place that encourages autonomy, respect, and accountability through active participation with our diverse environment. [My classroom] values what one thinks, cares how one feels, and supports student learning experiences. . . . Let the children develop the life skills authentically. Respect is giving it, expecting it, not about writing a poem. You can write a poem, yes, but live it! The ones I really insist they have from day one are *respect, responsibility, cooperation,* and *caring.*

This excerpt reveals the primary emphasis on social and academic success of the individuals within the classroom as well as for the collective in general, which is a central tenet of the construct of collective classroom efficacy. In addition, this construct consists of a goal orientation, which Ms. Falls facilitates among the students in the collective by encouraging autonomy, building respect, and expecting accountability at both the individual and collective levels. The way in which she claims to promote achievement of these goals is by having students actively participating in authentic activities that foster life skills. This is brought forward in her statement that respect is not just talked about and enacted but actually lived throughout their school experience. Expectations are that students will live this within her classroom as well as in other academic and social contexts. Ms. Falls's claims and expectations that emanate from her philosophy are evidenced throughout the following analytic segments.

Norms and Work Ethic Rubric

From a prior ethnographic study of this classroom (Putney, 2007), we recognize that Ms. Falls commonly established a social structure in which students made responsible choices about how they would work to become productive classroom citizens. Through the norms and work ethic rubric, she established a social framework or set of practices that required students to demonstrate responsibility toward self and others while becoming academically proficient.

Following her own philosophy and as the classroom community organizer, Ms. Falls co-constructed classroom norms with her students beginning the first day of the school year. As she stated to students at the onset of the norm construction activity, "We don't have rules, boys and girls, we have norms. Norms are ways that people live and work together. These become our guidelines for how we will act in this classroom community" (Field notes, Day 2 of school). When she began the discussion about what the norms might be, she reminded students of her "bottomliners" of respect, responsibility, caring, and collaboration. They constructed norms related to listening with respect; being responsible, organized, and persevering; and respecting opinions of others and believing that you can do whatever you need to do if you follow through (Putney, 2007).

The norms constructed by the students in this case highlighted the notion of continuing to work toward their goals by emphasizing "persevere at all times" to Norm 2 that related to being responsible and organized from the previous year. Recall that a central tenet of efficacy is one's belief in the ability to attain a goal, no matter how challenging. By emphasizing the notion of perseverance, the students were establishing the foundation for developing academic efficacy through their everyday work together. Although the norms were individually directed, they also became collectively oriented as students used them to encourage one another to respect everyone's opinions and to carry on when the work was difficult. The following excerpts make visible how the teacher continued in her role of community organizer to foster a sense of collective efficacy among the individual members of the group.

Self-Worth, Unity, and Interdependence

"Take an intelligent risk ... we should learn and stretch ourselves. Is that what I hear you saying?" (Ms. Falls, field notes, Day 2 of class). Ms. Falls consistently encouraged her students to take academic risks as a central feature of building collective efficacy in this classroom. In her role of classroom community organizer, Ms. Falls set the expectation that students would take an intelligent risk when participating in learning activities. At the same time, she held the expectation that students would contribute to the knowledge base by helping each other solve common issues.

The first example is one that we deemed typical of the type of interactions that took place in this classroom over the year. A common classroom practice was for students to review their norms each morning to monitor their progress in constructively working together. A new student, Jordan, had just transferred in to the school. In this excerpt the discourse reveals a common practice of students inviting each other to take a risk and participate in the learning activity with the more knowledgeable other offering assistance. The excerpt begins with the Mayor, Jaz, calling on a new student, Jordan, to explain one of the norms that they review in class each morning.

In leading the discussion, Jaz encouraged Jordan to take a risk and make sense of one of the norms (Table 2, Lines 105–108) and then offered assistance from a more experienced other in the class if he could not provide an answer (110–111). Once Jordan offered an explanation (112–113), David acknowledged Jordan's response (114) and offered additional information for the class (115–117). From a Vygotskian perspective, this is an example of intersubjectivity as classroom members offered explanations for the benefit of all in the collective to take up and use individually in making meaning from the text under discussion.

In the beginning days of constructing this classroom culture, this type of incident would have been initiated by the teacher in her role as classroom community organizer. By the time that this example occurred (six weeks into the first semester), the students were enacting the expectations established collectively during the first days of school. When the new student, Jordan, struggled to answer a question, Jaz encouraged him to ask for "a lifesaver." To be a lifesaver, you would first have to be actively listening so that you could offer a potential answer to the relevant question put before the class. As a lifesaver, it was expected that you would not say that a person was wrong because that would stop them from learning. Instead, students (as in the case of David above) were expected to build on what the other person said so that their answer added to the discussion while taking nothing away from the other students.

The concept of lifesaver utilizes three of the features of community organizers. It serves the purpose of upholding students' sense of self-worth and dignity while also

Table 2 Taking a Risk

Actor	Line	Dialogue	Vygotskian construct
Jaz	105	Jordan	Personalizing the learning; invoking historicity in reviewing the norms each day; connecting learning day to day
	106	can you please explain norm number two	
	107	don't say can't	
	108	you can do it if you put your mind to it	
Jordan	109	[hesitates before attempting an answer]	New student maybe has not yet internalized completely
Jaz	110	you can ask for a lifesaver Jordan	More knowledgeable other may assist if needed
	111	but first try it on your own	
Jordan	112	if you say you can do it	Offers explanation to the extent he has made sense of the idea
	113	you can	
David	114	adding to what Jordan just said	Offers additional information to be considered; puts ideas in the intersubjective space for all to access if they choose
	115	if you say you can't do something	
	116	then you send a message to your mind	
	117	that stops you from learning	

promoting unity and motivating interdependence in solving shared issues (Bandura, 1997). What is evident in this interchange among Jaz, Jordan, and David is that the students have embraced the concept of lifesaver and used it themselves in their discussions. They acknowledged that a newer student might not have a complete understanding of the question posed; however, they encouraged him to take an intelligent risk while still offering the option to request assistance (lifesaver) from another student. In addition, David extended the answer given by Jordan, thus he upheld the others' sense of trust while working interdependently in solving shared issues. The discourse suggests that taking intelligent risks and striving to establish and maintain trust during classroom activities contribute to the development of collective classroom efficacy.

The developmental aspect of collective classroom efficacy is made visible by following the concept of lifesaver throughout the academic year as a tracer unit (Putney et al., 2000). In the following excerpt, we further illustrate how the concept of lifesaver actually occurred during a classroom academic discussion (in the 10th week of school) surrounding a topic that had been introduced the day prior. In this example, a question was posed to the students related to a new word, *perpetrator*. The teacher posed the question, and when the answers given were acknowledged as approaching the appropriate answer, a female student (Tanya) suggested that a lifesaver was perhaps in order (Table 3).

As in the previous example, we recognize that the students have accepted the concept of lifesaver as being an appropriate way to answer a question when someone is searching for the meaning of the question. In this excerpt, the student, Tanisha, acknowledged that Matthew's answer is approaching the meaning of the word, perpetrator (Line 233). Ms. Falls encouraged Matthew (234–236) to continue his line

of thinking by rephrasing the question (237–239). When he hesitated to answer, Tanya offered the possibility of using a lifesaver (240). The teacher acknowledged the request for a lifesaver and sought someone to take on the role (241). When Adriana raised her hand, Tanya called on her to offer an answer (242), with the teacher offering encouragement (246).

The interchange between Adriana and Tanya illustrates how the teacher as community organizer motivated interdependence among students as they solved the shared problem of understanding the concept of perpetrator. From a Vygotskian perspective, this happens in the zone of proximal development when a more experienced other provides hints or suggestions or prompts to assist in the learning. In this case, the students were taking on the role rather than relying completely on the teacher to initiate such a form of scaffolding. This handing over of the role of more knowledgeable other by the teacher was part of her classroom management plan that stems from her value system.

In addition, this example suggests that the teacher helped students maintain their sense of dignity and self-worth as they took risks, asked for a lifesaver, and then shared their ideas about this new vocabulary word. As community facilitator, the teacher kept the discussion student centered rather than teacher directed to encourage students to work together to solve the common issue. As the school year progressed, students were more willing to take intelligent risks and to ask for or offer lifesavers to help the individual and the collective reach their academic goals.

Self-Improving and Self-Directing Collective

In the following excerpt we look at additional roles of the teacher as community organizer: developing self-improvement capabilities, constructing a self-directing collective,

Table 3 Calling for a Lifesaver in Week 10

Actor	Line	Dialogue	Research comments
Ms. Falls	225	What's a perpetrator?	Teacher linking back to prior day's discussion
Jamal	226	Is that a traitor?	Jamal attempts although absent day prior
Ms. Falls	227	Not quite, not quite	Teacher signaling need for another response, nods toward Matthew
	228	A perpetrator	
Matthew	229	What I think a perpetrator is	Matthew uses terms from prior day's discussion but not quite the correct answer, tries to self-correct, still not quite the right answer
	230	is a person who crosses the	
	231	uh his own boundary	
	232	his or her own boundary	
Tanisha	233	Almost	Tanisha encouraging Matthew
Ms. Falls	234	Almost	Teacher reiterates encouraging response of Tanisha and adds to it
	235	you're real close	
	236	you're real close	
Ms. Falls	237	What other boundary do they cross	Teacher reiterates the question with a hint about the other boundary
	238	the perpetrator?	
	239	There's another boundary they cross	
Tanya	240	Lifesaver	Tanya suggests that student can ask for help from another student
Ms. Falls	241	Who wants to be a lifesaver?	Teacher calling for student to help
Tanya	242	Adriana	Adriana and others with hands raised
Adriana	243	A perpetrator is somebody who	Adriana responds with her definition using the prior day's terms
	244	will cross their own boundary	
	245	plus another person's boundary	
Ms. Falls	246	Right, great	Teacher verifying response

while continuing to promote unity and motivate interdependence. In addition we examine the tracer unit of lifesaver as a telling case of development of collective classroom efficacy. The classroom activity, Visible and Invisible Walls, was initiated by the teacher to have students investigate the meaning of tolerance by examining the acts of intolerance represented by the walls. Several walls were discussed in class and chosen by the students for in-depth research projects to be presented by the citizens in February, Week 25 of the school year. Examples of the physical walls that were to be studied through use of the Internet over the course of the next month were the Berlin Wall, the Great Wall of China, and the Vietnam Memorial in D.C. The invisible walls were examples of discrimination such as the Aboriginal Wall and the Nelson Mandela Wall (see, e.g., Talking Walls Software).

For the Visible and Invisible Walls project, students were assigned to small groups and chose which particular wall they intended to study. Over the course of several weeks, they used nonfiction texts, almanacs, the Talking Walls Software, and Internet resources to construct a poster or PowerPoint presentation. Their presentation was to contain information about the wall they researched as well as the process they used to conduct the research. On the day of presentations, Ms. Falls set expectations for participation of all students during the activity. Ms. Falls had asked for students in the audience to be "critical friends." In her words, she asked them to "listen with a critical ear, not a criticizing ear, a researcher's ear." After each presentation Ms. Falls asked the other students to offer feedback in the form of helpful critique.

One group finished their presentation, answering questions about the topic from fellow students as well as the teacher. When the next group proceeded with their presentation on the Aboriginal Wall, it quickly became apparent that they were not as well prepared with their topic knowledge.

With each advancing point in their presentation, questions from fellow students went unanswered by the group members.

The teacher asked for constructive feedback from the class members who had been listening to the presentation. Given that one of the common teaching practices in this classroom was to ask "probing questions, ones that make you answer why," it was not surprising that a female student, Anna, suggested, "You should have known Ms. Falls was going to ask questions. You should have spent more time studying your notes and looking over your presentations, and you should have worked together so that everyone knew what was being talked about." Other students offered productive critiques of the group's knowledge base. For example, Tomas stated, "You needed to understand the meanings of the words you presented." Shaylon offered, "You should have helped each other with pronunciation. When one of you didn't know how to say a word, another should have helped." Another female student, Cristina, offered, "Why don't you do another presentation, so go home and study over track break."

The discussion then moved to reflection on the part of the group members who made the Aboriginal Walls presentation. As with each presentation, the students rated themselves on a rubric of zero to four, with zero meaning that they interfered with someone's learning and a four meaning that they worked together collaboratively to improve their learning. The group rated themselves a one, meaning that they were working individually with not much comprehension. One student observer gave them credit for making an attempt and suggested that a two was more appropriate; however, Barbara stated that she respected their decision to give themselves a one and praised them for not attempting to rate themselves a three. The class settled on a one and one half effort grade but suggested that the group be allowed to present again after their upcoming break from school to improve their score.

Ms. Falls restated, "You did show some effort, but you have lots of work to do, don't you? You had suggestions from the community . . ." The Aboriginal Walls group members responded, "We need to work together and help each other," "We should help each other with the words," and "We should study over track break." In this example, the role of the classroom community organizer was to help students develop self-improvement capabilities by refocusing their efforts to improve their understanding of their particular topic and how it related to the larger focus on tolerance.

What is interesting is that the students themselves offered specific and productive input and encouraged the group to work together and try again to improve on their presentation so that all could be successful. This encouragement illustrates the development of the concept of lifesaver as well as the development of collective classroom efficacy. During the initial days of school, lifesaver took the form of taking intelligent risk and being offered help from another. Further into the school year, the use of lifesaver developed into explicitly requesting assistance from others. Toward the end of the school year, students commonly used lifesaver implicitly as part of their interactional discourse during classroom activities.

This collaborative effort suggests that students were likely to be focused on the academic success of the entire class since they strongly encouraged their peers to achieve the academic goal of the collective. As explained previously, a central tenet of Ms. Falls's teaching philosophy was to construct a self-directed classroom collective. Ms. Falls initiated this goal by positioning students as audience members to be critical friends and offer constructive feedback to one another.

The feedback from the other class members provides further evidence of the developing self-directed classroom collective. For example, the classmates in the audience suggested to the small group members that they should have been better prepared to present their work and to work together over school break so that they could present again on return to school. This suggestion gave the group an opportunity to improve on their presentation and also to improve their grade for the project. Ms. Falls supported the audience members in encouraging the small group to work on their project during school break. She, in turn, supported the small group by taking up the audience suggestion of giving them a second opportunity. She reminded them that they still have work to do and that they can be successful if they follow the suggestions given.

Discussion and Implications

Bandura's (1997) construct of collective efficacy was initialized at a global community level. As shown in our review of the literature, researchers narrowed the field to examine collective efficacy at the schoolwide level. Our intention is to extend the literature by further narrowing the field in examining collective efficacy at the classroom level by placing classroom in the center of the construct. In applying the construct in this way, the classroom teacher takes on Bandura's community organizer role, thus facilitating classroom interdependence as an avenue for developing collective classroom efficacy.

In this article, we bring forward the notion of collective classroom efficacy as a social construct that can be developed over time as opposed to being viewed as a dichotomous variable. From a Vygotskian (1986) perspective, development is not a phased phenomenon but rather a dynamic and reciprocal process in which individuals utilize thoughts and ideas placed into the intersubjective space through interactive classroom activities, thus making personal sense through interactions with others. Through her role as community organizer, the teacher paved the way for the social and academic interplay among students of various skill levels. Over time their interactions resulted in a shared sense of efficacy across the different learning activities.

Our purpose in examining this telling case of one elementary classroom is to provide an understanding of how collective classroom efficacy evolves over time through classroom interaction and how classroom teachers may act as community organizers in actuating the developing collective classroom efficacy. From this perspective, collective classroom efficacy, much like classroom literacy, "is not a generic process or state of being but a continual expansion of practices, a continual dynamic development" (Putney, 1996, p. 130). A further goal was to provide a perspective that teachers and researchers can use to examine the local and historical practices that shape collective classroom efficacy.

Through the data analysis, in particular the dialogic triangulation of social skill building and academic knowledge building, we illustrated how the construct of collective classroom efficacy can be co-constructed as a reciprocal process. The sense of collective classroom efficacy that we illustrated went beyond the social aspect of belonging to a group because the sense of belonging was also related to academic goals. The teacher actively encouraged students to take intelligent risks as they worked to achieve their academic and interpersonal goals, which has been established as a cornerstone of self-efficacy (Bandura, 1997). She further fostered capabilities of the members by promoting self-worth and dignity through the use of the classroom norms. As local leaders, students took on the role of uniting the collective for a common cause of encouraging autonomy, respect, and academic accountability. This synergistic unification of academic and social accountability mirrors the synergy of teacher efficacy and student efficacy that can lead to collective classroom efficacy.

In a society steeped in the individual race to the top with proof of ability testing, the notion of collective classroom efficacy exemplifies the need for more research examining a community-oriented notion of efficacy. The existing literature on teacher efficacy and self-efficacy, and even collective efficacy, is individually oriented (Wheatley, 2005). However, it is possible that research on efficacy can involve a more inclusive approach to determine how classroom participants view themselves in relation to others in developing collective classroom efficacy. The examination of teacher as efficacious community organizer via the characteristics offered by Bandura (1997) led us to theorize the unification of teacher and student self-efficacy in dialogic reciprocal relationship as the foundation of collective classroom efficacy. More research is warranted to establish this relationship definitively and to examine the influence of collective classroom efficacy on student achievement.

A limitation of this study was that it involved data collected from one elementary classroom. As such, it could be inferred that collective classroom efficacy was the result of the work of an exemplary teacher and cannot be generalized to other classrooms. However, as we worked through the data and saw an ever-increasing example of how this teacher took up the role that Bandura (1997) recognized as community organizer, we could not help but consider that these data could be reminiscent of other classrooms as well. This suggests that further research needs to be conducted for cases from other classroom settings, grade levels, and types of schools to investigate further the role of teachers and students in constructing collective classroom efficacy.

As Renshaw (2007) argued, in a commentary related to similar types of studies, this format of addressing teachers and practitioners in this way invites them "to draw upon their own recollections of similar voices and experiences" (p. 244). In addition, he noted that such studies "are designed to persuade teachers that it is possible to transform any classroom into a relational learning community" (p. 244). In a similar vein, we add to this commentary that this study of Ms. Falls's classroom is designed to illustrate what it takes for classroom teachers to transform their classrooms into ones that develop a sense of collective classroom efficacy.

The implications of this study indicate that, as Bandura (1997) suggested for schoolwide collective efficacy, the role of community organizer becomes a critical aspect for development of collective classroom efficacy as well. In conjunction with Bandura's perspective, Vygotsky's (1978, 1986) view of individual and collective development provided the lens for us to illustrate how classroom members can develop a sense of collective classroom efficacy. They do so as they work together to construct common knowledge in the intersubjective public classroom space and to set and achieve academic goals. Based on the findings of this investigation, some ways in which teachers can serve as community organizers in pursuit of collective classroom efficacy include encouraging informed risk taking by (a) creating a sense of belonging, (b) setting and working toward personal and academic goal attainment, (c) taking responsibility for self and others' learning, and (d) believing in individual and collective capabilities.

References

Ashton, P. T., & Webb, R. B. (1986). *Making a difference: Teacher's sense of efficacy and student achievement.* New York, NY: Longman.

Bandura, A. (1993). Perceived self-efficacy in cognitive development and functioning. *Educational Psychologist, 28,* 117–148.

Bandura, A. (1997). *Self-efficacy: The exercise of control.* New York, NY: W.H. Freeman & Co.

Bruner, J. (1986). *Actual minds, possible worlds.* Cambridge, MA: Harvard University Press.

Castanheira, M. L., Crawford, T., Green, J., & Dixon, C. (2000). Interactional ethnography: An approach to studying the social construction of literate practices. *Linguistics and Education, 11*(4), 295–420.

Dweck, C. S. (2000). *Self-theories: Their role in motivation, personality, and development.* Philadelphia, PA: Taylor & Francis.

Dweck, C. S., & Leggett, E. L. (1988). A social-cognitive approach to motivation and personality. *Psychological Review, 95,* 256–273.

Edwards, D., & Mercer, N. (1987). *Common knowledge: The development of understanding in the classroom.* Cambridge, MA: Routledge.

Goddard, R. D. (2001). Collective efficacy: A neglected construct in the study of schools and student achievement. *Journal of Educational Psychology, 93*(3), 467–476.

Goddard, R. D. (2002). A theoretical and empirical analysis of the measurement of collective efficacy: The development of a short form. *Educational and Psychological Measurement, 62*(1), 97–110.

Goddard, R. D., & Goddard, Y. L. (2001). A multilevel analysis of the relationship between teacher and collective efficacy in urban schools. *Teaching and Teacher Education, 17,* 807–818.

Goddard, R. D., Hoy, W. K., & Hoy, A. W. (2004). Collective efficacy beliefs: Theoretical developments, empirical evidence, and future directions. *Educational Researcher, 33*(3), 3–13.

Goddard, R. D., Hoy, W. K., & Woolfolk Hoy, A. (2000). Collective efficacy: Its meaning, measure, and impact on student achievement. *American Educational Research Journal, 37,* 479–508.

Gumperz, J. J. (2003). Interactional sociolinguistics: A personal perspective. In D. T. D. Schiffrin & H. E. Hamilton (Eds.), *The handbook of discourse analysis* (pp. 215–228). Malden, MA: Blackwell.

John-Steiner, V. P., & Meehan, T. M. (2000). Creativity and collaboration in knowledge construction. In C. D. Lee & P. Smagorinsky (Eds.), *Vygotskian perspectives on literacy research. Constructing meaning through collaborative inquiry* (pp. 31–50). New York, NY: Cambridge University Press.

Lave, J., & Wenger, E. (1991). *Situated learning: Legitimate peripheral participation.* Cambridge, UK: Cambridge University Press.

Mercer, N. (2000). *Words and minds: How we use language to think together.* London, UK: Routledge.

Mitchell, J. C. (1984). Case studies. In R. F. Ellen (Ed.), *Ethnographic research: A guide to general conduct* (pp. 237–241). San Diego, CA: Academic Press.

Moll, L. (2000). inspired by Vygotsky: Ethnographic experiments in education. In C. D. Lee & P. Smagorinsky (Eds.), *Vygotskian perspectives on literacy research: Constructing meaning through collaborative inquiry* (pp. 256–268). New York, NY: Cambridge University Press.

Pajares, F. (1996). Self efficacy beliefs in academic settings. *Review of Educational Research, 66,* 543–578.

Pajares, F. (2001). Toward a positive psychology of academic motivation. *Journal of Educational Research, 95,* 27–35.

Pajares, F., & Valiante, G. (2006). Self efficacy beliefs and motivation in writing development. In C. A. MacArthur, S. Graham, & J. Fitzgerald (Eds.), *Handbook of writing research* (pp. 158–170). New York, NY: Guildford.

Putney, L. G. (1996). You are it: Meaning making as a collective and historical process. *Australian Journal of Language and Literacy, 19,* 129–143.

Putney, L. G. (2007). Discursive practices as cultural resources: Formulating identities for individual and collective in an inclusive classroom setting. *International Journal of Educational Research, 46,* 129–140.

Putney, L. G., & Broughton, S. H. (2007, April). *Exploring collective efficacy opportunities available through juxtaposition of primary and secondary data analysis.* Paper presented at the American Educational Research Association annual conference, Chicago, IL.

Putney, L. G., Green, J. L., Dixon, C. N., Duran, R., & Yeager, B. (2000). Consequential progressions: Exploring collective-individual development in a bilingual classroom. In C. D. Lee & P. Smagorinsky (Eds.), *Vygotskian perspectives on literacy research: Constructing meaning through collaborative inquiry* (pp. 86–126). New York, NY: Cambridge University Press.

Renshaw, P. D. (2007). A commentary on the chronotopes of different "cultures of learning": Transforming classrooms from trading-places into relational-places of learning. *International Journal of Educational Research, 46,* 240–245.

Schunk, D. H. (1990). Goal setting and self efficacy during self-regulated learning. *Educational Psychologist, 25,* 71–86.

Schunk, D. H. (1995). Self-efficacy and education and instruction. In J. E. Maddux (Ed.), *Self-efficacy, adaptation, and adjustment: Theory, research, and application* (pp. 281–303). New York, NY: Plenum.

Schunk, D. H. (2003). Self efficacy for reading and writing: Influence of modeling, goal setting, and self-evaluation. *Reading & Writing Quarterly, 19,* 159–172.

Souza L. E. (1995). Culture revisited: Vygotsky's ideas in Brazil. *Anthropology and Education Quarterly, 26*(4), 443–457.

Talking Walls Software Series [Computer software]. Redmond, WA: Edmark.

Tschannen-Moran, M., Woolfolk Hoy, A., & Hoy, W. K. (1998). Teacher efficacy: Its meaning and measure. *Review of Educational Research, 68,* 202–248.

Vygotsky, L. S. (1978). *Mind in society: The development of higher psychological processes.* Cambridge, MA: Harvard University Press.

Vygotsky, L. S. (1986). *Thought and language.* Cambridge, MA: MIT Press.

Vygotsky, L. S. (1997). *Educational psychology* (R. Silverman, Trans.). Boca Raton, FL: St. Lucie Press.

Wertsch, J. V., del Rio, P., & Alvarez, A. (1995). Socio-cultural studies: History, action, and mediation. In J. V. Wertsch, P. del Rio, & A. Alvarez (Eds.), *Socio-cultural studies of mind* (pp. 1–36). Cambridge, UK: Cambridge University Press.

Wheatley, K. F. (2005). The case of reconceptualizing teacher efficacy research. *Teaching and Teacher Education, 21,* 747–766.

Woolfolk, A. E., & Hoy, W. K. (1990). Prospective teachers' sense of efficacy and beliefs about control. *Journal of Educational Psychology, 82,* 81–91.

Critical Thinking

1. What do conversations contribute to classroom communities?
2. How does the teacher serve as organizer?
3. What techniques can the teacher use?
4. Why are promoting and participating important in shared efficacy?

LeAnn G. Putney coauthored *A Vision of Vygotsky,* a book relating Vygotskian theories to pedagogy for teachers. Her ethnographic research of diverse classroom activity has been published in *Journal of Classroom Interaction, International Journal of Educational Research,* and *TESOL Journal,* among others. Suzanne H. Broughton researches emotion's influence on conceptual, attitude, and belief change. Her investigations of refutational text interventions for conceptual change are published in the *Journal of Educational Research.*

She also researches development of collective classroom efficacy through classroom community practices.

Funding—The author(s) received no financial support for the research and/or authorship of this article.

Declaration of Conflicting Interests—The author(s) declared no potential conflicts of interests with respect to the authorship and/or publication of this article.

Meeting ACTFL/NCATE Accreditation Standards: What World Language Teacher Candidates Reveal about Program Preparation

FREDDIE A. BOWLES

Introduction

Future teachers of a foreign language must know how to speak another language well, but speaking another language is only one aspect of teaching it. Future teachers must also know how to teach their language for candidate learning. Foreign language teachers use language to teach language, so they are learning a language and learning how to teach it.

Foreign language teacher candidates in one mid-south state have several K-12 licensure options. They can complete a traditional four-year program, a fifth-year masters program, or a state sponsored non-traditional two-year program. Licensed teachers may also add foreign language to their initial license through the ALP, Additional Licensure Plan. A traditional licensure program with four years of undergraduate classes combines content, pedagogy, and candidate teaching. The practical experience of candidate teaching lasts one semester for the undergraduate degree. A fifth-year program combines pedagogy with a year-long internship or with a concurrent program that offers pedagogy classes to employed teachers. In this state, the state department of education offers a non-traditional two-year program in which candidates enroll in an intensive pedagogy program for two three-week sessions in two summers and nine Saturday sessions for two years during the academic years with on-the-job training as in-service practicing teacher. The institution hosting this investigation offers a fifth-year Master of Arts in Teaching (MAT) degree, which entails a three-semester program combining classes in pedagogy and methods of instruction with a two-semester, three-rotation internship. Teacher candidates spend a total of 33 weeks in a public school level at three different locales including middle, junior, and senior high schools in two large school districts and one rural school district.

The state requires national accreditation for tertiary institutions that offer programs of study for licensure. Every seven years, the National Council on Accreditation of Teacher Education (NCATE) assesses all college or university programs of study for any area of public school teaching, prekindergarten/elementary to secondary, in all content areas. The state department of education wants to know if future teachers are prepared to be highly-qualified, effective public school teachers.

In order to verify that candidates are indeed well-versed in their content areas and graduate with strong pedagogical and practical foundations, NCATE visits tertiary campuses every seven years to collect evidence that programs are meeting the standards established by their Specialized Professional Associations (SPAs). This evidence is the "joint responsibility of foreign language and education faculty if these are in different departments/colleges" (Phillips, ArACTE, 2008), which is the case at this institution.

In 2002, the American Council on the Teaching of Foreign Languages (ACTFL), the Specialized Professional Association (SPA) for foreign languages, established the Program Standards for the Preparation of Foreign Language Teachers to ensure that teacher candidates meet NCLB's requirements of "highly qualified," which include a bachelor's degree and "competence in all the academic subjects in which the teacher teaches based on a high objective uniform state standards of evaluation" set by the state and aligned with the state's student academic achievement standards (Berk, 2005, p. 16). NCATE approved the standards the same year.

Six assessments are required as evidence for meeting the ACTFL/NCATE standards. At the researcher's university, two of these assessments are generated from the content areas of French, German, and Spanish in the World

Languages, Literatures, and Cultures Department (WLLC) housed in the College of Arts and Sciences. The remaining four assessments originate from the Department of Curriculum and Instruction, housed in the College of Education and Health Professions (COEHP). Two additional assessments are optional and may be collected from either department.

The two ACTFL program standards that apply to the foreign language content areas are Standard 1: Language, Linguistics, Comparisons; and Standard 2: Cultures, Literatures, Cross-Disciplinary Concepts. Standard 1 includes three sub-standards: 1a) Demonstrating Language Proficiency, 1b) Understanding Linguistics, and 1c) Identifying Language Comparisons. Standard 2 also includes three sub-standards, but only two are applicable for the WLLC department: 2a) Demonstrating Cultural Understandings and 2b) Demonstrating Understanding of Literary and Cultural Texts and Traditions.

Because of the recent implementation of the ACTFL/NCATE standards, the research is mostly limited to collaboration and data collection between departments (Glisan, Smith-Sherwood, McDaniel, & Brooks, 2007; Colville-Hall, Fonseca-Greber, Cavour, 2007; McAlpine & Dhonau, 2007; McAlpine & Shrum, 2007).

An overlooked and critical component of the teacher preparation process concerns many undergraduate candidates who want to become foreign language teachers. Specifically, do they consider their undergraduate preparation sufficient for teaching a foreign language at the secondary level? To find out more about what candidates know, the researcher created a survey based on the two ACTFL/NCATE assessment standards for the WLLC Department asking for candidates' perceptions on how well they consider their program of study to meet the ACTFL standards for preparing candidates to teach a foreign language.

Methodology

This investigation helps determine how well a WLLC department prepares future teachers in the three common languages: French, German, and Spanish. A self-report, Likert-scaled instrument was designed to assess participants' knowledge of their undergraduate preparation in addressing ACTFL teacher preparation program standards 1 and 2. Survey results were informally compared and contrasted to candidate scores on their Oral Proficiency Interviews and Praxis II content scores. Because the surveys were collected anonymously, all analyses were examined and reported as aggregate numbers.

Research Question

How do pre-MAT candidates perceive their programs of study prepare them for teaching a foreign language in K-12 settings? Candidates were asked to consider how well their programs of study prepared them to meet the ACTFL/NCATE program standards for teaching a foreign language using the first two ACTFL assessment

standards for reporting content knowledge in the ACTFL/NCATE accreditation report.

Limitations

- The data were not disaggregated by the program areas of French, German, and Spanish.
- The sample size (n = 7) was small. However, this number of FL majors in one year is considered a generous number of majors for the size of the state. In the previous two years, the total number was six, with three candidates each year. This is the first year in the researcher's program for German representation.
- The data were collected as self-reported.
- Variables such as age, gender, and years out from graduation were not considered. The sample number was too small to add additional variables.
- Dispositions for teacher candidates were not considered.

Delimitations

- External validity: Because the sample represents only graduates from one university, the findings may not be generalized to other foreign language departments. The program is also a fifth-year program, whereas many programs use a traditional four-year model.
- Internal validity: Responses might have been affected by the language used in the survey that is peculiar to education and brief self-reporting protocol used in this instrument. The survey was administered at the beginning of their first semester in the Master of Arts in Teaching (MAT) program. However, the participants had a sufficient amount of time to consider their responses. It was also assumed that each candidate would answer the questions honestly without consulting with their classmates.

Participants

Nine candidates, eight female and one male, began their MAT program of study in July. Four candidates graduated with degrees in Spanish, three in French, and two in German. One candidate graduated from another university, so that survey was not included in the statistical analysis. One candidate failed to return the survey. Prior to July, the candidates' pedagogical knowledge consisted of five credit-hours of prerequisite courses including a one credit-hour pre-observation course consisting of 60 hours of classroom observation, a one credit-hour capstone course in which candidates created portfolios to show evidence of target language proficiencies in the fours skills of learning a foreign language, i.e., reading, writing, listening, and speaking, and in culture., and a three credit-hour course titled, "Teaching Students in an Inclusive Setting."

Instrument

A self-report, Likert-scaled instrument was designed to assess participants' knowledge of their undergraduate preparation in addressing ACTFL teacher preparation program standards 1 and 2. Thirty-one questions were constructed based on the two assessment standards required for content areas. The researcher, who was also the instructor of the course, created the questions based on her expertise in teacher education preparation and knowledge of the standards. The WLLC department chair read the first draft for appropriateness and quality of the items based on her expertise as a Spanish instructor and a foreign language methods teacher for tertiary instruction. The survey questions were divided into two groups as follows. Standard 1: Language, Linguistics, Comparisons had three sub-standards (21 questions) and Standard 2: Cultures, Literatures, Cross-Disciplinary Concepts had two sub-standards (10 questions). Participants were asked to assess their perceptions of how each language program addressed the standards using a 0-3 scale: *0 = don't know, 1 = not at all, 2 = sufficient, 3 = very well.* Participants were also given the opportunity to write comments after completing the survey instrument (see Appendix A). Four of the participants added comments.

Administration of Instrument

Approval was obtained from the Institutional Review Board to conduct the research. The instructor described the research project to the candidates on the first day of their methods class and asked them to take the survey home to complete it for the next class. One candidate was not included in the statistical analysis because the participant matriculated from another institution. Taking the survey implied consent to participate in the project. Seven surveys were returned the following class. Surveys were anonymous, coded 1-7, and used as aggregated data.

Analysis of Data

Once the surveys were collected, data were entered into an Excel file according to the participants' codes. Questions were coded according to the standard, sub-standard, and question number. For example, Standard 1, Sub-standard b, question six was coded as S1b.6. Scores were entered by numbers 0-3 with *0 = don't know, 1 = not at all, 2 = sufficient,* and *3 = very well.*Calculations were determined for the percentage and frequency of responses for each standard, sub-standard, and question. Only one question was unanswered, so the "n" for that question was lowered to six to calculate the mean.

Data were not disaggregated by language (French, German, Spanish) due to the limited number of participants and because the ACTFL standards apply to all languages. This report will focus on frequencies, percentages, means, and standard deviations for all questions (see Appendix B).

Results

The survey included 31 questions divided between two standards—Standard One: Language, Linguistics, Comparisons and Standard Two: Cultures, Literatures, and Cross-Disciplinary Concepts—and five sub-standards, distributed as follows:

- Standard 1, sub-standard a, Demonstrating Language Proficiency: 10 questions,
- Standard 1, sub-standard b, Understanding Linguistics: 8 questions,
- Standard 1, sub-standard c, Identifying Language Comparisons: 3 questions,
- Standard 2, sub-standard a, Demonstrating Cultural Understandings: 4 questions, and
- Standard 2, sub-standard b, Demonstrating Understanding of Literary and Cultural Texts and Traditions: 6 questions.

The *Very Well* category received the highest percentages for each sub-standard. However, less than half the candidates felt *very well*-prepared to demonstrate their language proficiency (S1a-45%) or to understand linguistics (S1b-38%). Yet, over half the candidates felt *very well*-prepared to identify language comparisons (S1c-52%) and to demonstrate cultural understandings (S2a-56%). The majority of candidates, 83%, had the opinion that their programs of study prepared them *very well* in demonstrating their understanding of literary and cultural texts and traditions (S2b).

In the *Sufficiently* category, S1a: Demonstrating Language Proficiencies received the highest percentage with 39% of the candidates responding. Twenty-three percent of the candidates felt *sufficiently* prepared to understand linguistics (S1b), 29% felt prepared to identify language comparisons (S1c), and 25% felt *sufficiently* prepared to demonstrate cultural understandings (S2a). Only 17% felt *sufficiently* prepared to demonstrate understanding of literary and cultural texts and traditions (S2b).

In the *Not At All* category, the data reveal that 12% of the candidates felt unprepared to demonstrate language proficiency (S1a), but almost one-fourth of the candidates, 23%, felt that they were not prepared to understand linguistics (S1b). Fourteen percent felt unprepared to identify language comparisons (S1c), and 21% marked unprepared to demonstrate cultural understandings (S2a). No one marked *Not At All* for Substandard 2b: Demonstrating Understanding of Literary and Cultural Texts and Traditions

Candidates reported *Don't Know* in three sub-standards and the percentages were miniscule: 4% for S1a, 2% for S1b, and 5% for S1c. No one responded to *Don't Know* in Sub-standards 2a and 2b (see Table 1).

Average mean scores ranged from a low of 2.10 for Standard 1b: Understanding Linguistics, to a high of 2.83, 2b: Demonstrating Cultural Understandings out of a possible 3.0. The average mean scores for the remaining three standards include 2.22 for 1a: Demonstrating Language Proficiencies, 2.29 for 1c: Identifying Language Comparisons, and 2.32 for 2a: Demonstrating Cultural Understandings. Standard deviations ranged from .40 on Standard 2b: Demonstrating Understanding of Literary and Cultural Texts

Table 1   Percentages for ACTFL Sub-Standards

Sub-Standard	n	Percentage Very Well	Percentage Sufficiently	Percentage Not At All	Percentage Don't Know
1a: Demonstrating Language Proficiencies*	6	45.0	39.0	12.0	4.0
1b: Understanding Linguistics	7	38.0	23.0	23.0	2.0
1c: Identifying Language Comparisons	7	52.0	29.0	14.0	5.0
2a: Demonstrating Cultural Understandings	7	56.0	25.0	21.0	0.0
2b: Demonstrating Understanding of Literary and Cultural Texts and Traditions	7	83.0	17.0	0.0	0.0

* One student did not respond to one question in this sub-standard.

Table 2   Mean Scores and Standard Deviations for Each ACTFL Sub-Standard

Sub-Standard	n	M	SD
1a: Demonstrating Language Proficiencies*	6	2.22	.65
1b: Understanding Linguistics	7	2.10	.81
1c: Identifying Language Comparisons	7	2.29	.92
2a: Demonstrating Cultural Understandings	7	2.32	.81
2b: Demonstrating Understanding of Literary and Cultural Texts and Traditions	7	2.83	.40

* One student did not respond to one question in this sub-standard.

Table 3   ACTFL Standard Rating / OPI Results

ACTFL /NCATE Standard 1a1.1	n	OPI	n
Very Well	0	Advanced Low	2
Sufficiently	2	Intermediate High	2
Not At All	2	Intermediate Mid	2
Don't Know	2	Intermediate Low	1

* One student did not respond to survey question in this sub-standard.

and Traditions to .92 on 1c: Identifying Language Comparisons. A standard deviation of .65 was the median for 1a: Demonstrating Language Proficiencies. Standards 1b: Understanding Linguistics and 2a: Demonstrating Cultural Understandings both received a .81 standard deviation (see Table 2).

In comparing and contrasting the survey results to other benchmark assessments, two assessments were used: the Oral Proficiency Interview (OPI) and the Praxis II Content and Productive tests. Individual survey questions were examined to seek similarities of candidate perceptions and actual scored data.

Standard 1a1.1 asked candidates if their programs of study prepared them to score an advanced low on the OPI. One candidate failed to answer this question, so the mean response for six candidates was 1.00 with a standard deviation of .89. Two candidates marked *Don't Know,* two candidates marked *Not At All,* and two candidates marked *Sufficiently.* No candidate marked "3" or *Very Well.* The actual scores on the OPI point out the variance in this answer. Three candidates scored in the advanced range: one advanced mid and two advanced low. However, one of these candidates was a bilingual Spanish speaker and the other two candidates had extensive immersion experiences. The remaining five candidates who had matriculated from the university all scored in the intermediate range: one high, three mid, and two low. The latter scores would seem to indicate a more realistic representation of a 2 + 2 program model in which candidates study two years of language followed by two years of literature and have little or no immersion experiences. The WLLC does not require an immersion experience of its graduates (see Table 3).

Benchmark Test Data

The other benchmark tests include the Praxis II Content and Productive tests. Teacher candidates in this mid-south state must pass the Praxis II series of test for licensure. Only Spanish candidates must pass three tests in their content area: Spanish Content Knowledge, Spanish Productive Language Skills, and Spanish Pedagogy. French candidates have two content tests to pass: French Content Knowledge and French

Table 4 ACTFL Standard Rating / Praxis II Test Range Scores for Listening*

ACTFL / NCATE Standard 1a2.3	n	ACTFL / NCATE Standard 1a.2.4	n	Praxis II Content Test Listening Comprehension	n
Very Well	4		5	Upper Range	3
Sufficiently	3		2	Mid Range	0
Not At All	0		0	Low Range	1
Don't Know	0		0	Below Range	1

* German language candidates were not required by the state to take the Praxis II test.

Table 5 ACTFL Standard Rating / Praxis II Test Range Scores for Reading*

ACTFL /NCATE Standard 1a2.2	n	Praxis II Content Test Reading Comprehension	n
Very Well	4	Upper Range	1
Sufficiently	3	Mid Range	2
Not At All	0	Low Range	0
Don't Know	0	Below Range	2

* German language candidates were not required by the state to take the Praxis II test.

Table 6 ACTFL Standard Rating / Praxis II Test Range Scores for Speaking

ACTFL / NCATE Standard 1a3.6	n	ACTFL / NCATE Standard 1a3.7	n	Praxis II Productive Test Speaking	n
Very Well	5		3	Upper Range	1
Sufficiently	2		3	Mid Range	2
Not At All	0		1	Low Range	2
Don't Know	0		0	Below Range	0

* German language candidates were not required by the state to take the Praxis II test.

Productive Language Skills. German candidates do not have a normed content test in this state at this time. French and German candidates must also pass the Principles of Learning and Teaching (PLT) test to indicate their pedagogical knowledge. For this study, five candidates took content tests in Spanish and French, each consisting of four sub-sets: listening, structure, reading, and culture. The Spanish and

Table 7 ACTFL Standard Rating / Praxis II Test Range Scores for Writing

ACTFL /NCATE Standard 1a4.9	n	ACTFL / NCATE Standard 1a4.10	n	Praxis II Content Test Writing	n
Very Well	4		5	Upper Range	2
Sufficiently	3		2	Mid Range	1
Not At All	0		0	Low Range	2
Don't Know	0		0	Below Range	0

* German language candidates were not required by the state to take the Praxis II test.

French Productive tests included two sub-sets: speaking and writing. The data are grouped according to ACTFL/NCATE questions and sub-scores results.

In Standard 1a: Demonstrating Language Proficiency, survey questions 1a2.2, 1a2.3, and 1a2.4 relate to the reading and listening portions of the Praxis II Content tests. Candidates reported feeling better prepared in these areas with mean scores and standard deviations reflecting an agreement respectively of 2.57, 2.57, and 2.66 and standard deviations of 0.53, 0.53, and 0.49. Three of the five candidates scored in the upper range on the listening section, one in the lower range, and one below range (see Table 4).

On the reading section, one of the candidates scored in the upper range, two mid-range, and two below the range (see Table 5).

Questions 1a3.6 and 1a3.7 addressed speaking skills that compared and contrasted to the Productive test sub-section on speaking. Candidates reported feeling prepared in this category with mean scores respectively at 2.71 and 2.29 with standard deviations of 0.49 and 0.76 respectively. However, the Praxis results indicate a disconnect between perception and reality. On the speaking portion of the Praxis tests, two candidates scored in the low range, two in the mid range, and one high (see Table 6).

The last two questions in Standard 1a relate to the writing section of the Productive test. Candidates indicated sufficiently prepared in this section with mean scores of 2.86 and 2.00 with standard deviations of 0.38 and 0.82 respectively. On the writing portion, two candidates scored in the low range, one mid, and two high (see Table 7).

Linguistic questions were addressed in Standard 1b: Understanding Linguistics. Candidates felt least prepared in this standard with an overall mean score of 2.10 and a standard deviation of 0.81. Questions 1b1, 1b2, 1b3, 1b4, and 1b5 relate to the Structure section on the Praxis II Content tests. Candidates' mean scores respectively stand at 1.71, 1.85, 2.29, 2.14, and 2.71 with standard deviations of 0.76, 0.90, 0.76, 0.90, and 0.49 respectively. On the Praxis tests,

Table 8 ACTFL Standard Rating / Praxis II Test Range Scores for Structure

	ACTFL /NCATE Standard					Praxis II Content Test	
	1b1	1b2	1b3 (n = 7)	1b4	1b5	Structure (n = 5)	
Very Well	1	2	3	3	5	Upper Range	1
Sufficiently	3	2	3	2	2	Mid Range	2
Not At All	3	3	1	2	0	Low Range	2
Don't Know	0	0	0	0	0	Below Range	0

* German language candidates were not required by the state to take the Praxis II test.

Table 9 ACTFL Standard Rating / Praxis II Test Range Scores for Culture

	ACTFL /NCATE Standard				Content Test	
	2a.1	2a.2 (n = 7)	2a.3	2a.4	Culture (n = 5)	
Very Well	5	4	3	3	Upper Range	1
Sufficiently	2	1	2	2	Mid Range	3
Not At All	0	2	2	2	Low Range	1
Don't Know	0	0	0	0	Below Range	0

* German language candidates were not required by the state to take the Praxis II test.

two candidates scored in the low range, two in the mid-range, and one above range (see Table 8).

Culture questions were addressed in Standard 2a: Demonstrating Cultural Understandings. Candidates reported feeling better prepared in this area with an overall mean score of 2.32 and a standard deviation of 0.81. Questions 2a1, 2a2, 2a3, and 2a4 relate to the Culture section of the Praxis II Content tests. Candidates' mean scores respectively stand at 2.71, 2.29, 2.14, and 2.14 with standard deviations of 0.49, 0.95, 0.90, and 0.90 respectively. This section had the most variance with the second highest individual standard deviation in the entire survey of 0.95. The Praxis scores were also distributed with one each in the low and upper range and three in the mid range of scores (see Table 9).

Discussion

For candidates in this mid-south university, their program of study is completed in the college of arts and sciences. Candidates most likely graduate with a BA before applying for the fifth year MAT program. Most language education candidates do not take the five hours of pre-MAT courses until their senior year, with three of the courses delivered on-line. Teacher education frequently appears as much a mystery to the candidates as it is to the world language faculty. Candidates enter the MAT program with vague notions of how teachers are licensed and how classroom teachers use standards-based instruction. However, this group of candidates was enrolled in a one credit-hour pilot capstone course during the preceding spring semester, so they brought some background knowledge regarding the ACTFL standards for learning the "five Cs" of foreign language standards (Communication, Cultures, Connections, Comparisons, and Communities) and some background knowledge regarding state frameworks.

The mean scores of each standard indicate that the candidates felt sufficiently prepared in both standards. Standard deviations for each substandard also indicated little variation in the scores. It was no surprise to find the highest score with the least standard deviation fell to Standard 2b: Demonstrating Understanding of Literary and Cultural Texts and Traditions with a mean of 2.83 and a standard deviation of 0.40.

Based on the 2 + 2 model of undergraduate preparation (two years of language preparation and two years of literature and culture courses), the literary focus of the course work during the last two years of a language major prepare candidates more strongly in the receptive skills of reading and analysis. Candidate comments support these scores: "The (name of language) program . . . focuses on literature first and foremost," and "The program focuses purely on writing proficiency and knowledge of culture and civic/history," and "The program was very focused on literature and reading in the target language."

The lowest score, found in Standard 1b: Understanding Linguistics with a 2.10 and a 0.81 standard deviation, was also expected. Candidates in the three language programs do not take a required linguistic course. The WLLC department offers an introductory course in linguistics but only Spanish has a language-specific linguistics course. Again, candidate comments support their assessment: "I learned (name of language) outside of the classroom in an immersion experience. Therefore, my formal education mostly dealt with culture and literature and not with grammar," and " . . . I don't recall ever learning about phonology, semantics, morphology, or syntax in any of my undergrad classes," and "All of my understanding of linguistics is the result of our linguistics paper (research) for the capstone course. I did not learn any of this info in actual FLAN classes . . ."

Only 38% of the respondents felt *very well*-prepared for this standard with 23% marking *sufficiently* and 23% *not at all.* Of the eight individual questions on the survey, four questions received less than "2." Praxis scores also support this rating. Of the six candidates taking the test, only two candidates scored above the range. Three scored in the lower range and one in the mid range.

Standard 1c: Understanding Language Comparisons showed the highest standard deviation of 0.92. The mean score of 2.29 was also the median score of the five mean substandard scores (2.10-2.83), so the higher standard deviation indicates some disagreement in the overall average regarding this standard. Question 1c.2, Sociolinguistic Variation, also had the highest standard deviation in the survey of 1.20 further supporting the greater variance in this standard.

Implications

Prior to the development of the ACTFL/NCATE standards, NCATE accreditation for foreign language teacher education programs involved minimal participation on the part of the content language instructors. Faculty usually provided evidence for the report in the form of syllabi and curriculum vitae. However, with the adoption of the *ACTFL/NCATE Program Standards for Foreign Language Teacher Preparation* by NCATE in 2002, cooperation between colleges becomes critical for accreditation. Evidence for the accreditation report is now performance-based. Programs must also include documentation in the report that they use this evidence to improve instruction in their own programs of study.

Regardless of the need for collaboration, little incentive exists for collaboration between colleges other than altruism due to time constraints, limited faculty commitment to teacher education, and issues with regard to teaching distribution (Colville-Hall, Fonseca-Greber, & Cavour, 2007). Another issue regards the value placed on research in the social sciences by liberal arts colleges (Hopkins, 2005). Hopkins found that "too often faculty members from arts and sciences or professional schools who express interest in collaborating with education faculty on research are advised that their efforts will not count toward tenure or promotion" and "Too often research in teaching is seen as extraneous to career advancement" (p. 162).

In preparing for the ACTFL/NCATE report, the researcher found some similarities between the research and the context for her own institution although the small number of

surveys with self-reported data narrows the implications to this locale. Most language faculty were unaware that program standards had been established for teacher preparation. Faculty were also disinterested in making curricular changes to provide assessment evidence for the report. They were satisfied with the state's Non-Traditional Licensure (NTL) program for preparing foreign language teachers. It must be pointed out that the state-supported non-traditional licensure program does not require participants to take the OPI or any methods course in teaching a foreign language K-12.

Conclusion

In order to better prepare our candidates at the undergraduate level for a teaching profession, the survey results suggest three areas of improvement: oral proficiency, understanding of linguistics, and demonstrating cultural understandings. Candidate results on the OPI and the portfolio assessments also support the candidates' perceptions of the strengths and weaknesses of their undergraduate language preparation. However, faculty in the world language department are reluctant to make curricular changes at this time to better prepare candidates for a career in teaching foreign languages at the K-12 level.

However, in order to prepare for the NCATE accreditation visit, faculty did agree to two changes: 1) teacher candidates must take the Oral Proficiency Interview to assess their language proficiency, and 2) they must enroll in a capstone course to create a portfolio of their abilities to understand linguistics, identify language contrasts and comparisons, demonstrate cultural understandings, and understanding of literary and cultural texts and traditions. The capstone course was instituted one year ago in order to provide evidence in a portfolio of the two standards discussed in this article.

Four faculty, one each from French and German and two from Spanish, assisted with assessing the portfolios. Their comments supported the evidence found in the survey: candidates were weak in understanding linguistics (sub-standard 1c) and in demonstrating understanding of language comparisons (sub-standard 2a). World language faculty pointed out that candidates who wanted to be teachers were often weaker academically, yet the same group of candidates had overall average GPAs from their college above 3.0. Ideally, the world language department faculty would take a greater interest in teacher education standards and use this data to implement greater curricular changes that would benefit all language candidates as some programs have done (Colville-Hall, Fonseca-Greber, & Cavour, 2007; Glisan, Smith-Sherwood, McDaniel, & Brooks, 2007; McAlpine & Dhonau, 2007).

Further research regarding tertiary candidates' perceptions of how well they are prepared to teach a foreign language would also benefit the profession as we seek to provide highly effective teachers for K-12 candidates.

Language programs should reconsider how candidates view language learning in the 21st century and how their perceptions shape their expectations for a curriculum that is interactive and communicative. Immersion opportunities should be integrated into the requirements for majors so that all candidates can exit a program with a minimum OPI score of Advanced Low as required by the ACTFL/NCATE standards.

This researcher would like to see the survey administered to all language candidates. Perhaps the candidates' input would alert faculty that a new paradigm for language learning is in the wind, one that emphasizes knowing and using the language along with learning about the greater and smaller cultures of the target language countries. The ACTFL/NCATE standards are reasonable guidelines for creating a well-rounded program of language learning for any candidate who wishes to communicate in another language and learn about another culture.

References

Berk, R.A. (2005). *Test alignment and balancing with state standards: Every six months or 50 items, whichever comes first.* In National Evaluation Systems, Inc. (Ed). *After student standards: Alignment (*pp. 15–27). Amherst, MA: National Evaluation Systems, Inc.

Colville-Hall, Fonseca-Greber, & Cavour. (2007). Preparing for the ACTFL/NCAT program report: Three case studies. In A. J. Moeller & J. Theiler, (Eds.), *Learning languages in a digital world: Selected papers from the 2007 Central States Conference* (39–53). Eau Claire, WI: RMT.

Glisan, Smith-Sherwood, McDaniel, & Brooks (2007). *Using assessment to mend the lang/lit split in higher education.* Presentation ACTFL. San Antonio, Texas.

Hopkins, D. (2005). *Aligning academe: Achieving success in Texas.* In National Evaluation Systems, Inc. (Ed). *After student standards: Alignment (*pp. 161–175). Amherst, MA: National Evaluation Systems, Inc.

McAlpine, D., & Dhonau, S. (2007). Creating a culture for the preparation of a ACTFL/NCATE program review. *Foreign Language Annals, 40*(2), 247–259.

McAlpine, D., & Shrum, G. (2007). ACTFL/NCATE program review. Workshop presentation. ACTFL conference. San Antonio, TX.

McAlpine, D., & Shrum, G. (2007). ACTFL/NCATE program review. Workshop presentation. ACTFL conference. San Antonio, TX.

Phillips, J. (2007). *NCATE/SPA program review.* Workshop presentation. ArACTE conference. Russellville, AR.

Critical Thinking

1. What do world language teachers say they need to meet standards?
2. How does cultural competence impact world language teachers?
3. What can other teachers learn from this study?
4. Why is multicultural education essential for all teachers and students?

Appendix A
Survey Instrument

Connect or Disconnect?
Meeting the Needs of Pre-Service Foreign Language
Teachers in a Master of Arts in Teaching Program
Part II

The National Council for Accreditation of Teacher Education (NCATE) sets standards of compliance for all state-supported institutions of higher learning teacher education programs in order to assure quality instruction and preparation of teacher candidates. NCATE works closely with specialized professional associations (SPAs) to establish standards for preparing teachers such as the American Council on the Teaching of Foreign Languages (ACTFL). The state of Arkansas only grants licensure to teacher candidates from NCATE accredited institutions.

Researchers in CIED and FLAN are also investigating the alignment of the ACTFL program standards for the preparation of foreign language teachers with program preparation. ACTFL holds that preparing foreign language teachers is the joint responsibility of both teacher education programs and foreign language departments and lists eight requirements for teacher education programs and foreign language departments for preparing future teachers with the skills, knowledge, and dispositions necessary for this career. Please indicate your opinion regarding how well **you consider your program of study in French, German, or Spanish** meets the ACTFL requirements in preparing our students to teach foreign languages. **Circle** your assessment of each statement using the following scale: 1 = not at all; 2 = sufficiently; 3 = very well. If you don't know the answer, mark DK = Don't Know.

Arkansas has a critical shortage of foreign language teachers. Without highly effective teachers in the classroom, students enter the tertiary classroom poorly or inadequately prepared for the rigor of learning second languages. It behooves us in both the Foreign Language Department and in Curriculum and Instruction to collaborate in preparing the next generation of foreign language teachers. Your comments on this issue will be helpful.

Standard 1: Language, Linguistics, Comparisons				
Standard 1a: Demonstrating Language Proficiency:				
Candidates demonstrate a high level of proficiency in the target language, and they seek opportunities to strengthen their proficiency.				
Candidates exhibit evidence of ability in the following areas.				
1: Interpersonal Communication: Speaking				
1a1.1. Advanced Low on ACTFL Oral Proficiency Interview	1	2	3	DK
1a2: Interpretive Communication: Listening and Reading				
1a2.2. Infer meaning of unfamiliar words and phrases in new contexts	1	2	3	DK
1a2.3. Infer and interpret author's intent	1	2	3	DK
1a2.4. Offer personal interpretations of message	1	2	3	DK
1a3: Presentational Communication: Speaking				
1a3.5. Deliver oral presentations extemporaneously	1	2	3	DK
1a3.6. Topics are of personal interest, familiar literary and cultural topics	1	2	3	DK
1a3.7. Able to speak in connected discourse using a variety of time frames and vocabulary	1	2	3	DK
1a3.8. Extralinguistic support to facilitate audience comprehension (PowerPoint, posters, etc.)	1	2	3	DK
1a4: Interpersonal and Presentational Communication: Writing				
1a4.9. Advanced Low on ACTFL scale; routine social correspondence	1	2	3	DK
Willingness/openness for acquiring proficiency:	1	2	3	DK
1a4.10. Candidates seek out opportunities to strengthen proficiency by interacting in the target language outside the classroom.				
Standard 1b: Understanding Linguistics:				
Candidates know the linguistic features of the target language system, recognize the changing nature of language, and accommodate for gaps in their own knowledge of the target language system by learning on their own.				
Candidates exhibit evidence of ability in the following areas.				

1b1. Phonetics	1	2	3	DK
1b2. Morphology	1	2	3	DK
1b3. Syntax	1	2	3	DK
1b4. Semantics	1	2	3	DK
1b5. Rules for word and sentence formation—Example: Where does the object pronoun go?	1	2	3	DK
1b6. Discourse, sociolinguistic, and pragmatic knowledge (Basic Interpersonal Communication Skills)	1	2	3	DK
1b 7. Changing nature of language—historical linguistics	1	2	3	DK
1b 8. Willingness/openness for accommodating for gaps in knowledge of target language system. Example: Student asks for grammar reference book	1	2	3	DK
Standard 1c: Identifying Language Comparisons:				
Candidates know the similarities and differences between the target language and other languages, identify the key differences in varieties of the target language, and seek opportunities to learn about varieties of the target language on their own.				
Candidates exhibit evidence of ability in the following areas.				
1c1. Comparisons between target language and first language	1	2	3	DK
1c2. Sociolinguistic variation—Example: gender, economic differences, etc.	1	2	3	DK
1c3. Willingness/openness for learning about target language varieties	1	2	3	DK
Standard 2: Cultures, Literatures, Cross-Disciplinary Concepts				
Standard 2a: Demonstrating Cultural Understandings				
Candidates demonstrate that they understand the connections among the perspectives of a culture and its practices and products, and they integrate the cultural framework for foreign language standards into their instructional practices. Note. The foreign language standards for teachers have been established by ACTFL and are also used for the Arkansas K-12 foreign language standards.				
Candidates exhibit evidence of ability in the following areas.				
2a1. Cultural knowledge: Candidates cite key cultural perspectives (ex. Easter celebration) and provide through description of products (egg decorations) and practices (custom of celebration)	1	2	3	DK
2a2. Cultural experience: Candidates have spend time in target culture; personal experience connects to academic studies (Bastille Day, St. Nicolas Day, Dia de los Muertos)	1	2	3	DK
2a3. Process of analyzing cultures: Candidates demonstrate ability to analyze and hypothesize about unfamiliar or unknown cultural issues.	1	2	3	DK
2a4. Willingness/openness for cultural learning: Candidates integrate cultural insights into communicative functions and work to extend their knowledge of culture through interactions with native speakers	1	2	3	DK
Standard 2b: Demonstrating Understanding of Literary and Cultural Texts and Traditions				
Candidates recognize the value and role of literary and cultural texts and use them to interpret and reflect upon the perspectives of the target cultures over time.				
Candidates exhibit evidence of ability in the following areas:				
2b1. Knowledge of Literary and Cultural Texts:	1	2	3	DK
2b2. Interpretation literary texts that represent defining works in the target cultures	1	2	3	DK
2b3. Identify themes in a variety of texts that the cultures deem important in understanding the traditions of the cultures.	1	2	3	DK
2b4. Identify authors in a variety of texts that the cultures deem important in understanding the traditions of the cultures.	1	2	3	DK
2b5. Identify genres in a variety of texts that the cultures deem important in understanding the traditions of the cultures.	1	2	3	DK
2b6. Willingness/openness toward exploring literatures and other texts and media.	1	2	3	DK

Appendix B
Percentages and Frequencies for Standards One and Two and Sub-Standards 1a, 1b, 1c and 2a, 2b.

Standard 1: Language, Linguistics, Comparisons
1a: Demonstrating Language Proficiency

Candidates demonstrate a high level of proficiency in the target language, and they seek opportunities to strengthen their proficiency.

1a.1: Interpersonal Communication: Speaking

Candidates exhibit evidence of the ability to...   Interns 2009

1a.1.1. . . . *Score Advanced Low on ACTFL Oral Proficiency Interview.*

	Frequency	Percent
DON'T KNOW	2	33.0%
NOT AT ALL	2	33.0%
SUFFICIENTLY	2	33.0%
VERY WELL	0	0.0%
No response	1	

1a:2: Interpretive Communication: Listening and Reading

1a.2.2. . . . *Infer meaning of unfamiliar words and phrases in new contexts.*

	Frequency	Percent
DON'T KNOW	0	0.0%
NOT AT ALL	0	0.0%
SUFFICIENTLY	3	43.0%
VERY WELL	4	57.0%

1a.2.3. . . . *Infer and interpret author's intent.*

	Frequency	Percent
DON'T KNOW	0	0.0%
NOT AT ALL	0	0.0%
SUFFICIENTLY	3	43.0%
VERY WELL	4	57.0%

1a.2.4. . . . *Offer personal interpretations of message.*

	Frequency	Percent
DON'T KNOW	0	0.0%
NOT AT ALL	0	0.0%
SUFFICIENTLY	2	29.0%
VERY WELL	5	71.0%

1a3: Presentational Communication: Speaking

1a.3.5. . . . *Deliver oral presentations extemporaneously.*

	Frequency	Percent
DON'T KNOW	0	0.0%
NOT AT ALL	2	29.0%
SUFFICIENTLY	4	57.0%
VERY WELL	1	14.0%

1a.3.6. . . . *Discuss topics that are of personal interest, familiar literary and cultural topics.*

	Frequency	Percent
DON'T KNOW	0	0.0%
NOT AT ALL	0	0.0%
SUFFICIENTLY	2	29.0%
VERY WELL	5	71.0%

156

1a.3.7. . . . *Speak in connected discourse using a variety of time frames and vocabulary.*	Frequency	Percent
DON'T KNOW	0	0.0%
NOT AT ALL	1	14.0%
SUFFICIENTLY	3	43.0%
VERY WELL	3	43.0%

1a.3.8. . . . *Use extra-linguistic support to facilitate audience comprehension (PowerPoint, posters, etc.).*	Frequency	Percent
DON'T KNOW	1	14.0%
NOT AT ALL	1	14.0%
SUFFICIENTLY	4	57.0%
VERY WELL	1	14.0%

1a4: Interpersonal and Presentational Communication: Writing

1a.4.9. . . . *Score Advanced Low on ACTFL scale; routine social correspondence.*	Frequency	Percent
DON'T KNOW	0	0.0%
NOT AT ALL	0	0.0%
SUFFICIENTLY	1	14.0%
VERY WELL	6	86.0%

1a.4.10. . . . Seek out opportunities to strengthen proficiency by interacting in the target language outside the classroom.	Frequency	Percent
DON'T KNOW	0	0.0%
NOT AT ALL	2	29.0%
SUFFICIENTLY	3	43.0%
VERY WELL	2	29.0%

1b: Understanding Linguistics

Candidates know the linguistic features of the target language system, recognize the changing nature of language, and accommodate for gaps in their own knowledge of the target language system by learning on their own.

Candidates exhibit evidence of ability in . . .

1b.1. . . . *Phonetics*	Frequency	Percent
DON'T KNOW	0	0.0%
NOT AT ALL	3	43.0%
SUFFICIENTLY	3	43.0%
VERY WELL	1	14.0%

1b.2. . . . *Morphology*	Frequency	Percent
DON'T KNOW	0	0.0%
NOT AT ALL	3	43.0%
SUFFICIENTLY	2	29.0%
VERY WELL	2	29.0%

1b.3. . . . *Syntax*	Frequency	Percent
DON'T KNOW	0	0.0%
NOT AT ALL	1	14.0%
SUFFICIENTLY	3	43.0%
VERY WELL	3	43.0%

1b.4. . . . *Semantics*	Frequency	Percent
DON'T KNOW	0	0.0%
NOT AT ALL	2	29.0%
SUFFICIENTLY	2	29.0%
VERY WELL	3	43.0%

1b.5. . . . *Rules for word and sentence formation.*	Frequency	Percent
DON'T KNOW	0	0.0%
NOT AT ALL	0	0.0%
SUFFICIENTLY	2	29.0%
VERY WELL	5	71.0%

1b.6. . . . *Discourse, sociolinguistic, and pragmatic.*	Frequency	Percent
DON'T KNOW	1	14.0%
NOT AT ALL	0	0.0%
SUFFICIENTLY	5	71.0%
VERY WELL	1	14.0%

1b.7. . . . *Changing nature of language—historical linguistics.*	Frequency	Percent
DON'T KNOW	0	0.0%
NOT AT ALL	3	43.0%
SUFFICIENTLY	2	29.0%
VERY WELL	2	29.0%

1b.8. . . . *Willingness/openness for accommodating for gaps in knowledge of target language system.*	Frequency	Percent
DON'T KNOW	0	0.0%
NOT AT ALL	1	14.0%
SUFFICIENTLY	2	29.0%
VERY WELL	4	57.0%

1c: Identifying Language Comparisons

Candidates know the similarities and differences between the target language and other languages, identify the key differences in varieties of the target language and seek opportunities to learn about varieties of the target language on their own.

Candidates exhibit evidence of ability in . . .

1c.1. . . . *Comparisons between target language and first language.*	Frequency	Percent
DON'T KNOW	0	0.0%
NOT AT ALL	1	14.0%
SUFFICIENTLY	2	29.0%
VERY WELL	4	57.0%

1c.2. . . . *Sociolinguistic variation.*	Frequency	Percent
DON'T KNOW	1	14.0%
NOT AT ALL	1	14.0%
SUFFICIENTLY	1	14.0%
VERY WELL	4	57.0%

1c.3. . . . *Willingness/openness for learning about target language varieties.*	Frequency	Percent
DON'T KNOW	0	0.0%
NOT AT ALL	1	14.0%
SUFFICIENTLY	3	43.0%
VERY WELL	3	43.0%

Standard 2: Cultures, Literatures, Cross-Disciplinary Concepts
2a: Demonstrating Cultural Understandings

Candidates demonstrate that they understand the connections among the perspectives of a culture and its practices and products, and they integrate the cultural framework for foreign language standards into their instructional practices.

Candidates exhibit evidence of ability in the following areas . . .		Interns 2009	
2a.1. . . . Cultural knowledge: Candidates cite key cultural perspectives.		Frequency	Percent
	DON'T KNOW	0	0.0%
	NOT AT ALL	0	0.0%
	SUFFICIENTLY	2	29.0%
	VERY WELL	5	71.0%
2a.2. . . . Cultural experience: Candidates have spent time in target culture; personal experience connects to academic studies.		Frequency	Percent
	DON'T KNOW	0	0.0%
	NOT AT ALL	2	29.0%
	SUFFICIENTLY	1	14.0%
	VERY WELL	4	57.0%
2a.3. . . . Process of analyzing cultures: Candidates demonstrate ability to analyze and hypothesize about unfamiliar or unknown cultural issues.		Frequency	Percent
	DON'T KNOW	0	0.0%
	NOT AT ALL	2	29.0%
	SUFFICIENTLY	2	29.0%
	VERY WELL	3	43.0%
2a.4. . . . Willingness/openness for cultural learning: Candidates integrate cultural insights into communicative functions and work to extend their knowledge of culture through interactions with native speakers.		Frequency	Percent
	DON'T KNOW	0	0.0%
	NOT AT ALL	2	29.0%
	SUFFICIENTLY	2	29.0%
	VERY WELL	3	43.0%

2b: Demonstrating Understanding of Literary and Cultural Texts and Traditions

Candidates recognize the value and role of literary and cultural texts and use them to interpret and reflect upon the perspectives of the target cultures over time.

Candidates exhibit evidence of ability in. . .		FLAN INSTRUCTORS	
2b.1. . . . Knowledge of literary and cultural texts.		Frequency	Percent
	DON'T KNOW	0	0.0%
	NOT AT ALL	0	0.0%
	SUFFICIENTLY	1	14.0%
	VERY WELL	6	**86.0%**
2b.2. . . . Interpretation of literary texts that represent defining works in the target cultures.		Frequency	Percent
	DON'T KNOW	0	0.0%
	NOT AT ALL	0	0.0%
	SUFFICIENTLY	2	29.0%
	VERY WELL	5	**71.0%**

2b.3. . . . *Identify themes in a variety of texts that the cultures deem important in under-standing the traditions of the cultures.*	Frequency	Percent
DON'T KNOW	0	0.0%
NOT AT ALL	0	0.0%
SUFFICIENTLY	1	14.0%
VERY WELL	6	**86.0%**

2b.4. . . . *Identify authors in a variety of texts that the cultures deem important in under-standing the traditions of the cultures.*	Frequency	Percent
DON'T KNOW	0	0.0%
NOT AT ALL	0	0.0%
SUFFICIENTLY	1	14.0%
VERY WELL	6	**86.0%**

2b.5. . . . *Identify genres in a variety of texts that the cultures deem important in under-standing the traditions of the cultures.*	Frequency	Percent
DON'T KNOW	0	0.0%
NOT AT ALL	0	0.0%
SUFFICIENTLY	1	14.0%
VERY WELL	6	**86.0%**

2b.6. . . . *Willingness/openness toward exploring literatures and other texts and media.*	Frequency	Percent
DON'T KNOW	0	0.0%
NOT AT ALL	0	0.0%
SUFFICIENTLY	1	14.0%
VERY WELL	6	**86.0%**

Examining Second Language Literacy Development in an Urban Multi-Age Classroom

SHARON H. ULANOFF ET AL.

This paper describes a multi-year ethnographic study of literacy instruction for English language learners (ELLs) in a multi-age classroom in Los Angeles. This study was undertaken by three university professors and one of the two teachers of the multi-age classroom. Data collection began in July 2003 and initially focused on exploring the nature of literacy instruction in this classroom. Second-year data collection explored teacher and student discourse during classroom activities, focusing on teacher-student discourse and student-student discourse. This study is guided by the following question: *How does the multiage experience impact second language literacy learning for urban elementary school students in Los Angeles?*

This work is situated in a growing body of research that describes benefits and challenges for multi-age education (Anderson and Pavan, 1993; Chase and Doan, 1996; Guitierrez and Slavin, 1992; 1994; Lauer, 2000; Lloyd, 1999) and explores the implications for English literacy instruction for ELLs. Given the recent incarnation of the reading wars nationwide (Allington, 2002; Allington and Woodside-Jiron, 1999; Coles, 2000; Foorman, Fletcher, Francis, and Schatschneider, 2000; Garan, 2002) and a political move toward an English only ideology in the United States (see Crawford, 2000; García and Curry-Rodriguez, 2000; Ulanoff and Vega-Castaneda, 2003), it is important to look at ways to provide opportunities for social interaction that embed literacy instruction in context for those students learning to read and write in their second language L2.

It is also influenced by the literature that explores the ways in which teachers' and students' discourse patterns in classroom lessons and other interactions influence student learning (Cazden, 1988; Gutierrez, Rymes, and Larson, 1995). Within the framework of sociolinguistics and sociocognitive theory, it is argued that student learning is positively related to students' "... appropriation of social discourses" (Hicks, 1996, p. 105), which occurs as they participate in classroom interactions. Hicks (1996) suggests that "discourse is a central means through which new understandings are negotiated among participants" (p. 105). Gee (1996) further argues that students use language as a social tool to help them accomplish interactional tasks in order to internalize learning (p. 274). As students are scaffolded through the learning process by either teachers or more capable peers (Vygotsky, 1962) they are able to make meaning out of the interactions.

In addition to providing a variety of opportunities for teacher and student interactions, multi-age classrooms may have positive implications for English literacy learning and instruction for ELLs. Peer teaching and cross-age tutoring have been shown to be highly effective approaches for ELLs because they allow them to utilize language in a social and academic context thereby enhancing their overall language skills while maintaining a high degree of age-appropriate content area instruction (Johnson, 1988). They further allow for students to interact in multiple ways related to classroom discourse, specifically student and teacher talk.

Methodology

Data were collected at La Nieta School, an urban elementary school on a multi-track year-round calendar. La Nieta School has a student population of 96% Latinos, 3% African American and the rest a mix of other ethnicities. Seventy-nine percent of the students are labeled English language learners (ELLs) and 98% of the students at La Nieta receive free and reduced lunch. The neighborhood consists of both single-family homes and multiple family dwellings that were built decades ago. La Nieta School has an active relationship with a local university. There is also a Parent Center on campus. Many of the teachers at La Nieta are bilingual and others hold certification that allows them to teach ELLs.

Data were collected by three researchers from a local university who served as non-participant observers in the classroom as well as by the two classroom teachers who acted as complete participants (Gold, 1958; Junker, 1960) for a period of three years beginning in July 2003 and ending in April 2006. Instruction was provided in English at all times, although Spanish was used as needed to clarify concepts or explain unknown vocabulary. Students generally enter the class in kindergarten and exit at the end of second grade. The classroom teachers had worked together in the multi-age classroom for nine years at the time the research study began.

At the beginning of the first year of study there were thirty-six students (29 English language learners and 7 English only learners) in the classroom community, 22 boys and 14 girls. There were twelve five-years olds, eight six-years olds and sixteen seven-years olds. Although the students were technically divided between the two teachers into separate class rosters, they functioned as one classroom with students moving fluidly between two connecting rooms to form the multi-age classroom. While the demographics of the class at the beginning of the second and third years of study were similar, there was a dramatic shift in the classroom population throughout the second and third years.

Beginning in July 2003, the classroom was observed once weekly by one or more of the researchers for a minimum of two hours to a maximum of the full day. Second year data collection included twice-monthly observations. Third year data collection consisted of sporadic observations to collect data to support data gathered during the first two years. Multiple data sources were collected to develop an in-depth understanding of the culture of the multi-age classroom. Ethnographic field notes, audio and video recordings, and student artifacts were collected (Emerson, Fretz, and Shaw, 1995) during each observation. Students were interviewed periodically as deemed necessary. The researchers met with the teachers formally and informally throughout the project, as a means of conducting member checks during the data collection and analysis phase of the study, allowing the researchers to clarify and/or modify any interpretations and conclusions they had drawn. The interview data served to enrich and triangulate the findings (Merriam, 1995).

The data were analyzed, categorized, compared, and contrasted using a methodology that seeks to "elicit meaning from the data" (LeCompte & Preissle, 1993, p. 235), rather than codifying and computing it, as well as the construction of categories or domains (Spradley, 1980). A domain analysis was used to sort the data into multiple categories, allowing a portrait to emerge that is reflective of the "big picture" of the literacy practices being utilized in the classroom (Frank, 1999).

Initial data collection focused on examining the construction of practice in the classroom. The second year of the study focused on the collection and analysis of the discourse taking place within the classroom between the student/s and teacher/s, the teacher and teacher and the student/s and other student/s. Using a meaning-based definition of discourse "as

a socially and culturally organized way of speaking through which particular functions are realized" (Schriffen, 1994, p. 32), allowed the researchers to move from a strict analysis of conversation to a view of discourse as socially-situated within a particular time, place and context adding richness to the data. While sociocultural theory (Jennings and Di, 1996; Rommetveit, 1974; Vygotsky, 1962; Wertsch, 1984) formed the foundation for the study, activity theory (Engestrom and Middleton, 1996; Leont'ev, 1978; Rogoff, 1990) provided a lens through which to view and understand the interactions and activities taking place within the learning situation.

Findings

Several overarching themes serve as the context for instruction in this multi-age classroom. First, Susan and Richard focus on allowing students to make meaning of school activities, learn and use literacy in meaningful ways, while connecting new learning to prior knowledge. By design they create spaces for L2 literacy development by creating a safe classroom environment where students are free to take risks with their learning and become valuable members of the classroom community. The following themes emerged that describe the structures in place that impact the creation of that community.

Community and Respect

Students in this multi-age classroom develop a sense of community and belonging from the first day they enter the classroom. There is an instructional focus on community and respect. Returning students are expected to be role models for newcomers. There is an equal level of respect for all community members, whether they are newcomers, teachers or returning students; everyone is important rather than no one is important. For example, during one lesson, Susan was listening to a student talk when Richard walked over to ask her a question. Susan looked at Richard and said, "Excuse me, but I am listening to Viviana (a pseudonym for one of the multiage students) now so I can't talk to you at this moment," indicating to students their equal status. This incident is only one example. Similar events take place throughout the school day. Furthermore, the class members consistently demonstrate respect and value for the diversity of languages, ethnicities and cultures in the classroom.

Communication

There is a high degree of communication between the two teachers; it is almost as if they function as one person. There are differences, for example, Susan is referred to by her first name and Richard is called Mr. Rogers, acknowledging each individual teacher's preferences and culture. Throughout the day, decisions are made by both teachers as to the direction they will take both procedurally and instructionally, with continual efforts to take both perspectives into account. It is always a discussion rather than a mandate. Moreover, parents are kept in the information loop. Not only do notes go home related to class activities, parents, teachers and students consistently communicate with one another.

Print-Rich Environment

The classroom provides the students with a print-rich environment in which all of the objects are labeled with English vocabulary. This environment emerges during the first few weeks of every school year school as the classroom community works to construct a literate environment. Student work is prominently displayed and changed throughout the school year. There is a library with several bookshelves and other book containers filled with both fiction and non-fiction texts in English at a variety of reading levels. There are charts and lists with important classroom information displayed throughout the room. All classroom print is in English, but as noted above, notes go home to parents in Spanish. . . .

High Expectations in a Safe Environment

Both teachers and students have high expectations for the quality of work students are expected to complete in class. These expectations include behaviors that students exhibit in class and on the playground. Everyone looks out for one another and there is no hesitation to step in and refocus a student as needed. It seems as if the students feel responsible for the group rather than just for themselves. These expectations are consistently communicated to students and parents. As part of these high expectations Susan and Richard create an atmosphere where students are called upon to actively engage in all classroom activities. Support is provided through the use of modeling, questioning and prompting as needed, and students are free to use their native language when they do not have the English skills to participate.

Integrated Curriculum

Music, literature, writing, and science are often integrated into weekly lessons. Both teachers spend time activating the students' background knowledge when introducing a new concept, unit or book. Beginning in kindergarten, reading and writing are presented across the curriculum with a focus on strategy instruction. This is interesting in light of the fact that teachers in this public school are required to follow the district's adopted scripted reading program that is heavily based on phonics and phonemic awareness instruction. Both teachers have adapted their use of the basal materials in order to present a thematic approach that embeds their instruction in context and supports the students. Rather than engage the students in decontexualized tasks throughout the day, the teachers emphasize metacognitive awareness and students are asked to verbalize the strategies they have or will use when reading, writing or approaching a specific task.

The Role of Teacher Talk

The teachers use language in ways that not only communicate, but also teach language and usage. Susan and Richard use targeted procedural and instructional talk aimed at both classroom management and instruction. They further work to "teach" students to use both procedural and instructional talk during classroom activities, through "self-talk," aimed at helping students internalize instructional and behavioral procedures. Teachers use a "questioning mode" to impel students to search for answers to instructional and procedural questions.

Throughout the day, both teachers use "teacher talk" in ways that both describe classroom procedures and also model those very procedures. Lessons consist of direct instruction but also allowed for independent activities on a daily basis. In addition to the direct instruction students engage in inquiry activities. The first few days of the school year are spent on group building and teaching appropriate classroom behaviors to the new students in class. Newcomers are paired with returning students in newcomer/role model pairs and returning students are expected to take on expert roles in acclimating the new students to the classroom culture.

Both teachers teach and use what they call self-talk with the students. This consists of specific phrases that help students know how to behave in the classroom. The teachers model the specific behaviors that they expect of students and then students create "posters" of these statements, which are then posted throughout the room. . . . Furthermore, teachers and students engage in choral self-talk chants at the beginning of the year to help the students learn the classroom procedures. At first they chant with prompting, but after a while students are asked to repeat the self-talk without prompts.

Susan and Richard are active participants in instruction, modeling behavior and "thinking aloud" as they engage in classroom activities. They both use questioning to get students to think about classroom activities and model vocabulary usage throughout instruction, posing critical questions and often responding with questions that hold students accountable for learning. It is through the use of questions that both Susan and Richard guide the students to take ownership for their learning as well as developing a sense of collaboration within the classroom community. This is evident during reading instruction when Susan reads aloud to the class. She consistently checks for understanding and then models the use of new vocabulary, embedding it in the context of the story being read. During lessons, Susan models the expectations she has for student behavior, including turn taking behavior during lessons and discussions. While students are expected to raise their hands when guest teachers and other visitors work with the whole class during lessons, Susan focuses on holding conversations with the class where students are free to participate without waiting for recognition. She often provides wait time allowing students to chime in when they have something to say. "Show me, don't tell me." is one of the mantras frequently heard in class by both students and teachers. The expert role models are quite adept at appropriately scaffolding the procedural information for the newcomers so that they are relatively indistinguishable by the end of the first month of school.

The Role of Student Talk

Despite the fact that all instruction in this class takes place in English, the second language of most of the students in this class, students use Spanish when they are working together, especially when they are giving instructions to other students, telling them what to do. While at first glance this appeared to be little more than translating to support one another and clarify instructions, upon further examination it appears that the students are operating within their comfort zone, using their first language for communication. It may also be used as a means of forming more personal relationships with other students in the class.

However, students consistently appropriated the self-talk used by Susan and Richard in the classroom and this self-talk was in English. What is interesting is that while this type of discourse was similar to that used by Susan and Richard, there were differences, demonstrating the students' ability to internalize and modify the self-talk to meet their communication needs. For example, one student, exasperated at another student who appeared to be critiquing his work, yelled, "I did it to the best of my ability, ok, huh?" This seems to mirror a question that Susan might have asked (Did you do it to the best of your ability?) but is slightly different. Students also appropriated teacher talk when they took on leadership roles in the classroom. It was not uncommon to hear [Ivonne as she leads the calendar] say, "We have about one minute left. . . ." or "Hey, raise your hand if you know" much as Susan or Richard might say to the class.

Conclusions

The present ethnographic research study documents the use of a multi-age K-1-2 classroom situation for educating and supporting ELLs within the public school system of California. The goal of the three-year study was to make visible those processes that allow ELLs to not only acquire English, but to excel within the educational system thus allowing them access to the same occupational and educational opportunities of their English only peers. During year one of the study, researchers collected data pertaining to the instructional practices in place within the classroom.

The findings indicated that the teachers spent time developing a classroom learning community that promoted respect for one another based on a high degree of communication between teachers and students, students and students, parents and teachers, and parents and students. At all times teachers and students maintained high academic and behavioral expectations for one another, generally holding each other accountable for fulfilling these standards. Additionally,

instruction was provided in a safe, well-maintained print-rich environment through the use of a high interest, literature-rich integrated curriculum. Students were encouraged to take ownership of their learning, beginning within the first few weeks of entering kindergarten and increasing as they progressed into higher grade levels.

Over the course of the study Susan and Richard consistently engaged the students in the learning process through the use of higher-level questions, student-led lessons and activities, group-building strategies and genuine dialogue. In year two, the researchers explored the notion that students were appropriating and modifying "teacher self-talk" into conversations with their peers. It became apparent that the students had internalized much of the teacher self talk modeled and reinforced over time because they were able to alter the language and use it within different academic situations. Through this process, the students were able to create their own self-talk. This is an important finding as it shows that ELLs in the early stages of English language acquisition are able to understand and appropriate complex English language concepts through the use of scaffolded instruction by skilled teachers when it is reinforced across a period of 3 years.

These findings support the notion that students of diverse linguistic, economic and cultural backgrounds have opportunities to engage in "a continuum of teaching strategies that involves them in motivating, meaningful reading (and learning) experiences" (Au, 2002, p. 409). These experiences should take place within a safe learning environment with high academic expectations and a high degree of support from parents, teachers and students. The current study adds to the research literature by providing further support for the use of relevant instruction that promotes the active engagement of ELLs in academic dialogue within the classroom. Because students need time to acquire and internalize this language, the use of a multi-age classroom experience in the early stages of English language acquisition is suggested.

Implications

The debate over appropriate initial literacy instruction for ELLs in California is ongoing despite demonstrated success for properly implemented primary language programs (Krashen and Biber, 1988; Willig, 1985). Further arguments describe challenges to effective literacy instruction as a result of restrictions based on how and what is taught in reading (Moustafa and Land, 2002). Presently ELLs in California are being taught to read in English, most often through the use of scripted programs that do not always focus on the construction of meaning.

This study attempts to examine the impact of one multi-age experience on ELLs' literacy acquisition during their initial years of schooling in the hopes of describing ways to imbed literacy instruction within the classroom context. This study specifically explores the impact of student and teacher discourse on second language literacy learning. Advocates of multi-age education believe that the presence of older and younger children allows them to engage in meaningful literacy activities by encouraging collaboration and promoting a climate of "expected cooperation" (Katz, Evangelou, and Hartman, 1991, p. 10). It is during these exchanges that children learn to problem solve and negotiate alternative responses to the problems they encounter thereby scaffolding each other's learning experiences (Pontecorvo and Zucchermaglio, 1990). It is during these interactions that literacy learning takes place. Multi-age classrooms encourage and promote collaborative learning experiences, and provide the context-rich environment needed to support ELLs as they acquire English.

References

Allington, R. L. (2002). *Big brother and the national reading curriculum: How ideology trumped evidence. Portsmouth*, NH: Heinemann.

Allington, D. and Woodside-Jiron, H. (1999). The politics of literacy teaching: How "research" shaped educational policy. *Educational researcher,* Vol. 28, No. 8, pp. 4–13.

Anderson, R. H. and Pavan, B. N. (1993). *Nongradedness: Helping it to happen.* Lancaster, PA: Technomic Publishing.

Au, K. (2002). Multicultural factors and the effective instruction of students of diverse backgrounds. In A.E. Farstrup & S.J. Samuels (Eds.), *What research has to say about reading instruction* (pp. 392–413). Newark, DE: International Reading Association.

Cazden. C. B. (1988). *Classroom discourse: The language of teaching and learning.* Portsmouth, NH: Heinemann.

Chase, P. (1994). Valuing. In P. Chase and J. Doan (Eds.). *Full circle: A new look at MULTI-AGE education.* Portsmouth, NH: Heinemann.

Chase, P. and Doan, J. (1994). *Full circle: A new look at MULTI-AGE education.* Portsmouth, NH: Heinemann.

Chase, P. and Doan, J. (1996). *Choosing to learn: Ownership and responsibility in a primary multi-age classroom.* Portsmouth, NH: Heinemann.

Coles, G. (2000). *Misreading reading: The bad science that hurts children.* Portsmouth, NH: Heinemann.

Crawford, J. (2000). *At war with diversity: US language policy in an age of anxiety.* Clevedon, UK: Multilingual Matters.

Doan, B. (1996). The option of choice. In P. Chase and J. Doan, (Eds.). *Choosing to learn: Ownership and responsibility in a primary multi-age classroom.* Portsmouth, NH: Heinemann.

Emerson, R., Fretz, R., and Shaw, L. (1995). *Writing ethnographic fieldnotes.* Chicago, IL: University of Chicago Press.

Engestrom, Y. and Middleton, D. (1996). *Cognition and communication at work.* New York, NY: Cambridge University Press.

Fitzgerald, J. (1995). English-as-a-second language instruction in the United States: A research review. *Journal of Reading Behavior, 27,* 115–132.

Foorman, B. R., Fletcher, J.M., Francis, D. J., and Schatschneider, C. S. (2000). Response Misrepresentation of research by other researchers. *Educational researcher,* Vol. 29, No. 6, pp. 27–37.

Frank, C. (1999). *Ethnographic eyes: A teacher's guide to classroom observation.* Portsmouth, NH: Heinemann.

Garan, E. M. (2002). *Resisting reading mandates: How to triumph with the truth.* Portsmouth, NH; Heinemann.

García, E. E. and Curry-Rodriguez, J. E. (2000). The education of limited English proficient students in California Schools: An assessment of the influence of Proposition 227 on selected districts and schools. *Bilingual Research Journal,* Vol. 24, Nos. 1 & 2., pp. 1–21.

Gee, J. P. (1996). Vygotsky and current debates in education: Some dilemmas as afterthoughts to *Discourse, learning and schooling.* In D. Hicks (Ed.). *Discourse, learning and schooling.* New York: Cambridge University Press.

Gold, R. (1958). Roles in sociological field observation. *Social Forces,* Vol. 36, pp. 217–223.

Guiterrez, R. and Slavin, R. E. (1992). Achievement effects of non-graded elementary schools: A best evidence synthesis. *Review of educational research,* Vol. 62, No. 4, pp. 333–376.

Hicks, D. (1996). Contextual inquiries: A discourse-oriented study of classroom learning. In D. Hicks (Ed.). *Discourse, learning and schooling.* New York: Cambridge University Press.

Jennings, C. and Di, X. (1996). Collaborative learning and thinking: The Vygotskian approach. In L. Dixon Krause (Ed.), *Vygotsky in the classroom: Mediated literacy instruction and assessment* (pp. 77–92). White Plains, NY: Longman.

Johnson, D. M. (1988). ESL children as teachers: A social view of second language. *Language arts,* February, 1988.

Junker, B. (1960). *Field work.* Chicago, IL: University of Chicago Press.

Katz, L., Evangelou, D., and Hartman, J. (1991). *The case for mixed-age grouping in early education.* Washington, D.C. : National Association for the Education of Young Children.

Krashen, S. and Biber, D. (1988). *On course: Bilingual education's success in California.* Sacramento, CA: CABE.

Lauer, P. A. (2000). *Instructional practices and implementation issues in multi-age classrooms.* Aurora, CO: Mid-continent research for education and learning.

LeCompte, M. and Preissle, J. (1993). *Ethnography and qualitative design in educational research.* San Diego, CA: Academic Press.

Leont'ev, A.N. (1978). *Activity, consciousness, personality.* Englewood Cliffs, NJ: Prentice Hall.

Lloyd, L. (1999). Multi-age classes and high ability students. *Review of educational research,* Vol. 69, No. 2, pp. 187–212.

Lodish, R. (1992). The pros and cons of mixed-age grouping. *Principal,* Vol. 7, No. 5, pp. 20–22.

Merriam, S. (1995). *Qualitative research and case study applications in education.* San Fransisco, CA: Jossey-Bass.

Miller, B. A. (1996). A basic understanding of multi-age grouping: Teacher readiness, planning, and parent involvement required for successful practice. *The school administrator,* Vol. 53, No. 1, pp. 12–17.

Moustafa, M. and Land, R. (2002). The reading achievement of economically-disadvantaged children in urban schools using Open Court vs. comparably disadvantaged children in urban schools using non-scripted programs. *2002 Yearbook of the Urban Learning, Teaching and Research Special Interest Group.* Los Angeles, CA: CSULA.

Ogbu, J.U. (1981). School ethnography: A multilevel approach. *Anthropology & Education Quarterly,* 12, 3–29.

Pontecorvo, C. and Zucchermaglio, C. (1990). A passage to literacy: Learning in a social context. In Y. Goodman (Ed.), *How children construct literacy: Piagetian perspectives* (pp. 59–98). Newark, DE: International Reading Association.

Rogoff, B. (1990). *Apprenticeship in thinking-cognitive development in social context.* San Francisco, CA: Jossey-Bass.

Rommetveit, R. (1974). *On message structure: A framework for the study of language and communication.* New York, NY: Wiley.

Schriffin, D. (1994). *Approaches to discourse.* Malden, MA: Blackwell Press.

Spradley, J. (1980). *Participant observation.* Orlando, FL: Harcourt, Brace and Jovanovich.

Ulanoff, S. H. and Vega-Castaneda, L. (2003). The sociopolitical context of bilingual instruction in 21st century California. *Proceedings of the annual meeting of the Hawaii International Conference on Education,* Honolulu, HI.

Valdes, G. (1998). The world outside and inside schools: Language and immigrant children. *Educational Researcher, 27,* 4–18.

Vygotsky, L. (1962). *Theory and language.* Cambridge, MA: MIT University Press.

Wertsch, J.V. (1984). *Culture, communication and cognition.* New York, NY: Cambridge University Press.

Willig, A.C. (1985). A meta-analysis of selected studies on the effectiveness of bilingual education. *Review of educational research,* Vol. 55, No. 3, pp. 269–317.

Critical Thinking

1. What are the three major themes of this study?
2. How can teachers improve the literacy development among their second language learners?
3. What techniques from this article are essential for teaching all young learners?
4. Why is risk-taking with vocabulary critical for all classrooms?

SHARON H. ULANOFF, California State University, Los Angeles.
AMBIKA GOPALAKRISHNAN, California State University, Los Angeles.
DIANE BRANTLEY, California State University, San Bernardino.
SUSAN COURTNEY, Los Angeles Unified School District. With
RICHARD ROGERS, Los Angeles Unified School District.

From *International Journal of Early Childhood Education,* 2007, pp. 53–62. Copyright © 2007 by Sharon Ulanoff. Reprinted by permission of the author.

Celebrating Diversity through Explorations of Arab Children's Literature

TAMI AL-HAZZA AND BOB LUCKING

Incidents of terrorism and other forms of heinous violence around the world are so dramatic and painfully wrenching that they often dictate change: in politics, in social convention, in battle, and in the classroom. The five years since the 9/11 attacks, in particular, have brought about huge shifts in the collective global view of Arabs, and it is certainly timely to examine how educators treat the literature of the people in that part of the world. While language arts teachers may feel like throwing up their arms in frustration at being asked to learn about yet another body of children's literature, it has never been more important to represent a clear-headed and balanced view of a people, their culture, and their literature. In the United States, Arabs and Arab Americans have become a minority of suspicion (Al-Hazza & Lucking, 2005), and enormous misconceptions and biases exist about these people and their culture. Mindful of all teachers' efforts to establish cultural pluralism in their classrooms (Banks, 1991), we hope to offer some guidance in defining these issues relative to children's literature that accurately reflects some of the cultural norms of the Arab world.

To begin, many educated Americans do not even know what the term *Arab* means, and many confuse the terms "Arabs" and "Muslims." People who describe themselves as Arab speak Arabic or claim the Arabic language as their ancestors' mother tongue, possess Semitic roots, and trace their lineage to the descendants of Abraham and Hagar (Goldschmidt, 1989). The majority of Arabs are from Africa and the Middle East, in a region that stretches from Mauritania, positioned on the Atlantic coast of Africa, to Oman, which is situated on the Indian Ocean coast of the Arabian Peninsula. This territory encompasses 22 countries, located in three regions: countries in northern Africa, countries situated on the Mediterranean but not in Africa, and countries located in the heart of Arabia, on the Arabian Peninsula. All Arab countries combined constitute an Arab world population of approximately 300 million people (Elmandjra, 2004). The geographic area of the Middle East is also home to Pakistani, Kurds, Turks, Iranians, Afghans, and Armenians, who are not considered Arabs. They each have their own distinct language, traditions, and cultures.

One of the most persistent points of misunderstanding is that all Muslims are Arabs and that all Arabs are Muslim. The two terms are not interchangeable. The majority of Muslims are from Indonesia; only 20 percent of the world's Muslim population is Arab (Suleiman, 2000). Arab communities also contain significant populations of Copts, Melokites, Christians, Jews, Druze, and Maronites; this diversity of faith is due, in part, to the fact that the majority of Arab countries place no restrictions on freedom of worship.

All of these nuances are lost in popular culture as there is a constant search for formulaic villains. Movies and television have prominently featured Arab villains in recent years; not since the days of "cowboys and Indians" has such a dichotomous portrayal of good and evil been more apparent. Arab extremists or Muslim fundamentalists bent on destroying the world populate contemporary films. This formulaic portrayal of villainy also can be found in comic books and action computer games (Khan, 2004).

Therefore, Arab Americans are sometimes viewed through the scrim of misconception. They often are assumed to be impoverished and lacking in education, when this is quite untrue. Whereas 24 percent of all Americans hold college degrees, 41 percent of Arab Americans are college graduates. Furthermore, the median annual income of an Arab American family living in the United States in 1999 is $47,000, compared with $42,000 for all U.S. households. More than half of such families own their own home. Seventy-three percent of people of Arab descent in the United States work as managers or professionals, while the overall U.S. average is 34 percent (Arab American Institute, 2005).

One of the reasons that Americans have a distorted view of Arabs is the dramatic and often negative image that popular culture frequently projects of the Middle East. What is missing in the images that Americans receive from, and about, the Middle East is a realistic and humanistic portrayal of a people and their culture as told from an indigenous perspective. To promote an acceptance of diverse individuals, teachers can introduce good-quality Arab children's literature that accurately depicts Arab culture, creates positive images, and credibly represents Arabs in the plots, descriptions, and illustrations (Bishop, 1997). It is essential that children are exposed to stories that describe everyday events and the thoughts and feelings of Arab children.

Traditional Literature

While teachers can select from many genres of Arab children's literature, fairy tales from the Arab world are a wonderful place to begin since these stories, as is the case of many stories from traditional cultures, are designed to transmit cultural values and mores as well as entertain readers and listeners. *Sitti and the Cats: A Tale of Friendship* (Bahous, 1999) is an excellent example of a children's fairy tale that exemplifies traditional Arab values. This fairy tale relates behavior and values that are socially acceptable for survival in a small village in Palestine. The main character, an elderly widow called Sitti who has outlived her family, is rewarded for her benevolent nature, good heart, and kind deeds to others by a gift from a family of magical cats.

Sitti's experiences offer insight into the traditional beliefs and values inherent in the Arab culture, such as generosity, fulfilling one's role in society, caring for others before oneself, and hard work. The predominant theme throughout this story is thinking of one's responsibility to the group before considering individual wants. This theme is explored as the neighbors share their crops, firewood, and other necessities with Sitti and with each other, thus caring for each other to ensure the survival of the entire village.

The importance of generosity is emphasized when Sitti is given a magical gift of gold and silver, and her immediate response is to purchase items for others. Only after she has bestowed gifts on significant individuals does she consider her own needs. Generosity is a common theme throughout Arab children's stories and is predominant in Arabs' everyday lives.

Another bedrock value in Arab societies is respect and concern for the elderly. In *Sitti and the Cats,* these traits are manifested by the neighbors who care for Sitti in a respectful fashion. They do not just give her the supplies she needs; they allow her to perform small but important services, such as babysitting or mending clothes, in exchange for her daily staples. This type of exchange allows Sitti to maintain her dignity and save face, while ensuring that she is able to sustain her standard of living and her place in society. Saving face, or preserving one's personal dignity within the social order, is a motivation common throughout the Middle East and the Far East. Losing face would involve being embarrassed or being viewed as capable of committing acts considered unacceptable by the larger society. These social strictures are deeply rooted in traditional and modern Middle Eastern culture, and it is imperative that individuals maintain a level of decorum in public in order to maintain face.

Numerous other fairy tales are available to classroom teachers that can open new doors and broaden children's cultural horizons. These tales can be found in such books as *The Golden Sandal* (Hickox, 1998), *Aladdin* (Johnson-Davies, 1995), *The Animals of Paradise* (Durkee, 1996), *Goha the Wise Fool* (Johnson-Davies, 1993), *Sindbad: From the Tales of the Thousand and One Nights* (Zeman, 1999), and *The Storytellers* (Lewin, 1998). *The Golden Sandal* is an Iraqi version of the Cinderella story, dating back thousands of years. Elementary-age children will enjoy comparing and contrasting the American and Arab versions of this story. And while most American children will be familiar with the story of *Aladdin,* Arab versions differ somewhat from Americanized versions (especially the Disney movie by that name). Children will delight in discussing the differences and how the Disney version was made to fit an Americanized image of Arabs.

Contemporary Realistic Fiction

Rich teaching opportunities about Arab cultures are not limited to fairy tales, of course. Children's books that offer unique insight into realistic, contemporary Arab life are also available and are invaluable resources. An example of this category of children's literature is *The Day of Ahmed's Secret* (Heide & Gilliland, 1990). This story is set in the bustling Egyptian city of Cairo. The colorful narrative offers a glimpse into unique aspects of Arab life with which most American children will be unfamiliar, such as the typical clothing worn by Egyptians, the exotic image of vendors selling their wares in the streets, and buildings designed in ancient Arab Islamic architecture. The plot of *Ahmed's Secret* revolves around a young boy who is brimming with glee in anticipation of telling his family that he has learned to write his name. American children will be able to relate to Ahmed's excitement as they learn about a new world, full of a rich diversity of uniquely Arab characters engaging in traditions and occupations typical of the early 20th century and no longer seen in more modern Arab cities.

Fulfilling one's role in society is a common theme throughout Arab stories. Although Ahmed is young, he is expected to work and help support his family. While the concept of child labor is quite alien to most American youngsters, Ahmed is proud that he is old enough and physically strong enough to perform the traditional work of his father and grandfather. This pride in carrying on the family trade is an excellent point of discussion for American teachers and can be related to historical fiction from many cultures.

Another key value emphasized in this book is the centrality of the family. The recurring theme of putting the needs of others (in this case, the family) above the needs of the individual is clear as Ahmed spends his days working, instead of playing like most American children. Yet, this book also allows young readers to see the commonality between cultures and to reach across borders to share the excitement of Ahmed's day.

The strong emphasis that Arab cultures place on the cohesiveness of the family is found in this story, as Ahmed honors his family by saving his special secret to reveal first to his parents, not to the other people he meets during the day. This tradition of telling important news to the most honored members of the family first is often found in Arab society. The importance of family time together also is evident as the family waits for all members to gather at the conclusion of the day to discuss significant events of the day. This tradition can be found throughout Arab literature and among Arab families of today. Other realistic contemporary fiction books that portray the same themes are *Sami and the Time of the Troubles* (Heide & Gilliland, 1992), *Samir and Yonatan* (Carmi, 2000), *A Stone in My Hand* (Clinton, 2002), and *Habibi* (Nye, 1999).

Historical Fiction

Another genre of Arab children's literature is historical fiction. *A Peddler's Dream* (Shefelman, 1992), one such example, focuses on Arab immigration to America. This book enables teachers to introduce to students a segment of the population that historically has been distorted or excluded from the elementary school curriculum. *A Peddler's Dream* relates how Mediterranean Arabs came to America in the early 1900s to pursue an economic livelihood. Because of widespread prejudice and subsequent limited opportunities, many could only find work as peddlers, traveling from farmhouse to farmhouse selling their wares.

This book presents a realistic portrayal of an immigrant from Lebanon, through the experiences of Solomon Azar. Students will be able to explore the similarities of Solomon's perspectives and experiences to those of other immigrants. The underlying theme of Arab life found throughout this book is the value of hard work and thrift. Solomon leaves his country and the woman to whom he is betrothed to come to the United States to establish a better future. He arrives with only the dream of owning a store, his ambition to succeed, and very little money. However, Solomon is a good man whose kindness and honesty help him to prosper in his endeavors, reaping the rewards of virtue.

Other books that offer a broader understanding of Arab culture and introduce young readers to historical people and events are: *Traveling Man: The Journey of Ibn Battuta* (Rumford, 2001), *Saladin: Noble Prince of Islam* (Stanley, 2002), *The House of Wisdom* (Heide & Gilliland, 1999), and *The Shadows of Ghadames* (Stolz, 2004).

Choosing Arab Children's Literature

Folktales, contemporary realistic fiction, and historical fiction are invaluable sources for teaching children about the Arab culture and traditions. Aside from the list presented here, many other wonderful works of Arab children's literature are available (refer to Al-Hazza, 2006, for a more comprehensive list), yet it can be difficult for the educator who does not have direct experience with the culture to choose stories that accurately represent the Arab culture. Guidelines that educators utilize when selecting Arab children's books for inclusion into the elementary language arts curriculum should be based on clear criteria.

In selecting multicultural children's literature, both the author's and the illustrator's credentials must be examined (Bishop, 1997; Temple, Martinez, Yokota, & Naylor, 1998).

While being a native of the Arab culture is one of the best qualifications to write about that culture (Sleeter & Grant, 2003), others may derive their legitimacy from traveling or residing in the area. If the storyline is written from the perspective of an insider or a native viewpoint, it rings with authenticity (McMahon, Saunders, & Bardwell, 1996/1997) and thus will be more likely to capture the hearts of young readers. Additionally, Sleeter and Grant contend that the books should authentically depict well-rounded characters, rather than portraying them as terrorists, religious fanatics, or polygamists. Educators also should pay attention to the relationships between characters in the story (Manning & Baruth, 2004). Ideally, the Arab characters would exert personal power in the story and not merely serve subservient roles in the work.

Careful examination should not be limited to thematic elements alone; the images included in the book should be brought under scrutiny as well. For example, the illustrations or art in the book should reflect details of dress, setting, and physical environment in ways that do not reinforce stereotypes. The issue of Arab women covering their heads with *hijabs* (head coverings) and *burqas* (veils) and Arab men wearing long flowing robes is potentially contentious and incendiary. The majority of Arab men from the Persian Gulf region still dress in the traditional robes called *dishdashas;* however, Arabs from the Mediterranean and North Africa wear a different type of attire. Many women throughout the Arab world choose to wear a veil over their face, but significant numbers of women do not (Al-Hazza, 2004). An open discussion with youngsters is likely the best path to true acceptance.

Photos or illustrations should accurately portray Arab people, their lifestyles, and the living circumstances of these diverse people. An immediate point of examination should be the physical representations of the people themselves. While the stereotypes shown in B-grade movies would have viewers believing that all Arabs have dark complexions, black hair, and black eyes, significant numbers of Arabs who have light skin, freckles, and brown or blond hair reside throughout the world. A modern storyline depicting Arabs living in tents in the desert and riding camels would likely be inappropriate. In a historical novel this depiction would be accurate; today, however, only a small percentage of Arabs reside in the desert and live a nomadic lifestyle.

Finally, the date of publication bears examination. Books published in the mid-1960s were often written from an Anglo-American perspective (Manning & Baruth, 2004). Books with a more recent publication date are more likely to be accurate.

Carefully choosing Arab children's literature, using such clear criteria as outlined here, will yield selections that provide avenues into the hearts and culture of Arabs and the various nationalities that constitute this ethnic group. Through exploration of the above-mentioned works of literature, and similar ones, students can reach beyond the mainstream culture. Young readers may come to appreciate the diversity represented by Arabs, which is especially important in these times of suspicion and misinformation. These literary experiences hold the power to free children from the damaging effects of premature, inaccurate, and prejudiced interpretations of a different culture

(Spindler, 1987). Literature about Arab peoples reflects both the universal qualities of human experience and the unique dimensions of another part of the world, where social mores and cultural norms differ from those of mainstream American life. Teachers who show respect for ethnic and cultural pluralism are more likely to have students who are similarly inclined. Such instruction integrates an examination of attitudes, accurate information, and literary exploration, involving both teacher and students in developing a broader appreciation of the potential of all cultural groups. And it is only when people of all cultures believe that they have a place in the world order that we are likely to see an end to senseless acts of violence.

Children's Books Cited

Bahous, S. (1997). *Sitti and the cats: A tale of friendship.* Boulder, CO: Roberts Rinehart Publishers.

Carmi, D. (2000). *Samir and Yonatan.* New York: Arthur A. Levin Books.

Clinton, C. (2002). *A stone in my hand.* Cambridge, MA: Candlewick Press.

Durkee, N. (1996). *The animals of paradise.* London: Hood Hood Books.

Heide, F. P., & Gilliland, J. (1999). *The house of wisdom.* New York: DK Publishing.

Heide, F. P., & Gilliland, J. (1992). *Sami and the time of the troubles.* New York: Clairon Books.

Heide, F. P., & Gilliland, J. (1990). *The day of Ahmed's secret.* New York: Lothrop, Lee & Shepard Books.

Hickox, R. (1998). *The golden sandal.* New York: Holiday House.

Johnson-Davies, D. (1993). *Goha the wise fool.* Dokki, Cairo: Hoopoe Books.

Johnson-Davies, D. (1995). *Aladdin.* Dokki, Cairo: Hoopoe Books.

Lewin, T. (1998). *The storytellers.* New York: Lothrop, Lee & Shepard.

Nye, N. S. (1999). *Habibi.* New York: Simon Pulse.

Rumford, J. (2001). *Traveling man: The journey of Ibn Battuta.* Boston: Houghton Mifflin.

Shefelman, J. (1992). *A peddler's dream.* Austin, TX: Houghton Mifflin.

Stanley, D. (2002). *Saladin: Noble prince of Islam.* New York: HarperCollins.

Stolz, J. (2004). *The shadows of Ghadames.* New York. Delacorte Press.

Zeman, L. (1999). *Sindbad: From the Tales of the Thousand and One Nights.* Toronto, Ontario: Tundra Books.

References

Al-Hazza, T. C. (2004). Women in the Gulf Arab region: A historical perspective and present day comparison. In A. Gupta & S. Sinha (Eds.), *Empowering Asian women: Language and other facets* (pp. 76-94). Jaipur, India: Mangal Deep Publications.

Al-Hazza, T. C. (2006). Arab children's literature: An update. *Book Links, 15*(3), 11-17.

Al-Hazza, T., & Lucking, R. (2005). The minority of suspicion: Arab Americans. *Multicultural Review, 14*(3), 32-38.

Arab American Institute. (2007). *Arab Americans.* Retrieved January 2007, from www.aaiusa.org/arab-americans/22/ demographics.

Banks, J. A. (1991). A curriculum for empowerment, action, and change. In C. E. Sleeter (Ed.), *Empowerment through multicultural education* (pp. 125-142). Albany, NY: SUNY Press.

Bishop, R. S. (1997). Selecting literature for a multicultural curriculum. In V. J. Harris (Ed.), *Using multiethnic literature in the K-8 classroom* (pp. 1-19). Norwood, MA: Christopher-Gordon.

Elmandjra, M. (2004). *How will the Arab world be able to master its own independent developments?* Retrieved November 12, 2005, from www.transnational.org/forum/meet/2004/El-mandjra_ ArabWorld.html

Goldschmidt, A., Jr. (1989). *Concise history of the Middle East.* Cambridge, MA: Westview Press.

Khan, A. (2004). Teens slam "racist" game, but still love it. *Reuters News Agency.* April 22, 2004. Retrieved January 2, 2006, from www.mafhoum.com/press7/191T44.htm

Manning, M. L., & Baruth, L. G. (2004). *Multicultural education of children and adolescents.* Boston: Pearson.

McMahon, R., Saunders, D., & Bardwell, T. (1996–1997). Increasing young children's cultural awareness with American Indians. *Childhood Education, 73,* 105–108.

Sleeter, C. E., & Grant, C. A. (2003). *Making choices for multicultural education: Five approaches to race, class and gender.* New York: John Wiley & Sons.

Spindler, G. D. (1987). *Education and cultural process: Anthropological approaches* (2nd ed.). Prospect Heights, IL: Waveland Press.

Suleiman, M. (2000). *Teaching about Arab Americans: What social studies teachers should know.* (ERIC Document Reproduction Service No. ED442 714)

Temple, C., Martinez, M., Yokota, J., & Naylor, A. (1998). *Criteria for evaluating multicultural materials.* Retrieved February 1, 2006, from the North Central Regional Educational Laboratory Web site: www.ncrel

Critical Thinking

1. What are the benefits of featuring children's literature from around the world?

2. How does literature help share a person's cultural background and heritage?

3. What do the authors recommend for showcasing multicultural children's literature?

4. Why is all literature multicultural literature?

TAMI AL-HAZZA is Assistant Professor and **BOB LUCKING** is Professor, Darden College of Education, Old Dominion University, Norfolk, Virginia.

From *Childhood Education,* Spring 2007, pp. 132–135. Copyright © 2007 by the Association for Childhood Education International. Reprinted by permission of Tami Al-Hazza and Bob Lucking and the Association for Childhood Education International, 17904 Georgia Avenue, Suite 215, Olney, MD 20832.

Chica Lit: Multicultural Literature Blurs Borders

Marie Loggia-Kee

With chick lit, it's all about the attitude: Think of the original *Diary of Bridget Jones,* a tell-all of the dating life of a singleton. Chica lit takes that sass and combines it with culture.

Alisa Valdes-Rodriguez, author of the genre-setting bestseller *The Dirty Girls Social Club,* quickly dismisses the term "Latina lit." That's not what her novels are. They're *Chica lit.* "There has been a rich tradition of Latina literature out there, most of it quite literary and heavy. Chica lit, by contrast, is bubbly, fun, irreverent, modern, and fashionable," Valdes-Rodriguez says. "I think of Chica lit as being like the *Seinfeld* show, whereas traditional Latina literature is more like *ER.*"

> **There has been a rich tradition of Latina literature out there, most of it quite literary and heavy. Chica lit, by contrast, is bubbly, fun, irreverent, modern, and fashionable.**

In May 2006 Valdes-Rodriguez joined Mary Castillo, author of *Hot Tamara: What's Life Without a Little Spice,* among others, in Miami Beach at the first Chica Lit Club. While Valdes-Rodriguez usually sets her novels on the East Coast, Castillo captures the essence of Los Angeles. Together the two authors are helping to define a new genre of writing.

When Castillo submitted her manuscript for publication, editors told her the same thing over and over again: "It's not Latina enough." Often Chica literature breaks the traditional roles and forges a new identity; the protagonist of the new fiction is not just a woman of Latina heritage, she's a strong, and strongly identified, Latina-American woman.

In *Hot Tamara's* closing notes, Castillo said that she learned more about herself and her heritage while working on the book:

> Writing *Hot Tamara* was a journey for me to realize how much of a Latina I really am. In my family we didn't speak Spanish or even identify ourselves as Mexican. I was a fourth-generation American on my dad's side, who happened to be Mexican. ("Avon's Little Black Book on Mary Castillo," cited in *Hot Tamara*)

Castillo and other writers reach a segment of the population eager for role models that reflect some of the realities and obstacles they face in real life. Authors such as Valdes-Rodriguez and Castillo touch a growing mainstream population that often relates to more than one culture.

Industry Trends

One way to distinguish the direction of the publishing industry is to look at what the major houses solicit. Chica lit is showing up on the request list. Selina McLemore, a former editor at Harper-Collins Publishers who now acquires for Harlequin, credits not only literary writers such as Isabel Allende and Sandra Cisneros for changing the voice of the literature, but contemporary writers such as Valdes-Rodriguez and Castillo as well.

"We're seeing fiction that is truly intended for the commercial market," McLemore explains. "These writers and books are a reflection of the way Latino culture has become, in the last ten years, a much more accepted part of mainstream pop culture, as has been proven in music, movies, and TV."

Rather than assimilating her characters into mainstream culture, Valdes-Rodriguez notes that they and their stories reflect the lives of her readers. "I had no idea my work would resonate with so many people—more than half a million books sold to date," Valdes-Rodriguez says. "Again and again I hear that my work has affirmed the life choices many Latinas have made, like college and a professional career, choices that none of us have yet seen reflected in the mainstream media very well."

Cultural Identity

The recently published anthology *Border-Line Personalities: A New Generation of Latinas Dish on Sex, Sass and Cultural Shifting* explores the concept of self-defining that surfaces in many of the Chica lit novels. Michelle Herrera Mulligan, one of the anthology's editors, said that her mother accused her of not staying true to the culture. "Even though I'm half white," she said, "I thought I'd bridged the gap between my mother and me. If I didn't fit into her world, where did I belong?" (xxvi). Through the process of putting together the anthology, Herrera

Mulligan said that the contributors developed a "pathology of being Latina" (xxxi):

> We realized that ultimately, it is up to us to decide if we are Latina, to individually determine what the term means. We grappled with the implications of this on our greater cultures, and argued about the word's ability to entirely define us. At the end of this process, we realized that no matter how loaded, conflicted, and difficult the term may be, we are Latinas. Through heritage and by choice. (xxxi)

Hot Latinas

Rather than falling victim to the traditions of its readers' heritage, Chica lit forges new ground. The female characters in the literature follow their dreams and take on new roles: Women can be strong, and they don't have to be dependent on or subservient to a man. McLemore says that current stories are "more reflective of real Latina women."

The female characters in the literature follow their dreams and take on new roles.

"We're not just maids anymore, nor the salacious vixens of telenovelas," McLemore explains. "These stories often reflect the lives of first- and second-generation Latinas who have grown up in the United States, who may or may not even speak Spanish. They are about blending cultures, living in what can sometimes seem to be two very different worlds."

In the opening of Castillo's debut novel, *Hot Tamara,* the protagonist forgoes the traditional values of settling down with the "right" guy—by her family's standards—in order to pursue her dream of working for an art gallery. Like Tamara, the characters of Chica lit are not necessarily disrespectful, but that doesn't mean that their elders see them as respectful. In *Hot Tamara,* Tamara's mother expresses her feelings about modern girls:

> "You're so self-centered that you can't see how your idiotic decisions hurt everyone around you." Her mom's voice cracked. "We do these things for you because you can't. You're making a mistake, and as far as I'm concerned, I want nothing to do with it. You want to move to L.A.? Fine. Go. There's nothing for you here, and when you fall on your face, don't bother to come running to us." (72)

But Tamara is willing to go against the wishes of her mother and pursue her interests. Rather than taking the safe choice, this Latina embraces the diversity within her own heritage and the wider culture that enables her freedom.

Described by *New York* magazine as "the Hispanic version of *Waiting to Exhale*" (on the back cover of the book), *The Dirty Girls Social Club* also breaks through the multicultural barrier to address stereotypes about identity and gender roles. *The Dirty Girls* follows six Latina women who come from different cultural backgrounds. Lauren, the opening narrator, is a Cuban woman who learned Spanish for a reporting job; Amber is Californian Mexican; Usnavys is Puerto Rican; Rebecca aligns herself as "Spanish," not "Mexican"; Sara is Cuban; and Elizabeth is a black Colombian. Valdes-Rodriguez shows the cultural diversity of the characters' milieu in her descriptions, but although all of these women hail from a different heritage, they are still considered "Latina" women.

While Valdes-Rodriguez says she's very much in touch with her own heritage, she admits that she learned much while writing her novel. "I'm not Colombian, but for Elizabeth's character, [I] had to learn about Colombia. In that sense, writing has broken down a lot of barriers for me," she explains. "I think all writers should stretch to include people whose backgrounds are different from their own. Just because I'm Latina doesn't mean I speak for all Latinas. We are a diverse group. The books that succeed will be those that reflect this diversity."

Fiction also touches on some of the same language and terminology issues addressed in the nonfiction anthologies; even though the women are "Latinas," they don't truly know what the word encompasses. In *The Dirty Girls Social Club,* Valdes-Rodriguez writes, "Nobody knew that we had no idea what a Latina was supposed to be, that we just let the moniker fall over us and fit in the best we could" (34).

In a recent interview, Castillo said that the new Chica fiction doesn't necessarily get pigeonholed into the "often hard-to-find Latino" section at Barnes & Noble. Instead, her readers vary from those who happen to be Mexican Americans to those who are not. At its heart, Chica fiction touches on a reality shared by many cultures. While the market has seen changes with the acceptance of a more "mainstream" Latina lit, Castillo implied that there is still a ways to go.

"I think they need to be honest portrayals of Latinas in all their cultural, racial, and economic diversity. Readers aren't dumb and they can sniff out a faker and stereotypes," Castillo said. "This is where authors and publishing houses can experience some tension. A friend of mine was asked to make the title of her new book 'more ethnic.' That is not only confusing to us authors, but also a bit demeaning. How much do you want to bet that Janet Evanovich isn't asked to make her titles 'more white' or 'more New Jersey'?"

Chica lit shows the main characters not only embracing their culture, but also accepting the diversity that comes along with it. Rather than following the traditional roles imposed within the Hispanic culture, writers such as Castillo show that sometimes a woman's got to stay true to herself.

"Chica lit is filling a void in commercial women's fiction in the United States and elsewhere by portraying Latinas as diverse, modern, funny, smart, educated, independent, and professional," Valdes-Rodriguez offers. "Many of my Latina readers also enjoy Sophie Kinsella and Jennifer Weiner, so in a sense it's not imperative that a reader identify with the ethnicity of a character. Many of my readers, too, are not Latina at all. The most important thing a writer can offer readers is believable characters who are fundamentally human, flawed like the rest of us.

"It is the universal appeal of character that hooks readers," she continues, "regardless of the racial, cultural, or ethnic background of the reader, writer or characters. That said, it is of course important for people to feel like their own life is somehow validated and accepted in popular culture."

References

Castillo, Mary. "Re: Answers to your questions." E-mail to the author. May 23, 2005.

Castillo, Mary. *Hot Tamara.* New York: HarperCollins, 2005.

McLemore, Selina. "Re: Latina Lit Trends." E-mail to the author. May 18, 2005.

Moreno, Robyn and Michelle Herrera Mulligan, eds. *Border-Line Personalities: A New Generation of Latinas Dish on Sex, Sass and Cultural Shifting.* New York: HarperCollins, 2004.

Valdes-Rodriguez, Alisa. *The Dirty Girls Social Club.* New York: HarperCollins, 2003.

Valdes-Rodriguez, Alisa. E-mail to the author. October 26, 2005.

Critical Thinking

1. What is Chica lit?
2. How is Chica lit unique from multicultural literature?
3. What do young girls want to read in literature written for them?
4. Why is it important to cater to adolescents' interests?

With a mother who was adopted from Mexico at the age of 12 and an Italian-American father, **MARIE LOGGIA-KEE** understands growing up between cultures. In addition to writing, she teaches English and popular culture and the University of Phoenix and National University.

From *Multicultural Review,* Spring 2007, pp. 46–48. Copyright © 2007 by Multicultural Review. Reprinted by permission of The Goldman Group, Inc.

UNIT 6

Strengthen and Weave Together Complexities and Controversies

Unit Selections

Learning Outcomes

After reading this unit, you will be able to:

- Retell the experiences of Hindu, Muslim, and Sikh students in U.S. schools and classrooms.

- Describe the challenges that English language learners face and how educators can help.

- Expand upon the influences of Asian American teachers for today's students.

- Discuss the perceptions and realities for teaching about religion with K-12 students.

- Summarize the difficulties that non-Anglo teachers face in contemporary classrooms and communities.

- Explain the importance to reach and teach each student.

Student Website

www.mhhe.com/cls

Internet References

Association for Moral Education
www.amenetwork.org
Center for Social Justice
http://csj.georgetown.edu
Human Rights Watch
www.hrw.org/
Hunger and World Poverty
www.poverty.com

A phrase commonly used in multicultural education circles references "talking the talk and walking the walk." It is one endeavor to become knowledgeable about the multitude of topics and issues related to multicultural education and cultural competency; it is an entirely different endeavor to take steps and get involved to do something positive and productive for multicultural education. For many teacher candidates, classroom teachers, school administrators, and teacher educators, merely becoming acquainted with the vocabulary, concepts, resources, and practices informing and supporting multicultural education so they can talk the talk presents an overwhelming challenge.

Walking the walk requires a different focus.

Far too many educators do not know what multicultural education is, how it is practiced, and why it is vital for every student and educator. Unfortunately, far too many educators of all ages and in all stages continue to resist multicultural education and cultural competence. Thoughts, words, actions, and interactions that are biased, stereotypical, and prejudicial are displayed in schools and classrooms across the United States. Some educators continue to demonstrate acts of power and control in order to promote selected individuals and groups of people while demoting other individuals and groups of people. Public displays of disenfranchisement and discrimination are far too common in educational settings. By chance and by choice, these disingenuous displays communicate harsh messages to both the victims and the witnesses that resonate across the community.

The actions can be both overt and covert. When actions are overt, they are not only visible and acknowledged, they are substantiated by false statements and extremely difficult to overturn due to popular support. The actions have long become ingrained into the school's traditions and local customs. For example, the names of athletic teams or schools' mascots. When the actions are covert, the actions are less visible and conducted in private; they tend to be denied as existing. The individuals responsible for the covert actions may or may not even be fully aware of their offenses. For example, schools that refer to the men's sports and the girl's sports are not using gender equal terminology. Examples of both overt and covert acts of discrimination are endless. Taking action against social injustice requires intelligence, courage, energy, determination, and support. As the famous quote stated by Margaret Mead (1901–1978), "Never doubt that a small group of thoughtful, committed citizens can change the world."

The questions of taking the best steps to overcome social injustice especially as an educator and with young people present serious challenges for everyone. Most educators can recognize inequality and are prepared in their teacher education programs to ensure that all students are treated fairly, and most educators comply with this expectation. As these educators work hard to ensure cultural competence throughout their curricular development, instructional strategies, assessment techniques, community building, and classroom management, frequently they discover that they place their students or themselves in jeopardy. For example, a teacher may supplement the content with additional resources, engage the students in non-traditional learning experiences, administer alternative classroom assessments, rearrange the classroom seating, or practice innovative reward systems. These actions may be viewed as too extreme and threatening to other educators and some families. Classroom teachers are strongly encouraged to discuss endeavors that may

© Getty Images

be considered extreme with their school administrators, share them with colleagues, and send them in writing to the students' families so everyone is informed well in advance.

Some teachers are more attuned to social injustice found in schools and society; their goal is to get their students involved in becoming part of the change. These teachers definitely should visit with their school administrators, colleagues, and community. When they are based on academic standards, grounded in learning theory, exemplifying student-centered activities and assignments, and assessed through a multitude of instruments, most activities will be approved wholeheartedly and supported profusely. Many school administrators seek mechanisms to increase attendance, achievement, and completion so the reported data are strong for their schools.

School administrators also recognize that constructivist classrooms tend to produce more responsible and respectful students who serve as positive and productive role models for their peers. Initiating activities related to educational inequities and social injustice range from classroom simulations followed by self-reflection to historical examinations accompanied with community involvement. Every aspect of the curriculum can contribute to learning the concepts of multicultural education and engaging in the practices applicable both inside and outside the classroom.

Unit 6 articles guide the reader to strengthen and weave together the complexities and controversies associated with cultural competence. All students should be engaged in grappling with complex topics and issues related to the curriculum and instruction to increase higher-order thinking skills and practical application in the world. Students must be provided authentic opportunities to participate in critical thinking, problem solving, and decision making related to their curriculum and their communities. Students want multiple experiences to discuss culturally based controversial topics and issues that impact their learning and living. The reader should practice curricular mapping to connect appropriate controversial issues to their curriculum and classrooms. By meeting with a mentor, the reader can learn more about conducting classroom meetings effectively with their students when discussing controversial topics and issues.

One Nation, Many Gods

Seven years ago, Modesto, Calif., became the only school district in the country to require a world religions course for graduation. Now, research shows the course helps reduce religious intolerance among students without undermining students' religious beliefs. The lessons learned in Modesto may provide a helpful roadmap for schools across the nation.

CARRIE KILMAN

In West Virginia, a public high school refuses to remove a painting of Jesus that hangs outside the principal's office. In Georgia, legislators vote to include the Bible in a statewide public school curriculum. And in New York, officials prohibit the scheduling of standardized tests on religious holidays, after protest over a statewide exam held on a Muslim holy day.

For decades, educators have wrestled with how to handle the increasingly diverse religions of an increasingly diverse student body. Sometimes, the line between church and state—what schools can and cannot do under the Constitution—can feel confusing and slippery.

Today, religion has become a subject one high school teacher calls even more controversial than teaching sex-ed. Teachers feel ill-equipped to talk about it. In a post-9-11 world, students increasingly face harassment for what they believe.

And yet, today's students will interact with a far more pluralistic society than their parents or grandparents did. Some educators see in this a call for urgency. If faith-based intolerance is ever to be confronted, they say schools are exactly the place religion should be addressed.

"Schools are the one place where all of these different religions meet," said one educator. "It follows that religious diversity must be dealt with in school curriculum if we're going to learn to live together."

For the past seven years, the school district in Modesto, Calif., has done just that.

After a divisive, public battle over the role of tolerance in the city's schools, a small group of teachers developed a world religions curriculum for every 9th-grade class in the district. Now, Modesto stands out as the only school district in the country that mandates a world religions course for high school graduation.

New research shows the course has increased students' respect for religious diversity. And teachers here hope their efforts will encourage other districts across the country to follow their lead.

California's "Bible Belt"

Modesto was a surprising birthplace for such a risky venture.

The city of about 200,000 sprawls across Northern California's Central Valley, about 90 miles east of San Francisco. Residents call the area the "Bible Belt of California," for its conservative roots and vocal evangelical community. But a growing immigrant population has infused Modesto with a jolt of religious diversity, adding to the mix growing numbers of Buddhists, Hindus, Muslims and Sikhs.

Several years ago, a move to add gay and lesbian students to the school district's safe-schools policy, titled "Principles of Tolerance, Respect and Dignity," caused an uproar among local religious leaders. The conflict lasted for months. Finally, district officials turned to Charles Haynes, director of the Arlington, Va.-based First Amendment Center, for help.

"I thought I was meeting with the committee appointed to deal with this issue," Haynes said. "I went into the school cafeteria, and there was a 'committee' of about 115 people. Everyone wanted a voice in this issue–gay and lesbian students, local pastors, teachers, administrators—but people were speaking past one another."

He suggested they abandon the word "tolerance"—many religious conservatives thought it meant the school district was "taking a stand on homosexuality." Instead, Haynes asked the group whether all students, regardless of their beliefs or lifestyle, had the right to be safe at school and free from bullying.

Everyone agreed.

"The pastor who was in charge of the opposition stood up and said, 'If this is what the district means, we're fully for that. We're Christians—we don't want anyone beat up or hurt'," Haynes recalled. "A gay student stood up and said, 'Well, that's all we want, too.'"

Together, they crafted a new safe-schools policy grounded in the First Amendment right of free expression, and the responsibility to safeguard that right for others.

The school board unanimously adopted it.

From the policy stemmed many new initiatives, such as a character education course and human rights clubs. Among them was a new focus on teaching about religious diversity.

"When you don't know about something, you fear it—and when you fear something, you become more likely to strike out against it," said Modesto teacher Yvonne Taylor. "We wanted students to understand that even if we disagree with a group of people, they still have the right to be here."

"You Can't Teach Religion"

Modesto requires that every 9th-grader in the district enroll in a semester-long world religions course. Ninth grade made sense—students were old enough to handle the subject material, and the emphasis on religious diversity happened to coincide with the district's desire to enhance the 9th-grade history and social studies curriculum. Since then, state standards have changed—the world religions course no longer fulfills specific state curricular requirements, but it's been so successful in changing attitudes that school officials decided to keep the course in place.

"(At the beginning of) every semester, the kids say, 'You can't teach about religion!'" said Jennie Sweeney, the curriculum coordinator who organized the course's development. "And we say, 'Yes, we can—we're going to teach *about* religion, we're not going to *teach* religion.' There's a big difference."

By law, public schools cannot show preference to one religion [although, in implicit ways, many do—see "Because I Had a Turban,"]. Yet they can legally address religion in ways that are both fair and neutral.

Modesto's world religions course is modeled after the same First Amendment principles that guided the safe-schools policy. "You can be staunch in your own personal beliefs, yet also staunch in respecting and protecting the religious liberties of other people," said Sherry Sheppard, who teaches the course at Modesto's Johansen High.

The class begins with an overview of First Amendment rights and responsibilities. Teachers emphasize the importance of respectful inquiry, and students learn catch-phrases for keeping each other in check to minimize disrespectful remarks.

Next, students delve into six religious units, covering Buddhism, Christianity, Hinduism, Islam, Judaism and Sikhism. The class spends equal time on each unit, studying the history of each faith, the basic tenets, and examples of each religion's societal significance (i.e., Hinduism's influence on Gandhi and the concept of nonviolence).

For the sake of neutrality, teachers aren't allowed to share their own faith backgrounds during the semester, nor are outside speakers welcome. Every class in the district reads the same textbook, watches the same videos and follows the same scripted lesson plans. "It can almost feel prescribed," Sheppard said, "but it prevents teachers from sliding in their own biases."

Students, though, are encouraged to share their own beliefs and ask questions.

As a result, the course provides a safe space to talk about sensitive issues in ways that otherwise might be inappropriate or impolite. It's not unusual, for example, for students to come to class with questions about the man wearing a turban in the grocery store, or a person sporting some other form of religious garb.

"They get excited as the course goes on, because they realize it's something they've never learned about before," said Taylor, who also teaches the course at Johansen.

During the course's inaugural semester, a student who was Buddhist left school on a Friday afternoon with a full head of hair and, to everyone's surprise, returned Monday with a shaved head. His uncle had died, and, in his honor, the student became a Buddhist monk over the weekend, committing to six weeks of service to the temple.

The world religions course became a forum where the student could speak openly about his experience. Because the class had spent weeks exploring different aspects of multiple faiths, classmates viewed the student's decision with interest and respectful curiosity instead of derision.

"For a lot of non-Christian kids, they feel validated at school for the first time," Taylor said. "They say, 'I have a voice now, I'm proud of who I am, and now I can share that and talk about it in a safe environment.'"

The district provides an opt-out policy for parents uncomfortable with the curriculum. Since the program's launch seven years ago, fewer than ten parents have taken advantage of the policy.

"My parents thought it was really interesting," said Lakhbir Kaur, now a senior. "They asked a lot of questions and talked about it at dinner. There was some stuff I learned (during the class) about my own religion that I didn't know, and I went home and asked my mom about it. It was eye-opening."

"Not Different after All"

In May 2006, researchers from the First Amendment Center released the results of a comprehensive study of Modesto's world religions course. They wanted to know if teaching

Toolbox
10 Tips for Starting a World Religions Curriculum

1. **Involve the community.** Teachers in Modesto invited community members to review the curriculum, hosted a meeting with local faith leaders during the curriculum's development, and toured several local houses of worship. "It gave people a voice in the process, which helped create community buy-in," says one teacher.

2. **Engage diverse voices.** Make sure every religion represented in your area has a place at the table. Be sure to make space for atheism, too.

3. **Build trust.** "People can be suspicious of schools," says one Modesto teacher. "You need to build trust with different key constituencies before you attempt something like this."

4. **Be sensitive.** Religion is a touchy subject. For many people, it's directly connected to culture, language and ethnicity. Recognize and respect the multiple layers of identity at play.

5. **Get district buy-in.** "This cannot be done by one teacher at one school," says another Modesto teacher. Support from the district—in time, money and resources—is key.

6. **Training, training, training.** Recognize that you can never have enough training. Provide it before the semester starts and throughout the year.

7. **Opt-in for teachers.** Some teachers might not feel comfortable teaching about religion, and classes should by taught by teachers who volunteer to teach them.

8. **Communicate with parents.** "At the open house every year, I give parents a briefing," says teacher Sherry Sheppard, at Modesto's Johansen High. "I assure them that my job is to teach and not preach. It has been such an easy thing."

9. **Lay the groundwork for respect.** "I am adamant (in the beginning of the semester) that if students have a comment that may come across as hurtful, they think about it first," says another Johansen teacher. "I get a lot of 'wow, that's interesting.' What they might be thinking is, 'wow, that's weird,' but they don't dare say it."

10. **Maintain neutrality.** "It made a big difference that teachers didn't take sides," says Edward Zeiden, now a senior at Johansen High. Added classmate Amy Boudsady: "It made me feel safe to share my own beliefs. I didn't feel like someone was judging me."

---

about diverse religions had any impact on students' religious tolerance.

"We've never really known what effect it would have if we taught more about different religions in public schools," Haynes said. "We've always said it was a good idea—but in terms of empirical evidence, what it does for our kids, this study is the first indication of what it might do."

Researchers interviewed students before, during and immediately after the semester, and again six months after the course ended. Over and over, they found that students had become more tolerant of other religions and more willing to protect the rights of people of other faiths.

In their own words, students say the course broadened their views and empowered them to fight back against faith-based bullying.

"I didn't know anything about any religion other than mine," said Kristin Busby, now a senior. "By the end [of the semester], we were all much more accepting toward one another. You realize that we're all not that different after all. We all have these necessities, and these religions provide for those necessities, just in different ways."

By the end [of the semester], we were all much more accepting toward one another.

Added Ishmael Athneil, a freshman: "If some of my friends are talking about someone and saying, 'Wow that's weird,' now I can jump in and say, 'Well, actually, this is why he does that.'"

However, this increase in religious tolerance was not accompanied by a change in students' personal religious beliefs, a finding of huge interest to researchers. "This is important," Haynes said. "It means that learning about different religions will not undermine the faith of the family."

Students who began the semester with strong religious convictions ended the semester with the same beliefs.

"My mom and dad were biased against this course," said 9th-grader Richard Dysart. "They were afraid I'd convert and get confused about what my family believes. But if you're part of a culture, you won't switch just by learning about how other people live."

The course's ability to offset religious intolerance was put to the test at the beginning of its second year.

"We had just made it through the first year without a single complaint from a parent," Sheppard said. "We walked into that September feeling kind of cocky. Then 9-11 happened."

The training for the world religions course prepared teachers to handle the issues and questions that arose that year.

"We realized we'd have to be very delicate with this, making sure the difference was explicit between Islam as a religion and the people who committed that act," Sheppard recalled. "We still emphasize that point when we get to Islam."

Across the country, reports of schoolyard harassment against Muslim students escalated in the months immediately following 9–11. In Modesto, not a single act of harassment was reported against a Muslim student during the 2001–2002 school year.

Not in This Alone

These results, teachers said, didn't happen by accident.

The teacher-led committee that created Modesto's curriculum worked closely with the local community during the course's development. First, teachers identified each religion that would comprise the curriculum; next, they worked in teams to research the different faiths.

Part of that research involved field trips. Teachers toured several houses of worship and invited religious leaders from multiple faith backgrounds to attend a meeting at the school, to explain the purpose of the curriculum and ask for input.

Before the course launched, teachers asked local religious representatives to review the textbook. "There are an equal number of pages given to each religion," Sweeney said. "We knew they would count."

In addition, the book contains a section on nonbelievers; whether teachers delve into atheism (some do, some don't) seems to be one of the few ways that different classes deviate from the curriculum.

For all of its successes, researchers did identify some curricular shortcomings. They faulted the Modesto course for failing to address the negative aspects of religions, to give students a more accurate picture. Researchers questioned the policy of forbidding guest speakers, and they suggested that Modesto's teachers would benefit from more robust training.

Teachers, for their part, questioned these criticisms. "They weren't sensitive to what we were trying to do and the limitations we faced," Sweeney said.

Currently, teachers who volunteer to instruct the course must first attend a 30-hour workshop on how to teach about religion. In addition, the district tries to provide time and space throughout the year for the world religions teachers from each campus to meet, share ideas and discuss concerns.

While this in-service training isn't as frequent as the researchers would like, it does add value to teachers' experiences. "We know we're not in this alone," explained Taylor. "I think this is one of the best things I've done in 35 years of teaching."

If Here, Anywhere

The moral of Modesto's success isn't that every district should rush to create its own world religions requirement. "Not all districts can, because there simply isn't room in the curriculum," Haynes said.

But schools *can* reconsider how and what they teach when it comes to religion. More schools could offer world religion electives, improve the religion sections of their social studies curricula, or implement school policies that are more inclusive of diverse faiths (i.e. not scheduling tests on religious holidays).

Specifically, Modesto's success suggests more schools should do the following:

- **Improve teacher training.** "The biggest barriers (to teaching about religion) are not parents or the community or the law," said Haynes. "The biggest barriers are that teachers do not feel prepared to teach about religion."

  Researchers at the First Amendment Center suggest a world religions requirement for every pre-service social studies teacher in the country, religious studies courses incorporated into teacher training programs, and improved in-service training for teachers already on the job.

- **Understand the law.** Many school districts still think it's constitutionally problematic to discuss religion in schools. Some districts think neutrality means silence. Others address some religions but exclude others (i.e. an elective on the Christian Bible, but no equivalent for other religions).

  "Neutrality, in a word, means 'fairness,'" said Haynes. "School officials are supposed to be the fair, honest, neutral brokers who allow various voices to be heard."

- **Work with communities, not against them.** Parents and religious leaders can be seen as the enemies of efforts to address religious pluralism in schools. But teachers in Modesto attribute their success, in part, to how well they worked with the community.

  As a result, Sweeney said, parental complaints have been minimal: "Because we have support from the religious community, I think they've told their members not to worry about this."

- **Consider it a core mission.** "Students *need* to learn these things," said Modesto student Edward Zeiden, of his school's world religions course. "It should be required, just like history."

Resources

The First Amendment Center works to preserve and protect First Amendment freedoms through information and education. The Center serves as a forum for the study and exploration of free-expression issues, including freedom of speech and religion. www.firstamendmentcenter.org

Sponsored by the First Amendment Center, **First Amendment Schools** represent a national initiative designed to transform how schools teach and practice the rights and responsibilities of citizenship that frame civic life in our democracy. www.firstamendmentschools.org

A collaboration of NPR's "Justice Talking" and The New York Times Learning Network, **Justice Learning** uses multimedia, including audio and news articles, to engage high school students in informed political discourse. The website also offers curricular materials and other age-appropriate classroom resources. The "Religion in Schools" section offers an interactive timeline and student quiz.
www.justicelearning.org

The Pew Forum offers a variety of resources that explores the relationship between religion and public schools, including reports, event transcripts, polling data and the latest news.
www.pewforum.org/religion-schools

Critical Thinking

1. What are the guidelines for classroom teachers when teaching about religion?

2. How is teaching about religion a part of a balanced history and social studies education?

3. What do teacher education programs need to do to improve teaching religion in middle level and high school classrooms?

4. Why is teaching about religion vital for today's young people?

From *Teaching Tolerance*, Fall 2007, pp. 38–46. Copyright © 2007 by Southern Poverty Law Center. Reprinted by permission.

"Because I Had a Turban"

In almost every public school in the United States, attitudes and behaviors in the classroom presume an unacknowledged, yet pervasive, Christian norm. How does this affect students who are not Christian?

KHYATI Y. JOSHI

In American society, as in many others, religion shapes and informs everything from our language to our social habits. For us, one particular religion plays the hegemonic role: Christianity.

It is celebrated both in our calendars—where school breaks often coincide with Christmas and Easter, but rarely with the major holidays of other religions—and in our curricula, through "seasonal" art projects and activities like Easter egg drawings and "holiday" pageants.

Christianity is present in the turns of phrase from "turning the other cheek" and being a "good Samaritan," to being a "sacrificial lamb."

Taken together, these activities and experiences cause students who identify with Christianity to find their identity affirmed in school. Yet today, our classrooms include students from many religious backgrounds, and this "Christian normalcy" causes those who are not Christian to feel just the opposite.

My research into the life experiences of Hindu, Muslim, and Sikh students of Indian American backgrounds uncovered the hidden cost of this "normalcy" in public schools.

Many students reported school experiences in which their religious identity was ignored, marginalized, or actively discriminated against in a host of ways. The intense turmoil caused by these experiences threatened their ethnic identity development, their relationships with peers and family members, and their academic outcomes.

Their experiences offer insight and guidance for schools and educators.

Family Ties and Feelings of Exclusion

Classroom conversations about going to church, celebrating holidays, or participating in Christian youth group activities produced extreme anxiety for students interviewed during my study.

For many Hindu, Muslim, and Sikh students, religion is intrinsically tied to ethnic identity. Frequently their immigrant parents use religious activities and organizations as a way to gather with people like themselves and transmit culture to their children.

And yet, faced with Christian normalcy and feeling the normal childhood yearning to fit in with peers, many students were embarrassed to be associated with their own families and ethnic communities. Some avoided learning about their home religions.

"I remember at Christmastime having to lie about what my parents got me," said Priti, a Hindu student. Her parents "wouldn't get me too much, because they really didn't have the concept of" Christmas. Priti felt that describing the small gifts she received would emphasize her differentness from her Christian peers.

Priti also described how "on many occasions, when we would celebrate Christian holidays [in class], I definitely get the feeling that I was not a part of that celebration. . . . There wasn't one solitary event, but a string of events for many years that made me feel that I was not part of this group."

Over time, this exclusion caused many students to feel self-conscious and even ashamed of coming from a faith tradition that was not perceived as "normal" by their teachers and classmates.

These feelings often had long-term ramifications—not only in diminished self-esteem, but also in the loss of knowledge about rituals and traditions, of aptitude with the home language, and even of connections with family.

Targets for Discrimination

But Christian normalcy, like religious dominance in many countries, is only one facet of religious oppression, which is not about theology so much as power. A religion becomes oppressive when its followers use it to subordinate the beliefs of others, to marginalize, exclude and deny privileges and access to people of other faiths.

The Indian Americans in my study shared stories of being targeted for discrimination and mockery because of their religions. One young Muslim reported that his homeroom teacher would often duck when he entered the classroom, saying, "You don't have a bomb in that backpack, do you?" The rest of the class had a good laugh, and this student felt compelled to laugh along throughout the school year.

Harpreet, a male Sikh who wears a turban, recalled his high school's annual tradition of hosting a Christmas Dinner for the homeless, where students dressed up as different characters.

His teacher asked Harpreet to dress up as Jafar, the villain from the Disney film *Aladdin*, he said, "because I had a turban." The teacher treated Harpreet's turban as something cartoonish, ignoring its religious significance to Sikhs and conflating it with an Arab cultural emblem.

Other students were told they were "going to hell" or that they and their families needed to "be saved." When teachers overheard comments like these and did not intervene, many students took their silence as an endorsement of religious discrimination.

It's Academic

While many school districts make accommodations for students who are not Christian—for example, by excusing students for certain religious holidays—these accommodations can result in educational experiences that are unequal.

Consider the voice of a 13-year-old Hindu girl from Ohio:

I hate skipping school to celebrate Diwali. After we celebrate, I still have to do all the in-class assignments and the homework for the next day. Now I tell my parents I'd rather just go to school.

"Making up" for religious observances is a burden Christian students do not carry. This reality can make it difficult for some non-Christian students to stay on equal footing with Christian peers, socially and academically.

Another Hindu student, Nikhil, faced a different kind of academic challenge.

Since elementary school, Nikhil had experienced being teased for "praying to cows" and being "reincarnated from a dog." Like many Indian Americans, he developed the habit of keeping his home life separate from his school life.

When his public school's National Honor Society chapter decided to visit different churches to learn about religious diversity, Nikhil offered to share his religious life with his NHS peers.

"I told them that we should go to one of the Hindu services," Nikhil said, "and the NHS faculty sponsor said, 'No, we're not going to do that.'" When his offer was rejected, Nikhil decided he would stop attending Christian services with the honor society. As a result, he was dismissed from the NHS for "inadequate participation."

Nikhil feared academic retribution if he did anything about the expulsion. "[The NHS advisor] was also my English teacher," he said, "and I was afraid . . . it would reflect on my grade, so I never said anything."

When I interviewed him more than a decade later, Nikhil's voice still quivered with emotion as he recalled feeling "very,

very mad. I was graduating in the top five of my class. Everybody around me had the honor stole on except for me—and the only reason was because I refused to go to church."

Making Religion Matter

As practitioners of multicultural education, we must recognize and respond to religion's importance as a cultural marker for many students, Christians and non-Christians alike. We must acknowledge and correct Christian normalcy in our classrooms and curricula. The answer is not to ignore or exclude Christianity; in fact, the opposite is true.

Consider these suggestions:

1. **Know our own students.** There are a lot of religions in the world. Start with the ones present in your classroom.
2. **Learn our ABCDs.** We don't need to be theologians, but we can at least learn the:

   - **A**rchitecture: Know what the house of worship is called, like *mandir* (Hindu), *masjid* or *mosque* (Muslim), and *gurdwara* (Sikh).
   - **B**ooks: Know the name(s) of the religion's holy text(s).
   - **C**ities: Know the names and locations of the religion's holiest cities, like Amritsar (Sikhism), Mecca and Medina (Islam), and Varanasi/Benares (Hinduism).
   - **D**ays: Know the names and meanings of the religion's major holidays, like Diwali and Holi (Hinduism), Ramadan and Eid ul' Fitr (Islam), and Vaisaki (Sikhism).

3. **Recognize religion as part of students' social identities.** Religion and religious institutions are one of the major ways ethnic communities—particularly immigrant communities—organize and gather. Understand how this makes religion especially salient for some students, and how the family's religion may be important even to students who don't see themselves as "religious."
4. **Avoid the urge to "Christianize" religions and holidays.** Observe religious holidays in their own context and their own time, instead of lumping them all together in December. Don't assume holidays that fall close to a Christian holiday on the calendar share the same social or theological meaning. Likewise, don't diminish other religions by drawing analogies to Christian holidays–*e.g.,* saying "Ramadan is like Lent" or "Janmastami is like Christmas."
5. **Include religion in our curricula whenever it's appropriate.** Knowledge about religions is important for students living in our religiously pluralistic democracy, and in our global community. Religions influence the behavior of individuals and nations and have inspired some of the world's most beautiful art, architecture, literature, music, and forms of government. When discussing these subjects, it's okay to acknowledge religion and its impact. Discuss how different religions deal with the concept at hand.

Understanding religious differences and the role of religion in the contemporary world—and in our students' lives—can alleviate prejudice and help all students grow into the thoughtful global citizens our world requires.

Critical Thinking

1. What do Indian Americans experience in the United States?

2. How are Indian Americans' experiences similar to and different from other marginalized students in U.S. schools and classrooms?

3. What are five practices suggested by this article that will benefit teachers and their students?

4. Why should classroom teachers take time to incorporate these five practices?

KHYATI Y. JOSHI is an assistant professor in the Peter Sammartino School of Education at Fairleigh Dickinson University in Teaneck, New Jersey. The interviews quoted in this article are also the subject matter of her first book, *New Roots in America's Sacred Ground: Religion, Race and Ethnicity in Indian America* (Rutgers University Press, 2006).

Asian American Teachers

Do they impact the curriculum? Are there support systems for them?

HEMA RAMANATHAN

Introduction

The significance and importance of global education and a culturally relevant curriculum have been thrown into relief by the events of Sept. 11, 2001, emphasizing the urgency to understand and be accepting of diverse cultures. This has a strong bearing on the "enculturation" role of schools, as agents of cultural reproduction.

The traditional curriculum transmits Euro-American norms that are seen as the primary American culture. The possible positive effects of a culturally responsive and diverse curriculum (CDC) have been detailed, including affirming the value of cooperation, helping students and teachers build an identity by comparing what they have learned in the classroom with their own experiences, and the importance of a caring community (Gay, 2000; Ladson-Billings, 1992b; Sleeter & Grant, 1991; Zimpher & Ashburn, 1984).

There is little doubt that schools should be more inclusive and that school-based personnel should appreciate and affirm what minority teachers bring to facilitate the development of a culturally relevant curriculum that is academically rigorous (Quiocho & Rios, 2000) but there is no systemic effort to genuinely shift from a Western perspective to include other perspectives and materials (Foster, 1994, cited in Quiocho & Rios, 2000; Gay, 2000).

However, adopting CDC or culturally congruent approaches to teaching has its own pitfalls. They can render teachers suspect by the broader school community since such approaches do not conform to the mainstream (Conner, 2002; Foster, 1994; Lipka, 1994, cited in Quiocho & Rios, 2000). Further, race and race-related pedagogy are not considered appropriate topics for discussion among faculty members, and issues regarding them are not raised in faculty forums (Foster, 1994, cited in Quiocho & Rios, 2000).

Where there is no self-examination, there is unlikely to be an expectation of overt support. The result is that the voices of minority teachers have been silenced and many of them do not have a role as decision-makers beyond the everyday decisions that teachers make in the classroom (Goodwin, Genishi, Asher, & Woo, 1997; Irvine, 2002; Quiocho & Rios, 2000).

These issues as they relate to Asian Americans have other features that complicate the matter. The term "Asian American,"

classed as one group for purposes of census and political policy, embraces sub-groups that differ widely in matters of language, religion, and cultural practices and beliefs. This multicultural, multi-ethnic, multi-literate profile engenders a lack of coherent cultural identity so that only a narrow slice is represented in the broad spectrum of the curriculum (Gay, 2000).

In the past three decades, the Asian-American population has been overlooked in terms of the demographic profile in spite of a dramatic increase of about 63%. Of Asian Americans, nearly a fourth is under 17 and of school-going age, accounting for about 3% of the total K–12 student population (Smith, Rogers, Alsalam, Perie, Mahoney, & Martin, 1994) while accounting for only 1.2% of the nation's teaching force (Snyder & Hoffman, 1994). Their low visibility is compounded by the fact that they are not evenly represented across the country in all regions; clustered along the East and West coasts, they are largely "missing in action" in the Midwest and South (U.S. Census Bureau, 2000).

Unlike other minority communities, there is no scarcity of qualified persons in this community in which 37% aged 25 or older is college educated. Yet, specifically among Asian-American women who hold degrees, only 1% goes into teaching, a profession still dominated by women. Many of the rest opt for jobs in technical and scientific fields which are higher-paying and where discrimination is perceived to be less of a barrier to advancement (Rong & Preissle, 1997; Su, Goldstein, Suzuki & Kim, 1997).

Emerging literature on Asian Americans shows that perceptions about the community are often at odds with reality. Asian Americans desire to be 'normal,' to fit in (Gordon, 2000). Whether it is to be accepted as "honorary Whites" so as not to remain "forever foreigners," or to get by in a racist society by staying quiet and behaving so that nobody would bother them (Tuan, 1998), Asian Americans indicate a desire to assimilate and to nullify their Asian roots. Their integration seems to depend on how mainstream they are, which argues for assimilation not accommodation.

Viewed as a "model minority," self-esteem issues that are cited in support of African-American and Hispanic profiles in the curriculum may not appear to be applicable to Asian-American students. While it is true that Asian-American students by and large are academic achievers and the Asian-American community appears to be successful economically, second- and third-generation Asian-American students in schools have to contend with cultural, social, and emotional issues like any other minority group (Siu, 1996).

Among all ethnic groups, the extremely limited research that is available on Asian-American teachers is a matter of deep concern (Quiocho & Rios, 2000). The available data focus on issues of motivation, explaining why Asian Americans are drawn to teaching and what may keep them in the profession (Goodwin, Genishi, Asher, & Woo, 1997; Gordon, 2000; Rong & Preissle, 1997; Su, Goldstein, Suzuki, & Kim, 1997). There are few studies that address the effect Asian-American teachers could have on the curriculum or the issues they may have to deal with in their work environment (Gay, 2000; Goodwin, Genishi, Asher, & Woo, 1997; Quiocho & Rios, 2000).

The purpose of this descriptive study was: (1) to understand problems Asian Americans may face as minority teachers; (2) to examine any impact they may have on curricula and academic experiences at the building level; and (3) to identify support systems available to them to implement desired changes.

Methodology

A survey of 23 items based on the research questions was designed. Of the 15 of these items that dealt with issues of identity of the Asian-American teachers and other professionals in the building, five explored the respondents' perceptions of the effect of their ethnicity on the curriculum and related activities in school. Seven items focused on how peers, administrators, students, and their parents related to issues of acceptance of their identity, and support that was or could be offered. Three items questioned the respondents about their awareness of and membership in professional ethnic support groups. Since the sampling frame of Asian-American teachers available was small, the survey was piloted with African-American teachers to test for a minority perspective.

The Midwestern state chosen for study mirrored the changing national demographics with regard to the Asian-American population (U.S. Bureau of Census, 1997). A list of all Asian-American teachers, obtained from the state Department of Education, provided an initial sampling frame of 106. Deletion of those no longer teaching and additions of names suggested by respondents defined a final sample of 96.

The final survey, with a cover letter and a stamped envelope for returning the completed survey, was mailed to all participants. Reminders over a period of two months included postcards, phone calls, and duplicate surveys. Forty participants responded to the survey for a return rate of 41.7%. Four of them declined to participate; they felt their ethnic identity as Asian Americans was not relevant to their identity as teachers. Another respondent stated that since he was mistaken for a Caucasian, his responses were not relevant. A sixth respondent chose not to complete the survey since the questions dealt with "delicate issues." Eventually 34 surveys were deemed useable. The data were coded and categorized by the researcher using open coding techniques (Strauss & Corbin, 1990).

Findings and Discussion
Curricular Issues

The presence of Asian-American teachers appears to have little effect on the curriculum or the academic experiences of students, and core content courses are not affected by the presence of Asian-American teachers in schools. Given that five of the respondents stated that they did not see themselves as Asian American, it is likely that their curriculum is not affected by ethnic perspectives.

Of the 34 usable responses, only three related their ethnicity to the content formally. Two taught Japanese and Chinese languages in their schools, supporting Ladson-Billings' (1992a) statement that there is a distinct ethnic-specific cultural preference for language that teachers bring into the classroom. The Japanese language teacher was also in charge of an after-school Japanese club. A music teacher incorporated a few Japanese songs into the repertoire.

Three other respondents brought their experience and knowledge of "otherness" into the curriculum informally, reflecting the findings of Goodwin, Genishi, Asher, and Woo (1997). They referred to world literature and global issues while discussing their content; this was not a requirement of the curriculum but was made possible by their wide experience. For example, a teacher from India compared Third World conditions to the U.S. to illustrate differences in life styles and to inculcate sensitivity to environmental issues.

Any other references to the ethnicity of the Asian-American teachers were sporadic and "add-ons." Four respondents said they incorporated activities related to their culture in their classroom but were not specific about the purpose or the learning expected from the students. Eight of the 34 responded that they had been used as resource persons by other teachers in the building.

In a scenario that is easily recognized, they were invited to talk to other classes about their culture, ethnicity, and country of origin or affiliation. The topics most often included the "visible" features of culture such as food, festivals, customs, and rituals, especially of marriage. On a more personal and serious note, a Japanese American was invited to talk about the experiences of Japanese Americans interned in concentration camps in the U.S. during World War II.

Decision-Making

Asian-American teachers are curriculum deliverers (Twisleton, 2004), not involved in defining the curriculum and with no opportunity to influence either the structures or the people in their working environment.

The Japanese language teacher stated that he wished that he were included in decisions regarding establishing or abolishing a foreign language department or offering Japanese but seemed to have no belief that his wish would be granted. A second respondent was both skeptical and cautious about her presence on any decision-making body. She believed that there was a danger of "being tokenized or less than appreciated because the teachers may have little understanding of non-mainstream experiences."

With the exception of one school building which had three Asian-American teachers, all the other respondents were the only Asian Americans in their schools. This lack of critical numbers may preclude their having an impact on decision-making at the building level.

The teachers were cautious about establishing an alternative culturally-responsive pedagogy and curriculum, unlike those studied by Su (1997). Except for two respondents, none of the others expressed a desire to be involved in re-designing the curriculum with a view to incorporating Asian-American elements. Rather than see schools as sites for diversity, anti-racism, social justice, and transformation (Feuerverger, 1997; Foster, 1994; Klassen & Carr, 1997, cited in Quiocho & Rios, 2000), most of these Asian-American teachers appear to want to maintain the status quo.

Issues of Support

Administrators and Peers

Asian-American teachers appreciated the support they receive from both administrators and their peers and detailed generic teacher needs in the areas of teaching, curriculum, and discipline.

Of the 34 usable responses to this set of questions, 15 respondents stated that they were supported by their peers in two areas—professional and personal—while 12 felt that they were not. Like all teachers, they looked to the administration for help with planning and implementing their teaching responsibilities and with student discipline.

Peripheral experiences of sharing information related to their ethnicity were seen as acknowledgement by peers and administrators of their uniqueness. Thus, most of the support they asked for was not curricular re-alignment, representation in the curriculum, or cultural mores of expectation and behavior that might distinguish them from their 'mainstream' peers.

Students

Asian Americans are proud of their ethnicity and yet wish to blend in with the dominant group (Gordon, 2000b). This dichotomy of appearance and perception was clearly noticeable in their interpretation of student appreciation. Asian-American teachers were pleased both when students noticed their ethnicity and when they did not. They welcomed being treated like all other teachers regardless of their ethnicity. On the other hand, they enjoyed the attention students paid to their different cultural background.

Fully a third of the respondents indicated that their ethnic identity did not impinge itself on the students. They believed that they were successful teachers because they were like any other teachers and exhibited the same characteristics of concern and caring. As one respondent colorfully phrased it, "I could be purple and still (the students) would enjoy my class, hopefully because I teach with caring and love." Another respondent commented,

> More than 80% of my students and parents like and appreciate the things I'm doing to help my students learn. I use my lunch hour to help the slow students. I always find time to help my students.

Yet students were not entirely blind to their teachers' differences. Their curiosity was piqued by their teachers' ethnicity and the respondents saw this as an indication of a positive attitude. Students questioned their teachers about their personal background and culture. The respondents felt that sometimes students "look(ed) to me as a source of information about Asia." Students are also curious about the country of origin of the Asian-American teachers. "They love to see some real samples from China/Taiwan and hear about the Chinese zodiac."

Some respondents were also subliminally conscious that students' perceptions of race and ability are influenced by the teacher's ethnicity. Beyond seeing the teachers as sources of trivia, two clear statements made by the respondents point to their belief that minority students are conscious and appreciative of the teachers modeling a minority status. They "appreciate the fact that (the teacher) can connect with them in different ways . . . can talk about skin color and speaking languages other than English with a certain depth of understanding."

As another respondent said, "My students realize that teachers don't just come in Black and White background. Anyone with the right qualifications (education) can become a teacher."

Professional Support Groups

Eighteen of the respondents indicated that they would join a group that addressed Asian-American issues related to teaching and teachers while nine did not wish to be part of any group. There are two professional organizations already in existence that are based on Asian-American ethnicity: the Chinese Language Teachers Association and an organization for music teachers founded by one of the respondents.

Yet, except for two respondents who each identified one organization, the others were unaware of the existence of these organizations. However, respondents felt the need for such support systems that would help them in their professional life, which are not available to them at present.

Role as Interlocutors

Falling outside the "color lines" of traditional racial discourse provides Asian-American teachers a role not obviously available to African-American or European-American teachers in a school building: interlocutors in a racially-charged incident. Being neither Black nor White, they are seen either as neutral, "colorless," or as either color, as may suit the students. "I can be seen as White by White students and as Black by Black students," a participant stated.

At the very least, Asian-American teachers see themselves as a "bridge between worlds and between people." This seems to be a great advantage with parents who are not hostile or wary of their 'allegiance.' As one respondent said,

> I'm in a high-minority population school and being non-White is an advantage with African Americans, Hispanic, and Asian parents. I don't sense the immediate mistrust that I see directed towards White educators. I've been asked to sit in on conferences where the educators were all White and the parents were non-White, for that very reason.

Their strength is derived from their being perceived as impartial. As mediators, they have been able to explain grading issues to minority students, defusing potential problems. Since they do not "belong" to the "other side," their words have veracity and carry weight with all stakeholders in a school building. As two respondents said,

> (Being an Asian American helps) with my students simply because it aids me in discussing fairness of rules, policies, treatment of minorities, or any related issues from a minority perspective.

> Some of my African-American students have accused other White teachers of giving out low grades to Black students because they are prejudiced. Since I'm not White, I was able to play neutral ground and explain to them how mistaken the students were, since grades are *earned* and not *given* by the teachers.

Non-Responses

Four respondents declined to participate; they felt that their ethnic identity as Asian Americans was not relevant to their identity as teachers. Another respondent stated that since he was often mistaken for a Caucasian, his responses would not be relevant. A significant third of them are either not conscious of their ethnicity or choose not to bring them into play. Their claim to be Caucasian or mainstream distinguishes them from those who would like to see their ethnicity as a strength and would like to have active support from their peers to explore it.

A sixth respondent chose not to complete the survey though she was repeatedly assured that her anonymity and that of the school would be maintained. As she explained in a telephone conversation, the questions dealt with "delicate issues" that she did not want to talk about.

Discussion

Asian-American teachers in this study appear to be well-integrated into the school system with regard to a teacher's life, role, and responsibilities, unlike the teachers in Goodwin, Genishi, Asher, and Woo (1997). They feel accepted and supported by peers and students and believe that their concerns are heard. Their problems relating to issues of curriculum, student discipline, and professional support are no different from other teachers in U.S. schools in most respects. Thus, the Asian part of their identity does not seem to count with them at all or to be an issue, and they do not seem to be overly concerned about being underrepresented in their schools or in the curriculum.

For change to be effected a critical mass has to be achieved. The desire on the part of Asian-American teachers to maintain the status quo may be prompted by a lack on numbers in their school buildings. In most cases, as the sole representative of their community, the desire to make a change in the curriculum may not seem feasible to them and therefore may not be entertained.

Calls for a wider, more multicultural curricula have not gone unheard. It is clear that students of today will need to know more about Asia than was required of the previous generation.

The economic growth of India and China make it apparent that in the future students will have to be more familiar with the present histories and cultures of such countries.

With this in mind, schools should be more deliberate about diversifying the curriculum. It should be apparent that teaching Asia in two weeks in a high school Social Studies class will not meet these needs, and that a more equitable distribution of time, addressing various cultures, is necessary (Conner, 2002).

Content teachers should become more knowledgeable about Asian cultures and a growing body of Asian literature in English. It seems natural that Asian-American teachers would be more intentionally involved in such curricular decisions about internationalizing the curriculum and making it more globally focused.

Recent world events have shown the need for foreign language expertise in this country and that promoting a functionally monolingual education is totally inadequate. Schools could offer an Asian language as part of its curriculum. Apart from the need for students to become well-rounded adults with knowledge of the world, the growth of India and China as global economic forces make it important for them to learn about Asia. It then would seem to follow that Asian-American teachers would be a rich resource.

With minority teachers a rarity in the teaching force and growing scarcer, attracting Asian Americans into the teaching profession will require that certain features such as salaries be amended (Su, 1997). Perhaps they could be offered inducements and bonuses and differentiated contracts as is offered to math and science teachers in some school districts. Calls for increasing teacher pay have come from a wide spectrum of society (Blair, 2001; Bond, 2001; Johnson, 2000). Whether this will come to pass is a question but until the monetary benefits are appreciably increased, Asian Americans are unlikely to enter the teaching profession in any substantial numbers.

The variety of roles that teachers play in a school in providing support for each other could be limited if they are not aware of their own strengths. The ability to offer differing viewpoints and perspectives on issues so that they can act as interlocutors in race-related matters could be significant to the well-being and growth of school and society. For example, Asian-American teachers could mediate in racially-charged situations where trust is challenged and communication lines are broken. They could explicate to minority students the nuanced perspectives of the educational system and, on appropriate occasions, advocate for the perceptions of beleaguered minority students.

The larger question is about teacher professional identity in which ethnicity is assimilated or absorbed. The most common way minority groups address conflicts in identity is either by adopting the dominant mode of identification and ignoring or relegating to the background their own ethnic features.

Ethnic organizations may exist in part because of the desire of the community to maintain its identity (Barth, 1969; Gordon, 1964). The case in point of a teacher being unwilling to respond to an anonymous survey is deeply disturbing and is a telling comment on the insecurity that some Asian-American teachers deal with in their work environment. The reluctance to address what is probably an unpleasant situation may indicate a peer group or administration that could be deliberately vindictive at being portrayed in unflattering terms.

Professional support groups could help Asian-American teachers identify and retain their cultural and ethnic features without jeopardizing their career or professional persona. Exploring and affirming their identity, and in turn finding ways of understanding and valuing it, will mitigate the marginalization of Asian-American teachers. However, the practically nonexistent research on the formation of an ethnic professional identity precludes a detailed discussion in an empirical study.

Conclusion

It is increasingly apparent that the conversations about race in the U.S. cannot continue to be a Black-White issue but must include Asian Americans and Hispanic Americans. The violence inflicted on Asian Americans in the aftermath of Sept. 11 was only one in a long line of attacks on them. The incidents by the "dot-busters" in Jersey City dating from the 1980s to the ransacking of Korean shops in 1992 were unfortunately not isolated occurrences (Zia, 2000).

Asian-American teachers appear to be an untapped resource; they should recognize that they are a "salient marker" (Tuan, 1998) to their students and other stakeholders, making it essential for them not to make their ethnic identity a private affair.

The U.S. perceives itself as a unique multiracial and multi-ethnic society. Schools claim to help their students value and celebrate diversity. Raising the profile of the largely invisible Asian-American teachers in schools is a viable starting point in achieving these objectives. It remains to be seen what the map of a school would look like if Asian-American teachers were to emphasize their ethnicity and not conform to the generic role that a teacher is expected to play in a school.

References

American Association of Colleges of Teacher Education. (1994). *Teacher education pipeline III: Schools, Colleges and Departments of Education enrollments by race, ethnicity, and gender.* Washington, DC: Author.

Banks, J. A. (1994), Transforming the mainstream curriculum. *Educational Leadership, 51*(8), 4–8.

Banks, J. A. (Ed.) (1996). *Multicultural education, transformative knowledge, and action: Historical and contemporary perspectives.* New York: Teachers College Press.

Barth, F. (1969). *Ethnic groups and boundaries: The social organization of cultural differences.* London, UK: Allen & Unwin.

Blair, J., (2001, February 21), Lawmakers plunge into teacher pay. *Education Week.* Retrieved September 2005, from http://www.edweek.org

Bond, C. K. (2001). Do teacher salaries matter? Unpublished doctoral dissertation, Teachers College, Columbia University, New York.

Gay, G. (2000). *Culturally responsive teaching: Theory, research and practice.* New York: Teachers College Press.

Goodwin, A. L., Genishi, C., Asher, N., & Woo, K. A. (1997). Voices from the margins: Asian American teachers' experiences in the profession. In D. M. Byrd & D. J. McIntyre (Eds.) *Research on the education of our nation's teachers. Teacher education Yearbook V.* Thousand Oaks, CA: Corwin Press.

Gordon, J. (2000a). Asian-American resistance to selecting teaching as a career: The power of community and tradition. *Teachers College Record, 102*(1), 173–96.

Gordon, J. (2000b). *The color of teaching.* New York: Routledge Falmer

Gordon, M. (1964). *Assimilation in American life.* New York: Oxford University Press.

Irvine, J. J. (Ed.) *In search of wholeness: African-American teachers and their culturally specific classroom practices.* New York: New York University, Institute for Education and Social Policy.

Johnson, S. M. (2000, June 7). Teaching's next generation. *Education Week.* Retrieved September 2005, from http://www.edweek.org

Kincheloe, J. L & Steinberg, S. R. (1997). *Changing multiculturalism.* Philadelphia: Open University Press.

Ladson-Billings, G. (1992a). Culturally relevant teaching: The key to making multicultural education work. In C. Grant (Ed.), *Research and multicultural education.* London, UK: Falmer Press.

Ladson-Billings, G. (1992b). Reading between the lines and beyond the pages: A culturally relevant approach to literacy teaching. *Theory into Practice, 31,* 312–320.

Ladson-Billings, G. (1994). *The dreamkeepers: Successful teachers of African American children.* San Francisco: Jossey-Bass.

Morishima, J. K., & Mizokawa, D. T. (1980). *Education for, by, and of Asian/Pacific Americans, II.* ERIC Documents. ED199356.

Phinney, J. (2000). Ethnic identity. In A. Kazdin (Ed.), *Encyclopedia of psychology. 3.* Washington, DC: American Psychological Association.

Quiocho, A., & Rios, F. (2000). The power of their presence: Minority group teachers and schooling. *Review of Educational Research, 70*(4), 485–528.

Rong, X. L., & Priessle, J. (1997). The continuing decline in Asian-American teachers. *American Educational Research Journal, 34*(2), 267–93.

Shain F. (2003). *The schooling and identity of Asian girls.* Sterling, VA: Trentham Books.

Siu, S-F. (1996). *Asian-American students at risk: A literature review. Report No. 8.* ERIC Reproduction Services ED404406.

Sleeter, C. E., & Grant, C.A. (1991). Mapping terrains of power: Student cultural knowledge versus classroom knowledge. In C. E. Sleeter (Ed.), *Empowerment through multicultural education.* Albany, NY: State University of New York Press.

Smith, T. M., Rogers, G. T., Alsalam, N., Perie, M., Mahoney, R. P., & Martin, V. (1994). *The Condition of education, 1994.* Washington, DC National Center for Education Statistics, Department of Education. ED371491.

Snyder, T. D., & Hoffman, C. M. (1994). *Digest of education statistics, 1994.* Washington, DC National Center for Education Statistics, Department of Education. ED377253.

Strauss, A. L., & Corbin, J. M. (1998). *Basics of qualitative research: Techniques and procedures for developing grounded theory.* Thousand Oaks, CA: Sage.

Su, Z. (1997). Teaching as a profession and as a career: Minority candidates' perspectives. *Teaching and Teacher Education, 13*(3), 325–40.

Su, Z., Goldstein, S., Suzuki, G., & Kim, J. (1997). Socialization of Asian Americans in human services professional schools: A comparative study *Urban Education, 32*(3), 279–303.

Tuan, M. (1998). *Forever foreigners or honorary whites: The Asian American experience today.* New Brunswick, NJ: Rutgers University Press.

Twisleton, S. (2004). The role of teacher identities in learning to teach primary literacy. *Educational Review, 56*(2), 157–164.

U.S. Census Bureau. (2000). *Statistical abstract of the United States: 2000* (120th Edition). Washington DC: United States Department of Commerce.

Ware, F. (2002) Black teachers' perceptions of their roles and practices. In J. J. Irvine (Ed)., *In search of wholeness: African-American teachers and their culturally specific classroom practices.* New York: New York University, Institute for Education and Social Policy.

Waters, M. C. (1990). *Ethnic options: Choosing ethnic identities in America.* Berkeley, CA: University of California Press.

Yon, D. (1996). Identity and differences in the Canadian diaspora: Case study from Metropolitan Toronto. In A. Ruprecht & C. Tiana (Eds.), *The re-ordering of cultures: Caribbean, Latin America, and Canada in the hood.* Ottawa, ON: Carleton Press.

Zia, H. (2000). *Asian American dream: The emergence of an American people.* New York: Farrar, Strauss & Giroux.

Critical Thinking

1. What percent of teachers and students are Asian American?

2. How are Asian American teachers and students treated in U.S. society, schools, and classrooms?

3. What contributions have Asian Americans made to U.S. history and society?

4. Why are Asian teachers and students treated differently from other groups?

HEMA RAMANATHAN is an associate professor in the Department of Curriculum and Instruction of the College of Education at the University of West Georgia, Carrollton, Georgia.

UNIT 7

Waken Compassion and Commitment

Unit Selections

Learning Outcomes

After reading this unit, you will be able to:

- Summarize the author's position related to his statement that good intentions are not enough.

- Describe some of the issues associated with educational inequity.

- Expand upon the approaches for overcoming educational inequity.

- Retell how Black educators promote success with Black students.

- Discuss the procedures and positive outcomes for using cross-country simulations.

- Explain the benefits of featuring popular music to explore social justice with today's learners.

Student Website
www.mhhe.com/cls

Internet References

Education World
www.education-world.com

Infonation
www.un.org/Pubs/CyberSchoolBus/infonation/e_infonation.htm

National Association of Social Workers
www.socialworkers.org/pressroom/features/issue/peace.asp

Becoming an accomplished multicultural educator is never easy or achieved. Like all parts of education and life, multicultural education entails a process, a never-ending journey. For most educators, pursuing cultural competence encompasses the most exciting aspect of being an educator. During our teacher preparation programs, we learned what is required for us to become teachers to fulfill the state and university expectations.

Our minds were opened as we completed series of courses in our academic content areas such as math and science, then we launched into a series of courses about pedagogy, the science of teaching and learning, as we embarked on the path in learning how to teach.

We put it altogether once we arrived in a classroom during practica and internships. At last we could connect theory, research, and practice to focus on when and where to teach. We began to align the curriculum, instruction, and assessment while we struggled to manage our new classrooms. For most of us, we were amazed at the amount of responsibilities and number of decisions for which classroom teachers are accountable. And we zipped through each day hoping to keep one breath ahead of the students' interests and energies.

As we reflected upon our classrooms, we suddenly became much more aware of the learners both as individuals and as members of various groups. We became attuned to each class and the group's ability to function as a community of learners. As we became acquainted with individual students, we realized that each student is unique and special; each student is the manifestation of nature and nurture connected with family, friends, community, school, and life. During our reflections and connections, many of us discovered that truly getting to know our students is indeed the multicultural education journey.

Helping each student to find strengths, success, and satisfaction requires the teacher to know the individual student. Teachers must explore every avenue possible to understand how each student processes the cognitive, physical, social, and affective domains of learning. Teachers must talk with prior teachers; read cumulative folders; visit with parents and family members; assess prior knowledge, skills, and dispositions through speaking and writing; hold conversations and listen as each student shares formally and informally before, during, and after class. Getting to know the students takes time, energy, and patience. Yet, each student is entitled to and deserves an education that is equitable and excellent.

Professional development equips teachers with opportunities to provide the most efficient and effective learning experiences for every student in honor of and respect for each student's heritage, needs, and interests. Novice teachers tend to be concerned with classroom management techniques and the teacher's abilities to keep students on task. Few novice teachers recognize that by getting to know their students both as members of the learning community and, more important, as individuals, classroom management will no longer pose such great challenges. All teachers, novice and veteran, who are stymied by their classroom management techniques would benefit from redirecting their expectations on changing the students to changing the teacher.

© moodboard/Corbis

This type of transformation is difficult for teachers to comprehend and to trust. Teachers have come to believe that they need to be the commanders of their classrooms. However, teachers will soon discover that they get more power by giving power away. By collaborating with their students, constructing a sense of shared governance in the classroom, getting to know one another personally, and connecting the academic expectations with the local and global environments, teachers soon realize that classroom management is no longer a major issue and greater attention can be placed on learning and achievement. Staff developments should recognize that professional development must be powerful and worth teachers' time and energies. Teachers readily express that school administrators may not honor their responsibilities or provide them with the tools and techniques that will help them become more efficient and effective. Most efforts to promote multicultural education as professional development are avoided or resisted; frequently, the professional development has not been prepared or facilitated appropriately.

School administrators, especially staff developers, are strongly encouraged to find professional developers who can quickly connect with and engage teachers in identifying the specific challenge(s), accessing resources, and implementing change based on theory, research, and practice. Many accomplished teacher educators are available to provide effective professional development.

The articles in Unit 7 compel the reader to waken compassion and commitment by teaching all students the concepts and practices of care and compassion in the context of both the curriculum and the community. Students need opportunities to organize and participate in meaningful service learning projects that they initiate and manage. Students benefit by learning the concepts and practices of commitment necessary for future learning and living. The reader will benefit by attending seminars emphasizing compassion for a community concern and reading biographies about individuals who displayed compassion and commitment that changed the world.

Building the Movement to End Educational Inequity

Teach for America is working, Ms. Kopp argues. And studies show that TFA teachers do as well as or better than teachers with traditional certification.

WENDY KOPP

T each for America exists to address educational inequity—the stunning reality that in our nation, which aspires so admirably to be a land of equal opportunity, where one is born still largely determines one's educational outcomes. Despite plenty of evidence that children growing up in poverty can do well academically—when given the opportunities they deserve—the stark reality in our nation today is that the 13 million children growing up below the poverty line are already three grade levels behind children in high-income communities by the time they are 9 years old. Moreover, even the half of low-income children who do manage to graduate from high school are performing, on average, at the level of eighth-graders who live in affluent communities.

Why do we have this problem? We believe that the foremost reason is that children in low-income communities face extra challenges of poverty that other children don't face, including lack of adequate health care and housing and lack of access to high-quality preschool programs. The situation is compounded by the fact that the schools they attend were not designed to put children facing extra disadvantages on a level playing field with students in other areas. These circumstances persist because our national policies and practices, driven by our national priorities, have not been sufficient to tackle either the socioeconomic challenges or the inadequacies in our school systems.

At Teach for America, we know we can solve this problem because we see evidence in classrooms across the country that, when students growing up in poverty are given the opportunities they deserve, they excel. Knowing that we cannot expect every teacher to go above and beyond traditional expectations to the extent necessary to compensate for all the weaknesses of the system, however, we believe our best hope for a lasting solution is to build a massive force of leaders working from inside and outside education who have the conviction and insight that come from teaching successfully in low-income communities. We need such leadership working at every level of our school systems, working outside the system to address the socioeconomic factors that contribute so significantly to the problem, and working in policy and the sectors, such as journalism and business, that influence policy. In order to provide more students growing up in poverty today with excellent teachers and also to build this force of leaders, Teach for America recruits our nation's most promising future leaders, invests in the training and professional development necessary to ensure their success as teachers in our highest-poverty communities, and fosters their ongoing leadership as alumni.

The evidence indicates that our approach is working. Last year, more than 35,000 graduates of top universities competed for the opportunity to teach in urban and rural communities. Our incoming corps of 4,100 members achieved an average GPA of 3.6; 89% of them held at least one leadership position in a campus activity. Thirty percent of the corps members identify as people of color, and 32% are male. They come to this effort with a desire to reach the nation's most disadvantaged students, and based on the results of the most rigorous evaluation conducted to date, they are in fact teaching students who begin the year, on average, at the 14th percentile against the national norm.

The research actually does not show that our teachers have less impact than fully certified teachers, as Megan Hopkins seems to suggest. Multiple rigorous studies, such as the one she cites by Thomas Kane, Jonah Rockoff, and Douglas Staiger, have actually found that certification is a weak predictor of effectiveness and that Teach for America teachers do as well as or better than those from traditional preparation routes.

Moreover, the "small study" to which she refers was conducted by Mathematica Policy Research; the random-assignment methodology used in that study is widely considered the "gold standard" in research. This rigorous study found that students taught by Teach for America corps members made more progress in both reading and math than would typically be expected in a single year. In math, the impact of hiring a Teach for America teacher over another new teacher was the equivalent of reducing class size by eight students (as in the Tennessee class-size reduction experiment). The study found that Teach for America teachers produced gains in math that were not only larger than those of other beginning teachers but also larger than those of veteran and certified teachers.

The preponderance of evidence shows that corps members effect greater academic gains than other teachers in their schools. And while fewer than 10% of corps members report that they might have taught even if Teach for America hadn't been an option, more than 60% of our 17,000 alumni are working full-time in education. While they are still in their twenties and thirties, they are pioneering vital reforms, modeling excellence as teachers, serving as school principals and district administrators, and even getting appointed to superintendencies. They are making a tangible difference in communities across the country where we have been placing corps members for a decade or more. In our nation's capital, for example, Teach for America alumni serve as the schools' chancellor, deputy chancellor, 10% of school principals, one of two newly elected state board members, a policy advisor to the mayor, and the only national teacher of the year in the city's history. Other Teach for America alumni work from the social services and the legal profession to mitigate the pressures on schools in the first place, and still others work from corporations to marshal additional resources toward the effort.

In our program's 19-year history, we have engaged in ongoing research to continuously improve our program. In the process, we have given extensive thought to the suggestions made by Ms. Hopkins and have made decisions based on evidence of what is likely to maximize the impact of our model. For example, we have not moved to a three-year commitment because of evidence that doing so would significantly decrease the size, diversity, and quality of our corps, particularly in such key areas as math and science. We weigh this information against the reality that most of our corps members do, in fact, remain in education over the long term, despite the two-year commitment. We have also remained committed to enabling corps members to make first-year teacher salaries, knowing that asking them to work for a stipend or reduced salary would reduce the socioeconomic—and in turn racial and ethnic—diversity of the corps.

While we do remain committed to placing corps members in schools where they can reach our country's most underserved children, we have also made an unprecedented investment in their professional development. This is hard work, but by investing in measuring corps members' academic impact and in the continuous improvement of the training and professional development we provide, we aim to produce a corps of first- and second-year teachers who move their students forward significantly more than would typically be expected in a year.

It is also worth noting that principals in our partner schools give consistently high ratings to the preparation of our corps members. In a recent nationwide survey of principals with corps members in their schools, nearly all reported that corps members' training is at least as good as the training of other beginning teachers, and nearly two-thirds rate the training of corps members as better than that of other new teachers.

In very recent years, to increase the impact of our alumni, we have launched initiatives to support those who aim to pursue educational leadership through continued teaching, principalships, launching new social enterprises, policy and advocacy, and securing elected office. In some ways this development is responsive to Ms. Hopkins' suggestion that we offer incentives to entice members to remain in teaching, though, as outlined above, we continue to believe that it is important to foster the efforts of Teach for America alumni to effect change from other professions as well.

We laud the efforts of the local programs that Ms. Hopkins highlights. These programs show much promise for meeting the national need for qualified teachers. As we see evidence of their success, we look to such programs to help us identify good practices, and we incorporate those practices into our approach when applicable. Still, Teach for America is not beginning to meet the demand from districts and education reformers for our corps members and alumni, and this continuing demand fuels our commitment to grow even as we strengthen our program model and even as others experiment with new approaches to meeting the need for talent.

Finally, we are grateful to the university partners who work with us in pursuit of our mission. You can read about some of these partnerships elsewhere in this special section. We hope this conversation will open more opportunities for collaboration with others in the higher education community, and we appreciate Ms. Hopkins' willingness to bring this discussion to a broader audience.

Critical Thinking

1. What is Teach for America?
2. How are Teach for America teachers prepared for classrooms?
3. What is the emphasis for Teach for America teachers?
4. Why are alternative teacher preparation programs ideal for some schools and classrooms?

WENDY KOPP is founder and chief executive officer of Teach for America, New York, NY.

The Promise of Black Teachers' Success with Black Students

H. RICHARD MILNER, IV

In this article, I discuss African American[1] researchers' perspectives on the experiences, impact, and success of Black teachers with Black students in public schools. This study builds on an earlier study that focused specifically on these researchers' insights about the impact of the *Brown versus the Topeka Board of Education* decision on Black teachers, Black students, and Black communities (see Milner & Howard, 2004). In that work, the interviewed researchers focused on the experiences and impact of Black teachers in improving the learning opportunities of Black students, both past and present. In short, based on that study with a focus on *Brown,* the researchers who participated in the study pointed to a need for the recruitment and retention of Black teachers in public schools to improve the academic, cultural, and social experiences of all students but particularly African American students. In this study, I attempt to focus on what we know about successful Black teachers of Black students to (a) contribute to the ever-growing literature about successful teachers of Black students for the benefit of teachers from various ethnic backgrounds; and (b) outline several salient suppositions that may help us in advancing the research and theory about successful teachers of Black students. Clearly, outlining some of the practices of Black teachers and their success with Black students can be insightful for all teachers interested in teaching Black students.

For the purposes of this study, I focus specifically on the following questions:

- From what features of successful Black teachers and their teaching might others learn and benefit? and
- What types of questions should we investigate and address in order to improve the learning opportunities for Black students?

It is critical to note that it is not my intent to engage in a form of what Gay (2000) called "professional racism"—

> by underscoring the need for more teachers of color. The need for more Latino, Asian, Native, and African American teachers in U.S. schools is unquestionable. But to make improving the achievement of students of color contingent upon fulfilling this need is based on a very fallacious and dangerous assumption. It presumes that

membership in an ethnic group is necessary or sufficient to enable teachers to do culturally competent pedagogy. This is as ludicrous as assuming that one automatically knows how to teach English to others simply because one is a native speaker . . . (p. 205)

Engaging in this professional racism is not my goal or mission in this article. I agree with Gay and believe her perspectives here around the danger in assuming that Black teachers, for instance, carry all the knowledge, skills, and commitments necessary to successfully teach African American students. To the contrary, there is a huge range of diversity even within groups, and we cannot oversimplify the characteristics of any group of teachers. I have observed some less than successful and knowledgeable teachers from various ethnic backgrounds, including Black teachers. Moreover, as Gay explained,

> . . . knowledge and use of the cultural heritages, experiences, and perspectives of ethnic groups [of students] in teaching are far more important to improving student achievement than shared group membership. Similar ethnicity between students and teachers may be potentially beneficial, but it is not a guarantee of pedagogical effectiveness. (p. 205)

Still, based on the findings of my study, I want to focus on Black teachers' experiences and success both pre and post desegregation for insights about how all teachers can deepen and broaden their knowledge and understanding to better meet the needs and situations of students at present, particularly among Black students. In addition, I hope to encourage and inspire other researchers to continue investigating what we know about successful teachers of Black students. By outlining several central suppositions that emerged from this study and from the literature, more research is needed to build on what we know (theoretically) and how we know it (empirically).

Black teachers and their multiple roles, identities, and contributions have been the focus of many research articles, commentaries, and conceptual analyses (Foster, 1997; Milner, 2003; Mitchell, 1998). The seminal work of Michele Foster, Jackie Irvine, and Vanessa Siddle-Walker, for instance, has helped shape the field for the study of and implications for Black teachers and their teaching. The literature on Black teachers and their teaching is conceptualized in several important ways: It spans the pre-desegregation era to the present and focuses on P-12 schools as well as higher education. The research is clear that having more Black teachers in the teaching force could potentially improve a wide range of situations and needs of Black students. However, we must not focus exclusively on the recruitment and retention of Black teachers in P-12 classrooms. Rather, I argue that understanding Black teachers and Black students' situations and needs are also important to equip teachers from various ethnic backgrounds with the knowledge and skills necessary to become successful teachers of Black students. In other words, what teacher education programs and teachers do until more Black teachers are recruited is perhaps just as important as recruiting teachers of color for public school classrooms. Thus, what can we learn about Black teachers and their teaching of Black students to benefit all teachers, regardless of their ethnic, cultural, and racial background?

Black Teachers and Their Teaching

Much has been written about Black teachers, their experiences, their curriculum development, and their teaching in public school classrooms (Dixson, 2002; Foster, 1990, 1997; Holmes, 1990; Hudson & Holmes, 1994; Irvine & Irvine, 1983; King, 1993; Milner, 2003; Milner & Howard, 2004; Monroe & Obidah, 2004), and this literature is not limited to public schools but also highlights Black teachers' experiences in higher education, namely in teacher education programs (Baszile, 2003; Ladson-Billings, 1996; McGowan, 2000; Milner & Smithey, 2003). Agee (2004) explained that a Black teacher "brings a desire to construct a unique identity as a teacher . . . she [or he] negotiates and renegotiates that identity" (p. 749) to meet their objectives and to meet the needs and expectations of their students.

hooks (1994) makes it explicit that Black female teachers carry with them gendered experiences and perspectives that have been (historically) silenced and marginalized in the discourses about teaching and learning. Although teaching has often been viewed as "women's work," Black women teachers and their worldviews have often been left out of the discussions—even when race was the topic of discussion (hooks, 1994). Similarly, in colleges of education and particularly preservice and inservice programs, the programs are largely tailored to meet the needs of White female teachers (Gay, 2000), and Black teachers along with other teachers of color (male and female) are left out of the discussion. Where curricular materials were concerned in her study, Agee (2004) explained that "the teacher education texts used in the course made recommendations for using diverse texts or teaching diverse students based on the assumption that preservice teachers are White" (p. 749). Still, Black teachers often have distinctive goals, missions, decision making, and pedagogical styles that are important to understand.

In her analyses of valuable African American teachers during segregation, Siddle-Walker (2000) explained,

consistently remembered for their high expectations for student success, for their dedication, and for their demanding teaching style, these [Black] teachers appear to have worked with the assumption that their job was to be certain that children learned the material presented. (pp. 265–266)

Clearly, these teachers worked overtime to help their African American students learn; although these teachers were teaching their students during segregation, they were also preparing their students for a world of integration (Siddle-Walker, 1996). Moreover, as Tillman (2004) suggested, "these teachers saw potential in their Black students, considered them to be intelligent, and were committed to their success" (p. 282). There was something authentic about these Black teachers. Indeed, they saw their jobs and roles to extend far beyond the hallways of the school or their classroom. They had a mission to teach their students because they realized the risks and consequences in store for their students if they did not teach them and if the students did not learn. An undereducated and underprepared Black student, during a time when society did not want nor expect these students to succeed, could likely lead to destruction (drug abuse, prison, or even death).

Pang and Gibson (2001) maintained "Black educators are far more than physical role models, and they bring diverse family histories, value orientations, and experiences to students in the classroom, attributes often not found in textbooks or viewpoints often omitted" (pp. 260–261). *Thus, Black teachers, similar to all teachers, are texts themselves, but these teachers' text pages are inundated with life experiences and histories of racism, sexism, and oppression, along with those of strength, perseverance, and success.* Consequently, these teachers' texts are rich and empowering—they have the potential to help students understand the world (Freire, 1998; Wink, 2000) and to change it.

However, as evident from the literature, these African American teachers still often felt irrelevant and voiceless in urban, rural, and suburban contexts—even when the topic of conversation was multicultural education (see, Buendia, Gitlin, & Doumbia, 2003; Ladson-Billings, 1996; Milner & Woolfolk Hoy, 2003; Pang & Gibson, 2001). These experiences are unfortunate given the attrition rate of Black teachers in the teaching force. Black teachers are leaving the teaching profession and quickly (Howard, 2003; Hudson & Holmes, 1994).

Pre and post desegregation, Black teachers have been able to develop and implement optimal learning opportunities for students—yet in the larger school context, they were often ridiculed for being too radical or for not being "team players." As evident in my own research (Milner, 2003) and this study, Black teachers can feel isolated and ostracized because they often offered a counter-story or counternarrative (Ladson-Billings, 2004; Ladson-Billings & Tate, 1995; Parker, 1998; Solorzano & Yosso, 2001; Tate, 1997) to the pervasive views of their mostly White colleagues. Black teachers' ways of connecting with their students were successful—yet often inconsistent with their non-Black colleagues. In short, different does not necessarily mean deficient, wrong, or deficit.

Black teachers can have a meaningful impact on Black students' academic and social success because they often deeply understand Black students' situations and their needs. For instance, Mitchell (1998), in her qualitative study of eight recently retired African American teachers, reminded us of the insight Black teachers can have in helping us understand the important connections between the affective domain and student behavior. Building on lessons learned from Black teachers, Mitchell explained that in order for teachers to establish and to maintain student motivation and engagement, they should be aware of the students' feelings and their social needs. Students' feelings and emotions matter in how they experience education; Black students often bring a set of situations that have been grounded in racism, inequity, and misunderstanding (Milner, 2002). Racism and inequity can emerge not only through their daily interactions but also through institutional and structural circumstances.

The teachers in Mitchell's study "were critically aware of the experiences of the students, both in and out of school, and of the contexts shaping these experiences" (p. 105). The teachers in the study were able to connect with the students in the urban environments because they understood that the students' behaviors (whether good or bad) were often a result of their out of school experiences. There were reasons behind the students' behavioral choices. In Mitchell's words,

> . . . [The teachers] recalled situations in which factors outside of the school adversely affected students' behavior. They described students listless because of hunger and sleepy because they worked at night and on weekends to help support younger siblings. They described students easily distracted and sometimes belligerent because of unstable living environments. (p. 109)

Thus, these retired teachers understood the important connections between the students' home situations and school, and they were able to build on and learn from those out of school experiences and situations in their teaching. The Black teachers understood that many of their students were doing drugs, living in poverty, and were acting as adults in their homes in terms of bringing in money to support their families. However, the teachers did not use these realities as an escape. The teachers still put forth the effort necessary teach and to teach well.

It is easy for teachers to grant students "permission to fail" (Ladson-Billings, 2002) when they consider the complex and challenging lives of their students outside of the classroom. However, successful teachers of Black students maintain high expectations for their students (Siddle-Walker, 1996) and do not pity them but empathize with the students (McAllister & Irvine, 2002) so that students have the best possible chance of mobilizing themselves and empowering their families and communities. To explain, teachers who are committed to improving the lives of their students do not accept mediocrity, and they encourage and insist that their students reach their full capacity, mainly because these teachers understand that allowing students to "just get by" can surely leave them in their current situation or even worse. Thus, teachers cannot adopt approaches that do not push their students—high expectations, as Siddle-Walker

(1996) explained, are necessary to help the students emancipate themselves and to move beyond their current situations. Irvine (1998) described an interaction between a student and teacher below by borrowing James Vasquez' notion, "warm demanders," a description of teachers of color "who provide a tough-minded, no-nonsense, structured, and disciplined classroom environment for kids whom society has psychologically and physically abandoned" (p. 56):

> "That's enough of your nonsense, Darius. Your story does not make sense. I told you time and time again that you must stick to the theme I gave you. Now sit down." Darius, a first grader trying desperately to tell his story, proceeds slowly to his seat with his head hanging low. (Irene Washington, an African American teacher of 23 years; from Jacqueline Irvine's (1998) *Warm Demanders*)

An outsider listening and observing the Black teacher's tone and expectations for Darius may frown upon the teacher's approach. However, this teacher's approach is grounded in a history and a reality that is steeped in care for the student's best interest. In short, the teacher understood quite deeply the necessity to help Darius learn. She understood the necessity to "talk the talk." There is a sense of urgency not only for Irene to "teach her children well but to save and protect them from the perils of urban street life" (p. 56). Indeed, Black teachers often have a commitment to and a deep understanding of Black students and their situations and needs because both historically and presently these teachers experience and understand the world in ways similar to their students. In addition, the teachers have a commitment to the students because they have a stake in the African American community. Students often do not want to let their teachers down because the teachers are concerned for the students (Foster, 1997), and this concern has been described as other mothering (Collins, 1991), and I would add other fathering. The students sense this care of the teachers, and this care pushes them to do their best in the teachers' classroom.

Method

In an attempt to understand some of the impact of *Brown* for Black teachers, for Black students, and for Black communities, I invited six experts (educational researchers) to participate in an interview. For the purposes of this study, I focus specifically on these researchers' perspectives of the experiences and impact of Black teachers[2] to provide information for other teachers, teachers from various ethnic backgrounds, on successful teaching of Black students and to think about a research agenda that points to some central suppositions for future study. The six experts that I selected and invited to participate in the interview met several criteria: (a) They had engaged in research and writing about *Brown* (and in some cases taught courses that highlighted *Brown* from various perspectives); (b) they were experts and researchers who had been in their respective fields of study for longer than five years; and (c) they were willing to participate in the interview and follow-up interviews if necessary. I found it necessary to have conversations with experts around the country who had studied these and similar issues to get their viewpoints at the 50-year anniversary of *Brown* in order to assess where we have been, to think about where we are presently, and to chart a research agenda about where we are going.

From the six invitations extended, three experts agreed to participate in the study. I conducted the phone interviews, which lasted approximately 45 minutes to an hour. Participants in the study were asked several questions. As themes and issues emerged throughout the interviews, follow up questions were posed. Thus, these interview questions (listed below) are not exhaustive. Rather, they represent the thrust of questions posed: (a) what happened to Black teachers after the *Brown* decision (e.g., morale, dedication, self-concept, and retention)? (b) What impact might the *Brown* decision have on Black teachers leaving the profession? (c) How might *Brown* have influenced the education of Black students? (d) Why is it important to have Black teachers educating Black students? (e) How might we think about increasing the number of Black teachers in the teaching profession? (f) What types of questions should we be researching and addressing regarding the *Brown* decision around Black teachers, Black students, and Black communities? (g) In other words, where should we (researchers, teachers, and policy makers) go from here in order to reverse (Ford, 1996) the underachievement of Black students? Finally, the experts were given the opportunity to add additional comments at the end of the interview. Interestingly, consistent features and characteristics of successful teaching and teachers emerged in the interviews, which spoke to the question: What can we (teacher educators, other Black teachers, and teachers in general) learn about the teaching of successful Black teachers and their practice that can benefit others in the profession?

Analysis of Interviews

An interpretive perspective (Guba & Lincoln, 1994) was used to guide the interview analyses in this study. Interviews were tape-recorded and transcribed. Upon reviewing the interview transcripts, themes emerged from all three transcripts. In several instances, the themes overlapped, and I used them to guide much of the discussion in subsequent sections of this article. As themes emerged throughout the interviews, I developed coding categories to better understand the issues and to organize the data. These categories were named conceptually but were, in essence, themes that were stressed and pointed out by the participants to guide further inquiry. The posing of interview questions followed an inductive cycle, where a broad and general question was posed and experts were given the opportunity to expand upon those issues based on their perspectives and knowledge base.

The Participants

Participant one[3] (hereafter referred to as Barbara) is an endowed professor at a research university. She has been in the field of education for longer than 20 years. Participant two (hereafter referred to as Vince) is a lead researcher in a research institute. Vince has been in the field of education for seven years. Participant three (hereafter referred to as Peggy) is a professor at a research university who has been in the field of education for longer than 20 years. All three participants have written scholarly articles and/or book chapters about the *Brown* decision, Black teachers, and/or Black students. Moreover, in two cases, the researchers

have written books that focus (in some form and to some extent) on these important matters. The discussion shifts now to reveal the researchers' perspectives, offered in the interviews.

Researchers' Perspectives

In this section, I discuss several themes that emerged from the interviews with the researchers: Black teachers' importance and refocusing teacher education; roadblocks, barriers, and rolemodels; and culturally informed relationships.

Black Teachers' Importance and Refocusing Teacher Education

Among other issues, one theme that consistently emerged among the interviewed researchers when asked about the educational experiences of Black students as related to *Brown* was that of the need for more Black teachers. The participants all stressed the importance of having Black teachers in the teaching profession. In addition, the participants also stressed the importance of refocusing how teachers are educated. To illuminate, the researchers stressed the impact of, the relevance of, and the possibilities of having Black teachers teaching in public schools for the benefit of all students and especially Black students. All three experts reported the great need for an increase in the Black teaching force. For instance, Barbara and Vince stressed the importance of recruiting Black teachers, particularly for the benefit of Black students.

It is also important to note that Barbara stressed that White teachers [or teachers of any ethnic background] can be successful teachers of Black students. Barbara's perspective is consistent with that of other research that shows how teachers from any ethnic background can be successful teachers of Black students (Cooper, 2003; Ladson-Billings, 1994). However, Barbara also made it clear that in order for more meaningful learning to occur with Black students, "we're going to have to change dramatically the way we train teachers." Barbara's attention to the ways in which we educate Black teachers suggests that teacher educators, policy makers, principals, and teachers need to focus on more innovative ways to educate teachers as these teachers work to provide learning opportunities for students in P-12 classrooms; that is, we cannot focus all our attention on recruiting Black teachers but must (re)focus our attention on how teachers are educated such as building on successful features and characteristics of successful teachers from any background, including Black teachers.

While the interviewed researchers pointed out that many Black teachers serve as role models for their students, Barbara explained that there are too many barriers and roadblocks present that prevent Black teachers from entering the teaching profession.

Roadblocks, Barriers, and Role-Models

On one level, Vince explained that Black students need "to see other Black teachers" in order to have role models. He stated that, "What people experience day-to-day effectuates how they view and vision the possibility of their lives." Pre-*Brown*, Black students went from schools where all of their teachers and principals were Black to schools (post-*Brown*) where most, if not all, of their teachers were White. The magnitude of Black students "now being taught by White teachers" cannot be stressed enough, according to Vince. One can only imagine the quality of instruction that Black students received from White teachers, some of whom were opposed to the very notion of desegregation and teaching Black students from the very outset of the *Brown* decision. New Black teachers as well as Black students seemed to lose their Black teacher role models. Consequently, Black teachers, in large measure, started to select alternative fields. Whereas, historically, teaching, in the Black community was perceived as one of the most prestigious professions for Blacks (Foster, 1997), the perception of the teaching profession changes when this "equilibrium" is imbalanced according to Vince. Black students and new Black teachers need to see experienced, successful Black teachers. To illuminate, in Vince's words:

> . . . If students are growing up in schools that they don't see Black teachers, that they don't see Black principals or Black superintendents, how the hell are they going to imagine themselves being one?

Role models are critical in helping students decide on a profession and in helping students visualize the possibilities of their life. On another level, Barbara stressed that

> teacher education programs and states are going to have to eliminate or re-envision some of the barriers and road blocks that keep Black teachers out of the profession. And most of them [barriers and road blocks] come from the standardized tests of assessment that summarily declare that these Black candidates, in teacher education, aren't worthy or capable enough to become teachers.

Importantly, the push to recruit and to retain talented Black teachers is framed by these teachers' abilities to relate to and to connect to other Black students, socially, academically, pedagogically, and culturally. Barbara explained:

> And so Black teachers are important to have not because we want them [only] as role models, but that's important. But that's not the only reason we want [and need Black teachers]. We want them because they have a way of teaching [Black] kids that leads to achievement. They know how to come up with examples in the kids' lives that make the lessons come alive, and they [Black students] retain the material.

In essence, both Barbara and Vince stressed the importance of Black teachers' contributions as role modes for Black students. Further, Barbara pointed to some central reasons she believed many capable Black teachers are not making it into the classroom: roadblocks and barriers (primarily standardized tests). Still, if the researchers have found that teachers from various ethnic backgrounds can be successful teachers of Black students, we need to further investigate the extent to which teachers can become role models and how they develop and provide vivid examples to help Black students learn. Thus, successful teachers of Black students act as role-models and

develop pedagogical strategies that bring lessons to life through examples provided.

Barbara and Vince consistently referenced the importance of cultural connections between Black teachers and their Black students as a fundamental reason to increase the Black teaching force. At the same time, how do other teachers (Black) and teachers from various—different—ethnic backgrounds develop those connections with their Black students?

Culturally Informed Relationships

In many instances, there are cultural informed relationships that exist between Black teachers and Black students. In addition to Black teachers' having the ability to construct meaningful instructional examples with Black students, Peggy pointed to the connections between the hidden curriculum (or what students learn through the implicit nature of teaching and learning) and Black teachers. In other words, Peggy stressed the importance and benefits of Black teachers teaching Black students because there are inherent, unstated, lessons that emerge in classroom interactions that show up between teachers and students. For instance, she stressed that "cultural connections" are often prevalent in relationships with Black teachers and Black students. These culturally informed relationships allow Black teachers to develop meaningful, relevant (Ladson-Billings, 1994) and responsive (Gay & Kirkland, 2003) curricula and pedagogy in classrooms with Black students. To elaborate, Peggy stated,

> It comes in subtly [or through the hidden curriculum]; it comes in the talks that they [Black teachers] had with the students. It comes up in club activities . . . so the hidden curriculum was to explain what it means to be Black in American, to [be] role models . . . And I would add this deep understanding of culture. It's not just that I have high expectations of you and . . . believe in your capacity to achieve, and they're [Black teachers] willing to push you [Black students]. The teachers also had an intuitive understanding of the culture because they lived it . . . I [the teacher] live in the community. I go to church in the community. You know, in this segregated world . . .

Peggy discussed how Black teachers often expressed and demonstrated "high expectations, deep care for Black children, [and] beliefs in their [Black students'] capacity to succeed." These issues were inherent in the implicit curriculum as Peggy explained. Peggy goes on to explain what she refers to as the "bottom line":

> But the bottom line is that . . . teachers had the advantage of understanding the culture and being apart of it [during segregation]. They didn't have to be taught it. We [Black teachers] understood it. They understood you don't talk down to parents, okay?—That you don't treat people negatively. I mean they understood these things, wherein after desegregation, we're still trying to figure out how to understand it.

Thus, the idea is that Black teachers, by virtue of their out of school interactions and their deep cultural understanding of what it meant and means to be Black in America, often brought a level of knowledge and connectedness into the classroom that showed up in their teaching. Because Black teachers often interacted with Black students and parents outside of school (in the grocery stores, and at church, for instance) they had an insider's perspective on how Black students lived and experienced life outside of the classroom, and they were able to use this knowledge and understanding in the classroom with their students—to provide optimal learning opportunities for students. Black teachers were equipped to bring cultural understanding and connections into the classroom, partly because of how they lived their lives outside of the classroom. In essence, there were culturally informed relationships that existed in the classrooms between Black teachers and Black students that enabled success for all involved. We need to know more about how teachers can build cultural knowledge and how they can use that knowledge in the classroom.

Teaching and learning extended beyond the walls of the school as teachers found themselves sitting next to the parents of their students in church, for example. In Barbara's words,

> Many of the Black teachers were also Sunday school teachers at church. They lived in the community. And so they lived in the community and went to church with these [Black] kids; these things all connected in some interesting kinds of ways . . . it's not the building, necessarily. It's not the supplies, but it's the relationship between a teacher and a student that is the critical piece for Black kids. When you take that out of the equation, everything else fails. It doesn't matter how fine of a building, or how nice the books are, you've got to have a confident teacher who your kids all trust and care for. And if the teacher doesn't like the kids, it all falls apart.

The relationships that existed in the classroom enabled success for teachers and students alike. The researchers that I interviewed stressed the importance of teachers' ability to establish relationships with their students, and they believed that teachers from various backgrounds can develop these relationships to benefit Black students.

The discussion shifts to discuss, in more depth, some of the findings in this study. In particular, I discuss and conclude with features of successful teachers of African American students as I believe these features and characteristics can serve as data to assist all teachers in teaching Black students well. Moreover, what issues and perspectives as outlined in the previous section need additional attention through careful inquiry?

Discussion and Conclusions

Clearly, teachers from any ethnic background can be effective and successful teachers of Black students (Cooper, 2003; Gay, 2000; Ladson-Billings, 1994). As Gay (2000) stressed "the ability of teachers to make their instruction personally meaningful and culturally congruent for students account for their success, not their [ethnic] identity *per se*" (p. 205). However, much can be learned from the ways in which Black teachers have engaged and empowered Black students (both pre and post desegregation). Again, one of my goals in this article is to discuss some of the pervasive strategies, philosophies and characteristics of Black teachers that can help teachers, any teacher, become more

effective and successful pedagogues of Black students. As evident in this article, teachers can provide learning environments that foster student learning, and many Black teachers, historically, have succeeded in fostering optimal learning opportunities for students, especially for Black students.

In Figure 1, I attempt to outline some important features of successful Black teachers of Black students. The figure could prove useful in at least two interrelated ways: (1) the chart outlines a set of suppositions around practice that appear central to successful teachers of Black students, and other teachers—teachers from any ethnic background could benefit from the list; and (2) the chart provides a list of suppositions that surely need to be (re)visited, (re)searched, and (re)investigated. That is, replicate studies and studies that investigate the suppositions can possibly assist researchers, teachers, policy-makers, and teacher educators as they work collectively to improve the learning opportunities for Black students. It is important to note that the features in Figure 1 emerged from past and current research as well as other scholars' research (as outlined in previous sections of this article). It is my desire that teachers of any ethnic background would learn from what Black teachers often bring into the classroom as all teachers work to improve their practices with students.

In conclusion, the loss of African American teachers and the interactions Black students had with these teachers has been detrimental to the overall success of African American students. Hudson and Holmes (1994) explained that: ". . . the loss of African American teachers in public school settings has had a lasting negative impact on all students, particularly African American students and the communities in which they reside . . ."(p. 389). More than anything, Siddle-Walker (2000) concluded that because of the hard work and dedication of Black teachers "students did not want to let them down" (p. 265). The students put forth effort and achieved academically and socially because

> teachers held extracurricular tutoring sessions, visited homes and churches in the community where they taught, even when they did not live in the community, and provided guidance about "life" responsibilities. They talked with students before and after class, carried a student home if it meant that the child would be able to participate in some extracurricular activity he or she would not otherwise participate in, purchased school supplies for their classroom, and helped to supply clothing for students whose parents had fewer financial resources and scholarship money for those who needed help to go to college. (Siddle-Walker, 2000, p. 265)

In short, much can be learned from the success of Black teachers with Black students. While the increase in the Black teaching force could potentially be advantageous for Black students and all students, learning about how and what these teachers have done to be successful with Black students has the potential to assist us in thinking about the education of teachers (any teacher—from any ethnic background) at the present time. That is, what are some characteristics, philosophies, and insights about Black teachers that other teachers, from any ethnic background, can use to improve their experiences and impact with Black students? In addition, it is important for researchers to continue this line of inquiry to build on, substantiate, and redirect what we know and

Culturally Responsive (Gay, 2000) Classroom Management (Weinstein, Thomlinson-Clarke & Curran, 2004) Approaches: Teachers may be less likely to refer their Black student to the office for suspension and expulsion because they implement firm, no-nonsense management styles in their abilities to create optimal learning opportunities and spaces where learning can occur. They understand how to get students involved in lessons, and they have strict and successful classroom management approaches.

Culturally Informed Relationships: Teachers understand Black students and their experiences both inside and outside of school. They use cultural knowledge about the students' (home) community to build and sustain relationships with them.

Mentoring and Role-Models. Students often see the possibilities of their futures by the mentoring and role-modeling from their teachers. Black students often think: "If they (as Black teachers, principals, and superintendents) can be successful, I can too."

Parental Connections: They learn and deepen their knowledge, understanding, and awareness about Black parents and their concerns in many out of school contexts such as church or the beauty shop. They respect parents of their students; they do not insult or talk down to parents, and the parents respect the teachers. They work *together* for the benefit of the students.

Culturally Congruent (Gay, 2000) Instructional Practices: Teachers refuse to allow their students to fail (Ladson-Billings, 2002). They develop appropriate, relevant, responsive, and meaningful learning opportunities for students. Teachers have high expectations for students and push students to do their best work. Teachers often see expertise, talents, and creativity in their students, and they insist that students reach their full capacity to learn.

Counter-Narratives on Behalf of Black Students; Teachers offer a counter-story or counter-perspective on the situations that Black students find themselves dealing with in school. Because of their deep cultural knowledge about Black students, these teachers often advocate for Black students in spaces where others misunderstand their life experiences, worldviews, and realities.

Figure 1 Suppositions of successful teachers and teaching.

how we know it as we work to provide the very best learning opportunities for all students—and especially Black students.

Notes

1. Throughout this article, the terms "Black" and "African American" are used interchangeably.

2. It is important to note that these "experts" had studied *Brown* in some dimension of their research. In some cases, the experts may form speculative arguments about the nature of questions posed because they had not studied (with any depth) that particular issue. In such cases, I was sure to frame these speculative claims as such. That is, I trust the level of expertise that the experts shared but understood that in some cases the researchers were relying on a data set that *related to* an issue rather than focus *specifically on* that issue. Finally, the terms "experts" and "participants" will be used interchangeably throughout this article.

3. Pseudonyms are used to mask the identity of the participants and their institutional affiliations.

References

Agee, J. (2004). Negotiating a teaching identity: An African American teacher's struggle to teach in test-driven contexts. *Teachers College Record, 106*(4), 747–774.

Baszile, D.T. (2003). Who does she think she is? Growing up nationalist and ending up teaching race in white space. *Journal of Curriculum Theorizing, 19*(3), 25–37.

Buendia, E., Gitlin, A. & Doumbia, F. (2003). Working the pedagogical borderlands: An African critical pedagogue teaching within an ESL context. *Curriculum Inquiry 33*(3), 291–320.

Collins, P.H. (1991). *Black feminist thought: Knowledge, conscious, and the politics of empowerment: Perspectives on gender, Volume 2.* New York: Routledge.

Cooper, P.M. (2003). Effective white teachers of Black children: Teaching within a community. *Journal of Teacher Education 54*(5), 413–427.

Delpit, L. (1995). *Other people's children: Cultural conflict in the classroom.* New York: The New Press.

Dixson, A.D. (2002). "Let's do this!": Black women teachers' politics and pedagogy. *Urban Education, 37*(5) 670–674.

Ford, D.Y. (1996). *Reversing underachievement among gifted Black students: Promising practices and programs.* New York: Teachers College Press.

Foster, M. (1990). The politics of race: Through the eyes of African-American teachers. *Journal of Education, 172,* 123–141.

Foster, M. (1997). *Black teachers on teaching.* New York: The New Press.

Freire, P. (1998). *Pedagogy of the oppressed.* New York: Continuum.

Gay, G. (2000). *Culturally, responsive teaching: Theory, research, & practice.* New York: Teachers College Press.

Gay, G., & Kirkland, K. (2003). Developing cultural critical consciousness and self-reflection in preservice teacher education. *Theory into Practice 42*(3), 181–187.

Guba, E., & Lincoln, Y. (1994). Competing paradigms in qualitative research. In N. Denzin & Y. Lincoln (Eds.), *Handbook of qualitative research* (pp. 105–117). Thousand Oaks, CA: Sage.

Holmes, B. J. (1990). New strategies are needed to produce minority teachers. In A. Dorman (Ed.), *Recruiting and retaining minority teachers.* (Guest Commentary). Policy Brief No. 8. Oak Brook, IL: North Central Regional Educational Laboratory.

hooks, b. (1994). *Teaching to transgress: Education as the practice of freedom.* New York: Routledge.

Howard, T.C. (2003). Who receives the short end of the shortage?: America's teacher shortage and implications for urban schools. *Journal of Curriculum and Supervision, 18*(2), 142–160.

Hudson, M. J., & Holmes, B. J. (1994). Missing teachers, impaired communities: The unanticipated consequences of Brown v. Board of Education on the African American teaching force at the precollegiate level. *The Journal of Negro Education, 63,* 388–393.

Irvine, J. J. (1998, May 13). Warm demanders. *Education Week, 17*(35), 56+.

Irvine, R.W., & Irvine, J.J. (1983). The impact of the desegregation process on the education of black students: Key variables. *The Journal of Negro Education, 52,* 410–422.

King, S. (1993). The limited presence of African-American teachers. *Review of Educational Research, 63*(2), 115–149.

Ladson-Billings, G. (1994). *The dreamkeepers: Successful teachers of African American children.* San Francisco: Jossey-Bass Publishers.

Ladson-Billings, G. (1996). Silences as weapons: Challenges of a Black professor teaching White students. *Theory into Practice, 35,* 79–85.

Ladson-Billings, G. (2002). Permission to fail. In L.Delpit & J.K. Dowdy (Eds.), *The skin that we speak: Thoughts on language and culture in the classroom.* (pp. 107–120). New York: The New Press.

Ladson-Billings, G. (2004). Landing on the wrong note: The price we paid for *Brown. Educational Researcher, 33*(7), 3–13.

Ladson-Billings, G., & Tate, B. (1995). Toward a critical race theory of education. *Teachers College Record, 97,* 47–67.

McAllister, G., & Irvine, J. J. (2002). The role of empathy in teaching culturally diverse students: A qualitative study of teachers' beliefs. *Journal of Teacher Education, 53*(5), 433–443.

McGowan, J.M. (2000). Multicultural teaching: African-American faculty classroom teaching experiences in predominantly White colleges and universities. *Multicultural Education, 8*(2), 19–22.

Milner, H.R. (2002). Affective and social issues among high-achieving African American students: Recommendations for teachers and teacher education. *Action in Teacher Education, 24*(1), 81–89.

Milner, H.R. (2003). A case study of an African American English teacher's cultural comprehensive knowledge and (self) reflective planning. *Journal of Curriculum and Supervision 18*(2), 175–196.

Milner, H.R., & Howard, T.C. (2004). Black teachers, Black students, Black communities and *Brown:* Perspectives and insights from experts. *Journal of Negro Education 73*(3) 285–297.

Milner, H.R., & Smithey, M. (2003). How teacher educators created a course curriculum to challenge and enhance preservice teachers' thinking and experience with diversity. *Teaching Education 14*(3), 293–305.

Milner, H. R., & Woolfolk Hoy, A. (2003). A case study of an African American teacher's self-efficacy, stereo-type threat, and persistence. *Teaching and Teacher Education 19,* 263–276.

Mitchell, A. (1998). African-American teachers: Unique roles and universal lessons. *Education and Urban Society, 31*(1), 104–122.

Monroe, C. R., & Obidah, J. E. (2004). The influence of cultural synchronization on a teacher's perceptions of disruption: A case study of an African-American middle-school classroom. *Journal of Teacher Education, 55*(3), 256–268.

Pang, V.O., & Gibson, R. (2001). Concepts of democracy and citizenship: Views of African American teachers. *The Social Studies, 92*(6), 260–266.

Parker, L. (1998). Race is . . . race ain't": An exploration of the utility of critical race theory in qualitative research in education. *Qualitative Studies in Education 11*(1), 45–55.

Siddle-Walker, V. (1996). Their highest potential: An African American school community in the segregated south. Chapel Hill: University of North Carolina Press.

Siddle-Walker, V. (2000). Valued segregated schools for African American children in the South, 1935–1969: A review of common themes and characteristics. *Review of Educational Research, 70*(3), 253–285.

Solorzano, D.G. & Yosso, T.J. (2001). From racial stereotyping and deficit discourse toward a critical race theory in teacher education. *Multicultural Education 9*(1), 2–8.

Tate, W. F. (1997). Critical race theory and education: History, theory, and implications. In M. Apple (Ed.), *Review of research in education* (Vol. 22, pp. 195–247). Washington, DC: American Educational Research Association.

Tillman, L.C. (2004). (Un)Intended consequences? The impact of Brown v. Board of Education decision on the employment status of Black educators. *Education and Urban Society, 36*(3), 280–303.

Weinstein, C. S., Thomlinson-Clarke, S., & Curran, M. (2004). Toward a conception of culturally responsive classroom management. *Journal of Teacher Education, 55*(1), 25–38.

Wink, J. (2000). Critical pedagogy: Notes from the real world. (2nd Ed.). New York: Longman.

Critical Thinking

1. What are the benefits of Black teachers for Black students?

2. How are Black teachers' accomplishments effectively conveyed to Black students?

3. What does the research report about Black teachers' contributions for all teachers?

4. Why should additional research about Black teachers be conducted and shared among educators?

H. Richard Milner, IV, is Betts Assistant Professor of Education and Human Development, Peabody College, Vanderbilt University, Nashville, Tennessee.

Good Intentions Are Not Enough: A Decolonizing Intercultural Education

PAUL C. GORSKI

I remember the invitations: red text on a white background, the title of the event in a curly bold typeface surrounded by a crudely drawn *piñata,* a floppy sombrero, and a dancing *cucaracha.* A fourth grader that year, I gushed with enthusiasm about these sorts of cultural festivals—the different, the alien, the other—dancing around me, a dash of spice for a child of white flighters. Ms Manning distributed the invitations in mid-April, providing parents a few weeks to plan for the event, which occurred the first week of May, on or around Cinco de Mayo.

A few weeks later my parents and I, along with a couple of hundred other parents, teachers, students, and administrators crowded into the cafeteria for Guilford Elementary School's annual Taco Night. The occasion was festive. I stared at the colorful decorations, the papier maché *piñatas* designed by each class, then watched as my parents tried to squeeze into cafeteria style tables built for eight-year-olds. Sometimes the school hired a Mexican song and dance troupe from a neighboring town. They'd swing and sway and sing and smile and I'd watch, bouncing dutifully to the rhythm, hoping they'd play *La bamba* or *Oye como va* so I could sing along, pretending to know the words. If it happened to be somebody's birthday the music teacher would lead us in a lively performance of *Cumpleaños feliz* and give the kid some Mexican treats.

¡Olé!

Granted, not a single Mexican or Mexican American student attended Guildford at the time. Although I do recall Ms Manning asking Adolfo, a classmate whose family had immigrated from Guatemala, whether the Taco Night tacos were 'authentic.' He answered with a shrug. Granted, too, there was little educational substance to the evening; I knew little more about Mexico or the Mexican American experience upon leaving Taco Night than I did upon arriving. Still, hidden within Taco Night and the simultaneous absence of real curricular attention to Mexicans, Mexican Americans, Chicanos, and other Latinos, were three critical and clarifying lessons: (1) Mexican culture is synonymous with tacos; (2) 'Mexican' and 'Guatemalan' are synonymous, and by extension, all Latino people are the same, and by further extension, all Latino people are synonymous with tacos (as well as sombreros and dancing *cucarachas*); and (3) white people really like tacos, especially the kind in those hard, crunchy shells, which, I learned later, nobody eats in Mexico.

Thus began my intercultural education: my introduction to the clearly identifiable 'other.'

And I could hardly wait until Pizza Night.

Introduction

As I look back, 26 years later, through my educator and activist lenses, what I find most revealing—and disturbing—about Taco Night and my other early experiences with intercultural education is intent. Or, more precisely, lack of intent. I assume that the adults at Guilford Elementary School believed that this event had educational merit. I am sure they believed that events like Taco Night were more age-appropriate for fourth graders than, say, a critical examination of US imperialist intervention in Latin America. And I am equally certain that they intended for my classmates and me to leave that evening with an appreciation for Mexican or Mexican-American culture. I am certain, as well, that they did not intend to inflate the stereotypes about Chicana/os and Latina/os into which the media and my parents had been socializing me since birth. I am equally certain that they did not purposefully reify my growing sense of racial and ethnic supremacy by essentializing the lives and diverse cultures of an already-oppressed group of people, then presenting that group to me as a clearly identifiable 'other.' But that is exactly what they did.

Unfortunately, my experience and a growing body of scholarship on intercultural education and related fields (such as multicultural education, intercultural communication, anti-bias education, and so on) reveal a troubling trend: despite overwhelmingly good intentions, most of what passes for intercultural education practice, particularly in the US, accentuates rather than undermines existing social and political hierarchies (Aikman 1997; Diaz-Rico 1998; Gorski 2006; Hidalgo, Chávez-Chávez, and Ramage 1996; Jackson 2003; Lustig 1997; Nieto 2000, 1995; Schick and St. Denis 2005; Sleeter 1991; Ulichny 1996). This is why the framework we construct for examining and encouraging intercultural education reveals, among other things, the extent and limits of our commitments to a genuinely intercultural world. The questions are plenty: do we advocate and practice intercultural education so long as it does not disturb the existing sociopolitical order?; so long as it does not require us to problematize our own privilege?; so long as we can celebrate diversity, meanwhile excusing ourselves from the messy work of social reconstruction?

Can we practice an intercultural education that does not insist first and foremost on social reconstruction for equity and justice without rendering ourselves complicit to existing inequity and injustice? In other words, if we are not battling explicitly against the prevailing social order with intercultural education, are we not, by inaction, supporting it?

Such questions cannot be answered through a simple review of teaching and learning theory or an assessment of educational programs. Instead, they oblige all of us who would call ourselves intercultural educators to re-examine the philosophies, motivations, and world views that underlie our consciousnesses and work. Because the most destructive thing we can do is to disenfranchise people in the name of intercultural education.

In this essay—my response to a request from the International Association for Intercultural Education (on whose Board of Directors I sit) to share my philosophy of intercultural education—I offer my continuously evolving, perpetually incomplete reflections on these questions. I organize these reflections into two primary arguments. First, any framework for intercultural education that does not have as its central and overriding premise a commitment to the establishment and maintenance of an equitable and just world can be seen as a tool, however well-intentioned, of an educational colonization in which inequity and injustice are reproduced under the guise of interculturalism. Secondly, transcending a colonizing intercultural education requires in educators deep shifts in consciousness rather than the simple pragmatic or programmatic shifts that too often are described as intercultural education.

I begin by providing a brief contextualization for these arguments and how US and world socio-politics inform them. I then contend that the softening of socio-political context in the dominant intercultural education discourse (Gorski 2006)—particularly that context related to economic exploitation through racism, sexism, xenophobia, and other oppressions–results, too often, in unintentionally colonizing intercultural education. I end with a series of shifts of consciousness that, I argue, may inform a more authentic intercultural education.

As a point of clarification, although 'multicultural education' is a much more common term and movement in the US (my present national context) than 'intercultural education,' and although I define the objectives of both of these movements very similarly–as the establishment and maintenance of equity and social justice in education contexts and, by extension, society—I choose to focus here specifically on the latter. I do so because multicultural education tends to refer more rigidly to formal schooling environments, whereas intercultural education, in my conceptualization, is broader in scope, unconstrained to formal education.

Socio-political Context

The world may be flat, as Friedman (2006) wrote, for the corporate elite, but for the rest of us—the workers, the teachers, the wage-earners, those of us without stock options and lobbyists—the world is as round and inhibiting as ever. Even while economic power brokers invite us into unabashed celebrations of globalization, corporate elites—often with help from legislators—demonstrate greater and greater propensities for expanding their markets and finding ever-cheaper labor. They demonstrate, as well, propensities for accelerating economic inequality worldwide (Chossudovsky 2003); and so globalization, although pitched as the pathway toward economic growth and stability, even in the poorest countries in the world, has proven to be little more than a contemporary form of mass economic exploitation–a vehicle for what Harvey (2005) calls the 'new imperialism' and what Chossudovsky (2003) calls the 'globalization of poverty.'

Corporations and their government allies employ a variety of techniques to maintain among the people something on a continuum between compliance and complicity with this exploitation. In Colombia, US corporations such as Chiquita Brands International fund paramilitaries to protect their interests, often through physically and psychologically violent means (Bussey and Dudley 2007). It is not uncommon for Colombian teachers who dare voice an opinion about, for example, their government's complicity with US corporate interests, to be assassinated (Klein 2004). Within the US, where federal education policy is firmly under the thumbs of corporate elites in the form of the Business Roundtable, the public education system itself (along with increasingly conglomerated corporate media) is becoming, more and more explicitly, a vehicle for socializing citizens into compliance and complicity (Chomsky 2003; Gabbard 2003). We can observe this infestation of corporate influence on education in one of its most disturbing manifestations in the emerging educational hegemony in the US. Although the idea has long existed (however contested) that education's primary purpose is to prepare people for employment and economic stability, only recently has the language commonly used to describe this attitude—preparing students 'to compete in the global marketplace'—become so explicitly market-centric.

As corporations and their lobbyists garner greater control over all manner of policy and legislation, they gain more access to the systems, such as education, that facilitate access to knowledge and popular perception. A clear and complex illustration of this process can be found in the weakening over the last decade of laws prohibiting the very sort of media super-conglomeration happening today in the US. The outcome of these processes is the centralization of control of virtually every mainstream newspaper, magazine, film studio, television station, and radio station in the country into the hands of five corporations (Bagdikian 2004). As a result, these media, like the education system, have become tools for socializing a compliant and complicit populace into a market hegemony that normalizes consumer culture (with the help of a president insisting that we respond to the 9/11 attacks by shopping), glorifies corporate imperialism (with language such as 'liberating the Iraqi people'), and conflates capitalism with democracy. The ideals underlying and driving these shifts often are described as neo-liberalism.

One of the key neo-liberal strategies for socializing the masses into complicity with corporate interests is the propagation of deficit theory—an approach for justifying inequality that is enjoying resurgence in the Western world today. Deficit theory, a remnant of colonial and imperial history (Shields, Bishop, and Mazawi 2005), holds that inequality is the result, not of systemic inequities in access to power, but intellectual and ethical deficiencies in particular groups of people (Collins 1988). Deficit theorists draw on stereotypes already well-established in the mainstream psyche (Osei-Kofi 2005; Rank 2004; Tozer 2000)—such as through television shows that paint African Americans as urban thugs or gay men as promiscuous—in order to pathologize oppressed communities rather than problematizing the perpetrators of their oppressions (Shields et al. 2005; Villenas 2001).

Deficit theory has been used throughout history to justify imperial pursuits. For example, European colonialists justified Native American genocide and slavery in the US in part by painting native peoples and African slaves as 'savages' who required civilizing–the white man's burden. Deficit theory is used in similar ways today, such as to justify imperial US intervention in the Middle East.

But it is used, as well, to justify the dissolution of human rights and the quickening transfer of power from the people to corporations. In order to accomplish this justification, capitalist elites use their access to the media and schools to effectively blame certain groups of people, such as the poor and indigenous communities, for a plethora of social ills and the general decay of society, rendering them, in the public's eye, undeserving of economic or social justice (Gans 1995). In the US, economically disadvantaged people, from the homeless to undocumented immigrants, have become particularly vulnerable targets for deficit theorists. The capitalist fruits of this process are two-fold: (1) the deterioration of support for public policy meant to alleviate political and economic marginalization, which, among other things, helps justify the erosion of welfare programs in the US; and (2) the diversion of the public's attention away from increasing corporate empowerment and toward a perceived need to eradicate inequality by 'fixing' deficient people. 'Fixing' in this case often means assimilating—as in assimilating poor students into the very structures and value systems that oppress them, as today's dominant discourse on poverty and education in the US calls on educators to do.

No Child Left Behind (NCLB)—President Bush's landmark federal policy for US schools, composed largely by the Business Roundtable and other corporate cooperatives—epitomizes the deficit approach. Its reliance on a largely corporate model of standardization and accountability demonizes schools (and as a result, students and teachers) based on a narrow conception of student performance even while it ignores the structural conditions—including those within the system, such as inequitable school funding, and those outside the system, such as the scarcity of living wage jobs—that so heavily influence students' educational opportunities. Meanwhile, several aspects of the legislation, such as mandated testing and an insistence that schools use so-called 'scientifically-based' reading programs, provide additional economic pipelines from a supposedly public education system to the corporations that provide these materials and services.

As I explained in a previous essay (Gorski 2006), most of what people refer to as intercultural or multicultural education—including scholarship, teacher preparation courses, or educational programs—fails to take this sort of context into account. As a result, we expend much energy fighting symptoms of oppressive conditions (such as interpersonal conflicts) instead of the conditions themselves; and this is exactly what we are socialized to do. The powers that be are thrilled that we host Taco Night instead of engaging in authentic antiracism; that we conduct workshops on a fictitious 'culture of poverty' instead of holding corporations and governments responsible for the growing economic inequities that inform educational inequities.

As an intercultural educator in the US, the journey toward acknowledging this sociopolitical context leads me daily into a corridor with two doors. I see most people who call themselves intercultural educators stepping through the first door—the one, easiest to reach, that allows access to a space where they can avoid this cynicism and concern over power and oppression; a space where these conditions are accepted as normal or inevitable; a space where we communicate interculturally and resolve conflict

without spending an ounce of energy on reconstructing society at any fundamental level. I am tempted to follow suit, to participate in intercultural dialogue and skim along the surface of cultural awareness.

I see few people and even fewer organizations choosing the second door—the one, heavy and inconveniently placed, that leads to a space of personal and institutional vulnerability. Like every intercultural educator, I must choose: will I comply, practicing an intercultural education that does not disturb these sociopolitical realities? Or will I choose vulnerability, practicing intercultural education for nothing less than social reconstruction? And what does my decision reveal about me?

Colonizing Intercultural Education: To Whose Benefit?

I have spent—continue to spend—countless agonizing hours in that corridor, slipping in and out of both doors. And I have arrived at this conclusion: the practice of intercultural education, when not committed first and foremost to equity and social justice—to the acknowledgement of these realities and the disruption of domination—might, in the best case, result in heightened cross-group awareness at an individual level. But in many cases, such practice is domination. And in any case, ignoring systemic oppression means complying with it. And to whose benefit? Who or what are we protecting?

In her discussion of intercultural education in Latin America, Aikman (1997) observes that it 'developed out of concern and respect for indigenous knowledge and practices, but primarily in response to the exploitation, oppression and discrimination of indigenous peoples' (p. 466). With this conception in mind, Aikman reports, indigenous organizations throughout the region lobbied extensively for intercultural education. Governments responded and began codifying their commitments to intercultural education—or, more precisely, to candy-coated versions of it. For example, Foro Educativo (as cited by Aikman), an NGO hired to help the Peruvian government conceptualize intercultural education, offered this definition:

> Interculturality in education is a space for dialogue which recognises and values the wealth of cultural, ethnic and linguistic diversity in the country, promotes the affirmation and development of different cultures which co-exist in Peru and constitutes an open process towards cultural exchange with the global society. (Aikman 1997, 469)

This vision echoes most conceptualizations of intercultural education—especially those from people and organizations in positions of power. Cushner, a leading US voice in the field, offers a similar vision, explaining that intercultural education

> recognizes that a genuine understanding of cultural differences and similarities is necessary in order to build a foundation for working collaboratively with others. It also recognize[s] that a pluralistic society can be an opportunity for majority and minority groups to learn from and with one another, not a problem as it might be viewed by some. (Cushner 1998, 4)

These views synthesize the goals most often identified in definitions of intercultural education: the facilitation of intercultural dialogue, an appreciation for diversity, and cultural exchange. But they also demonstrate why intercultural education quickly became a target of scorn and scrutiny by many of the indigenous communities who once enthusiastically supported it (Aikman 1997; Bodnar 1990). This sort of framework for intercultural education, they argued, according to Aikman (1997), 'maintains the distribution of power and forms of control which perpetuate existing vertical hierarchical relations . . . Thus, this intercultural-ity remains embedded in relations of internal colonialism' (469). In other words, an intercultural education constructed on the basis of these visions is a tool for the maintenance of marginaliza-tion (Gorski 2006; Lustig 1997; Sleeter 1991)—marginalization that supports the interests of the powerful at the expense of the oppressed.

Take, for example, the goal of intercultural dialogue—a hall-mark of intercultural education. Research indicates that par-ticipation in such experiences can result, in the short-term, in changes to individual attitudes and cross-group relationships (Dessel, Rogge, and Garlington 2006; Rozas 2007; Vasques Scalera 1999). However, absent from this scholarship is evidence that intercultural dialogue contributes in any way to eliminat-ing, or even mitigating, systemic inequities (DeTurk 2006). But this body of scholarship does include several studies that reveal the colonizing outcomes of intercultural dialogue when it is not grounded in an acknowledgement of inequities in access to power—including imbalances of power among the participants themselves—and a bigger movement toward social reconstruc-tion (DeTurk 2006; James 1999; Jones 1999; López-Garay 2001; Maoz 2001; Wasserman 2001).

This sort of colonization and domination through intercultural dialogue reveals itself in a variety of ways. For example, such dia-logues usually involve groups that, according to Maoz,

> are involved in asymmetrical power relations. Such are the planned contacts between Whites and African Americans in the United States, Whites and Blacks in South Africa, and . . . representatives of the Jewish majority and Palestin-ian minority in Israel. (Maoz 2001, 190–1)

But far too often these experiences are facilitated—controlled—in ways that assume that all participants sit at an even table (Jones 1999), one at which all parties have equitable access to cultural capital. According to Jones, such dialogue experiences tend to focus on the goal of mutual empathy—requiring dominated people to empathize with people who are, or who represent, their oppres-sors. Jones asks,

> What if 'togetherness' and dialogue-across-difference fail to hold a compellingly positive meaning for subordinate ethnic groups? What if the 'other' fails to find interesting the idea of their empathetic understanding of the powerful, which is theoretically demanded by dialogic encounters? (Jones 1999, 299)

Which people and systems do we protect when we request empa-thy from dominated groups without first demanding justice from the powerful?

Dialogue experiences and other intercultural education practices reinforce prevailing colonizing hegemony as well when, absent a central focus on social reconstruction, the rules of engagement require disenfranchised participants to render themselves more vulnerable to the powerful than they already are. Jones explains

what she calls the 'imperialist resonances' of such conditions for cross-cultural exchange:

> In attempting, in the name of justice, to move the boundary pegs of power into the terrain of the margin-dwellers, the powerful require them to 'open up their territory'. (Jones 1999, 303)

The powerful—who, as individuals or institutions, usually con-trol (implicitly or explicitly) rules of engagement in intercultural education experiences—tend to leave unacknowledged the reality that the marginalized voices they invite into dialogue do not need organized opportunities to hear the voices of the powerful. They are immersed in these voices (Jones 1999) through the media, edu-cation, and so on. So in addition to being ill-conducive to a move-ment for real social change, this brand of intercultural education actually reifies power hierarchies (Maos 2001).

Worst of all participants from dominant groups, according to Vasques Scalera (1999), enjoy personal growth and fulfillment from these practices at higher rates than those from subordinate groups. And isn't this—the powerful gaining cultural capital on the backs of the oppressed, who often, regardless, are compelled to participate (as they are in school curricula, teacher education courses, or staff development workshops)—the epitome of colo-nizing education?

This brand of intercultural education, in which we focus on inter-personal relationships and cultural awareness, the power hierarchy firmly in place even within our intercultural practice, is exactly the kind of diversion that serves the colonizing and neo-liberal inter-ests of the powerful. We can call ourselves authentic intercultural educators only when we ensure that our work—every moment of it—pushes against, rather than supporting, these interests.

Decolonizing Intercultural Education

One of the most dangerous dimensions of educational hegemony in the US is a culture of pragmatism. Exacerbated by a flood of education policy that requires assessment of student and teacher performance on the basis of standardized test scores, the culture of pragmatism dissuades theoretical or philosophical discourses among educators in favor of those focused on immediate, practical strategies. I find that educators who attend my workshops increas-ingly resist discussions aimed at deepening theoretical understand-ing and consciousness. Many seem to want, instead, a series of lesson plans they can implement immediately in their classrooms. I do not blame them for this desire. After all, we are all victims of this culture of pragmatism; of its de-professionalization of the teaching professions; of its power to lure us away from a discourse of what 'could be' in education; of how it limits the education reform discourse to minor shifts in practice—Taco Night—that, despite good intentions, colonize more than they liberate.

Unfortunately, perhaps because we, as educators, are socialized into this culture, there seems to be little resistance to it. This is why the first step toward authentic intercultural practice is undertaking shifts in consciousness that acknowledge sociopolitical context, raise questions regarding control and power, and inform, rather than deferring to, shifts in practice. It is difficult work—transcending hegemony, turning our attention away from the cultural 'other' and toward systems of power and control. Those of us who choose this door must acknowledge realities we are socialized not to see. We must admit complicity. But how can we do otherwise, risking the possibility that our work may devolve into sustenance for the status quo, and still call ourselves intercultural educators?

I describe here several shifts of consciousness that, I propose, are fundamental to preparing a larger shift from a colonizing to a decolonizing intercultural education. Many of these shifts, in the most basic terms, refer to seeing what we are socialized not to see and pushing back against hegemony; against its diversions from dominance and our complicity with it.

I see these shifts as developmental. I continue to struggle, from my place of relative privilege, with all of them.

Shift No. 1: Cultural Awareness Is Not Enough

Rather than focusing on cultural awareness or understanding differences, I must expose hegemonic meaning-making regarding difference (as compared with hegemony's appointed 'norm') and how it informs my worldview. Culture and identity differences may affect personal interactions, but more importantly, they affect one's access to power. The powerful exploit differences from the hegemonic norm to justify dominance and oppression. I especially must avoid the sorts of cultural awareness activities that other or essentialize non-dominant groups or that, absent a commitment to social justice, require dominated groups to make themselves ever more vulnerable for the educational benefit of the privileged.

Shift No. 2: Justice First, Then Conflict Resolution

Too often, intercultural educators conflate conflict resolution and peace with justice. When equity and social justice are not in place, peace and conflict resolution merely reify the existing social order. I must not allow intercultural education to become yet another vehicle for the maintenance of order by resolving conflict, meanwhile leaving injustices unresolved.

Shift No. 3: Rejecting Deficit Theory

Any approach to intercultural education that explains inequality by demonizing disenfranchised communities must be abandoned. I must be wary of any supposed intercultural paradigm that, like the 'culture of poverty' myth, attributes values or worldviews to anyone based on one dimension of identity. I must recognize deficit theory as a diversion from the goal of dismantling oppression.

Shift No. 4: Transcending the Dialogic Surface

Like conflict resolution, intercultural dialogue rarely occurs among people with equal access to power. So instead of facilitating such experiences with the false assumption of an even table, I must acknowledge the power imbalances, both individual and systemic, in play. In addition, I must avoid facilitating dialogue experiences in which I expect the least powerful participants to teach their privileged counterparts about oppression. Similarly, I must not focus exclusively on commonalities between the powerful and oppressed, minimizing disenfranchisement.

Shift No. 5: Acknowledging Sociopolitical Context

A few years ago I attended a symposium on globalization intended for corporate CEOs and upper-level managers. Between presentations I stood in the hallway with a group of attendees as they debated the optimum unemployment level–the optimum, that is, not for securing living wage jobs for all workers, but for maximizing their profits. One attendee argued that 'his people' insisted that 'the current level of unemployment is perfect–just enough to ensure sufficient demand for jobs.' Another attendee explained that 'his people' informed him that a 'half-percentage or so rise in the unemployment rate would help keep wages down and curb workers' bargaining power for better benefits.' I stood, jaw agape, while these men, polished from head to toe, argued over how many of their fellow citizens should be sacrificed to their corporate greed.

Today, as I attend symposia on class and poverty, I find an equally troubling reality: a dominant discourse that, ignoring this sociopolitical context, centers on ending poverty by 'lifting' individual people into the middle class through job skills and education. If I, as an intercultural educator, fail to see how ludicrous such propositions—like the idea that we can end poverty without dismantling a class hierarchy that sustains itself on un- and underemployment—are, then I am doomed, despite good intentions, to doing the bidding of the powerful in the name of intercultural education.

Shift No. 6: 'Neutrality' = Status Quo

People often ask me why I make education so political. Shouldn't I, as an intercultural educator, be more neutral, appreciative of all opinions? But I must remember that I practice colonizing education when I claim or attempt neutrality. In fact, the very act of claiming neutrality is, in and of itself, political, on the side of the status quo. As such, my intercultural work must be explicitly political, against domination and for liberation; against hegemony and for critical consciousness; against marginalization and for justice.

Shift No. 7: Accepting a Loss of Likeability

Practicing decolonizing intercultural education requires that I speak truth to power, challenging hegemony and hierarchy. I cannot undertake these challenges authentically without being disliked by many individuals and most institutions. In fact, I must acknowledge that, as a white, heterosexual, first-language-English-speaking man in the US, I have access to a degree of institutional likeability that most people of color, lesbians and gay men, people who speak first languages other than English, and women, do not enjoy, and that this discrepancy is based on nothing more than unearned privilege. So I, in effect, must be willing to 'spend' my likeability, to take on oppression so vigorously that I risk being disliked by the powerful. If my educational practice is not seen by the powerful as threatening to their dominance, as terrifying to their sense of entitlement and control, then I am not an intercultural educator.

Conclusion

I have not intended in this essay to question the commitments of those of us who refer to ourselves as intercultural educators. To the contrary—much of my analysis begins with my own struggles to abandon the path of least resistance and to choose a more authentic intercultural education.

This analysis has led me to a philosophy of intercultural education that insists, first and foremost, on the establishment and maintenance of an equitable and just world. It has led me, as well, to the conclusion that such a philosophy cannot be achieved through intercultural programs or slight curricular shifts. I cannot effectively enact authentic intercultural education so long as I—in mind and soul—am colonized; so long as I do the bidding of the powerful through well-intentioned, colonizing practice. I begin by liberating myself, determined to deepen my consciousness about the sociopolitical contexts and implications of my practice. And only then—when I can say that my work decolonizes instead of colonizes; that my work challenges hegemony rather than reifying it; that my work transcends prevailing intercultural discourses of cultural awareness, conflict resolution, and celebrating diversity—can I call myself an intercultural educator.

References

Aikman, S. 1997. Interculturality and intercultural education: A challenge for democracy. *International Review of Education* 43, no. 5: 463–79.

Bagdikian, B. 2004. *The new media monopoly.* Boston, MA: Houghton.

Bodnar, Y. 1990. Aproximación a la Etnoeducación como elaboración teorica. In *Etnoeducación: Conceptualización y ensayos,* ed. Ministry of Education, Colombia. Bogota: Programa de Etnoeducación PRODIC.

Bussey, J., and S. Dudley. 2007. U.S. companies under scrutiny for payoffs to terrorists. *Miami Herald.* http://www.miamiherald.com/949/story/75255.html.

Chomsky, N. 2003. The function of schools: Subtler and cruder methods of control. In *Education as enforcement: The militarization and corporatization of schools,* ed. K. Saltman and D. Gabbard, 25–35. New York, NY: RoutledgeFalmer.

Chossudovsky, M. 2003. *The globalization of poverty and the new world order.* Pincourt, Quebec, Canada: Global Research.

Collins, J. 1988. Language and class in minority education. *Anthropology & Education Quarterly* 19, no. 4: 299–326.

Cushner, K. 1998. Intercultural education from an international perspective: An introduction. In *International perspectives on intercultural education,* ed. K. Cushner, 1–14. Mahwah, NJ: Lawrence Erlbaum Associates.

Day, R. 2001. Who is this *we* that gives the gift? Native American political theory and the western tradition. *Critical Horizons* 2, no. 2: 173–201.

Dessel, A., M.E. Rogge, and S.B. Garlington. 2006. Using intergroup dialogue to promote social justice and change. *Social Work* 51, no. 4: 303–15.

DeTurk, S. 2006. The power of dialogue: Consequences of intergroup dialogue and their implications for agency and alliance building. *Communication Quarterly* 54, no. 1: 33–51.

Díaz-Rico, L.T. 1998. Toward a just society: Recalibrating multicultural teachers. In *Speaking the unpleasant: The politics of (non) engagement in the multicultural education terrain,* eds. R. Chávez Chávez and J. O'Donnell, 69–86. Albany, NY: State University of New York Press.

Friedman, T. 2006. *The world is flat: A brief history of the twenty-first century.* New York, NY: Farrar, Straus and Giroux.

Gabbard, D. 2003. Education *is* enforcement!: The centrality of compulsory schooling in market societies. In *Education as enforcement: The militarization and corporatization of schools,* eds. K. Saltman and D. Gabbard, 61–80. New York, NY: RoutledgeFalmer.

Gans, H.J. 1995. *The war against the poor: The underclass and antipoverty policy.* New York, NY: BasicBooks.

Gorski, P.C. 2006. Complicity with conservatism: The de-politicizing of multicultural and intercultural education. *Intercultural Education* 17, no. 2: 163–77.

Harvey, D. 2005. *The new imperialism.* New York, NY: Oxford University Press USA.

Hidalgo, F., R. Chávez-Chávez, and J. Ramage. 1996. Multicultural education: Landscape for reform in the twenty-first century. In *Handbook of research on teacher education,* 2nd edn, ed. J. Sikula, T. Buttery, and E. Guyton, 761–78. New York, NY: Macmillan.

Hooks, B. 1994. *Teaching to transgress: Education as the practice of freedom.* New York, NY: Routledge.

Jackson, C.W. 2003. Crystallizing my multicultural education core. In *Becoming multicultural educators: Personal journey toward professional agency,* ed. G. Gay, 42–66. San Francisco, CA: Jossey-Bass.

James, M.R. 1999. Critical intercultural dialogue. *Polity* 31, no. 4: 587–607.

Jones, A. 1999. The limits of cross-cultural dialogue: Pedagogy, desire, and absolution in the classroom. *Educational Theory* 49, no. 3: 299–316.

Klein, R. 2004. Teachers under fire in war-torn Colombia. *Times Educational Supplement,* Issue 4574, 21.

López-Garay, H. 2001. Dialogue among civilizations: What for? *International Journal on World Peace* 18, no. 1: 15–33.

Lustig, D.F. 1997. Of Kwanzaa, Cinco de Mayo, and whispering: The need for intercultural education. *Anthropology & Education Quarterly* 28, no. 4: 574–92.

Maoz, I. 2001. Participation, control, and dominance in communication between groups in conflict: Analysis of dialogues between Jews and Palestinians in Israel. *Social Justice Research* 14, no. 2, 189–207.

Nieto, S. 2000. *Affirming diversity: The sociopolitical context of multicultural education.* New York, NY: Longman.

Nieto, S. 1995. From brown heroes and holidays to assimilationist agendas. In *Multicultural education, critical pedagogy, and the politics of difference,* ed. C. Sleeter and P.L. McLaren, 191–220. Albany, NY: State University of New York Press.

Osei-Kofi, N. 2005. Pathologizing the poor: A framework for understanding Ruby Payne's work. *Equity & Excellence in Education,* 38, 367–75.

Rank, M.R. 2004. *One nation, underprivileged: Why American poverty affects us all.* New York, NY: Oxford University Press.

Rozas, L. 2007. Engaging dialogue in our diverse social work student body: A multilevel theoretical process model. *Journal of Social Work Education* 43, no. 1, 5–29.

Schick, C., and V. St. Denis. 2005. Troubling national discourses in anti-racist curricular planning. *Canadian Journal of Education* 28, no. 3: 295–317.

Shields, C.M., R. Bishop, and A.E. Mazawi. 2005. *Pathologizing practices: The impact of deficit thinking on education.* New York: Peter Lang.

Sleeter, C. 1991. Introduction: Multicultural education and empowerment. In *Empowerment through multicultural education,* ed. C. Sleeter, 1–23. Albany, NY: State University of New York Press.

Tozer, S. 2000. Class. In *Knowledge and power in the global economy: Politics and the rhetoric of school reform,* ed. D. Gabbart, 149–159. Mahway, NJ: Lawrence Erlbaum Associates.

Ulichny, P. 1996. Cultures in conflict. *Anthropology and Education Quarterly* 27, 331–64.

Vasques Scalera, C.M. 1999. Democracy, diversity, dialogue: Education for critical multicultural citizenship. Unpublished doctoral dissertation, University of Michigan

Villenas, S. 2001. Latina mothers and small-town racisms: Creating narratives of dignity and moral education in North Carolina. *Anthropology & Education Quarterly* 32, no. 1: 3–28.

Wasserman, H. 2001. Intercultural dialogue in recent Afrikaans literary texts: A discourse of identity. *Pretexts: Literary and Cultural Studies* 10, no. 1: 37–49.

Critical Thinking

1. What does decolonizing intercultural education mean?

2. How does most intercultural education contribute to dominant hegemony and power rather than challenge inequities and social structures?

3. What are the effects of subtle shifts in personal relationships and professional practices?

4. Why do outlooks and attitudes about intercultural education need to change?

Advancing Cultural Competence and Intercultural Consciousness through a Cross-Cultural Simulation with Teacher Candidates

NANCY P. GALLAVAN AND ANGELA WEBSTER-SMITH

Teacher education programs accredited by the National Council for the Accreditation of Teacher Education are expected to incorporate curricula and guide instruction for teacher candidates to acquire meaningful knowledge and experiences with regard to diverse cultures and cultural characteristics (NCATE, 2008). Through their courses, particularly their multicultural education courses, candidates explore topics and issues focused on educational equity (Darling-Hammond, 2007) that impact teaching, learning, schooling, families, and society.

Using effective pedagogical strategies, teacher educators introduce and model the constructs of valuing diversity naturally, authentically, and holistically (Gallavan, 2007) so candidates can help all P-12 students learn and achieve.

Ideally, candidates are provided ample opportunities to apply new concepts, principles, and practices in their coursework and field experiences so they can better appreciate diversity within themselves, in classrooms, and across communities. Ultimately, candidates are expected to understand and demonstrate appropriate knowledge, skills, and dispositions for interacting with other people in many different contexts (Shulman, 1987). In essence, they are expected to be well-prepared, possessing the competence and confidence to demonstrate readiness (Gallavan, 2007) for their future teaching careers.

In order to afford teacher candidates in classroom assessment courses the opportunity to engage in unfiltered, authentic, and inclusive experiences, they participate in an intercultural simulation that cultivates their skills in connecting multicultural concepts with classroom practices. The simulation also advances their cultural competence (ATE, 2007) and intercultural consciousness (Karim, 2003) in an experiential context (Achenbach, & Arthur, 2002; Fowler, 1986). As Barnga, the simulation used in this study, distinctively fosters these objectives (Steinwachs, 1990; Thiagarajan, 1984), this study captures teacher candidates' thoughts, feelings and interactions as they occurred during this cross cultural simulation.

Conceptual Framework

The conceptual framework for this project stems from three primary sources. The first is the rarity that teacher candidates are taught the purposes, processes, and philosophies of reflecting in multiple contexts of education. Even though teacher educators routinely ask candidates to reflect on their practices, candidates are oftentimes missing the essential understandings, the necessary tools, and the refined techniques that ensure that reflection is principled, productive, and positive. To wit, they must receive guidance in analyzing and discerning their growth and development.

With that, Gallavan's Critical Components and Multiple Contexts of Self-Assessment Model (Gallavan & Webster-Smith, in press) guides teacher educators and candidates through the processes of reflecting thoughtfully, completely, and productively. The procedures provide the necessary scaffolding candidates need to examine both the strengths and the weaknesses of their principles and practices so they become more purposeful and positive in all contexts of teaching. Each of the three critical components of self assessment—reaction, response and reflection—is explored through multiple contexts of education that afford philosophical connections to teacher candidates' idealistic, realistic, pragmatic, and existential beliefs.

The second framework is important as it offers assumptions about human tendencies and inclinations associated with developing an intercultural consciousness (Karim, 2003) to include that: people are culturally encapsulated and ethnocentric in their world view; people feel cognitively, emotionally, and behaviorally challenged in unfamiliar situations and settings; people attempt to reduce cognitive dissonance; people prefer to avoid uncertainty and reduce anxiety; and people tend to behave in self-protective ways if they perceive threats to their psychosocial identity. Therefore, providing opportunities for candidates to connect their practical behaviors to their philosophical beliefs can prove to be enlightening.

The third framework is rooted in Achenbach and Arthur's (2002) cultural schema that represent three different dimensions of cultural awareness: self, other, and conditions. The perceptions associated with developing cultural schema are validation, evaluation, adjustment, negotiation, and incongruence. During experiential, intercultural learning situations the aforementioned sentiments are triggered. When students are unable to understand and reflect upon their own emotions and how they are represented in their behaviors, they are more challenged in interpreting the intended meaning of the overall experience. Hence, affording candidates reflective opportunities regarding culture is critical.

As teacher candidates build their funds of knowledge (Moll, Armanti, Neff, & Gonzalez, 1992) related to culturally responsive (Gay, 2000) and responsible content, pedagogy, and context, they should be developing cultural competence (ATE, 2007), raising their intercultural consciousness (Karim, 2003) and becoming reflective practitioners (Schön, 1987). One's cultural competence is developed by interacting with other people, like and unlike oneself, to increase one's comfort and understanding of people who are different in thoughts, beliefs, words, and actions.

Cultural competence (Gallavan, in press) is evident through interactions and through expressions individuals make about themselves as well as about and to other people individually and as members of various groups. Intercultural consciousness is more than comfort and understanding of cultural differences. Rather it requires intentional inquiry of others, patience, tolerance and flexibility in behaviors and thinking, along with the critical dimension of ethical and moral responsibility. Both cultural competency and intercultural consciousness promote local and global acumen.

Cultural competence and intercultural consciousness can be developed by providing safe opportunities for close proximity and positive interactions. In these environments, the propinquity effect manifests (Festinger, Schachter, & Back, 1950); that is, as individuals spend more time engaged in meaningful activities with new people unlike themselves, the more likely they will understand, accept, and become friends with the new people. Thus, harmonious outcomes (Dixon, 2006) and social cohesion (Friedman, 2004) occur between people and across groups building positive relationships and friendships between and among people who do not interact or converse regularly.

In classroom assessment courses, it is instructive to integrate a class activity that builds intercultural bridges. Such strategies help teacher candidates become more aware of potentially disparate and unfair assessment practices that may have an impact on the ability of diverse students to learn and develop in a psychologically safe, academic environment. Employing such an exercise might also help teachers gain a better understanding of the role their background plays in their teaching as well as cultivate skills in comparing and contrasting general curricular principles with culturally specific knowledge (Webster-Smith, 2008).

Purpose of the Study

The purpose of the study is to examine the three critical incidences (reactions, responses, and reflections) that teachers experience (Arthur, 2001) before, during, and after cross-cultural encounters. The benefit of using the simulation, Barnga is that it affords candidates perspective taking opportunities to question their beliefs about the certainty, source and structure of knowledge (Sleeter, 2009) as it allows them to grapple with multiple perspectives. Barnga also affords the instructor the expediency of closely observing teachers as they journey through the three critical incidences of self assessment and the ability to collect data in a controlled environment. As the authors have facilitated this simulation at least 30 times during the last 15 years with various groups of educators and are well-acquainted with the procedures and outcomes, their experience gave them a keen understanding of the potential power of the simulation to advance the conversation on diversity. In addition, the authors have researched and published findings on many topics and issues related to cultural competency.

The Research Questions

The classroom assessment course was selected so candidates would be exposed to similar cross-cultural experiences that contemporary P-12 students might encounter daily. Using Barnga, they would gain further understandings and representations of their beliefs as they relate to the impact of cross-cultural experiences on teaching, learning, and assessment.

Three research questions framed the study to examine candidates' cultural competency: (1) What are candidates' reactions when introduced to a new cross-cultural experience? (2) What are candidates' responses while involved in the cross-cultural experience? (3) What are candidates' reflections following the cross-cultural experience? Each research question in this study aligns with each of three critical incidences (reaction, response and reflection) associated with cross-cultural experiences.

Participants

Teacher candidates enrolled in three different sections of a classroom assessment course participated in this study. All 64 candidates had identified that they were aspiring to become middle level and high school teachers midway through their programs. Demographics of the participants showed that there were 46 females and 16 males. The racial distribution among the females included 7 African American, 2 Asian American, 31 Caucasian, and 3 Latino candidates. The racial distribution among the males included 5 African American, 0 Asian-American, 11 Caucasian, and 0 Latino candidates. The candidates ranged in age from 22 to 49 years.

Procedures

The professor facilitated Barnga early during the course to establish the importance of realizing the presence and power of possible preconceptions and prejudices that may influence a teacher's ability to assess students fairly. First, teacher candidates were guided through the simulation Barnga. Next the candidates participated in an interactive debriefing. Then a 10-item open-ended survey (which is embedded in the survey findings) was administered to collect feedback. Finally, a class conversation was held with each section of candidates following the data collections using the ten open-ended items as prompts allowing candidates to share their individual experiences and insights.

The mixed methodology combined non-experimental approaches during the simulation and debriefing. Narrative inquiry (Connelly & Clandinin, 1990) and naturalistic inquiry (Lincoln & Guba, 1985) data were collected during the survey. Category 1 Questions (1-5) probed initial reactions relating to preconceived notions expressed as candidates anticipated descriptions, rules and contexts of the upcoming cross-cultural interactions. Category 2 Questions (6-8) examined ongoing responses that candidates used to justify their behaviors and changes experienced during cross-cultural interactions. Category 3 Questions (9-10) investigated candidates' transformative processes after participating in the cross-cultural simulation and debriefing.

Survey Findings

Responses to Category 1 and Category 2 Questions (1-8) were analyzed and organized into groups based on a five-point range of emotions with the following descriptions: A-acceptance; B-curiosity; C-apprehension; D-irritation, and E-fury. These responses are aligned with foundations of the conceptual framework in terms of Achenbach and Arthur's (2002) perceptions associated with developing cultural schema and Karim's (2003) assumptions about human tendencies and inclinations. Each of these assumptions was perceived by study participants and revealed in the data. Category 3 Questions (9-10) were analyzed into a narrative summary. Whereas candidates' responses to every question fit into the prescribed categories, most of their responses were classified as expressing acceptance, curiosity, and apprehension. Sample responses are provided to authenticate the results.

Answering the "what" questions, the candidates' reactions (immediate, raw and nervous retorts offered without the benefit of deliberation and consideration) captured their immediate, emotional reactions about the simulation before it began.

Category 1 Questions: What were your feelings when . . .

1. you were assigned to a table without any choice?

A-acceptance	I trusted the teacher. I didn't care. We are all friends.
B-curiosity	It was a new adventure.
C-apprehension	We were not given a reason or explanation. I didn't have a choice.
D-irritation	Uneasy. I like sitting with my friends and choosing where I want to sit.
E-fury	I didn't want to move. I don't like change.

2. you were told to place all of your personal items to the side of the room?

A-acceptance	This classroom is a safe place.
B-curiosity	Now I began to wonder what we were going to do.
C-apprehension	What if there was going to be a quiz?
D-irritation	I wanted to keep my sweater, so I did. I felt uncomfortable and a little mad.
E-fury	I don't like being told what to do.

3. you learned the importance of the number on your table?

A-acceptance	Lucky! I landed at the top number.
B-curiosity	I wanted to know how I could move and move quickly.
C-apprehension	I thought the numbers were too competitive for our usual class activities.
D-irritation	Focusing on the card game was difficult since all I wanted to do was move up.
E-fury	I wanted to be at the best table. I kept moving to a lower number.

4. you were informed there would be no talking at any time or you would be told to leave the room?

A-acceptance	I figured we would have to be creative. This was just a game and I didn't care. Hooray, it would be a quiet time.
B-curiosity	I wondered what the reason was for this rule.
C-apprehension	I don't like to gesticulate and I don't read people well.
D-irritation	This rule frustrated me; I need to talk.
E-fury	This seemed extremely unfair. The facilitator was a dictator.

5. you read the directions and were told to put them back into the envelope?

A-acceptance	Fine; I play cards all the time. The rules seemed easy.
B-curiosity	This made the game more intriguing and exciting.
C-apprehension	It made me think something was going to be tricky. I read them much more closely than I usually read new information.
D-irritation	I was concerned that I could not remember them clearly.
E-fury	I wanted to keep the rules out to reread. This was too much pressure. I got worried.

While answering the "how" questions, the candidates' responses (perfunctory replies that occur with some attention and deliberation) captured their representations of their feelings and behaviors during the simulated cross-cultural interactions.

Category 2 Questions: How did you feel when . . .

6. you got to move to the table with the higher number after you had won a round at your table?

A-acceptance	Great! I won. I remembered the rules. Success!
B-curiosity	I don't play cards so I couldn't identify with the game.
C-apprehension	Moving into a new group made me nervous.
D-irritation	I didn't move; I didn't like it when new people came to my table.
E-fury	The new table seemed to have different rules that I didn't know. I wanted to ask questions, but we weren't allowed to talk.

7. you had to move to the table with the lower number after you had lost a round at your table?

A-acceptance	That's the way it happens. I lost the practice rounds so I expected to move down. This was just a game.
B-curiosity	I wondered about the rules at each table.
C-apprehension	I was fearful that I would continue moving down and never move up. Embarrassed.
D-irritation	Distressed!
E-fury	I didn't like being the lowest. Bummer! I felt like a loser. I was determined to move back up to a higher numbered table.

8. you discovered that the rules were different for different tables?

A-acceptance	The light bulb went off immediately! Enlightened! Thought provoking!
B-curiosity	I kept trying to think of a plan to overcome the differences so I could win. I thought it was funny thinking how the players

C-apprehension	I felt better knowing that it was the rules and not me. I wanted everyone to play by my rules and for my way to be respected.
D-irritation	I realized how competitive I am and I didn't like this discovery.
E-fury	I was frustrated. How can we play fairly if the rules are different?!? I just wanted to know THE rules.

behaved. It was amazing that I didn't figure this out sooner.

Answering the "why" questions, the candidate's reflections (pensive interpretations that are punctuated with integrative connections) captured their understanding of the simulation's connections to prior lessons in diversity as well as to its larger purpose, meaning and significance to their role as 21st century educators.

Category 3 Questions: Why does this simulation . . .

9. apply to living?

This game is just like life: different rules for different people. You have to know the rules to play . . . and win. Sometimes it is hard to communicate. Every group has its own set of rules; other people interpret the rules the best they can. You have to adjust your way of thinking in order to be successful in other people's worlds. Life changes all the time; we must adjust or we'll be run over. We all must be able to move in and around all cultures with knowledge and comfort. We all need to be considerate of one another's differences and to be nice by playing by the same rules. We are a world that plays by different rules. We never know all of the rules or which rules are needed to win. The rules constantly change and are changed by the winners to ensure there is chaos and people can't win—to take away their power.

10. apply to teaching?

Teachers must explain the rules and keep them the same for everybody. Teachers should involve their students in establishing the rules. Teachers have to figure out how to communicate with every group of student and every student. Teachers cannot always have their own way in the school or the classroom. Students come from different backgrounds and need to understand their teachers and other students. The confusion and frustration experienced in this game is exactly what students experience every day. New teachers experience these too. Teachers must teach tolerance in every subject area. They must listen and connect with students. Teachers must model consideration, conservation, and cooperation with and among the students. All teachers should have this experience so they will remember the confusion of not knowing and wanting to be accepted and win.

Limitations of the Study

The simulation was facilitated by the course instructor. Candidates were well-acquainted with the instructor, and the instructor had established high levels of trust with the candidates during both formal and informal interactions. Survey responses occasionally referenced the candidates' sense of trust in their instructor. Further research will be conducted to examine feedback in environments where the candidates are not acquainted with the simulation facilitator.

Implications

The findings from this study imply that engaging in simulations with candidates opens their eyes about themselves, their outlooks toward and interactions with others, and their perspectives related to developing long-range goals and reasons for incorporating similar learning experiences in their own future classrooms. This is an important implication considering that most teachers are comfortable in schools and society, perceive that learning and achievement are available to everyone, and tend to deliver instruction from their own narrow viewpoints void of opportunities for students to exchange multiple perspectives (Ford, 2004).

Effective cross-cultural simulations result in four important outcomes for teachers and their students: self knowledge, acceptance of group conventions, multiple perspectives, and their passion or indifference toward equity and change (Delany-Barmann, & Minner, 1996; Pedersen, 2003). This study shows that as candidates progress through their coursework, especially their multicultural education courses, they benefit from

1. student-centered conversations extending honest investigations and analytical perceptions of all peoples and inequities in schools and societies— locally and globally (Marbley, et al., 2007); candidates can discuss the relationships between worldwide current events and the curricular content that they will be teaching.

2. controlled investigations of disenfranchised P-12 students and their families who do not feel valued, visible, or viable in today's classrooms; candidates can write questions probing connections between the curricular content and specific populations.

3. frequent examinations of one's own personal values (Harry, 2008) that reveal growth and changes

related to self knowledge, acceptance of group conventions, multiple perspectives, and passion or indifference toward equity and change; candidates can record their reflections in journals noting their personal changes over time from multiple perspectives (Capella-Santana, 2003) as experienced by the propinquity effect and its importance when teaching their own students.

Conclusions

To develop cultural competency and intercultural consciousness, teacher candidates need opportunities to interact with people like and unlike themselves to experience the propinquity effect within a learning environment that allows for safe and supportive dissection and discussion of critical incidents. Simulations, such as Barnga, offer these benefits through experiential learning. Candidates engage in dynamic, interactive processes increasing their self knowledge, acceptance of group conventions, multiple perspectives and their passion or indifference toward equity and change by expressing and exchanging their reactions, responses, and reflections. Ultimately, the goal is for each candidate to experience a sense of cultural transformation (Banks & Banks, 2006) that becomes visible through the learners' successes, classroom support of students and colleagues, and their own professional satisfaction.

These three components of self-assessment capture the critical incidents (reaction, response, and reflection) of cultural competency and intercultural consciousness that teacher candidates should understand and demonstrate personally in preparation for their professional teaching careers. Then, as professional practicing teachers, they will be ready to guide their own P-12 learners with appropriate pedagogy to understand and demonstrate cultural competency and intercultural consciousness in their classrooms and communities.

References

Achenbach, K., & Arthur, N. (2002, Winter). Experimental learning: Bridging theory to practice in multicultural counseling. *Guidance and Counseling, 17*(2), 39–45.

Arthur, N. (2001). Using critical incidents to investigate cross-cultural transition. *International Journal of Intercultural Relations, 25*, 41–53.

Association of Teacher Educators. (2007). *Standards for teacher educators.* Retrieved from http://www.ate1.org/pubs/uploads/tchredstds0308.pdf

Babbie, E. R. (1990). *Survey research.* Belmont, CA: Wadsworth Publishing.

Banks, J. A., & Banks, C. A. M. (2006). *Multicultural education; Issues and perspectives* (6th ed.). Belmont, CA: Wadsworth Publishing.

Barrera, I., & Corso, R. M. (2002). Cultural competency as skilled dialogue. *Topics in Early Childhood Special Education, 22*(2), 103–113.

Capella-Santana, N. (2003, Jan/Feb). Voices of teacher candidates: Positive changes in multicultural attitudes and knowledge. *The Journal of Educational Research, 96*(3), 182–190.

Connelly, F. M., & Clandinin, D. J. (1990). Stories of experience and narrative inquiry. *Educational Researcher, 19*(5), 2–14.

Darling-Hammond, L. (2007). The flat earth and education: How America's commitment to equity will determine our future. *Educational Researcher, 36*(6), 318–334.

Delany-Barmann, G., & Minner, S. (1996, Summer). Cross-cultural workshops and simulations for teachers. *The Teacher Educator, 32*, 37–47.

Dixon, J. C. (2006, June). The ties that bind and those than don't: Toward reconciling group threat and contact theories of prejudice. *Social Forces, 84*(4), 2179–2204.

Festinger L., Schachter S., & Back, K. W. (1950). *Social pressures in informal groups: A study of human factors in housing.* New York: Harper.

Ford, M. (2004). Considering the standpoints of differently situated others: Teachers and arrogant perception. *Philosophy of Education Yearbook,* 337–345.

Fowler, S. M. (1986). Intercultural simulation games: Removing cultural blinders. *New Directions for Continuing Education, 30*, 71–81.

Friedkin, N. E. (2004). Social cohesion. *Annual Review of Sociology, 30*, 409–425.

Gallavan, N. P. (in press). *Navigating cultural competence.* Thousand Oaks, CA: Corwin Press.

Gallavan, N. P. (2007). Seven perceptions that influence novice teachers' efficacy and cultural competence. *Praxis: The Center for Multicultural Education, 2*(1), 6–22.

Gallavan, N. P., & Webster-Smith, (in press). Self-assessment: Analyzing reflectivity with candidates. In Association of Teacher Educators (Eds.) *The purposes, practices, and professionalism of teacher reflectivity: Insights for 21st century teachers and students.* Lanham, Maryland: Rowman & Littlefield.

Gay, G. (2000). *Culturally responsive teaching: Theory, research, & practice.* New York: Teachers College Press.

Harry, B. (2008, Spring). Collaboration with culturally and linguistically diverse families: Ideal versus reality. *Exceptional Children, 74*(3), 372–388.

Karim, A. (Sept/Oct 2003). A developmental progression model for intercultural consciousness: A leadership imperative. *Journal of Education for Business, 79*(1), 34–39.

Lincoln, Y. S., & Guba, E. G. (1985). *Naturalistic inquiry.* Beverly Hills, CA: Sage.

Marbley, A. F., Bonner, F. A., McKisick, S., Henfield, M. S., Watts, L. M., & Shin, Y-J. (2007). Interfacing cultural specific pedagogy with counseling: A proposed diversity training model for preparing preservice teachers for diverse learners. *Multicultural Education, 14*(3), 8–16.

Moll, L. C., Armanti, C., Neff, D., & Gonzalez, N. (1992). Funds of knowledge for teaching: Using a qualitative approach to connect homes and classrooms. *Theory into Practice, 31*(2), 132–141.

National Council for Accreditation of Teacher Education. (2008). *Professional standards for the accreditation of teacher preparation institutions.* Washington, DC: Author.

Pedersen, P. B. (2003). Multicultural training in schools as an expansion of the counselor's role. In P. B. Pedersen & J. C. Carey (Eds.), *Multicultural counseling in schools,* (pp. 190–210). Boston: Pearson Education.

Schön, D. A. (1987). Educating the reflective practitioner. Paper presented at the annual meeting of the American Educational Research Association. Washington, DC.

Shulman, L. S. (1987b). Knowledge and teaching: Foundations of the new reform. *Harvard Educational Review, 57,* 1-22.

Sleeter, C. (2009). Developing teacher epistemological sophistication about multicultural curriculum: A case study. *Action in Teacher Education, 31,* 1, 3–13.

Thiagarajan, S. (1984). BARNGA: *A flexim on cultural clashes.* Bloomington, IN: Instructional Alternatives.

Volkema, R., & Rivers, C. (2008, Jan/Feb). Negotiating on the Internet: Insights from a cross-cultural exercise. *Journal of Education for Business, 83*(3), 165–172.

Webster-Smith, A. (2008). Examining the role of diversity in school dynamics: An internship that helps to meet NCATE Standard 4. *International Journal of Educational Leadership Preparation.* http://cnx.org/content/m16317/latest/.

Webster-Smith, A. (2008). Roots and wings: A self examination of familial influences that ground diversity leadership and an assignment that lifts it. *International Journal of Educational Leadership Preparation.* http://cnx.org/content/m16315/1.1/.

Webster-Smith, A. (2008). Monitoring teacher knowledge, skills and dispositions for culturally responsive pedagogy: An internship experience that helps to meet NCATE Standard 4. *International Journal of Educational Leadership Preparation.* http://cnx.org/content/m16607/latest/.

Critical Thinking

1. What is Barnga?

2. How do the participants express their learning outcomes?

3. What are some of participants' discoveries related to their classrooms?

4. Why is cross-cultural simulation helpful for learning about people unlike yourself?

NANCY P. GALLAVAN, Ph.D, is a professor at the University of Central Arkansas in the Department of Teaching and Learning teaching performance-based assessment in the MAT program. An active member of Association of Teacher Education, the National Association of Multicultural Education, and the National Council for the Social Studies, Nancy has authored more than 100 publications. **ANGELA WEBSTER-SMITH,** Ph.D, is an assistant professor at the University of Central Arkansas in the Department of Leadership Studies teaching in the School Leadership Program working with public and open enrollment charter schools. Angela has taught in the United States and abroad; she is active in the National Council for Professors of Educational Administration.

UNIT 8

Nurture and Welcome Challenges and Changes

Unit Selections

Learning Outcomes

After reading this unit, you will be able to:

- Discuss the approaches for analyzing the community to promote social justice in schools and classrooms.

- Expand upon the rewards and processes for sustaining multicultural educators.

- Describe culturally relevant pedagogy and strategies that help all students learn about themselves, one another, and all of society.

- Summarize some key issues in multicultural education that educators encounter in P-12 and higher education.

- Explain the benefits for diversifying the teaching workforce both in P-12 classes and teacher education.

- Retell forms of resistance that multicultural educators encounter.

Student Website

www.mhhe.com/cls

Internet References

Centers for Disease Control and Prevention/National Center for Health Statistics
www.cdc.gov/nchswww
Demographic and Healthy Surveys
www.measuredhs.com
State of the World's Children
www.unicef.org/apublic
The World Bank
http://web.worldbank.org

The challenges in multicultural education connect directly with teachers; sadly, there is a tendency to blame the victim. Many people are unable or unwilling to think that education and life could or should change. There are strong beliefs voiced in words like, "It was good enough for me when I was a kid; it is good enough for today," "Why can't they (or those people) do things the way we have always done it here?" and "If you don't like it here, go away."

None of these statements make sense, and most people would not want to hear these statements said to or about them; yet, words like these are spoken or acted upon every day across our nation, whether the reference is school or society. Laws and attitudes have changed over time; they will continue to change as new challenges are acknowledged.

Cultural competence means having the will to do good, to do right, and to do well. Through your journeys, reflect upon your own thoughts, beliefs, words, actions, and interactions as an individual, as an educator in general, and as a classroom teacher responsible for a particular content with a specific age group of students in a particular community. Your commitment to welcoming cultural competence into your personal life, professional demeanor, and pedagogical expertise may occur across all three aspects of your existence simultaneously or in discrete steps separated from one another. Many teachers begin acknowledging their challenges and changes through personal reflections and discoveries. Your challenges and changes may be stimulated through your desire to influence the educational system as a professional educator or throughout your intentions to impact the students in your own classes throughout your pedagogical expertise.

The four overarching goals of multicultural education and cultural competence are to teach democratic principles, to endure educational equity, to champion human rights, and to promote social justice. In a democracy, everyone is accepted, everyone has a vote, and everyone's thoughts and beliefs are honored and respected through accommodation. Your classroom does not operate a true democracy; however, you can teach about democratic principles, incorporate them into your classroom procedures, and create an environment framed on democracy. Teaching about democratic principles is essential before practicing them with your students regardless of the content of your curriculum. You want your students to understand not only what you are doing, but why you ascribe to a different set of procedures than the students may have experienced in other classrooms. Then you want to identify the presence of democratic principles, such as letting each student speak or taking a vote, so students connect the concept with a practice.

Your classroom must offer a high-quality education for everyone, multiple perspectives evident across the curricular content, multiple strategies of experiencing and connecting content to personal lives evident in the instruction, multiple techniques for expressing one's progress, and full acceptance and participation in the learning community. You want the classroom to be one that your student will call their own.

To ensure educational equity, move around the classroom so you connect with each student and give each one an opportunity

© MBI/Alamy

to talk with you during class. When you sit, make sure all of your students feel safe and comfortable meeting at your desk or table. Spend the same amount of time or an equitable amount of time with each student. You are encouraged to keep a checklist of your students and mark how often you interact with each of them formally and informally.

Delve the same with each student. Use appropriate levels of follow-up questions with all students. Again, keep a checklist and notice your patterns. Positively reinforce all students with the same enthusiasm. You want to be sure that all students feel welcomed and wanted.

- Is your humor neutral, or is it prejudicial or sarcastic? Some teachers err in thinking that their students will respond to sarcasm. Most likely, your students will not understand your sarcasm and may not trust you when you are sarcastic.

- Are you extending the same opportunities to all students? Some teachers select the same students to participate in special events. These teachers base their selections on academic and social qualities that some students cannot achieve.

- Are you disciplining your students fairly and equitably? Be aware of the students who are punished and how they are punished.

- Are you making references to special services equitably? Note the patterns of which students are referred to special services and the reasons for the referrals.

You may want to review these questions of educational equity on your own practices or you may want to discuss them with a school administrator. There may be some issues that the whole school needs to research and discuss.

Everyone in the United States is entitled to a set of human rights that must be honored, respected, taught, and modeled in your classroom. You can begin by teaching about the changes in human rights since the founding of the United States. You also can talk about how the United States is a model for the rest of the world and that not all students have the same rights as the students in your classroom. However, your primary goal is to eradicate bias, discrimination, and stereotyping among your students. You want to begin by teaching your students about these words and how the words are detected in words and actions. There are many selections of children's literature that you can use to introduce this discussion. You also are encouraged to guide your students in using the phrase, "*I know someone who . . .*" when the students wants to tell you what a person you all know says or does. You do not want to establish an environment where students report on one another.

Social justice involves helping every student to become a good citizen and to help other students to be good citizens. Through your conversations about social justice, point out that getting along with other people means being to disagree pleasantly. People should be able to state their opinions at appropriate times and places. Likewise, a person should be able to question an action if the person feels an injustice has occurred. Promoting social justice also helps to reduce intimidation and bullying that may occur among your students overtly or covertly in your classroom and around the school. Reading and writing about social justice will empower your students.

The word *commitment* generates a list of descriptors that includes (in alphabetical order) allegiance, assurance, dedication, dependability, duty, faithfulness, loyalty, obligation, pledge, promise, responsibility, and trust. These words capture what some people claim is the single most important characteristic of success: commitment. Most people want commitment from other people, but most people tend to avoid making commitments. We like the flexibility of changing our minds in the moment. This dichotomy does not translate well to your students. Students need to be able to depend on you to learn about making commitments themselves. When you make a commitment to your students, you need to follow through so your students learn from your words and actions. And like learning about compassion, you want to articulate your actions so your students make strong and lasting connections.

Teaching commitment involves critical thinking, clear communication, problem solving, and decision making to establish a shared or common foundation from which everyone is working. Commitment means interacting with all kinds of other people. It also means maintaining self-respect by being honest, showing courage, and developing self control. Throughout your curriculum and instruction, capture the teachable moments to highlight individuals and acts of public commitment. Your students will benefit greatly when they hear and see commitment as part of literature, movies, and in the lives of researchers in all content areas. Invite guest speakers to visit your classroom to share their stories of commitment to their work and passions.

In Unit 8, the articles motivate the reader to nurture and welcome the challenges and changes associated with multicultural education. The reader should teach all students how challenges exist in all parts of the curriculum coupled with skills related to decision making and conflict management. Students want to be taught the change process and to engage in authentic opportunities to practice the change process. The reader should locate a mentor who has experiences with challenges and changes in one professional practices. Additionally, the reader is encouraged to reflect on his or her personal life to identify a challenge related to cultural competence and to practice making changes personally to better understand the change process professionally.

Sustaining Ourselves under Stressful Times: Strategies to Assist Multicultural Educators

PENELOPE WONG AND ANITA E. FERNÁNDEZ

Resistance that educators face in teaching multicultural education courses, particularly from preservice teachers, is well documented (Carpenter, 2000; Cochran-Smith 2004; Cruz-Janzen & Taylor, 2004; Horton & Scott, 2004; McGowan, 2000, O'Donnell, 1998; Valerio, 2001). Much of the literature around resistance tends to focus on strategies that multicultural educators can employ in overcoming preservice teacher resistance (Young & Tran, 2001).

However, preservice teacher resistance is not the only kind of resistance to multicultural education. Less well documented is the resistance to multicultural education from fellow educators who sometimes exhibit the same kinds of resistance as preservice teachers (Ahlkvist, Spitzform, Jones, & Reynolds, 2005; Ghosh & Tarrow, 1993). While there is little literature concerning teacher/faculty resistance to multicultural education, even more sparse is any literature concerned with *the effects* of such resistance on multicultural educators.

The small body of literature in this area, more often than not, has focused on multicultural educators of color and the resistance they face in teaching such topics and the strategies they used to counter such resistance (Boutte, 1999; McGowan, 1996, 2000; Valverde, 2003). Rarely has there been any discussion on how multicultural educators cope and sustain themselves in the face of continual resistance. In fact, there is virtually no literature on *how* multicultural educators address these effects and the *strategies* they employ to sustain themselves on a daily basis.

The purpose of this article to address this void in the field by providing a theoretical framework of the ways in which multicultural educators might address such resistance so as to preserve themselves and keep from suffering some of the negative effects of continual resistance, such as despair, hopelessness, and burnout.

Rationale/Motivation behind the Creation of the Framework

The development of this framework occurred over a period of three years when the authors, two women of color teaching in a predominantly White rural northern California teacher

preparation program, were hired to address multiculturalism and diversity, which was lacking in the program. We soon came to the realization that a number of stakeholders, not only students but also fellow faculty and administrators, thought that the *idea* of multiculturalism and multicultural education was more appealing than the actual practice of it.

This discomfort from various stakeholders manifested itself in the forms of passive resistance on one hand (e.g., not wanting to address or engage on multicultural education topics at all) to outright hostility on the other (e.g., denouncing various multicultural education concepts). As a result of these reactions, we were forced to develop strategies to help us continue to be effective and healthy educators.

As we struggled to figure out strategies and any means to handle the effects of such resistance (i.e., frustration, anger, sadness, etc.) we began to systematically identify dimensions of our personal and professional lives that were impacted by the resistance we encountered. Specifically, we identified five aspects of our lives that we felt were most directly impacted by resistance to our work. They were the intellectual, emotional, physical, ethical, and spiritual dimensions of ourselves.

Methodology and Overview of the Framework of Sustainment

The development of the framework evolved as we encountered various incidents of resistance and collected data in the form of personal journal entries, notes from conversations and meetings, minutes from meetings, and other documents. It was only after months of reflection that the framework assumed its present form. During the first year, there was no framework because we realized that we were individually addressing each instance of resistance as a unique event seemingly unrelated to any other events of resistance. It was only over time were we able to detect patterns.

For example, fairly early on (in the first year) it was clear that one of the most pervasive and immediate types of resistance we encountered was in the intellectual realm when the credibility of the content we were teaching was questioned. Once we recognized this pattern, we came up with systematic ways to address this intellectual challenge.

Another area in which the resistance was extremely challenging was the emotional arena. While we could intellectually rationalize the resistance we encountered toward the various multicultural issues, such as sexual orientation, it was much more difficult to deal with the *feelings* of anger, hurt, and frustration associated with addressing these issues. The emotional energy expended on handling conflicts in the classroom, hostility, and passive resistance was at times almost overwhelming, and we had to come up with concrete psychological strategies to ensure we did not lose hope and simply give up in despair.

Another area of our lives that was showing signs of stress during this time was our physical health. We both realized early on that being constantly challenged intellectually and emotionally did take a physical toll on our health. In short, we were more vulnerable to being sick, suffering from fatigue and lacking vitality precisely because our positive energy was being diverted to addressing the intellectual and emotional resistance we encountered. When we realized what was happening, we came up with some very specific and personal strategies to make sure that we maintained our physical health, so we could continue working.

While it was incredibly helpful to specifically identify the kinds of resistance (i.e., intellectual, emotional, and physical) we encountered so we could address each type of resistance with specific strategies, sometimes we still felt we needed something more. It was at these moments we turned to the spiritual dimension of our lives. This dimension provided a rather unique lens through which to examine our experiences. For one of the authors, the spiritual dimension was the most significant and critical one in enabling her to affirm *why* she continued to be engaged in such demanding work.

Finally, we considered the ethical dimensions of our work. Unlike the other above-mentioned dimensions, we found the ethical dimensions of who we are as educators raised more questions than provided answers. However, it was the process of deliberating the ethical aspects of the various incidents of resistance we experienced that helped reaffirm our work and purpose.

In providing this brief overview of the framework we want to stress a few points. First, these dimensions are perhaps best visually seen as interconnected rings, much like the symbolic Olympic rings. Or, as some people recommended, as slices of a pie. Others saw the dimensions as separate boxes all leading to one bigger box of overall health. The point is that the framework can take any form, but what matters is that it works for the individual who is using it.

Second, these dimensions are not necessarily equal in significance or presence to one another. In other words, for one of the authors, the spiritual dimension was the most prominent dimension in her overall health for awhile, and for the other author it was the physical dimension. The point is that these dimensions are somewhat fluid. At different times, different dimensions will offer the answers sought at just the right time and will be prominent in one's exploration of how to address and overcome resistance. At other times, other dimensions will

be foregrounded. To this end, even though the dimensions will be individually discussed in a linear fashion, we are in no way implying that there is a hierarchy of importance.

Finally, by using ourselves as models, we provide a case example to concretely illustrate how a particular incidence of resistance seemed to speak to a specific dimension of our health; then we discuss how we addressed the resistance using strategies and resources that enabled us to directly draw on this dimension and work through the resistance. This framework is based on the unique experiences of two multicultural educators and is offered as a strategy to current educators and future educators alike to help them proactively think about how they will handle resistance they potentially or are currently encountering.

Expressions of Resistance

While the purpose of this article is not to discuss resistance per se, it is necessary to briefly identify the common types of resistance that have been discussed among multicultural educators because sometimes one type of resistance falls in the province of one of the dimensions we discuss and thus requires a specific set of strategies to be addressed.

Dittmar (1999) and Tatum (1994) have documented facing resistance and outright hostility when addressing multicultural issues in teacher education. Griffin (1997) divides resistance into four types: anger, immobilization, distancing, and conversion. While anger tends to be the kind of resistance that is most uncomfortable for educators, all four of these types of resistance contribute to the overall feelings of stress and disequilibrium which we attempt to provide strategies for preventing.

The Intellectual Dimension

The situation: Having completed her doctoral work in anti-racist, multicultural education, one of the authors accepted a position at an institution seeking a faculty member with expertise in the area of multicultural education. She accepted the position expecting to continue the work she had been doing over the last several years. Once her new role of teacher educator began, it became quite clear that not only were many of the students she worked with completely skeptical of and resistant to multicultural education, but also most faculty and administers as well. This assistant professor was faced with the reality that her new colleagues were much more prone to "talking the talk" than "walking the talk" and she found herself constantly having to explain, defend, and justify multicultural teacher education to a variety of stakeholders.

This scenario was not all that unusual as multicultural educators around the country face similar challenges when trying to teach about issues that challenge students' preconceived notions of diversity. The surprising element was the resistance on the part of faculty and administration to understanding the need for students to engage in addressing difficult and challenging multicultural topics. As students complained, some faculty members started to question the need for such a course. In essence the very existence of multicultural education was being questioned.

Naturally, in an attempt to defend the validity of multicultural education as a body of knowledge and justify the need for future teachers to study it, she employed an intellectual response. She realized it was important to speak the language of the context — in this case the academy. Students, faculty, and administration would only ever be convinced of the legitimacy of multicultural education if it could be presented in terms they knew: theory, statistics, current literature, and research results.

With regard to the above mentioned scenario, the author realized that the intellectual dimension was the most tangible way to sustain herself as a multicultural educator. Thus, the strategies she employed in this realm were to strengthen her theoretical framework by remaining current in the literature and learning ways to use this intellectual information in such a form that was not threatening or radical to her colleagues or students.

More specifically, when confronted with resistance, she would reach into her intellectual side to ask the question *what does the literature say about this?* By doing so, she found that her ideas were affirmed because she could use state law, current research, and testimonies as intellectual rationalizations for the topics being addressed.

A second intellectual response to the situation above was to find allies who shared the same intellectual philosophy concerning multicultural education and diversity. In this case, it was the authors of this article supporting one another. Without the support of a colleague to discuss multicultural issues, and the resistance that comes with those issues, there is a danger of being worn down and overwhelmed by the resistance.

Intellectual allies were another source of critical information that could be used in countering the resistance. They can play the role of "devil's advocate," or in this case "resister to multicultural education," and provide sound counsel on how to handle various situations. Just as importantly, intellectual allies were those individuals who were willing to publicly support multicultural education and faculty who taught such courses.

All of these elements of the intellectual dimension of sustaining ourselves were deeply interconnected with the emotional dimensions as well. As our intellect supported us in *what* kind of work we did (i.e., the content), our emotions often determined how we did the work (i.e., the teaching approaches and strategies).

The Emotional Dimension

The situation: After viewing the film Color of Fear *a class of preservice teachers were asked to write down their immediate reactions on an index card. As the instructor read through the cards she came across one that said, "If White culture is the dominant culture, then it is meant to be that way, for it has been for centuries. If non-White people have a problem with that get off your butts and do something about it. Change the system, SHOW ME YOU ARE BETTER THAN ME!" Although not completely surprised by this comment, this incident, combined with recent local hate crimes and a lack of support for multicultural education in her college, put this instructor in an emotionally drained state.*

We defined the emotional dimension of the framework as the feelings or the affective responses we had to the work we did as multicultural educators. The emotional output that one engaged in during the course of teaching a multicultural education course was unlike that of many other disciplines. As we heard about the

daily injustices that not only occured in larger society but also in schools, it is easy to feel emotionally taxed.

However, this situation, combined with the resistance from our students and colleagues to either not acknowledge and/or not be willing to address such issues made a difficult situation even more challenging and we often feel "burned out" or completely emotionally exhausted.

One of the ways we have attempted to sustain ourselves emotionally was to recognize when we were reacting emotionally versus when we were reacting intellectually. We noticed that when students made comments, such as the one above, our immediate reactions were emotional ones (i.e., anger, frustration, etc.). The author in this scenario engaged in a strategy that focused on reacting with empathy rather than anger or disgust at such beliefs. bell hooks referred to this as engaged Buddhism. In other words, the work of multicultural educators is built on loving kindness and it is this loving kindness that can prevail in times of deep emotional crisis.

A second strategy was to train oneself to never react immediately to something that triggered a negative reaction. We found that participating in a cool-down period enabled us to respond to faculty and student comments in a purposeful and controlled manner and prevented further escalation of an already emotionally trying situation. By spending some time thinking about why the resistance occurred, we could be more rational and less emotional when actually responding to an individual.

Finally, it was crucial for our emotional well-being to celebrate the small victories rather than becoming overwhelmed by the big picture or the constant state of inequity around the world and in many schools. When a student reached an epiphany about diverse perspectives or an administrator seemed to better understand why it is we feel so strongly about the work we do, such was a small victory to be applauded and it raised our spirits immeasurably.

The Physical Dimension

The situation: Four young males of large stature were becoming increasingly volatile during a conversation about gay and lesbian issues in education. As the discussion proceeded, they became physically agitated: They were red in the face, postured defensively, raised their voices, and gestured aggressively. At the height of the outburst, one of the males yells, "What do those fags expect parading around the Castro [the location of an annual gay pride parade in San Francisco]?" The instructor immediately addressed the language that was used but was cut off and interrupted by the other three males. At this point she noticed that her heart was racing, she was breathing heavily, perspiring, and physically distancing herself from them.

We define the physical dimension as the "bodily" realm of the work we do as multicultural educators. For the the purposes of this article, we define "bodily" as literally our physicality. In this situation, the author was caught off guard by the violent reactions of the students, precisely because they were expressions of physical resistance rather than the more traditional emotional and intellectual forms of resistance we were accustomed to experiencing. This was not a situation one would expect in a classroom setting, particularly in a university. An immediate strategy the author employed in this "fight or flight" situation was to defuse the tension by switching topics.

While changing the topic achieved the immediate effect of defusing a potentially volatile physically violent reaction, it was clear the issue could not end on this note. In the days before the next class meeting the instructor agonized over her next course of action and felt physically ill (i.e., stomach cramps) at the thought of having to face the same students in class. She had trouble sleeping and suffered physical signs of stress.

In reflecting on the class, the instructor wondered if any of the students themselves were also suffering physical signs of stress due to disruptive nature of the previous class meeting. So the instructor began the subsequent class by asking students to respond in writing to the situation that had taken place the week before. In reading the responses, it became clear that many of the students, mostly the females, felt physically intimidated to come to class.

To handle such situations, we developed a set of strategies to address the physical nature of this aspect of our work. When facilitating tense classroom situations, we made a point of explicitly monitoring and being aware of our own and our students' physical reactions to the situation.

For example, we monitored our breathing (i.e., took a few deep breaths), monitored our facial expressions, and spoke in a calm and quiet voice. However, we also held on to the role of teacher-leader by staying on our feet and moving about the room when necessary. With respect to our students, we became much more adept at reading body language and taking short breaks if students exhibited signs of physical stress.

Finally, at the beginning of new classes, we discussed with students this scenario and how it was (1) inappropriate behavior, (2) what they should do if they feel themselves being physically stressed out, and (3) that to some degree such physical stress will likely happen in reaction to some topics discussed over the course of the semester.

Along with these in-class strategies, we also recognized the importance of stress-reducing practices to maintain our own physical health in order to avoid illness. For example, both of us began practicing yoga, which conferred a number of benefits, such as stress-reduction, breathing techniques, and an overall sense of well being. Additionally, one of the authors engaged in more physically active and intensive activities, such as horseback riding.

Multicultural educators must engage in some physical activity that provides an outlet for the intensity and stress they experience. Although the physical dimension of teaching was not commonly considered, we found that it had a great impact on our overall well-being as well as our teaching both in and out of the classroom.

The Spiritual Dimension

The situation: After several years of teaching the department's multicultural education course, one of the authors noticed a gradual but definite change in attitude among preservice teachers. There was clearly less tolerance for diversity, let alone acceptance, and more and more students were emboldened to immediately denounce the concept of multicultural education
from the beginning, whereas several years earlier, students were just questioning its legitimacy. Perhaps most disturbing, the usual responses to such challenges were failing. Intellectual responses grounded in statistical, empirical, and other data were ignored by unwilling intellects. Affective approaches highlighting personal stories of individuals who had experienced a life different from the status quo fell on deaf ears. Even ethical explorations that asked students to examine for themselves current injustices (let alone past injustices) could not penetrate their hearts. It was at this point that one of the authors realized she was on the brink of despair and turned to the spiritual dimension of her life to look for answers that could address this professional crisis.

The spiritual dimension was perhaps the most elusive and difficult to articulate of all the dimensions of the framework we have discussed so far. To begin with, the "spiritual" aspect of education is a topic infrequently discussed (Noddings, 1992). While a universal definition of the spiritual dimension of teaching would be impossible to articulate, Parker Palmer, who has written extensively on this subject, offers a definition of spirituality in the context of teaching which is helpful. He defines spirituality as "the eternal human yearning to be connected with something larger than our own egos" (Palmer, 2003, p. 377). It is this definition that we use as a departure point for exploration of the spiritual dimension of teaching.

In addition to being difficult to define, it is also difficult to articulate exactly how the spiritual dimension of education functioned in the lives of educators because this was often a very personal endeavor. Some strategies that worked for one of the authors in exploring this aspect of her professional life included three main activities: (1) meditation, (2) journaling, and (3) identifying role models and mentors (not necessarily in education) who drew on their spirituality to sustain them.

In terms of meditation, the author explored this activity by learning as much as possible about it (i.e., reading and instruction) and incorporating it into her daily life. In terms of journaling, the author wrote daily to engage in consistent and deeper self-reflection about her experiences. It provided a safe place to explore any ideas. Finally, the author sought role models and mentors who engaged their spiritual side as a source of inspiration and instruction for the work they did. For example, she read about ordinary individuals who engaged in activist causes, such as antiracist work, and learned how spirituality sustained them (Thompson, 2001).

For one of the authors, the above mentioned strategies were extremely beneficial precisely because strategies in the other dimensions were failing her. By utilizing non-educational sources of guidance, such as spiritual texts (Tolle, 2005), Buddhist and Taoist works, and other alternative information sources, she was able to view her work as a multicultural educator in unique, non-traditional, non-academic ways that helped her reaffirm her commitment to multicultural education.

The Ethical Dimension

The situation: A student was seeking admission into a teacher preparation program. The candidate was not atypical from many of her peers: She was from a small town and had little experience working and interacting with individuals culturally different from herself (i.e., racially, religiously, linguistically, politically, etc.). She was not a particularly strong student academically but expressed a sincere desire to be a teacher. Over the course of the semester in a multicultural education course, the student's comments during class discussions, in various papers, and in journal reflections revealed some disturbing features: racism and homophobia. When the candidate was asked to examine the beliefs and values that undergirded these apparent tendencies, she became a bit withdrawn and shut down in class. In effect, she refused to examine her belief system and its possible impact on the children she would be teaching. The faculty denied her admission to the program, using the same criteria used for all other candidates. However, due to parental pressure, the denial of admission reached the highest administrative levels of the University, who overturned the faculty's decision despite protests from some of the faculty.

Of all the scenarios discussed thus far, the above-mentioned one was perhaps the most challenging to us as multicultural educators because the action that should have been taken seemed so clearly unequivocal—the student should not have been admitted. However, as the vignette clearly illustrated, not all the parties who had the power to take action were in agreement.

In this very complex situation there are two salient ethical dilemmas. When, if at all, is it ethical to deny a candidate admission to a teacher preparation program based on his/her dispositions? How do multicultural educators maintain their ethical integrity (i.e., commitment to social equity and justice) in the face of institutional pressure asking them to do otherwise? We will not discuss the first dilemma (though it is extremely significant) because it is beyond the scope of this article and because it does not directly pertain to the issue of sustainment of multicultural educators.

So, what strategies might multicultural educators/faculty who find themselves in a similar situation do to maintain their own sense of ethical integrity under seemingly impossible circumstances? Our first strategy was to garner all the professional and institutional codes of ethics we could find that demonstrated that there are credible professional bodies that do consider the ethical dispositions of future teachers to be a critical criterion for admission.

In our case, we had the National Education Association and American Federation of Teachers' "Codes of Ethics." We also had the California Standards of Teacher Practice and our own Department's mission statement concerning democratic education. In short, there was no lack of ethical codes of conduct to support our decision not to admit the candidate in this regard.

We quickly learned that ethical codes or frameworks were just that. They were not binding documents; they were not legal mandates. In essence, they held no weight. They were regarded as "helpful guides" but if necessary could be ignored when they interfered with a desired administrative decision.

What we realized in hindsight was that ethical codes, and even our own Department's mission, meant nothing if the faculty as a group was not clear about the values they held regarding critical multicultural issues. The faculty initially voted to not admit the candidate; it only took some external pressure for

individual faculty members to cave and submit to the administration's overturning of the decision. While some faculty stuck to their original vote, others were willing to compromise and/or abandon ethical principles under duress.

It was in hindsight that we realized there should have been ongoing and sustained discussion about cases such as this one, where faculty were given the time and space as a group to converse and clarify the multicultural and social justice values they believed future teachers should possess. Additionally, use of a systematic ethical framework to shape discussions (Strike & Soltis, 1998) would have also helped individual faculty members clarify their positions on various issues and allow the faculty as a group to reach consensus, not mere agreement of the majority, on key issues.

It was unlikely in this particular case that even if the faculty had been unequivocal, clear, and strong in their reasons for nonadmission, that the outcome would have been different. The administrative pressure at the highest institutional levels was just too strong. At the very least, however, the case would have generated much needed discussion and possible future action to prevent another similar event from occurring.

So, what are multicultural educators to do when they want to "walk the talk" and maintain their ethical commitment to social justice and equity but in the end are forced to compromise such principles due to political and legal power? There seemed to be only two viable choices: Accept the decision and continue to do the work we were doing, or resign. We both chose to resign from the institution. One of us resigned immediately and the second one a year later.

Many may have viewed this situation as "giving up." Others pointed out that if change agents keep leaving then change will never occur. But as we have hopefully and convincingly demonstrated throughout this article, multicultural educators must also be very protective about sustaining themselves. In this particular context, sustainment meant knowing that we had done all that was professionally possible to maintain our ethical integrity in terms of multicultural issues. Our ethical response as multicultural educators was to recognize the point at which we had effected as much change as possible at that particular institution at that particular time.

Most important, when we realized it would be impossible to maintain any sort of individual ethical integrity concerning our beliefs about multicultural education and social justice, we realized we had to separate ourselves from that particular institution. In hindsight we both felt we made the correct decision because it reinforced our commitment and beliefs in multicultural education and allowed us to sustain ourselves not only ethically but also in the other dimensions we have described in this article, and thereby continue our work elsewhere.

Conclusion

As stated earlier, this framework can take many forms and include different dimensions, depending on the individual. In presenting this framework at a recent National Association for Multicultural Education annual conference, one participant recommended that we consider the "political" dimension in future research. The framework suggested here is the one that fit our individual needs at the time and should be altered as necessary.

While some of the dimensions for either of us might have taken on different levels of significance at different times, we both felt that these five dimensions were at work at some level for both of us and strategies of how to take care of each of these dimensions of our teaching lives were necessary to achieving balance and thus overall "good health" in dealing with the resistance we encountered.

References

Ahlkvist, J., Spitzform, P. Jones, E., & Reynolds, M. (2005). Making race matter on campus. In N. Peters-Davis & J. Shultz (Eds.), *Challenges of multicultural education: Teaching and taking diversity courses.* Boulder, CO: Paradigm Publishers.

Boutte, G. (1999). Higher education. In G. Boutte (Ed.), *Multicultural education raising consciousness* (pp. 199–227). Menlo Park, CA: Wadsworth.

Carpenter, A. (April 2000). An ethnographic study of preservice teacher resistance to multiculturalism: Implications for teaching. Paper presented at the annual meeting of the American Educational Research Association, New Orleans, LA.

Cochran-Smith, M. (2004). *Walking the road: Race, diversity, and social justice in teacher education.* New York: Teachers College Press.

Cruz-Janzen, M., & Taylor, M., (2004). Hitting the ground running: Why introductory teacher education courses should deal with multiculturalism. *Multicultural Education, 12*(1), 16–23.

Dittmar, L. (1999). Conflict and resistance in the multicultural classroom. In J.Q. Adams & J.R. Welsch (Eds.), *Cultural diversity: Curriculum, classroom, & climate.* Macomb, IL: Western Illinois University.

Ghosh, R., & Tarrow, N. (1993). Multiculturalism and teacher educators: Views from Canada and the USA. *Comparative Education, 29*(1), 81–92.

Griffin, P. (1997). Facilitating social justice education courses. In M. Adams, L. A Bell, & P. Griffin (Eds.), *Teaching for diversity and social justice. A sourcebook.* New York: Routledge.

Horton, J., & Scott, D. (2004). White students' voices in multicultural teacher education preparation. *Multicultural Education 11*(4).

McGowan, J. (1996). African American faculty challenges in the classroom at predominately White colleges and universities. Paper presented at Kansas Regents Diversity Conference, October, University of Kansas, Lawrence, KS.

McGowan, J. (2000). Multicultural teaching: African-American faculty classroom teaching experiences in predominantly White colleges and universities. *Multicultural Education, 8*(2), 19–22.

Noddings, N. (1992). *The challenge to care in schools: An alternative approach to education.* Teachers College Press: New York.

O'Donnell, J. (1998). Engaging students' recognition of racial identity. In R.C. Chavez, & J. O'Donnell, (Eds.), *Speaking the unpleasant: The politics of (non) engagement in the multicultural education terrain* (pp. 56–68). Albany: State University of New York Press.

Palmer, P. (2003). Teaching with heart and soul: Reflections on spirituality in teacher education. *Journal of Teacher Education, 54*(5), 376–385.

Strike, K., & Soltis, J. (1998). *The ethics of teaching.* New York: Teachers College Press.

Tatum, B. D. (1994). Teaching White students about racism: The search for White allies and the restoration of hope. *Teachers College Record, 95*(4), 462–476.

Thompson, B. (2001). *A promise and a way of life: White anti-racist activism.* Minneapolis, MN: University of Minnesota Press.

Tolle, E. (2005). *A new earth: Awakening to your life's purpose.* New York: Penguin.

Valerio, N.L. (2001). Creating safety to address controversial issues: Strategies for the classroom. *Multicultural Education, 8*(3), 24–28.

Valverde, L. (2003). *Leaders of color in higher education: Unrecognized triumphs in harsh institutions.* Walnut Creek, CA: Rowman & Littlefield.

Young, & Tran, (2001). What do you do when your students say "I don't believe in multicultural education"? *Multicultural Perspectives 3*(3), 9–14.

Critical Thinking

1. What are the causes of resistance among educators to using effective multicultural education?

2. How can educators overcome resistance?

3. What are the benefits for teachers to overcome resistance to multicultural education for schools, classrooms, and students?

4. Why does resistance to using effective multicultural education still exist among educators?

PENELOPE WONG is a professor in the Department of Education at Centre College, Danville, Kentucky, and **ANITA E. FERNÁNDEZ** is a professor in the Department of Education at Prescott College, Prescott, Arizona.

Toward a Conceptual Framework of Culturally Relevant Pedagogy

An Overview of the Conceptual and Theoretical Literature

SHELLY BROWN-JEFFY AND JEWELL E. COOPER

Introduction

The United States is a diverse country with constantly changing demographics. In 1980, the U.S. was 83.1 percent White, 11.7 percent Black, and 6.4 percent Hispanic. Over a quarter of a century later, the U.S. Census documents that 75.0 percent of the population of the United States is White, 12.4 percent is Black or African American, and 15.4 percent is Hispanic or Latino (U.S. Department of Census, 2008). The noticeable shift in demographics is even more phenomenal among the school-aged population. Racial/ethnic minority students consisted of 44 percent of the total public school population in 2007; this percentage is a 22 percent increase from 1972 as the percentage of White students in public schools showed a 22 percent decrease from 78 to 56 percent of the population (NCES, 2009).

The increase of ethnic-minority student presence is largely credited to the national growth of the Hispanic population, which exceeded the growth of all other ethnic minority group students in public schools (NCES, 2009). The racial/ethnic composition of the teaching force, however, is substantially less diverse than that of the student population. The U.S. Department of Education recognizes that knowledge of the changing demographic conditions in schools, though challenging, can aid such institutions in their response to this change (NCES, 2000). More specifically, while the process of schooling is fraught with challenges, a notable one is the preparation of teachers who can effectively teach students whose cultural backgrounds are different from their own (Banks, 2000; Gay, 2000; Gollnick & Chin, 2004; Irvine, 2001; Ladson-Billings, 1994, 2001; Riley, 1999).

Scholars have pondered over strategies to assist teachers in teaching about diversity (multiculturalism, racism, etc.) as well as interacting with the diversity found within their classrooms in order to ameliorate the effects of cultural discontinuity. One area that has developed in multicultural education literature is culturally relevant pedagogy (CRP). CRP maintains that teachers need to be non-judgmental and inclusive of the cultural backgrounds of their students in order to be effective facilitators of learning in the classroom. For more than a quarter of a century, scholars have written extensively on the role that the intersection between school and home-community cultures does and should play in the delivery of instruction in schools (e.g., Gay, 2000; Jordan, 1985; Ladson-Billings, 1992, 1994, 1995; Nieto, 1999, 2004). While CRP focuses on the importance of culture in schooling, it does not focus on race and racism as they relate to the sociohistorical pattern of schooling in the U.S. In an effort to understand and change how culture and race interact in the educational system, scholars (Chapman, 2008; Dixson & Rousseau, 2006; Howard, 2008; Ladson-Billings & Tate, 1995; Lynn, 2004; Lynn & Parker, 2006; Milner, 2008) have written about the relationship or connection among race, racism, and power as critical race theory (CRT). The plethora of literature on CRP, however, has not been presented as a testable theoretical model nor has it been systematically viewed through the lens of CRT. By examining the evolution of CRP among some of the leading scholars, we broaden this work through a CRT infusion which includes race and indeed racism as normal parts of American society that have been integrated into the educational system and the systematic aspects of school relationships.

Significance of the CRP Approach to Teaching and Learning

Equality of Educational Opportunity (1966) by Coleman and his colleagues was the first major post-*Brown v. Board of Education* study to establish that the achievement of Black children was lower than that of White children. This racial gap in achievement has been documented as early as kindergarten/first grade and continues to grow as students matriculate through the public school system (Coleman, Campbell, Hobson, McPartland, Mood, Weinfeld, & York, 1966; Entwisle & Alexander, 1992, 1994; Lee & Burkham, 2002; Vanneman, Hamilton, Baldwin Anderson, & Rahman, 2009). By the time racial/ethnic minority students (particularly Black, Hispanic, and Native American students) reach high school, their achievement significantly lags behind that of White and Asian students. The most recent National Assessment of Educational Progress (NAEP) reading and math results showed that across the 4th and 8th grades, White and Asian/Pacific Islander students continued to score higher, on average, than Black, Hispanic, and American Indian/ Alaska Native students (NCES, 2005).

The problem embracing the American educational system is how to ensure that all students, especially racial/ethnic minority students, achieve. However, how the problem is defined dictates the actions taken to address the issues. Moreover, theories which focus on the problem as originating within the schools will look to the schools for resolution. Theories which focus on home-community factors such as racial/ethnic heritage, family composition, and socioeconomic status as the causes of failure will look for solutions there. Theories and research which argue that students, especially those from status-oppressed minority groups, are sensitive to their treatment in school by teachers, administrators, and peers will look for answers in these social relationships. We believe, however, the latter focus has value in explaining differences in student outcomes. Educational processes and structures, especially those related to teaching or pedagogy, can make a difference in student achievement.

Examining this match, or more often the mismatch, between teaching styles and the home-community culture of students originated in the anthropology-of-education literature and has been given many designations. Early works that advocated connections between home-community and school cultures in developing viable teaching and learning environments described this phenomenon in a variety of ways: (a) *culturally appropriate* (Au & Jordan, 1981); (b) *culturally congruent* (Mohatt & Erickson, 1981); (c) *mitigating cultural discontinuity* (Macias, 1987); (d) *culturally responsive* (Cazden & Legget, 1981; Erickson & Mohatt, 1982); and (e) *culturally compatible* (Jordan, 1985; Vogt, Jordan, & Tharp, 1987). For our purposes, we use the term *culturally relevant pedagogy* (coined by Gloria Ladson-Billings in 1995), which places emphasis on the needs of students from various cultures. Ladson-Billings (1995) specifically defined culturally relevant pedagogy as:

> a pedagogy of oppression not unlike critical pedagogy but specifically committed to collective, not merely individual, empowerment. Culturally relevant pedagogy rests on three criteria or propositions: (a) students must experience academic success; (b) students must develop and/or maintain cultural competence; and (c) students must develop a critical consciousness through which they challenge the current status quo of the social order. (p. 160)

Thus, culturally relevant pedagogy is a way for schools to acknowledge the home-community culture of the students, and through sensitivity to cultural nuances integrate these cultural experiences, values, and understandings into the teaching and learning environment.

When the discussion is about culturally relevant pedagogy— one that "teaches to and through the strengths of ethnically diverse students" (Gay, 2000, p. 29)—the discussion is also about the connection between school and culture. For many years, scholars observed that not all students who enter schools come from the same culture—i.e., not all schools are a homogenous environment. Just as the student body is not homogenous, teachers may come from a culture quite different from that of their students, resulting in cultural clashes that can potentially lead to gaps in learning. For viable teaching and learning to take place, there must be connections between the home-community and school cultures. This connection demonstrates the value of cultural and social capital that students bring with them to school. Such intentional inclusion of students' backgrounds becomes a direct demonstration of the distinction between difference and deficiency. In other words, difference does not imply nor translate as deficit. Furthermore, acknowledging the home-community environments of students in teaching and learning supports tenets of critical race theory in its critical, constructive analysis of how race relations in the United States informs the study and implementation of education in schools. More directly, CRP and CRT can inform the delivery of pedagogy in America's schools.

Historical Evolution of CRP

Before Ladson-Billings coined culturally relevant pedagogy, several authors discussed the concept. Au and Jordan (1981) maintained that knowing the difference between school learning and informal learning is important in facilitating academic success for students. As specifically related to CRP, they asserted: "The context of school learning is often different from that of informal learning and often unrelated to the child's culture. Bringing the relevance of the text to the child's own experience helps the child make sense of the world" (pp. 149–150). This illustrates the importance of the teacher as a bridge between home-community and school cultures.

Mohatt and Erickson, in their 1981 study of native Indians in Odawa, Canada, concluded that (a) student and teacher behaviors need to be taken into context because they are culturally patterned behavior, and (b) research needs to focus on understanding the effect of teachers' behaviors on students. The authors listed several factors that teachers must consider when dealing with the culture of Canadian Indian students, specifically behaviors that teachers should interpret based not upon the teachers' cultures but in the context of the students' cultures.

Macias (1987), in an examination of the Papago Indian tribe's early learning environment, found that when the home culture is radically different from that of the social mainstream, there is a way to introduce the mainstream that does not erode the child's appreciation of his or her own culture. Though beneficial when the ethnicity, race, or culture of the teacher matches that of the students, culturally competent teachers, regardless of race, can learn enough of the child's home-community cultural context to be able to properly interpret behavior and structure curriculum to be an effective facilitator of the student's learning.

Cazden and Legget (1981) noted that teachers need to recognize differences in interactional style (preference for learning style and demonstrating what was learned) as well as differences in cognitive style (cognitive information processing). They stressed that the teacher should be actively involved in ascertaining the learning styles of his or her students. In 1982, Erickson and Mohatt examined the cultural organization of social classrooms where the teacher was of either a similar or different race/ethnicity from the students. They found that the learning environment in the class where the teacher and students were of the same culture was more beneficial for the students, as the teacher "developed adaptive ways of teaching" (p. 168).

Jordan's 1985 work showed that the Kamehameha Elementary Education Program (KEEP) was an aspect of cultural continuity because it incorporated an educational environment compatible with the culture of the native Hawaiian children. Jordan found that continuities or discontinuities between the home-community and school cultures could affect the quality of learning that took place. Discontinuity has often been viewed as a deficit of the racial/ethnic minority children or as cultural deprivation (Jensen, 1969). Jordan, however, maintained that to deal with cultural difference, teachers need to get a feel for the students' cultures and then make adjustments in teaching. Such adjustments would lead to the creation of a culturally compatible program. Vogt, Jordan, and Tharp (1987) further noted that cultural incompatibility is one explanation for school failure.

One significant point to note is that these earlier works were with populations where cultural differences were easier to see and accept because the White middle class teachers were immersed in different (new) cultures that were foreign to them. Because there were no White middle class students in these classes, the teachers needed to do something to ensure that their culturally homogenous students achieved. Hence, the focus had to be on teaching the culturally "different" (i.e., non-White, middle class) student. Too, these earlier works focused on the broader concept of culture versus the more defined concept of race. Nonetheless, it is important to include race and race consciousness in the multicultural classroom, especially in environments where race and culture could be dismissed as student deficiency.

In contrast to earlier works, Irvine (1990) focused on the racial aspect of culture. Irvine dealt with the lack of cultural synchronization, an anthropological and historical concept that recognizes "that Black Americans have a distinct culture founded on identifiable norms, language, behaviors, and attitudes from Africa" (p. 23), between teachers and students. Manifestations of this culture can be most vividly seen in lower-income Black communities "where racial isolation persists and assimilation into the majority culture is minimal" (p. 24). This distinct culture is "incongruous and contradictory" (p. 24) to European American culture. Therefore, cultural misunderstandings and cultural aversions can result among teachers, administrators, students, and parents within our nation's classrooms. While culture and race share some similarities, we propose that focusing solely on culture negates the reality of race and racism in American society. Moreover, we expand the work on culture and race to be inclusive of more than just Black Americans.

Significance of Critical Race Theory

Race must be considered in how culturally relevant pedagogy is enacted. The delivery of CRP is, in part, the acknowledgement of who children are, how they perceive themselves, and how the world receives them. Therefore, the complexities of the social construction of race in the United States must also be explored. One of the central reasons for the development of CRP is to respond to school "settings where student alienation and hostility characterize the school experience" (Ladson-Billings, 2001, p. 112). Some of this alienation can be attributed historically to racism with certain groups being categorized as biologically, culturally, and academically competent or inferior. A continuing and significant factor in explanations of academic and sociocultural deficiency, racism persists in being "endemic and deeply ingrained in American life" (Ladson-Billings & Tate, 1995, p. 55).

Ladson-Billings and Tate (1995) argued for a critical theory of race in education that was related to the one created in legal scholarship; thus emerged the concept of critical race theory (CRT) in education, which is used to analyze social inequity that is covertly demonstrated through racist practices within academic institutions. According to Solorzano and Yosso (2000) critical race theory in education is defined as

> . . . a framework or set of basic perspectives, methods, and pedagogy that seeks to identify, analyze, and transform those structural, cultural, and interpersonal aspects of education that maintain the marginal position and subordination of [Black and Latino] students. Critical Race Theory asks such questions as: What roles do schools, school processes, and school structures play in the maintenance of racial, ethnic, and gender subordination. (pp. 40–42)

Critical race theory brings attention directly to the effects of racism and challenges the hegemonic practices of White supremacy as masked by a carefully (re)produced system of meritocracy. CRT is built on the five tenets of: (1) racialized power; (2) the permanence or centrality of race; (3) counter storytelling as a legitimate critique of the master narrative; (4) interest convergence; and (5) critique of liberalism. These CRT tenets and the themes that flow from them challenge the existing ways of knowing and doing. Using the analytical lens of CRT in education would certainly lead to reviewing the ways that, for instance, curriculum is designed, the delivery of instruction is executed, classes are composed and grouped, assessment is determined and processed, school funding is allocated, and redistricting lines are drawn (Ladson-Billings, 1998; Lynn, 2004).

While the social construction of race is a complex factor that permeates the fabric of the American lived experiences, culturally relevant pedagogy does not explicitly problematize race. Yet, the theory and praxis of culturally relevant pedagogy should include a critical analysis of race and racism. CRP, like critical race theory, recognizes the value of lived experience by marginalized groups in understanding and making meaning of the world. In other words, the oral and written master narrative, a reality that is created, interpreted, and accepted by those in power (Stanley, 2007), is not the only voice of truth. Nonetheless, CRP does not question or critically examine the structures that feed into the cultural incongruence perspective. This is where critical race theory updates the CRP framework. The broadness of race (and consequently racism) can be seen in the way that it focuses specifically on how privilege has been given and truncated in American society, something culture does not do. The history of the U.S. has informed us that race is very central to how people perceive and relate to the world. While CRT provides a framework and for some a tool of analysis for examining educational practices and structures that continue to subordinate groups of people, culturally relevant pedagogy offers a model of theory to practice and examples of how such instruction can be delivered. When CRT is related to CRP, the centrality of race to American culture is acknowledged.

In our evaluations of the literature, we have found some universal truths that we believe are applicable to any and all cultural groups and could lead to the development of a conceptual model of pedagogical strategies with wide application. Our presentation is not an exhaustive literature review, and we recognize that a limitation of this work is that we did not attempt to create a comprehensive review of all the research on CRP. Nonetheless, we did include the major scholars who influenced the evolution of CRP and therefore informed the development of our conceptual framework: Banks, Cookson, Gay, Hawley, Irvine, Nieto, Schofield, & Stephan, 2001; Delpit, 1988, 1995; Foster, 1997; Gay, 1994, 2000; Gordon, 1999; Irvine, 1990, 2001; Irvine & York, 1995; Irvine, Armento, Causey, Jones, Frasher, & Weinburgh, 2001; Ladson-Billings, 1992, 1994, 1995, 2001; Nieto, 1999, 2004; Sleeter & Grant, 2002; and Tatum, 1992, 1997. Their contributions are discussed in the next section of this paper. We reasoned that most of the work not included here has been launched from the works of the included scholars. Even so, our purpose here is to infuse the tenets of CRT into an overview of the literature that supports a conceptual framework for understanding and studying culturally relevant pedagogy.

Conceptual Framework of CRP

In developing our conceptual framework of CRP teaching behaviors, we used Gay's (1994, 2000), Ladson-Billings' (1994), and Nieto's (1999) principles of culturally relevant teaching to flesh out five themes: identity and achievement, equity and excellence, developmental appropriateness, teaching the whole child, and student-teacher relationships. Initially we developed a list of 35 broad themes of culturally relevant pedagogy. After grouping similar concepts among the authors, we were left with five major themes. We used these five themes of CRP to guide the discussion. Additionally, we also incorporated CRT to show the importance of race and racism. The five themes of CRP, along with the specific, definitive concepts that are aligned with each theme are presented in Figure 1.

Identity and Achievement

The following concepts are aligned with identity and achievement: identity development, cultural heritage, multiple perspectives, affirmation of diversity, and public validation of home-community cultures which includes the social and cultural capital that students bring to school with them. In addressing the theme of identity and achievement, both student and teacher identities are considered. As such, identity is defined as a cultural construct. If culture is defined as the ways in which persons perceive, believe, relate to, and evaluate the world around them (Goodenough, 1981), then how people see themselves can be viewed through these same lenses. Language, behavioral expressions, interpretations of actions, and societal expectations are all culturally borne and implemented. Culture includes ethnicity and race, as well as gender, class, language, region, religion, exceptionality, and other diversities that help to define individuals. Participating as a member of these microcultures makes each individual a multicultural being. In addition, these microcultures help shape a person's multicultural identities. As Tatum (1997) pointed out:

> The parts of our identity that do capture our attention are those that other people notice, and that reflect back to us. The aspect of identity that is the target of others' attention, and subsequently of our own, often is that which sets us apart as exceptional or 'other' in their eyes. (p. 21)

Teachers should realize that students who are racial or ethnic minorities see, view, and perceive themselves and others differently than those who are of the majority group. Because race is visual and has all too often been viewed as the determinant of intelligence (for example see the works of Arthur Jensen), teachers should understand their own biases when they see their class. As part of American culture, racism prevails in American life. As such, race is not to be ignored in the picture of identity development.

In order for teachers to be culturally attuned to the identities of their students, they should be aware of their own identities, as well as how those identities may be divergent from the identities of their students. Nieto (1999) acknowledged that "by reconnecting with their own backgrounds, and with the sufferings as well as the triumphs of their own families, teachers can lay the groundwork for students to reclaim their histories and voices" (p. 3). This interest convergence, as defined by CRT, acknowledges "the legitimacy of cultural heritages of different ethnic groups, both as legacies that affect students' dispositions, attitudes, and approaches to learning and as worthy content to be taught in the formal curriculum" (Gay, 2000, p. 29). CRT clearly lets students know that individually and collectively their voices are heard, that they matter, and their presence and contributions are valued. Once this is accomplished, then it is possible to hear, acknowledge, and accept the legitimate voices of people of color as they exist in the society in which we live. Furthermore, even teachers who have not been aware of their own unique identities need to recognize the diversity of cultural heritages within the classroom. The reality of today's classrooms is that a teacher will encounter students with identities different from his or her own (e.g., a middle class White

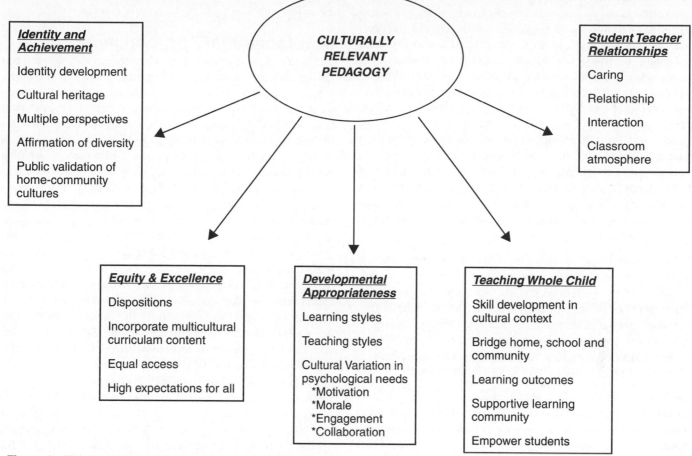

Figure 1   The Principles of Culturally Relevant Pedagogy

woman teaching a class of Native American/American Indian students), or, the classroom itself will be culturally diverse (i.e., composed of Black, Hispanic, Asian, Native American and White students).

Critical race theory adds that cultural awareness does not and should not include colorblindness or race-neutral policies. Liberalism does not mean that teachers should be colorblind or race neutral because these two approaches ignore the centrality of race and racism within American society. Colorblindness would devalue the experiences and realities of students of color by denying that race preferences and racism exists. Instead, teachers need to be aware of the White power and privilege system in American education. When teachers acknowledge that the system is racist, they can move forward to not only avoid socially reproducing the racism, but also to rethink the system, recognize their actions in it, change them if need be, and embrace all cultures as equally important.

Identifying variation of cultures within the classroom is key to becoming a teacher who practices culturally relevant pedagogy. Thus, by embracing the reality of diversity through such an identification is critical in creating an environment for equitable learning. Additionally, embracing diversity is not just acknowledging or seeing it, but also affirming it as an asset. Embracing diversity and affirming it as an asset begins to diminish the idea that the non-White model is wrong or inferior.

It forces one to understand that non-White is as important or is as significant as White; all races are valuable. As Delpit (1995) explained,

> . . . rather than think of diverse students as problems, we can view them instead as resources who can help all of us learn what it feels like to move between cultures and language varieties, and thus perhaps better learn how you become citizens of the global community. (p. 69)

Therefore, home-community cultures are used as learning tools for both students and teachers. In addition, students feel validated as their cultures are publicly acknowledged as valuable.

Equity and Excellence

We addressed the following concepts related to the theme of equity and excellence: dispositions, incorporation of multicultural curriculum content, equal access, and high expectations. Simply stated, equity involves giving students what they need. It is not the same as equal opportunity. More specifically, equal opportunity does not acknowledge that students have needs that require differentiation. Giving children what they need means believing (a) difference is good, (b) differentiated instruction is essential for some, and (c) CRP practices can enhance learning. In treating students equitably, teachers accept students through affirmations of their cultural capital (Gay, 2000). Claiming to be color-blind is not an equitable approach to teaching and learning, and is certainly not a disposition conducive to CRP practices. In fact, teachers can no longer pretend not to see racial and ethnic diversity. The notion of equity as sameness only makes sense when all students are exactly the same. Various children have different needs; addressing those needs dictates that some teaching methods may not be applicable. Therefore, when teachers do not see diversity, they truly do not see the students at all and therefore greatly limit their abilities to meet students' diverse educational and social needs (Gay, 1994).

Equity and excellence also includes the incorporation of multicultural content in curriculum and instruction. Students may not see themselves in a positive light in the traditional material that is usually presented in schools. As Banks et al. (2001) concluded:

> In curriculum and teaching units and in textbooks, students often study historical events, concepts, and issues only or primarily from the point of view of the victors. The perspectives of the vanquished are frequently silenced, ignored, or marginalized. This kind of teaching privileges mainstream students—those who most often identify with the victors or dominant group—and causes many students of color to feel left out of the American story. (p. 198)

The teachers in Foster's (1997) and Ladson-Billings' (1994) studies implemented this idea that the content of the curriculum needs to be inclusive of all cultures represented in the classroom. However, Ladson-Billings and Tate (1995) warned that the acknowledgement of racial, ethnic, or cultural difference should not be reduced to simplistic, symbolic, and meaningless tasks such as eating ethnic or cultural foods, dancing and singing songs, and reading folktales; instead it should incorporate "bringing both student and faculty from a variety of cultures into the school (or academy environment)" (p. 61). They also admonished teachers and administrators that recognition of cultural diversity must also be inclusive of the maintenance and sustenance of high expectations of both students and teachers.

Critical race theory adds that equity and excellence clearly focus on realizing that race is a significant factor in inequality. Some would argue that it is the "central construct for understanding inequality" (Ladson-Billings & Tate, 1995 p. 50). Too, multiculturalism in the curriculum can turn racism on its head and use race as the springboard for equality. In particular, multiculturalism is not simply stating that some cultures are different, which in American society has also meant deficient, wrong, or bad. CRT debunks the belief that equity and excellence are solely defined as the property interest of Whites and highlights the exclusionary practices of the educational system (Ladson-Billings & Tate, 1995). It uses counter storytelling as a legitimate critique of the mainstream master narrative. The focus will not be on cultural inclusions during a specific time of year (such as Black History Month), but interweaving the acknowledgement and inclusion of culture throughout the entire academic process. More explicitly, Whiteness should not be the only determinant of entry into high-level courses and programs because equity and excellence are not the exclusive ownership of Whites. Thus, the

practice of CRP serves to recognize that equity and excellence are and should be enjoyed by students of color as well.

Developmental Appropriateness

The theme of developmental appropriateness includes the following concepts: learning styles, teaching styles, and cultural variation in psychological needs (motivation, morale, engagement, collaboration). As such, developmental appropriateness acknowledges the importance of knowing where children are in their cognitive development. It also involves knowledge of children's psychosocial development. While there is a global developmental appropriateness for children, as conceptualized by theorists such as Elkind, Erickson, and Piaget, their theories have usually been applied to the very young learner. Thus, we recognize the importance of student age in development, but we also believe that the process should carry on through the higher grades as it moves from considering *is this appropriate for a student at a certain age to how does diversity of culture impact developmental appropriateness*. In addressing developmental appropriateness, the teacher should be interested in what is culturally appropriate or relevant for the culturally diverse students in her or his classroom. Knowledge that students bring with them to school must be acknowledged, explored, and utilized (Ladson-Billings, 1994).

CRT adds that developmental appropriateness must also focus on where the student is when he enters school and whether it can be a direct remnant of racism. Students of color may already believe that the educational system is stacked against them, leading them to a defeatist relationship with the educational process. The student may have already learned lessons that devalued her or his worth based solely upon race, ethnicity, or culture. More than 70 years ago, Woodson (1933) made this apparent in *The Mis-education of the Negro*. Part of developmental appropriateness is taking students where they are and getting them to where they need to be with innovative teaching methods and assessments.

Not only does developmental appropriateness focus on the implementation of activities designed to meet the cognitive, emotional, social and psychological needs of students, it also integrates teaching styles and student learning styles. In this arena, teachers should realize that the psychological needs of students may vary and that students do have different motivations to learn. The key is generating teaching styles that incorporate the vast differences in culturally-based learning styles and learning preferences of students.

Developmental appropriateness also means that teachers are cognizant of the dominant and sometimes racist, non-inclusive ideology that has been institutionalized and legalized in American education. Critical race theory forces teachers to critique liberalism and challenge the dominant ideology. This includes the development and use of diverse assessment opportunities which begins with high standards and expectations for all. CRP teachers have to advocate for and perform a paradigm shift in assessment.

While teachers must practice in the context of this standardized curriculum, they can also embrace the opportunity to incorporate or cultivate additional views of achievement that will allow those who do not experience achievement through the standard curriculum to obtain success through these additional methods, ones that recognize and value who children are and how they learn best. When teachers respond to developmental appropriateness, they, in effect, cultivate students who want to learn instead of the students who will just engage in rote memorization and regurgitation. Good pedagogy is more than just teaching the content information; what is important is to teach students so that they are able to learn and to transfer such learning in various environments.

Teaching the Whole Child

Closely related to developmental appropriateness is teaching the whole child, a theme that includes the concepts of skill development in a cultural context, home-school-community collaboration, learning outcomes, supportive learning community, and empowerment. When attempting to achieve the goal of practicing CRP, teachers must remember the needs of the total child. Influences from initial cultural socialization experiences in the family and community shape the academic identity of students who enter our classrooms. These cultural influences affect how students and their families perceive, receive, respond to, categorize, and prioritize what is meaningful to them. Therefore, teachers should be sensitive to how culture, race, and ethnicity influence the academic, social, emotional, and psychological development of students.

Culture resides in the individual (Goodenough, 1981). While a student can be guided in many ways by cultural group identification, his or her ways of believing and perceiving can also be influenced by individual understandings and conceptualizations. In other words, teachers cannot solely base an individual's behavior on what s/he believes his or her group culture to be, for those beliefs may be stereotypical. Teaching the whole child will require not only that teachers recognize, understand, and intentionally acknowledge cultural group behaviors, but also observe and interact with students as individuals. Thus, it is crucial for teachers to learn about all of their students, especially those who are culturally different from the teachers themselves. Additionally, students' recognition of teachers' desires to learn about them beyond the classroom can have tremendous power to motivate and invite learning. The CRP practice of teaching to the whole child expands teachers' knowledge base of instructional strategies and also heightens their cultural sensitivity and recognition of the definitive link between culture and schooling. Moreover, through the lens of CRT, CRP supports the child as an integrated human being where culture and schooling are key to his/her development.

Furthermore, the whole child is nurtured from his/her home and community before s/he enters the school setting. Children bring with them to school culturally-based ways of doing, seeing, and knowing; in response, culturally relevant teachers find ways to scaffold those cultural experiences in order for the students to gain additional meaning and ultimately be successful. By so doing, the culturally relevant teacher emphasizes the "funds of knowledge" (Moll, 1992) or cultural capital (Gordon, 1999; Bourdieu, as cited in Lareau, 2001) developed

in students' homes and communities, thereby encouraging academic achievement. Not only are ethnic minority students able to see their cultures in the classroom, but also other students comprehend the value of various cultures.

Student-Teacher Relationships

Our last CRP theme, from Figure 1, addresses the relationship between the students and the teacher in the classroom. This theme includes the concepts of caring, relationships, interaction, and classroom atmosphere. According to Nieto (1999), "the nature and the extent of the relationships between teachers and their students are critical in promoting student learning" (p. 167). The teacher is an important significant other in the lives of students because of the amount of time spent in schools. Students need to know teachers care and teachers should recognize and respect their students for who they are as individuals and as members of a cultural group. Too, students want to be recognized for their different ways of knowing that are reflective of their own cultures. With this recognition, positive responses from both students and teachers to diversity enhance the student-teacher relationship. Students see teachers as real and teachers broaden their knowledge base of how students respond to the world around them.

Understanding the synergistic linkages between culture, communication, and cognition is crucial to successful student-teacher relationships (Gay, 2000). According to Gay (2000), "communication is strongly culturally influenced, experientially situated, and functionally strategic. It is a dynamic set of skills and performing arts whose rich nuances and delivery styles are open to many interpretations and instructional possibilities" (p. 109). We communicate with others as a means of expressing thoughts, sharing our experiences, and creating and accessing knowledge, both general and situated. Awareness, appreciation, and acceptance of different discourse patterns and styles of verbal and nonverbal communication, those which go beyond speaking and writing, help to bridge the gap between the home-community and school culture. In other words, CRP teachers' knowledge and translation of different cultural communications styles can avert misinterpretations of behavior, demonstrations of disrespect, and conflicts in schools (Irvine, 2001, 1990).

Ladson-Billings (1994) defined student-teacher relationships as ones that are "fluid and equitable and extend beyond the classroom. [Culturally relevant teachers] demonstrate a connectedness *with* all their students and encourage that same connectedness *between* the students" (p. 25). Teachers should not only recognize students' individual value and importance, but they should also consciously recognize what their students have in common. Together, students and teachers need to build classroom community, making it a safe place in which to nurture everyone's cultural identity. Foster (1997) concluded that teachers need to expand their individual classrooms to be inclusive of the entire school community through collaborations with colleagues as well as the surrounding community. This outreach will strengthen student-teacher interactions in the classroom community because CRP teachers accept that the community is a vital partner in students' learning.

Providing caring interpersonal relationships is a hallmark of CRP teachers (Gay, 2000). Caring is demonstrated through patience and persistence with learners. These teachers facilitate learning, validate learners' knowledge construction, and empower learners' individual and collective learning capacity. In doing so, these teachers maintain high standards for excellence and equity. More specifically, CRP teachers are "demanding but facilitative, supportive and accessible, both personally and professionally" (Gay, 2000, p. 48). The culturally relevant teacher simply does not accept failure, but begins where students are and works hard to help them succeed. As one teacher in Foster's (1997) book affirmed: "In order to teach well . . . you have to think about students as if they belonged to you. If teachers showed the same concern, interacted with their students and treated them as if they were their own children, schools would have more success with greater numbers of students" (p. 98).

CRT informs and can be infused into CRP where student-teacher relationships are concerned in various ways. In order to form better relationships with students, teachers should consider and value their students' counterstories, for their perceived realities of lived experiences can unveil the historic and continuing presence of racism and its effects on students' and families' lives. In other words, through counterstories, teachers are provided a vehicle by which they can see what has, in some cases, been consciously invisible to them before. Additionally, educational theory reminds us of the importance of relating disciplinary content to students' lives. However, CRT cautions teachers to more closely examine and scrutinize the programming of educational systems, curricular development, and resulting barriers to equal education access and opportunity that could occur because of the permanence of racism in our society. CRT also requires that teachers of CRP question students' learning and placement in programs or classes (i.e., academically gifted, exceptional children, etc.) that have been historically defined by the dominant culture. Additionally, CRT informs these teachers to maintain high expectations of all students no matter what the placement is and to negate the belief that students who are not in the highest academic programs are "less than." In other words, teachers who are in tune with their students are knowingly and sometimes unknowingly aware of the tenets of CRT and work hard to "make it right" for all children, not just those perceived to be more privileged than others.

Conclusion

One of the major concerns in the education of students has been how to address the race/ethnicity-based achievement gap between mainstream and minority children. This gap has persisted among various groups throughout the history of the NAEP assessment and is likely to persist as the U.S. becomes increasingly more culturally diverse. Thus, a goal of educational research is to find a way to teach all students regardless of their ethnicity, race, cultural background, or community of origin. Culturally relevant pedagogy is a promising area of research in determining the actual effects of the mismatch of the culture of particular populations within the educational system and the effects of schooling on the learning outcomes of these children. It could be that CRP is an effective way to address these issues.

In this article, we integrated selected writing on culturally relevant pedagogy to address overlap and divergence within the conceptual and theoretical literature. We have taken the CRP literature that was couched in culturally specific domains (e.g., Foster's work on African Americans and Nieto's work on Hispanics) and brought it together in one location. Our aim was to collect and categorize the themes that are evident across major works on CRP. Through our investigation of CRP, we became critically aware that culture does not always take into account the permeating thread of racism in the fabric of American life. We acknowledged that the delivery of CRP includes knowledge of who children are, how they perceive themselves, and how the world receives them. Therefore, the complexities of the social construction of race in the United States must also be explored because people in American society are often viewed in terms of racial characteristics. As such, we extended CRP by integrating the tenets of CRT to incorporate the significance of race and racism within the discussion of culture.

What we have presented here is a conceptual framework of culturally relevant pedagogy that is grounded in over a quarter of a century of research scholarship. By synthesizing the literature into the five areas and infusing it with the tenets of CRT, we have developed a collection of principles that represents culturally relevant pedagogy. We believe that culturally relevant pedagogy is distinguishable based on the principles of teaching to the whole child, equity and excellence, identity and achievement, developmental appropriateness, and student-teacher relationships. Even though we believe that working independently on any one of these areas is a necessary step toward adopting a culturally relevant pedagogical style, the combination of these elements is what truly makes one engaged in and a more comprehensive practitioner of CRP. While culturally relevant pedagogical behaviors are factors that help students, Foster (1997) and Ladson-Billings (1994) found that not all culturally relevant teachers use similar techniques within their classrooms. The common thread among the teachers was their philosophies of teaching; the observed behaviors were manifestations of their teaching philosophies.

The reasoning behind the development of *No Child Left Behind* (NCLB) included the knowledge that some categories of students were not receiving quality education when they should have been. This 2001 national educational reform legislation provides a structured guidepost in responding to needs of students who most frequently fall within the persistent achievement gap in America's public schools. Critics maintain that while implementation of NCLB appears to have improved student achievement and narrowed the achievement gap (Sack, 2005), these gains mask continued inequities in the education of culturally diverse students.

Despite its shortcomings, NCLB has focused attention on the ideal that every child is entitled to learn. Unequivocally, CRP also focuses on the fact that every child is entitled to learn. As such, one way to assure that each child learns is for teachers to deliver instruction that is relevant to all of the diverse population that inhabits our schools. In light of the

NCLB initiative, this CRP framework, one that is inclusive of the tenets of CRT, is valuable because it is useful for pre-service teachers as well as in-service teachers. However, it must be explicitly taught and modeled in our schools of education by teacher educators. Therefore, teacher educators must be knowledgeable of the framework in order to teach it to their students and demonstrate it in their professional practice as well as in professional development offerings in our nation's school systems; for such intentional pedagogy is a clear, indisputable signal that we must and can prepare teachers with responsive tools and strategies to make sure that *all* students learn.

Note

1. The authors' names are listed in alphabetical order, but they share first author status for the article.

References

Au, K., & Jordan, C. (1981). Teaching reasoning to Hawaiian children: Finding a culturally appropriate solution. In H. Trueba, G. Guthrie, & K. Au. (Eds.), *Culture and the bilingual classroom: Studies in classroom ethnography* (pp. 139–152). Rowley, MA: Newbury House.

Banks, J. A. (2000). *Cultural diversity and education: Foundations, curriculum, and teaching.* Boston: Allyn & Bacon.

Banks, J. A., Cookson, P., Gay, G., Hawley, W. D., Irvine, J. J., Nieto, S., Schofield, J. W., & Stephan, W. G. (2001). Diversity within unity: Essential principles for teaching and learning in a multicultural society. *Phi Delta Kappan,* November, 196–203.

Cazden, C., & Legget, E. (1981). Culturally responsive education: Recommendations for achieving Lau remedies. In H. Trueba, G. Guthrie & K. Au. (Eds.), *Culture and the bilingual classroom: Studies in classroom ethnography* (pp. 69–86). Rowley, MA: Newbury House.

Chapman, T. K. (2008). Desegregation and multicultural education: Teachers embracing and manipulating reforms. *The Urban Review, 40*(1), 42–63.

Coleman, J. S., Campbell, E. Q., Hobson, C. J., McPartland, J., Mood, A. M., Weinfeld, F. D., & York, R. L. (1966). *Equality of educational opportunity.* Washington DC: U.S. Government Printing Office.

Delpit, L. D. (1988). The silenced dialogue: Power and pedagogy in educating other people's children. *Harvard Educational Review, 58*(3), 280–298.

Delpit, L. D. (1995). *Other people's children: Cultural conflict in the classroom.* New York: The New Press.

Dixson, A. D., & Rousseau, C. K (2006). *Critical race theory in education: All God's children got a song.* New York: Routledge.

Erickson, F., & Mohatt, C. (1982). Cultural organization and participation structures in two classrooms of Indian students. In G. Spindler (Ed.), *Doing the ethnography of schooling* (pp. 131–174). New York: Holt, Rincholt, & Winston.

Entwisle, D., & Alexander, K. L. (1992). Summer setback: Race, poverty, school composition, and mathematics achievement in the first two years of school. *American Sociological Review, 57,* 72–84.

Entwisle, D., & Alexander, K. L. (1994). Winter Setback: The racial composition of schools and learning to read. *American Sociological Review, 59,* 446–460.

Foster, M. (1997). *Black teachers on teaching.* New York: New Press.

Gay, G. (1994). *The essence of learning.* Bloomington, IN: Kappa Delta Pi.

Gay, G. (2000) *Culturally responsive teaching: Theory, research, and practice.* New York: Teachers College Press.

Gollnick, D., & Chin, P. (2004). *Multicultural education in a pluralistic society* (6th ed). Upper Saddle River, NJ: Pearson.

Goodenough, W. H. (1980). *Culture, language and society.* Menlo Park, CA: Benjamin/Cummings Publishing.

Gordon, E. W. (1999). *Education and justice: The view from the back of the bus.* New York: Teachers College Press.

Howard, G. (2006). *We can't teach what we don't know: White teachers, multiracial schools* (2nd ed.). New York: Teachers College Press.

Howard, T. E. (2008). Who really cares? The disenfranchisement of African American males in preK-12 schools: A critical race theory perspective. *Teachers College Record, 110*(5), 954–985.

Irvine, J. J. (1990). *Black students and school failure: Personnel, practices, and prescriptions.* Westport, CT: Greenwood.

Irvine, J. J. (2001). The critical elements of culturally responsive pedagogy: A synthesis of the research. In J. J. Irvine, Armento, J. B. Causey, V. E., Jones, J. C., Frasher, R. S., & Weinburgh, M. H. (Eds.), *Culturally responsive teaching: Lesson planning for elementary and middle grades.* New York: McGraw-Hill.

Irvine, J. J., & York, D. E. (1995). Learning styles and culturally diverse students: A literature review. In J. A. Banks & C. A. M. Banks (Eds.), *Handbook of research on multicultural education* (pp. 484–497). New York: Macmillan.

Irvine, J. J., Armento, J. B., Causey, V. E., Jones J. C., Frasher, R. S., & Weinburgh, M. H. (Eds.). (2001). *Culturally responsive teaching: Lesson planning for elementary and middle grades.* New York: McGraw-Hill.

Jensen, A. R. (1969). How much can we boost IQ and scholastic achievement? *Harvard Educational Review, 19,* 1–123.

Jordan, C. (1985). Translating culture: From ethnographic information to educational program. *Anthropology and Education Quarterly, 16,* 105–123.

Ladson-Billings, G. (1992). Culturally relevant teaching: The key to making multicultural education work. In C. A. Grant (Ed.), *Research and multicultural education* (pp. 106–121). London, UK: Falmer Press.

Ladson-Billings, G. (1994) *The dreamkeepers: Successful teaching for African-American students.* San Francisco: Jossey-Bass.

Ladson-Billings, G. (1995). But that's just good teaching! The case for culturally relevant pedagogy. *Theory into Practice, 34*(3) 159–165.

Ladson-Billings, G. (1998). Just what is critical race theory and what's it doing in a nice field like education? *International Journal of Qualitative Studies in Education, 11*(1), 7–24.

Ladson-Billings, G. (2001). *Crossing over to Canaan: The journey of new teachers in diverse classrooms.* San Francisco: Jossey-Bass.

Ladson-Billings, G., & Tate, W. F. (1995). Toward a critical race theory of education. *Teachers College Record, 97*(1), 47–68

Lareau, A. (2001). Linking Bourdieu's concept of capital to the broader field: The case of family-school relationships. In B. J. Biddle (Ed.), *Social class, poverty, and education: Policy and practice* (pp. 77–100). New York: Routlege/Falmer.

Lee, V. E., & Burkham, D. T. (2002). *Inequality at the starting gate: Social background differences in achievement as children begin school.* Washington, D.C.: Economic Policy Institute.

Lynn, M. (2004). Inserting the 'race' into critical pedagogy: An analysis of 'race-based epistemologies.' *Educational Philosophy and Theory, 36*(2), 153–165.

Lynn, M., & Parker. L. (2006). Critical race studies in education: Examining a decade of research on U. S. schools. *The Urban Review, 38*(4), 257–290.

Macias, J. (1987). The hidden curriculum of Papago teachers: American Indian strategies for mitigating cultural discontinuity in early schooling. In G. Spindler & L. Spindler (Eds.), *Interpretive ethnography at home and abroad* (pp. 363–80). Hillsdale, NJ: Lawrence Erlbaum Associates.

Milner, H. R. (2008). Critical race theory and interest convergence as analytic tools in teacher education policies and practices. *Journal of Teacher Education, 59*(4), 332–346.

Mohatt, G., & Erickson, F (1981). Cultural differences in teaching styles in an Odawa school: A sociolinguistics approach. In H. Trueba, G. Guthrie, & K. Au. (Eds.), *Culture and the bilingual classroom: Studies in classroom ethnography* (pp. 105–119). Rowley, MA: Newbury House.

Moll, L. C. (1992). Bilingual classroom studies and community analysis. *Educational Researcher, 21*(2), 20–24.

National Center for Educational Statistics (2000). *The condition of education 2000*. NCES 2000-062. Washington, DC: U.S. Government Printing Office.

National Center for Educational Statistics. (2005). *Nation's report card*. Retrieved October 25, 2005 from http://nces.ed.gov/nationsreportcard/nrc/reading_math_2005/.

National Center for Educational Statistics. (2009). *The condition of education 2006*. Retrieved January 21, 2010 from http://nces.ed.gov/programs/coe/2009/section1/indicator07.asp.

Neito, S. (1999). *The light in their eyes: Creating multicultural learning communities*. New York: Teachers College Press.

Nieto, S. (2002/2003). Profoundly multicultural questions. *Educational Leadership*. December/January, 6–10.

Nieto, S. (2004). *Affirming diversity: The sociopolitical context of multicultural education* (4th ed.). New York: Longman.

No Child Left Behind (NCLB) Act. (2001). Enacted by the Senate and House of Representatives of the United States of America in Congress assembled. Retrieved September 10, 2003 from http://www.ed.gov/nclb/landing.jhtml?src=pb and http://www.ed.gov/policy/elsec/leg/esea02/107-110.pdf

Riley, R. (October. 1999). Improving America's schools. (A speech delivered at the Improving America's Schools Conference, Tampa, FL.)

Sack, J. L. (2005, March 23). Progress report on "No Child" law shows hits and misses. *Education Week, 24*(28), 9.

Sleeter, C. E., & Grant, C. A. (2002). *Making choices for multicultural education: Five approaches to race, class and gender* (4th ed.). Upper Saddle River, NJ: Prentice-Hall.

Solorzano, D., & Yosso, T. (2000). Towards a critical race theory of Chicano and education. In C. Tejada, C. Martinez, & Z. Leonardo (Eds.), *Charting new terrains in Chicana(o)/Latina(o) education* (pp. 35–66). Cresskill, NJ: Hampton Press

Stanley, C. A. (2007). When counter narratives meet master narratives in the journal editorial-review process. *Educational Researcher, 36*(1), 14–24.

Tatum, B. D. (1992). Talking about race, learning about racism: The application of racial identity development theory in the classroom. *Harvard Educational Review, 62*(1), 1–24.

Tatum, B. D. (1997). *"Why are all the Black kids sitting together in the cafeteria?" And other conversations about race*. New York: Basic Books.

U.S. Department of Census. (2008). *ACS demographic and housing estimates: 2007*. Retrieved January 21, 2010, from http://factfinder.census.gov/servlet/ADPTable?_bm=y&-qr_name=ACS_2008_1YR_G00_DP5&-geo_id=01000US&-ds_name=ACS_2008_1YR_G00_&lang=en&-_caller=geoselect&-redoLog=false&-format=

Vanneman, A., Hamilton, L., Baldwin Anderson, J., & Rahman, T. (2009). *Achievement gaps: How Black and White students in public schools perform in mathematics and reading on the National Assessment of Educational Progress* (NCES 2009-455). Washington, DC: National Center for Education Statistics, Institute of Education Sciences, U.S. Department of Education.

Vogt, L., Jordan, C., & Tharp, R. (1987) Explaining school failure, producing school success: Two cases. *Anthropology and Education Quarterly, 18*, 276–286.

Woodson, C. G. (1933). *The mis-education of the Negro*. Washington, DC: Associated Publishers.

Critical Thinking

1. What is culturally relevant pedagogy (CRP)?

2. How can you transform your practices so they are feature CRP?

3. What are the benefits of CRP for today's students?

4. Why do you need to continue your professional development in CRP?

SHELLY BROWN-JEFFY is an associate professor in the Department of Sociology and JEWELL E. COOPER is an associate professor in the Department of Teacher Education and Higher Education, both at the University of North Carolina at Greensboro, Greensboro, North Carolina.

Approaches to Diversifying the Teaching Force

Attending to Issues of Recruitment, Preparation, and Retention

Ana María Villegas and Danné E. Davis

The widening cultural chasm between teachers and students in elementary and secondary schools is a serious problem in American education demanding concerted action. As the works in this special issue of *Teacher Education Quarterly* make clear, the shortage of teachers of color has real consequences for all students, but especially for students of color. Despite the urgency, programs of teacher education are not giving this matter the attention it deserves. In this context of relative inattentiveness to the need for teachers of color, it is encouraging to read a collection of articles that feature a variety of carefully designed and well documented approaches to diversify the teaching force. Our goal in this commentary is to place the approaches described in this issue within the broader discussion of recruiting, preparing, and retaining prospective teachers of color.

Bringing People of Color into Teaching

Programs of teacher education have historically played a passive role in student recruitment. It has generally been assumed that the market need for teachers will automatically draw students into teacher education. The passage of the Civil Rights Act of 1964 inadvertently challenged this approach to recruitment, however. Prior to the enactment of this legislation, teaching was one of the few careers available to women and people of color. As a result, programs of teacher education—whether at Predominantly White Institutions (PWIs) or Historically Black Colleges and Universities (HBCUs)—had a captive pool of talented people from which to draw students. As professional opportunities opened up in this country for women and racial/ethnic minorities, undergraduates from these groups began to defect in large numbers from education to other fields such as business, engineering, and the health professions (Carter & Wilson, 1992; Urban, 2000). The declining popularity of teaching, coupled with increased demand for teachers over the past fifteen years, has pushed programs of teacher education to take on a more

active and thoughtful role in recruiting students. Below we discuss the major approaches used during this time to bring candidates of color into teaching, weaving throughout our discussion the approaches described in this issue. Such approaches are distinguished primarily by the population targeted for recruitment, as we explain below.

Enrolled Undergraduates with Undeclared Majors

Teacher education programs seeking to diversify their enrollments often recruit undergraduates of color at their institutions with undeclared majors. An advantage of this approach is that potential recruits are on campus already and generally eager to give direction to their professional futures. Unfortunately, because the number of students of color who matriculate directly at four-year colleges is limited, programs of teacher education must compete aggressively with other fields on campus for this small population. To promote interest in teaching, recruitment efforts are crafted to help identified students understand the valuable contributions that educators make to society, the many opportunities available to someone with a teaching credential, and the type of preparation and support the teacher education program is ready to provide.

This recruitment approach is exemplified by the teacher preparation program Wong, Murai, Avila, White, Baker, Arellano, and Echandia describe in this issue. Although the Multilingual/Multicultural Teacher Preparation Center (M/M Center) at California State University, Sacramento, was designed as a fifth-year credential program, the recruitment of potential students begins as early as their freshman year in college. The Freshman Seminar, sections of which are taught by M/M Center faculty, exposes students to the merit of a teaching career. Faculty from the M/M Center also offer an undergraduate minor in Multicultural Education (into which the pre-requisites to the teacher credential program are built) and teach capstone courses for Social Science majors with an interest in teaching. These contacts enable program faculty to effectively nurture the young people's interest in a teaching career and to help them begin to envision themselves as the type of social justice teacher the program aims to prepare.

Once admitted to the program, participants receive support services designed to help them navigate the intricacies of the higher education bureaucracy, such as connecting student to sources of financial aid, providing assistance with their application to the teacher education program, tracking their progress through the program to ensure the timely completion of requirements, and creating a built-in network of peer support through the use of cohort groups. Beyond recruitment and support services, students benefit from exposure to a coherent, race- and language-conscious curriculum that is thoughtfully designed to prepare teachers to create learning opportunities for poor students from diverse racial and ethnic backgrounds and to advocate on their behalf. In fact, one of the more important contributions of this article to the literature is the attention it gives to the content of the preparation participants receive in the program to enable them to act as agents of change in schools. In so doing, the authors move the discussion about the diversification of the teaching force beyond the customary focus on issues of recruitment and support services needed.

Targeting students of color already admitted into four-year colleges/universities for recruitment is an approach best suited for institutions that serve large numbers of racially and ethnically diverse students, such as HBCUs and Hispanic Serving Institutions (HSIs). Because the overwhelming majority of teacher education programs in this country are housed in PWIs, settings with consistently low enrollments of students of color, this recruitment approach alone—while helpful—is not likely to alter the overall racial/ethnic composition of the U.S. teaching force in any appreciable way. To significantly increase the representation of people of color in teaching, the pool of potential candidates must be expanded beyond those who are already enrolled in four-year colleges/universities. It is not surprising, then, that most efforts to diversify the ranks of teachers recruit non-traditional candidates—pre-college students who might not otherwise go to college, community college students, paraprofessionals in elementary and secondary schools, and people of color who already hold a bachelor's degree and are open to making a career switch. The literature shows that such recruitment approaches are tailored to the targeted population and provide recruits with the necessary support to experience success, as we describe below.

Pre-College Students

One way of expanding the pool of potential teachers of color is to identify likely candidates prior to their senior year in high school, even as early as the middle grades, and involving them in intervention programs that aim both to cultivate the students' interest in teaching and to facilitate their admission to college. Project FUTURE, described in this issue by Stevens, Agnello, Ramirez, Marbley, and Hamman, is illustrative of the early recruitment approach. This Texas Tech University initiative targets students enrolled in sixth grade through senior year in high school and involves them in an array of activities over the years to strengthen their resolve to go on to college

and to promote their teaching self-efficacy. As Stevens et al. detail, Project FUTURE advances these two goals by bringing students on campus frequently to give them a window into college life, involving them in exercises that allow them to better understand the relationship between having a college degree and earning potential, providing information about financial aid for college as well as the college application process, offering workshops that focus on the development of test-taking strategies, engaging students in teaching simulations to give them practice with instructional strategies, and exposing them to different teaching styles and having them reflect on those experiences. As described by the authors, this initiative builds on the collaboration of members from the university community, the school districts in which the participants are enrolled, and the broader communities in which those schools are located. Other types of activities used in early recruitment efforts, as reported in the literature, include Future Educators Clubs, introductory teacher education courses that offer college credit to high school juniors and seniors, inspirational speakers who give students information about the teaching profession and encourage them to become part of it, summer programs that provide students intensive teaching experiences in addition to academic support, and work study programs in which upper high school students of color tutor younger children in community programs (Zapata, 1998).

While teacher cadet programs, such as Project FUTURE, have the potential to bolster the pool of racial/ethnic minorities for teaching, they are long-term efforts that take minimally five to eight years to produce results, and typically much longer. Equally important, while such programs have been shown to increase the number of racially and ethnically diverse college entrants, they do not necessarily guarantee that college recruits will actually seek admission into teacher education or that those who are admitted continue in this field through graduation (Clewell et al., 2000).

Community College Students

Community college students represent another important, yet largely untapped pool of prospective teachers of color (Hudson, Foster, Irvine, Holmes, & Villegas, 2002). After all, the overwhelming majority of people of color who pursue a postsecondary education first enroll in community colleges. Since teachers must earn a bachelor's degree before they can be certified, students who start at community colleges must transfer to four-year colleges or universities to become teachers. Sadly, the transfer rate from two- to four-year institutions is disappointingly low (Nettles & Millet, 2004). As discussed in the literature, part of the problem is the lack of clear articulation agreements between the partnering institutions that establish which community college credits will be accepted at the four-year institution. As a result, community college students often lose credits upon transfer. The difficulty of the transfer process is confounded further by a general lack of support services to facilitate the students' successful integration into the teacher education program at the four-year institution once the transfer occurs.

The Teacher Academy Learning Community at the University of Texas, San Antonio—featured in the Busto Flores,

Riojas Clark, Claeys, and Villarreal article—typifies initiatives that focus recruitment efforts on the community college student population. This program was designed primarily to meet the needs of students transferring into teacher education from San Antonio College, the largest two-year college in the geographic area serving a largely Latino population. (The University of Texas component of the program is also open to incoming freshmen and students with undeclared majors at the institution.) The article focuses on the support structures put in place to facilitate the integration into the university system of transfer students pursuing teacher education. A key element of the support structure is a collaborative network of student service offices at the partner institutions through which transfer students are identified for program participation. Support begins with careful advisement of students at the community college to ensure they take the appropriate courses prior to their transfer into teacher education at the University of Texas. Upon transfer, students are involved in a Summer Bridge Institute that gives them an orientation to university life and exposes them to other activities intended to strengthen the academic and problem-solving skills they will need to succeed at the university.

Once on campus, participants receive a variety of supports including monitoring of their progress through the teacher education program; referrals for assistance with time management, study skills, and tutoring when such needs are identified; counseling with personal issues that present a threat to their persistence in college; activities that guide them through an exploration of their professional dispositions; and mentoring and coaching on professional matters both throughout the teacher education program and during their initial year of teaching. These support services not only smooth the transfer process to the university, but also enhance the capacity of the teacher education program at the University of Texas, San Antonio, to produce teachers of color who will persist in the profession. Particularly noteworthy in this initiative is the mentoring and coaching support graduates of the teacher education program receive during their initial year of teaching, a time in which teachers are most vulnerable to attrition. There is little in the literature about the mentoring of new teachers of color.

Residents of Communities of Color

Partnerships between teacher education programs at colleges and universities and various types of organizations/agencies in communities of color have been established with the goal of increasing the supply of certified teachers of color for schools in those communities. This "grow your own" recruitment approach builds on the belief that people of color who live in the community are particularly well suited to teach children from that community. These individuals are said to bring to teaching personal insight into the lives of the students and a commitment to improving the young people's academic performance. Indeed, there is much evidence in the literature to support these claims (Villegas & Davis, in press). Most of this work has focused on paraprofessionals in schools. Programs of teacher education that recruit paraprofessionals work closely with the school districts that employ them. As part of these "career ladder" initiatives, paraprofessionals continue their

salaried positions while enrolling in courses each semester toward the completion of requirements for teaching certification, and usually a bachelor's degree as well. Such programs, which typically take a minimum of three years to produce teachers, offer a variety of support services to enable participants to make it through graduation and obtain their certification (Villegas & Clewell, 1998).

The Pathways Program at Armstrong Atlantic State University (AASU), described by Lau, Dandy, and Hoffman, is a good example of a career ladder program for paraprofessionals. In this initiative, AASU collaborates with the Savannah-Chatham County Public School District (SCCPS) to select participants for the program. The selection process gives attention to a variety of indicators of ability and future success as teachers, including exemplary track records as paraprofessionals in schools and commitment to teaching in high need school environments. Because one of the goals of the program is for completers to be hired as teachers in the partner district, recommendations from SCCPS teachers and administrators carry special weight in selection decisions. To address the needs of paraprofessionals—many of whom bring academic lags resulting from inequitable schooling, have children to support, and shoulder major financial responsibilities for their households—the program offers various services. These include tight monitoring of participants' academic progress, tutorials and other academic supports for those experiencing difficulties in courses, a system of peer support promoted by the use of cohort groups, test-taking preparation for certification exams, and financial assistance in the form of tuition scholarships and textbook vouchers. Among the many salient features of this nationally recognized program, two stand out. One is the creative arrangement that the partnering school district and institution of higher education have worked out to secure release time with pay for paraprofessionals to attend classes at the university, thereby shortening the time they would otherwise need to complete the required coursework. The second is the successful restructuring of the student teaching experience so that participants can complete this certification requirement without having to lose salary and benefits during this time.

Two other initiatives featured in this issue—the Hopi Teacher for Hopi Schools (HTHS) program described by White, Bedonie, De Groat, Lockhard, and Honanie, and Project TEACH described by Irizarry—also use the grow your own recruitment approach. But instead of limiting recruitment efforts to paraprofessionals, these two programs targeted adults in the community with an interest in teaching, including paraprofessionals. This broader reach was possible because the partnership involved formal relationships with the community beyond the local schools. A community-based organization committed to creating pathways into higher education for community residents was a key collaborator in Project TEACH, helping to identify potential participants and securing funding to cover the cost of tuition for some of them. Similarly, the HTHS program was planned and implemented with direct input from representatives of the Hopi Nation. Given the sense of program ownership on the part of the communities involved, the strong critique of the university curriculum evident in both articles is not surprising. In the university/tribal collaboration, for example, the program was pushed to make the coursework for participants more inclusive by adding elements of "red pedagogy" to the curriculum. In Project TEACH, participants were offered "supplemental" professional development activities to compensate for the relative lack of attention given to issues of diversity and social justice in the teacher education courses they took.

Readers of the Irizarry article, in particular, walk away with a clearer understanding of the difficulties involved in respectfully integrating into existing programs of teacher education people from historically oppressed groups who are committed to returning to their communities to work toward changing the many inequities built into the everyday fabric of schools. For this to happen, programs of teacher education need to attend to issues of recruitment and provide support services to see the recruits through graduation. But equally important, if not more so, programs must be willing to rethink the curriculum in fundamental ways. As Irizarry astutely explains, recruiting people of color into teacher education, while "failing to prepare them to promote educational equity does little to alter a system of education characterized by significant disparities in opportunity and achievement. Solely focusing on the representation of teachers of color in university or K-12 classrooms is tokenism and not transformative. Representation, while important, is not enough." Unfortunately, most of the literature on diversifying the teaching force continues to focus on representation, without giving sufficient attention to the type of preparation new recruits of color need to serve as agents of change in schools. We were pleased to see that the Wong et al. article in this issue dealt squarely with this topic.

Holders of Bachelor's Degrees

People of color who already hold bachelor's degrees in fields other than education comprise another important pool from which to draw new teachers. In fact, schools with severe teacher shortages, overwhelmingly urban schools, routinely fill vacant positions with candidates from this pool, either by issuing them provisional certificates or bringing them into teaching through an alternative route program. The latter option generally allows recruits to take on instructional positions in subject areas with teacher shortages, contingent on their successful completion of a program that provides some preparation in pedagogy and an internship experience in classrooms. The provisional certificate approach allows individuals without preparation in pedagogy to work as teachers for a period of time, usually three to six years, during which they are expected to complete the requirements for certification. While these two pathways into teaching receive a fair amount of criticism in the literature, they are nevertheless used widely to fill vacancies in urban schools. In fact, without them, teacher shortages in those settings would be even more severe than they currently are. Clearly, traditional programs of teacher education must work harder to produce more teachers for urban schools, regardless of their race/ethnicity. In addition, they need to assume some responsibility for ensuring that those who enter teaching in urban schools with provisional certification or through alternative routes have the preparation they need to teach students successfully. Project 29,

highlighted in the Sakash and Chou article, is an example of such an effort.

The goal of Project 29, a collaborative initiative involving the University of Illinois at Chicago and the Chicago Public Schools (CPS), was to enable provisionally certified bilingual (Latino) teachers in the partner district to secure their standard teaching credentials while receiving in-class support to speed their development of pedagogical skills for teaching English language learners (ELLs). Several elements of the program contribute to its documented success over the past 13 years. To begin with, participants are carefully selected based on attributes that program staff have found predictive of future success as teachers, such as parenting experience, involvement in activism and leadership activities, and perseverance in overcoming problems, in addition to having an acceptable grade point average. Participants receive an individualized plan of study after a careful review of their transcripts. They meet regularly throughout the program in small "advisory" groups for peer support on academic, professional, and personal issues of concern to them. The curriculum focuses on assisting the Scholars, as participants are called, to see connections between what they learn at the university and what they experience daily as teachers of ELLs in urban schools.

Ongoing observations of the Scholars' performance in their classrooms by university field instructors serve two critically important functions in the program. They provide participants support and guidance for improving their pedagogical skills and enable the faculty to continuously modify the content of the education courses to address the specific difficulties Scholars are experiencing in their teaching. The redesigned "student teaching" experience—which calls for participants to complete inquiry projects in their own classrooms and to conduct a project on issues related to the education of ELLs jointly with a general education monolingual teacher from the school—provides a more authentic learning experience for this population of teacher candidates than the traditional student teaching. This curricular modification also allows participants to complete the "student teaching" requirement without experiencing an interruption in salary and benefits. In brief, the article by Sakash and Chou shows how a teacher education program committed to improving the conditions of urban schools can do so.

It is interesting to note that the majority of people of color entering teaching over the past 15 years did so either as provisionally certified teachers or through some form of alternate route (Allen, 2003). This is explained, at least in part, by the challenges involved in getting candidates of color from nontraditional teacher pools into and through traditional teacher education programs. We suspect, however, that another explanation is the blasé attitude toward diversifying the ranks of teachers that prevails in many programs of teacher education. Even when publicly claiming to be committed to that goal, little energy is actually devoted to making this happen.

Looking across the Approaches

From reading this collection of articles, several conclusions can be drawn about how best to diversify the teaching force, all of which are consistent with the existing literature on this topic.

Collectively, these works suggest that to increase the proportions of teachers of color will require more than luring college-bound students of color away from financially profitable fields into teacher education. A true expansion will necessitate developing the potential of others who might not otherwise go on to four-year colleges. A comprehensive recruitment approach, one that targets different pools of potential talent—pre-college students, community college students, and others who serve children and families within the community in addition to college students with undeclared majors—is needed. The article by Landis and colleagues, in this issue, underscores this conclusion.

Another lesson learned is that programs of teacher education seeking to diversify the teaching force must collaborate with different organizations/agencies to successfully recruit candidates from diverse racial and ethic backgrounds. To recruit from the pre-college student population calls for the involvement of the school districts in which those students are enrolled. Partnerships with school districts are also needed to recruit employed paraprofessionals. Clear articulation agreements that spell out which community college courses will be accepted by the partnering four-year college are essential to tap the large pool of students of color in two-year colleges. Collaborations with organizations based in communities of color—including churches, civic organizations, and various types of service agencies—are also helpful in identifying potential recruits with an interest in teaching and a commitment to return to their communities as teachers. (For a detailed explanation of the central features of such partnerships, see Clewell & Villegas, 2001.)

To successfully recruit teacher candidates of color from non-traditional pools, tuition assistance is essential. Several articles in this collection emphasize this point. Without financial incentives, few candidates from non-traditional teacher pools can afford to complete an undergraduate program of study. To address this need, teacher education programs could secure scholarships through grants from private foundations and/or government agencies. Forgiveness loans that are erased after graduates have taught in schools for a specified period of time are similarly helpful. The recent difficulty finding funding sources for this purpose presents a major obstacle to diversifying the teaching force, as the authors of several articles in this issue rightly point out.

From the works published in this issue of *Teacher Education Quarterly* we also learn that teacher education programs must work diligently to retain students of color from non-traditional pools through graduation and certification. As the authors explain, this involves offering a comprehensive network of academic and social support services, including orientation to the college/university, a strong advisement and monitoring system, prompt referrals to academic support services for students experiencing difficulties with their coursework, workshops designed to help participants develop test-taking skills, and the use of structured groups or cohorts to promote peer-support.

Looking Ahead

Upon reflecting on the literature, it is clear to us that we already know much about how to recruit people of color into teacher education and how to support them through graduation and certification. We know relatively little, however, about how to adequately prepare prospective teachers of color and how to facilitate their successful transition into the profession. Part of the rationale for increasing the diversity of the teaching force is that people of color bring to teaching knowledge about the lives of students of color and insider experiences that enable them to relate well to students of color and to build the necessary bridges to learning for them. However, unless teacher candidates of color are appropriately prepared to draw on this unique knowledge and insight to shape their pedagogy, the yield of those resources will be limited at best. Similarly, unless teacher candidates of color are appropriately prepared to act as change agents, their commitment to making schools more equitable and just for students of color is not likely to produce the desired results. Unfortunately, there is little in the literature that speaks directly to these two important topics.

We have argued elsewhere that the addition of large numbers of teachers of color represents our best chance to make schools in this country more democratic and just (Villegas & Davis, in press). But to maximize the benefits that could be derived from having a diverse teaching force, programs of teacher education must go beyond issues of recruitment and retention and attend to the preparation candidates of color need for the task. That is the immediate challenge ahead for those who are truly committed to diversifying the ranks of teachers.

References

Allen, M. B. (April 2003). *Eight questions on teacher preparation: What does the research say?* Denver, CO: Education Commison of the States.

Carter, D. J., & Wilson, R. (1992). *Minorities in higher education: Tenth annual report.* Washington, DC: American Council on Education.

Clewell, B. C., Darke, K., Davis-Googe, T., Forcier, L., & Manes, S. (2000). *Literature review on teacher recruitment programs.* Washington, DC: The Urban Institute.

Clewell, B. C., & Villegas, A. M. (2001). *Ahead of the class: A handbook for preparing new teachers from new sources: Design lessons from the DeWitt-Reader's Digest Fund's Pathways to Teaching Career Initiative.* Washington, DC: Urban Institute. http://www.urban.org/url.cfm?ID=310041.

Hudson, M., Foster, E., Irvine, J.J., Holmes, B., & Villegas, A.M. (2002). *Tapping potential: Community college students and America's teacher recruitment challenge.* Belmont, MA: Recruiting New Teachers.

Nettles, M., & Millett, C.M. (2004). *Student access in community college* (Issue Paper). Washington, DC: American Association of Community Colleges.

Urban, W. J. (2000). *Gender, race, and the National Education Association: Professionalism and its limitations.* New York: Routledge-Falmer.

Villegas, A. M., & Clewell, B. C. (1998). Increasing teacher diversity by tapping the paraprofessional pool. *Theory Into Practice, 37*(2), 121–130.

Villegas, A. M., & Davis, D. (In press). Preparing teachers of color to confront racial/ethnic disparities in educational outcomes. In M. Cochran-Smith, S. Feiman-Nemser, & J. McIntyre (Eds.), *Handbook of research on teacher education: Enduring issues in changing contexts* (3rd ed.). Mahwah, NJ: Lawrence Erlbaum.

Zapata, J. (1998). Early identification and recruitment of Hispanic teacher candidates. *Journal of Teacher Education, 39,* 19–23.

Critical Thinking

1. What are the unfortunate consequences for all students with a shortage of teachers of color?

2. How can teachers of color be recruited?

3. What specific steps must be taken to support teachers of color?

4. Why is having teachers of color essential for all students?

ANA MARÍA VILLEGAS is a professor of curriculum and teaching and **DANNÉ E. DAVIS** is an assistant professor of early childhood, elementary education, and literacy education, both with the College of Education at Montclair State University, Montclair, New Jersey.

Realizing Students' Every Day Realities: Community Analysis as a Model for Social Justice

You can't guide your students to overcome challenges of social injustice if you cannot relate material to the lives of your students outside of the classroom. And in my opinion, the most important reason for a teacher to understand the challenges facing their students outside the classroom is so that the teacher can become motivated to promote social justice in their own daily life as well as within their classroom and to not be naïve to the problems that truly exist in our society. —Darren, pre-service teacher

JEANETTE HAYNES WRITER AND H. PRENTICE BAPTISTE

This article examines the implications and effect of the Community Analysis (CA) Project assignment that we utilize in the Multicultural Education (MCE) course[1] at New Mexico State University, located in Las Cruces, New Mexico. The CA enables pre-service teachers to critically examine, through a social justice lens, the manifestations and intersectionalities of race, class, gender, sexual orientation, language, ability, and religion in PreK-12 students' communities, which may be rejected and ignored, or embraced, serving to connect students' lives to learning contexts and opportunities in their schools. The CA compels pre-service teachers to analyze systemic inequities and inequalities in communities which impact the everyday lives of students. They discover organic knowledge possessed by students and families to bridge students' knowledge and the knowledge promoted within the school curriculum. Pre-service teachers also contemplate how their privileged or disadvantaged identity statuses intersect with their future students' privileged or disadvantaged statuses, or impact how they read communities.

The ultimate goal of the CA, through this reflective practice, is to prepare pre-service teachers to provide equitable and just learning environments for all students.

With the examination and discussion of the CA, we offer educational professionals knowledge and information that can assist them in the implementation of multicultural education from a critical analysis perspective. We maintain that MCE must be formulated within a social justice framework, which purposefully transcends the "heroes and holidays," or what we refer to as the "food, fun, festivals, and foolishness" approach. It is only from multicultural education practice anchored to a social justice theoretical framework that we establish and maintain equitable and just learning environments.

The Conceptualization and Facilitation of the Course— Situating Our Teaching Context

Our teaching context is in Las Cruces, New Mexico. We are located at the south end of the state, approximately forty-two miles from the Texas border and approximately an hour's drive from Juarez, Mexico and the Mexico/US border. We are in the "borderlands" in terms of political boundaries, as well as in metaphorical, social, and cultural borderlands in regard to how various identities (race, citizenship, sexual orientation, religion, etc.) often times intersect in a confrontive manner. Our pre-service teacher population is typically one-half white and one-half Mexican American/Hispanic, the latter being divided into those who have immigrated to the area recently, either in their own or their parents' lifetimes, and those whose families have lived in the US for generations. We have a richness to draw from in linguistic ability and experience. Undergraduate courses host a higher percentage of women; the presence of men tends to increase in graduate courses. In terms of socio-economic class, white pre-service teachers typically occupy the middle class status; those who are Mexican American/Hispanic come from a mix of middle-class and working-class backgrounds.

Jeanette has been a faculty member in the Department of Curriculum and Instruction since fall of 1996; her primary teaching responsibility is the undergraduate and graduate MCE courses. Prentice has been with the department since 1997; previous to his teaching responsibility of the MCE course, he served as College of Education Dean for two years. Prentice began using the CA with his undergraduate and graduate courses in the 1980's during his tenure at the University of Houston. The community analysis module emerged from an activity called the Princeton Game. It was first modified by James Anderson for a course and further modified by Prentice at the University of Houston and Kansas State University before Prentice introduced it at New Mexico State University. He shared the assignment with Jeanette and she has been using the assignment for approximately five years. Previously, Jeanette had employed the community service option for her pre-service teachers, using the CA first in the graduate MCE course.[2] However, she extended the CA to all of her MCE courses because of the deep understandings obtained from the assignment.

Theoretical Underpinnings

Although a significant amount of literature has been developed in the field of MCE (Banks & Banks, 2001; Baptiste, 1986; Bennett, 2001; Boyer & Baptiste, 1996; May, 1999; Nieto & Bode, 2008; Sleeter & Grant, 1987), scholars have not settled on a specific definition. For our purposes, we utilize the following definition:

> Multicultural Education is a comprehensive philosophical reform of the school environment essentially focused on the principles of equity, success, and social justice for all students. . . . Social justice in schools is accomplished by the process of judicious pedagogy as its cornerstone and focuses on unabridged knowledge, reflection, and social action as the foundation for social change. (Baptiste, 1995, as cited in Boyer & Baptiste, 1996, p. 5)

May (1999) contends the MCE movement "promised much and delivered little" (p. 1). Recently, Jeanette visited a kindergarten teacher at a local elementary school. Within the conversation the teacher remarked that a fellow teacher planned to have the children "dress up like Indians and pilgrims for Thanksgiving." We know that the "heroes and holidays" form of MCE is happening in public schools, so we strategically work to move pre-service teachers from the "celebrating diversity" frame of reference to one of social justice.

Bell (1997) describes social justice as "both a process and a goal" (p. 3). Social justice interrogates the manifestations of power and the dynamics of oppression, such as in individuals' and groups' access to resources and the experiences those individuals and groups have due to their status that either advantage or disadvantage them. From this interrogation, a plan of action is developed to transform systems of oppression. Along with social justice, critical pedagogy is a vital aspect of our work in the MCE courses because it involves the teaching of critical analysis. As expressed by Oakes and Lipton (2007), critical pedagogy "links knowledge of diversity and inequality with actions that can make the culture more socially just" (p. 100).

The CA is a critical pedagogical tool to transform the awareness and consciousness of our pre-service teachers to recognize oppressions and to strategize circumventions for those oppressions. The CA encompasses these ideas by moving social justice from "words on a page" into a tangible, hands-on learning opportunity.

Constructing the Course Syllabus and Assignments

The background, goals and vision of the MCE course establishes that:

> Students from a variety of language, cultural, class, gender, and exceptionality backgrounds attend school everyday and interact with each other in academic, social and personal ways. Besides academic learning, the school environment fosters socio-cultural learning - be it positive or negative, implicit, or explicit.

The teacher's role can maximize or minimize the positive or negative multicultural learning that unfolds. This role develops through the teacher's personal knowledge, awareness, sensitivity, and critique of diversity and pluralism in a democratic context. The teacher is encouraged to create a sense of self that will promote a nurturing respect for self and others in order to genuinely promote equal and accessible education (EDUC 315 Syllabus).

In the first class meeting, Jeanette clarifies that this is not a "how to do MCE" course, it is a conceptual, research-based course where pre-service students develop awareness, skills, and abilities to intellectualize what MCE is and what social justice looks like. She explains that after reading the course texts and other readings, struggling with the concepts, and conducting their CA, pre-service teachers will be able to read communities and the educational terrain to be effective in various teaching locations and situations.

Banks (1994) and Vavrus (2002) maintain that teacher education programs should facilitate pre-service teachers' understanding of their cultural heritages before expecting them to understand those of their students. Other scholars (Artiles & McClafferty, 1998; Haynes Writer, 2002a; Mahlios & Maxson, 1995; Stachowski & Frey, 2003) articulate the value of surveys, inventories, and other methods of assessment of pre-service teachers' conceptualizations, beliefs, and attitudes in teacher education programs and teacher development. Jeanette does this by having the pre-service teachers conduct an analysis of their socialization employing Harro's (2000) "Cycle of Socialization." Pre-service teachers work though their seven core identities (race, class, gender, sexual orientation, language, ability, and religion/spiritual orientation) to identify their dominant or subordinate identities and identify how their identities intersect with each other. Haynes Writer (2002a) asserts, "After 'inventorying' one's own conceptualizations, attitudes, and beliefs, a student must then find her or his own courage for critical transformation as a critical multicultural teacher, to change what is incorrect and inequitable" (p. 13).

Utilizing Harro's Cycle of Socialization, each pre-service teacher presents her or his identities and socialization process to the class; Jeanette presents her Social Identity Project to the pre-service teachers first to serve as both a model for the presentation and as reciprocal disclosure of her socialization. As the pre-service teachers present, they bring in knowledge that all can access; they provide counterstories to the oppressions found in the dominating society; and they confront assumptions they had of colleagues. The assignment assists pre-service teachers to become aware of and name their subordinate statuses, as well as their privileged statuses that may "blind them" to the realities of students, families, and communities that are situated in subordinated identities or contexts. At the end of the semester, pre-service teachers write an "Epilogue" to discuss how their colleagues' presentations added to their knowledge base or how the CA transformed their understandings of community as they position themselves as critical educators; most students write about the impact of the CA.

Community Analysis Project Assignment

Too often a school and its staff constitute an island, which is physically within, but culturally and epistemologically removed from the surrounding community. The need is for direct experiences to give pre-service teachers knowledge and understanding of the problems and the strengths of the people in the kind of community in which she or he may teach. The CA develops in the pre-service teachers a critical lens as they examine communities in ways they have not before.

Each individual selects a school site, but is instructed not to go into the school; the pre-service teacher is to learn about the community around the school, not the school itself. The CA purposefully de-centers the authority of the school, while centering the authority of the community. The everyday realities of the students who go to the school are examined, as is the organic knowledge they bring to the school context. The pre-service teachers have to imagine themselves as future teachers at their particular school, asking these questions: How are the core identities manifested in the community? What are their intersections? How is power played out? What are the issues in the community that serves as obstacles for the students? What are the strengths and resources of the community? How will I bridge school curriculum with the organic knowledge that students bring to school? The CA is an overarching, culminating project that encompasses several assignments.

Activities within the CA Project Assignment

Pre-service teachers construct a Descriptive Map of their selected school community, including the names of the specific areas, villages, streets, or roads in the community; they may use the school district's boundaries or construct a purposeful boundary of their own. Using a color and number code to fill in the map, the following are designated: schools; federal/public community service agencies; religious/spiritual or political organizations; substandard housing; places where children and teenagers play or gather; places where the unemployed gather; major industries/businesses; and condemned buildings or areas.

Pre-service teachers also complete two Observation Logs regarding the presence or absence of two core identities that Jeanette selects; the logs coincide with the readings at that point in the semester. The logs are developed as ethnographic observations with accompanying personal reactions/questions, grounded with course readings and readings outside of class. Pre-service teachers are instructed to use this formula to examine the remaining core identities as a means to generate analyses and references for the Critical Analysis Paper. In addition, pre-service teachers collect various kinds of data concerning their community to complete the 20 question Questionnaire. The questionnaire focuses pre-service teachers' attention to such issues as quality and availability of food and housing, social issues, physical infrastructure viability, and perspectives of residents regarding the community.

The Critical Analysis Paper is developed based on the critical intellectual synthesis of information from community observations, interviews with residents and community service personnel, course readings, research articles, statistical data, and the information gathered for the questionnaire. The following questions are addressed: (1) What have you learned about the manifestations of race/ethnicity, socio-economic class, gender, sexual orientation, language, ability, and religion in the community?; (2) How are power and oppression connected to these identities displayed or played out in the community?; and (3) How will you circumvent the seven oppressions (racism or ethnocentrism, linguicism, classism, sexism, heterosexism, ableism, and religism) to address critical issues in the community through your work with students in the classroom and their caregivers?

The pre-service teachers share their new understandings with colleagues during the Community Analysis Reports. Each prepares a Power Point presentation and, taking turns in small groups of 3 to 4, discusses their communities with their "critical colleagues." As critical colleagues, the pre-service teachers listen, ask questions, provide feedback in comparison to what they have seen in their communities,

and ground the conversation to the Oakes and Lipton (2007) text and other course readings.

Several times during the semester progress checks are conducted in class, as scaffolding mechanisms, to see where pre-service teachers are in their CA. They have the opportunity to dialog with one another on what they are discovering, what difficulties they are having, and what resources they are tapping. In their research, pre-service teachers consult print and on-line research journals; governmental, community, and organization websites; US Census data; and talk to individuals in the community. The project is designed to expand pre-service teachers' resourcefulness in locating community information and resources.

The Pre-Service Teachers

Whereas, Jeanette has utilized the CA for a number of years, in Spring 2008 she collected papers from her undergraduate MCE course for the purpose of this article. Of the twenty-two pre-service teachers, sixteen described themselves as Hispanic, Mexican or Mexican American and six as White or Caucasian; fourteen were female and eight were male. Self-describing one's socioeconomic status, the class was comprised of a mix of socioeconomic classes, the majority claiming middle-class status with a few claiming working-class status. Of the twenty-two pre-service teachers, eighteen signed consent forms for the gathering of CA documents. Of these, seven Critical Analysis Papers and Epilogues were first selected for their completeness and depth; three were then analyzed further for discussion in this article.

After spending twelve weeks in their selected communities talking to students, parents/guardians, community members and personnel from community businesses, agencies and public services, frequenting various websites, and researching the scholarly literature to complete their Questionnaire, as well as constructing their Descriptive Maps, and completing Observation Logs, the pre-service teachers wrote their Critical Analysis Paper. This paper brings all the information together in a cumulative, intellectually-grounded, meaning-making paper. This is the opportunity, as Jeanette tells them, to "show what you know."

In the subsequent pages readers follow three students, Darren, Teresa, and Carlos, as they progress through their Critical Analysis Paper and Epilogue. Here, readers are introduced to the pre-service teachers and witness the transformation of their critical knowledge base, awareness of their dominant or subordinate identity statuses, and movement towards a social justice perspective.

Darren is a mono-lingual English-speaking, heterosexual, able-bodied white male in his early 20s, who was raised in a community that is a border town to the Navajo reservation. He described himself as middle-class, and came from a family that was economically sound and educated. His father is a veterinarian and he and his siblings were all expected and able to attend college. During his time in K-12 schools, he had Navajo classmates and related a story of being beat up because he was "a white boy." He also described himself as a person of strong Christian faith and at the beginning of the course inquired why evolution, which he did not support, was privileged over intelligent design. This was an issue of struggle within his trajectory of becoming a high school science teacher.

Teresa is a bilingual, able-bodied, middle-class, heterosexual Mexican American female in her early 20s. She is of the Catholic faith and was raised and went to school in the El Paso area. Teresa focused her examination on the community of Sierra Vista, located approximately twenty-five miles south of Las Cruces. Teresa stressed that the CA made her realize that teaching was not "a simple profession." As she studied her community, she found that interviews were important because of the sense of the community she gained from talking with residents, "The way the community members looked at the world is how their children, my students, were going to look at it as well." Teresa revealed that her point of challenge—and opportunity for transformation—revolved around the issues of homosexuality and heterosexism. She admitted that, "In order for me to try and confront homophobia in my classroom, . . . I had to really push my beliefs aside and take into consideration the discrimination against innocent individuals."

Carlos is a heterosexual, able-bodied Mexican male in his early 20s who is fluent in Spanish and English. He lives in Fairfield, which is a short drive north of Las Cruces. Instead of examining the immediate community surrounding one of the four schools in Fairfield, Carlos choose to study the entire community. Fairfield is a small, rural farming community. The backbreaking labor within the lucrative agricultural business in Fairfield comes from fieldworkers, many who are migrant laborers from Mexico, thus US citizenship and anti-immigrant sentiments play out in complex ways. Carlos was born in Mexico and has his US residency documents. He is a participant in the College Assistance Migrant Program at NMSU, which provides financial and educational support to students from migrant and seasonal farm working families. He described himself as being from a lower socioeconomic class; Carlos's mother works in the fields, as does he during the summer. Carlos was very quiet in class and rarely spoke in large group discussions. Jeanette sometimes wondered how and if he was making sense of the course content—was he engaged? His Critical Analysis Paper answered that question with a resounding "yes!" Carlos researched the community and deconstructed it along the seven core identities deeply and critically. As he analyzed the community, Carlos confronted some of his own oppressions—both what has been waged upon him and what he has participated in. He desires to become a bilingual teacher; he found that his linguistic skills benefited him in the CA Project, "Throughout my analysis I was able to make observations that a person that only spoke one language would either miss or not notice."

Question 1: Manifestations of the Seven Core Identities in the Community

Within the Critical Analysis Paper, the first question the pre-service teachers addressed was: What have you learned about the manifestations of race/ethnicity, socio-economic class, gender, sexual orientation, language, ability, and religion in the community? To discuss this question, we concentrate on specific identities, those with which the pre-service teachers personally struggled or those which stood out to them.

Becoming conscious of his strong Christian identity through the Social Identity Project, an identity he named as dominant for himself, Darren explored how religion manifested within the Las Cruces community around Sun View Elementary, specifically in the form of Christian religious organizations. Connecting course readings[3] and our class discussions to what he was observing in the community, Darren recognized how discrimination could be formulated due to historical biases and recent events.

> Within the city of Las Cruces there are over 180 religious organizations or churches. Of at least thirty-six religious institutions within one mile of the community, the majority of them are Catholic, Protestant, or other Christian-based churches. . . . The fact that the majority of churches in the Sun View community are either Catholic or Protestant may indicate that the discrimination against other religious views could be common. Following the attacks of September 11, 2001, a steep increase

in discrimination against Muslim people has occurred on a national level. Those events have most likely created similar feelings for some people living in the Sun View community.

He connected this to how religious groups outside of the Christian mainstream may be targeted, including students from those religions.

> Because young children are so easily influenced by parents, friends, the media, etc., many students have already developed negative stereotypes of people of certain religious groups or of non-religious people. This may lead to discrimination among these young people in schools based on religion by other students or even by faculty. . . .

Like Darren, Teresa also identified her religious identity, Catholic, as a dominant identity. Viewing discrimination as a moral and ethical issue, she challenged her beliefs to assess the homosexual presence, or rather, absence, in her community.

> There were no gay/lesbian groups or clubs that were easily detected. Fliers in stores and in restaurants had pictures of heterosexual couples. In asking around the community about homosexuality I did not get very many responses because some people did not wish to talk about it. The ones who did answer said that it was not common in Sierra Vista to see a gay or lesbian couple. Usually you see them at the gas station fueling up because they are just passers-by.

For Carlos, particular identities became very clear in Fairfield. Homes in the community illustrated a stark stratification based on the intersections between race, class, and citizenship or "arrival" in the US. Looking at various sections of the community, Carlos found a few "mansions" and "miniature mansions"; these were homes of Anglos who "owned or were related to people who owned the biggest money-making businesses in Fairfield." The areas where the poor lived reminded Carlos of what he had studied regarding the Hoovervilles from the Great Depression, homes that featured "doors made out of street signs," that were "literally falling apart," and apartments made of adobe that "seemed to have been built by the Spaniards themselves on their first conquistas." Whereas, the wealth and upper-class status in Fairfield was possessed by Caucasians, Carlos remarked that, "[M]ost of the middle-class . . . was Mexican American, while most of the lower-class was mostly of full Mexican descent. The middle-class seemed to be mostly second and third Mexican American generations."

Question 2: Examining How Power and Oppression are Displayed in the Community

The second question in the Critical Analysis Paper was: How are power and oppression connected to these diversities displayed or played out in the community? Carlos specifically examined race; he studied US Census data to establish the racial demographics of his community, which showed that Hispanics were numerically dominant. Carlos discovered that power did not, however, follow the numbers once socio-economics intersected with race in the power dynamic.

> Many may assume that the town is run by the Hispanic population because if you enter any business the managerial positions are all occupied by Hispanics. But after further investigation it slowly starts to become apparent that all of the businesses are managed by Hispanics but in reality they are owned by Anglos.

Driving around the community, Carlos found that most of the store signs and business advertisements were in English, however, the majority of the employees in the stores and businesses conducted business in Spanish. There was one exception:

> In the hardware store everyone only spoke English. The employees understood Spanish but they never spoke it. . . . I started to make the connection at the hardware store where the majority of customers were Caucasian; a few Hispanics would trickle in but it seemed that they were just in and out. . . . [I]t seemed that the whites almost used it as a clubhouse.

To critically analyze the intersections of race, class, and language, Carlos drew upon the course readings. He specifically cited Tatum's (2000) words that others are the mirror in which we often see ourselves, and Harro's (2000) Cycle of Socialization as to how Hispanic community members were collectively socialized to acquiesce to the Anglos' English. Carlos stated,

> [Tatum] kept making sense in my head because the reason I believe everything was in English was for adaptation purposes. The subordinate group in Fairfield is the Hispanic community and the dominant group is the Caucasian community. In this town the dominant group's population is more than doubled by the subordinate population, yet the language is adapted for the group whose population is smaller. . . . The Hispanics have gotten [so] used to always accommodating the whites that everything they do is to make life easier for the dominant group.

Teresa interrogated the power dynamic of heterosexism[4] in Sierra Vista; she affirmed that,

> Heterosexuality is dominant in Sierra Vista. The fact that some residents refused to talk about homosexuality is evidence that it is subordinate. . . . There are no support groups for adults or for children who are homosexual in Sierra Vista. Who are young gay and lesbian children going to run to if they have a problem? A child that is living in fear to come out is not healthy.

As she investigated her community to examine the power of heterosexuals, Teresa connected the absence of homosexuals as an issue of power and a position of invisibility, which may have the potential to place gay and lesbian individuals or students at risk in that community.

Question 3: Developing Strategies as Teachers to Circumvent Oppressions

The third question in the Critical Analysis Paper was: How will you circumvent the seven oppressions to address critical issues in the community through your work with students in the classroom and their caregivers? The three pre-service teachers had transformed themselves from being individuals unaware of their identities to "teachers-inprocess"; they were intellectually strategizing disruptions of discriminatory actions and discourses in their classrooms.

Darren transformed from being a young man who defended his privileged Christian identity, maintaining at the beginning of the course the need to present intelligent design on the same footing as or in place of evolution,[5] to a future educator who situated himself as being attentive to all of his students' religious orientations.

> One of the things that I will undoubtedly encounter in my science classroom will be the origin of life. I hope to explore various religious and non-religious views with my students that pertain to the origin of life, and to engage students in expressing their opinions about this. Religion is something that I do not

believe should be "taught" in any way in the classroom; however, I want to encourage my students to express their beliefs while being respectful and open-minded in learning about the beliefs of other people. I feel that my experiences with various religions and the information that I have learned from this project and in this class have prepared me to create an environment that is conducive to helping students develop respect for and diminish negative stereotypes of various religions.

Carlos situated himself as a social justice teacher by connecting to the everyday realities of his students. He would have them become active and see themselves as change agents.

> As an educator I will address these problems [that he found in his community] . . . I will strive to open the eyes of my students and help them see that the answer to their problems is right in front of them. I will not only promote equality but equity as well. . . . Oppression will always exist and I don't intend of abolishing it but I do intend on creating a socially just atmosphere in my classroom, home, and school.

Carlos began envisioning himself as a transformative educator, one whose work does not stay in the classroom but moves out into the community in an effort to create alliances and motivation for change.

> Always with great hope that my work will spill over to the community and create a bridge not only with myself and the school but with everyone in the community creating an interlaced network that fights for the same objectives with the same motives in mind.

"As a social justice educator I need to fight homophobia in my classroom because children are [placed] at risk." Teresa wrote extensively about what steps she would take to address homosexuality and homophobia in her classroom, from obtaining permission to show the film "It's Elementary: Talking about gay issues in school" (Cohen & Chasnoff, 1996), to putting up pictures in her classroom which portray families in various forms, to drawing upon suggestions from the book, Queering Elementary Education (Letts & Sears, 1999). She would also dialogue with her students regarding what homosexuality is because,

> I know that someday they will come across this word. I want to teach them before they are given a negative definition. . . . I also want my students to be aware of homophobia and the negative effects it has on individuals. I will certainly be open for any child who has a problem about coming out or just needs someone to talk to. I will make sure that bullying does not go unpunished, especially when it has to do with homophobia.

New Realizations and Understandings of Social Justice

James B. Boyer asserts that "The absence of instructional vision results in the absence of social and academic justice" (Boyer & Baptiste, 1996, p. 177). Darren, Teresa, and Carlos, through the CA, developed a new vision of their responsibility and possibility as teachers, moving them toward social and academic justice as they garnered new realizations and understandings about social justice.

Darren spoke of his transformation as a journey, "As a white, future educator, I have been on a journey to understand racism and white-privilege so that I am better prepared, as a strong believer and promoter of multicultural education, to challenge these problems in our schools." In his Epilogue, Darren wrote this regarding social justice:

ANNUAL EDITIONS

I learned from this project, and this class as a whole, the various factors that shape our identity, the fact that so much of who we are is not decided by us, and the importance of being an agent of change for social justice and equity. As teachers we are in the position to change the world by affecting the students that we come in contact with every day. This is a power that should not be wasted or abused. Teachers who are not in touch with the students in the classroom and are not aware of the struggles, disadvantages, and problems that students face in the community and home life will not be as able to integrate their curriculum into the real-life, situational type of education that students need to be able to confront and overcome the issues of social justice in their lives.

Carlos reflected on the impact of the CA as a catalyst to examine his home community through a social justice lens, revealing things he had not been aware of before, and facilitating realizations about himself:

[T]here was so much I never took the time to notice in my own home town. . . . This community analysis paper was an eye-opening experience to say the least. I have learned so much about myself and I have grown as an educator. I feel now that I am equipped with new tools to become a great educator. Learning about one's self may be hard sometimes because accepting the bad sides can be difficult, but this course has taught us social justice is not to be shown to other people, but to ourselves as well.

Teresa felt empowered to tackle oppressions as a teacher:

Observing the seven core identities in Sierra Vista has raised my awareness of what it really means to be a teacher. The observations really helped me open my eyes to things I never took the time to care about. I hope to take with me the knowledge I gained from this project and from my multicultural class when I enter the teaching field. One day I will confront these issues and I will have the tools to battle them.

Conclusion

In regard to our own praxis as critical multicultural educators, our work constantly reminds us of what we must do in MCE to advance the movement toward "'MCE as social justice,' to rid ourselves, our educational institutions, and ultimately the larger society from the 'food, fun, festivals, and foolishness' form of MCE" (Haynes Writer, 2008), to shift us into Baptiste's (1994) Typology of Multiculturalism, Level III, for social justice and social action. We must provide opportunities for our pre-service teachers to operationalize MCE concepts, not merely recall terminology from course texts, as a means to assist them in synthesizing theory and practice. As Teresa realized, "A book could not teach the students about their community and the injustices in it, but a teacher who has done her [or his] research could."

Assignments such as the CA facilitates the recognition of the core identities in lived contexts, enabling pre-service teachers to recognize the manifestations of power and oppression in the everyday, so those oppressions become part of the curricular content and social justice becomes a pedagogical imperative. The pre-service teachers addressed the metaphorical, social, and cultural borderlands that our location sustains, prompting the pre-service teachers' identification and understanding of the educational marginalization that often happens to diverse, less powerful students and communities.

In summary, this article examined the implications and effect of the CA Project assignment on pre-service teachers, providing them opportunity to critically examine the manifestations and intersectionalities of race, class, gender, sexual orientation, language, ability, and religion/spiritual orientation in PreK-12 students' communities. They identified organic knowledge from the communities, enabling them to envision and strategize curricular and pedagogical connections to students' lives. The CA required pre-service teachers to analyze systemic inequities in communities which impact the everyday lives of students, compelling them to intellectually analyze how their privileged or disadvantaged identity statuses impact how they read communities or will intersect with their students' privileged or disadvantaged identities. Because the CA is situated within a social justice framework, and functions as a critical pedagogical tool, it works to end or greatly challenge the educational marginalization that so many students experience. This engages the pre-service teachers with MCE teaching conceptualizations and strategies that purposefully transcend "food, fun, and festivals" approach as a means to establish and maintain equitable and socially just learning environments for all students.

Notes

1. All pre-service and in-service teachers must pass the MCE course to seek admission to NMSU's teacher education program. The MCE course is offered at both the undergraduate and graduate level. Whereas, the courses are similar in MCE content and emphasis on social justice, the courses differ in the texts utilized. Assignments may differ as well due to the professors or graduate assistants teaching the various course sections; up to seven sections are offered per semester at the undergraduate level and two at the graduate level.

2. Prentice uses the CA with graduate students, but they work in teams. For the purpose of this article, we examine the use of the CA at the undergraduate-level as an individual assignment.

3. Readings addressed the influence of media bias on the social constructions of the Muslim community (Haynes Writer, 2002b), and a teacher's pedagogical choices in working with a Muslim student (Karp, 2001).

4. Pre-service teachers completed the "Writing for Change" exercise which provided a definition of "compulsory heterosexism," and had them provide various examples of compulsory heterosexism and place themselves in scenarios. We also saw a portion of the film "It's Elementary: Talking about gay issues in school" (Cohen & Chasnoff, 1996).

5. With Darren's comment in class, Jeanette problematized the issue of presenting only "two sides of the story," the Biblical genesis story and the theory of evolution, by discussing that the over 575 federally recognized tribal nations in the US have their own "genesis" or origin stories. Thus, it was no longer a matter of two privileged sides, but hundreds of "sides."

References

Artiles, A. J., & McClafferty, K. (1998). Learning to teach culturally diverse learners: Charting change in preservice teachers' thinking about effective teaching. *The Elementary School Journal,* 98(3), 189–220.

Banks, J. A. (1994). *Multiethnic education:* Theory and practice. Boston, MA: Allyn and Bacon.

Banks, J. A., & Banks, C. A. M. (Eds.). (2001). *Multicultural education: Issues & perspectives* (4th ed.). New York: John Wiley & Sons, Inc.

Baptiste, H. P. (1986). Multicultural education and urban schools from a sociohistorical perspective: Internalizing multiculturalism. *Journal of Educational Equity and Leadership,* 6(4), 295–312.

Baptiste, H. P. (1994). A comprehensive multicultural teacher education program: An idea whose time has come. In M. M. Atwater, K. Radzik-Marsh, & M. E. Strutchens (Eds.), *Multicultural education: Inclusion of all.* Athens, GA: University of Georgia Press.

Bell, L. A. (1997). Theoretical foundations for social justice education. In M. Adams, L. A. Bell, & P. Griffin (Eds.), *Teaching for diversity and social justice: A sourcebook* (pp. 1–15). New York: Routledge.

Bennett, C. (2001). Genres of research in multicultural education. *Review of Educational Research,* 71(2), 171–217.

Boyer, J. B., & Baptiste, Jr., H. P. (1996). *Transforming the curriculum for multicultural understandings: A practitioner's handbook.* San Francisco, CA: Caddo Gap Press.

Cohen, H. (Producer), & Chasnoff, D. (Director). (1996). *It's elementary: Talking about gay issues in school* [Film]. San Francisco, CA: Women's Educational Media.

Harro, B. (2000). The cycle of socialization. In M. Adams, W. J. Blumenfeld, R. Castañeda, H. W. Hackman, M. L. Peters, & X. Zúñiga (Eds.), *Readings for diversity and social justice: An anthology on racism, anti-Semitism, sexism, heterosexism, ableism, and classism* (pp. 15–21). New York: Routledge.

Haynes Writer, J. (2002a). No matter how bitter, horrible, or controversial: Exploring the value of a Native American education course in a teacher education program. *Action in Teacher Education,* 24(2), 9–21.

Haynes Writer, J. (2002b, Fall). Terrorism in Native America: Interrogating the Past, Examining the Present, Constructing a Liberatory Future. *Anthropology and Education Quarterly,* 33(3), 1–14.

Haynes Writer, J. (2008). Unmasking, exposing, and confronting: Critical race theory, tribal critical race theory and multicultural education. *International Journal of Multicultural Education,* 10(2), 1–15.

Karp, S. (2001). Arranged marriages, rearranged ideas. In B. Bigalow, B. Harvey, S. Karp, & L. Miller (Eds.), *Rethinking our classrooms, volume 2: Teaching for equity and social justice* (pp. 188–193). Milwaukee, WI: Rethinking Schools, Ltd.

Letts, W. J., IV, & Sears, J. T. (1999). *Queering elementary education: Advancing the dialogue about sexualities and schooling (curriculum, cultures, and (homo)sexualities).* Lanham, MD: Rowman & Littlefield Publishers, Inc.

Mahlios, M., & Maxson, M. (1995). Capturing preservice teachers' beliefs about schooling, life, and childhood. *Journal of Teacher Education,* 46(3), 192–199.

May, S. (Ed.). (1999). *Critical multiculturalism: Rethinking multicultural and anti-racist education.* Philadelphia, PA: Falmer Press.

Nieto, S., & Bode, P. (2008). *Affirming diversity: The sociopolitical context of multicultural education* (5th ed.). Boston, MA: Allyn and Bacon.

Oakes, J., & Lipton, M. (2007). *Teaching to change the world* (3rd ed.). Boston, MA: McGraw-Hill College.

Sleeter, C. E., & Grant, C. A. (1987). An analysis of multicultural education in the United States. *Harvard Educational Review,* 57(4), 421–444.

Stachowski, L. L., & Frey, C. J. (2003). Lessons learned in Navajoland: Student teachers reflect on professional and cultural learning in reservation schools and communities. *Action in Teacher Education,* 25(3), 38–47.

Tatum, B. D. (2000). The complexity of identity: "Who am I?" In M. Adams, W. J. Blumenfeld, R. Castañeda, H. W. Hackman, M. L. Peters, & X. Zúñiga (Eds.), *Readings for diversity and social justice: An anthology on racism, anti-Semitism, sexism, heterosexism, ableism, and classism* (pp. 9–14). New York: Routledge.

Vavrus, M. (2002, October). *Connecting teacher identity formation to culturally responsive teaching.* Paper presented at the National Association of Multicultural Education in Washington, DC.

Critical Thinking

1. What are learning communities?

2. How does the Community Analysis (CA) Project combat inequities?

3. What steps are taken to bridge families and studies with the curriculum, instruction, and assessments?

4. Why is leveling privilege and power key to equity in education?

JEANETTE HAYNES WRITER is an associate professor in the Department of Curriculum and Instruction at New Mexico State University in Las Cruces, New Mexico. Her areas of specialization include critical multicultural teacher education, social justice and equity; Critical Race Theory and Tribal Critical Race Theory, and Indigenous education. She also serves as the department's coordinator of the multicultural education specialty. **H. PRENTICE BAPTISTE** is a professor in the Department of Curriculum and Instruction at New Mexico State University in Las Cruces, New Mexico. His areas of specialization include multicultural and science education. His research interests include the process of multiculturalizing educational entities and culturally diversifying science and mathematics instruction. His most recent research interest is an analysis of U.S. presidential domestic policies and actions through a multicultural lens. *(We would like to thank the students in Jeanette's Spring 2008, EDUC 315 course for providing us permission to use their papers for this article, especially, Carlos, Darren, and Teresa. The development of this article enabled us to think more deeply about our teaching.)*

Test-Your-Knowledge Form

We encourage you to photocopy and use this page as a tool to assess how the articles in *Annual Editions* expand on the information in your textbook. By reflecting on the articles you will gain enhanced text information. You can also access this useful form on a product's book support website at *www.mhhe.com/cls*.

NAME:

DATE:

_____

TITLE AND NUMBER OF ARTICLE:

_____

BRIEFLY STATE THE MAIN IDEA OF THIS ARTICLE:

_____

LIST THREE IMPORTANT FACTS THAT THE AUTHOR USES TO SUPPORT THE MAIN IDEA:

_____

WHAT INFORMATION OR IDEAS DISCUSSED IN THIS ARTICLE ARE ALSO DISCUSSED IN YOUR TEXTBOOK OR OTHER READINGS THAT YOU HAVE DONE? LIST THE TEXTBOOK CHAPTERS AND PAGE NUMBERS:

_____

LIST ANY EXAMPLES OF BIAS OR FAULTY REASONING THAT YOU FOUND IN THE ARTICLE:

_____

LIST ANY NEW TERMS/CONCEPTS THAT WERE DISCUSSED IN THE ARTICLE, AND WRITE A SHORT DEFINITION:

We Want Your Advice

ANNUAL EDITIONS revisions depend on two major opinion sources: one is our Advisory Board, listed in the front of this volume, which works with us in scanning the thousands of articles published in the public press each year; the other is you—the person actually using the book. Please help us and the users of the next edition by completing the prepaid article rating form on this page and returning it to us. Thank you for your help!

ANNUAL EDITIONS: Multicultural Education, 16e

ARTICLE RATING FORM

Here is an opportunity for you to have direct input into the next revision of this volume.
We would like you to rate each of the articles listed below, using the following scale:

1. **Excellent: should definitely be retained**
2. **Above average: should probably be retained**
3. **Below average: should probably be deleted**
4. **Poor: should definitely be deleted**

Your ratings will play a vital part in the next revision.
Please mail this prepaid form to us as soon as possible.
Thanks for your help!

RATING	ARTICLE
	1. Becoming Citizens of the World
	2. Colorblind to the Reality of Race in America
	3. "What Are You?" Biracial Children in the Classroom
	4. Beyond "Culture Clash": Understandings of Immigrant Experiences
	5. Metaphors of Hope
	6. A Letter Long Overdue
	7. Status of the Dream: A Study of Dr. King in Little Rock and Memphis Classrooms
	8. Teaching for Social Justice in Multicultural Urban Schools: Conceptualization and Classroom Implication
	9. The Human Right to Education: Freedom and Empowerment
	10. An Investigation of How Culture Shapes Curriculum in Early Care and Education Programs on a Native American Indian Reservation
	11. The Need to Reestablish Schools as Dynamic Positive Human Energy Systems That Are Non-Linear and Self-Organizing: The Learning Partnership Tree
	12. Promoting School Achievement among American Indian Students throughout the School Years
	13. Discarding the Deficit Model
	14. Arts in the Classroom: "La Llave" (The Key) to Awareness, Community Relations, and Parental Involvement
	15. Strengthening the Case for Community-Based Learning in Teacher Education
	16. As Diversity Grows, So Must We
	17. In Urban America, Many Students Fail to Finish High School
	18. A Critically Compassionate Intellectualism for Latina/o Students: Raising Voices above the Silencing in Our Schools
	19. Educating Vietnamese American Students

RATING	ARTICLE
	20. The Diversity Merry-Go-Around: Planning and Working in Concert to Establish a Culture of Acceptance and Respect in the University
	21. Developing Collective Classroom Efficacy: The Teacher's Role as Community Organizer
	22. Meeting ACTFL/NCATE Accreditation Standards: What World Language Teacher Candidates Reveal about Program Preparation
	23. Examining Second Language Literacy Development in an Urban Multi-Age Classroom
	24. Celebrating Diversity through Explorations of Arab Children's Literature
	25. Chica Lit: Multicultural Literature Blurs Borders
	26. One Nation, Many Gods
	27. "Because I Had a Turban"
	28. Asian American Teachers
	29. Building the Movement to End Educational Inequity
	30. The Promise of Black Teachers' Success with Black Students
	31. Good Intentions Are Not Enough: A Decolonizing Intercultural Education
	32. Advancing Cultural Competence and Intercultural Consciousness through a Cross-Cultural Simulation with Teacher Candidates
	33. Sustaining Ourselves under Stressful Times: Strategies to Assist Multicultural Educators
	34. Toward a Conceptual Framework of Culturally Relevant Pedagogy: An Overview of the Conceptual and Theoretical Literature
	35. Approaches to Diversifying the Teaching Force: Attending to Issues of Recruitment, Preparation, and Retention
	36. Realizing Students' Every Day Realities: Community Analysis as a Model for Social Justice

BUSINESS REPLY MAIL
FIRST CLASS MAIL PERMIT NO. 551 DUBUQUE IA

POSTAGE WILL BE PAID BY ADDRESSEE

McGraw-Hill Contemporary Learning Series
501 BELL STREET
DUBUQUE, IA 52001

NO POSTAGE
NECESSARY
IF MAILED
IN THE
UNITED STATES

ABOUT YOU

Name

Date

Are you a teacher? ☐ A student? ☐
Your school's name

Department

Address   City   State   Zip

School telephone #

YOUR COMMENTS ARE IMPORTANT TO US!

Please fill in the following information:
For which course did you use this book?

Did you use a text with this ANNUAL EDITION? ☐ yes ☐ no
What was the title of the text?

What are your general reactions to the Annual Editions concept?

Have you read any pertinent articles recently that you think should be included in the next edition? Explain.

Are there any articles that you feel should be replaced in the next edition? Why?

Are there any World Wide Websites that you feel should be included in the next edition? Please annotate.

May we contact you for editorial input? ☐ yes ☐ no
May we quote your comments? ☐ yes ☐ no